A Beginner's Guide to Digital Image Repair in Photoshop: Volume 2

Color Adjustments, Filters, and Animation

Jennifer Harder

apress®

A Beginner's Guide to Digital Image Repair in Photoshop: Volume 2: Color Adjustments, Filters, and Animation

Jennifer Harder
Delta, BC, Canada

ISBN-13 (pbk): 979-8-8688-0762-6   ISBN-13 (electronic): 979-8-8688-0763-3
https://doi.org/10.1007/979-8-8688-0763-3

Copyright © 2024 by Jennifer Harder

This work is subject to copyright. All rights are reserved by the Publisher, whether the whole or part of the material is concerned, specifically the rights of translation, reprinting, reuse of illustrations, recitation, broadcasting, reproduction on microfilms or in any other physical way, and transmission or information storage and retrieval, electronic adaptation, computer software, or by similar or dissimilar methodology now known or hereafter developed.

Trademarked names, logos, and images may appear in this book. Rather than use a trademark symbol with every occurrence of a trademarked name, logo, or image we use the names, logos, and images only in an editorial fashion and to the benefit of the trademark owner, with no intention of infringement of the trademark.

The use in this publication of trade names, trademarks, service marks, and similar terms, even if they are not identified as such, is not to be taken as an expression of opinion as to whether or not they are subject to proprietary rights.

While the advice and information in this book are believed to be true and accurate at the date of publication, neither the authors nor the editors nor the publisher can accept any legal responsibility for any errors or omissions that may be made. The publisher makes no warranty, express or implied, with respect to the material contained herein.

Managing Director, Apress Media LLC: Welmoed Spahr
Acquisitions Editor: Spandana Chatterjee
Development Editor: James Markham
Coordinating Editor: Kripa Joseph

Cover designed by eStudioCalamar

Cover image by Freepik (www.freepik.com)

Distributed to the book trade worldwide by Apress Media, LLC, 1 New York Plaza, New York, NY 10004, U.S.A. Phone 1-800-SPRINGER, fax (201) 348-4505, e-mail orders-ny@springer-sbm.com, or visit www.springeronline.com. Apress Media, LLC is a California LLC and the sole member (owner) is Springer Science + Business Media Finance Inc (SSBM Finance Inc). SSBM Finance Inc is a **Delaware** corporation.

For information on translations, please e-mail booktranslations@springernature.com; for reprint, paperback, or audio rights, please e-mail bookpermissions@springernature.com.

Apress titles may be purchased in bulk for academic, corporate, or promotional use. eBook versions and licenses are also available for most titles. For more information, reference our Print and eBook Bulk Sales web page at http://www.apress.com/bulk-sales.

Any source code or other supplementary material referenced by the author in this book is available to readers on GitHub (https://github.com/Apress). For more detailed information, please visit https://www.apress.com/gp/services/source-code.

If disposing of this product, please recycle the paper

Table of Contents

About the Author ix

Acknowledgments xi

Introduction xiii

Chapter 1: Adjustment Layers, Blending Modes with Masks for Photo Restoration: Part 1 1

Color Management, Color Correction, and Your Digital Image 2

Image Repair Review 15

Image Adjustment Options 17

Working with the Layers Panel Fill and Adjustment Layers 25

    Fill Options 25

    Layer Adjustments 63

    Additional Panels That Can Assist You While Working with the Adjustments Panel 68

    Properties Panel for Layer Adjustments 83

    Working with Multiple Adjustment Layers and the Adjustments Panel 226

Summary 232

Chapter 2: Adjustment Layers, Blending Modes with Masks for Photo Restoration: Part 2 233

Properties Panel and Adjustment Layer Masks 234

    Removing Gradients from Scan Using Several Layer Masks 236

    Properties Panel Layer Mask Settings for Normal and Adjustment Layers 240

TABLE OF CONTENTS

- Clipping Masks 250
- Applying an Additional Vector Mask with the Properties Panel 253
- Working in Combination: Layer Blending Modes and Adjustment Layers 278
  - Opacity, Fill, and Layer Styles 292
  - Layer Style Blending Options 297
  - Blending Options in the Layer Style Dialog Box 298
- Using Smart Filters to Make Certain Color Adjustments Nondestructive 308
  - Shadows/Highlights 313
  - Smart Filter Blending Options 320
- Advanced Adjustment Settings 323
  - Auto Correction 323
  - Equalize and Desaturate 325
  - Adjustments: Working with HDR Images 326
  - Advanced Color Adjustments 341
  - Match Color 342
  - Replace Color 347
- Advanced Image Adjustment Options 350
  - Apply Image 351
  - Calculations 357
- Notes on Out-of-Gamut Colors 359
- Working in Lab vs. RGB Color in Separate Channels 364
- Photo Project 364
- Summary 370

Chapter 3: Basic Filters for Photo Restoration 371
- Review: Creating a Smart Object Layer for Smart Filters 376
- Basic Filter Overview Specifically for Photo Correction 378

    Blur Filters 379

    Blur Gallery Filters 423

    Noise Correction Filters 453

    Sharpen Filters 475

    Render Filters 495

    Other Basic Filters to Consider for Image Restoration 511

Photo Project...521

Summary..523

Chapter 4: Advanced Filters for Photo Restoration: Part 1 525

    Liquify Filter Workspace...528

        Tools 529

        Liquify Properties Brush Tool Options..534

        Zoom Tool, Hand Tool, and Undoing steps 535

        Load Mesh Options 536

        Mask Options...537

        View Options..539

        Brush Reconstruct Options...541

        Face Tool and Properties 542

    Camera Raw Filter Workspace...560

        Workspace Overview...565

        Workspace Additional Panels 634

Other Advanced Filters to Consider Using with Camera Raw 689

        Lens Correction Filter 690

        Adaptive Wide Angle 706

What Are the Materials Parametric Filters? 719

Summary..725

TABLE OF CONTENTS

Chapter 5: Advanced Filters for Photo Restoration: Part 2................727
Neural Filters..728
Workspace Tools and Output..730
    Add to Selection (B)...730
    Subtract from Selection (E)...731
    Hand Tool (H)...732
    Zoom Tool (Z)..732
    Adding a New Filter..737
    Color..741
    Restoration..768
    Portrait (Facial Adjustments)..773
    Photography...788
    Creative (Filters for Artistic Work) Landscape Mixer and Style Transfer......795
    Filters to Come in the Future...806
Acquiring Other Filter Plug-Ins Through Adobe Creative Cloud...................807
Photo Project..812
Summary...812

Chapter 6: Creating a Parallax: Bring Your Vintage or Historical Photos to Life..813
Overview of the Timeline Panel..814
    Animations (And Preparation)..815
    GIF Animation Preparation Considerations...816
    Video Parallax Animation Preparation Considerations............................817
    Creating a New File for the Animation...820
    Timeline Panel and Considerations...821
    GIF Photo Gallery Project...822

Video Animation Parallax Project..880
Media Encoder Settings...967
Summary...985

Chapter 7: What Is the Next Step in Your Photo Restoration Project? 987

Photoshop 988
Saving RGB Files for the Web or Email 988
File Options and Tips for Saving Your Photo for Print 993
CMYK Filter Adjustments for a Specific Channel 997
Saving Your File for Print 1001
Additional Color Conversion Information 1002
Edit ➤ Color Settings 1003
Online Projects (PDF Presentation) 1006
InDesign 1019
Print Presentation 1021
PDF Interactive Presentation 1026
Microsoft PowerPoint Presentation..1029
Inserting an Image or GIF Animation 1029
Video Applications and Considerations 1033
Parallax and Animation 1034
Summary..1042

Index...**1043**

About the Author

Jennifer Harder has worked in the graphic design industry for over 15 years. She has a degree in graphic communications and is currently teaching Acrobat and Adobe Creative Cloud courses at Langara College. She is also author of several Apress books and related videos.

Acknowledgments

Because of their patience and advice, I would like to thank the following people, for without them I could never have written this book:

- My parents, for encouraging me to read large computer textbooks that would one day inspire me to write my own books and for their assistance in selecting photos for chapter projects
- My dad, for reviewing the first draft before I sent a proposal
- My program coordinator, Raymond Chow, at Langara College, who shares a similar interest in photography

I would also like to thank Spandana Chatterjee and Krishnan Sathyamurthy at Apress for showing me how to lay out a professional textbook and pointing out that even when you think you've written it all, there's still more to write. Also, thanks to the technical reviewer for providing encouraging comments and to the rest of the Apress team for being involved in the printing of this book and making my dream a reality again. I am truly grateful and blessed.

Introduction

Welcome to the book *A Beginner's Guide to Digital Image Repair in Photoshop: Volume 2*.

In today's digital world, with smartphones and cameras, we can easily transfer our photos from phone to computer. Then, with Photoshop, we do a few basic corrections using various healing tools in conjunction with adjustment layers and filters and then print out the picture with our inkjet printer or post it on our social media page. However, occasionally we are left with the old or damaged photos and slides from a loved one who lived before the age of digital cameras. Now we need to decide what to do with these old family treasures, whether they be a family portrait or a trip to a historical location, that we have been keeping in a shoe box for many years. Some are in good condition and others are very damaged. What can we do to restore them? Let's continue that discussion from where we left off in the first volume. Refer to Figure 1.

Figure 1. *Collection of photos, film slides, and negatives in a shoe box*

INTRODUCTION

Make sure to review Volume 1 before starting this next volume as we will explore how you can work with your old historical photos in Photoshop and digitally restore them so that you can print them out for family, as well as use them online as still photos or to animate select images. As we progress through the chapters, you will look at some of the many tools and filters that Photoshop has to offer, both old and new, that can assist you in your restoration project.

In Volume 1 we reviewed the following:

- Focused on preparation for working with old historical photos and reviewed scanner basics for your photo print, new information on how to work with film slides and negatives, some guidelines on what type of scanners and dialog box settings to use for them, and initial file formats that are created after the scan.

- Reviewed how to set up your Photoshop workspace, some of the tools and panels, and the basic file formats to save the files you are working on in.

- Looked at the basic Photoshop "healing tools" that are useful for very basic photo restoration as well as a few other additional tools that you incorporated for small touch-ups, color corrections, or cropping your artwork while working with the Layers panel on a personal project.

- Explored some more advanced features such as working with masks, selections, and other related commands and workspaces (old and new) that Photoshop has to offer. You saw that when there are gaps and details are not present in a photo, you can be creative and fill in the missing details.

INTRODUCTION

Now Volume 2 will continue to explore the following:

- Chapters 1 and 2: Explore various masks and how we can use them to color correct the entire scene or selected areas using the Adjustments panel, its new features, and related brushes. You will also review what the smart object layer is and how to apply smart filter adjustments to it that are nondestructive. Blending modes and other advanced color adjustment options will be looked at as well.

- Chapter 3: Review some of the main basic filters that are mostly used for blurring, sharpening, or removing noise from an image. These filters will be applied to various layers, but we will also look at situations where they could be applied to or in combination with a layer mask, smart object filter mask, or channels.

- Chapters 4 and 5: Explore some advanced filters as well as some new filters that you may not be aware of that can help you with your photo restoration project. We will also take a brief look at how you can go about acquiring additional filters from the Adobe Creative Cloud console if you have a subscription.

- Chapter 6: Focus on two possible ways that you can bring your images to life in Photoshop using the Timeline panel. One way is to create a basic slideshow GIF animation, and the second is to create a parallax video animation from components of a single or several images. The latter has in recent years become popular when no historical video footage is available. I will discuss and look at what kinds of photos do and do not lend themselves to a parallax and then how to render the video animation using Photoshop and Adobe Media Encoder.

INTRODUCTION

- Chapter 7: Conclude our discussion on Photoshop and digital image repair with some final color touch-ups you can do should you plan to print your images or save them for online use. I will also mention a few additional Adobe Creative Cloud and Microsoft apps that you may want to consider should you want to continue to work with your images for other multimedia projects.

At this point, I will just mention that though most photos we will be working with in this book will be historical or vintage, if you have modern digital photos, you can use them as well.

Note that in this book some of the images where people are present have had their faces altered (with blurs or mannequin faces) to protect their original identities, so that you can use them for practice. However, if you have similar photos of friends or family, then feel free to use the same techniques mentioned in this book and practice on them instead of mine.

Installation of Photoshop and Other Adobe Apps Review

This book assumes that you are using the Adobe Creative Cloud subscription. Currently, I am using an individual license, but you may have business/teams or a student license:

www.adobe.com/creativecloud.html

Make sure to install a copy of the Creative Cloud Desktop console on your computer.

Since the focus of this book is on Adobe Photoshop, if you have not already done so, make sure to download a copy of Photoshop from your Creative Cloud Desktop.

INTRODUCTION

Go to Apps ➤ All apps and choose the Desktop option from the list. Under Essential in your plan, locate Photoshop and click Install. Refer to Figure 2.

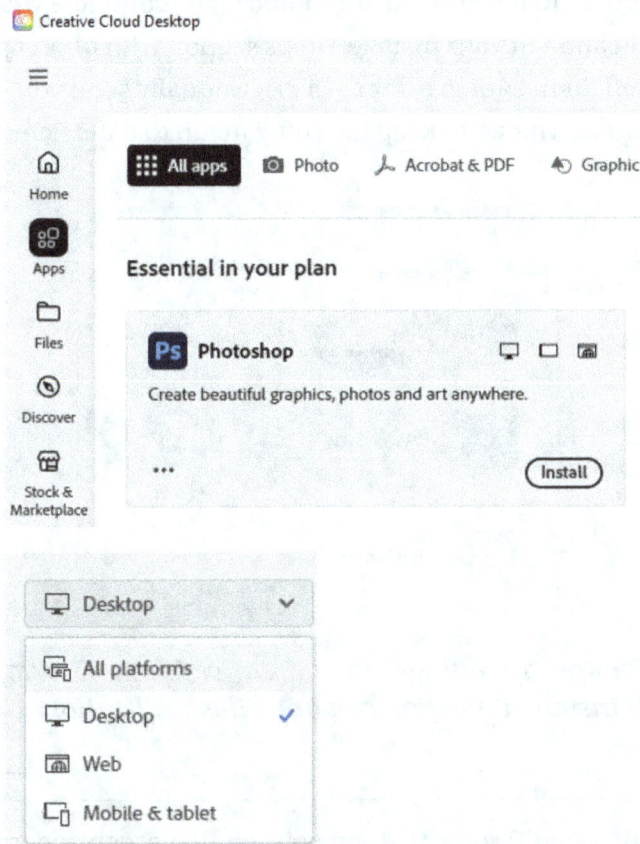

Figure 2. *Creative Cloud Desktop settings for installing Photoshop*

If you are not sure of your system requirements, you can check them here:
https://helpx.adobe.com/creative-cloud/system-requirements.html

INTRODUCTION

https://helpx.adobe.com/photoshop/system-requirements.html
I am currently using version 2024 (25.12).

It may take several minutes for the download to complete, and you may be prompted to restart your computer. Once complete you would find the application in your Installed apps section with other applications, if you installed them earlier. Adobe will occasionally send you updates, which you can download to keep the software up to date. Refer to Figure 3.

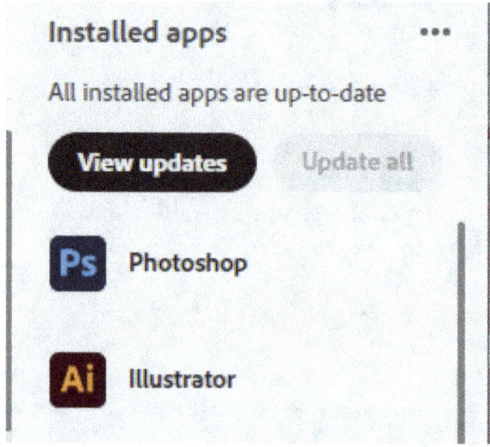

Figure 3. *Photoshop settings in the Creative Cloud Desktop to indicate it is installed and you can open the application*

Note that Adobe Bridge, to keep your photos organized, may also be downloaded. Though not used in this book, it will be briefly mentioned in Chapter 4 as it relates to the Camera Raw Filter. Camera Raw may also be installed with your Photoshop application. You may also want to download a copy of Media Encoder at the same time, but we will not require the application until Chapter 6. Refer to Figure 4.

INTRODUCTION

Figure 4. *Other Adobe applications that will be installed: Bridge, Media Encoder, and Camera Raw*

Now that Photoshop is installed, click the Open button in the Creative Cloud Desktop and then, after a minute, it will load and open. Refer to Figure 5.

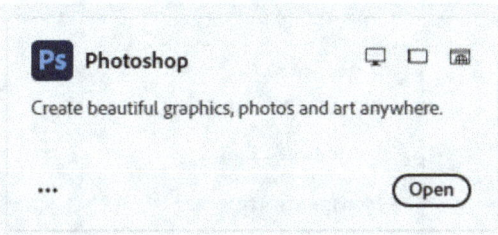

Figure 5. *Use the Creative Cloud Desktop to open the Photoshop application*

You can leave Photoshop open for now if you are planning to read Chapter 1 next and continue to use the Essentials (Default) Workspace as discussed in Volume 1. Or for now you can from the main menu choose File ➤ Exit (Ctrl/CMD+Q) if you need to exit the application.

Note that this book does not discuss the separate application Photoshop Express or Beta features unless they are installed in the current application.

Resources

Throughout this book I will be supplying a link for more details on various tools using the following link:

```
https://helpx.adobe.com/
```

INTRODUCTION

You can also access more information on various Photoshop-related topics from the Photoshop Help menu, Discover panel (magnifying glass icon), as well as the Creative Cloud console's Discover tab. Refer to Figures 6 and 7.

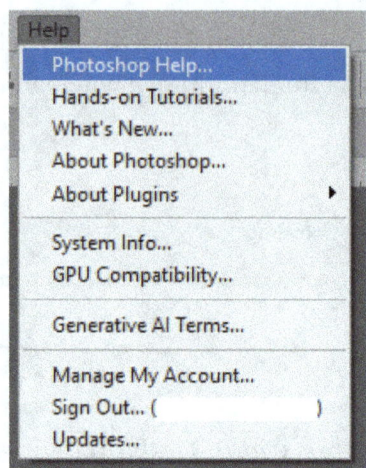

Figure 6. *Photoshop Help menu*

INTRODUCTION

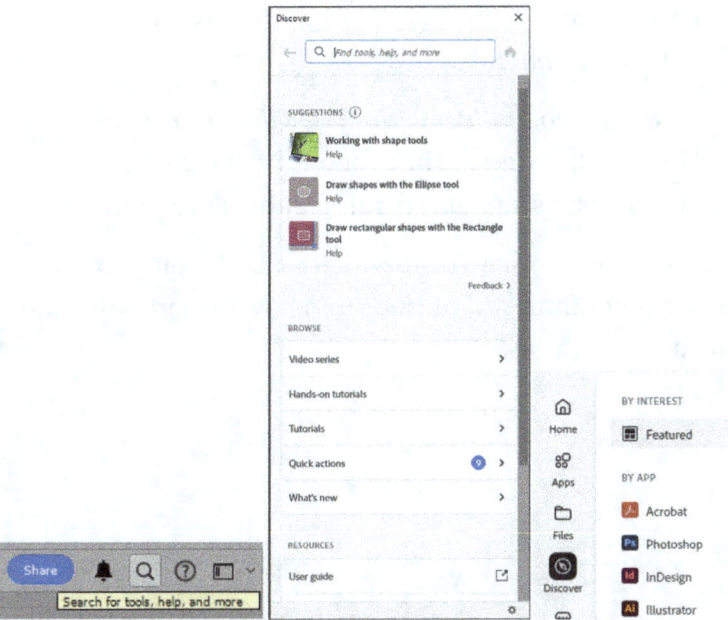

Figure 7. *Access to the Photoshop Discover panel along with the Creative Cloud Desktop gives access to Photoshop tutorials*

After you have finished this book, if you are interested in other Photoshop projects and working in combination with Adobe Illustrator, you can review some of my other Photoshop-related books should these topics be of interest to you:

- *Graphics and Multimedia for the Web with Adobe Creative Cloud*

- *Accurate Layer Selections Using Photoshop's Selection Tools*

xxi

INTRODUCTION

- *Perspective Warps and Distorts with Adobe Tools: Volumes 1 and 2*
- *Creating Infographics with Adobe Illustrator: Volumes 1, 2, and 3.* These books briefly discuss Photoshop as it relates to infographic development.

Projects for this book can be found here: Link from Apress.

So now let's continue our journey into how to work with your box of historical photo treasures.

CHAPTER 1

Adjustment Layers, Blending Modes with Masks for Photo Restoration: Part 1

In addition to working on damaged photos with the healing and selection tools, one of the other issues we discussed briefly in Volume 1 was color correction. Just because a scanner scans your film or print accurately does not mean that its appearance is color correct for printing purposes, especially if it has faded over time due to some environmental factors we discussed in Volume 1.

Likely, you will want to correct, balance, reduce, or even add more colors to an image. We talked breifly about other color modes in Volume 1 as well as how they related to images. However, in this chapter you will discover that Photoshop has a variety of options, whether for overall color correction or a selected masked area of an image. Photoshop within its Layers panel has various fill and adjustment layers to accomplish this task, and each of these unique layers can have blending modes and opacity altered.

CHAPTER 1   ADJUSTMENT LAYERS, BLENDING MODES WITH MASKS FOR PHOTO RESTORATION: PART 1

Later, in Chapter 2, you will also discover that you can use those adjustments and commands in combination with smart filters on smart object layers and their layer masks. We will also explore three other masking options that can be applied to layers, which include clipping masks, vector masks, and smart filter masks.

A brief mention will also be made on when to use layer styles to improve a photo for display.

Note this chapter does contain projects found in the Volume 2 Chapter 1 folder.

I have also mentioned some of the topics on smart layer objects in my book *Perspective Warps and Distorts with Adobe Tools: Volume 1*. However, that book is not required for this chapter.

In Chapter 2 we will also briefly look at a few additional selection-related tools as well as a few more advanced and automated blending options that you may want to use for specific projects and then use what we have learned from this chapter to continue with the photo project.

Color Management, Color Correction, and Your Digital Image

As a beginner using Photoshop, knowing which dialog boxes to use for color correction and adjustment can be a confusing and overwhelming topic. To begin with, it should be mentioned that whether scanning with a scanner, taking a digital photo, viewing your image on a monitor, or printing with a printer, the digital image is moving through various color modes and color profiles. Refer to Figure 1-1.

CHAPTER 1 ADJUSTMENT LAYERS, BLENDING MODES WITH MASKS FOR PHOTO RESTORATION: PART 1

Figure 1-1. *The photo print (CMYK) is scanned and enters the computer (RGB) colorspace and is then printed again on the CMYK printer. The digital camera RGB images are also stored on the computer*

When you buy new hardware such as a scanner, camera, monitor, or inkjet color printer, it is assumed that they are color correct or calibrated and displaying fairly closely to your intended print. Over time however, hardware ages and so you may need to get additional software updates to calibrate your hardware or replace the software and hardware altogether.

CHAPTER 1   ADJUSTMENT LAYERS, BLENDING MODES WITH MASKS FOR PHOTO RESTORATION: PART 1

> Note the topic of calibrating your monitor in this chapter is not discussed in this book as it is an advanced topic. However, I do recommend spending time doing your research when you plan to purchase a new monitor and looking at various reviews and models before you buy. Also do some online research on the topic of "monitor calibration tool."

In this book we are working in RGB color mode with the Working RGB sRGB profile that I mentioned in Volume 1, Chapter 2. In your case you may be working in a different RGB profile like Adobe RGB (1998). However, it should be noted that different profiles exist for different hardware and software. For example, some monitors have a larger range of display colors to display an image, but how the image displays is also dependent on the choice of mode if one switches from RGB to CMYK. If you study color theory, you will discover that you are in a sense limiting the amount of colors you can work with within a color space when you switch from RGB to CMYK.

RGB is known as an additive color mode. It displays the colors of light, and so it is visually closer to what your eyes see in the world around you. The presence of all colors is white, while the absence of all colors is black. Refer to Figure 1-2.

CHAPTER 1　ADJUSTMENT LAYERS, BLENDING MODES WITH MASKS FOR PHOTO RESTORATION: PART 1

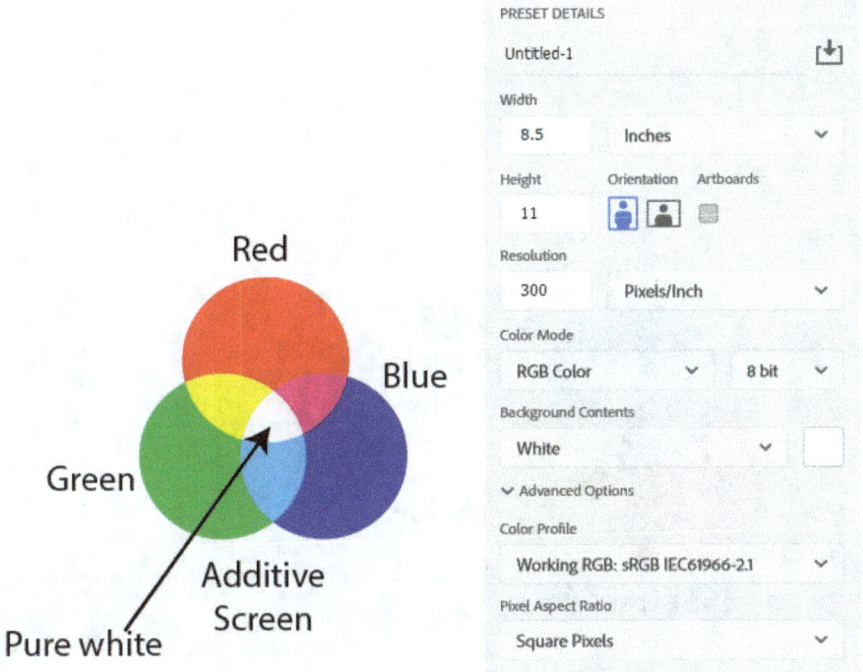

Figure 1-2. *Additive computer screen colors RGB create a pure white color when blended together (left) and Adobe color mode and profile in a new document set up (right)*

However, CMYK (cyan, magenta, yellow, and black) is known as subtractive color mode. It works with pigments and paper, both of which are impure. CMYK can never achieve the absolute purest of white (the paper substrate) or black as closely as an RGB monitor, which is closer to pure light, and so some colors that are in RGB color mode cannot be entirely reproduced simply by using CMYK pigments. Black (K) must be boosted with a separate black ink, as just using CMY creates a muddy dark gray. Refer to Figure 1-3.

CHAPTER 1   ADJUSTMENT LAYERS, BLENDING MODES WITH MASKS FOR PHOTO
            RESTORATION: PART 1

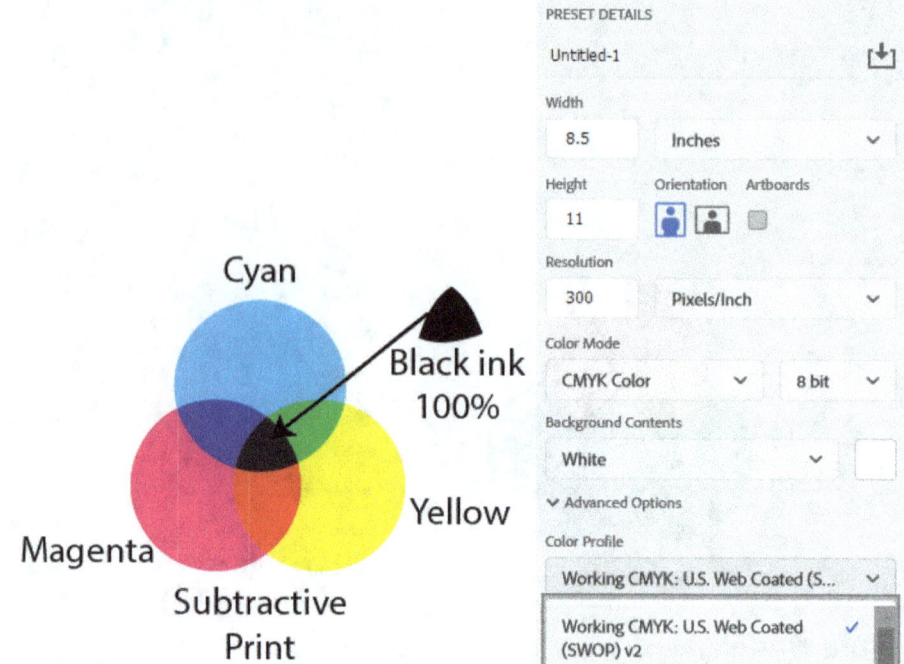

Figure 1-3. *Subtractive print colors CMY do not create a solid black color when blended together and need black ink as a booster (left) and Adobe color mode and profile in a new document set up (right)*

RGB has a wider gamut of color as the following example of a chromaticity compression chart can illustrate. Refer to Figure 1-4.

CHAPTER 1 ADJUSTMENT LAYERS, BLENDING MODES WITH MASKS FOR PHOTO RESTORATION: PART 1

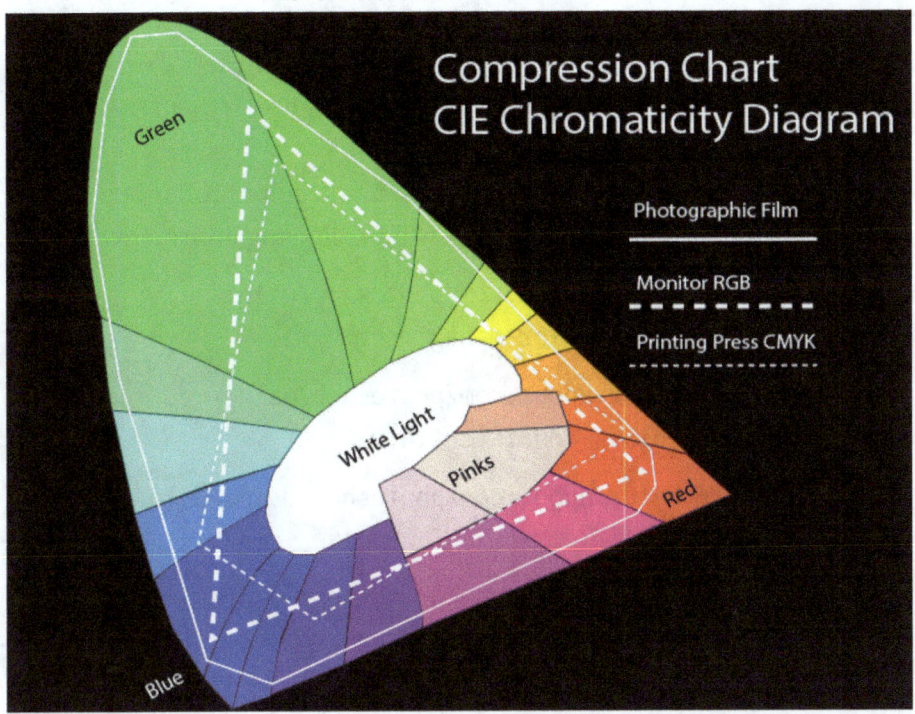

Figure 1-4. Compression chart for RGB and CMYK color spaces

In the case of an sRGB color space, the RGB color options are smaller than for Adobe RGB 1998.

I will not be discussing the topic of color theory in detail here, but you can explore that further in my book *Creating Infographics with Adobe Illustrator: Volume 1*. However, I will talk a bit more about how to check for out-of-gamut colors in Chapter 2 and later on how to make adjustments for your image in CMYK color mode in Chapter 7.

I'll just note now that, depending on the CMYK printer (offset, laser, or inkjet), you can have a slightly higher gamut, but this is dependent on the profiles and inks for your printer. In the case of an inkjet print, additional "booster inks" may be installed for blues and reds, and so this can slightly broaden the range of printed colors making it closer to what is seen in the real work and your screen.

7

CHAPTER 1   ADJUSTMENT LAYERS, BLENDING MODES WITH MASKS FOR PHOTO RESTORATION: PART 1

However, always keep in mind there will always be that gap between the colors captured from the real world and what is displayed on the screen and finally in print no matter how accurately you try to color manage or correct.

For more information on color management, color profiles, calibration, and working with Adobe, you can review the following information:

- `https://helpx.adobe.com/photoshop/using/understanding-color-management.html`

- `https://helpx.adobe.com/photoshop/using/keeping-colors-consistent.html`

- `https://helpx.adobe.com/photoshop/using/color-settings.html`

  `https://helpx.adobe.com/photoshop/using/working-with-color-profiles.html`

- `https://helpx.adobe.com/photoshop/using/color-managing-documents--printing.html`

- `https://helpx.adobe.com/photoshop/using/color-managing-imported-images.html`

- `https://helpx.adobe.com/photoshop/using/proofing-colors.html`

Even with an ideal color-managed environment, before you begin to color correct, you need to take three more factors into consideration.

First, in the context of the black-and-white photos, unless you were there on scene when the image was captured with the camera, how do you know what the color was of the people's clothing or what their eye color was? Unless it was written down somewhere or you later met that person or acquired a color image of them, you cannot know. Images that were

CHAPTER 1 ADJUSTMENT LAYERS, BLENDING MODES WITH MASKS FOR PHOTO RESTORATION: PART 1

taken in or before the 1890s and even sometime afterward lacked color. Often color was added by an artist, and this was called hand tinting or hand coloring. Refer to Figure 1-5.

Figure 1-5. *Example of hand tinting on a wedding photo from the 1950s*

For someone to hand-color then or use Photoshop to digitally color a black-and-white image, unless the artist can find those exact pieces of clothing or furniture, it is open to interpretation. It will never be 100% accurate. You can, for the grayscale, at best achieve a good tonal balance, and the black-and-white image should appear clean and viewable if you have used your healing and selection tools from Volume 1 chapters correctly. However, in this chapter you may want to also achieve some of the original sepia color or remove some stains, or maybe you want to add color to selected parts of the image. Refer to Figure 1-6.

CHAPTER 1   ADJUSTMENT LAYERS, BLENDING MODES WITH MASKS FOR PHOTO RESTORATION: PART 1

Figure 1-6. *Digitally hand-tinting the castle image in Photoshop*

Second, like the monochrome image, color images age and fade in similar ways. You then have to guess what the exact skin tone of that person was. In this case no amount of color management can help, only color correction. Refer to Figure 1-7.

CHAPTER 1   ADJUSTMENT LAYERS, BLENDING MODES WITH MASKS FOR PHOTO RESTORATION: PART 1

Figure 1-7. *Faded images make it difficult to recreate exact skin tones*

Color is also open to interpretation and people perceive color differently. How do you view color? If a person is older, with aging eyes, or has a form of color blindness or even is sitting in a room with different kinds of lighting, they will see and perceive color differently.

You need to consider the following:

- Do you want the color image to retain some of its original toning when it was photographed?

- Should it be as original as how you see color in the world around you?

- What was the weather like in that picture on that day? Is the green of the grass or the blue of the sky the same on a sunny summer day as it is on an overcast winter day? No, it is not. During the day light changes; sometimes light will take on a red hue during a sunset and other times it will be more blue or yellow.

CHAPTER 1   ADJUSTMENT LAYERS, BLENDING MODES WITH MASKS FOR PHOTO
            RESTORATION: PART 1

Thorough study of the colors around you in various lighting and weather can help you achieve better color balance in Photoshop. With practice, an accurate color correction is mostly achievable. However, if the scanned image color channels have been damaged drastically in some way, returning it to how you envision may take more effort, and it becomes much like the guessing game of the black-and-white photo. Refer to Figure 1-8.

Figure 1-8. *Images that have become discolored due to fading on prints and photos*

CHAPTER 1 ADJUSTMENT LAYERS, BLENDING MODES WITH MASKS FOR PHOTO RESTORATION: PART 1

Third, you may also be a person who likes very bright bold colors or likes the way the photo appears when it is muted and has low contrast. Our ideal perception of color correction while we want to repair the image may take on artistic or surreal looks as well. So each artist will come to various conclusions as to what is the ideal color repair. For your digital project you may also want to achieve a reverse effect of making a modern color photo appear "retro" with a color cast or in black and white overall or in selected areas, and this can also be achieved with adjustment layers. Refer to Figure 1-9.

CHAPTER 1 ADJUSTMENT LAYERS, BLENDING MODES WITH MASKS FOR PHOTO RESTORATION: PART 1

Figure 1-9. *Applying different color blends to the same image can add artistic interest*

CHAPTER 1 ADJUSTMENT LAYERS, BLENDING MODES WITH MASKS FOR PHOTO RESTORATION: PART 1

Image Repair Review

Before you start your color correction, it is always best to

- Ensure that you have scanned the image of a resolution of at least 300 dpi/ppi and that it is in RGB color mode. Scan at 600 dpi/ppi if you plan to do an enlargement later.

- Work on a duplicate of your image as you have been doing in the previous volume. Refer to Figure 1-10.

- Correct any major area of damage by removing as many of the dust particles, blemishes, and scratches as possible using your healing tools on a new layer.

- Crop and straighten your image.

- Use your selection tools as required to fill in gaps or missing details.

Then you can begin your color corrections with adjustment layers. However, because you are working on multiple layers, you still have the option of turning on and off the various layers' visibilities as you work, altering your setting at any time working in a nondestructive way. Remember that while using various healing tools, as you saw in Volume 1, Chapter 3, which included the Clone Stamp tool, you can turn on or off the adjustment layer option in the Options bar if you are worried that you might clone colors that you did not intend to from alternate adjustment layers as you work. Refer to Figure 1-10.

CHAPTER 1   ADJUSTMENT LAYERS, BLENDING MODES WITH MASKS FOR PHOTO RESTORATION: PART 1

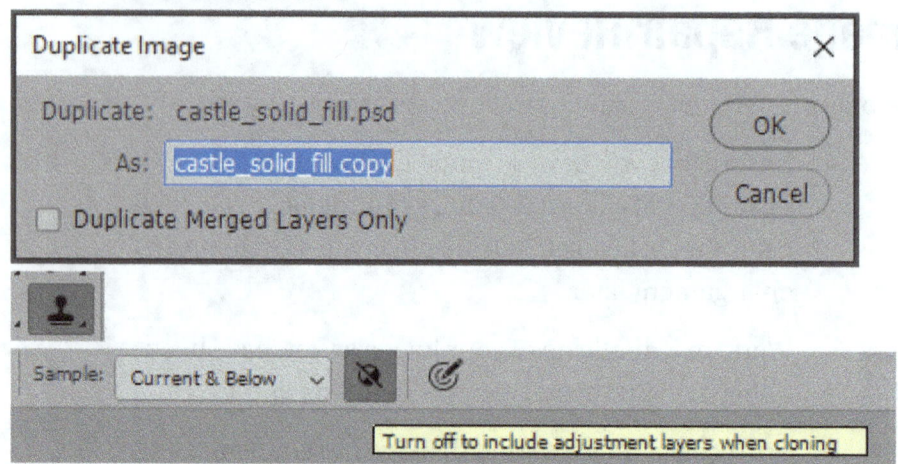

Figure 1-10. After using the Image ➤ Duplicate dialog box to create a duplicate file. Use the Clone Stamp tool Options bar panel to turn off adjustment layer settings when clone stamping certain areas above or below adjustment layers

Note   For advanced professional color correction of digital photos, Adobe does recommend working in 16 bits and not 8 bits. You can switch this using the Image ➤ Mode menu. However, you can remain in 8 bits as you work on a duplicate file, and we are working with scanned images. Refer to Figure 1-11.

CHAPTER 1 ADJUSTMENT LAYERS, BLENDING MODES WITH MASKS FOR PHOTO RESTORATION: PART 1

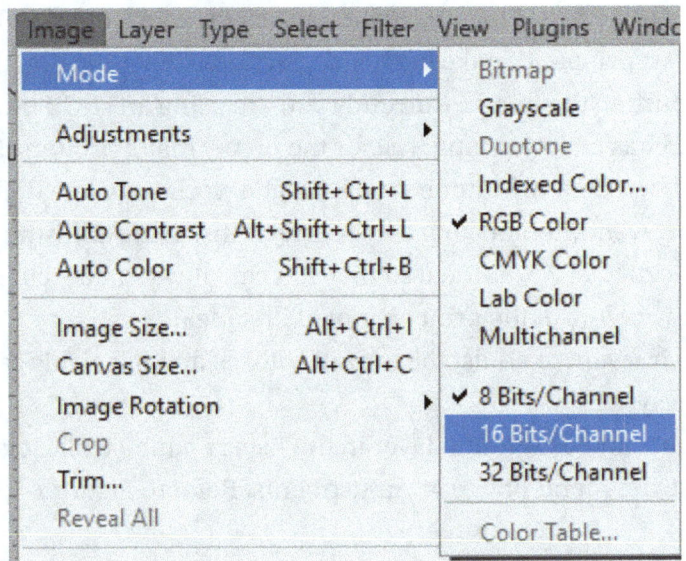

Figure 1-11. *Image ➤ Mode menu settings for bits/channel*

You can use 32 Bits/Channel when working with High Dynamic Range (HDR) photos, which I will mention briefly in this chapter and later in Chapter 2. However be aware that not all adjustment options are available for 32 Bits/Channel.

Image Adjustment Options

In this chapter we will begin by looking at which color correction adjustment layers to use for a specific project. This is important if you have not used any of these adjustment settings before. I will be giving you a basic overview of each as well as some ideas of when and how to apply these adjustment layers for my project examples. Ultimately it will be up to you to experiment with your settings as every project is different. If you are planning to print any of the images you have adjusted, you will ultimately have do a test print and make further corrections depending on the printer that is outputting the image. Currently you are using an sRGB profile, which I find has been working well for me on my inkjet printers. But as mentioned here and in Volume 1, you may be working with a different profile. However, when making color corrections, using adjustment layers in a nondestructive way is ideal so that you can always make changes quickly if the colors in the print are not at first ideal.

When you want to adjust the overall color of an image, this can be done in several ways.

First, on your background layer in the Layers panel, while it is selected you can use the menu Image ➤ Adjustments. Refer to Figure 1-12.

CHAPTER 1　ADJUSTMENT LAYERS, BLENDING MODES WITH MASKS FOR PHOTO RESTORATION: PART 1

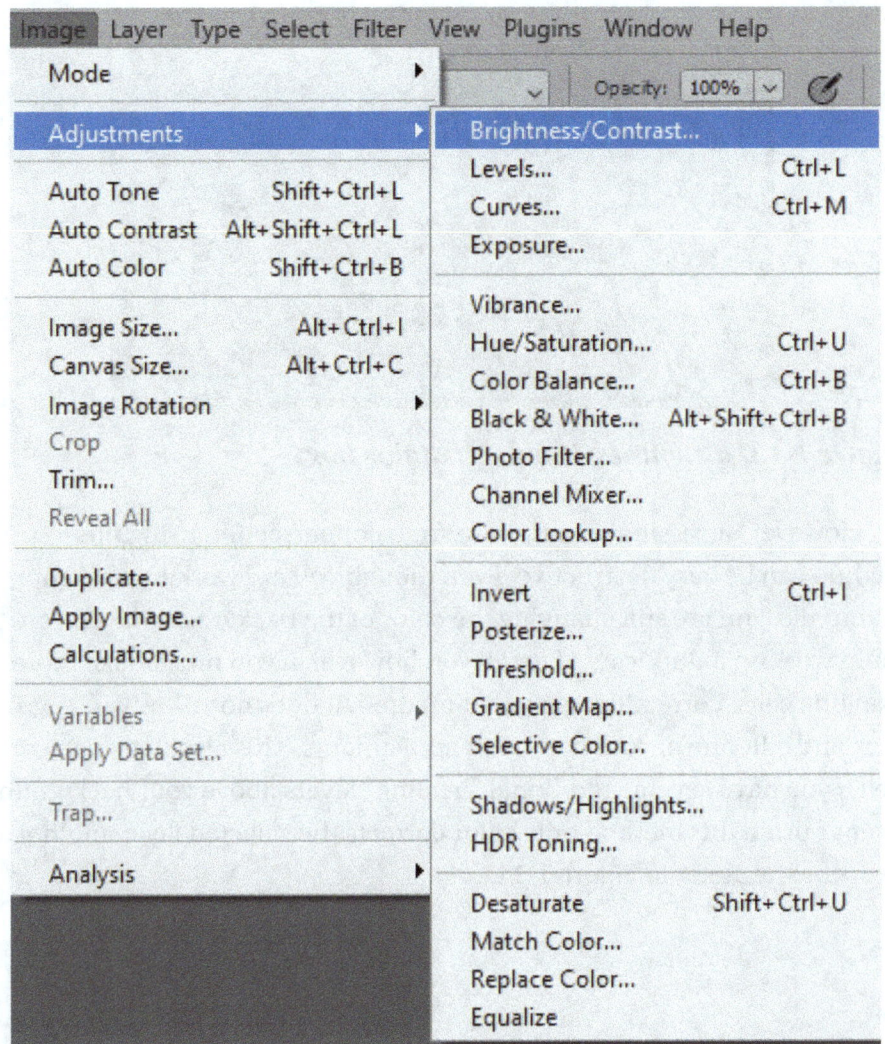

Figure 1-12. *Image ▶ Adjustments submenu*

Then choose an option from the menu like Brightness/Contrast or Levels and begin to use that dialog box to edit while the Preview option is enabled. Refer to Figure 1-13.

CHAPTER 1 ADJUSTMENT LAYERS, BLENDING MODES WITH MASKS FOR PHOTO RESTORATION: PART 1

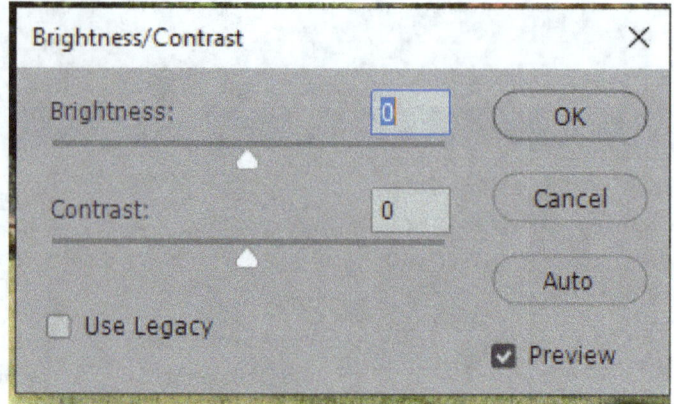

Figure 1-13. *Brightness/Contrast dialog box*

However, accessing your options for color correction using this method can be very destructive. Even though you are working on a copy of your file, you are still changing the color of the background layer. You could work on a duplicate of that layer; however, if you must make more than one color correction using that method, it does not allow you to go back and edit one of your past color adjustments. This also does not work well if you have several additional "healing" layers above your background layer as using this method only color corrects the selected layer and not all layers below. Refer to Figure 1-14.

CHAPTER 1 ADJUSTMENT LAYERS, BLENDING MODES WITH MASKS FOR PHOTO RESTORATION: PART 1

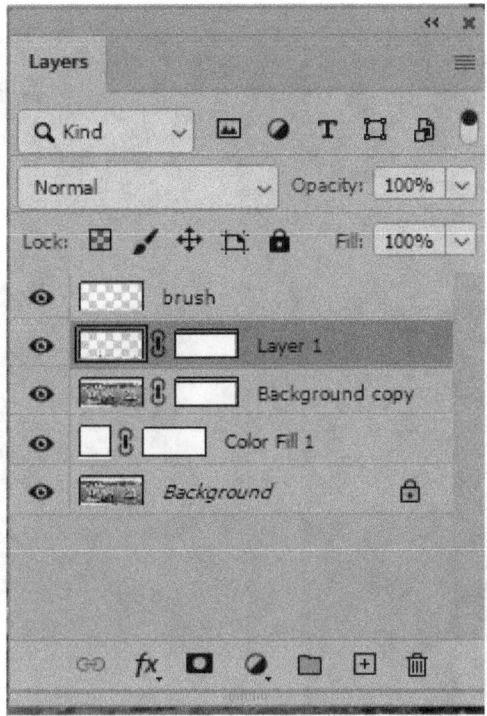

Figure 1-14. *Layers panel with Layer 1 selected*

To do color adjustments in a nondestructive manner, it is a better solution to work above all the current layers. To do that you must access the adjustments from the Layers panel via the fill and adjustment layers button to see the full list. Refer to Figure 1-15.

CHAPTER 1 ADJUSTMENT LAYERS, BLENDING MODES WITH MASKS FOR PHOTO RESTORATION: PART 1

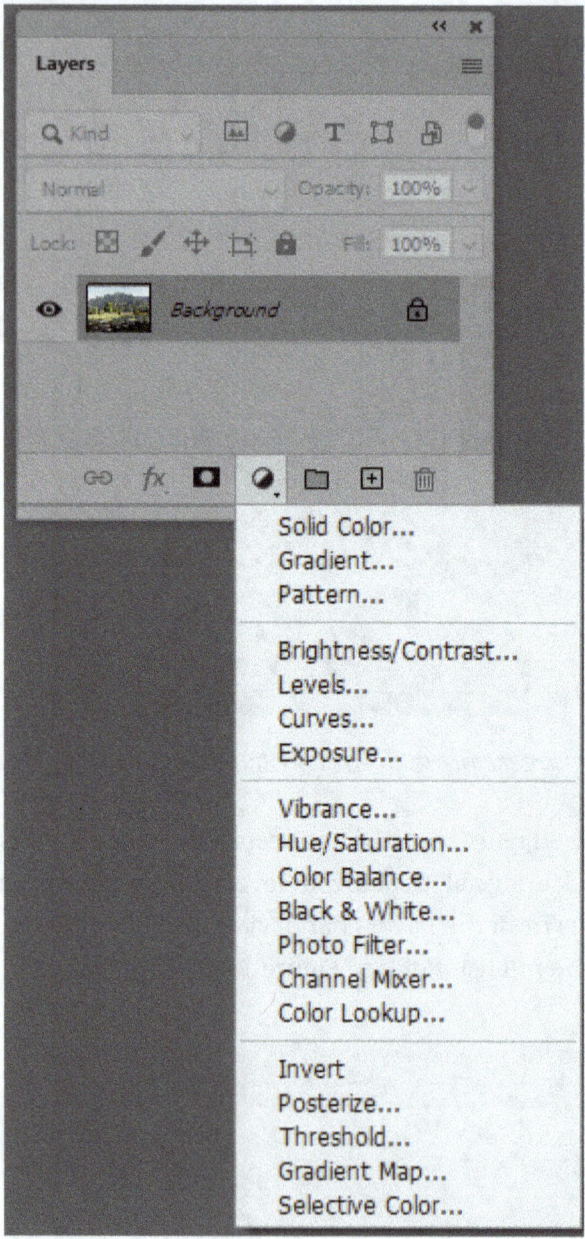

Figure 1-15. *Layers panel with the fill and adjustment layers dropdown list open*

CHAPTER 1   ADJUSTMENT LAYERS, BLENDING MODES WITH MASKS FOR PHOTO RESTORATION: PART 1

Even though doing so may increase the size of your .psd file, in the long term you will be able to adjust your colors at any time by clicking the fill and adjustment layers icon, which we will look at in more detail next along with its masks in the Properties panel. Refer to Figure 1-16.

CHAPTER 1   ADJUSTMENT LAYERS, BLENDING MODES WITH MASKS FOR PHOTO RESTORATION: PART 1

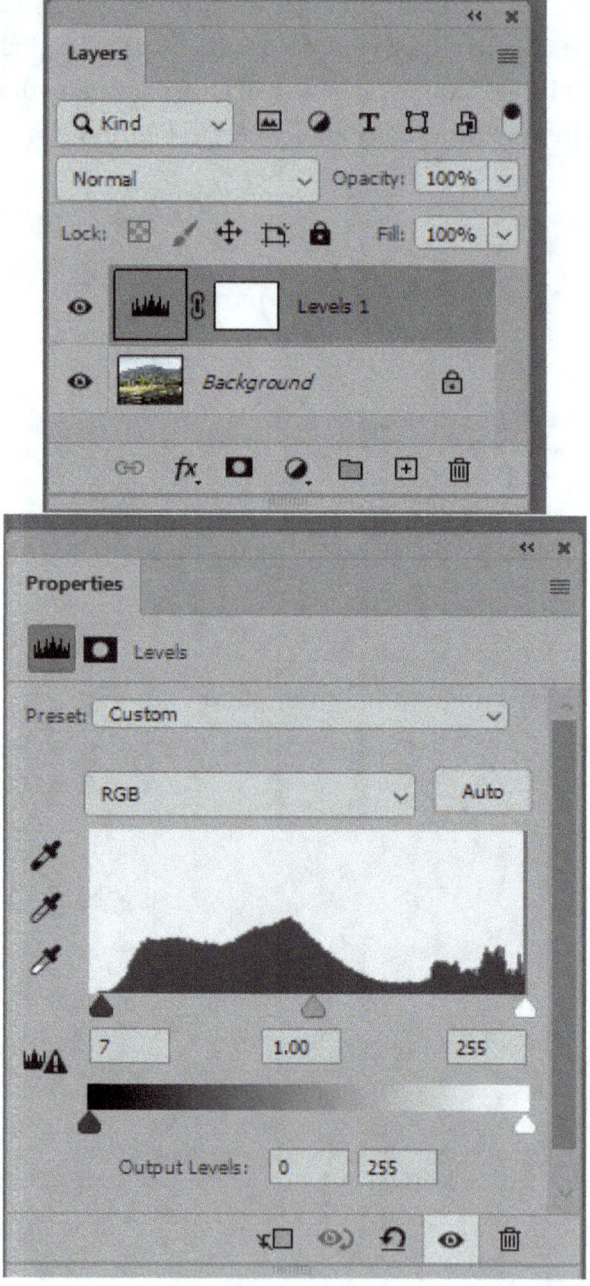

Figure 1-16. Layers panel with an adjustment layer and Properties panel displaying current settings

Note Later in Chapter 2 we will return to the Image ➤ Adjustments menu to discuss a third option so that we can access these same adjustment options and an additional command, while working with smart filters in a nondestructive way.

If you find that when you apply an adjustment layer, it is still below another layer, drag the adjustment layer in the Layers panel upward so that it is above the other normal layers. Refer to Figure 1-16 where the adjustment layer is above the background layer.

Working with the Layers Panel Fill and Adjustment Layers

We will now look at how to use and access the various fill and adjustment layers, which you can apply over your current background layer.

Fill Options

Let's begin with a review of the fill options, one of which you saw in Volume 1, Chapter 6, that was used to give the image a clean white background around the tower image (see **tower_solid_fill.psd**). Refer to Figure 1-17.

CHAPTER 1   ADJUSTMENT LAYERS, BLENDING MODES WITH MASKS FOR PHOTO RESTORATION: PART 1

Figure 1-17. *Layers panel with a Color Fill layer behind a vignette image with a layer mask*

While not found in the Adjustments panel, fill options can be very helpful for certain photo restoration projects. The three options are located in the Layers panel's lower bar in the half-circle icon. They are at the top of the list when you click the button to reveal the entire menu. They are Solid Color, Gradient, and Pattern. Refer to Figure 1-18.

CHAPTER 1 ADJUSTMENT LAYERS, BLENDING MODES WITH MASKS FOR PHOTO RESTORATION: PART 1

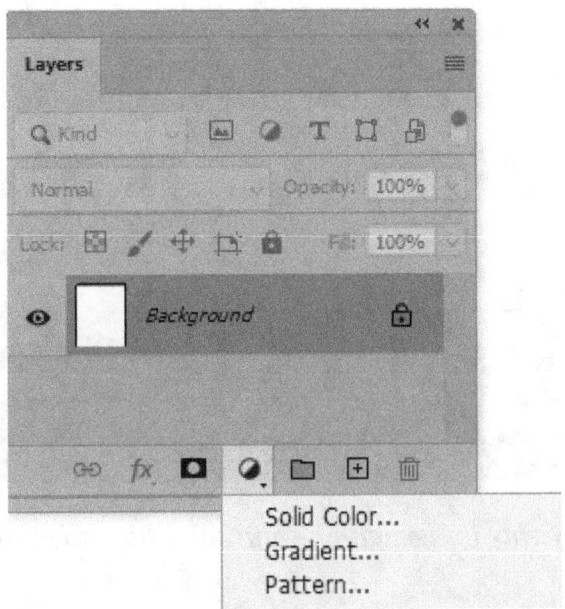

Figure 1-18. *Layers panel with the fill and adjustment layers dropdown list open, just displaying the fills*

Solid Color

Solid Color, also known as Color Fill, is ideal to use after you have completed working with a layer and applying a layer mask to a Layer 0 or a copy of your background. Then you can apply a solid color of white or whatever color you prefer behind your image. This creates a nice background border edge if you plan to frame your image. It is a great way to remove the stains and damage of rips and creases, especially if the original border is not worth restoring (see **army_healing_colorfill.psd**). Refer to Figure 1-19.

CHAPTER 1 ADJUSTMENT LAYERS, BLENDING MODES WITH MASKS FOR PHOTO RESTORATION: PART 1

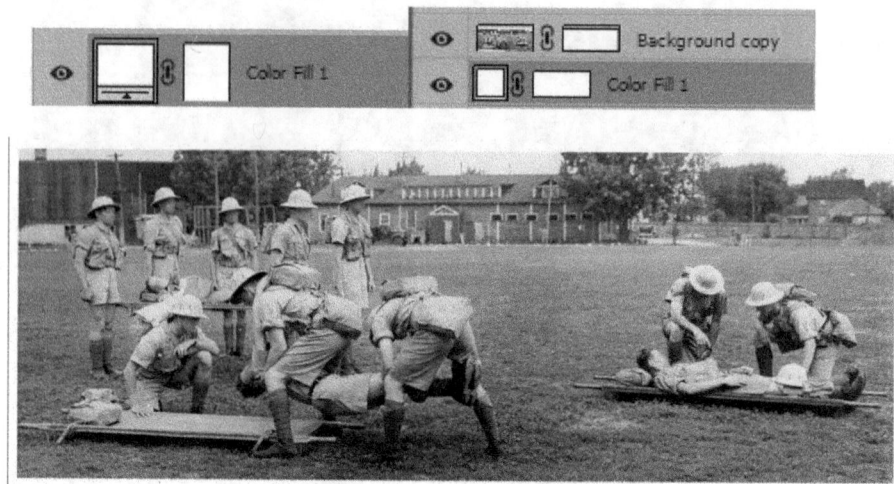

Figure 1-19. *Army image with a solid color fill added to the Layers panel*

Upon making this choice from the Layers panel list, use the color picker to choose a color and click OK. You can work with the color picker area, enter a color in various number settings, or use the eyedropper (Options bar panel) to select a color that may be somewhere in the image. In this example I set a color of white, which is R: 255, G: 255, B: 255. Note that the H or hue ratio button is enabled. Refer to Figure 1-20.

CHAPTER 1   ADJUSTMENT LAYERS, BLENDING MODES WITH MASKS FOR PHOTO RESTORATION: PART 1

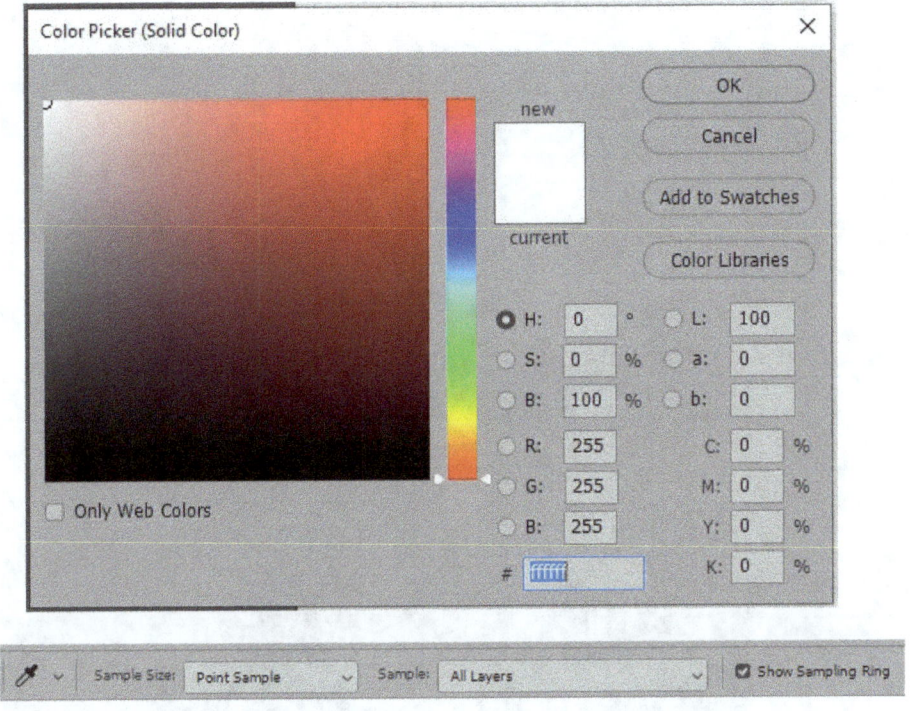

Figure 1-20. Solid Color color picker open with Options bar displaying the Eyedropper Tool

Ideally, in other situations, you may want to place the solid color over a layer to cover areas.

Either way, a layer mask is created so that you can paint on it to remove some of the color and reveal some of the background image. This is ideal when you have an older black-and-white image. In the following example of the **castle_solid_fill.psd**, I created a selection of my sky area as seen in quick mask mode (Q). I then exited quick mask mode and applied a solid color of blue, and this masked out my selection area as seen on the layer. Refer to Figure 1-21.

CHAPTER 1 ADJUSTMENT LAYERS, BLENDING MODES WITH MASKS FOR PHOTO RESTORATION: PART 1

Figure 1-21. *Using the Polygonal Lasso Tool to make a selection of the sky and then fill the selection with a solid color fill*

After you enter the color, in this case I used R: 209, G: 236, and B: 239 to create the blue, click OK, and the selection is automatically masked out. Refer to Figure 1-22.

CHAPTER 1 ADJUSTMENT LAYERS, BLENDING MODES WITH MASKS FOR PHOTO RESTORATION: PART 1

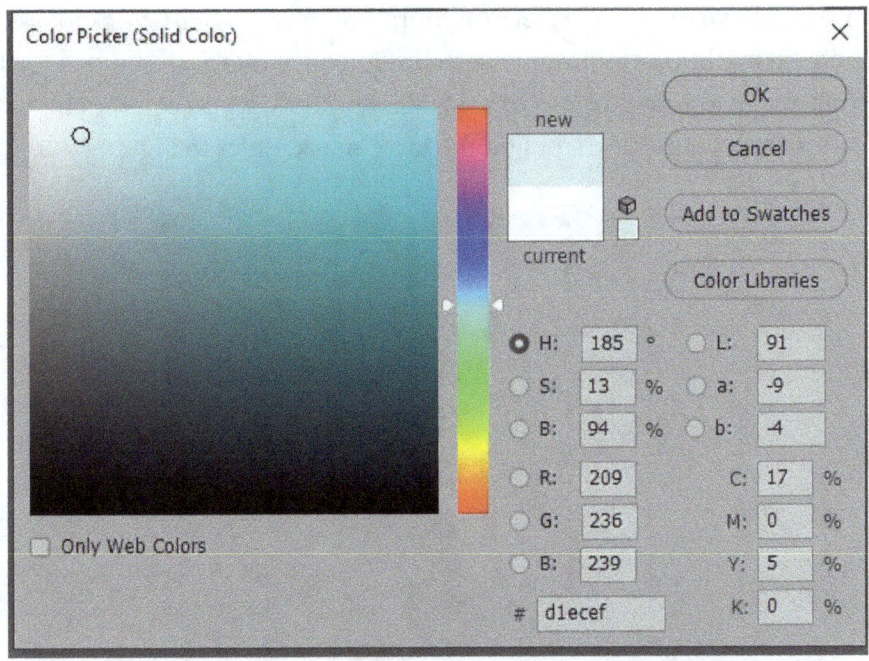

Figure 1-22. *Color picker solid fill dialog box settings and the Color Fill in the Layers panel and on screen*

CHAPTER 1 ADJUSTMENT LAYERS, BLENDING MODES WITH MASKS FOR PHOTO RESTORATION: PART 1

I could have made the selection more accurate while in quick mask mode with my Eraser tool. However, should you want to paint over areas in your image for the purpose of colorizing or tinting, you can touch up the selection with your Eraser tool on the layer mask. Refer to Figure 1-23.

Figure 1-23. *Use your Eraser tool on the layer mask of the Color Fill layer to hide and cover areas by toggling with the swatches Foreground and Background settings in the Tools panel*

CHAPTER 1 ADJUSTMENT LAYERS, BLENDING MODES WITH MASKS FOR PHOTO RESTORATION: PART 1

Remember, as you work with your Eraser with varying brush sizes and hardnesses on the mask, first press the D key to get your default black and white colors and then use the X key to switch between hiding and revealing the mask. You can do this for any fill or adjustment layer.

Tip If you are worried you might have missed covering something with the mask, Alt/Option + click the mask thumbnail on the layer itself to reveal just the mask and you can then, if you zoom in on an area, see if you left any black or white spots and use your Eraser tool to clean up. Refer to Figure 1-24.

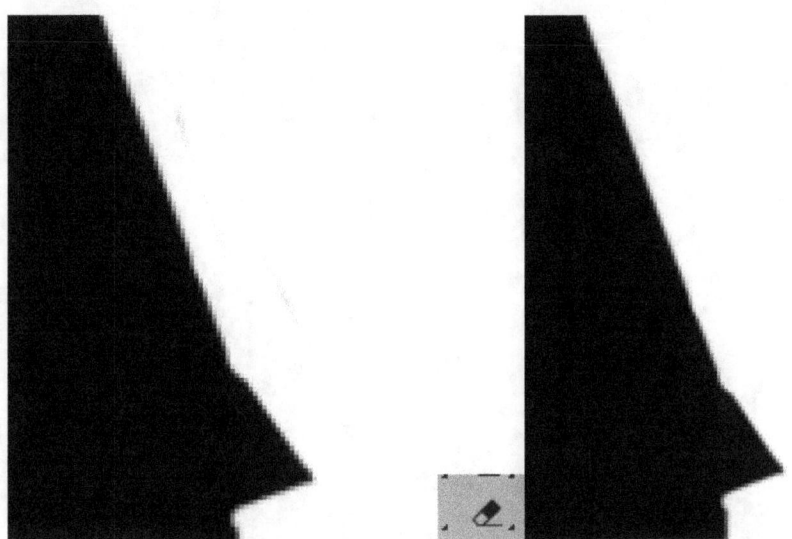

Figure 1-24. *Cleaning up areas of the mask with the Eraser tool*

Alt/Option + click the layer mask again when you want to exit, and you can continue to mask with the solid color visible again.

Likewise, after you finished masking, you can also reduce the opacity of the solid fill layer and change the blending mode if the color is overlaid over the background using Hue. This is a good way to work with solid color if you, for some reason, want to retain some of those background details or keep some of the original look of the image. Refer to Figure 1-25.

CHAPTER 1　ADJUSTMENT LAYERS, BLENDING MODES WITH MASKS FOR PHOTO RESTORATION: PART 1

Figure 1-25. *The Layers panel with Color Fill selected and the blue blending over the background*

CHAPTER 1   ADJUSTMENT LAYERS, BLENDING MODES WITH MASKS FOR PHOTO RESTORATION: PART 1

We will look at blending modes later in Chapter 2. However, I will just note that blending modes and opacity can be applied to any fill or adjustment layer, and they will alter the viewable colors of the underlying background layer.

I could add more solid color layers like a green for grass and some trees if I wanted to continue to colorize this image. In this case, while the layer mask is selected, you can use the command Ctrl/CMD + I to invert the mask if you want to start with the color not covering the layer until you paint. As I add more color, different details often reveal themselves that I can go back to and continue to edit. The color I used was R: 198, G: 229, and B: 211 with blending mode Multiply. Remember to remain on your mask as you erase or paint so that you do not rasterize the layer as you paint. Click Cancel on the warning message and return to the mask. Refer to Figure 1-26.

CHAPTER 1　ADJUSTMENT LAYERS, BLENDING MODES WITH MASKS FOR PHOTO RESTORATION: PART 1

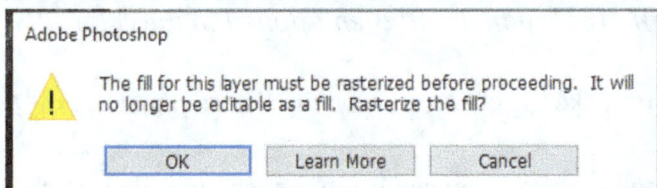

Figure 1-26. *As you work on the fill layers, only paint/erase on the layer mask, or you may get a warning to rasterize the layer*

Solid colors are also found and stored in the Swatches panel. Before you create a solid fill, you can always select one, and it will be stored in the Tools panel, and then create a solid color fill layer and that color will be added to the fill. Click OK to exit. Or when a solid color is active, you can click a swatch and automatically update the color fill without having to enter the color picker. Refer to Figure 1-27.

37

CHAPTER 1 ADJUSTMENT LAYERS, BLENDING MODES WITH MASKS FOR PHOTO RESTORATION: PART 1

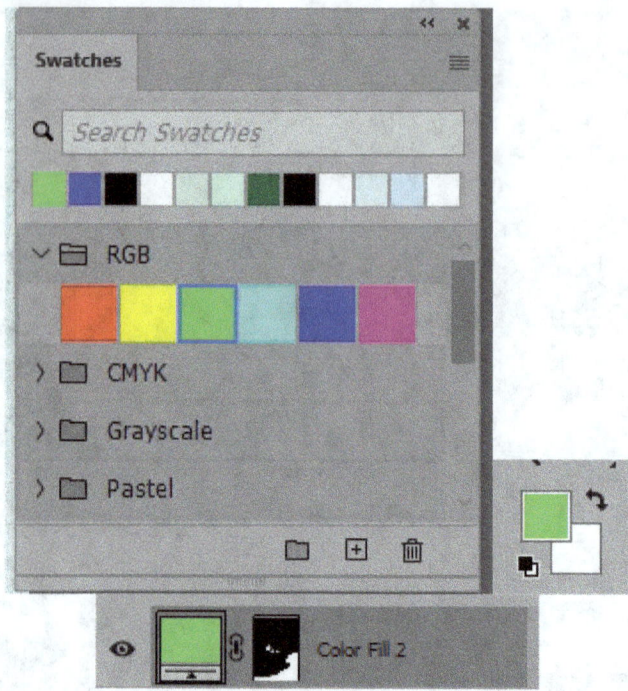

Figure 1-27. *Swatches panel with a swatch applied to the foreground swatch in the Tools panel and then applied to the color fill*

If you don't like the change, use your History panel or Edit ➤ Undo right away.

At any point in time, you can double-click the solid swatch in the Layers panel to adjust it and make a color update in the dialog box. Note that if you see any warning symbols as you work with your colors in the picker, for either out-of-gamut (triangle) or web safe colors (cube), you can ignore the web safe warning if you are planning to print the image and not put online. However, click the out-of-gamut (triangle) warning to ensure that you are using a color that is CMYK compatible. We will discuss gamut more in Chapter 2. Refer to Figure 1-28.

CHAPTER 1 ADJUSTMENT LAYERS, BLENDING MODES WITH MASKS FOR PHOTO RESTORATION: PART 1

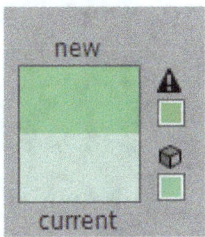

Figure 1-28. *Color picker dialog box warnings for out-of-gamut and web safe colors*

Refer to the file **castle_solid_fill_final.psd** if you want to see the completed work. We will come back to this image and add a bit more color later but in a different way (see "Hue/Saturation"). For now, let's look at the next fill layer.

Gradient

Gradients are good for applying graduated transitional colors or gradient effect. In recent years there have been improvements to the Gradients panel and its related dialog boxes. Refer to Figure 1-29.

CHAPTER 1 ADJUSTMENT LAYERS, BLENDING MODES WITH MASKS FOR PHOTO RESTORATION: PART 1

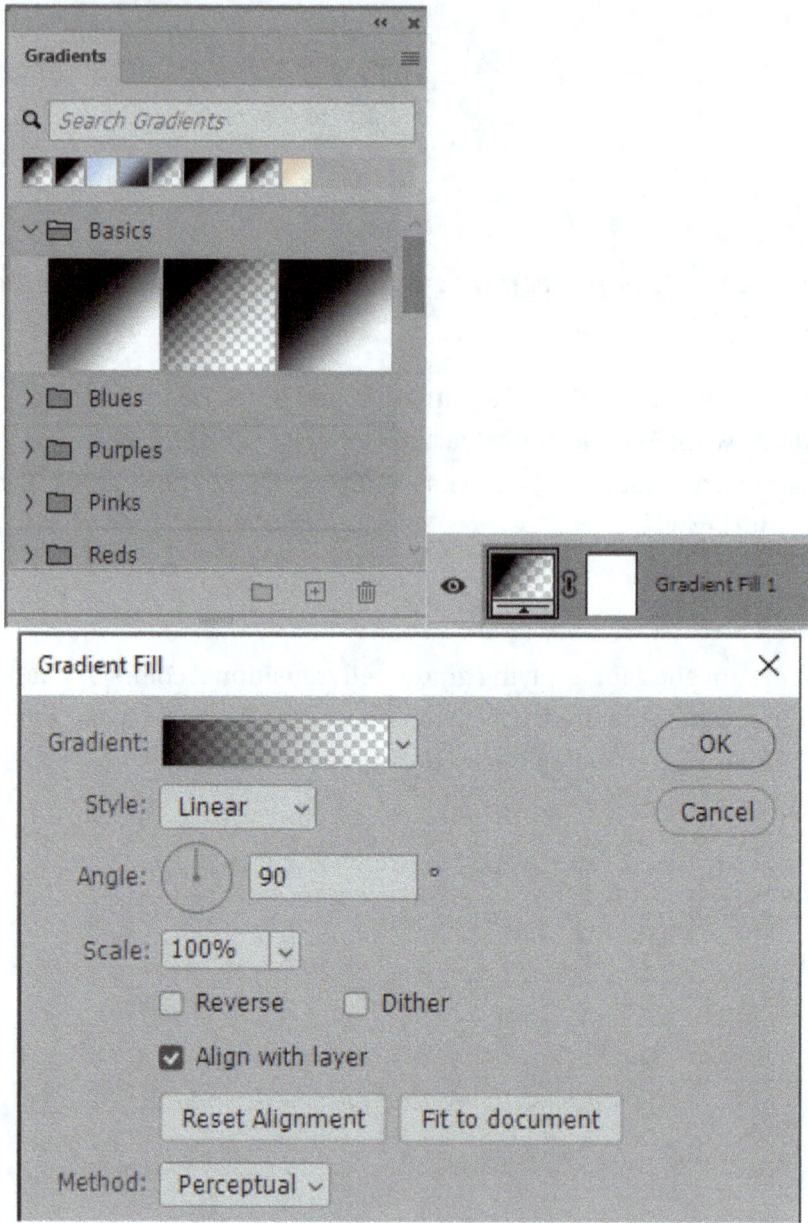

Figure 1-29. *Gradients panel, Gradient Fill layer, and its related dialog box*

CHAPTER 1 ADJUSTMENT LAYERS, BLENDING MODES WITH MASKS FOR PHOTO RESTORATION: PART 1

Now you can also use your Gradient Tool and a live annotation tool to create more accurate live gradients. The annotation tool can be dragged on the canvas to get a more accurate angle. Refer to Figure 1-30.

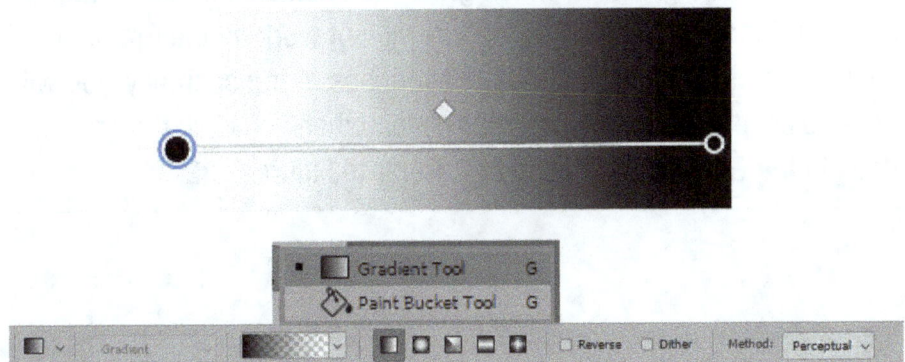

Figure 1-30. *Gradient annotator on the screen, Gradient Tool, and the Options bar panel settings*

The Gradient Tool without the annotator can also be used on the layer mask for creating vignettes on the layer mask. However, we will be looking at an easier way to accomplish this later in Chapter 2 when we review the Properties panel. Refer to Figure 1-31.

Figure 1-31. *Layer mask with a gradient applied*

Note that to see additional gradient options in the Options bar panel, you need to be on either a layer mask or normal layer, and you can switch to classic gradient, which gives the additional transparency and blend mode settings. This option will not work on the Gradient Fill layer itself; instead, for additional options of transparency, you will need to access the Gradient Editor dialog when you click the gradient itself in the Gradient Fill dialog box. Refer to Figure 1-32.

CHAPTER 1 ADJUSTMENT LAYERS, BLENDING MODES WITH MASKS FOR PHOTO RESTORATION: PART 1

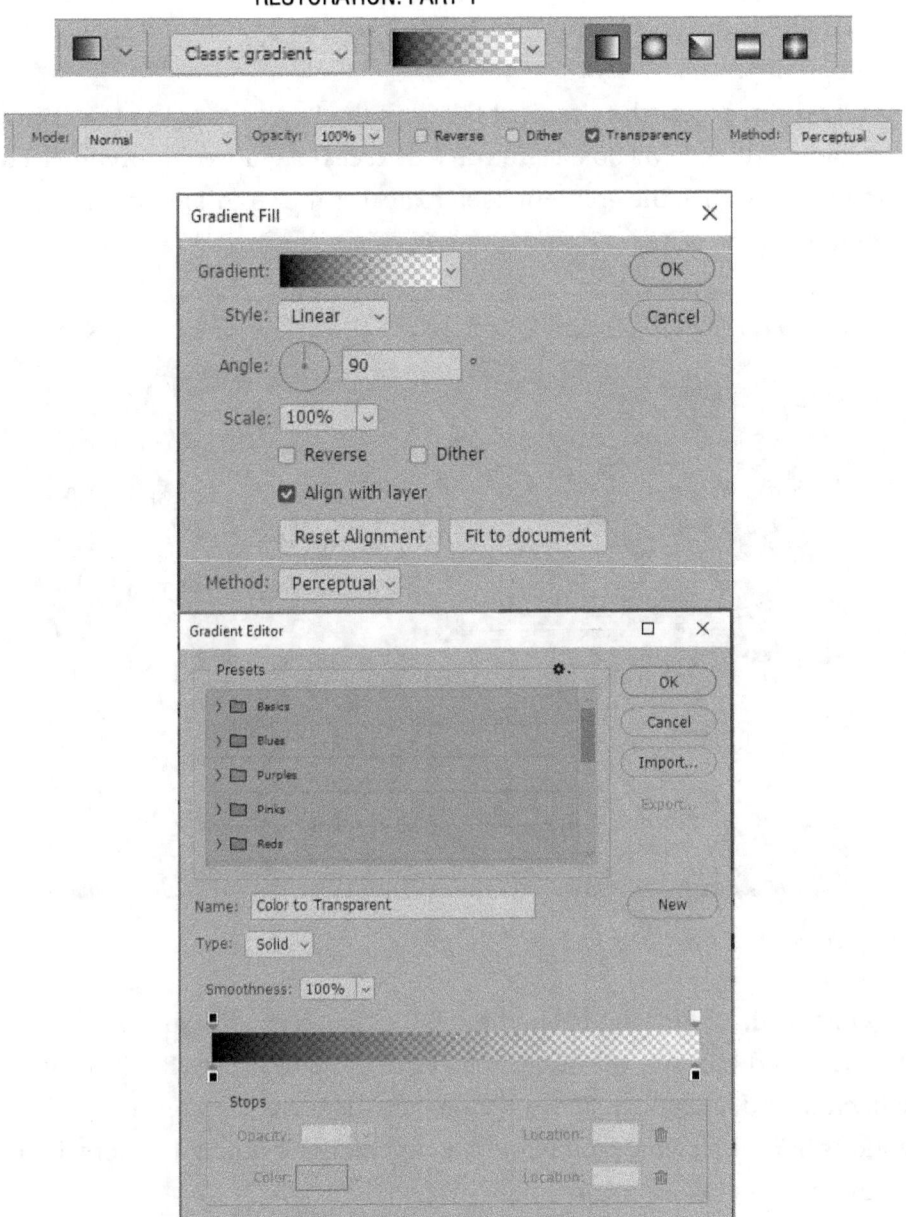

Figure 1-32. *Gradient Tool Options bar panel for classic gradient, Gradient Fill, and Gradient Editor dialog boxes*

CHAPTER 1 ADJUSTMENT LAYERS, BLENDING MODES WITH MASKS FOR PHOTO RESTORATION: PART 1

Later in this chapter, you will also see a related adjustment layer called Gradient Map.

When you access the Gradient Fill from the Layers panel, you will enter the Gradient Fill dialog box. Here you can access a gradient from the list or, as mentioned, click the gradient itself to access the Gradient Editor. Refer to Figure 1-33.

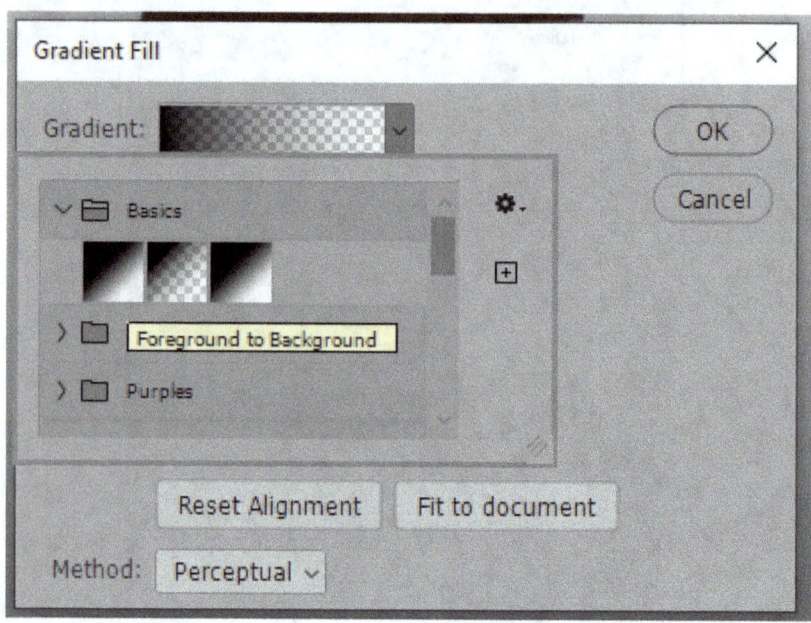

Figure 1-33. Gradient Fill dialog box

Outside the editor in the Gradient Fill dialog box, you can also choose a gradient style or shape, which can include Linear, Radial, Angle, Reflected, and Diamond. These options are displayed as icons in the Options bar menu when you later need to edit the gradient further with the Gradient Tool. Refer to Figure 1-34.

CHAPTER 1   ADJUSTMENT LAYERS, BLENDING MODES WITH MASKS FOR PHOTO RESTORATION: PART 1

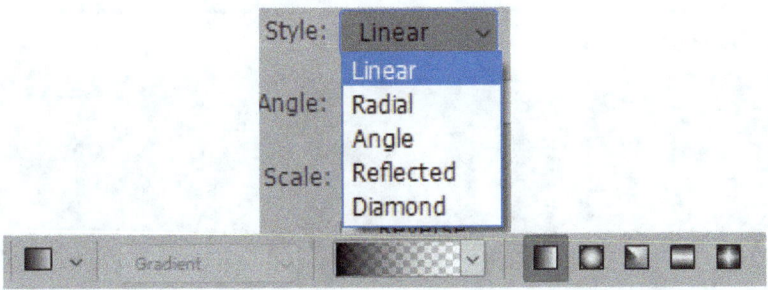

Figure 1-34. *Gradient Fill dialog box settings in the menu are the same as the icons on the Gradient Tool Options bar menu*

You can also adjust the

- Angle (-180°, 0°, 180°)
- Scale (1-1000%), to alter the size
- Reverse, to flip the gradient colors' order
- Dither, to smooth the gradient and make it appear not chopped up or banded
- Align with layer check box
- Reset Alignment button, for gradient
- Fit to document button

You can also set a method from the list choose (Perceptual, Linear, Classic, Smooth, Stripes). Refer to Figure 1-35.

CHAPTER 1   ADJUSTMENT LAYERS, BLENDING MODES WITH MASKS FOR PHOTO RESTORATION: PART 1

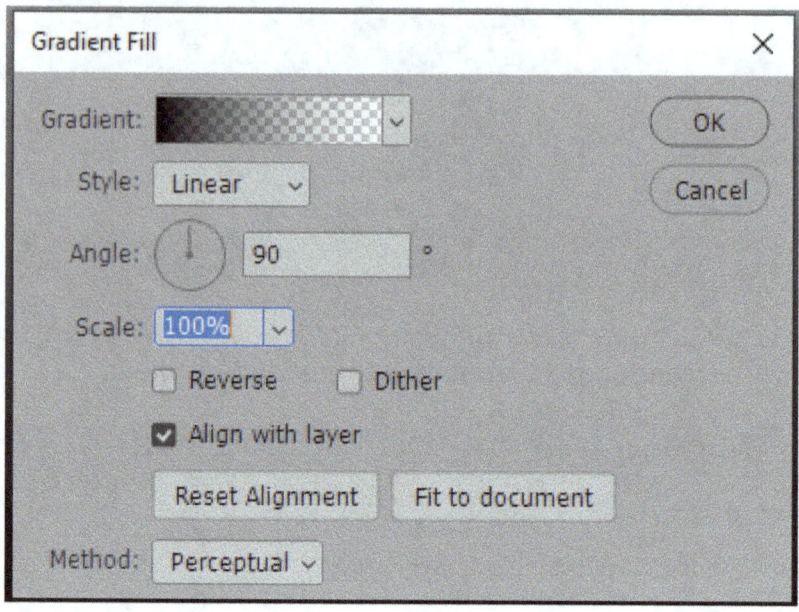

Figure 1-35. Gradient Fill dialog box with settings

A gradient interpolation method describes how the gradient colors will appear on canvas and transition from one color to the next. By default, it is set to Perceptual, which is often considered a good option for natural-looking gradients that would be perceived by the human eye. However, some artists may like a similar method like Linear, though this can give a banding, so Smooth may be a better choice, or the traditional way that Adobe used to interpolate gradients known as Classic. Stripes gives very banded gradients and is better for artistic effects.

More details on what a gradient interpolation method is can be found at the following link:

https://helpx.adobe.com/photoshop/using/gradient-interpolation.html

While the Gradient Fill dialog box is open, you can move the gradient around as mentioned in the Options bar panel. Refer to Figure 1-36.

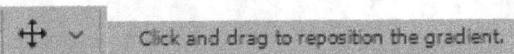

Figure 1-36. *Move tool in the Options bar panel when the Gradient Fill dialog box is active*

Gradient Editor

Creating a custom gradient using the Gradient Editor will let you choose from various presets found in the Gradients panel. Use the gear icon to adjust the viewing of the list. Refer to Figure 1-37.

CHAPTER 1 ADJUSTMENT LAYERS, BLENDING MODES WITH MASKS FOR PHOTO RESTORATION: PART 1

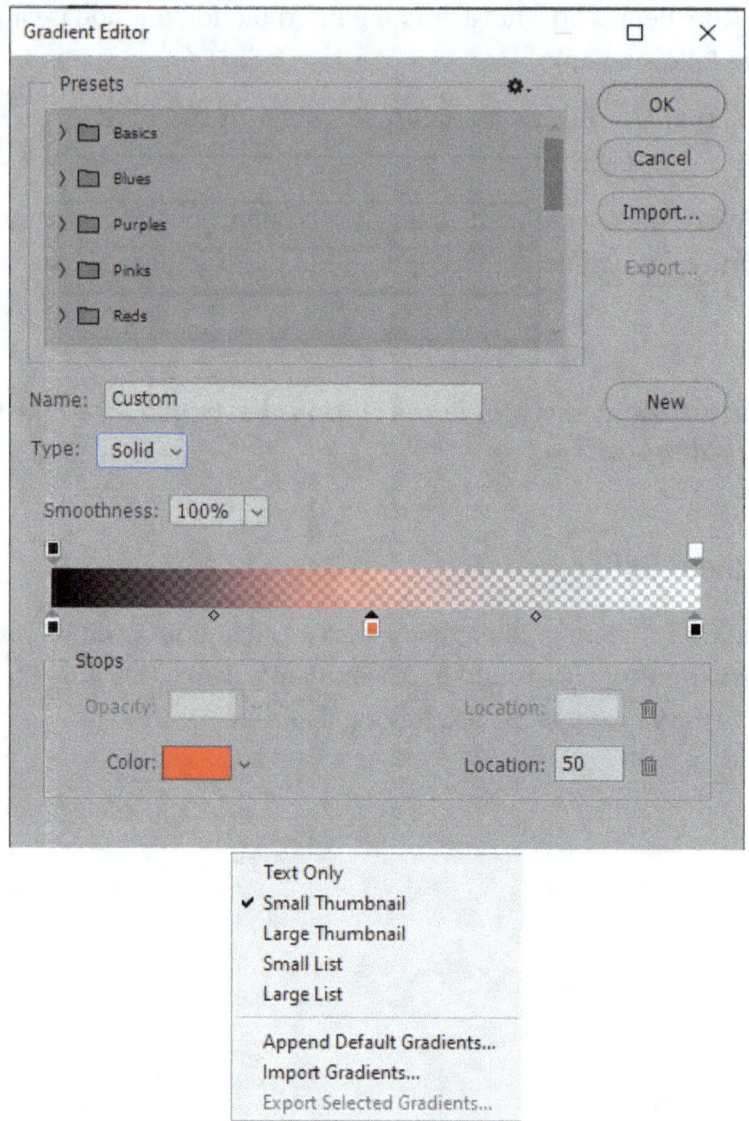

Figure 1-37. Gradient Editor dialog box and settings

You can then give the gradient a new name.

Set the type (Solid or Noise). Solid is the default smooth transition, while Noise can be used for more artistic design as it is very banded and has random bar patterns.

For a Solid type of gradient, set smoothness (0–100%) and stops with different opacity, color, and location.

For Type: Noise you would then adjust the roughness (0–100%) down to a number closer to 0% for a smoother appearance. You can then adjust the color range in various color model choices (RGB, HSB, and LAB) using the black and white sliders to adjust shadows and highlights. Other options allow you to restrict colors, add transparency, and randomize. Refer to Figure 1-38.

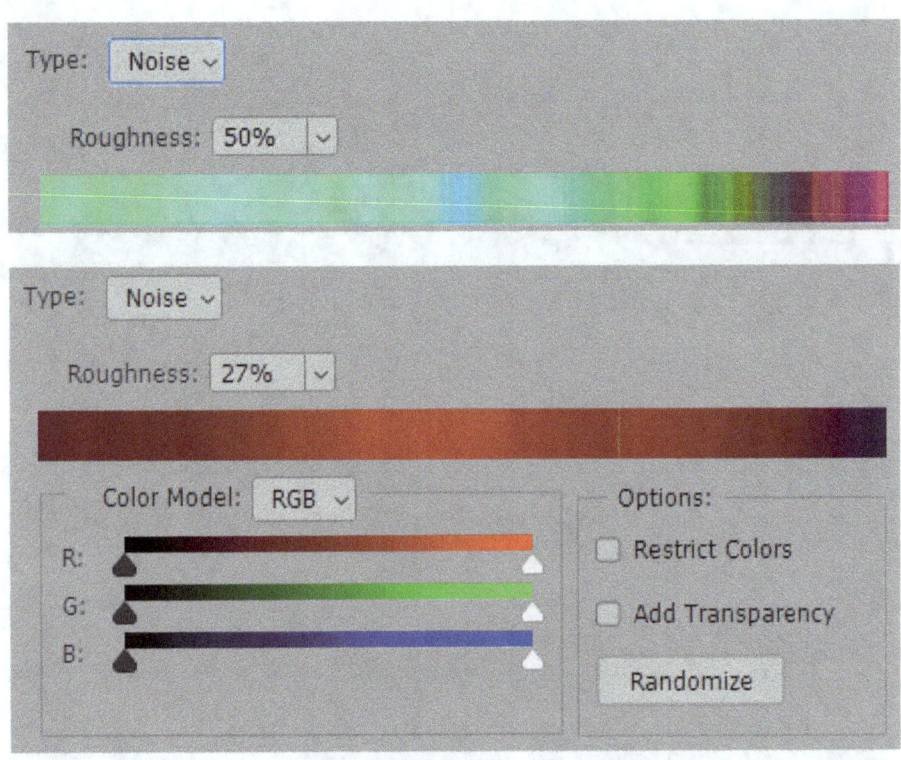

Figure 1-38. *Gradient Editor dialog box settings for Noise gradient*

Return to Type: Solid and note the slider stops above the gradient bar control. Each stop has different opacity (0–100%) where black is 100% and white is 0%. Between each slider is a diamond-shaped opacity midpoint, and both these sliders can be adjusted by dragging, or in the Stops area while selected, set the opacity and location. When a certain stop is not selected those areas are inactive in the dialog box. The bottom sliders are the color stops, which can be double-clicked to enter the color picker. Between these are diamond-shaped color midpoints. These can be dragged, or in the Stops area, while selected, you can set the color and location. To remove an opacity or color stop, you can either drag it off the bar or, while selected, click the trash can icon. Refer to Figure 1-39.

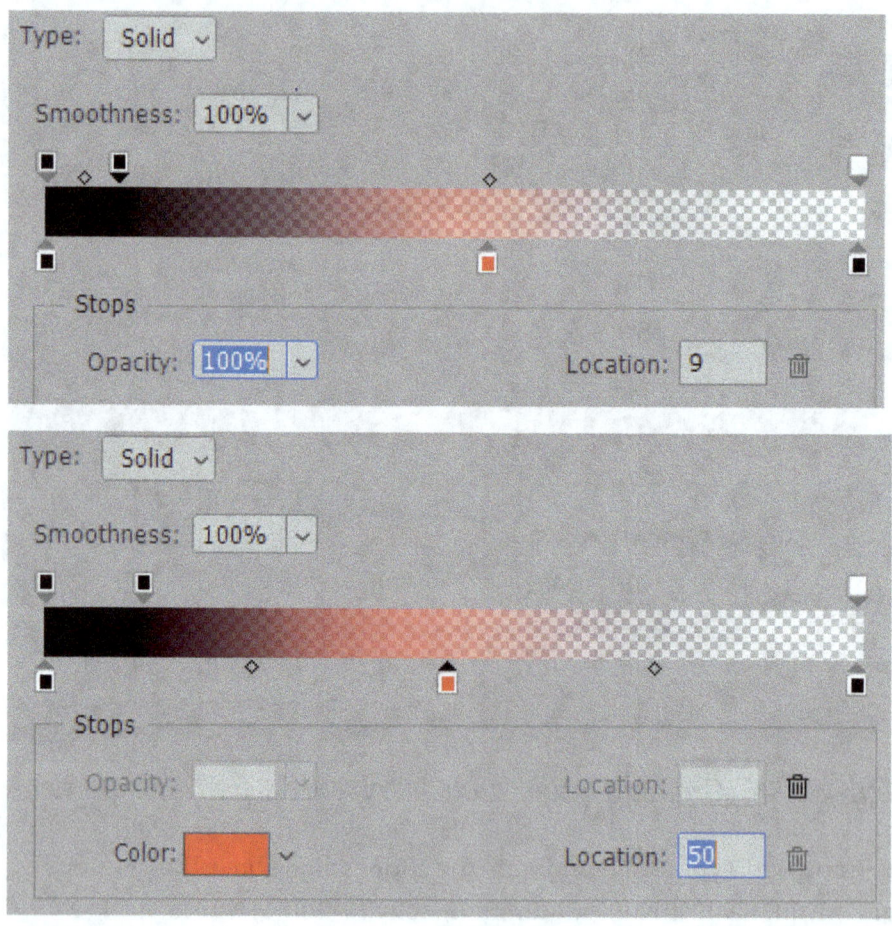

Figure 1-39. Gradient Editor dialog box settings for Solid gradient

CHAPTER 1 ADJUSTMENT LAYERS, BLENDING MODES WITH MASKS FOR PHOTO RESTORATION: PART 1

Gradients can also be imported and exported as (.GRD) files.

Then click OK to exit this dialog box and return to the Gradient Fill dialog box. Then click OK to commit the gradient. Refer to Figure 1-40.

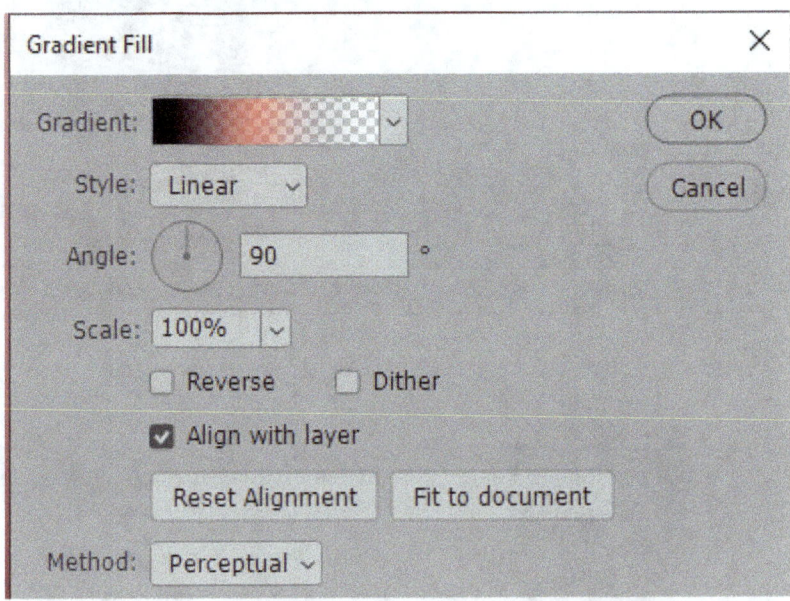

Figure 1-40. *Gradient Fill dialog box showing the gradient options*

Here you can see how this red gradient with transparency could be placed above or below a framed layer mask, affecting the way the image appears. Refer to Figure 1-41.

CHAPTER 1 ADJUSTMENT LAYERS, BLENDING MODES WITH MASKS FOR PHOTO RESTORATION: PART 1

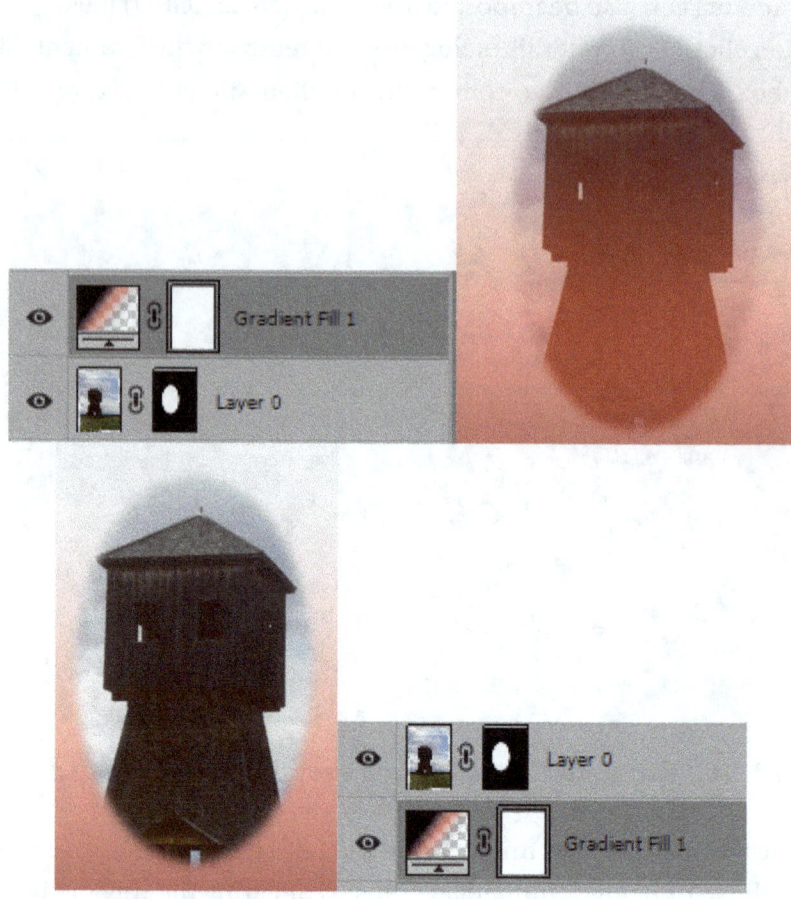

Figure 1-41. *Layer settings for Gradient Fill and how it appears above and below the image*

Gradient Tool and Properties Panel

While outside of the dialog box but while the Gradient Fill layer is selected, you can use the Gradient Tool and move the annotation sliders (gradient on canvas widget) on the board. At the same time you can access the Properties panel to control the gradient adjustments in more detail than

CHAPTER 1 ADJUSTMENT LAYERS, BLENDING MODES WITH MASKS FOR PHOTO RESTORATION: PART 1

using just the options found in the Gradient Editor, with a set of gradient and opacity controls. Quick Actions will allow you to reset the canvas controls and save a preset. Refer to Figure 1-42.

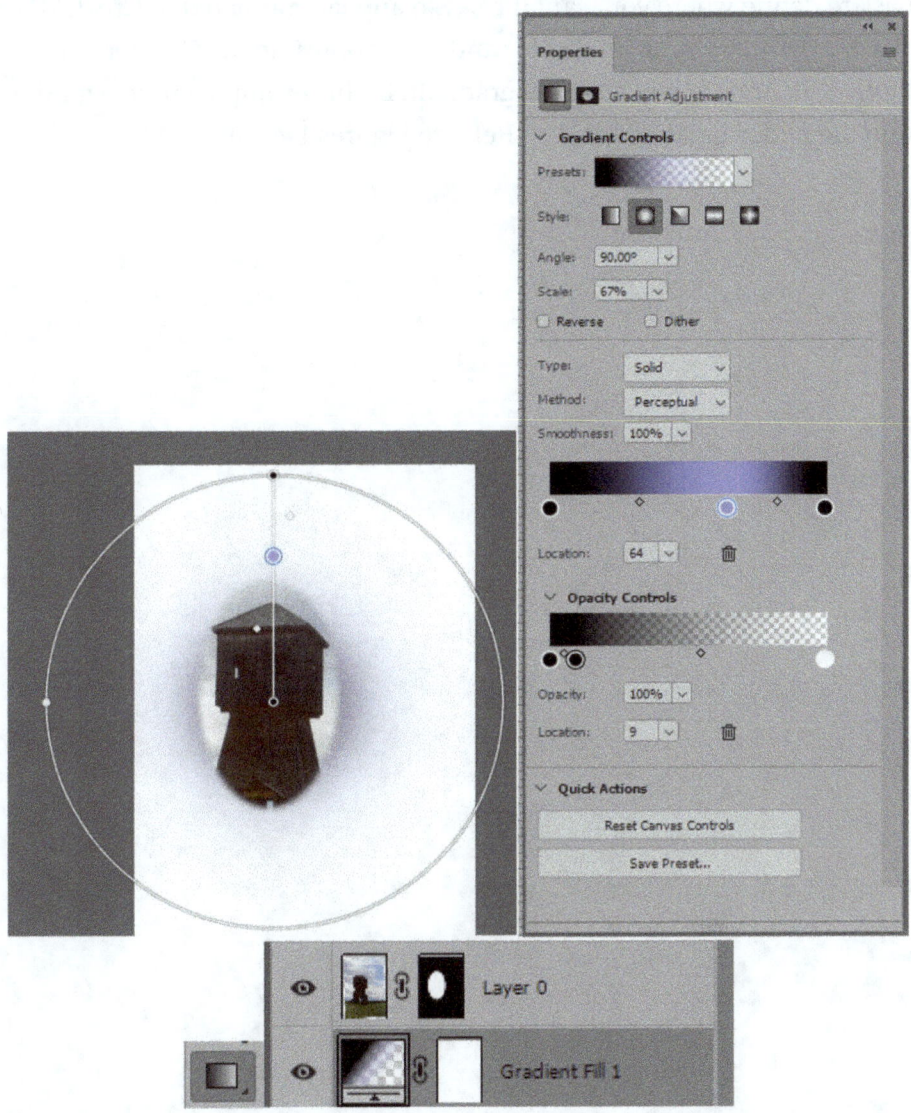

Figure 1-42. *Use the Gradient Tool annotator on canvas and the Properties panel while the Gradient Fill is active to edit the gradient*

Gradients can also be ideal for black-and-white images or even as basic skies when you do not want to incorporate clouds as you did in Volume 1, Chapter 8, with the sky replacement tool. You can again paint on your layer mask to define where you want the sky to appear graduated or Ctrl/CMD + click a mask from your solid color and then apply it to the Gradient Fill to duplicate it and then reverse the gradient. In this example I used a gradient from the folder Blues, "blue_02." Refer to Figures 1-43 and 1-44.

CHAPTER 1 ADJUSTMENT LAYERS, BLENDING MODES WITH MASKS FOR PHOTO RESTORATION: PART 1

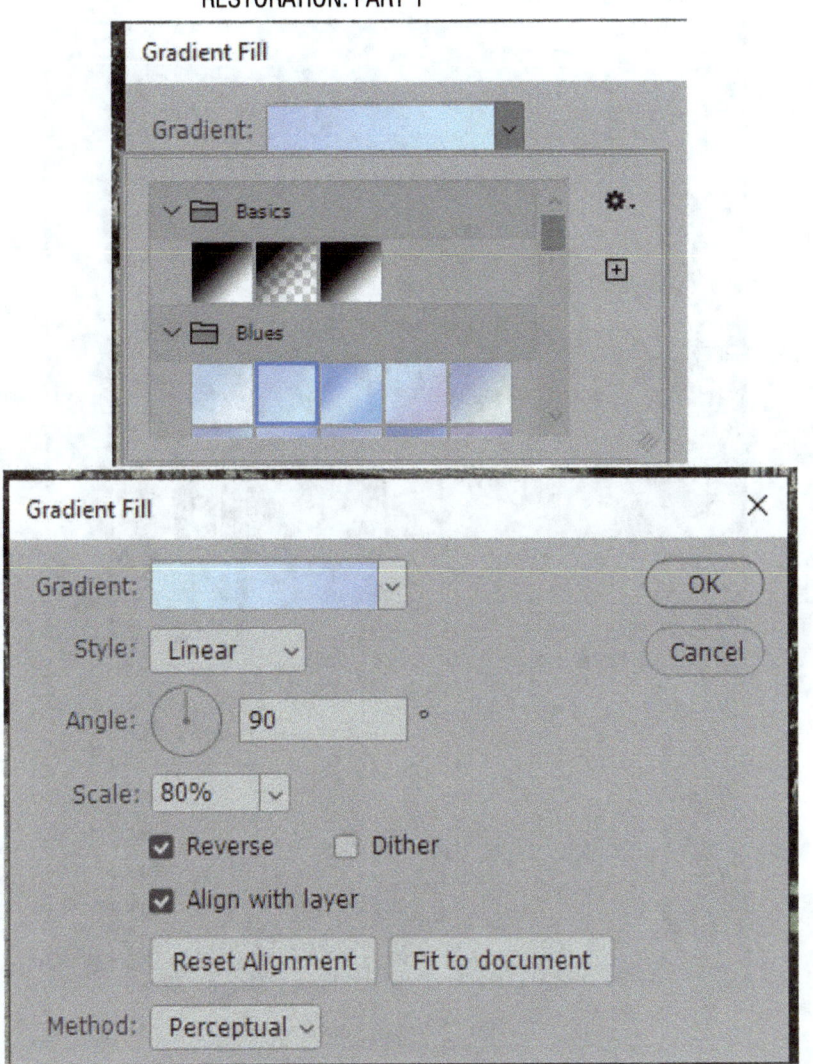

Figure 1-43. *Gradient Fill dialog box settings*

CHAPTER 1 ADJUSTMENT LAYERS, BLENDING MODES WITH MASKS FOR PHOTO RESTORATION: PART 1

Figure 1-44. *Gradient Fill applied to the sky area using a layer mask*

56

In this case I left the gradient at the Normal blend mode of 100% opacity to cover any artifacts in the sky. Refer to the files **castle_solid_fill_final.psd** and **tower_gradientfill.psd** for reference.

Pattern

Pattern is the third fill option, which you can use to fill an area, found in the Patterns panel. Refer to Figure 1-45.

Figure 1-45. *Patterns panel*

While not required for this book, it should be noted that you can create your own patterns in a variety of ways, which I mentioned in my book found in this chapter's introduction. Knowing how to do this is not

57

required for working in this book. However, for now, experiment with the patterns found in this panel using the Pattern Fill dialog box and the fill layer that is created. Refer to Figure 1-46.

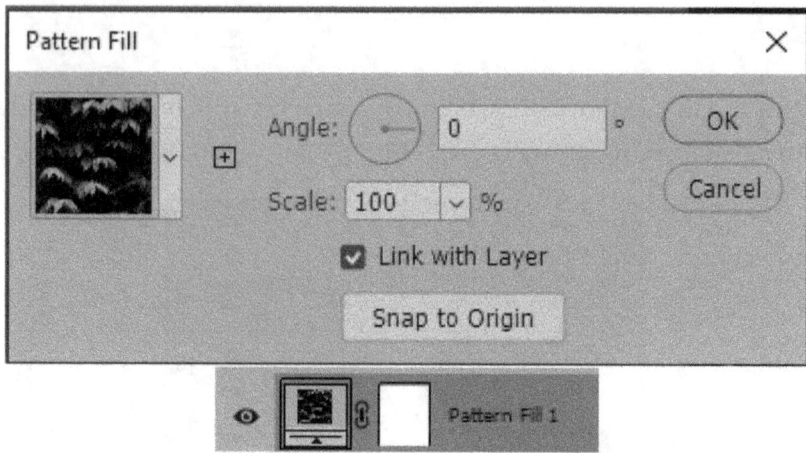

Figure 1-46. Pattern Fill dialog box and Pattern Fill layer

In the dialog box you can choose the pattern from the list, which is found in the Patterns panel. You can then set the angle (-180°, 0°, 180°) and scale (1-1000%), enable Link with Layer, and click the Snap to Origin button. The pattern can be moved while the dialog box is open, as mentioned in the Options bar panel. Refer to Figure 1-47.

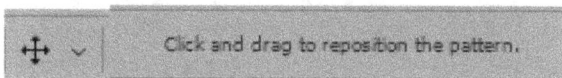

Figure 1-47. While the Pattern Fill dialog box is open, you have access to the Move tool in the Options bar panel

Click OK to commit your pattern. You can double-click the pattern icon thumbnail in the Layers panel at any time to edit it further.

Patterns, just like the solid fill or gradient, are ideal for creative borders when a layer mask is created or the pattern is placed behind the image. However, patterns could also be used for filling in gaps in an image where a wallpaper, stone, or even a wood pattern may add additional color and texture to an otherwise blank area. For example, in Volume 1, Chapter 3, recall the room where we edited the floor with our healing tools. If you wanted the glare of the floor to be even more faded, you could add a wood pattern, which would subtly add a bit of detail but still retain the natural reflection. Wood pattern is found in the Legacy Patterns and More ➤ 2019 Pattern folder ➤ Wood and could be used to add more texture to the floor and then brushed with a soft Eraser tool brush to feather the layer mask. Refer to Figure 1-48.

CHAPTER 1   ADJUSTMENT LAYERS, BLENDING MODES WITH MASKS FOR PHOTO RESTORATION: PART 1

Figure 1-48. *Multiple pattern fills in the Layers panel can be duplicated and modified and have their opacity reduced to blend more detail in the floor*

Because the floor, however, moves at slightly different angles of perspective, you may need to use several pattern fills set to various angles and scales to adjust. While in the dialog box you can also move the pattern if you need it to align better with the surrounding grains. I then lowered the opacity of the fill between 43% and 82% of the fill and set the blending mode to Overlay. Refer to Figure 1-48 and Figure 1-49.

CHAPTER 1 ADJUSTMENT LAYERS, BLENDING MODES WITH MASKS FOR PHOTO RESTORATION: PART 1

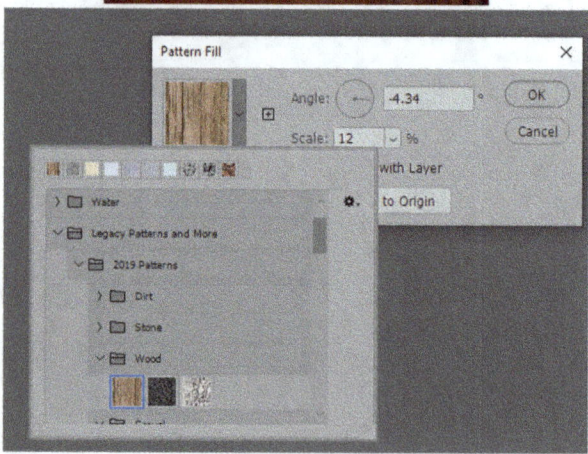

Figure 1-49. *A wood pattern chosen from the Pattern Fill dialog box for better blending*

You can move your Pattern Fill and mask together with the Move tool. To make a copy of the current fill, drag it over the Layers panel, click the Create a new layer button, and release to make a copy. Refer to Figure 1-48.

Refer to my file **big_room_healing_brush_pattern_fill.psd** to review my settings.

Later in Chapter 4, I will mention a new type of pattern option, which is also considered a filter.

Layer Adjustments

The next section of your fill and adjustment layers button in the Layers panel are the layer adjustments. There are 16 available. Refer to Figure 1-50.

CHAPTER 1 ADJUSTMENT LAYERS, BLENDING MODES WITH MASKS FOR PHOTO RESTORATION: PART 1

Figure 1-50. Layers panel fill and adjustments layers with all adjustments revealed

They are Brightness/Contrast, Levels, Curves, Exposure, Vibrance, Hue/Saturation, Color Balance, Black & White, Photo Filter, Channel Mixer, Color Lookup, Invert, Posterize, Threshold, Gradient Map, and Selective Color, which I will be describing next.

These adjustments apply the layer with a mask, and more can be added with the newly updated (see Modern view) Adjustments panel. Refer to Figure 1-51.

CHAPTER 1   ADJUSTMENT LAYERS, BLENDING MODES WITH MASKS FOR PHOTO RESTORATION: PART 1

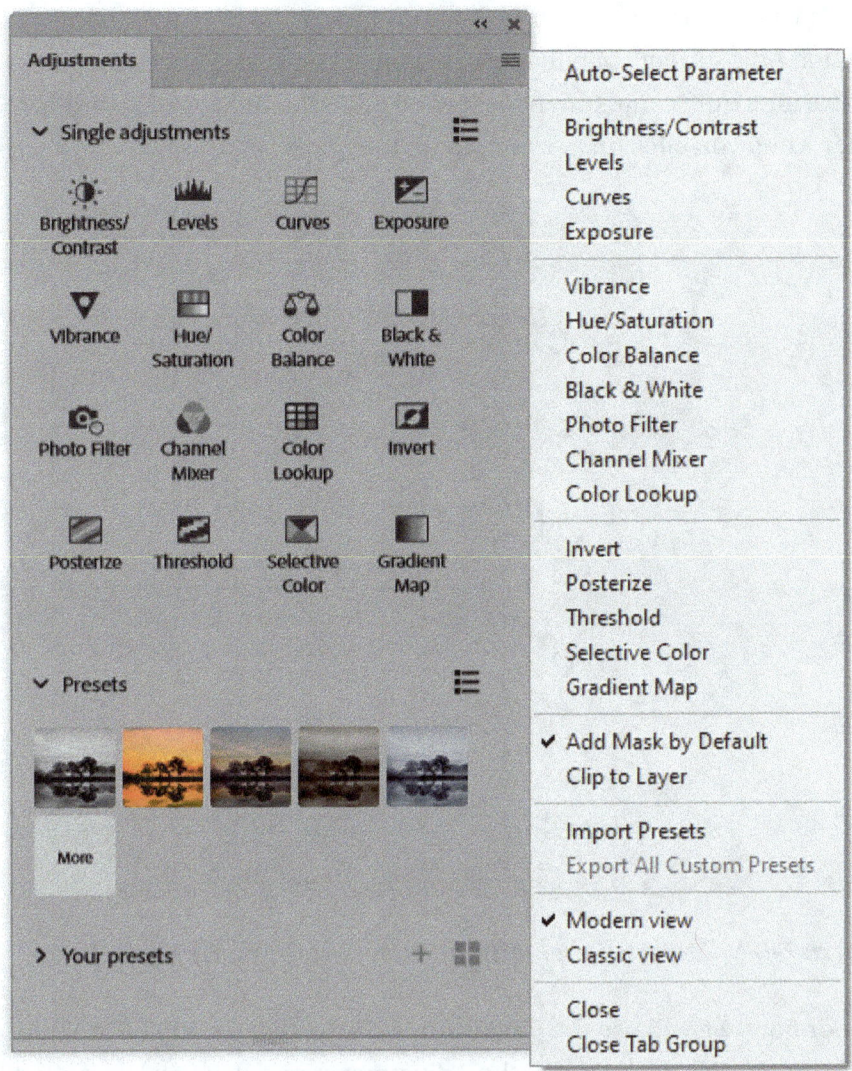

Figure 1-51. *Adjustments panel and options in the menu*

CHAPTER 1 ADJUSTMENT LAYERS, BLENDING MODES WITH MASKS FOR PHOTO
         RESTORATION: PART 1

We will now explore each of these options. I will note that in the updated Adjustments panel, you can choose to use the Adjustments presets for a quick adjustment of several adjustment layers in a group folder when you click on a preset. Refer to Figure 1-52.

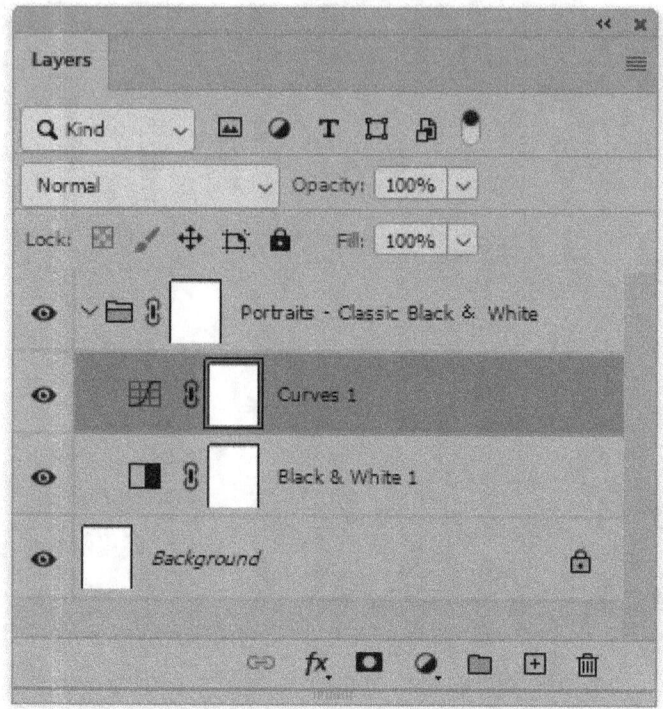

Figure 1-52. *Layers panel with adjustment layers applied*

For now, we will use the Single adjustments that we will be looking at next. As you click each icon in the Adjustments panel, it will be applied to the Layers panel. When you click the eye, you can turn that adjustment layer's visibility on or off as you work. Refer to Figure 1-53.

CHAPTER 1   ADJUSTMENT LAYERS, BLENDING MODES WITH MASKS FOR PHOTO RESTORATION: PART 1

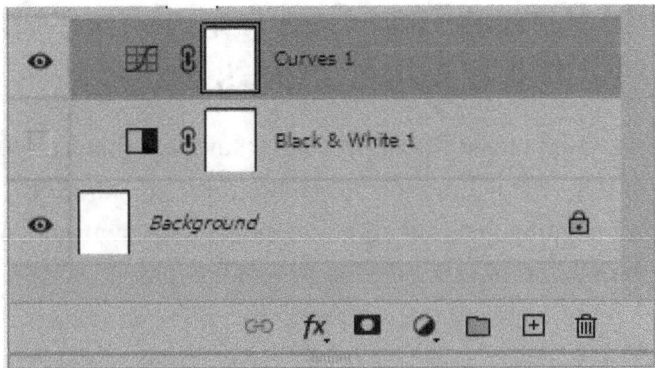

Figure 1-53. Layers panel with adjustment layers applied, one of which has the visibility eye turned off

Note that as you work through the book and gain skills, you will be able to create your own collection of custom presets, and you now have the option of storing these in the Adjustments panel as your presets. You can view your presets either as a list or icons. I will explain this more at the end of the chapter along with a link to information on the recently added Adjustment Brush Tool. Refer to Figure 1-54.

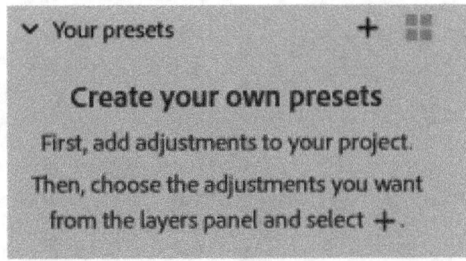

Figure 1-54. Adjustments panel now lets you create and store your custom presets

CHAPTER 1   ADJUSTMENT LAYERS, BLENDING MODES WITH MASKS FOR PHOTO RESTORATION: PART 1

Additional Panels That Can Assist You While Working with the Adjustments Panel

While working with your adjustment layers, several other helpful panels you may want to have visible are your Histogram, Info, and Properties panels as you inspect your images. You can use your own images or the **faded_image.psd** and **balanced_image.psd** if you need to follow along.

Histogram Panel

The Window ▶ Histogram panel is used for giving us an overview of how the channels are being affected. This will make more sense when we start looking at the adjustment layers. You can switch from Compact View to Expanded View or All Channels View using the panel's menu. This example shows Compact View, and I have clicked the Uncached Refresh option in the menu so that I can see the current histogram. Doing so in no way will alter the image, and clicking the cache data warning icon or refresh icon as you work will keep the histogram up to date. Refer to Figure 1-55.

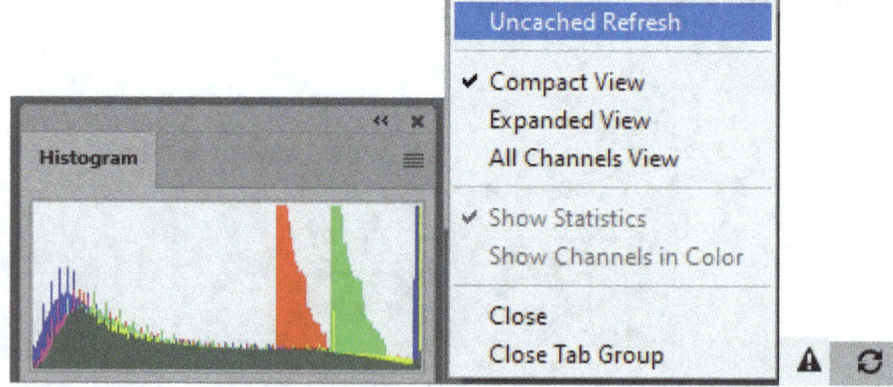

Figure 1-55. *Histogram panel and menu with alert and refresh icons*

CHAPTER 1　ADJUSTMENT LAYERS, BLENDING MODES WITH MASKS FOR PHOTO RESTORATION: PART 1

The Histogram displays how pixels in an image are distributed by graphing the number of pixels at each color intensity level for tonal dark (left) and light (right) value. While looking at the currently opened image, this can often give us clues as to in which channels the lack of or abundance of pixels might be occurring. A faded or overexposed image would show lack of pixels in shadows (left), some pixels in the midtone (middle) area, and some highlight (right) areas often shifted overall to the right. However, an underexposed image would show the reverse in distribution with high amounts of pixels in the shadows (left) and midtone (middle) and lack in highlights (right), the graph shifting to the left. If there is an extreme lack of pixels in one of these areas, that may make a complete image restoration difficult. Refer to Figure 1-56.

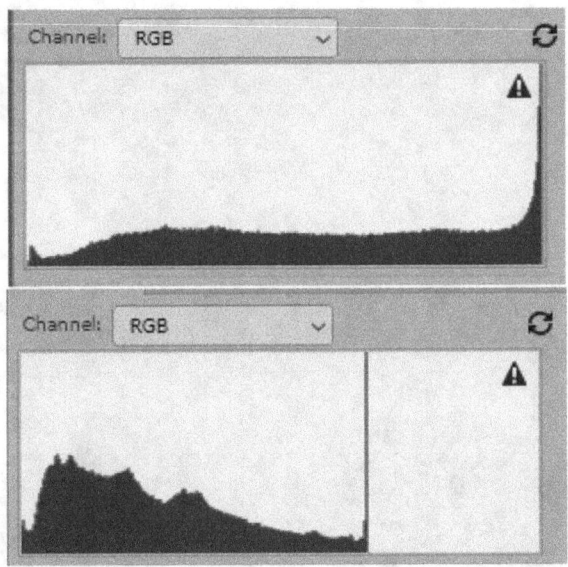

Figure 1-56. *Histogram panel settings for overexposed and underexposed images*

The grayscale color range for each RGB channel level can fall between 0 and 255. However, you will notice that some areas may have higher peaks than others extending off the graph, meaning that some pixels are being

CHAPTER 1 ADJUSTMENT LAYERS, BLENDING MODES WITH MASKS FOR PHOTO RESTORATION: PART 1

clipped and details in those areas are discarded, which can often happen in extreme areas of shadow and highlight.

Here is an example of a slide image that you might want to restore. It has faded overtime. You can see in All Channels View that there is lack of detail in the shadows. The midtones aren't bad for the red and green, but something has gone wrong for the blues. Refer to Figure 1-57.

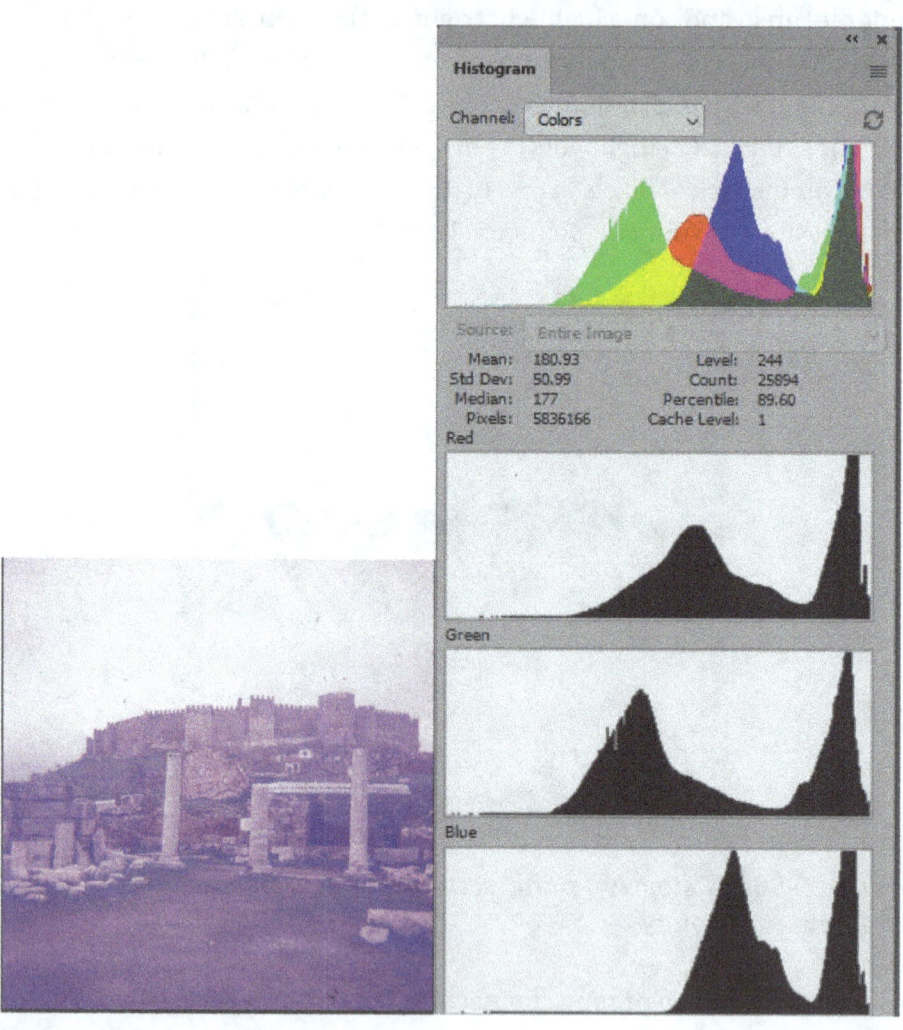

Figure 1-57. *Areas of the image have faded and are underexposed as revealed in the Histogram panel*

CHAPTER 1　ADJUSTMENT LAYERS, BLENDING MODES WITH MASKS FOR PHOTO RESTORATION: PART 1

In the highlights and midtone, you do have some detail in all channels that you can work with.

Ideally you would like to see a histogram with an even and full tonality in all areas, indicating proper exposure, which your modern digital camera may provide. Refer to Figure 1-58.

CHAPTER 1 ADJUSTMENT LAYERS, BLENDING MODES WITH MASKS FOR PHOTO RESTORATION: PART 1

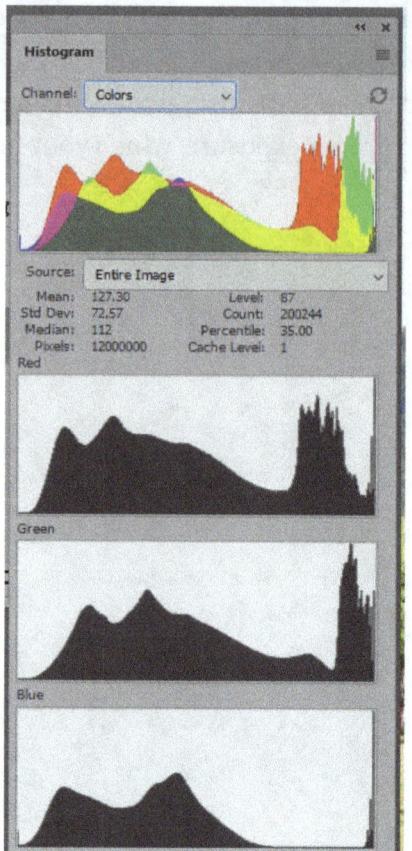

Figure 1-58. *Histogram panel shows a fairly balanced image*

However, there is no exact setting as to how this will appear. Every picture that you take will be different depending on what kind of subject matter the final image consists of. For example, if you took an image of just blue sky, you may not expect to see a lot of reds and greens in the image to correct for. In the case of the preceding image, there are a lot of greens and reds overall, but there are not a lot of blue midtones to highlight, except in the extreme highlight region. If there was you would have a blue cast, especially in the tree areas, which for this scene would not look natural.

If the image was originally black-and-white, you would only perhaps be able to adjust how the tone of the sepia or yellow tone of the paper or highlights, midtones, and shadows of the grayscale displayed as there may be a lack of blue in any channel or maybe all the channels appear very similar. Refer to Figure 1-59.

CHAPTER 1   ADJUSTMENT LAYERS, BLENDING MODES WITH MASKS FOR PHOTO RESTORATION: PART 1

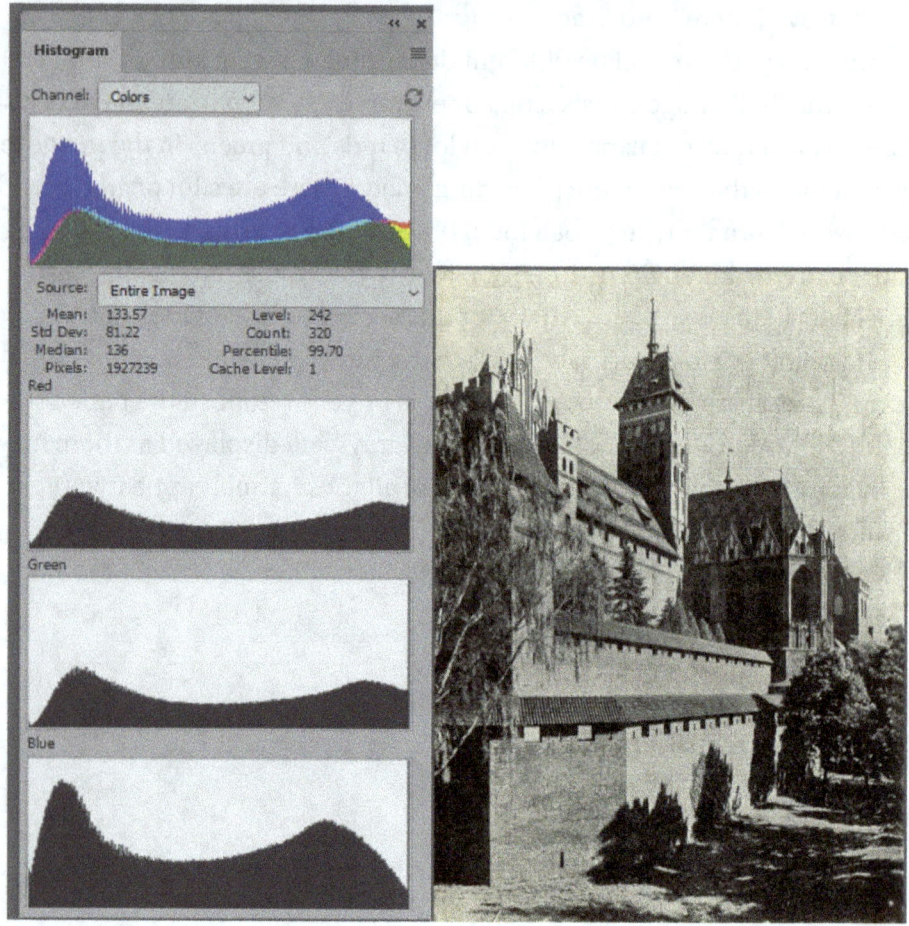

Figure 1-59. Histogram panel reveals fairly similar channels for the black-and-white image on yellowing paper

So, in essence, the histogram can only give us clues about the current scan. In a sense, we need to become "color detectives" so we can work with that information, using our adjustment layers to modify what we expect to see.

Info Panel

The Window ➤ Info panel is used for ideally finding the whitest and darkest areas in the image, which again will assist us with some of the different color adjustments. In this case you can sample in two different color modes, RGB and CMYK, to review the different values while using the Eyedropper Tool to hover over various locations and reading the information in the panel. Refer to Figure 1-60.

CHAPTER 1   ADJUSTMENT LAYERS, BLENDING MODES WITH MASKS FOR PHOTO RESTORATION: PART 1

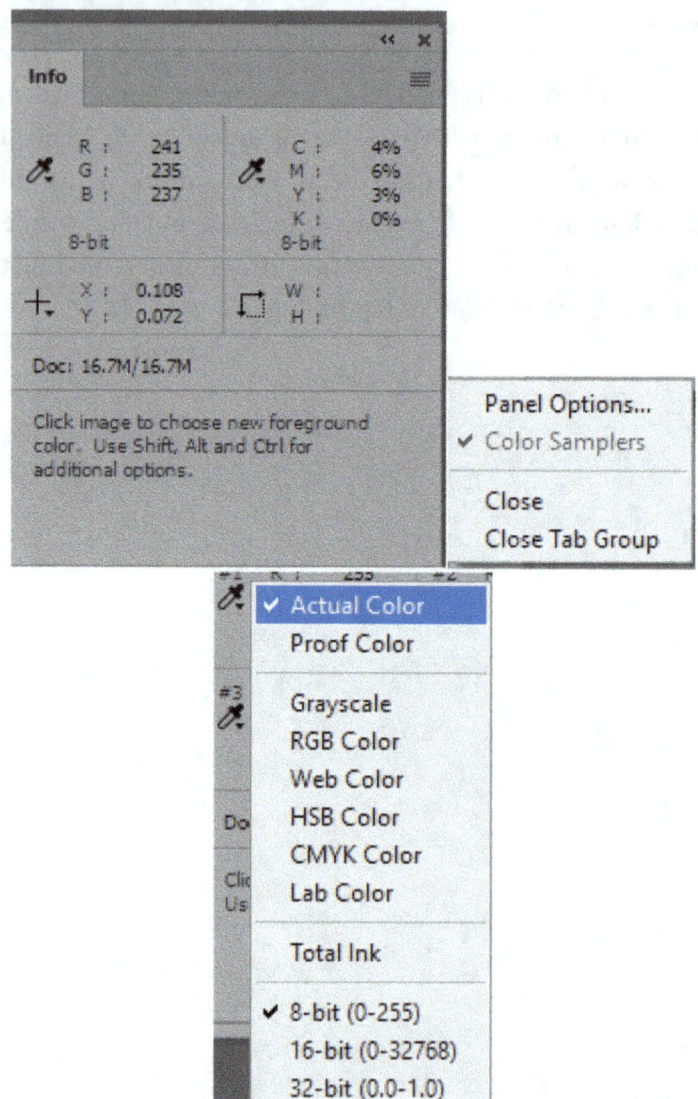

Figure 1-60. *Info panel with option menu*

While the Info panel can act similar to the Properties panel in giving guidance and information, the main thing to be aware of is completely white highlight areas for RGB will show up as R: 255, G: 255, B: 255, while areas of complete shadow black will appear as R: 0, G: 0, B: 0. All other tones will be a combination of numbers ranging from 0 to 255 in the three channels. Refer to Figure 1-61.

Figure 1-61. *Look for potential highlights and shadows in your image*

There is, however, no guarantee that in every image there will be a complete highlight or shadow. So, using adjustment layers, you may need to make choices as to what is truly the shadow or highlight in the image.

Note that as you hover over an area with your eyedropper, do not to hover over a small dust spot or scratch as this will affect your highlight or shadow options.

CHAPTER 1 ADJUSTMENT LAYERS, BLENDING MODES WITH MASKS FOR PHOTO RESTORATION: PART 1

Once you start working with the various adjustment layers, using the Properties panel, you will be able to use the Info panel to see a before (original) and after (new changes) of your current RGB and CMYK numbers with the new values. Refer to Figure 1-62.

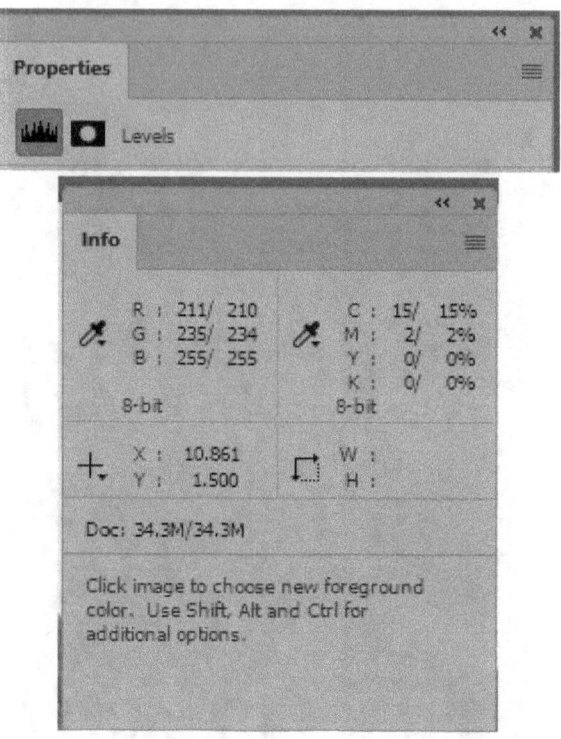

Figure 1-62. *Properties panel and Info panel*

Color Sampler Tool (I)

In your Info panel you can also set up to ten sampler markers on your canvas as you work for faster reference using the Color Sampler Tool, which looks similar to the Eyedropper Tool and is found with that tool in the Tools bar. Use the Options bar panel to set the tool's sample size. By default, it is set to Point Sample. Refer to Figure 1-63.

CHAPTER 1   ADJUSTMENT LAYERS, BLENDING MODES WITH MASKS FOR PHOTO RESTORATION: PART 1

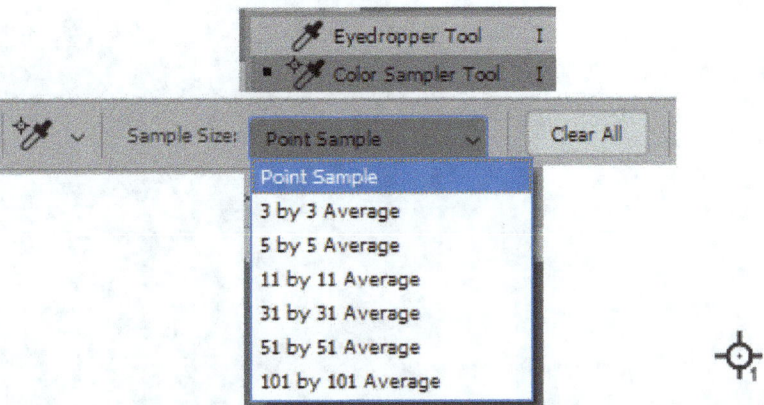

Figure 1-63. *Color Sampler Tool and settings in the Options bar panel*

Click the canvas where you want to add the numbered color sampler marker. They are saved in the document as you work but like guides, they do not print. Hold down the Ctrl/CMD key if you need to drag the marker to a new location. Refer to Figure 1-64.

CHAPTER 1 ADJUSTMENT LAYERS, BLENDING MODES WITH MASKS FOR PHOTO RESTORATION: PART 1

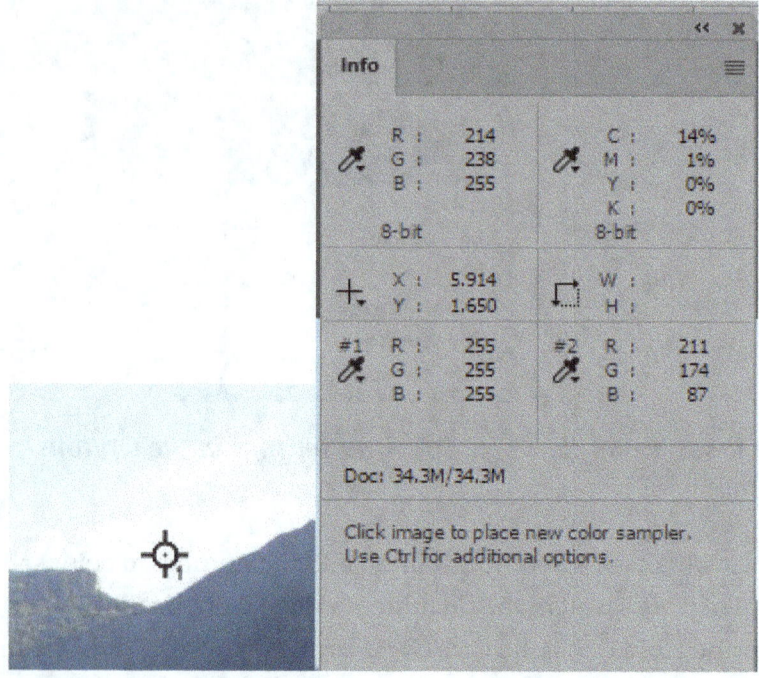

Figure 1-64. *Setting a sampler marker and viewing one in the Info panel*

As you work, for those you want to delete, you can either right-click the marker and choose Delete or use the Options bar panel to Clear All to remove all the markers at once. Refer to Figure 1-65.

CHAPTER 1 ADJUSTMENT LAYERS, BLENDING MODES WITH MASKS FOR PHOTO RESTORATION: PART 1

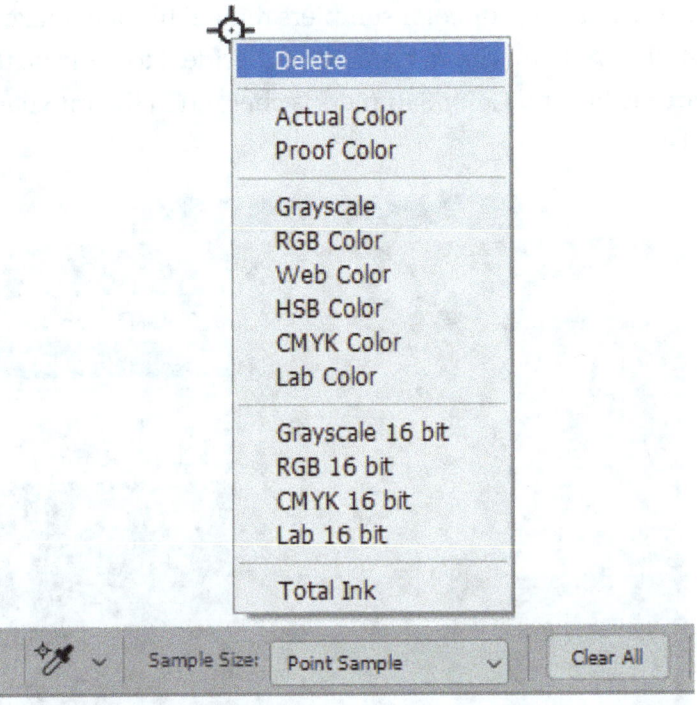

Figure 1-65. *Right-click to delete a single marker or use the Options bar panel to clear them all*

Note that if you switch to other tools in the Tools panel, the markers will temporarily hide until you return to the Eyedropper or Color Sampler Tool. However, the information will remain in the Info panel. Tools like Hand and Zoom will continue to display the markers on screen, and this will be helpful as you navigate to various markers on the canvas. Refer to Figure 1-66.

Figure 1-66. *Hand tool and Zoom tool*

CHAPTER 1 ADJUSTMENT LAYERS, BLENDING MODES WITH MASKS FOR PHOTO RESTORATION: PART 1

If for some reason your color samplers remain hidden, make sure to check that View ➤ Extras has a check mark beside it to indicate that the markers are visible and Color Samplers is checked in the Info panel. Refer to Figure 1-67.

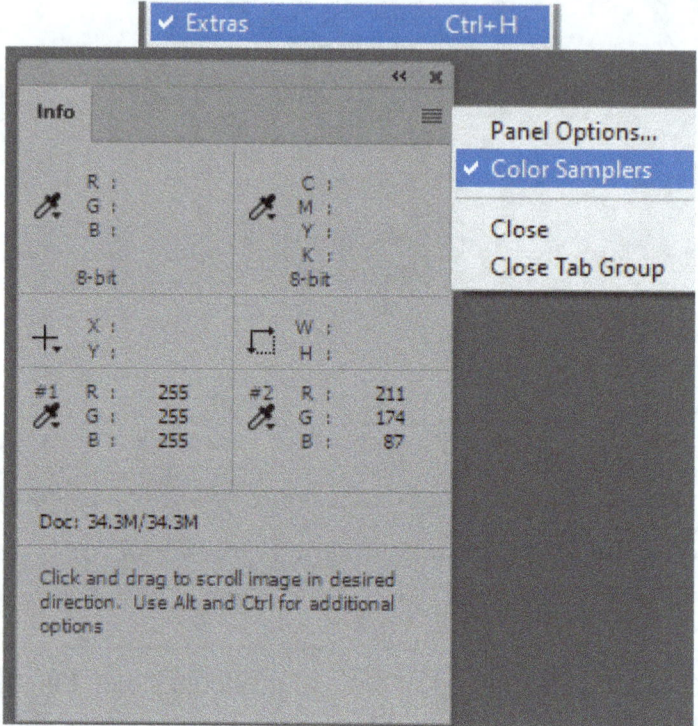

Figure 1-67. *View menu setting to view color sampler markers and Color Samplers setting in the Info panel*

In this case make sure that each of your color sampler markers is set to actual color. However, for your own projects you can change to other color sampler options and bit options using the dropdown menus. Refer to Figure 1-68.

CHAPTER 1 ADJUSTMENT LAYERS, BLENDING MODES WITH MASKS FOR PHOTO RESTORATION: PART 1

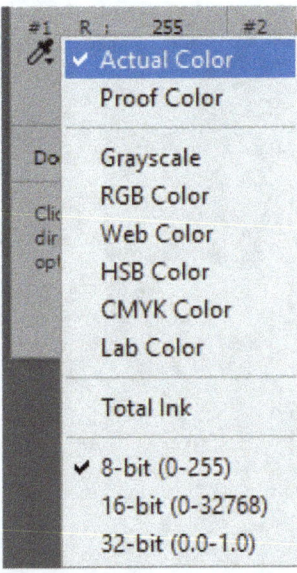

Figure 1-68. *Info panel settings*

For more advanced details on these two panels. visit the following link:

https://helpx.adobe.com/photoshop/using/viewing-histograms-pixel-values.html

Properties Panel for Layer Adjustments

The Properties panel will change options as you select a different adjustment layer rather than having to open different dialog boxes as you would if you had used the menu Image ➤ Adjustments. Refer to Figure 1-69.

CHAPTER 1 ADJUSTMENT LAYERS, BLENDING MODES WITH MASKS FOR PHOTO RESTORATION: PART 1

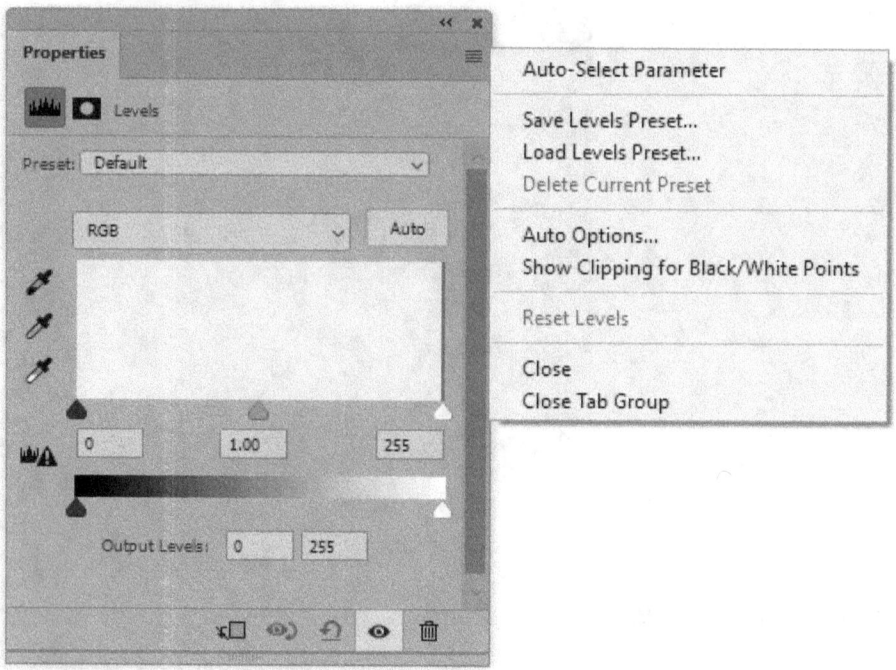

Figure 1-69. Properties panel and menu options for adjustment layers

I will now give a brief overview of each adjustment option. However, I will just note that for this chapter make sure that your file is in RGB color mode, or you may not have access to all the layer adjustment options, as is the case with CMYK, grayscale, and Lab color where certain adjustments are grayed out. Refer to Figure 1-70.

CHAPTER 1 ADJUSTMENT LAYERS, BLENDING MODES WITH MASKS FOR PHOTO RESTORATION: PART 1

CMYK	Grayscale	LAB
Brightness/Contrast... Levels... Curves... Exposure...	Brightness/Contrast... Levels... Curves... Exposure...	Brightness/Contrast... Levels... Curves... Exposure...
Vibrance... Hue/Saturation... Color Balance... Black & White... Photo Filter... Channel Mixer... Color Lookup...	Vibrance... Hue/Saturation... Color Balance... Black & White... Photo Filter... Channel Mixer... Color Lookup...	Vibrance... Hue/Saturation... Color Balance... Black & White... Photo Filter... Channel Mixer... Color Lookup...
Invert Posterize... Threshold... Gradient Map... Selective Color...	Invert Posterize... Threshold... Gradient Map... Selective Color...	Invert Posterize... Threshold... Gradient Map... Selective Color...

Figure 1-70. *There are fewer adjustment options for CMYK, grayscale, and Lab color modes*

Levels

Levels and the Histogram panel appear very similar. You can add the Levels to your Layers panel by either selecting the icon from the Layers panel or from your Adjustments panel under Single adjustments, by clicking the icon button. Hover over an icon if you are not familiar with it. Refer to Figure 1-71.

CHAPTER 1 ADJUSTMENT LAYERS, BLENDING MODES WITH MASKS FOR PHOTO
          RESTORATION: PART 1

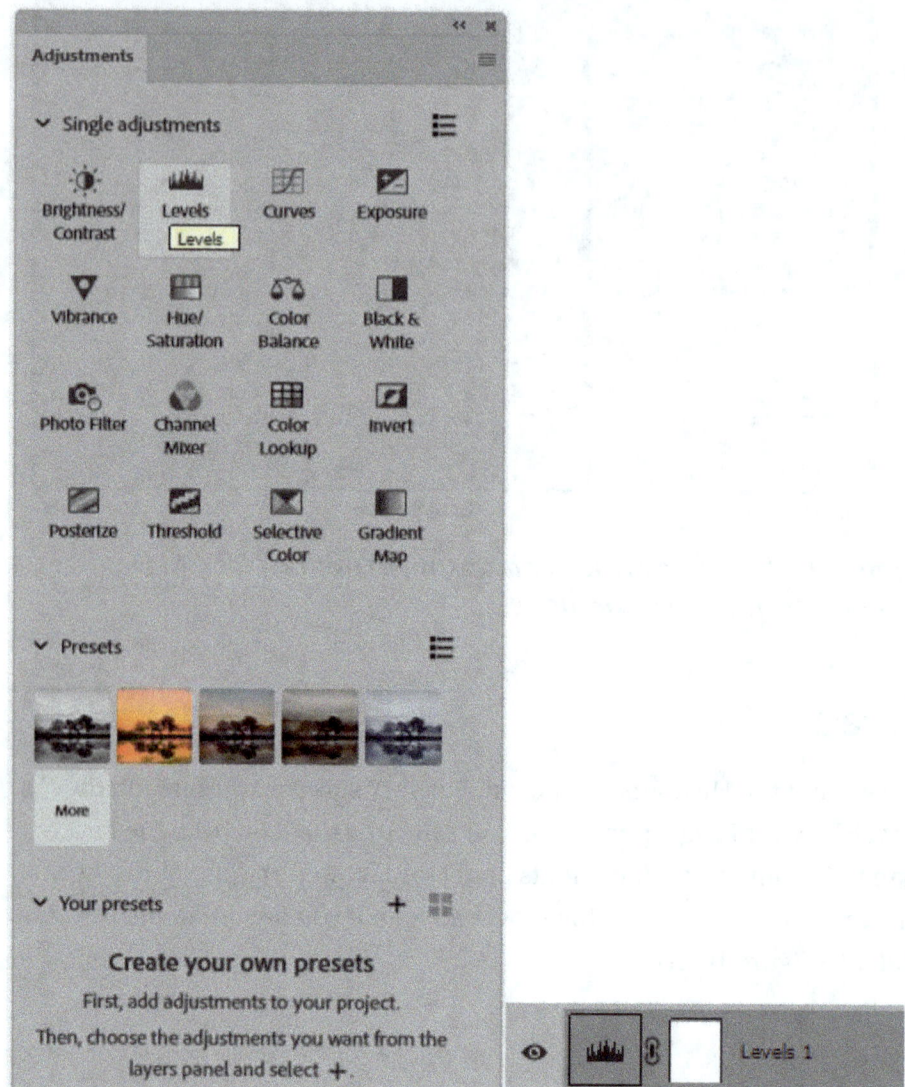

Figure 1-71. *Use the Adjustments panel to add an adjustment layer of Levels to the Layers panel*

This will then add the adjustment layer to the Layers panel. Then, when you select the adjustment, the options will be present in the Properties panel.

CHAPTER 1 ADJUSTMENT LAYERS, BLENDING MODES WITH MASKS FOR PHOTO RESTORATION: PART 1

Here we can see an example of an image (see **white_terrace_walls.psd**) with a lot of red in it. It was also printed on textured paper, but the main concern we want to work on right now is the color and see if we can restore it back to a more normal color. The histogram also gives us clues that in the red channel the shadows are very low but the midtone and highlights are high and the green and blue also show areas of imbalance in the midtone and highlights. Refer to Figure 1-72.

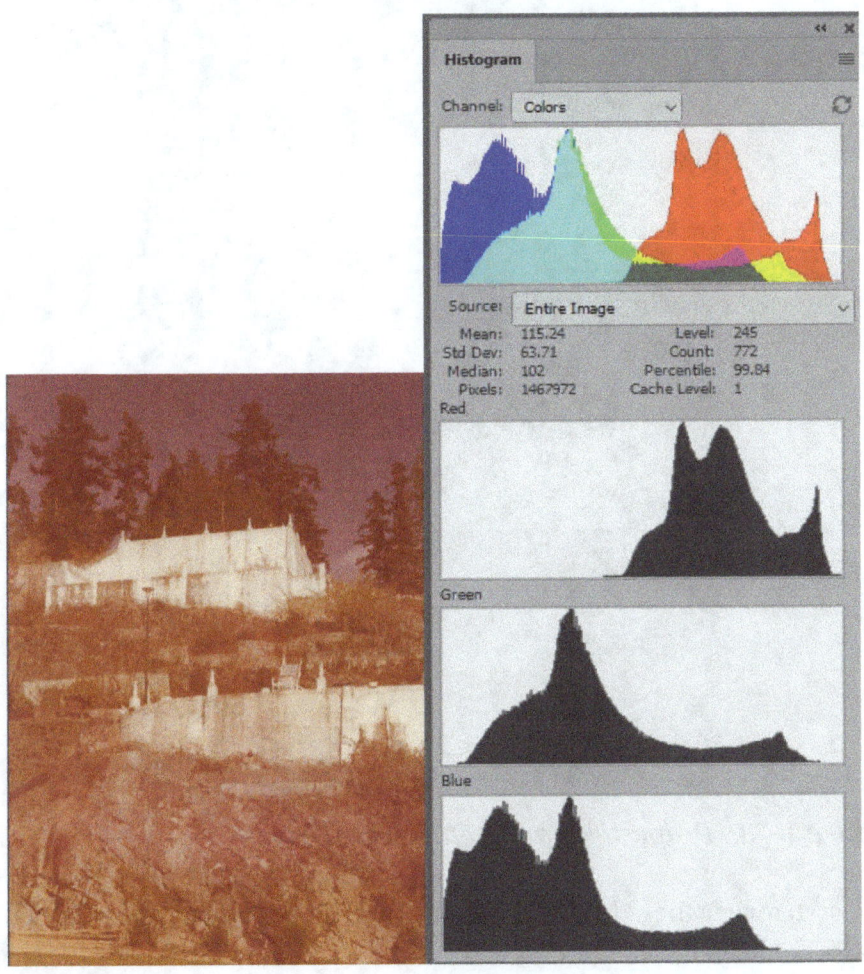

Figure 1-72. *Compare the opened image with the Histogram panel*

CHAPTER 1   ADJUSTMENT LAYERS, BLENDING MODES WITH MASKS FOR PHOTO RESTORATION: PART 1

Levels adjustments are ideal when you want to get better tonal corrections and color balance in the highlights, shadows, and possibly midtones. In essence, you should be able to balance and redistribute your pixels for a more realistic tonal range. You can affect the distribution overall or for individual color channels in the case of RGB. Refer to Figure 1-73.

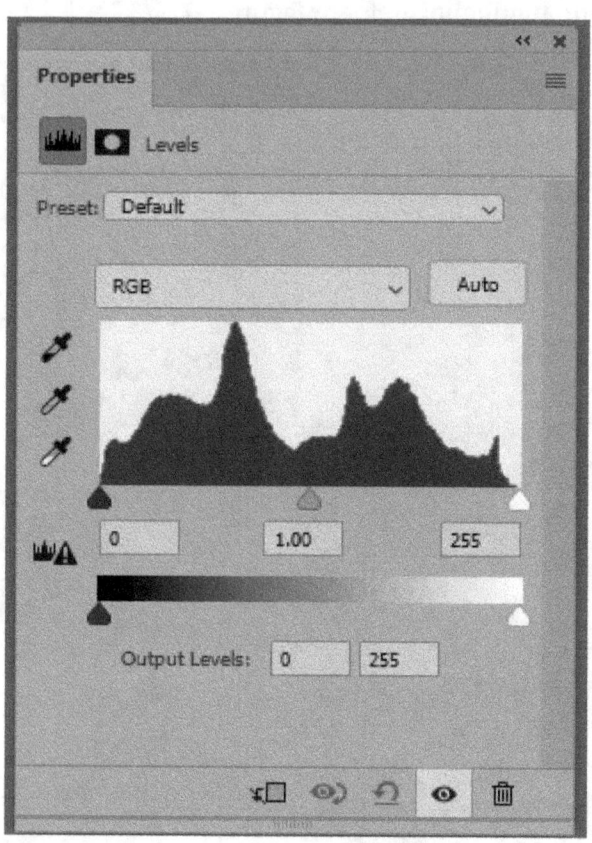

Figure 1-73. *Properties panel settings for Levels*

First, review the settings that appear in the Properties panel for this adjustment layer.

Preset: Select a Levels preset from the list of options. This is similar to using the Adjustments presets that are in the Adjustments panel. Once you have selected one, you can manually edit it, and it will display as Custom. When no changes have been made, it is set to Default. Refer to Figure 1-74.

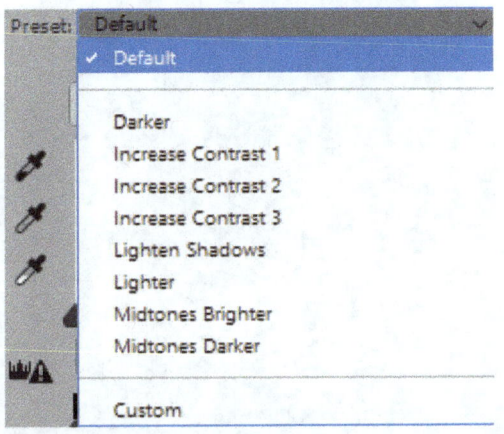

Figure 1-74. Properties panel settings for Levels presets

RGB: You can work with the RGB channels as a group or separately from the list when working with more challenging color corrections. Generally, I like to modify the composite RGB group first and adjust separate channels later. Refer to Figure 1-75.

Figure 1-75. Properties panel settings for Levels channels

Auto (quickly correct the auto balance in the image using a default setting; later, you can use the sliders to adjust manually): Click the button while holding down the Alt/Option key for access to more advanced

CHAPTER 1 ADJUSTMENT LAYERS, BLENDING MODES WITH MASKS FOR PHOTO RESTORATION: PART 1

options found in the Auto Color Correction Options dialog box. For now, leave at the default setting of Algorithms ➤ Enhance Brightness and Contrast.

Refer to Figure 1-76.

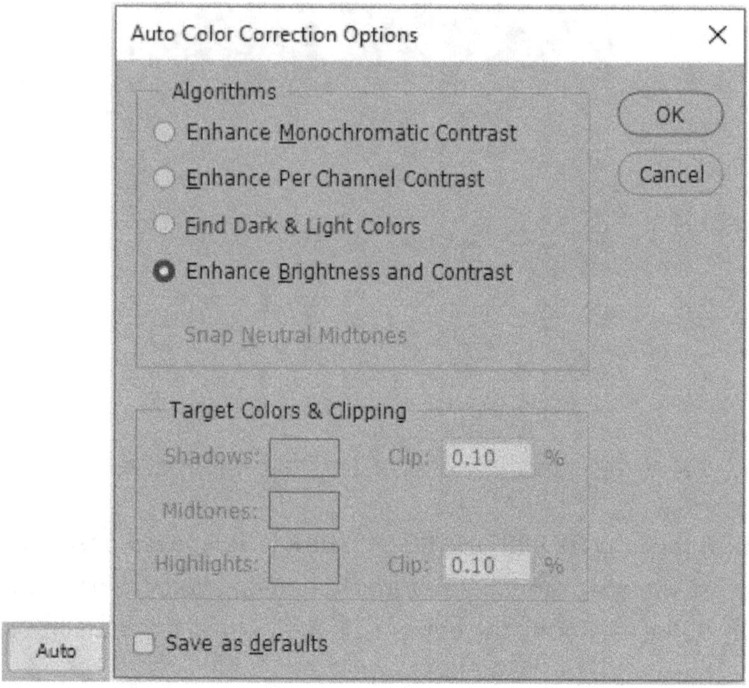

Figure 1-76. Properties panel settings for Levels Auto button and Auto Color Correction Options dialog box

As you advance in your color correction skill, you may want to adjust these settings depending upon your project, if it involves certain contrasts you want to enhance such as monochromatic. Some algorithms will allow you to access "Snap Neutral Midtones" and Target Colors & Clipping options.

Click Cancel to exit. Auto changes to these settings can also be used to affect other adjustment layers like Curves that access this dialog box. For more details about auto color, you can refer to the information and link in Chapter 2.

Use one of the three eyedroppers to sample in the image black point (press Alt/Option to display clipping preview), gray point, and white point. I will often select the specific eyedropper and click on the image to sample the white point first, then the black, and lastly the gray if I can find a gray stone in the image that I think should be neutral 50%. Refer to Figure 1-77.

Figure 1-77. *Properties panel settings for Levels, three eyedropper samplers*

However, in other projects you may prefer to start with the neutral gray point first and then work with the white or black eyedropper next. Your Info panel can help you find the darkest and lightest areas in the image. Select an eyedropper and then click a point somewhere on your image using the default target values. You can also preset some marker points using your Color Sampler Tool. Here, in the current image, I clicked what I felt was the whitest point on the right on the stone wall and very dark point near the rocks in the lower part of the page. Refer to Figure 1-78.

CHAPTER 1   ADJUSTMENT LAYERS, BLENDING MODES WITH MASKS FOR PHOTO
             RESTORATION: PART 1

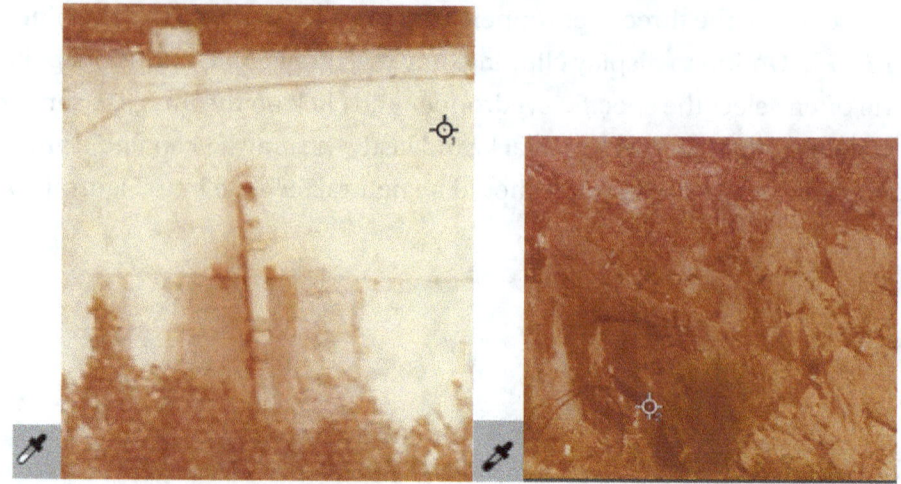

Figure 1-78. *Use the eyedroppers of the Levels and your color sampler marker points to accurately select colors for highlight and shadow*

The gray midpoint is rather difficult to find in this image right away so that is why I did not click it first, but is likely somewhere on the rock below the white lower wall. Refer to Figure 1-79.

CHAPTER 1 ADJUSTMENT LAYERS, BLENDING MODES WITH MASKS FOR PHOTO RESTORATION: PART 1

Figure 1-79. *Use the gray midpoint sampler and a color marker to find the ideal color point*

CHAPTER 1   ADJUSTMENT LAYERS, BLENDING MODES WITH MASKS FOR PHOTO RESTORATION: PART 1

After clicking with each dropper to sample each point, you can use Ctrl/CMD + Z as you work, if you do not pinpoint the color with your eyedropper as accurately as you hoped. See further tips on checking the default eyedropper values at the end of this section.

As changes are made, the Levels histogram will update, and on the image, you can see the color has vastly improved from what it once was. In this example, Auto could have done little to improve the image, so setting each point with the eyedropper was the best choice. Refer to Figure 1-80.

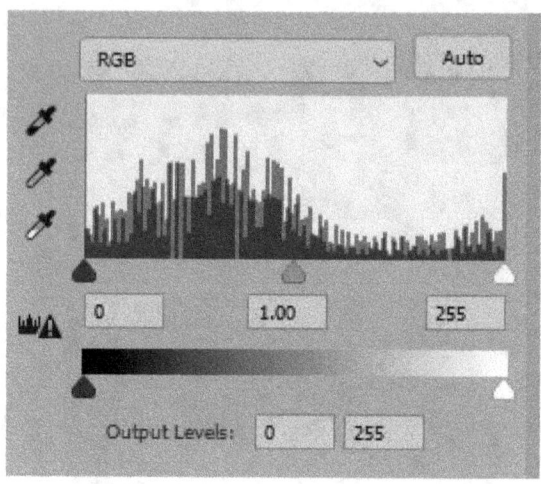

Figure 1-80. *Properties panel settings for Levels, histogram changes*

Shadow, midtone, highlight input level sliders: These you can adjust manually as you drag the sliders in the dialog box and the input values will update. The two outer sliders, which are black and white, are meant to map to the bottom corresponding output sliders. Likewise, they will also update when using the eyedroppers to set point values or clicking the Auto button. In the current example dragging the sliders in would not improve the image as the colors are fairly evenly distributed now. However, in the case of the image **garden_replace_sky.psd**, which was looked at in Volume 1, if we were to add a Levels layer, above the smart object layer, we would see that dragging the outer black and white input sliders inward might improve the overall color at least in the shadow areas. For the shadow slider any pixels on the left become black and for the highlight slider any pixels on the right are white. This is known as clipping. Refer to Figure 1-81.

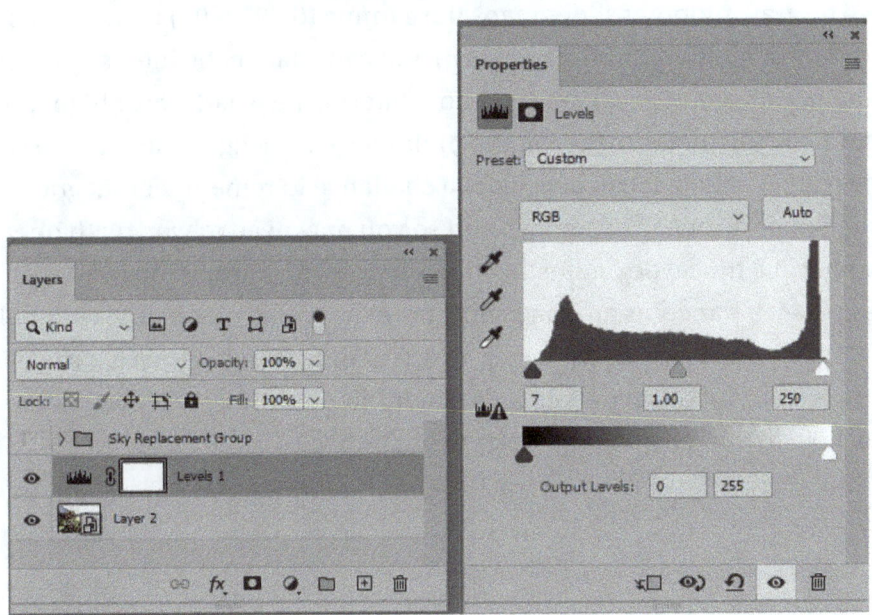

Figure 1-81. *Layers panel with adjustment layer Levels selected and settings adjusted in the Properties panel with the new changes displayed*

CHAPTER 1   ADJUSTMENT LAYERS, BLENDING MODES WITH MASKS FOR PHOTO
             RESTORATION: PART 1

In this example I turned off the visibility of my sky replacement folder while I worked so that I could focus on the color correction of the image below the sky.

The gray midpoint slider maps the gamma (9.99 - 0.01) in the image and is by default set to 1 (or level 128) and can change the intensity values of the middle gray (RGB) tones without altering the shadows or highlights. By moving this slider to the left the midtones will be lighter and to the right they will be darker. It can be a bit of a challenge to remember that gray is made up various RGB settings and so you may need to work with one channel at a time when adjusting the midpoint for certain images to get the correct balance, as an image may have an overall cast in one channel if fading has taken place. In the case of the white terraces image, I notice there is still a bit of a red cast, in the midtone, so shifting just that slider may help in the red channel. Refer to Figure 1-82.

CHAPTER 1   ADJUSTMENT LAYERS, BLENDING MODES WITH MASKS FOR PHOTO RESTORATION: PART 1

Figure 1-82. *Properties panel settings for Levels with sliders adjusted for the red channel and results in an image*

You can also type your values in manually. Holding down the Alt/Option key while dragging a slider can help you preview what colors are being clipped.

97

Shadow and highlight output level sliders: To make adjustments, move the sliders to adjust the values for either the shadows or highlights. Refer to Figure 1-83.

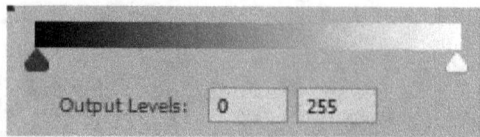

Figure 1-83. *Properties panel settings for Levels output sliders*

By default, they are set to 0 (black pixels) and 255 (white pixels), as seen in the Output Levels text boxes. You may not need to, in every case, adjust them. When you leave these output sliders in their default position, you can then move the earlier mentioned input sliders shadow (black) and highlight (white) to new locations, and they will map to the output slider values of 0 and 255. Any remaining input levels, including the midpoint slider, will also redistribute, based on these parameters. The point of the redistribution is to increase the tonal range or the overall contrast of the image, not to limit it and potentially make the color quality worse and cause it to lose contrast.

Be careful if you move any one of the sliders not to over-clip your highlights and shadows, thus eliminating important details. For the composite RGB I always just move the shadow and highlight input sliders to the point where I see the shadow or highlight starting or slightly back off from that point to ensure a good tonal range. Refer to the **garden_image_replace_sky_color_adjustments.psd** image.

For the midpoint slider, moving it a bit to the left or the right may help, but you need to observe how the histogram is formed or leave at 1.00. Just using the midtone eyedropper may be the best option in some circumstances. In this case I clicked near the edge of the barn roof near the middle. Refer to Figure 1-84.

CHAPTER 1 ADJUSTMENT LAYERS, BLENDING MODES WITH MASKS FOR PHOTO RESTORATION: PART 1

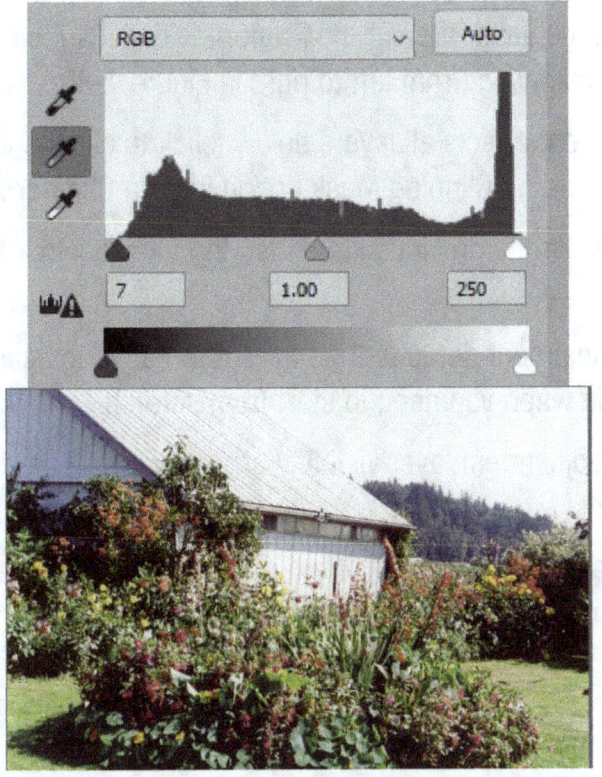

Figure 1-84. *Properties panel settings for Levels with shadow and highlight input sliders moved inward*

The "Calculate a more accurate histogram" icon will appear; you can click this to get a more accurate histogram reading and refresh the graph. The warning will then disappear. Refer to Figure 1-85.

Figure 1-85. *Properties panel settings for Levels histogram warning*

Note that in the lower area of the Properties panel are settings that include the following (from left to right in Figure 1-86):

This adjustment affects all layers below (click to clip the layer) (we will look at the Clipping Mask option later in Chapter 2).

Preview to view the previous state. Use the \ key on your keyboard to toggle.

Reset to adjustment defaults. This is an alternative to using Edit ➤ Undo when you need to start from scratch.

Toggle the adjustment layer visibility as you would in the Layers panel.

Delete the adjustment layer using the trash can icon rather than directly from the Layers panel. Click Yes or No if a warning message appears.

Figure 1-86. Properties panel settings at the bottom of the panel

An optional Properties panel menu will change depending upon the adjustment layer. However, you can use this menu when you need to save or load a Levels (.ALV) preset. This menu will be available for other adjustment presets as well. Refer to Figure 1-87.

CHAPTER 1 ADJUSTMENT LAYERS, BLENDING MODES WITH MASKS FOR PHOTO RESTORATION: PART 1

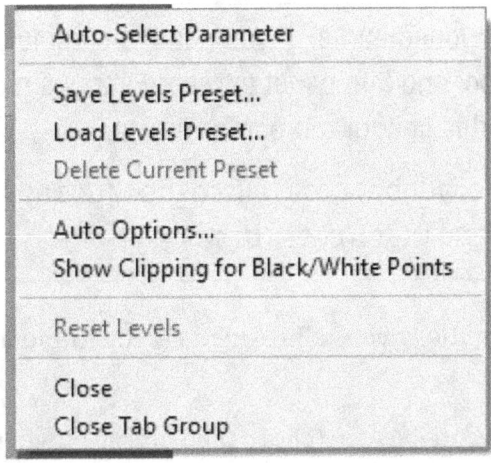

Figure 1-87. *Properties panel menu options of Levels*

One good tip to remember is that it is often best to use the eyedroppers first before you use your sliders to adjust the sliders for Levels or Curves. Double-clicking each eyedropper will open the color picker so that you can view and adjust the target values. White point is set to R: 255, G: 255, B: 255; gray point R: 128, G: 128, B: 128; and black point R: 0, G: 0, B: 0. I leave at the default values, but you may need to adjust for your projects. Click Cancel to exit without saving changes. Refer to Figure 1-88.

Figure 1-88. *Properties panel settings for Levels eyedropper and color picker*

101

Note that as mentioned earlier, if you need to sample colors, use your Color Sampler Tool and Info panel to record various marker points. You can refer to this link for more information:

https://helpx.adobe.com/photoshop/using/adjust-color-tone-levels-curves.html

---

More details on the Levels adjustment can be found at the following link:

https://helpx.adobe.com/photoshop/using/levels-adjustment.html

File ➤ Save your work at this point on both files. Refer to **garden_image_replace_sky_color_adjustments.psd** and **white_terrace_walls_final.psd** if you need to compare.

Curves

This adjustment has similar settings to the Levels but lets you, in this case, set up to 14 control points for highlights, shadows, and midpoints together or for each channel. The curve and its points will affect the entire image's tonal range. You may want this adjustment in combination with Levels for more accurate and balanced settings. I find the Curves ideal when I am trying to balance a set tonal range that is somewhere between the midpoint and the highlight and shadow that I can't quite pinpoint with the Levels options. You can set highlights and shadows and midtones in between (quartertone and three-quarter tone). In the case of the **white_terrace_walls.psd** image, it is still kind of dark overall, and so adjusting the midpoint by adding a Curves adjustment might help. Use Image ➤ Duplicate if you need to practice or continue with the file you used while you looked at Level adjustments earlier. Refer to Figure 1-89.

CHAPTER 1   ADJUSTMENT LAYERS, BLENDING MODES WITH MASKS FOR PHOTO RESTORATION: PART 1

Figure 1-89. *Image that needs some improvements made with Curves adjustments*

Use either your Adjustments panel (Single adjustments) or your Layers panel to set this adjustment layer. Initially, when you start, the tonal range will be represented by a straight diagonal line rising on the graph with a faded histogram in the background. Refer to Figure 1-90.

CHAPTER 1 ADJUSTMENT LAYERS, BLENDING MODES WITH MASKS FOR PHOTO RESTORATION: PART 1

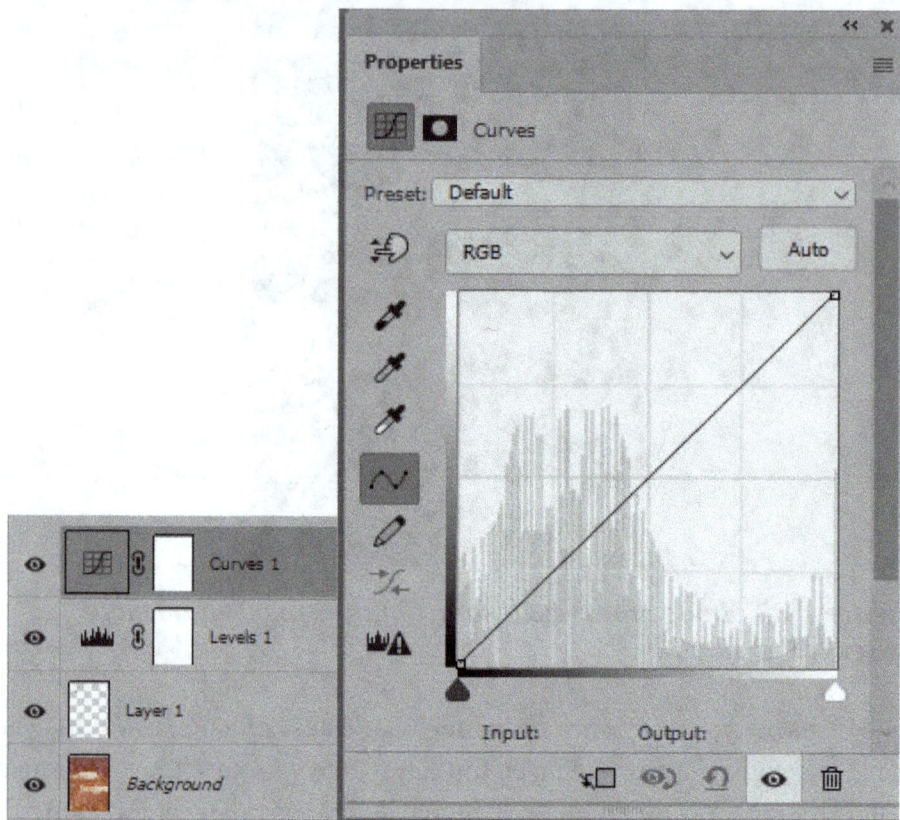

Figure 1-90. *Curves adjustment layer applied to the Layers panel and how settings appear in the Properties panel*

CHAPTER 1   ADJUSTMENT LAYERS, BLENDING MODES WITH MASKS FOR PHOTO RESTORATION: PART 1

While working on an image with the RGB composite channel, you will observe that the lower-left area of the graph represents shadows (black) and the upper-right area represent highlights (white). On the graph's grid the horizontal axis represents the input levels or original image values, and the vertical axis represents the output levels or new adjusted values. This becomes evident when as you add new control points to the line and move them, you begin to alter the shape of the curve. These alterations will reflect as color adjustments on your image. The steeper sections of the curve will represent areas of higher contrast, while flatter sections will represent areas of lower contrast. However, if you don't know how to alter the curve correctly, it can end in a messy surreal picture. Refer to Figure 1-91.

CHAPTER 1 ADJUSTMENT LAYERS, BLENDING MODES WITH MASKS FOR PHOTO RESTORATION: PART 1

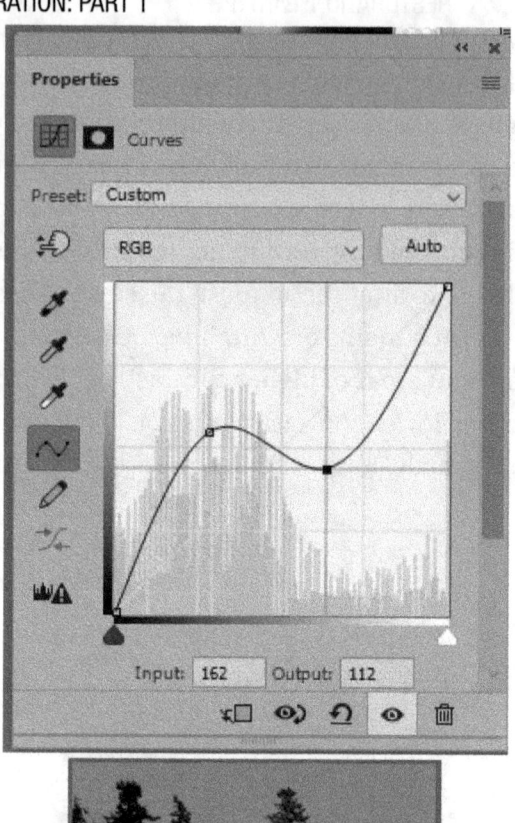

Figure 1-91. *Properties panel settings for Curves and an extreme curve that affects the color in the image*

CHAPTER 1   ADJUSTMENT LAYERS, BLENDING MODES WITH MASKS FOR PHOTO RESTORATION: PART 1

First, review the following Properties panel settings found for Curves when in RGB color mode:

Preset: Select a preset curve from the menu. This is similar to using the Adjustments presets that are in the Adjustments panel. Once you have selected one, you can manually edit it, and it will display as Custom. When no changes have been made, it is set to Default. Refer to Figure 1-92.

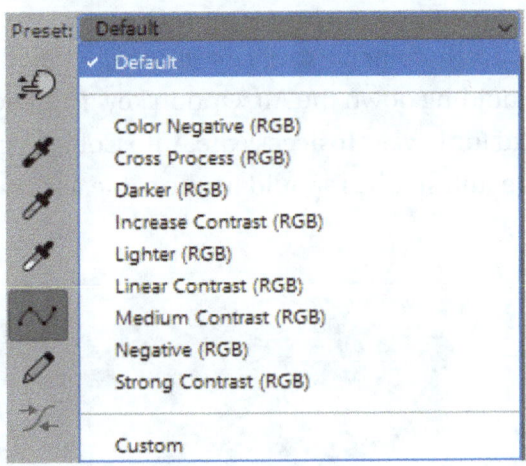

Figure 1-92. *Properties panel settings for Curves, presets*

RGB: When set to RGB you can adjust all the channels at once or select from the list each channel separately when you notice that one is more damaged than the others and is causing a distinct color cast in the image. To begin I will often work on my RGB channel collectively and then move to separate channels if I feel I'm not getting the exact results I want. Note that some presets will cause all RGB channel curves to appear on the graph itself. Refer to Figure 1-93.

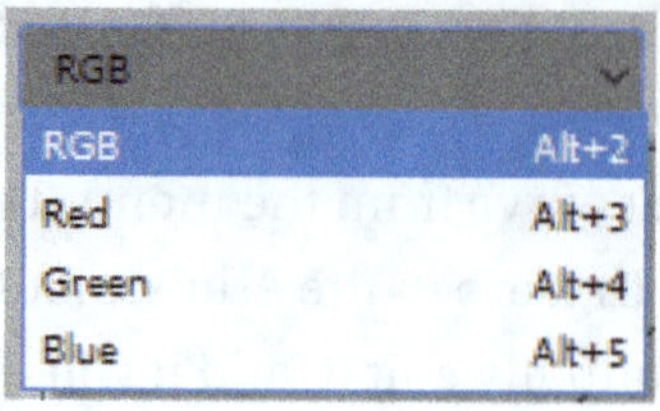

CHAPTER 1 ADJUSTMENT LAYERS, BLENDING MODES WITH MASKS FOR PHOTO RESTORATION: PART 1

Figure 1-93. *Properties panel settings for Curves, channels*

Auto: Automatically color correct Curves using a default setting. Click the button while holding down the Alt/Option key if you need to see more options, as you did for Levels, to access the Auto Color Correction Options dialog box. The default settings should be the same as the ones for Levels. Refer to Figure 1-94.

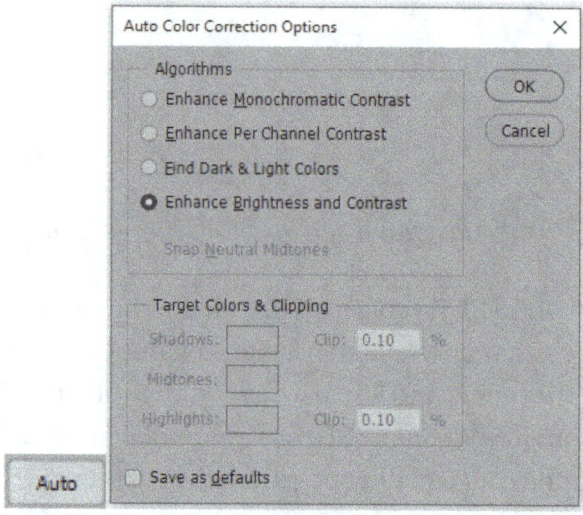

Figure 1-94. *Properties panel settings for Curves, Auto button and Auto Color Correction Options dialog box*

In this example, I just clicked Auto as soon as I added the adjustment layer, which was a good option as it continued to balance out the colors in the image and now the details in the trees are more visible and the sky is lighter. Refer to Figure 1-95.

CHAPTER 1 ADJUSTMENT LAYERS, BLENDING MODES WITH MASKS FOR PHOTO RESTORATION: PART 1

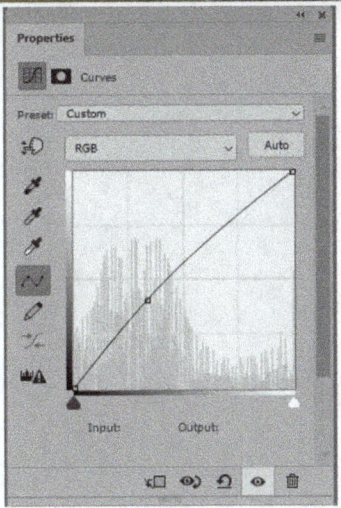

Figure 1-95. *The image's color alters when changes are made to the Curves in the Properties panel*

CHAPTER 1   ADJUSTMENT LAYERS, BLENDING MODES WITH MASKS FOR PHOTO RESTORATION: PART 1

On-image Targeted Adjustment Tool: With this button (hand) enabled, click and drag up or down on the canvas to modify the curve and add control points. This is ideal when you are visually trying to pinpoint an area that you feel is not correct in the tonal range and adjust the histogram. I usually enable this button when I want to adjust a setting somewhere in the midtones. Click the button again if you need to disable it. Refer to Figure 1-96.

CHAPTER 1 ADJUSTMENT LAYERS, BLENDING MODES WITH MASKS FOR PHOTO RESTORATION: PART 1

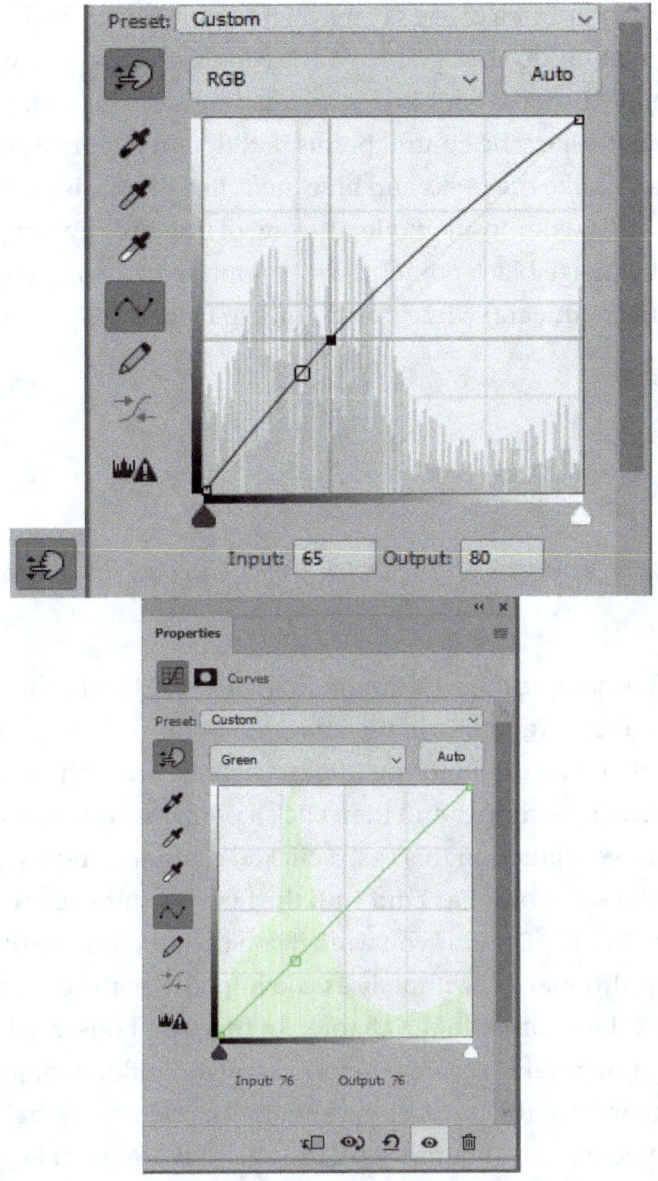

Figure 1-96. *On-image Targeted Adjustment Tool and Properties panel settings for Curves, channels RGB and just the green channel*

CHAPTER 1 ADJUSTMENT LAYERS, BLENDING MODES WITH MASKS FOR PHOTO RESTORATION: PART 1

Dragging in the area of the sky may lighten the image further and add more control points to your graph, which you may or may not want. Make sure to carefully observe your image as you drag across it with this tool. Observe, if you adjust the control points in different channels, which may affect gray areas like the rocks and blue areas like the sky in your image.

While in RGB composite mode, use one of the three eyedroppers to sample in the image black point (press Alt/Option to display clipping preview), gray point, and white point. Refer to Figure 1-97.

Figure 1-97. *Properties panel settings for Curves, three eyedropper samplers*

I will often sample the white point first, then the black, and lastly the gray, if I can find a gray stone in the image that I think should be neutral 50%. Your Info panel can help you find the darkest and lightest areas in the image. Click an eyedropper and then click a point on your canvas using the default target values. In this case I clicked again the color sampler markers in the same order as I did with the Levels: white, black, and gray. You can use Ctrl/CMD + Z as you work if you do not pinpoint the color with your eyedropper as accurately as you hoped. See the tip on Levels and eyedropper values earlier in the chapter. In this case I observed that doing so made my image take a more bluer tone and did reduce some of the red that remained in the lower stone and the sky. See how it balanced the curves and you can see differences in the channels. Refer to Figure 1-98.

CHAPTER 1 ADJUSTMENT LAYERS, BLENDING MODES WITH MASKS FOR PHOTO RESTORATION: PART 1

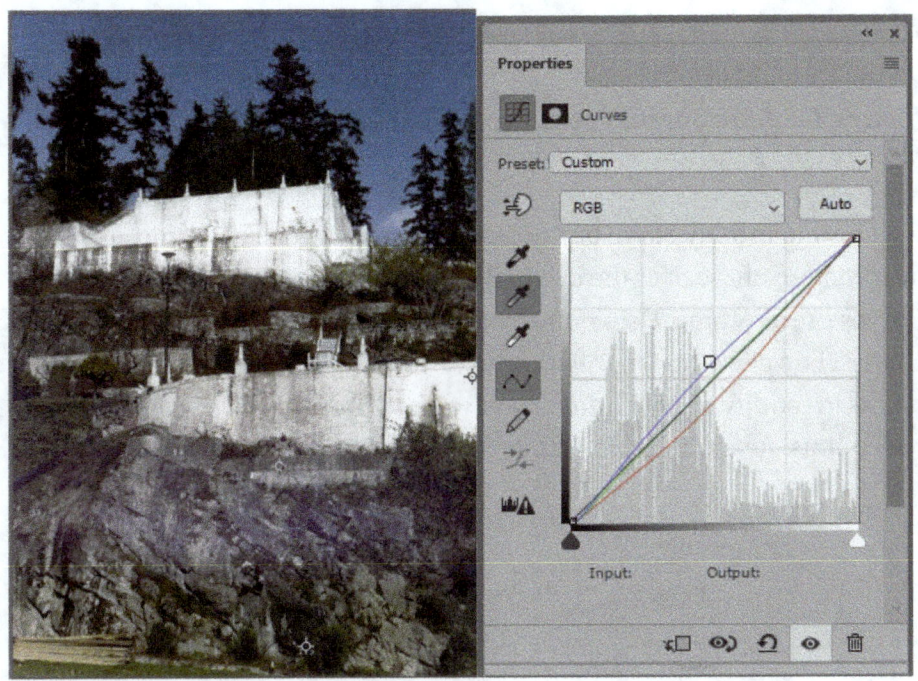

Figure 1-98. *Use the eyedroppers to sample the same areas of the image but this time with the Curves adjustments in the Properties panel*

Note Depending upon the image, it may have no neutral gray areas, so you still may need to adjust control point settings in each channel separately to improve the color correction.

Edit points to modify curve button: When enabled you can click and edit the point that you add to create your curve. This is set by default. Refer to Figure 1-99.

CHAPTER 1   ADJUSTMENT LAYERS, BLENDING MODES WITH MASKS FOR PHOTO RESTORATION: PART 1

Figure 1-99. *Properties panel settings for Curves, Edit points to modify curve button*

Draw to modify curve button: When enabled you can draw out your own custom curve over the original graph as you would with a pencil in the Curves preview area. Using this method may help you create a more ideal curve. Then click the Smooth the curve values button or return to the Edit points to modify curve button if you want to preview the curve with the new points. Refer to Figure 1-100.

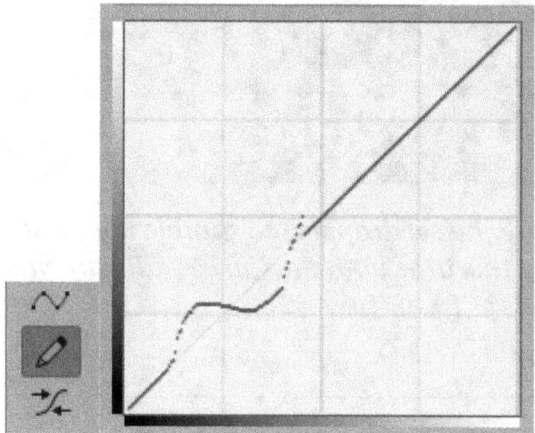

Figure 1-100. *Properties panel settings for Curves, Draw to modify curve button*

Smooth the curve values button: While working with the Draw to modify curve button, you can then click this Smooth the curve values button to smooth the curve and make it less jagged for better tonal blend. Steep curves create a stronger contrast. Click more than once to continue to smooth the curve. Then click the Edit points to modify curve button to see the results on the graph. Refer to Figure 1-101.

CHAPTER 1 ADJUSTMENT LAYERS, BLENDING MODES WITH MASKS FOR PHOTO RESTORATION: PART 1

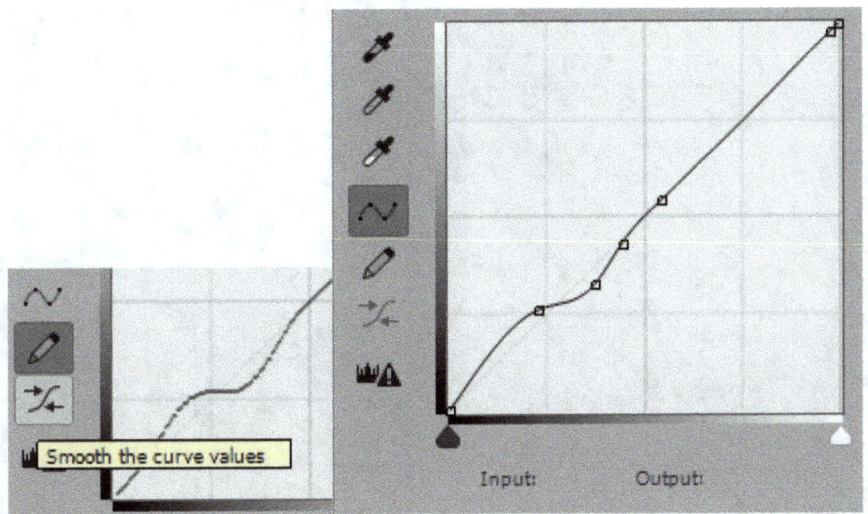

Figure 1-101. *Properties panel settings for Curves, Smooth the curve values button*

On the graph itself the lower-left control point is called the set white point, and moving this point upward can lighten the image. The upper-right control point is called the set black point, and moving this point downward can darken the image. Refer to Figure 1-102.

CHAPTER 1　ADJUSTMENT LAYERS, BLENDING MODES WITH MASKS FOR PHOTO RESTORATION: PART 1

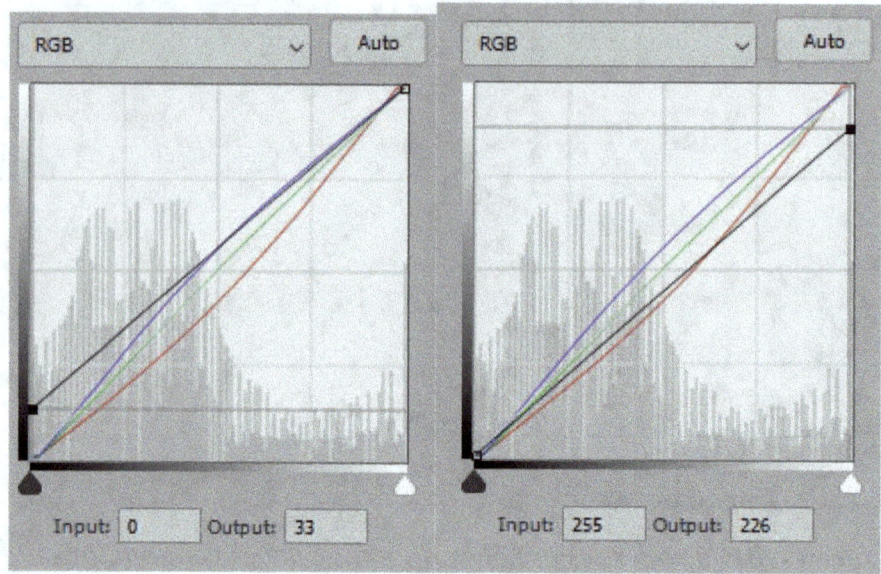

Figure 1-102. Properties panel settings for Curves, input/output for the selected control point

Generally, I leave these points in their set location, so I do not clip off important color details.

However, if a control point is set in the center of the two, that would be the set gray point and that is the point or points that, once added, are generally the ones I manipulate. Refer to Figure 1-103.

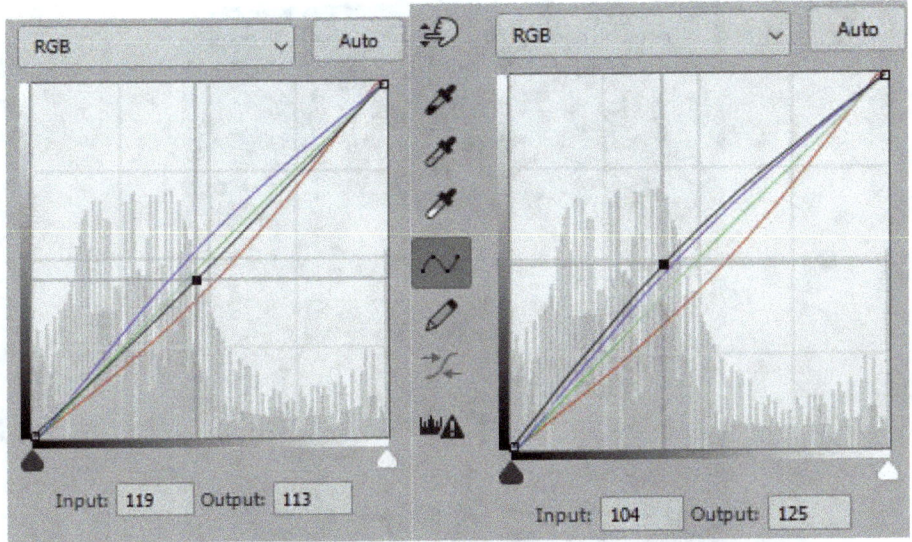

Figure 1-103. *Properties panel settings for Curves, adjusting control points*

Moving a point upward lightens, while moving a point downward darkens the tonal area. Moving a midpoint to the left can lighten and increase the contrast. Moving the midpoint to the right can darken or decrease the contrast. When you begin moving control points, test and observe how subtle or extreme movements affect the colors on the image. Refer to Figure 1-104.

CHAPTER 1   ADJUSTMENT LAYERS, BLENDING MODES WITH MASKS FOR PHOTO RESTORATION: PART 1

Figure 1-104. *Making adjustment to the color of the image with curves*

You can add up to 14 midpoint (gray) control points and then drag points off the graph/grid if you no longer want them or when you feel you have too many points. Often it is best just to have a few points and not the maximum. Control points remain anchored so you can move a single point without drastically affecting the other points or parts of your curve. Your original baseline will continue to display faded in the background. Refer to Figure 1-105.

CHAPTER 1 ADJUSTMENT LAYERS, BLENDING MODES WITH MASKS FOR PHOTO RESTORATION: PART 1

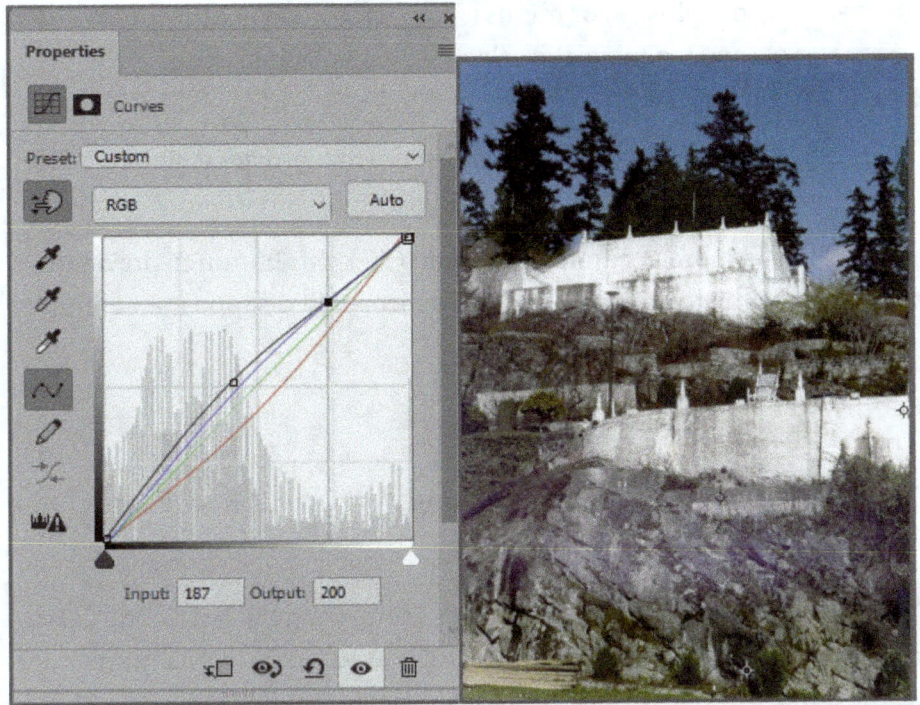

Figure 1-105. *Properties panel settings for Curves, control points and how they affect the current image*

Tips to remember while working with control points are as follows:

- If you need to make minor adjustment to a selected point, try using the up and down arrow keys to nudge it.

- Shift + click multiple points when you need to select more than one before you drag or nudge them.

- Ctrl/CMD + D will allow you to deselect all points.

- Use the plus (+) or minus (-) key on the keyboard when you need to move the selected control points up or down the baseline curve.

Additional tips can be found at the link provided at the end if this section.

Calculate a more accurate histogram: Click this button to preview a more accurate histogram setting, and the icon will disappear and refresh. Refer to Figure 1-106.

Figure 1-106. Properties panel settings for Curves, histogram alert icon

Move the black and white clipping sliders along the horizontal axis to adjust settings in the current (input) and new (output) intensity areas and set the darkest and lightest values in the image. Holding down the Alt/Option key as you drag can allow you to preview what is being clipped with black/white points. In my case I dragged the black slider back to avoid clipping off details. Refer to Figure 1-107.

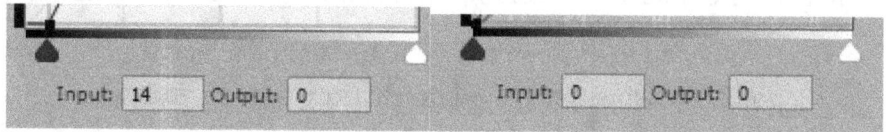

Figure 1-107. Properties panel settings for Curves, moving the clipping sliders

Input (current intensity of a selected point) and output (new intensity of a selected point): These will adjust as you move the various anchor points in the preview. These adjustments are based on light value (0–255). While a point is selected, you can enter new values in the Input and Output text boxes. Refer to Figure 1-108.

CHAPTER 1　ADJUSTMENT LAYERS, BLENDING MODES WITH MASKS FOR PHOTO RESTORATION: PART 1

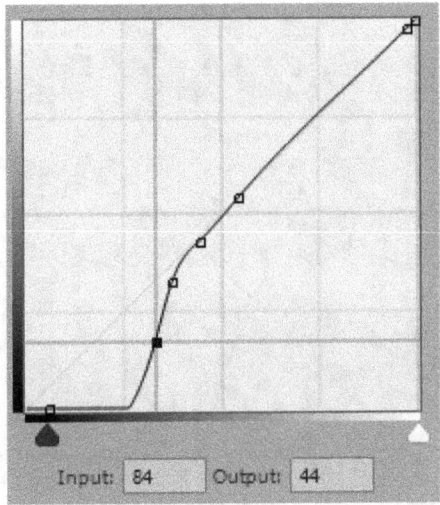

Figure 1-108. *Properties panel settings for Curves, with input and output settings*

Curves presets are saved and loaded as (.ACV) files.

Note　Besides RGB, if you are working in CMYK, Lab, or Grayscale color mode, you can also use the Curves adjustment layer. RGB will show amount of light (0–255) or intensity values (black is 0) in the lower left. Refer to Figure 1-108.

CMYK will be based on pigment/ink percentages, and so its slider setting will appear reversed in the Curves display with a range of 0–100%. Highlights are at 0% in the lower-left corner. Refer to Figure 1-109.

CHAPTER 1 ADJUSTMENT LAYERS, BLENDING MODES WITH MASKS FOR PHOTO RESTORATION: PART 1

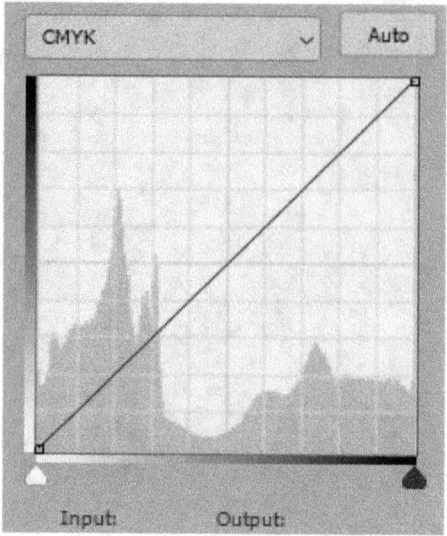

Figure 1-109. Properties panel settings for Curves, setting for CMYK

Grayscale and Lab will also be set to a setting of light. You can review Curves Display Options if you select that option from the Properties menu. This includes showing the channel overlays, histogram, baseline, intersection line (for better alignment of the control points with the histogram and grid), and type of grid increment of simple or detailed. Refer to Figure 1-110.

CHAPTER 1   ADJUSTMENT LAYERS, BLENDING MODES WITH MASKS FOR PHOTO RESTORATION: PART 1

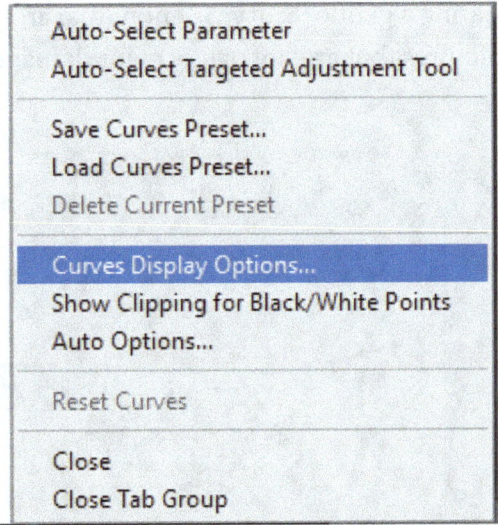
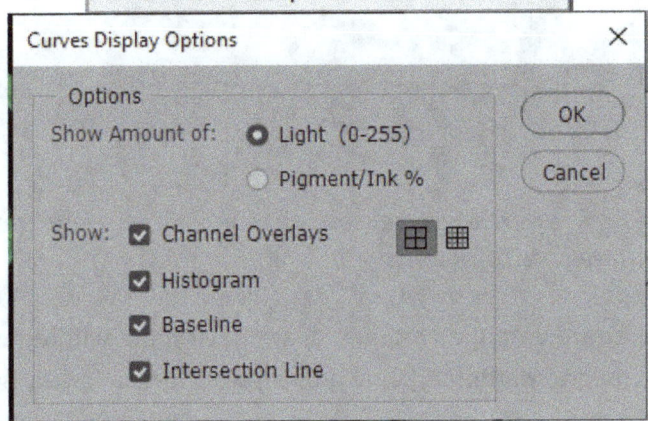

Figure 1-110. *Properties panel settings for Curves, menu options and Curves Display Options dialog box*

Tip   Alt/Option + clicking the preview grid can alter its increments outside of the dialog box.

Sometimes creating a gentle S curve is enough to create contrast in the midtones for pictures that are not overly color damaged. Refer to Figure 1-111.

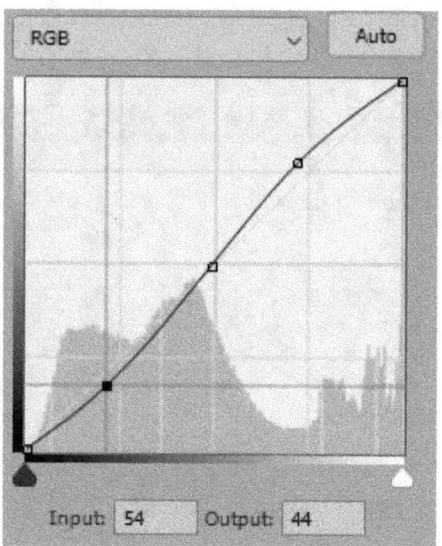

Figure 1-111. *Properties panel settings for Curves, creating an S curve with three control points*

However, more damaged images, as we have seen, will require additional work and patience. They may also require an additional adjustment layer to fine-tune your work. Refer to Figure 1-112.

In the case of the **garden_image_replace_sky_color_adjustments. psd**, for curves I just used the Auto setting. Refer to Figure 1-112.

CHAPTER 1   ADJUSTMENT LAYERS, BLENDING MODES WITH MASKS FOR PHOTO RESTORATION: PART 1

Figure 1-112. *Properties panel settings for Curves for the current garden image*

125

Adding the sky replacement visibility back in, we can see the colors in the image are now overall balanced. On your own project, this may reveal additional imperfections where you may want to use the Clone Stamp tool to correct inside of your smart object layer 2. Remember to do that (double-click) on the Layers thumbnail to open it and make your edits. When done save any changes inside the opened .psb file before you close it and return to the .psd file that shows your adjustment layers. Refer to Figure 1-112.

More details on Curves can be found at the following link:

https://helpx.adobe.com/photoshop/using/curves-adjustment.html

File ➤ Save any of your open files at this point. Refer to **garden_image_replace_sky_color_adjustments.psd** and **white_terrace_walls_final.psd** if you need to compare to your own work so far.

Hue/Saturation

This adjustment layer allows you to use the sliders to alter the hue, saturation, and lightness values of the entire image. However, alternatively you can also target and alter individual color components.

Use either your Adjustments panel (Single adjustments) or your Layers panel to set this adjustment layer. Refer to Figure 1-113.

CHAPTER 1 ADJUSTMENT LAYERS, BLENDING MODES WITH MASKS FOR PHOTO RESTORATION: PART 1

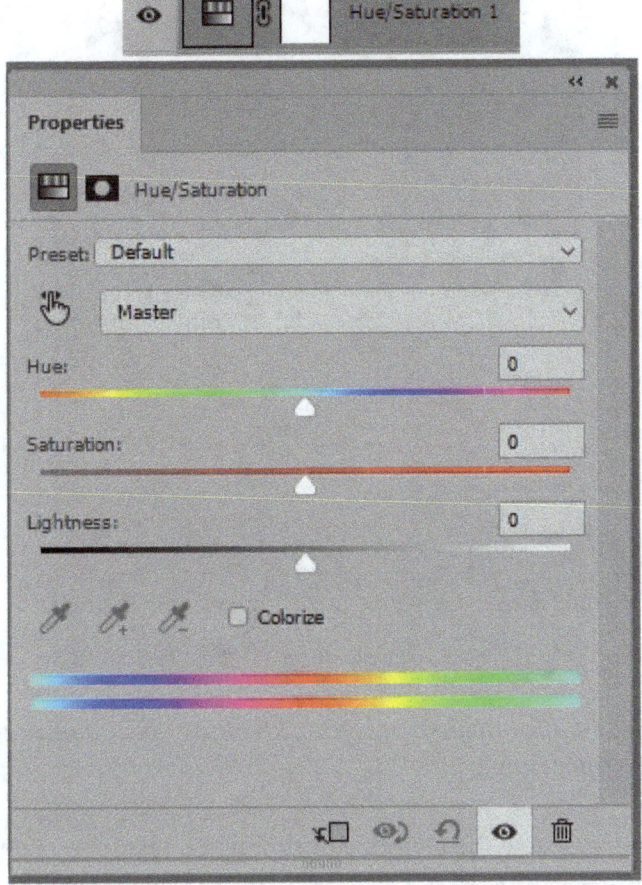

Figure 1-113. *Properties panel settings for Hue/Saturation and the Adjustment Layer*

Sometimes I will use this adjustment along with my Levels and Curves or even separately if I need to adjust clothing or in this case skin tones, which appear to be red or areas that need saturation reduced.

You can use this selection of an image called **accordion_hue_saturation.psd** as there is too much red in this image. Refer to Figure 1-114.

CHAPTER 1   ADJUSTMENT LAYERS, BLENDING MODES WITH MASKS FOR PHOTO RESTORATION: PART 1

Figure 1-114. *Color adjustments to skin tone can be made with Hue/Saturation adjustments*

Likewise, I also use the Colorize option when I want to create unique sepia tone images either as the original color or in new color tint options. I will show how this can be a great adjustment in combination with masks on separate adjustment layers when you want to colorize an image. It is a good alternative to the dodge, burn, and sponge tools mentioned in Volume 1, Chapter 4, and can be used in combination with your solid color fills as you saw earlier.

The Properties settings found for Hue/Saturation are as follows:

Preset: Select a preset hue/saturation. This is similar to using the Adjustments presets that are in the Adjustments panel. Once you have selected one, you can manually edit it and it will display as Custom. When no changes have been made, it is set to Default. Refer to Figure 1-115.

CHAPTER 1 ADJUSTMENT LAYERS, BLENDING MODES WITH MASKS FOR PHOTO RESTORATION: PART 1

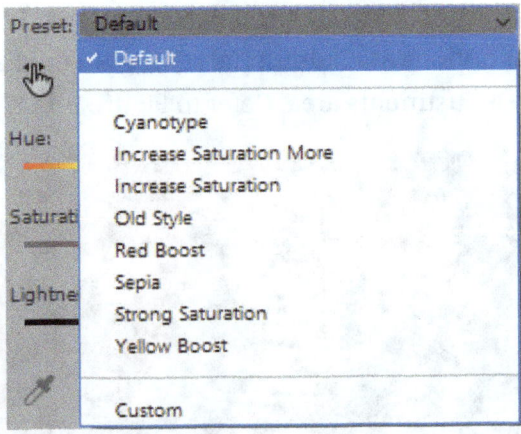

Figure 1-115. *Properties panel settings for Hue/Saturation, presets*

Master and other color options: Currently this list is set to Master to affect all colors. However, you can, from the list, choose other options such as reds, yellows, greens, cyans, blues, or magentas if you want to modify those colors in the image only. However, like channels for RGB Curves, note that individual settings in these areas may be different than the master. Refer to Figure 1-116.

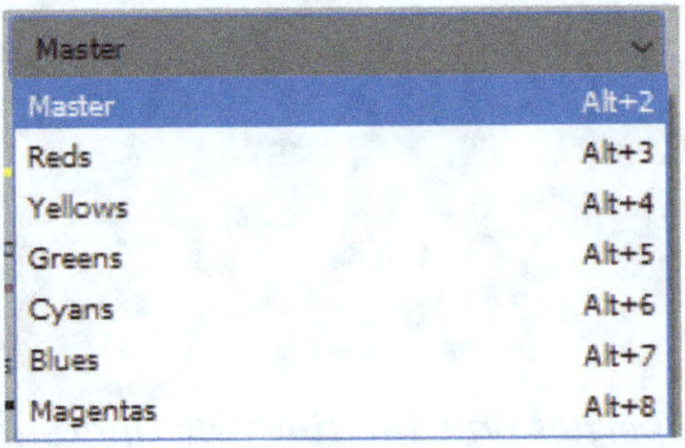

Figure 1-116. *Properties panel settings for Hue/Saturation, color options*

On-Image Adjustment Tool button: When enabled, click and drag on the canvas image to modify saturation or Ctrl/CMD + click and drag left or right to modify hue. As with Curves this can assist you when you are trying

CHAPTER 1 ADJUSTMENT LAYERS, BLENDING MODES WITH MASKS FOR PHOTO RESTORATION: PART 1

to adjust a specific set of colors. Using it will enable a different color as well as the eyedropper options and additional settings in the before/after color slider color range adjustments area. Refer to Figure 1-117.

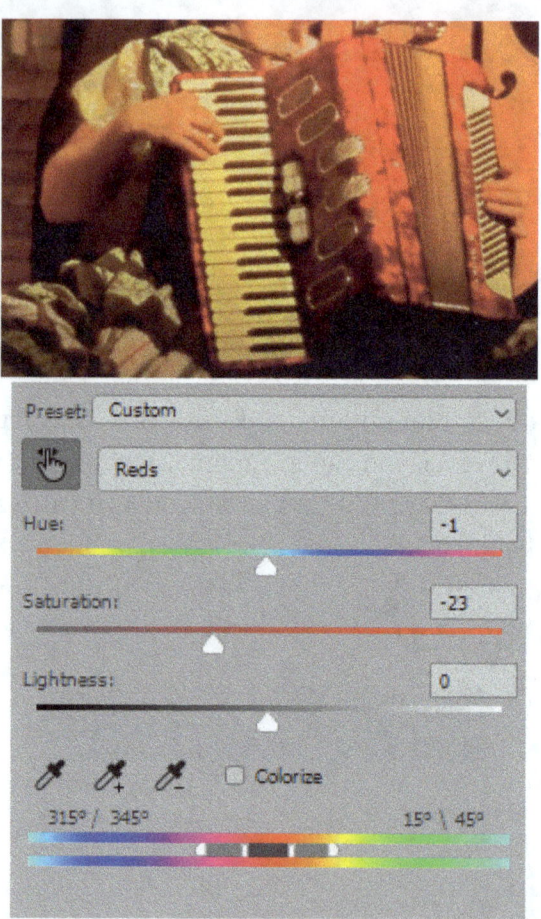

Figure 1-117. Properties panel settings for Hue/Saturation: the slider can reduce saturation in the image in the reds

Hue slider (–180, 0, +180): The values displayed in the box reflect the number of degrees of rotation around a color wheel from the original pixel's color. Each pixel will shift accordingly, which is why you get some

CHAPTER 1 ADJUSTMENT LAYERS, BLENDING MODES WITH MASKS FOR PHOTO RESTORATION: PART 1

unusual results if you move the sliders too drastically left (negative) or right (positive) while working with the master colors. A positive value indicates clockwise rotation; a negative value indicates counterclockwise rotation. Often, to color correct, a slight shift to the right or left is all that is needed. To affect just the Hue slider in a set color range, you can as mentioned hold down the Ctrl/CMD key and click and drag on the image with the On-image Adjustment Tool button enabled. Refer to Figure 1-117.

Saturation slider (–100, 0, +100): Dragging the slider to the left decreases the saturation or right increases the saturation. Beware that this can affect the colors in your image overall. To affect just the Saturation slider in a set color range, you can as mentioned click and drag on the image with the On-image Adjustment Tool button enabled; this will affect the set of pixels clicked. Refer to Figure 1-117.

Lightness slider (–100, 0, +100): Drag the slider left to decrease and add more black or right to increase the lightness adding more white. This is ideal when you want to create a faded or more shadowed area with a layer mask or overall. Refer to Figure 1-118.

Figure 1-118. Properties panel settings for Hue/Saturation, Lightness slider

CHAPTER 1 ADJUSTMENT LAYERS, BLENDING MODES WITH MASKS FOR PHOTO RESTORATION: PART 1

Eyedropper, Add to Sample, Subtract from Sample: These buttons only become active after you have started to use the On-image Adjustment Tool button or when you have switched to a color range other than the Master. Use an eyedropper to first select a color range and then, with the other eyedroppers, click and drag on the image to either add to or subtract from the sample. This will then display in the before and after color area with a specific color range and additional sliders. Subtract the range, such as selecting other areas, like around an instrument, which have a similar color to the original skin tone color. Refer to Figure 1-119.

Figure 1-119. *Properties panel settings for Hue/Saturation, eyedropper samplers with the On-image Adjustment Tool and color range*

CHAPTER 1 ADJUSTMENT LAYERS, BLENDING MODES WITH MASKS FOR PHOTO RESTORATION: PART 1

Colorize check box: This is an optional setting that creates a type of monochrome effect, when enabled for a specific color, which is ideal for creating sepia tone or hand-tinted prints as you did earlier with the solid color. With this setting enabled you still have access to the Hue, Saturation, and Lightness sliders to create an overall color adjustment. In the Tools panel, if the foreground color is black or white, the image is converted to a red hue or 0°. However, if the foreground color is neither black nor white, the image is converted to the hue of whatever the current foreground color is before the adjustment layer was created. The lightness value of each pixel will not change unless you manually adjust it along with your Hue and Saturation sliders. Also shown is a preview bar of the original and current color adjustments. Refer to Figure 1-120.

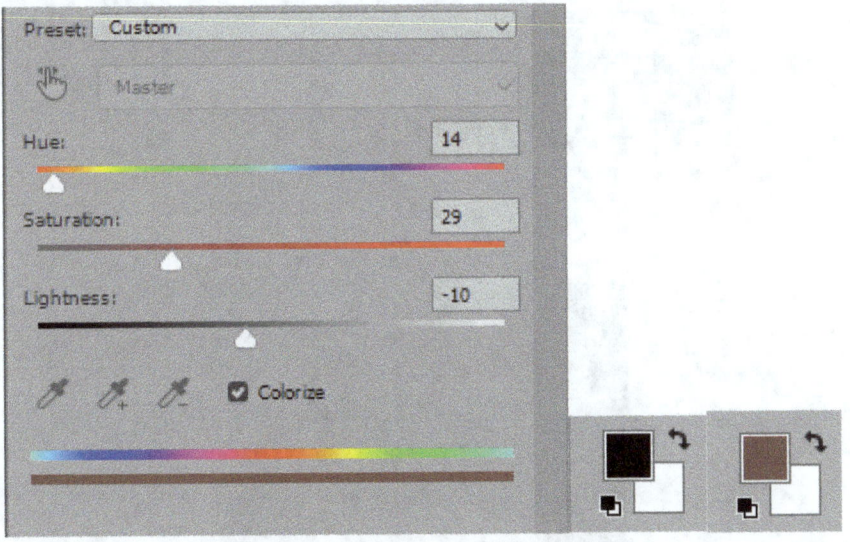

Figure 1-120. Properties panel settings for Hue/Saturation, using the Colorize setting and the Tools panel foreground color to alter the swatch

In the example of the castle image, notice that I used a brownish red tile color to colorize select areas of the image (Hue:14, Saturation: 29, Lightness -10), such as the roof, and painted on the layer mask with the Eraser tool. In this case I could leave the blending mode at Normal and still

133

CHAPTER 1 ADJUSTMENT LAYERS, BLENDING MODES WITH MASKS FOR PHOTO RESTORATION: PART 1

have the black-and-white details appear behind it. See **castle_solid_fill_final.psd**. Refer to Figure 1-121.

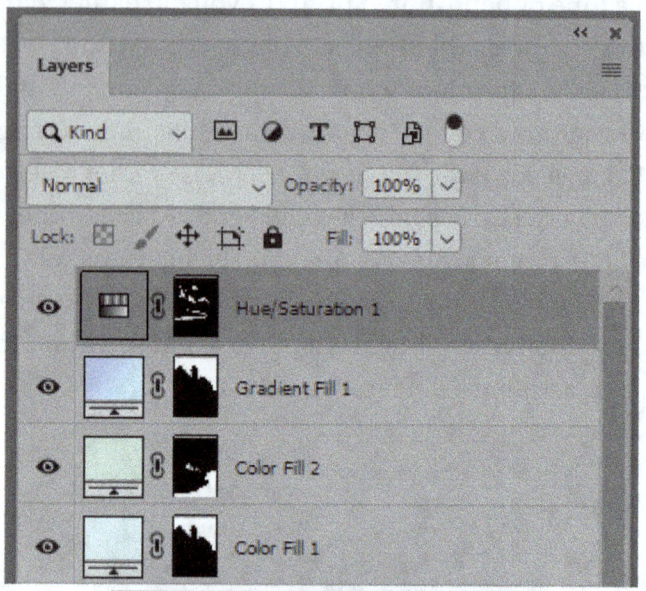

Figure 1-121. *Hue/Saturation adjustment layer added to the Layers panel and the roof of the castle is now colorized*

CHAPTER 1 ADJUSTMENT LAYERS, BLENDING MODES WITH MASKS FOR PHOTO RESTORATION: PART 1

Likewise, you could add more of these adjustment layers to colorize other areas as you did with the solid fills.

Tip With a color image you can also leave parts in color with a mask as I did with the following **bird.psd** image. Refer to Figure 1-122.

CHAPTER 1 ADJUSTMENT LAYERS, BLENDING MODES WITH MASKS FOR PHOTO RESTORATION: PART 1

Figure 1-122. *Properties panel settings for Hue/Saturation set to Colorize and a layer mask around areas of the bird that I want to remain in real color*

Note To avoid painting over another colored area, I will, when I first create the adjustment layer without a selection, then invert the selected layer mask right away (Ctrl/CMD + I), before I begin to paint on it.

Before/after color slider adjustments (color range): These are available when the Colorize check box is disabled and you are adjusting the colors in an image other than the master. It shows preview bar color adjustments as the sliders are moved. The lower horizontal bar will show after changes if you alter any of the sliders such as Hue. If your On-Image Targeted Adjustment Tool button has been used or you set a specific color range, this area will then have two sliders and two vertical bars that allow you to in degrees (hue values) adjust the color range for specific colors that correspond to the color values in the color wheel.

The inner sliders that appear as vertical bars define the color range; you can move them inward or closer to the outer fall-off sliders. Refer to Figure 1-123.

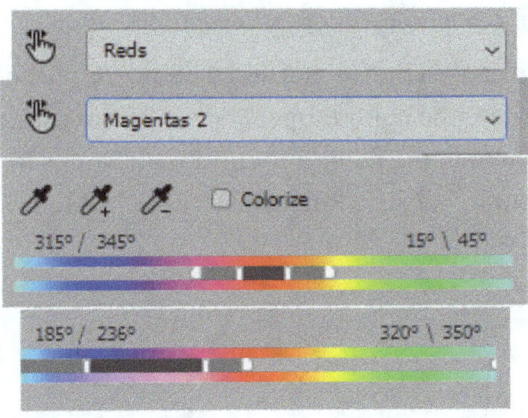

Figure 1-123. Properties panel settings for Hue/Saturation, sliders adjusted for a specific color range

CHAPTER 1   ADJUSTMENT LAYERS, BLENDING MODES WITH MASKS FOR PHOTO RESTORATION: PART 1

While the outer triangular sliders show where the adjustments on a color range "fall off," Adobe defines the "fall-off" as feathering or tapering of the adjustments instead of a sharply defined on/off application of the adjustments. A sharp tapering or low fall-off would be very abrupt or could have a posterizing or banding effect, which would not look natural. Dragging on these sliders will not affect the inner color range sliders.

You can also drag on an area between a triangle and a vertical bar slider to affect the size of the color range. Dragging in the center between the two vertical bars will move the entire slider set, and this may cause it to move into a different color range, and the name will appear in the color options menu. Refer to Figure 1-124.

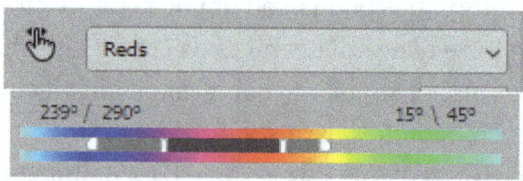

Figure 1-124. *Properties panel settings for Hue/Saturation, sliders adjusted for a specific color range such as reds in the color options menu*

However, you can set between 2 and 6 in individual color ranges or varieties within the same color range. They will have the color name and a number beside them in the color options menu. Notice in this example it is now called magentas 2 and no longer reds. Refer to Figure 1-125.

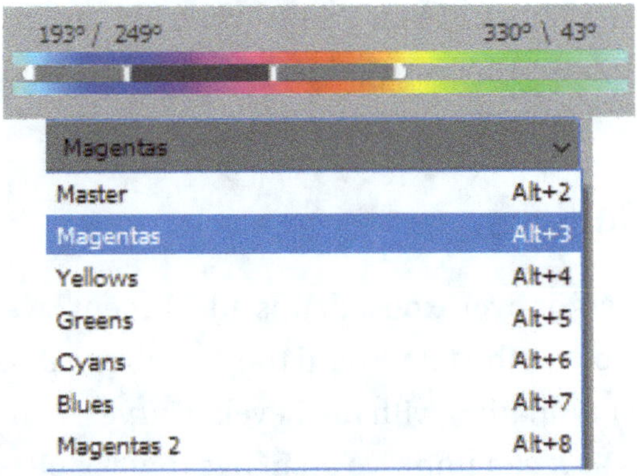

CHAPTER 1 ADJUSTMENT LAYERS, BLENDING MODES WITH MASKS FOR PHOTO RESTORATION: PART 1

Figure 1-125. Properties panel settings for Hue/Saturation, sliders adjusted for a specific color range such as a different magentas from the color options menu

By default, the settings are color range 30 degrees wide and 30 degrees fall-off on each side. In some images moving these sliders may have little or no effect.

Note to undo any settings in the master or individual colors, use the reset button in the Properties panel. Refer to Figure 1-126.

Figure 1-126. Properties panel settings, reset button in the panel

Hue/Saturation presets are saved and loaded as (.AHU) files.

You can also use Hue/Saturation for fine-tuning of colors in CMYK or Lab images but not for grayscale.

More details on Hue/Saturation can be found at the following link:

https://helpx.adobe.com/photoshop/using/adjusting-hue-saturation.html

CHAPTER 1 ADJUSTMENT LAYERS, BLENDING MODES WITH MASKS FOR PHOTO RESTORATION: PART 1

File ➤ Save your images so far and you can refer to the files **accordion_hue_saturation_final.psd**, **castle_solid_fill_final.psd**, and **bird final.psd** as you work.

Brightness/Contrast

If an image is under- or overexposed, this adjustment layer can make slight adjustments to improve the image and the overall tonal range. I like to use this filter in combination with my Levels, Curves, and Hue/Saturation adjustment layers as it can improve an image that is dull or with a low contrast.

In the file **white_terrace_walls.psd**, we looked at earlier, we can certainly add a bit of brightness and contrast so that areas in the midtone to highlight areas do not completely become washed out if your overall color adjustments cause this. Continue to work in your duplicate image. Refer to Figure 1-127.

CHAPTER 1 ADJUSTMENT LAYERS, BLENDING MODES WITH MASKS FOR PHOTO RESTORATION: PART 1

Figure 1-127. *Use Brightness/Contrast to affect the current image*

Use either your Adjustments panel (Single adjustments) or your Layers panel to set this adjustment layer. Refer to Figure 1-128.

CHAPTER 1 ADJUSTMENT LAYERS, BLENDING MODES WITH MASKS FOR PHOTO RESTORATION: PART 1

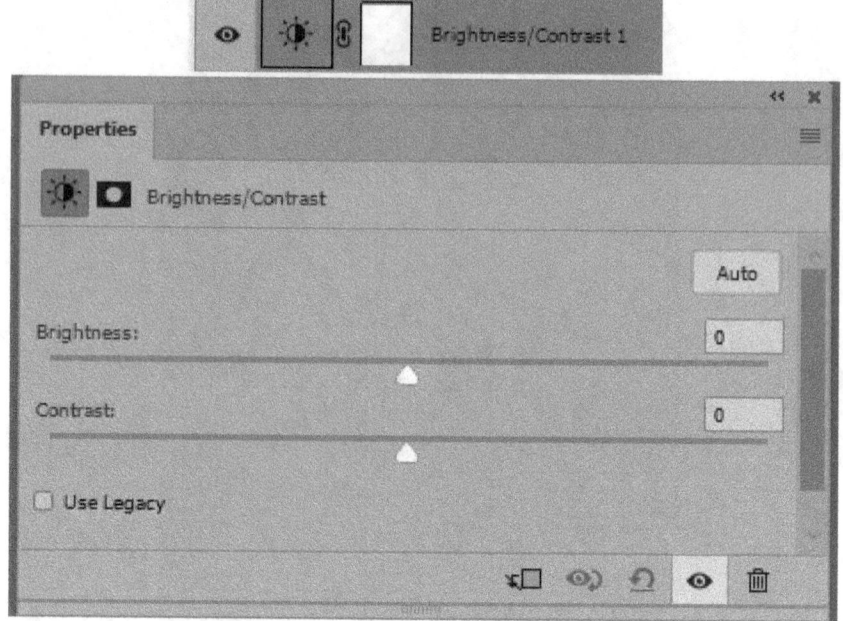

Figure 1-128. Properties panel settings for Brightness/Contrast and the adjustment layer

The Properties settings found for Brightness/Contrast are as follows:

Auto: Automatically correct brightness and contrast. Note that unlike the Levels and Curves, there is no extra dialog box that you can access from this button.

Brightness (–150, 0, +150): Control the brightness settings by dragging the slider. Moving to the left darkens the image shadows, while to the right it lightens the highlights.

Contrast (–50, 0, +100): Control the contrast setting by dragging the slider. Drag to the left for a lower contrast and to the right for a higher contrast. Move in small increments as you do not want to create extreme contrast settings even in black-and-white images.

Use Legacy: This check box when enabled uses the older legacy behavior of shifting the pixels (clips shadow/highlight detail). By default, it is disabled as it is not recommended for photographic images, only for editing a layer mask or certain scientific imagery as there could be a loss or clipping of details. When this setting is disabled, this is considered "Normal" mode where proportionate adjustments are applied as you would with Levels and Curves.

This adjustment layer does not allow you to save single presets.

Using the settings of brightness –4 and contrast –1 adds some slight detail back into the wall darkening some areas. Refer to Figure 1-129.

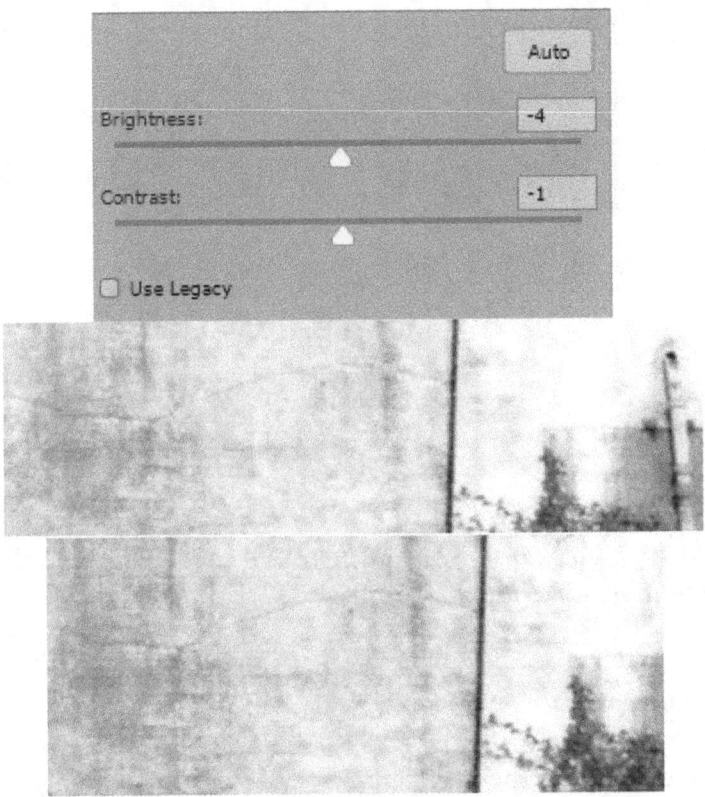

Figure 1-129. *Properties panel settings for Brightness/Contrast and the alterations in the color of the wall in the image*

CHAPTER 1 ADJUSTMENT LAYERS, BLENDING MODES WITH MASKS FOR PHOTO RESTORATION: PART 1

Refer to the file **white_terrace_walls_final.psd** for comparison.

More details on Brightness/Contrast can be found at the following link: https://helpx.adobe.com/photoshop/using/apply-brightness-contrast-adjustment.html

---

Note as you work with multiple adjustment layers, the order in which you add them can affect the overall color outcome as well. Reordering or sometimes just turning off and on an adjustment layer's visibility can help you discover if it still is required or not. Refer to Figure 1-130.

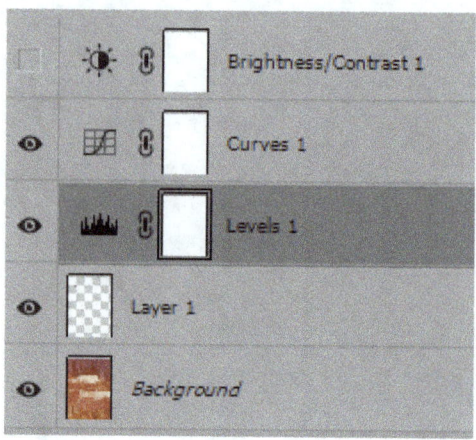

Figure 1-130. Check how your adjustments are affecting other adjustment layers in the Layers panel

Color Balance

Color Balance changes the overall mixture of colors in an image when moving the sliders. This can alter the colors if you feel that the image has too much of a cast in one channel. It has some similarities to the way Hue/Saturation works and may be a better option for certain color correction situations that require more intense conversion. In the case of the following pillar image, we can see that this stonework and the image overall have taken on a purplish pink cast. I first cleaned up the dust and scratches in the image surrounding the pillars using a layer mask and the dust and scratches filter, which we will see in Chapter 3. We need to balance the stonework, so it looks more natural. See file **pillars_color_balance.psd** for reference. Refer to Figure 1-131.

Figure 1-131. *This faded image of some pillars needs a color balance*

Use either your Adjustments panel (Single adjustments) or your Layers panel to set this adjustment layer. Refer to Figure 1-132.

CHAPTER 1 ADJUSTMENT LAYERS, BLENDING MODES WITH MASKS FOR PHOTO RESTORATION: PART 1

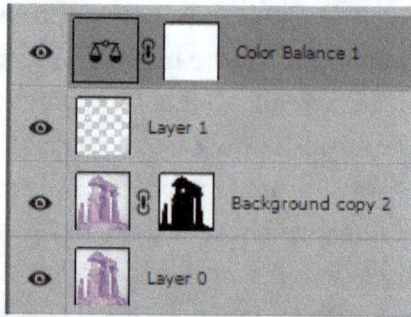

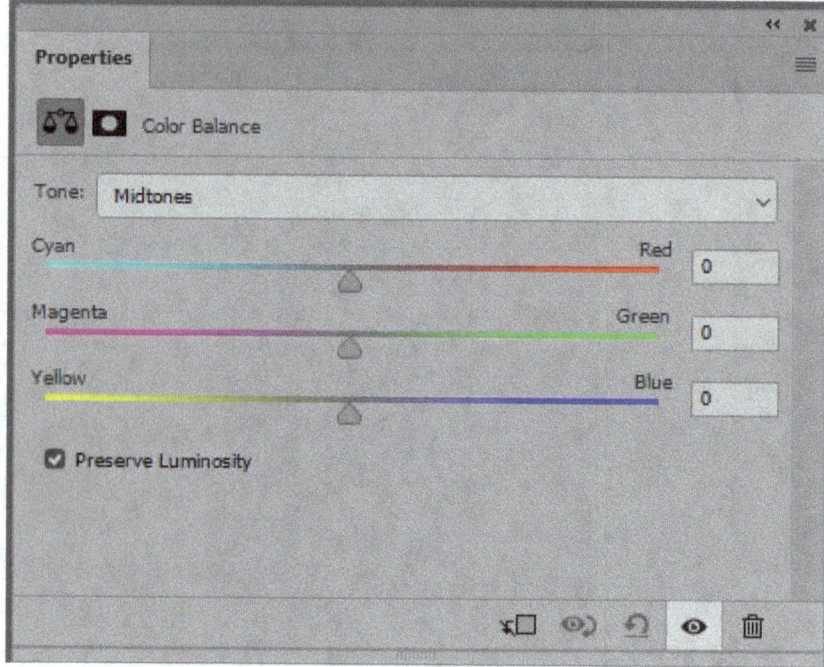

Figure 1-132. *Layers panel and Properties panel settings for Color Balance*

The Properties settings found for Color Balance are as follows:

Tone: Set your overall tonal range settings for either the Shadows, Midtones, or Highlights by selecting that tone balance setting from the list; by default it is set to Midtones. As you choose different options for the sliders, the image will change color to match what current tone setting you are altering. Refer to Figure 1-133.

CHAPTER 1 ADJUSTMENT LAYERS, BLENDING MODES WITH MASKS FOR PHOTO RESTORATION: PART 1

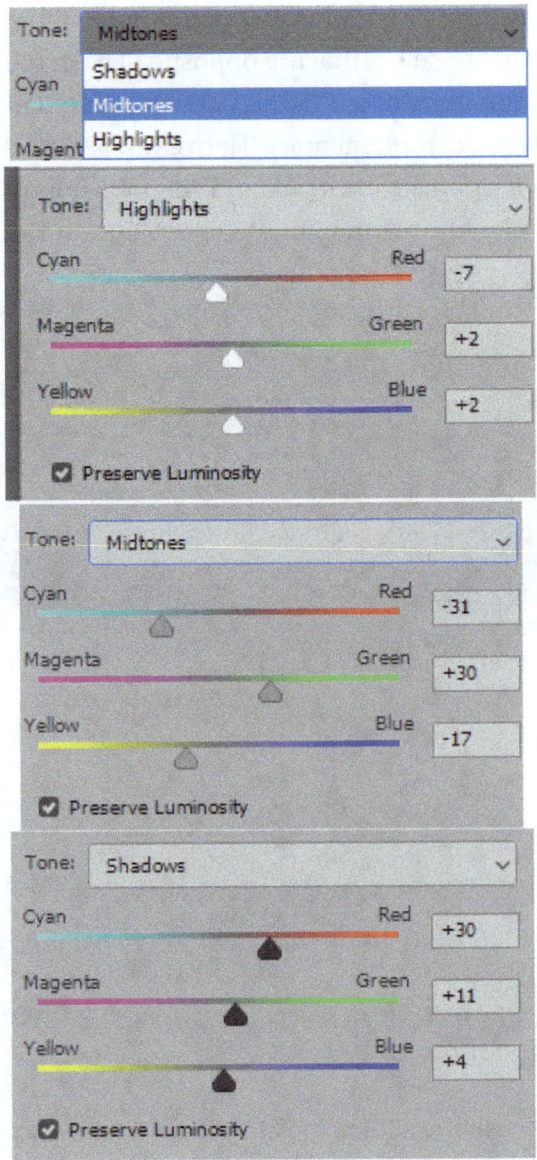

Figure 1-133. *Properties panel settings for Color Balance, Tone and slider settings*

CHAPTER 1   ADJUSTMENT LAYERS, BLENDING MODES WITH MASKS FOR PHOTO RESTORATION: PART 1

The reason that the sliders area is set up as such is that if we consider a color wheel there are colors that are opposite of each other, and they are known as complementary or in this case how the color falls on the wheel is an example of split complementary. Here Cyan is considered opposite to Red, Magenta is opposite to Green, and Yellow is opposite to Blue, balancing the cool to the warm hues. Refer to Figure 1-134.

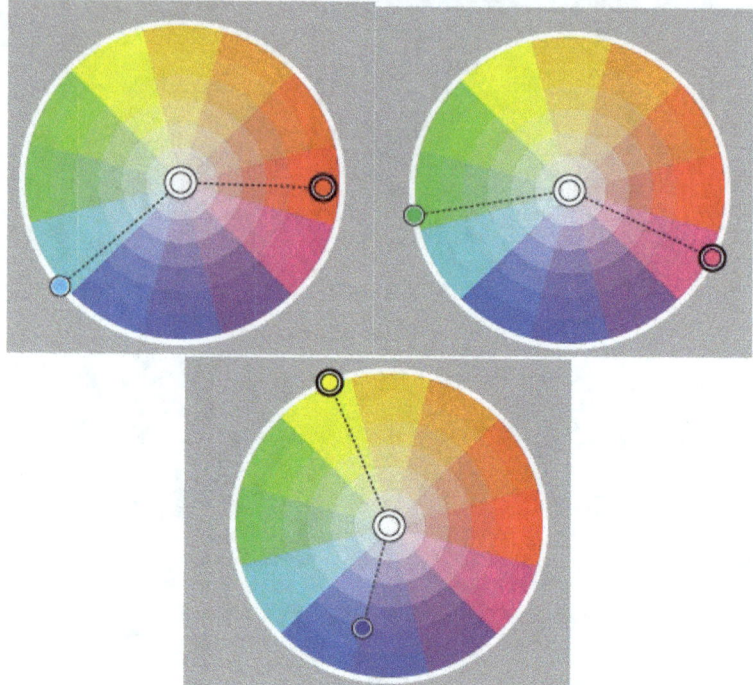

Figure 1-134. *An example of the color wheel displaying the distribution of the slider colors*

Therefore, we use the sliders to shift the balance between these split complementary pairs to achieve a more balanced result. Refer to Figure 1-135.

CHAPTER 1 ADJUSTMENT LAYERS, BLENDING MODES WITH MASKS FOR PHOTO RESTORATION: PART 1

Figure 1-135. *Improvements to the colors of the image made with color balance*

How colors exactly fall is not an exact science where one color begins in nature and ends; it's not abrupt but graduated. Observing the flat 2D color wheel is not the same as the 3D wheel or how it is displayed in nature. Also, from an art perspective, we would likely consider a red to green, blue to orange/yellow, and magenta to yellow/green to be actual complementary color sets. Yet, this is how Photoshop has arranged its simplified sliders to do the complex math calculations behind the scenes that affect hue, saturation, and brightness. Refer to Figure 1-136.

CHAPTER 1   ADJUSTMENT LAYERS, BLENDING MODES WITH MASKS FOR PHOTO RESTORATION: PART 1

Figure 1-136. *Colors in 3D on the color wheel*

The settings for the sliders are as follows:

Cyan–Red slider (–100, 0, +100): Use this setting to adjust your color in either the shadows, midtones, or highlights. You can shift from Cyan to Red tones to adjust the overall cast toward a color that you want to add to the image and away from the color you want to remove or reduce in the image.

CHAPTER 1   ADJUSTMENT LAYERS, BLENDING MODES WITH MASKS FOR PHOTO RESTORATION: PART 1

Magenta–Green slider (–100, 0, +100): Use this setting to adjust your color in either the shadows, midtones, or highlights. You can shift from Magenta to Green tones to adjust the overall cast.

Yellow–Blue slider (–100, 0, +100): Use this setting to adjust your color in either the shadows, midtones, or highlights. You can shift from Yellow to Blue tones to adjust the overall cast. Refer to Figure 1-137.

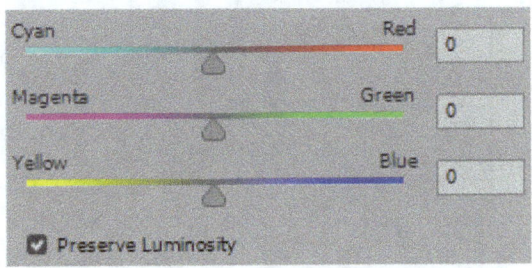

Figure 1-137. *Properties panel settings for Color Balance with sliders*

The values to the right of these sliders show the color value changes for the red, green, and blue channels. However, observe your Histogram and Info panels to get the full understanding of the shift.

Preserve Luminosity: This setting is enabled by default to maintain image brightness and overall tonal balance and prevent changing the luminosity values in the image while changing the color values.

Move the sliders in the various tones and observe the changes to the image.

Adobe also recommends using Color Balance in combination with Photo Filter for various adjustments.

However, in this case adding a Brightness/Contrast and even adjusting the levels of the image may also bring out certain color details. Refer to Figure 1-138.

CHAPTER 1 ADJUSTMENT LAYERS, BLENDING MODES WITH MASKS FOR PHOTO RESTORATION: PART 1

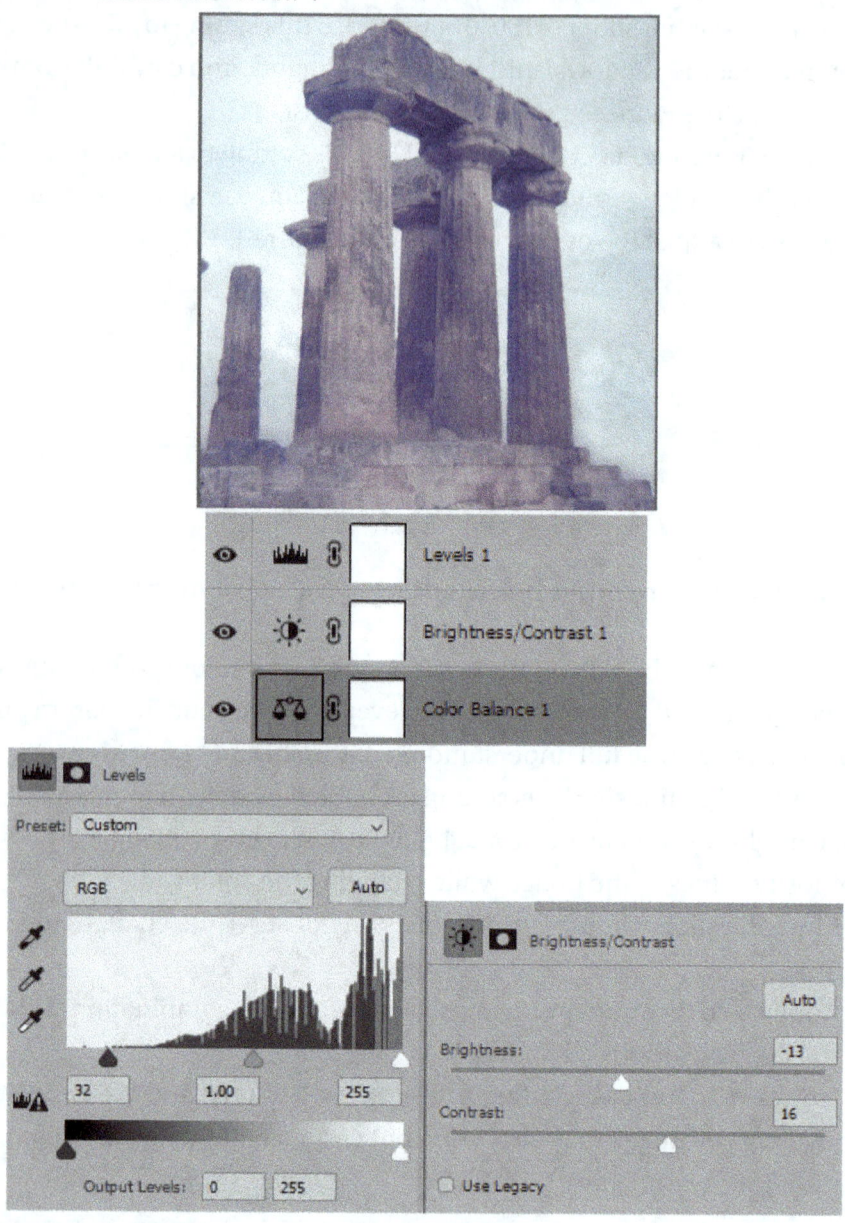

Figure 1-138. *Additional adjustments of Levels and Brightness/Contrast may need to be added to the Layers panel and adjusted using the Properties panel*

More details on Color Balance can be found at the following link:

https://helpx.adobe.com/photoshop/using/applying-color-balance-adjustment.html

File ➤ Save your work so far. Refer to the file **pillars_color_balance_final.psd** and Figure 1-133 for color balance settings used.

Black & White

This adjustment layer is great for when you want to create a black-and-white or sepia image. I like that you can use this to affect the layers overall but also, in combination with a layer mask, remove certain colors that may be caused by stains or discoloration.

In the case of the black-and-white image **castle_solid_fill.psd**, you could now use the adjustment layer to enhance the tone of the stone areas to a more sepia color. These are areas that were not tinted using solid color or Hue/Saturation. Note however that unless I mask out certain areas, this will give an overall yellower color to any adjustment layers above and solid color fills that had blending modes applied. Refer to Figure 1-139.

CHAPTER 1 ADJUSTMENT LAYERS, BLENDING MODES WITH MASKS FOR PHOTO RESTORATION: PART 1

Figure 1-139. *Altering color using the Black & White adjustment layers*

Use either your Adjustments panel (Single adjustments) or your Layers panel to set this adjustment layer. Refer to Figure 1-140.

CHAPTER 1 ADJUSTMENT LAYERS, BLENDING MODES WITH MASKS FOR PHOTO RESTORATION: PART 1

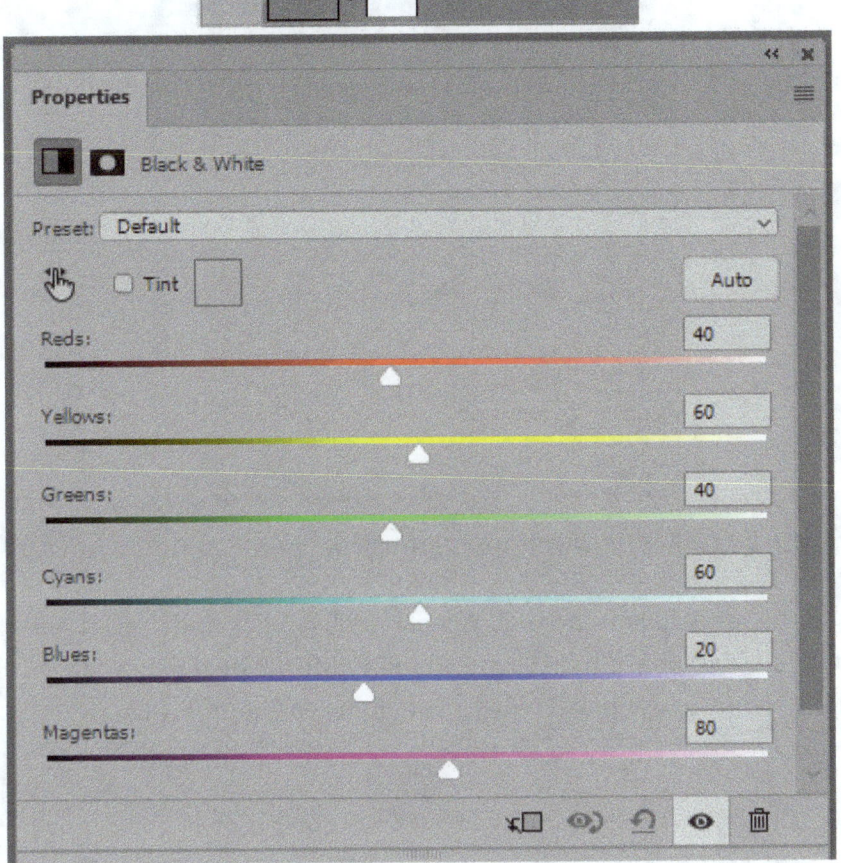

Figure 1-140. *Layers panel and Properties panel settings for Black & White*

The Properties settings found for Black and White are as follows:

Preset: Select a preset Black & White filter effect. This is similar to using the Adjustments presets that are in the Adjustments panel. Once you have selected one, you can manually edit it and it will display as Custom. When no changes have been made, it is set to Default grayscale conversion. Refer to Figure 1-141.

155

CHAPTER 1 ADJUSTMENT LAYERS, BLENDING MODES WITH MASKS FOR PHOTO RESTORATION: PART 1

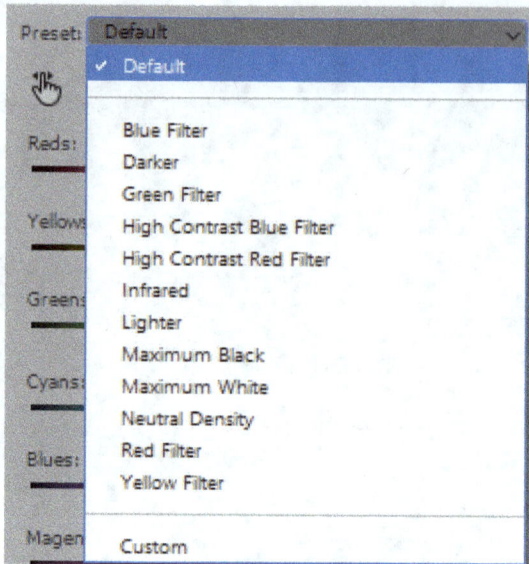

Figure 1-141. Properties panel settings for Black & White, presets

On-image Adjustment Tool: When enabled, click and drag on the canvas left (darken) or right (lighten) to modify the overall grayscale color and the sliders in the panel will update. Refer to Figure 1-142.

Figure 1-142. Properties panel settings for Black & White, On-image Adjustment Tool

Tint: When this is enabled, it allows you to access a swatch from the color picker rather than just use overall color sliders to adjust: R: 232, G: 221, B: 197. Refer to Figure 1-143.

CHAPTER 1 ADJUSTMENT LAYERS, BLENDING MODES WITH MASKS FOR PHOTO RESTORATION: PART 1

Figure 1-143. *Properties panel settings for Black & White for Tint and Auto button*

Auto: Auto sets the black and white settings based on the image's color values. Then you can adjust the gray values using the sliders. Unlike Levels and Curves, it does not have any additional settings. Refer to Figure 1-145.

Reds, Yellows, Greens, Cyans, Blues, and Magentas sliders have a range of (-200, 0, 300). They are often set to a default of Reds: 40, Yellows: 60, Greens: 40, Cyans: 60, Blues: 20, Magentas: 80. Refer to Figure 1-144.

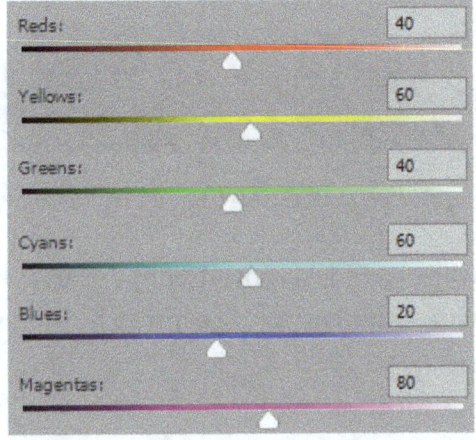

Figure 1-144. *Properties panel settings for Black & White for color sliders*

CHAPTER 1   ADJUSTMENT LAYERS, BLENDING MODES WITH MASKS FOR PHOTO
            RESTORATION: PART 1

Their main purpose is to adjust the gray tones of a specific color in your image. Drag the sliders to the left to darken and right to lighten the gray tones, which will correspond to the colors in your underlying image. However, you can move these sliders to clear up stains and color casts that may appear unwelcome in a black-and-white image. This could be overall or when using the layer mask in a specific area, as you will look at shortly and later in Chapter 2 when you continue with the army photo project.

Use the Save option in the Properties panel's menu if you want to save any settings you create. Black & White presets are saved and loaded as (.BLW) files.

Use the reset icon in the Properties panel if you need to reset any setting as you work. Refer to Figure 1-145.

Figure 1-145. Properties panel settings in the lower bar

We can see how the stain is removed from the area overall and around the car in the following tinted image. See image **home.psd**. Refer to Figure 1-146.

CHAPTER 1 ADJUSTMENT LAYERS, BLENDING MODES WITH MASKS FOR PHOTO RESTORATION: PART 1

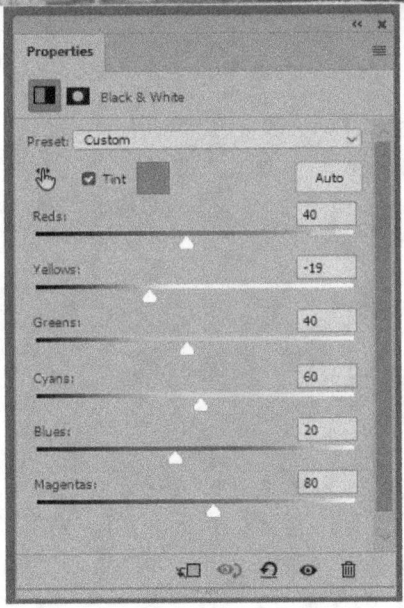

Figure 1-146. *Properties panel settings for Black & White can be used to reduce the stains in the image*

More details on Black & White can be found at the following link:

https://helpx.adobe.com/photoshop/using/convert-color-image-black-white.html

File ➤ Save any images you have open. Refer to file **castle_solid_fill_final.psd** for reference.

Exposure

This adjustment is ideal for working with HDR images to adjust tonality by performing calculations in linear color space.

HDR in photography refers to High Dynamic Range to capture an entire image scene that has both bright highlights and dark shadows. This is often common in digital photography where you may take several images (2-9) of one scene and some areas are overexposed and others underexposed. The images may then be blended together to create one properly exposed image with a complete tonal range. Refer to Figure 1-147.

CHAPTER 1   ADJUSTMENT LAYERS, BLENDING MODES WITH MASKS FOR PHOTO RESTORATION: PART 1

Figure 1-147. *Use the Exposure adjustment layer to adjust and make changes in your image*

However, when it comes to family photos, unless taken professionally, it is unlikely that you will have such a set of film prints or slide images like this, and this is more common with images that you take with a digital camera. However, using this adjustment layer you may be able to mimic that. I used the example of the tower image, which we looked at in Volume 1, Chapter 8, when we were working with the Content-Aware Fill workspace. However, even though the sky and grass are not bad, the tower is dark and underexposed, it could be lightened. Refer to the image **tower_exposure.psd.** Refer to Figure 1-148.

CHAPTER 1 ADJUSTMENT LAYERS, BLENDING MODES WITH MASKS FOR PHOTO RESTORATION: PART 1

Figure 1-148. *The tower in the image is dark and underexposed and could benefit from an exposure setting*

While Exposure and HDR Toning adjustments are primarily designed for 32-bit HDR images, you can also apply them to 16-bit and scanned 8-bit images to create HDR-like effects, as we will in this case.

Use either your Adjustments panel (Single adjustments) or your Layers panel to set this adjustment layer. Refer to Figure 1-149.

CHAPTER 1 ADJUSTMENT LAYERS, BLENDING MODES WITH MASKS FOR PHOTO RESTORATION: PART 1

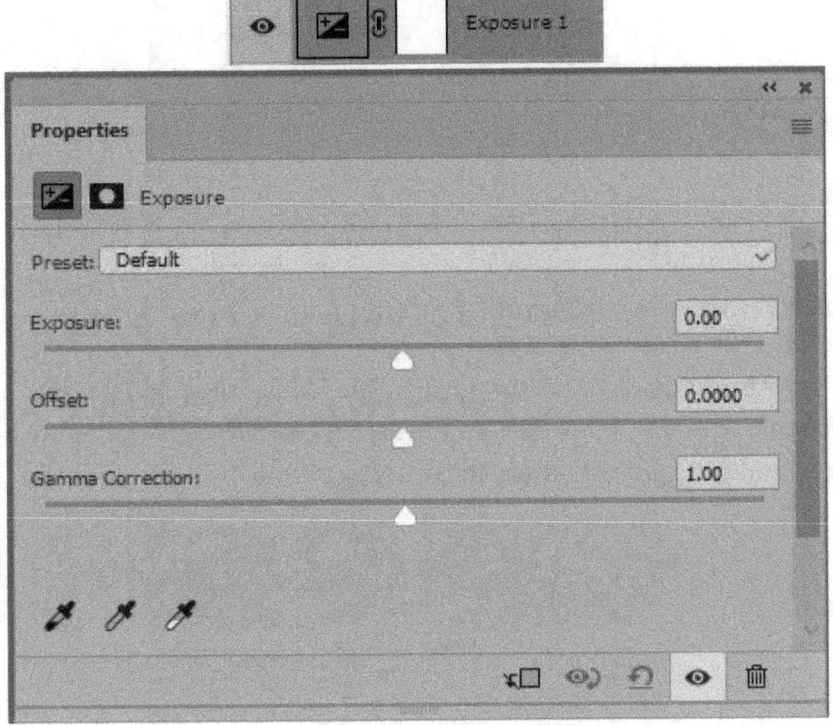

Figure 1-149. *Properties panel settings for Exposure*

The Properties settings found for Exposure are as follows:

Preset: Select a preset Exposure adjustment. This is similar to using the Adjustments presets that are in the Adjustments panel. Once you have selected one, you can manually edit it and it will display as Custom. When no changes have been made, it is set to Default. Refer to Figure 1-150.

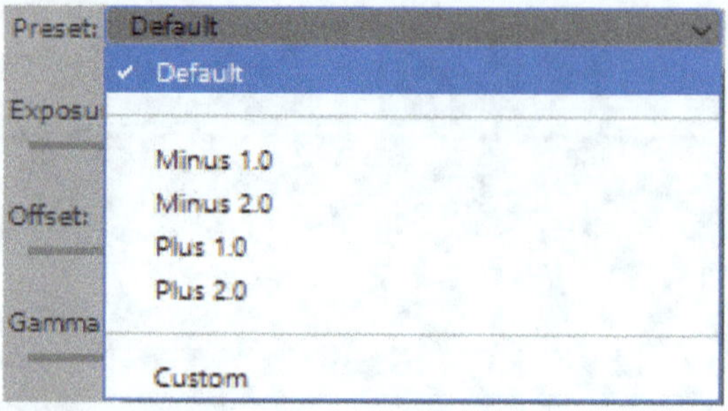

CHAPTER 1   ADJUSTMENT LAYERS, BLENDING MODES WITH MASKS FOR PHOTO RESTORATION: PART 1

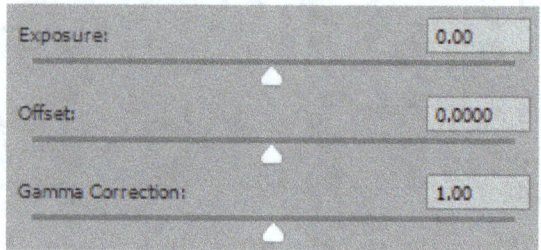

Figure 1-150. *Properties panel settings for Exposure, presets*

Exposure slider (–20.00, 0, +20.00): This adjusts the highlight end of the tonal scale with minimal effect on the extreme shadows. Move to the left to darken and the right to lighten. Refer to Figure 1-151.

Figure 1-151. *Properties panel settings for Exposure, slider settings*

Offset slider (–0.5000, 0, +0.5000): This darkens the shadows and midtones with minimal effect on the highlights. Moving to the left will cause the image to darken, and to the right it gradually becomes gray with lowered contrast.

Gamma Correction (9.99, 0.01): This adjusts the image's gamma range. Higher values lighten and lower values darken; by default it is set to 1.00.

Set black point, gray point, and white point: Clicking the canvas image in a specific point will sample and adjust the settings in the preceding sliders. Unlike eyedroppers found in Levels and Curves, these function a bit differently; they adjust the luminance values of images (unlike the Levels eyedroppers that affect all of the color channels). Refer to Figure 1-152.

CHAPTER 1 ADJUSTMENT LAYERS, BLENDING MODES WITH MASKS FOR PHOTO RESTORATION: PART 1

Figure 1-152. *Properties panel settings for Exposure, three eyedropper samplers*

Set black point eyedropper: Sets the Offset slider, shifting the pixel you click to zero or a negative number. Refer to Figure 1-153.

Figure 1-153. *Properties panel settings for Exposure, Offset slider, negative value*

Set white point eyedropper: Sets the Exposure slider, shifting the point you click to white or a positive number. Refer to Figure 1-154.

Figure 1-154. *Properties panel settings for Exposure, Exposure slider, positive value*

Set midtone (gray point) eyedropper: Sets the Exposure slider, making the value you click middle gray but now set to a negative number. Refer to Figure 1-155.

Figure 1-155. *Properties panel settings for Exposure, Exposure slider, negative value*

Note that none of the eyedroppers will alter the gamma correction and you must set this manually yourself.

Exposure presets are saved and loaded as (.EAP) files.

In this example I manually adjusted the sliders for exposure overall. Exposure is set to +0.17, Offset 0, and Gamma Correction 1.19. This lightened the image a bit. Refer to Figure 1-156.

CHAPTER 1   ADJUSTMENT LAYERS, BLENDING MODES WITH MASKS FOR PHOTO RESTORATION: PART 1

Figure 1-156. *Properties panel settings for Exposure with an overall Exposure adjustment in the Layers panel to lighten the image and second exposure required just to lighten the tower*

CHAPTER 1 ADJUSTMENT LAYERS, BLENDING MODES WITH MASKS FOR PHOTO
RESTORATION: PART 1

However, the tower was still a bit dark. In this case, loading the tower selection by Ctrl/CMD + clicking it in the Channels panel, I then added a second Exposure adjustment layer and then adjusted the tower so that it was lighter in color, this time only lightening Exposure to +0.57 but leaving Offset: 0 and Gamma Correction: 1.00 at the default settings. Refer to Figures 1-156 and 1-157.

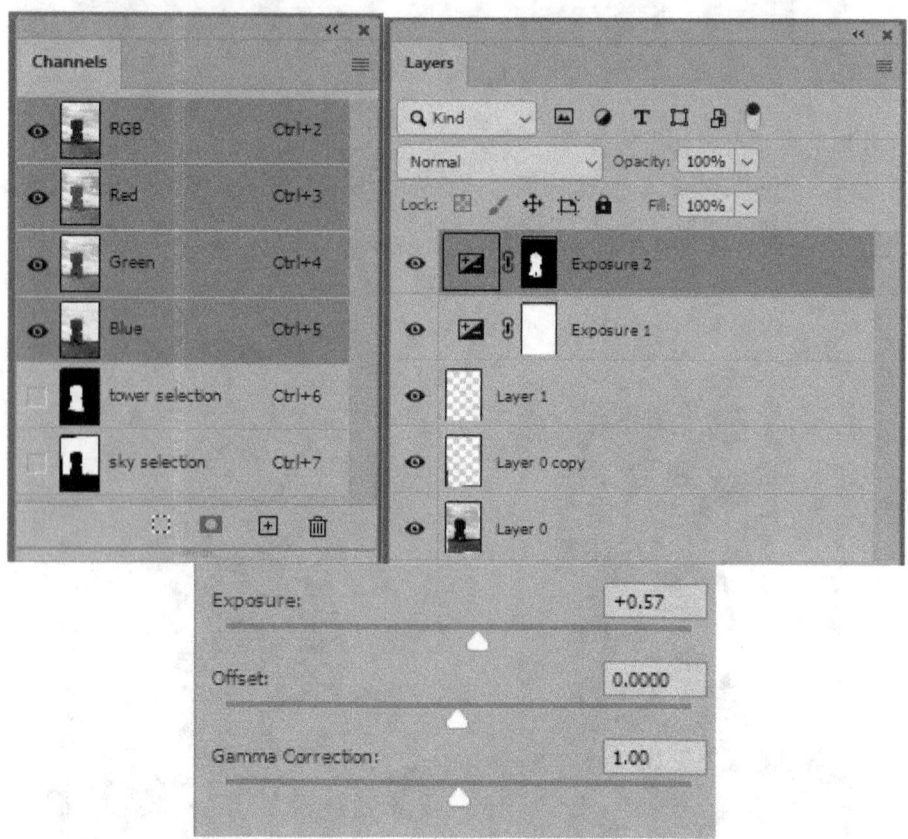

Figure 1-157. Properties panel settings for Exposure with a masked second Exposure adjustment in the Layers panel to lighten the tower further

CHAPTER 1　ADJUSTMENT LAYERS, BLENDING MODES WITH MASKS FOR PHOTO RESTORATION: PART 1

Later in Chapter 2, I will show you some commands and dialog boxes that you can use if you have some HDR images or just want to create an actual HDR effect.

More details on Exposure can be found at the following link:

https://helpx.adobe.com/photoshop/using/adjusting-hdr-exposure-toning.html

File ➤ Save any files you have open at this point. Refer to image **tower_exposure_final.psd** for reference.

Vibrance

This is meant to adjust color saturation so that clipping is minimized as color approaches full saturation. It can also be used to increase the saturation of less saturated colors and be used to prevent skin tones from becoming oversaturated. However, it may also be able to help images with over- or undersaturated greens. Refer to the **geese image_vibrance.psd** that was looked at in Volume 1, Chapter 4. Refer to Figure 1-158.

Figure 1-158. *This image needs some more vibrance added overall*

CHAPTER 1   ADJUSTMENT LAYERS, BLENDING MODES WITH MASKS FOR PHOTO RESTORATION: PART 1

Use either your Adjustments panel (Single adjustments) or your Layers panel to set this adjustment layer. Refer to Figure 1-159.

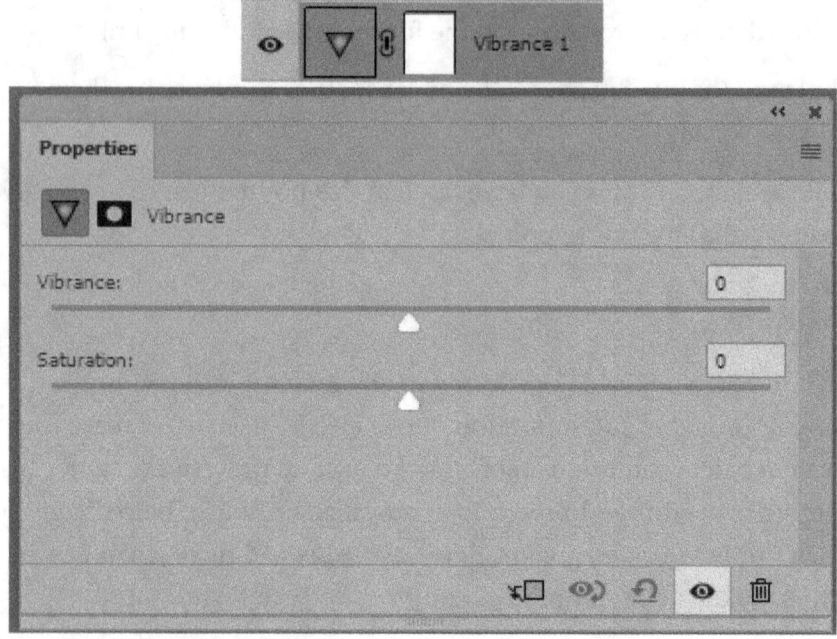

Figure 1-159.   Layer adjustment and Properties panel settings for Vibrance

The Properties settings found for Vibrance are as follows:

Vibrance (-100, 0, +100): Drag left to decrease or right to increase the vibrance without clipping when colors become more saturated or reach total saturation.

Saturation (-100, 0, +100): Drag to apply the same amount of saturation adjustment to all colors regardless of their current saturation; drag left to decrease or right to increase the saturation.

Vibrance can be added to an image. In this case I moved the Vibrance up to 64 so that the grass appeared less faded, but to reduce some of the yellow, I lowered the Saturation down to -2. Refer to Figure 1-160.

CHAPTER 1　ADJUSTMENT LAYERS, BLENDING MODES WITH MASKS FOR PHOTO RESTORATION: PART 1

Figure 1-160. *Properties panel settings for Vibrance and Saturation sliders*

While Vibrance can help, you may also want to add some Exposure and maybe try Color Balance, as I found working with Levels and Curves for this image caused the grass to become too blue-green or too yellow. Also keep in mind that it was a hot dry day in the park, possibly sometime in July. Refer to Figure 1-161.

CHAPTER 1   ADJUSTMENT LAYERS, BLENDING MODES WITH MASKS FOR PHOTO RESTORATION: PART 1

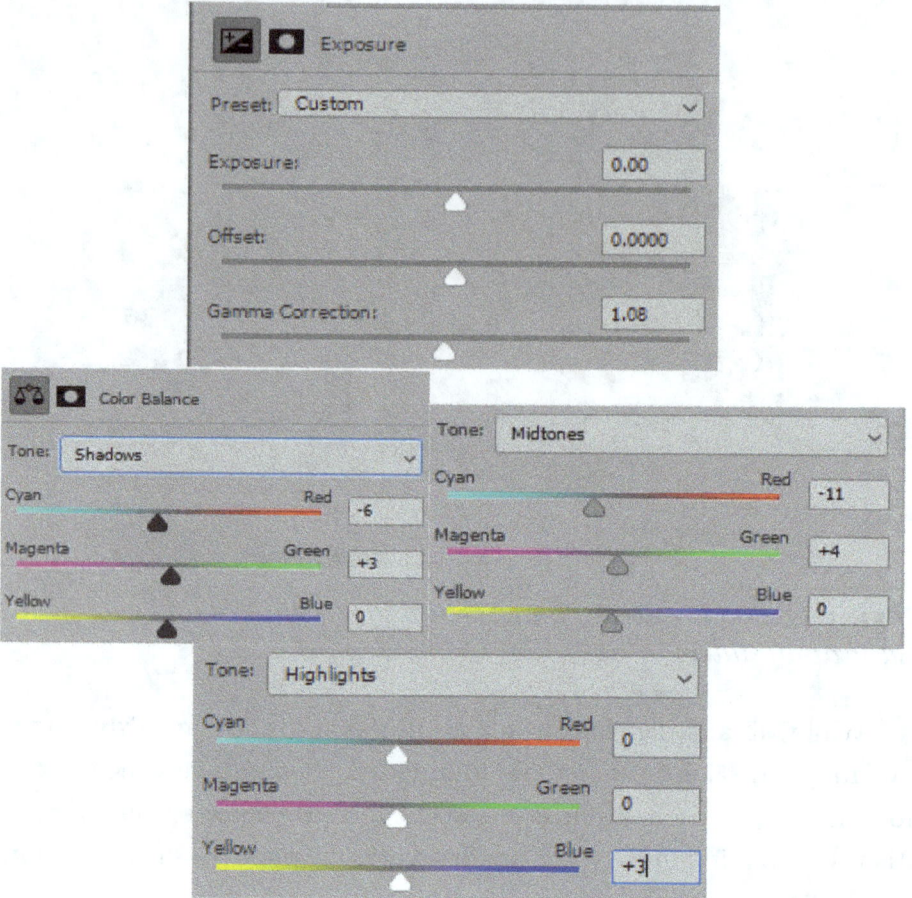

Figure 1-161. Properties panel settings for Exposure sliders and Color Balance in Shadows, Midtones, and Highlights

In this case I stored the layers above the background in a group folder for easier access to turn off and on at once. See **geese image_vibrance_final.psd** for reference to adjustment settings. Refer to Figures 1-161 and 1-162.

CHAPTER 1   ADJUSTMENT LAYERS, BLENDING MODES WITH MASKS FOR PHOTO RESTORATION: PART 1

Figure 1-162. *Use Vibrance along with other adjustment layers like Color Balance and Exposure*

Tip   Paint on the Vibrance layer mask with your Brush or Eraser tool when you want to affect select areas of the image.

More details on Vibrance can be found at the following link:

https://helpx.adobe.com/photoshop/using/adjust-vibrance.html

Photo Filter

This makes color adjustments or a type of color cast by simulating the effects of using a Kodak wratten or Fuji filter in front of a camera lens. This can create a feeling of warmth or coolness in the image, enhancing the colors overall. In color theory warm colors fall in the red–yellow range, while cool colors are generally green–blue. Note that some yellow-greens and magentas/violets could fall into either category. It shares some similarities to Hue/Saturation when the Colorize setting is added, but in this case the effect is not as monochrome, and some of the original colors remain.

As mentioned earlier, it can be used in combination with the Color Balance adjustment layer. However, its main purpose is either to reduce the cast or add a tint to the image.

Use either your Adjustments panel (Single adjustments) or your Layers panel to set this adjustment layer. Refer to Figure 1-163.

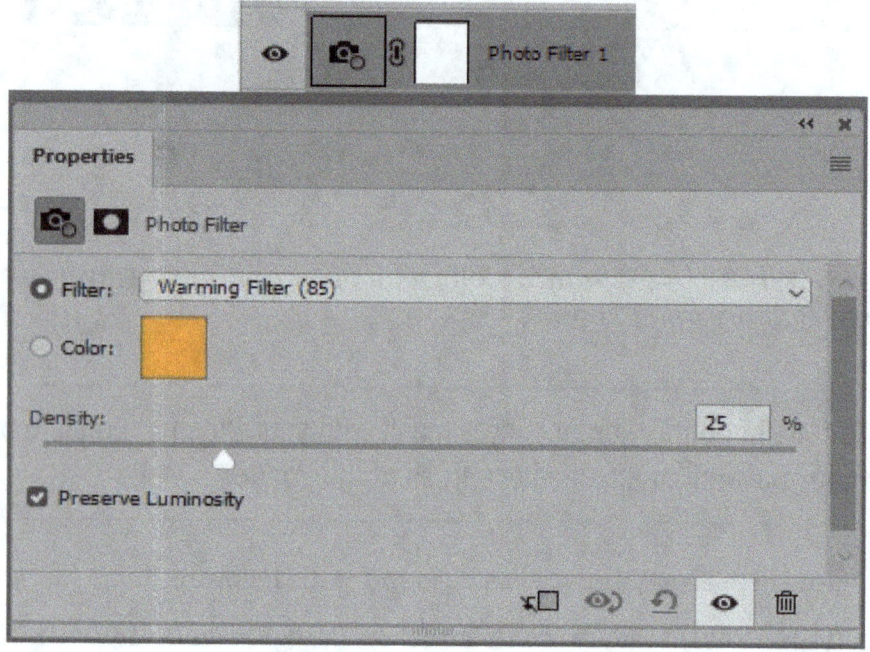

Figure 1-163. Layer adjustment and Properties panel settings for Photo Filter

The Properties settings found for Photo Filter are as follows:

Filter: Select a preset Photo Filter adjustment from the dropdown list. This is similar to using the Adjustments presets that are in the Adjustments panel. When no changes have been made, it is set to the default of Warming Filter (85). Refer to Figure 1-164.

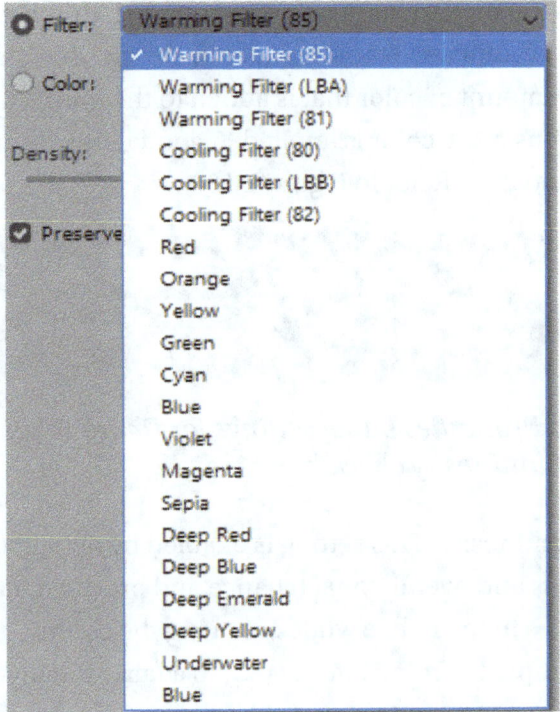

Figure 1-164. *Properties panel settings for Photo Filter, Filter menu list*

Color: If the custom color filter is not available, you can choose your own custom color by selecting this radio button option and clicking the swatch and choosing a setting in the color picker (Photo Filter Color). By default, it is set to an orange color, which is the same setting as Warming Filter (85). Refer to Figure 1-165.

Figure 1-165. *Properties panel settings for Photo Filter, custom color option*

Density (1–100%): Similar to an opacity setting, this is set by default to 25% but can be adjusted with the slider to change the filter effect and adjust the amount of color that is added to the image, and a higher percentage means more color is applied. A good range for subtle effects is between 10% and 25%. Refer to Figure 1-166.

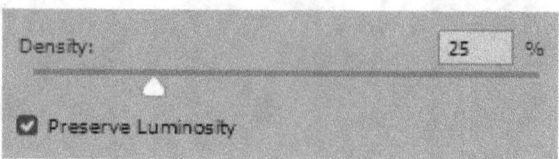

Figure 1-166. *Properties panel settings for Photo Filter, Density slider and Preserve Luminosity check box*

Preserve Luminosity: This setting is enabled by default to maintain image brightness and overall tonal balance and prevent changing the luminosity values in the image while changing the colors.

Adding a simple warming filter of (85) to a fairly tonally balanced image like the canoe example we saw in Volume 1, Chapter 3, when we used the Content-Aware Move tool can alter our mood about the image and the appearance of the cliffs. Trying a blue or cooling filter will change the tone of the image as well. Use the file **canoe_photo_filter.psd** if you want to experiment. Refer to Figure 1-167.

CHAPTER 1　ADJUSTMENT LAYERS, BLENDING MODES WITH MASKS FOR PHOTO RESTORATION: PART 1

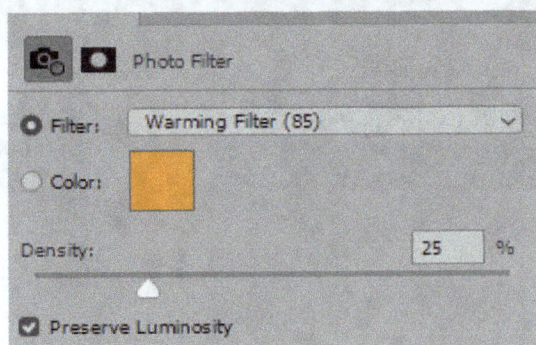

Figure 1-167. *Properties panel settings for Photo Filter and how it alters the current image's overall cast*

Turn on and off the visibility eye of the adjustment layer if you need to compare the before and after. See **canoe_photo_filter_final.psd** for reference.

More details on Photo Filter can be found at the following link:

https://helpx.adobe.com/photoshop/using/applying-color-balance-adjustment.html

Channel Mixer

This modifies a color channel and makes color adjustments not easily done with other color adjustment layers. It can also be used to create grayscale, sepia tone, and other tinted images, depending on how you drag the sliders for various artistic color effects. Use the **deer_group_ channelMixer.psd** image to practice. Refer to Figure 1-168.

Figure 1-168. *Use a Channel Mixer adjustment layer to alter colors in complex ways*

The Channel Mixer can be a more complex adjustment layer to understand. It modifies a single targeted (output) color channel using a mix of the existing (source) color channels in the image. As we have seen in the Channels panel, these color channels are grayscale images representing the tonal values of the color components in an image. In this case we are dealing with RGB channels. Refer to Figure 1-169.

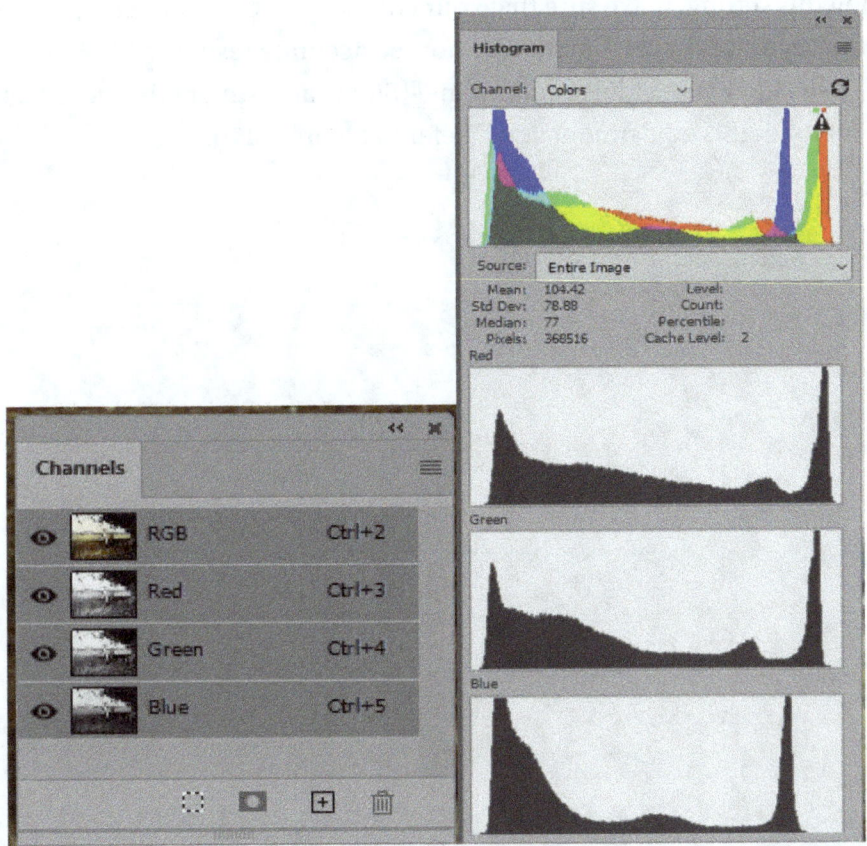

Figure 1-169. Observe your channels in the Channels panel and Histogram panel

CHAPTER 1　ADJUSTMENT LAYERS, BLENDING MODES WITH MASKS FOR PHOTO RESTORATION: PART 1

When you use the Channel Mixer, you are adding or subtracting grayscale data from a source channel to the targeted (output) channel. You are not adding or subtracting colors to a specific color component as you do with the Selective Color adjustment, which you will look at later. While working with this adjustment layer, I recommend watching your Histogram panel so you can observe how each channel shifts. Note, before using this setting, make sure that your composite RGB channel is selected in the Channels panel, or you may not see accurate results.

Use either your Adjustments panel (Single adjustments) or your Layers panel to set this adjustment layer. Refer to Figure 1-170.

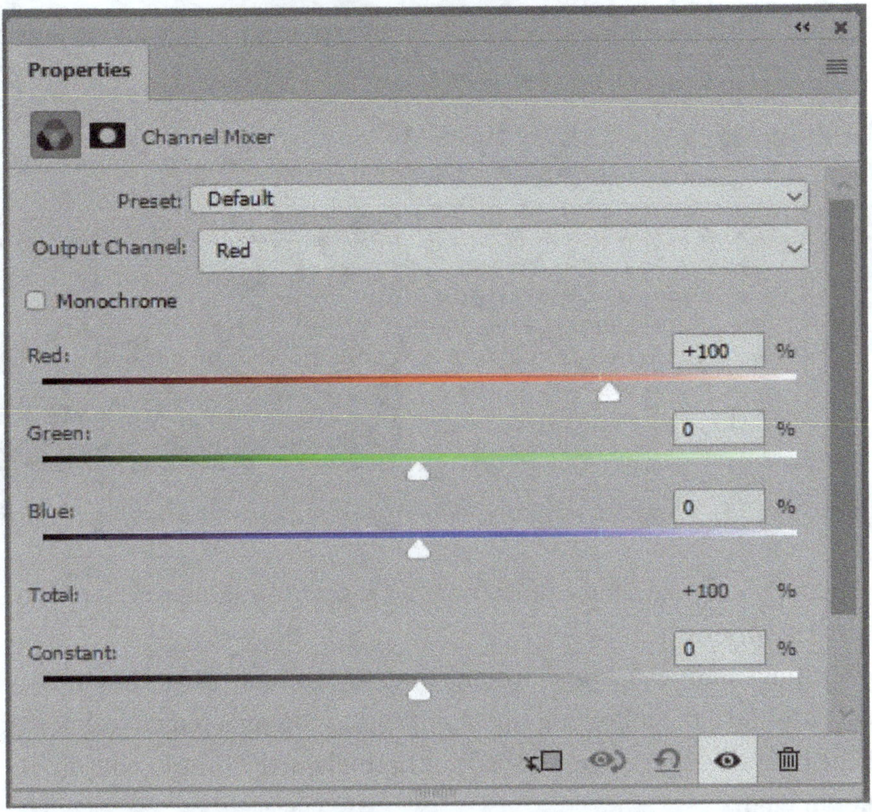

CHAPTER 1 ADJUSTMENT LAYERS, BLENDING MODES WITH MASKS FOR PHOTO RESTORATION: PART 1

Figure 1-170. Adjustment layer and Properties panel settings for Channel Mixer

The Properties settings found for Channel Mixer are as follows:

Preset: Select a preset Channel Mixer adjustment from the list. This is similar to using the Adjustments presets that are in the Adjustments panel. Once you have selected one, you can manually edit it and it will display as Custom. Any one of them may be helpful if you want to create a monochrome image quickly. However, some may give a better contrast than others, such as Black & White Infrared (RGB). Refer to Figure 1-171.

Figure 1-171. *Properties panel settings for Channel Mixer, preset list*

When no changes have been made, it is set to Default. And you can return to working in color.

Output Channel: Choose which channel to affect – Red, Green, or Blue – and save the following slider settings to the selected channel. You will be blending one or more existing channels to the output channel. Refer to Figure 1-172.

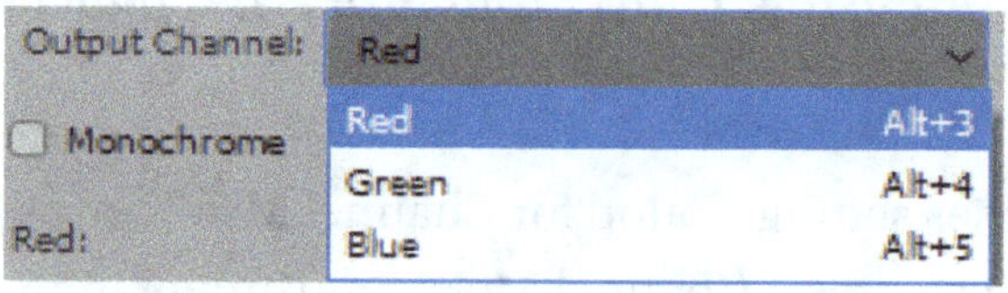

Figure 1-172. *Properties panel settings for Channel Mixer, Output Channel list*

When you choose an output channel, this sets the source slider for that channel to 100% and all other channels to 0%. In this example you can see how choosing Red as the output channel sets the source channel sliders for Red to 100% and to 0% for Green and 0% for Blue. Refer to Figure 1-173.

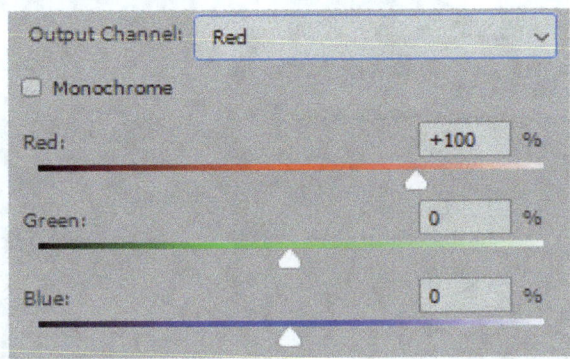

Figure 1-173. Properties panel settings for Channel Mixer, Red output channel and sliders

Monochrome: This changes the image to display color channels as gray value (Gray output channel) settings when the check box is enabled. Adjust the percentage of each source channel to fine-tune the overall grayscale image. As mentioned, while this setting is enabled you can still use one of the presets from the list. Refer to Figure 1-174.

CHAPTER 1   ADJUSTMENT LAYERS, BLENDING MODES WITH MASKS FOR PHOTO RESTORATION: PART 1

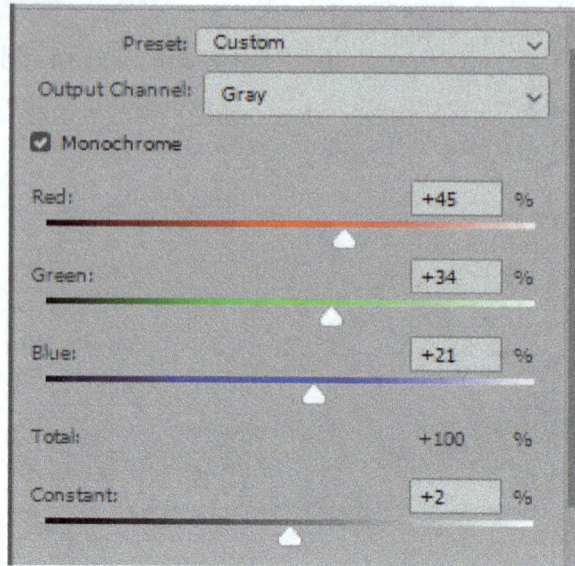

Figure 1-174. *Properties panel settings for Channel Mixer, set to Monochrome*

However, by default the check box is disabled and the RGB output channels are available.

You can then start to adjust the source channels.

To decrease a source channel's contribution to the preceding output channel, drag a source channel slider to the left. Refer to Figure 1-175.

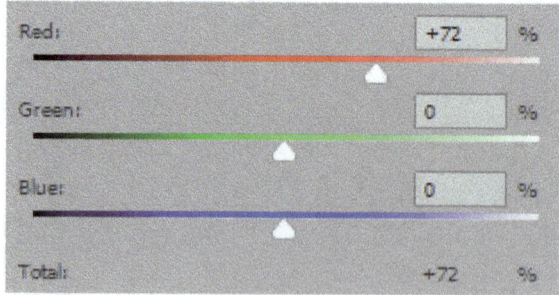

Figure 1-175. *Properties panel settings for Channel Mixer, RGB sliders*

184

To increase the source channel's contribution, drag a source channel slider to the right. Refer to Figure 1-176.

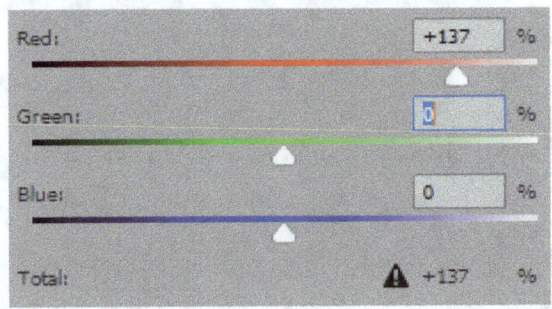

Figure 1-176. *Properties panel settings for Channel Mixer, RGB sliders and Total warning*

Red (–200, 0, +200%): Modify the influence of the red channel within the overall mix using the slider.

Green (–200, 0, +200%): Modify the influence of the green channel within the overall mix using the slider.

Blue (–200, 0, +200%): Modify the influence of the blue channel within the overall mix using the slider.

By setting the various sliders in the Reds, Greens, and Blues, you can create unusual effects. Refer to Figure 1-177.

CHAPTER 1   ADJUSTMENT LAYERS, BLENDING MODES WITH MASKS FOR PHOTO RESTORATION: PART 1

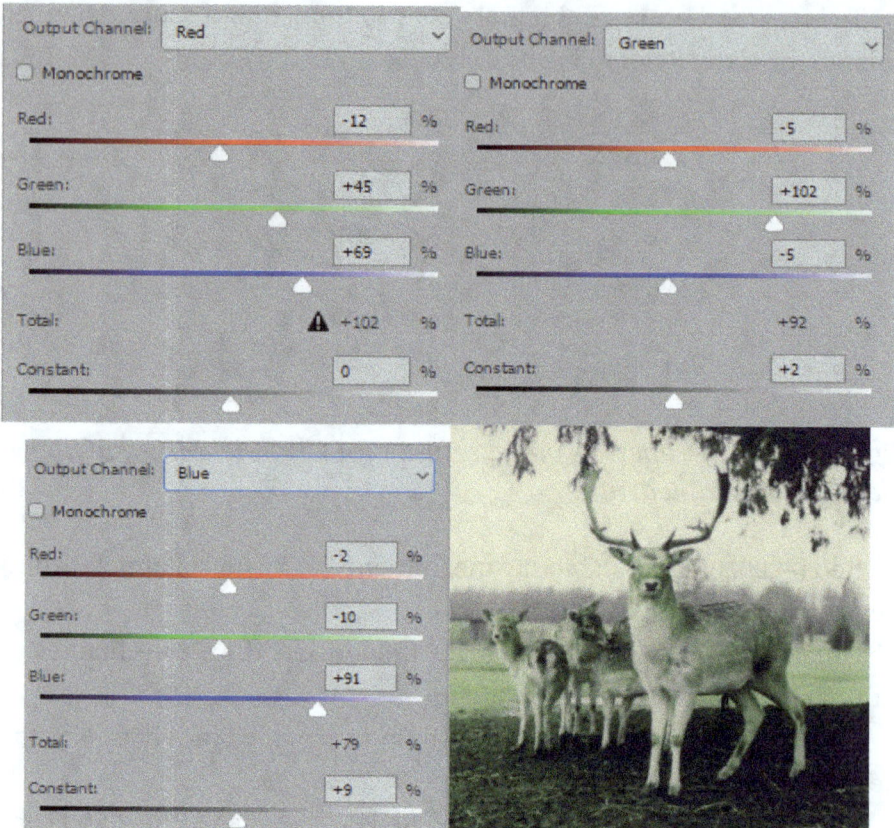

Figure 1-177. *Properties panel settings for Channel Mixer, resulting color in the image from adjusting various output channels and sliders*

Likewise, you can enter values between –200% and +200% in the text box.

Using a negative value will invert the source channel color before it is added to the output channel.

Total: After moving the sliders, the total value of the source channels displays in the Total field. If the combined channel values are above 100%, Photoshop displays a warning icon next to the total. Maintain the overall tone by keeping the total around 100%. When the number is above 100%, this can indicate that the processed image will be brighter than the original and some highlight detail may be lost. Refer to Figure 1-178.

CHAPTER 1 ADJUSTMENT LAYERS, BLENDING MODES WITH MASKS FOR PHOTO RESTORATION: PART 1

Figure 1-178. *Properties panel settings for Channel Mixer with Total alert and Constant slider*

Constant (–200, 0, +200%): Adjust brightness of the result saved to the output channel. Drag the slider or enter a value for the Constant option to adjust the grayscale value of the output channel. In Monochrome negative values will add black, and positive values will add white. A value of –200% or negative makes the output channel black or in this case not visible and a value +200% value makes the output channel white. In RGB color black negative percentage value in this case may refer to a specific color cast or shift, like toward cyan with a negative value or toward red when a positive value is chosen in the Red output channel. Refer to Figure 1-179.

Figure 1-179. *Properties panel settings for Channel Mixer with adjustment of Constant slider and results*

187

You can use this adjustment layer for CMYK images as well.

Tip: If you are planning to convert an image later from RGB to grayscale mode, you may want to use this adjustment layer first and work with the source channel sliders and move the slider to 100% to see how each channel is affected.

I also found that to achieve the more balanced monochrome total range, I wanted to add a Curves adjustment layer behind the Channel Mixer and adjust that, while the other adjustment layer was in the Layers panel and visible. Refer to Figure 1-180.

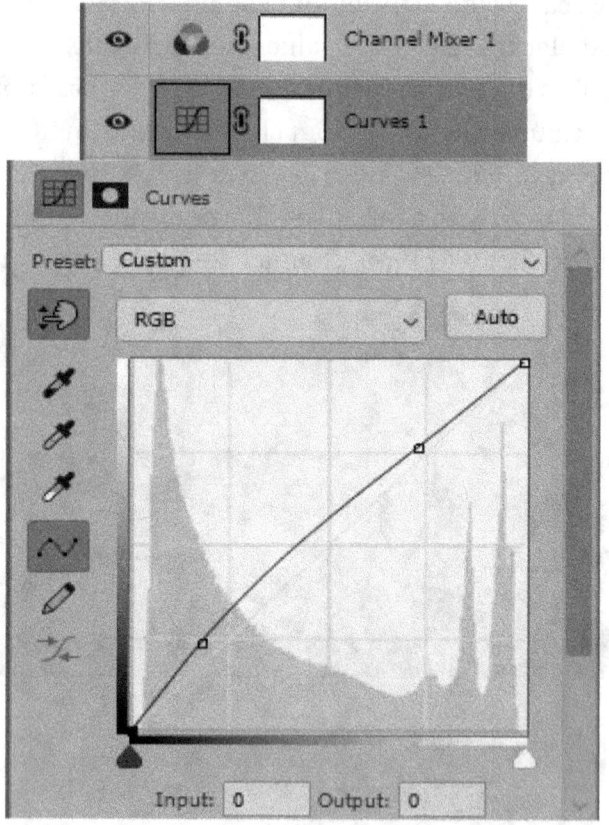

Figure 1-180. Combine the Channel Mixer with another adjustment layer, like Curves, and make changes in the Properties panel

CHAPTER 1   ADJUSTMENT LAYERS, BLENDING MODES WITH MASKS FOR PHOTO RESTORATION: PART 1

Channel Mixer presets are saved and loaded as (.CHA) files. You can access this option from the Properties panel menu.

As well, combining a second Channel Mixer layer can enhance the tint of the image, similar to the adjustment layer Black & White.

You may find this a good alternative when you work with slides that have gone completely red and no other color options are working and changing the file to monochrome is the only solution. Afterward you could always use various adjustment layers (Hue/Saturation) to add layer mask tints. Refer to Figure 1-181.

Figure 1-181. *Some images may only be improved to the point of making them black-and-white if too much of the other colors have faded away in the image*

File ➤ Save any files you have open at this point. Refer to the **deer_group_channelMixer_final.psd** and **pillars.psd** images for reference.

More details on Channel Mixer can be found at the following link:

https://helpx.adobe.com/photoshop/using/color-monochrome-adjustments-using-channels.html

Color Lookup

Color Lookup is more of a specialized adjustment that can be used to create unique tones and cast in an image. The initial concepts of this adjustment date back to the 1800s and 1900s when tinting of black-and-white images was a common and popular thing to do when there were none or few actual color photos produced with film. It is more of a complex filter that you can customize and create your own color filter effects from previously created adjustment layers.

People will sometimes sell Lumetri Look Up Tables (LUTs) as part of a collection for photographers to use in Photoshop but also for video use in applications like Media Encoder, After Effects, and Premiere Pro. The files store tables of data with color input and output information. However, you can use the ones available in this adjustment layer, but also buy ones provided by Adobe Creative Cloud Desktop via the Stock & Marketplace plugins. Or even better to save some money, you can use Photoshop to create your own. These are much like presets that you can save for other photo projects and create a similar color effect. You can use the file **light_house_lookup.psd** if you want to practice. Refer to Figure 1-182.

CHAPTER 1   ADJUSTMENT LAYERS, BLENDING MODES WITH MASKS FOR PHOTO RESTORATION: PART 1

Figure 1-182. *Color Lookup can alter the image's colors in a variety of subtle and dramatic ways*

Use either your Adjustments panel (Single adjustments) or your Layers panel to set this adjustment layer. Refer to Figure 1-183.

CHAPTER 1   ADJUSTMENT LAYERS, BLENDING MODES WITH MASKS FOR PHOTO RESTORATION: PART 1

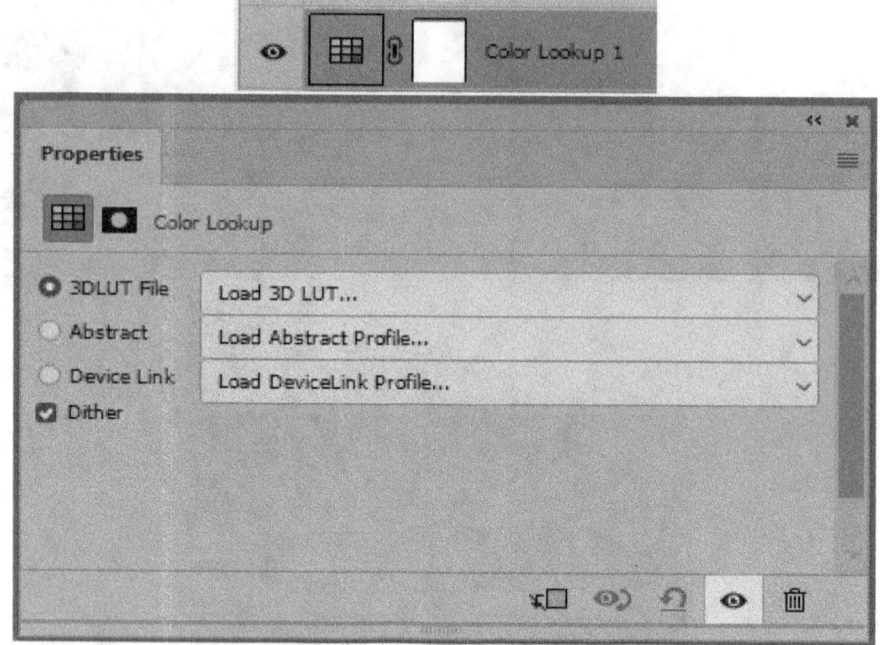

Figure 1-183. Adjustment layer and Properties panel settings for Color Lookup

The Properties settings found for Color Lookup are grouped into the following radio button and list selection options that contain various preset filters:

3DLUT File: Choose or load a 3DLUT file from the list. This is considered a 3D LUT file known as a CUBE file (*.CUBE). But other preset files in this section may also have different file formats such as 3DL (.3dl), 3DLS (.3dls), 1DLS (.1dls), IRIDAS Look (.look), and Cinespace 3DLUT (.CSP). Refer to Figure 1-184.

CHAPTER 1   ADJUSTMENT LAYERS, BLENDING MODES WITH MASKS FOR PHOTO RESTORATION: PART 1

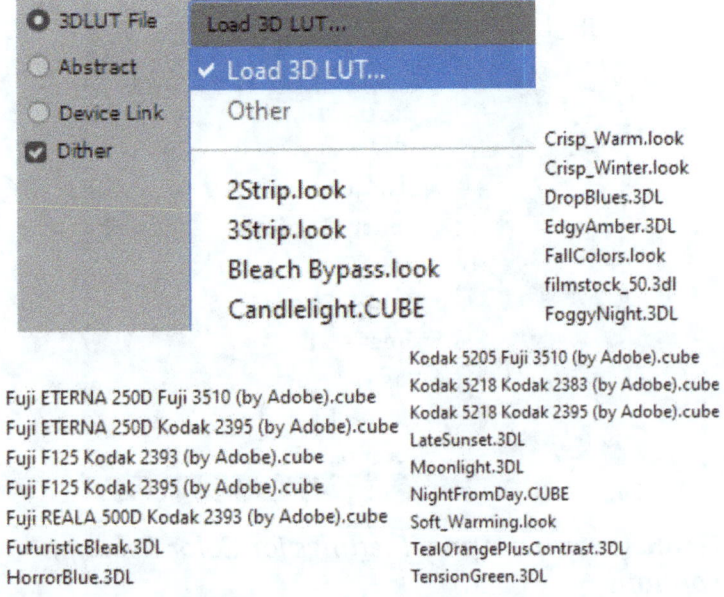

Figure 1-184. Properties panel settings for Color Lookup, 3DLUT options

---

Note   CUBE files often have additional Data and Table Order settings as well.

Abstract: Choose or load an abstract profile from the list. This is an ICC Profile (*.ICM, or *ICC) file. Refer to Figure 1-185.

CHAPTER 1 ADJUSTMENT LAYERS, BLENDING MODES WITH MASKS FOR PHOTO RESTORATION: PART 1

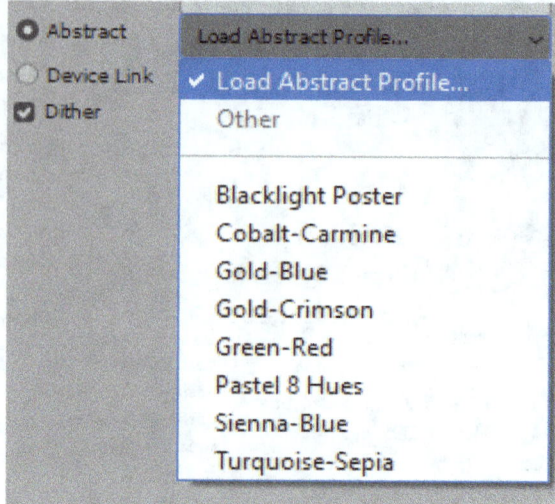

Figure 1-185. *Properties panel settings for Color Lookup, Abstract options*

Device Link: Choose or load a device link profile from the list. This is an ICC Profile (*.ICM, or *ICC) file. Refer to Figure 1-186.

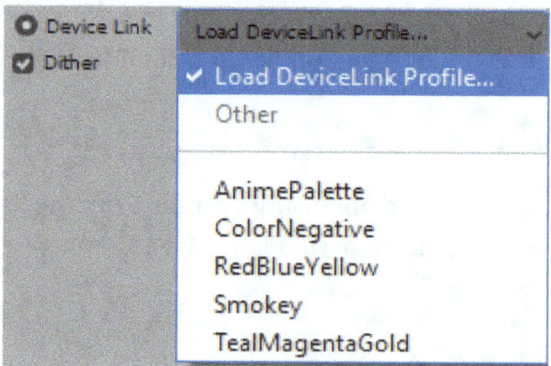

Figure 1-186. *Properties panel settings for Color Lookup, Device Link options and Dither setting*

CHAPTER 1   ADJUSTMENT LAYERS, BLENDING MODES WITH MASKS FOR PHOTO RESTORATION: PART 1

Dither: This is enabled by default for a smoother setting and breaks up potential banding in the image.

Once you select a file preset option. you can use your up and down arrow keys to cycle through them.

Optional: Some 3D LUT CUBE files will have additional Data Order and Table Order radio button settings. Refer to Figure 1-187.

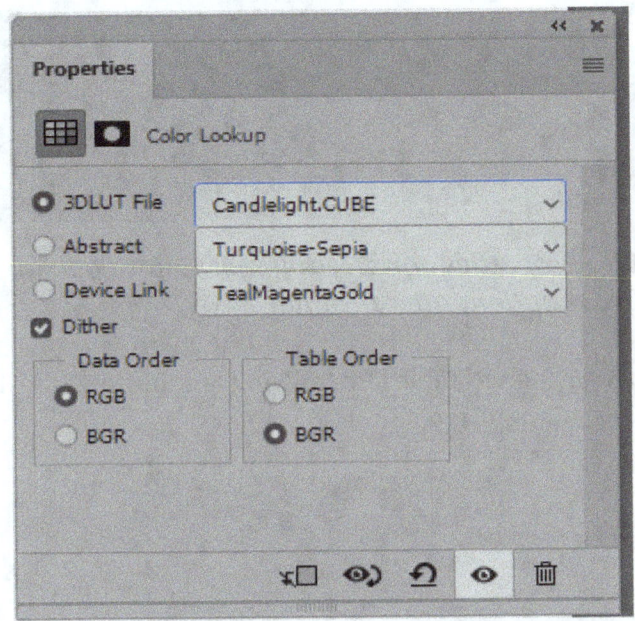

Figure 1-187. *Properties panel settings for Color Lookup, Data Order and Table Order options*

The default of the Data Order is usually RGB (Red, Green, Blue) and the Table Order is BGR (Blue, Green, Red), but you can try the other options, which, in this case, would give you complementary or opposite colors on the color wheel. For example, change the data order; if before a area was orange/yellow, now it is blue with BGR selected, and the tone becomes lighter or darker depending on what table order is chosen. Refer to Figure 1-188.

CHAPTER 1 ADJUSTMENT LAYERS, BLENDING MODES WITH MASKS FOR PHOTO RESTORATION: PART 1

Figure 1-188. *Properties panel settings for Color Lookup: Data Order and Table Order options alter the image*

Then you can change Table Order giving another slightly different look as well. Refer to Figure 1-189.

Figure 1-189. *Properties panel settings for Color Lookup: Data Order and Table Order options alter the image again*

In total you could have four different looks in one 3D LUT.

196

Color Lookup Table Creation

All adjustment layers can be used singly or collectively to create your own custom Color Lookup file. However, some will produce better results. I would avoid using fill layers like Gradient and Pattern, but using solid color is OK. Later you can apply blending modes (except for Dissolve) to the adjustment layer, as well as opacity, as we will talk about this later in the next chapter. If you adjust some of those settings prior to creating your own Color Lookup files, those results will also be displayed in the new custom adjustment preset.

You can export color lookup tables only from documents that have a background layer and additional adjustment layers to modify colors. However, make sure that the layer masks on any adjustment layers are clean and clear of painted effects as this can cause corruption when you try to create your file. The layer mask should be clean and white with no black erasing or brushing marks and no feathering (0 px) or change in density (100%) adjustment made in the Properties panel to the layer mask. Refer to Figure 1-190.

CHAPTER 1 ADJUSTMENT LAYERS, BLENDING MODES WITH MASKS FOR PHOTO RESTORATION: PART 1

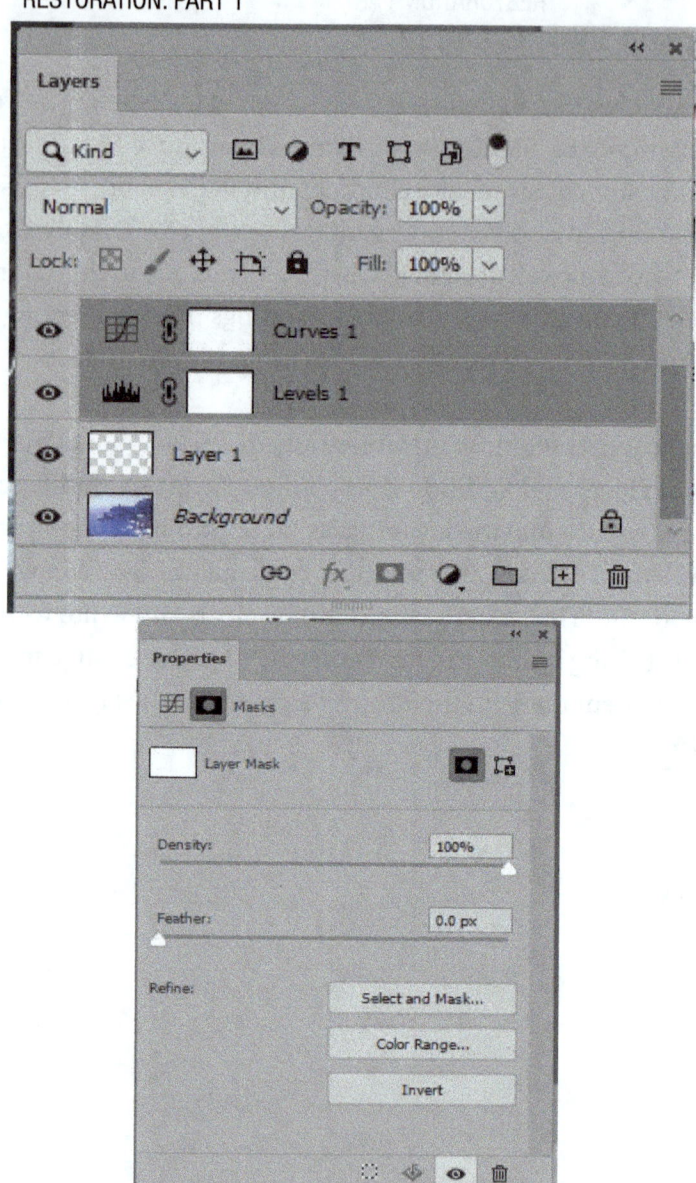

Figure 1-190. *Combine various adjustment layers in the Layers panel and check your layer mask in the Properties panel*

CHAPTER 1   ADJUSTMENT LAYERS, BLENDING MODES WITH MASKS FOR PHOTO RESTORATION: PART 1

It is tempting to create these kinds of modification to an adjustment layer like Levels or Hue/Saturation, but just like when using the Gradient or Pattern Fill, it creates, in the file's color table, missing information and corruption to the file. If you suspect that your adjustment layer mask may have some modifications, you can correct this by duplicating the layer and dragging it on to the Create a new layer button. Refer to Figure 1-191.

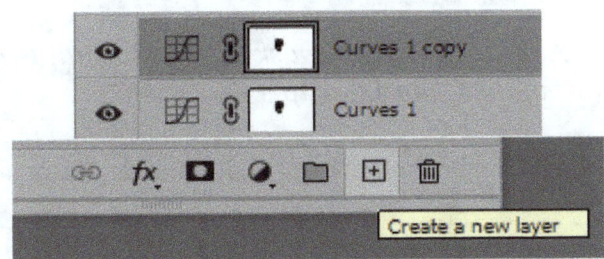

Figure 1-191. *Duplicate adjustment layers that you want to be part of the final Color Lookup file*

Then turn the eye off, on the original, should you need to keep that mask for something else. On the layer copy right-click the mask and choose Delete Layer Mask. Refer to Figure 1-192.

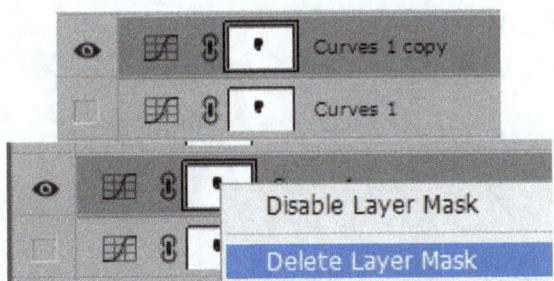

Figure 1-192. *Hide unwanted layers and delete the layer mask from the adjustment copy*

Then, while the adjustment layer is selected, click again the layer mask icon. Refer to Figure 1-193.

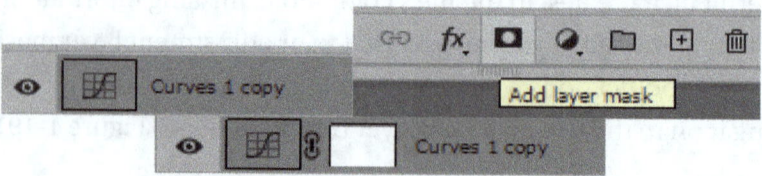

Figure 1-193. *Add a clean layer mask back to the adjustment layer that will be part of the Color Lookup*

This will apply a fresh white mask with no marks.

Tip Keeping adjustment layers for color lookup creation in separate folder groups is a good way to keep organized with a name and a color for identification. Then, when you're ready to create your Color Lookup, turn on only the visibility for that folder with the background images visible for review. Refer to Figure 1-194.

CHAPTER 1   ADJUSTMENT LAYERS, BLENDING MODES WITH MASKS FOR PHOTO RESTORATION: PART 1

Figure 1-194. *Store your adjustment layers in a group folder for better organization and turn off those that will not be part of the current Color Lookup*

Now just turn off the background layers and select just the folder that you want to create the color lookup table from. Refer to Figure 1-195.

CHAPTER 1 ADJUSTMENT LAYERS, BLENDING MODES WITH MASKS FOR PHOTO RESTORATION: PART 1

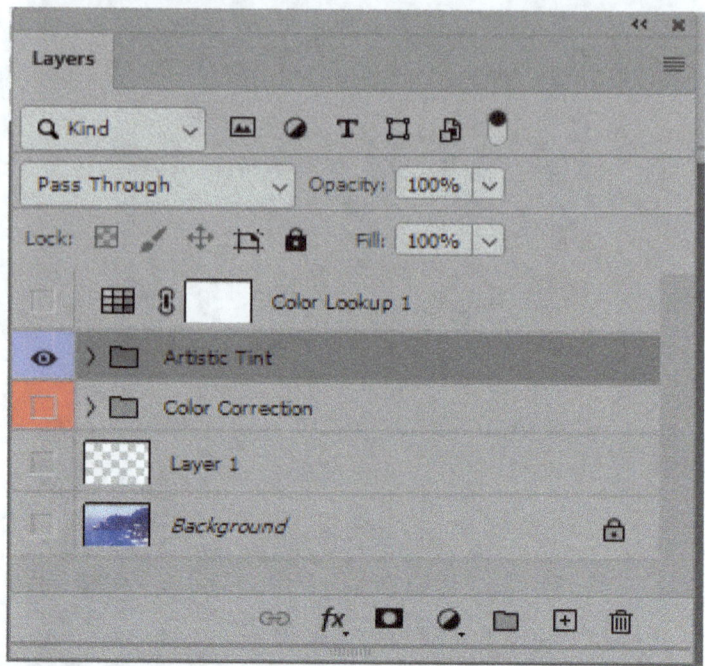

Figure 1-195. *Select only the group folder that you want as part of the Color Lookup files*

From the menu go to File ➤ Export ➤ Color Lookup Tables. Refer to Figure 1-196.

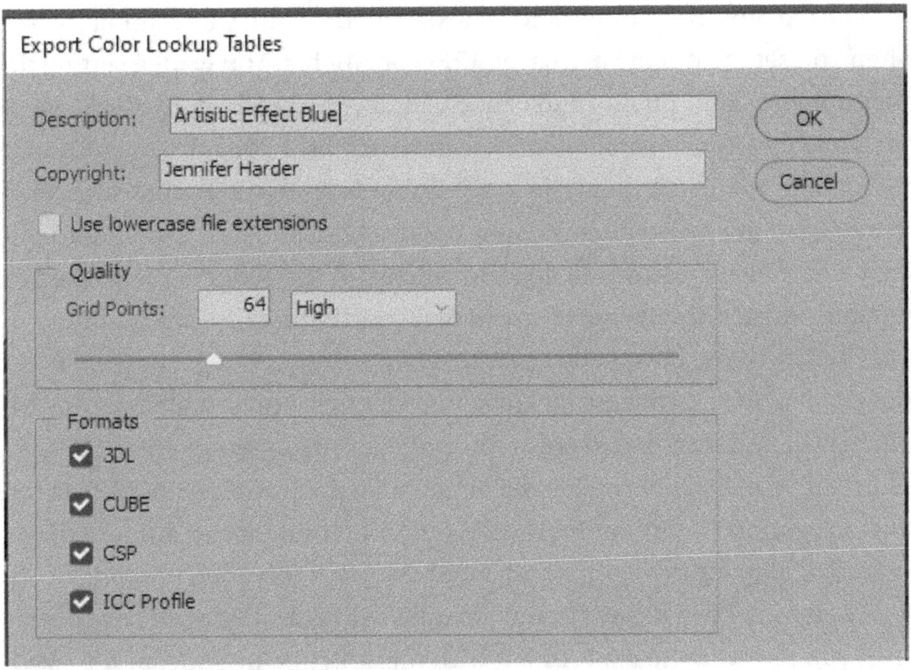

Figure 1-196. Export Color Lookup Tables dialog box

In the Export Color Lookup Tables dialog box, enter a description. The name or description of your saved file will appear on top, but you can retype it if required. This information is later embedded in the file. In this case I called it Artistic Effect Blue. Refer to Figure 1-196.

(Optional) Enter a copyright string, such as your name or the name of your company. Photoshop automatically prefixes © Copyright <current year> to your entered text. This data is found internally within the file.

You can then choose to enable the check box for Use lowercase file extensions. Some applications outside of Adobe may be very strict on whether you can use a .cube or a .CUBE (in lower- or uppercase). I am using Photoshop, which is not case sensitive, so I can leave this unchecked, and the file extension will be .CUBE (uppercase).

The Quality Grid Points field is next, which you may be familiar with when you set the quality of a saved JPEG or GIF file. You want a setting that does not lose color quality and cause banding, but at the same time does not allow the file to become too large and cause the program to crash when it is loaded. You can either type in a number from 0 to 256, choose a default setting from the menu ranging from Poor to Maximum, or use the slider to set the number; the lowest it goes down to with the slider is 7. File sizes can get quite large with several adjustment layers that require calculations.

The size of the files really starts to creep up once you get beyond 64 grid points. After some testing I discovered it may create a file over 400 MB, which is definitely going to crash an application. Remember that 3DLUT's main purpose is to interpolate using the table data; you do not have to map what every node or grid point should be. So I found that an amount of 64 or high quality for my photos and small video work is good enough.

Therefore, I will leave it at the default setting of 64. In your case over time, you may want to experiment with this and document your file sizes as you make various choices and experiment with quality. However, keep in mind files at the maximum setting can get very large.

Back to the Export Color Lookup Tables dialog box in Photoshop. We can see Formats as the last setting. Refer to Figure 1-196.

The options include

- 3DL
- CUBE
- CSP
- ICC Profile

Note that while Photoshop can load all these file formats, some Adobe programs like Media Encoder or Premiere Pro cannot support all of them. In most cases I check them all off, but for some projects certain formats may not be required, so the choice is up to you.

Now click the OK button to save the file. Refer to Figure 1-197.

Figure 1-197. *Export Color Lookup Tables dialog box, clicking OK*

Doing this brings you to the next Export Color Lookup dialog box, which allows you to find a place to save your file. When I am testing LUTs that I am not sure how they will appear, I save them usually in my Projects folder for later loading. Refer to Figure 1-198.

Figure 1-198. *Export Color Lookup files to a folder*

Select the location on your computer where you want to save the generated files. Also, enter a descriptive base filename to which Photoshop automatically appends the file extensions. Refer to Figure 1-199.

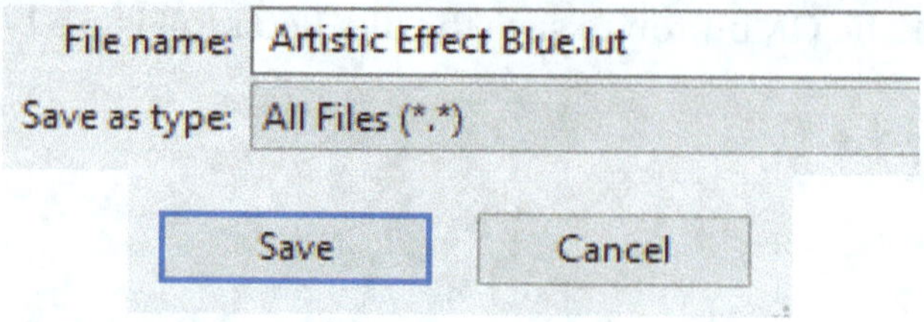

CHAPTER 1   ADJUSTMENT LAYERS, BLENDING MODES WITH MASKS FOR PHOTO RESTORATION: PART 1

Figure 1-199. Save your Color Lookup file with the .lut extension

Leave the .lut extension as this is because you are creating all four file types at once. Make sure Save as type is set to All Files. Then click Save and give Photoshop a moment to create the files and file formats.

It may turn your background layer back on afterward.

As they are saved, they are compiled, and you can view them when you open your file explorer for that folder. Refer to Figure 1-200.

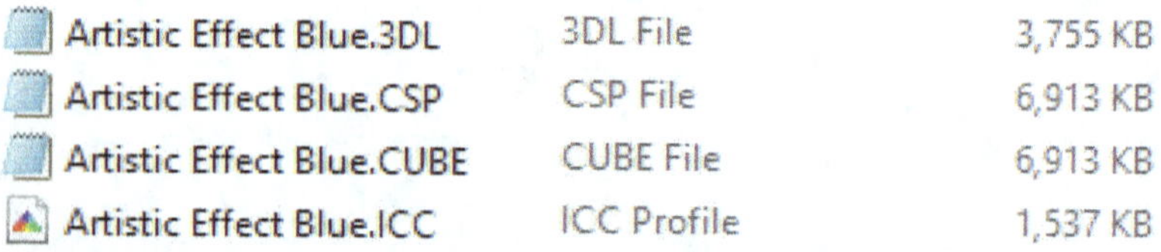

Artistic Effect Blue.3DL	3DL File	3,755 KB
Artistic Effect Blue.CSP	CSP File	6,913 KB
Artistic Effect Blue.CUBE	CUBE File	6,913 KB
Artistic Effect Blue.ICC	ICC Profile	1,537 KB

Figure 1-200. Color Lookup file created

Note   Color Lookup profiles can be used in various color modes including CMYK and Lab. However, RGB mode will allow you to use all the Color Lookup adjustment layer options.

More details on Color Lookup as well as file consideration for exporting different formats in color modes can be found at the following link: `https://helpx.adobe.com/photoshop/using/export-color-lookup-tables.html`

CHAPTER 1 ADJUSTMENT LAYERS, BLENDING MODES WITH MASKS FOR PHOTO RESTORATION: PART 1

Load the Color Lookup File

Now, if you want to load a Color Lookup that you created into Photoshop, apply a new Color Lookup adjustment layer and then, from the menu, choose Load 3D LUT and locate the file. Select the file from the folder and click Load. Refer to Figure 1-201.

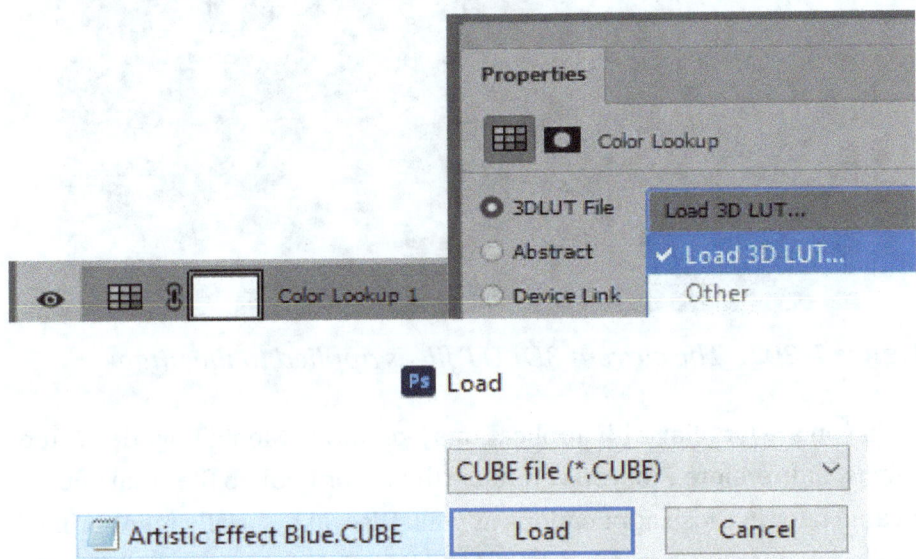

Figure 1-201. *Locate and load the Color Lookup file using the adjustment layer and Properties panel*

The new Color Lookup is applied, and this creates a compact color adjustment rather than having to have multiple adjustment layers. This is also a good way to share a specific color adjustment with your coworkers or apply a single adjustment to another file. Refer to Figure 1-202.

CHAPTER 1　ADJUSTMENT LAYERS, BLENDING MODES WITH MASKS FOR PHOTO RESTORATION: PART 1

Figure 1-202. *The current 3DLUT file is applied to the image*

If you are familiar with applications like Adobe Media Encoder, After Effects, or Premiere Pro, you can reuse the Color Lookup files that you created later in those applications as well. We will be briefly mentioning Media Encoder in Chapter 6 where I will mention the location where you can locate LUT files.

Note that if you want to keep all the adjustment layers separate, then saving them as a preset in the Adjustments panel may be a better option that we will look at in the end of this chapter.

File ➤ Save your document so far and refer to my file **light_house_lookup_final.psd**.

I have also included a text file in the chapter folder that you can review if you want information on how to store your profile files in a folder for regular use for the Photoshop application for Windows. See **Loading_Abstract_and_DeviceLink_Profiles.txt**.

Selective Color

This adjustment can be used to adjust the amount of process colors in individual color components. Ideally, when you need to affect colors in an image that is in CMYK color mode, you can use this layer to affect the Cyan, Magenta, Yellow, or Black color using the slider. You can use this adjustment to dramatically decrease the magenta in the red component of an image while leaving the magenta in the blue component unaltered. However, it can also be used to alter images that are in RGB mode. Use the **sunset_selective_color.psd** to practice. Refer to Figure 1-203.

CHAPTER 1 ADJUSTMENT LAYERS, BLENDING MODES WITH MASKS FOR PHOTO RESTORATION: PART 1

Figure 1-203. Set your Channels panel and make color adjustments using Selective Color

CHAPTER 1 ADJUSTMENT LAYERS, BLENDING MODES WITH MASKS FOR PHOTO RESTORATION: PART 1

Use either your Adjustments panel (Single adjustments) or your Layers panel to set this adjustment layer. Note: make sure that the composite RGB channel is selected in the Channels panel. Refer to Figure 1-204.

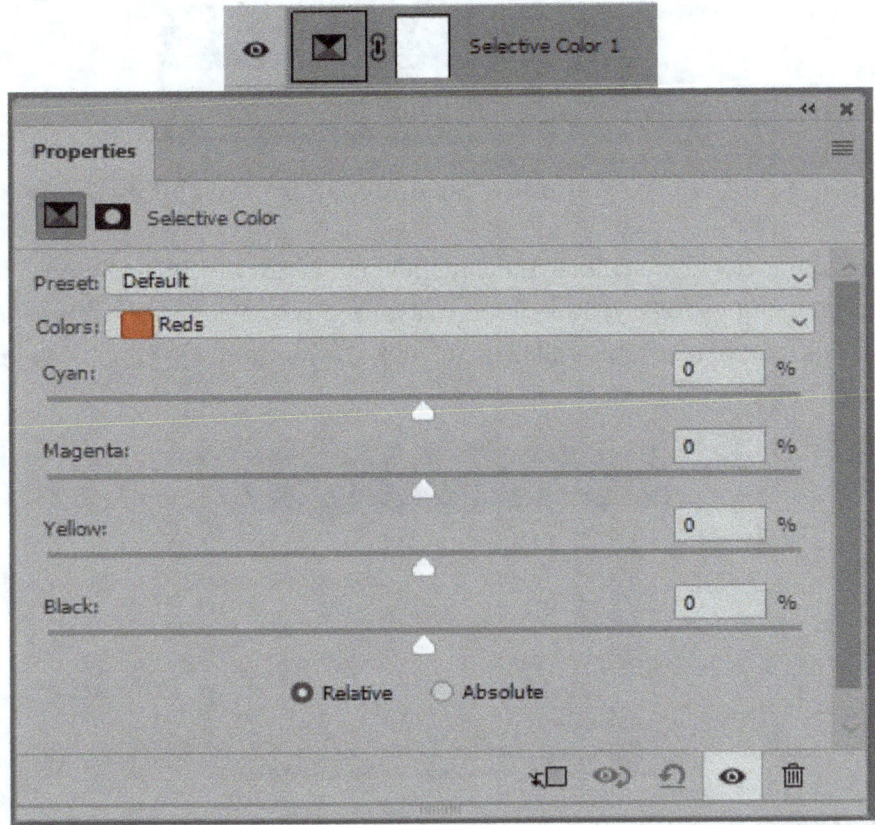

Figure 1-204. *Adjustment layer and Properties panel settings for Selective Color*

The Properties settings found for Selective Color are as follows:

- Preset: Select a preset Selective Color adjustment if one has been created. This is similar to using the Adjustments presets that are in the Adjustments panel. Once you have selected one, you can manually edit it

CHAPTER 1 ADJUSTMENT LAYERS, BLENDING MODES WITH MASKS FOR PHOTO RESTORATION: PART 1

and it will display as Custom. When no changes have been made, it is set to Default. Currently there are no additional presets in the list. Refer to Figure 1-205.

Figure 1-205. *Properties panel settings for Selective Color, presets*

Colors: These are colors you can affect later with the lower sliders. The list includes reds, yellows, greens, cyans, blues, magentas, whites, neutrals, and blacks. This will interact with the method you choose. Refer to Figure 1-206.

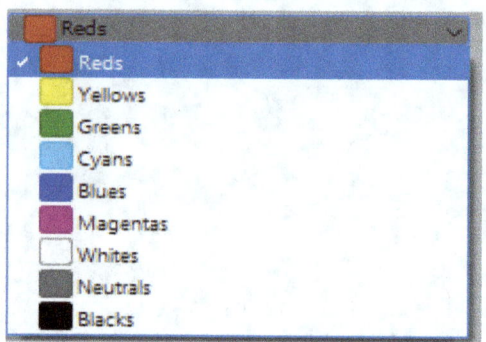

Figure 1-206. *Properties panel settings for Selective Color, color options*

Cyan, Magenta, Yellow, and Black sliders have a range of (-100, 0, +100%): Drag the sliders to decrease or increase the color components. Refer to Figure 1-207.

Figure 1-207. *Properties panel settings for Selective Color, CMYK color sliders*

A method radio button is either set to Relative or Absolute, and each affects the color slightly differently. Refer to Figure 1-208.

Figure 1-208. *Properties panel settings for Selective Color, method options*

Relative: This changes the existing amount of cyan, magenta, yellow, or black (CMYK) by its percentage of the total. For example, if you start with a pixel that is 50% cyan and add 10%, 5% is added to the cyan (10% of 50% = 5%) (1.1 × 0.5=0.55 for a total of 55% (0.55) cyan). However, this option cannot adjust pure specular white highlight, which contains no color components and is set to C=0, M=0, Y=0, K=0. Specular highlights are often a small single point on a person's forehead or shiny object like a fruit. Refer to Figure 1-209.

CHAPTER 1 ADJUSTMENT LAYERS, BLENDING MODES WITH MASKS FOR PHOTO RESTORATION: PART 1

Figure 1-209. *Example of specular highlights on an image of tomatoes*

However, as we have seen in this chapter, one or more channels could be damaged, and this could be due to an uncorrectable large glare without the use of some healing tool to add more pixels to fill in missing details.

Absolute: This adjusts the color in absolute values. For example, if you start with a pixel that is 50% cyan and add 10%, the cyan ink is set to a total of 60%. By default, the method is set to Absolute.

The adjustments are based on how close a color is to one of the options found in the Colors menu. For example, 50% cyan is midway between white and pure cyan and receives a proportionate mix of corrections defined for the two colors, in this case the whites and the cyans.

Selective Color presets are saved and loaded as (.ASV) files.

In my example I effected the following colors:

- Reds: C:0, M:0, Y:0, K:0
- Yellows: C:0, M:0, Y:0, K:–34
- Greens: C:0, M:0, Y:0, K:0
- Cyans: C:0, M:0, Y:0, K:+49
- Blues: C:+75, M:–13, Y:–45, K:–9

CHAPTER 1   ADJUSTMENT LAYERS, BLENDING MODES WITH MASKS FOR PHOTO RESTORATION: PART 1

- Magentas: C:-47, M:0, Y:0, K:+4
- Whites: C: -23, M:0, Y:0, K:0
- Neutrals: C:0, M:0, Y:0, K:-2
- Blacks: C:0, M:0, Y:0, K:-2

My method was set to Absolute as Relative was too subtle. Refer to Figure 1-210.

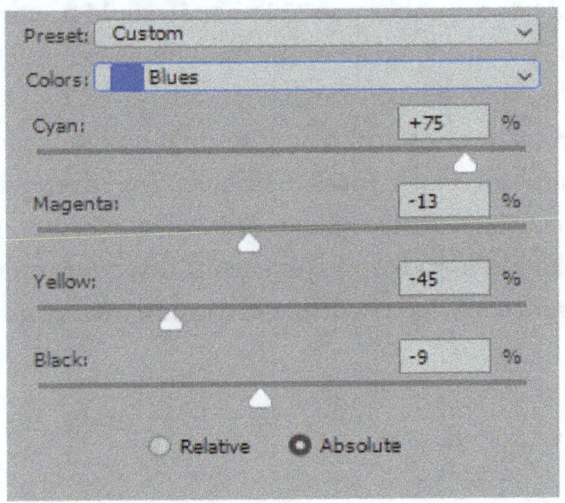

Figure 1-210. *Properties panel settings for Selective Color for Blues*

More details on Selective Color can be found at the following link:

https://helpx.adobe.com/photoshop/using/mix-colors.html

File ➤ Save your work so far and you can refer to my file **sunset_selective_color_final.psd**.

Keep in mind that for images with extreme blues and magentas on the screen, you may run into out-of-gamut issues when printing though it might look fine on the screen. So switching to the relative method may lead to better printing results.

CHAPTER 1 ADJUSTMENT LAYERS, BLENDING MODES WITH MASKS FOR PHOTO
RESTORATION: PART 1

Invert

Invert is ideal when you have scanned some negatives, but your older scanner did not automatically convert them into positives. This adjustment will automatically invert the colors. What this means is the brightness value of each pixel in the channels is converted to the inverse value on the 256-step color-values scale (0–255). For example, a pixel in a positive image with a value of 255 is changed to 0, and a pixel with a value of 5 is changed to 250. If the number was 250, then it would be changed to 5. Zero in this case is considered a number making there be actually 256 steps.

However, you should be aware that it is advisable, for ideal results, to use your film scanner's software and settings if possible because color print film contains an orange mask in its base. The Invert adjustment cannot make accurate positive images from scanned color negatives.

In the case of black-and-white film, using this adjustment layer should be fine as no orange mask is used. See **snowman_invert.psd**. Refer to Figure 1-211.

CHAPTER 1 ADJUSTMENT LAYERS, BLENDING MODES WITH MASKS FOR PHOTO RESTORATION: PART 1

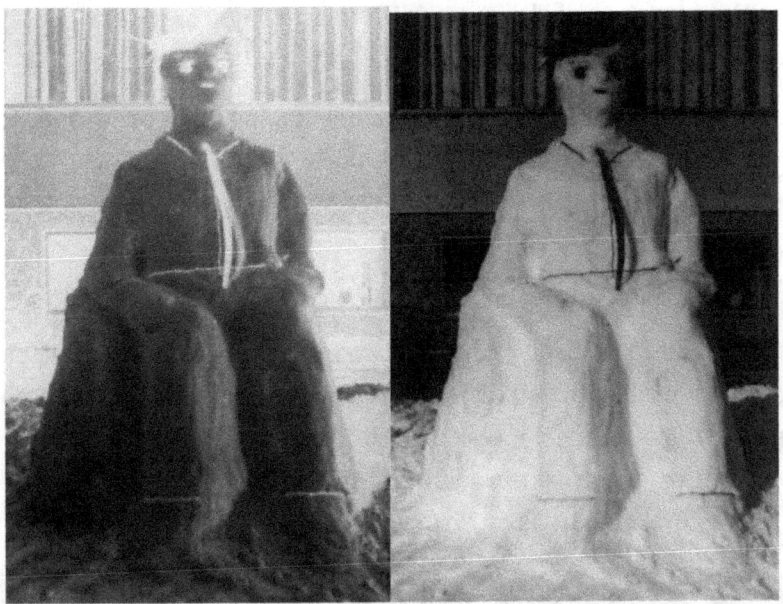

Figure 1-211. *A black-and-white image of a snowman inverted from negative to positive*

Use either your Adjustments panel (Single adjustments) or your Layers panel to set this adjustment layer. Refer to Figure 1-212.

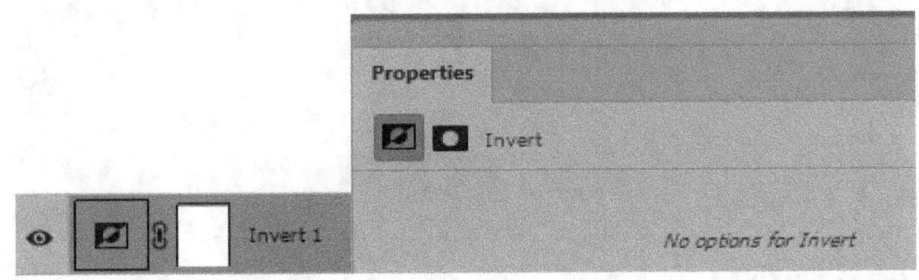

Figure 1-212. *Adjustment layer and Properties panel settings for Invert*

CHAPTER 1 ADJUSTMENT LAYERS, BLENDING MODES WITH MASKS FOR PHOTO RESTORATION: PART 1

The Properties panel has no additional settings for Invert.

More details on Invert can be found at the following link:

https://helpx.adobe.com/photoshop/using/applying-special-color-effects-images.html

Posterize

This adjustment layer allows you to specify the number of tonal levels (or brightness values) for each channel in an image and then maps pixels to the closest matching level. This will often give a more broken or segmented appearance to your image lowering or limiting the tonal range. We saw a similar result when we set the scanner in Volume 1, Chapter 1. It is not ideal for photo restoration and is more for artistic effects. Refer to Figure 1-213.

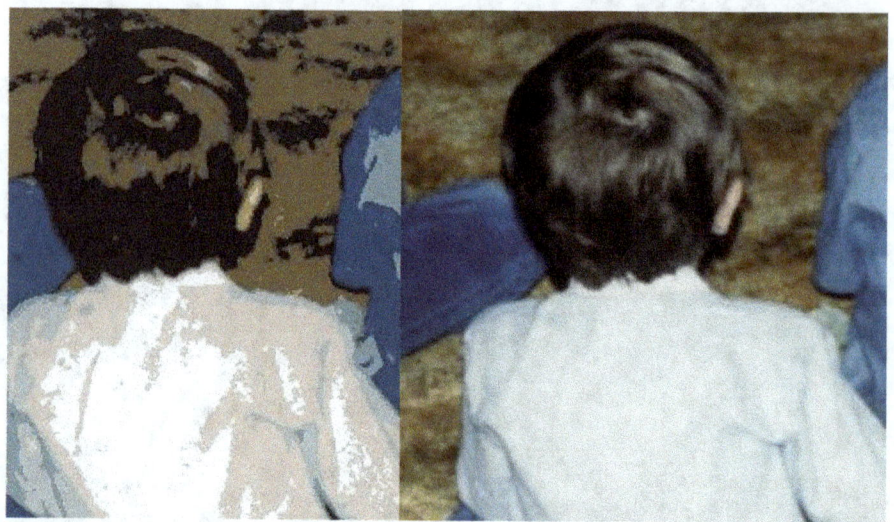

Figure 1-213. *A posterize effect and a non-posterized image created using the scanner*

To produce a similar effect in your photos, use either your Adjustments panel (Single adjustments) or your Layers panel to set this adjustment layer. Refer to Figure 1-214.

CHAPTER 1   ADJUSTMENT LAYERS, BLENDING MODES WITH MASKS FOR PHOTO RESTORATION: PART 1

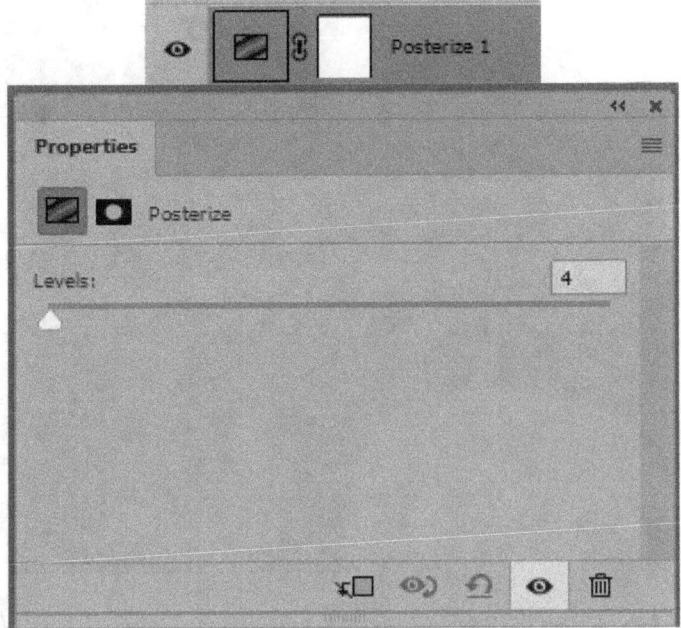

Figure 1-214. *Adjustment layer and Properties panel settings for Posterize*

The only Properties setting found for Posterize is as follows:

Levels (2–255): By default, this is set to 4. Move the slider or enter the number of tonal levels.

This produces a very similar effect to the scan option. A setting above 50 may show very little posterization on the image. Refer to Figure 1-215.

CHAPTER 1　ADJUSTMENT LAYERS, BLENDING MODES WITH MASKS FOR PHOTO RESTORATION: PART 1

Figure 1-215. *Posterize effect created using the adjustment layer*

Use this option for more artistic effects with a setting of 10.

Threshold

This converts grayscale or color images to high-contrast, black-and-white images. You can specify a certain level as a threshold. All pixels lighter than the threshold are converted to white, and all pixels that are darker are converted to black. I do not recommend using this adjustment layer for digital image repair. It is more for artistic effects if you are creating Color Lookup LUTs or with a blending mode applied.

Use either your Adjustments panel (Single adjustments) or your Layers panel to set this adjustment layer. Refer to Figure 1-216.

CHAPTER 1 ADJUSTMENT LAYERS, BLENDING MODES WITH MASKS FOR PHOTO RESTORATION: PART 1

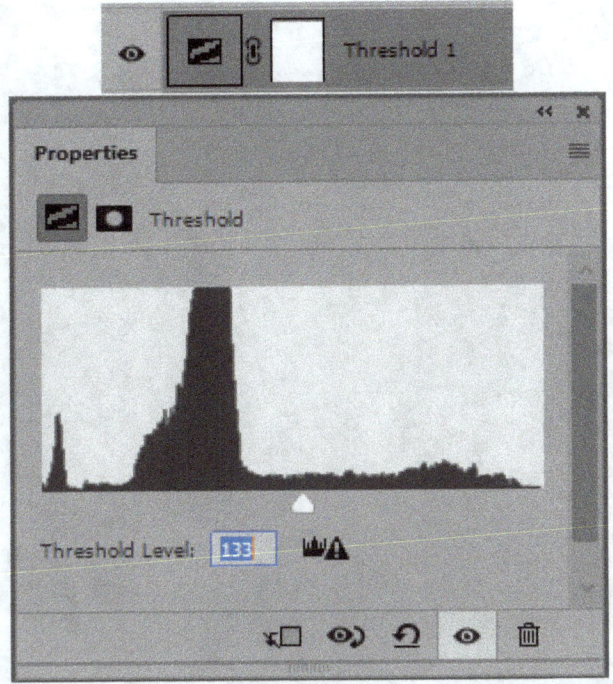

Figure 1-216. *Adjustment layer and Properties panel settings for Threshold*

The Properties settings found for Threshold are as follows:

The background displays a histogram of the selected pixel's luminance levels.

Threshold Level (1–255): By default, this is set to 128. Drag the slider to adjust the Threshold.

Calculate more accurate histogram: Click the warning to alter the setting display. Refer to Figure 1-216 and Figure 1-217.

221

CHAPTER 1 ADJUSTMENT LAYERS, BLENDING MODES WITH MASKS FOR PHOTO RESTORATION: PART 1

Figure 1-217. Threshold adjustments on a statue head

Gradient Map

Gradient Map is also a specialized adjustment that creates a gradient-like effect similar to a grayscale, the Black & White adjustment layer. It maps the equivalent grayscale range of an image to the custom colors of a specified gradient fill. If you specify a three-color gradient fill, for example, shadows in the image are mapped to one of the endpoint colors of the gradient fill, highlights are mapped to the other endpoint color, and midtones are mapped to the gradations in between. Refer to Figure 1-218.

CHAPTER 1 ADJUSTMENT LAYERS, BLENDING MODES WITH MASKS FOR PHOTO RESTORATION: PART 1

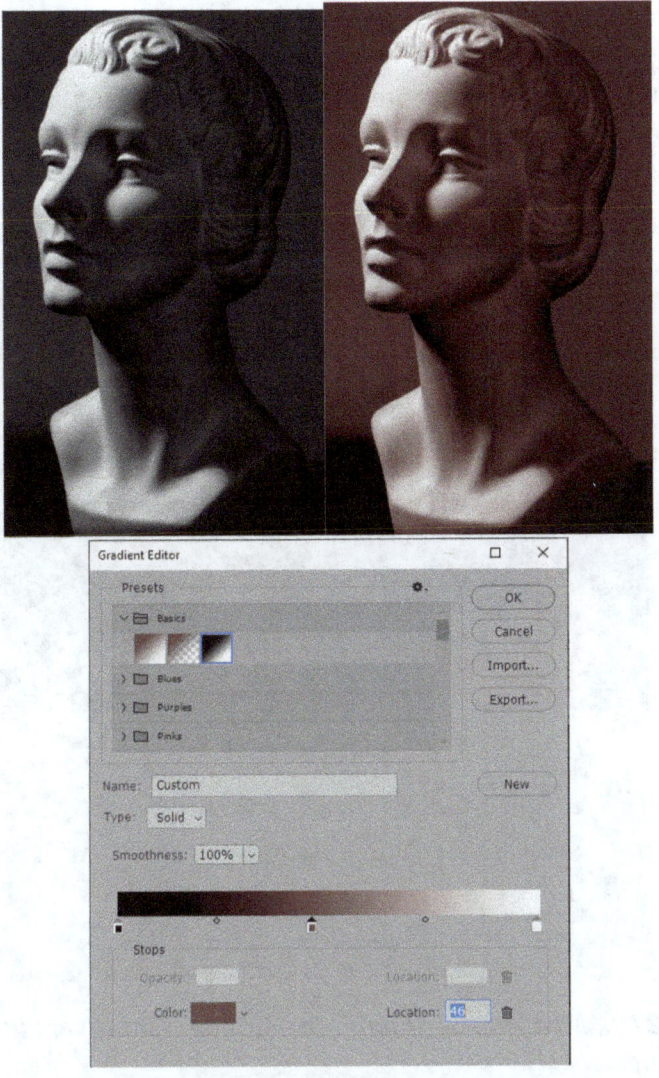

Figure 1-218. *Gradient Map effects on the statue head and adjustment with the Gradient Editor dialog box*

Adding more colors or even choosing a noise gradient can produce interesting effects much like a heat map, depending on how the colors are arranged. Or placing one or more on top of the other can produce darker effects like Film Noir. Refer to Figure 1-219.

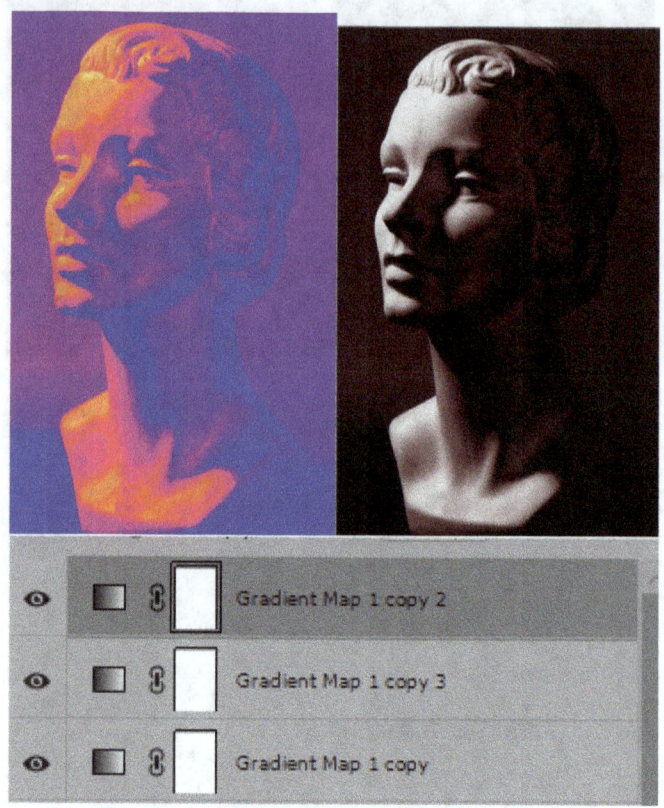

Figure 1-219. *Multiple Gradient Map adjustment layers in the Layers panel*

Use either your Adjustments panel (Single adjustments) or your Layers panel to set this adjustment layer. Refer to Figure 1-220.

CHAPTER 1   ADJUSTMENT LAYERS, BLENDING MODES WITH MASKS FOR PHOTO RESTORATION: PART 1

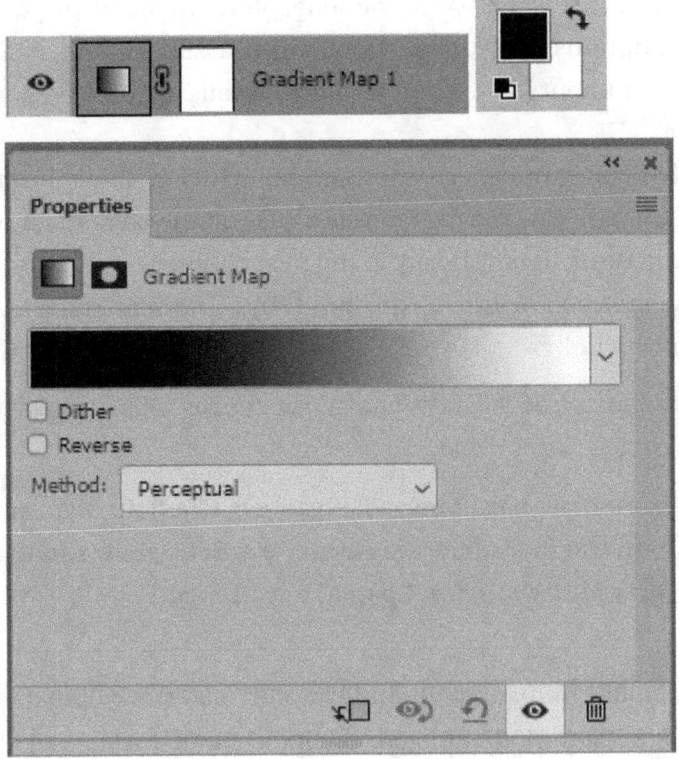

Figure 1-220. *Adjustment layer, black foreground in the Tools panel, and Properties panel settings for Gradient Map*

The Properties settings found for Gradient Map are as follows:

Gradient: Select a gradient from the list or click the list to enter the Gradient Editor, as you saw earlier with the Gradient Fill layer, and create a custom gradient. Shadows start by default at the left and highlights end on the right or if there is a darker foreground color in the Tools panel.

Dither: This is by default disabled but can have a smoothing effect. It adds random noise to smooth the appearance of a gradient fill and reduces the appearance of banding, which some color transitions may cause.

Reverse: This reverses the color order of the selected gradient fill and will reverse the order of the gradient map; by default this setting is disabled.

Method: This sets how your gradient colors will be displayed on the canvas. The options are Perceptual, Linear, Classic, Smooth, or Stripes. Refer to the Gradient Fill settings for more details. By default, it is set to Perceptual.

Note that you cannot access the Gradient Tool to affect the gradient map itself, but you can use the Gradient Tool on the layer mask, which we will review in more detail shortly in the next chapter.

More details on Posterize, Threshold, and Gradient Map can be found at the following link:

https://helpx.adobe.com/photoshop/using/applying-special-color-effects-images.html

To experiment with examples of Posterize, Gradient Map, and Threshold, you can look at my file **statue_gradient_map.psd** to review and see **statue_gradient_map_final.psd** as a reference.

Tip A Gadient Map adjustment layer can also have opacity and a different blending mode applied. Blending modes will be discussed in Chapter 2.

File ➤ Save your work at this point.

Working with Multiple Adjustment Layers and the Adjustments Panel

I conclude this chapter with discussing the following concerns: if you're not sure what kind of a combination to compose in the Adjustments panel. In the panel under the Adjustments presets, you can find other combinations for specific adjustments, such as Landscape and Photo Repair, when you click the More button. Refer to Figure 1-221.

CHAPTER 1 ADJUSTMENT LAYERS, BLENDING MODES WITH MASKS FOR PHOTO RESTORATION: PART 1

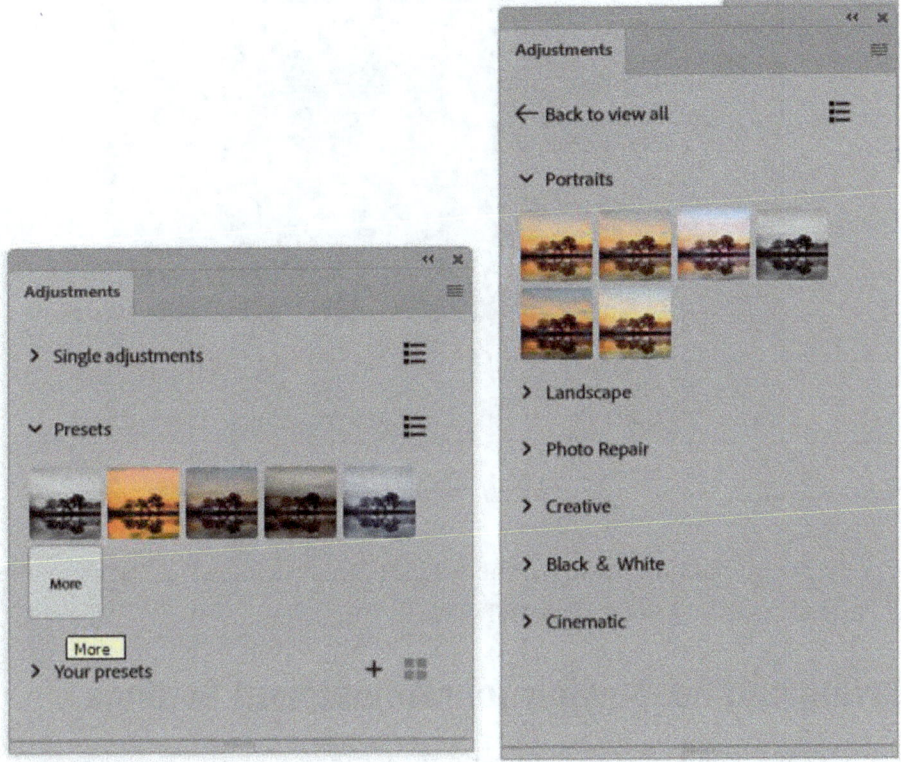

Figure 1-221. *Adjustments panel presets and more preset options*

You can hover over a button to preview on the canvas.

Clicking one of these buttons automatically applies several adjustment layers at once to create the described effect. You can then adjust each of these presets manually to fine-tune them to create the desired effect. Refer to Figure 1-222.

CHAPTER 1　ADJUSTMENT LAYERS, BLENDING MODES WITH MASKS FOR PHOTO RESTORATION: PART 1

Figure 1-222. *Layers panel with new Adjustments presets added*

When you need to return to the original presets, click the "Back to view all" arrow button. Refer to Figure 1-221.

Saving and Reapplying Your Adjustment Settings

If you have created your own adjustment settings, you can now save the combination, using the Adjustments panel, as well as under the section Your presets. Choose the adjustments (not fill layers) you want and then click the plus button on the right-hand side. Enter a preset name and click the Save button. Refer to Figure 1-223.

CHAPTER 1   ADJUSTMENT LAYERS, BLENDING MODES WITH MASKS FOR PHOTO RESTORATION: PART 1

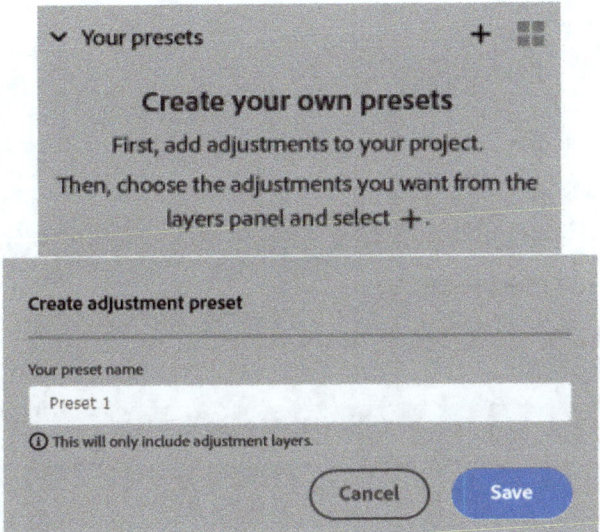

Figure 1-223. *Add your own presets to the Adjustments panel; name and save them*

The new preset will be added to your collection of presets, and then you have the additional options under the ellipsis (…) to rename, delete, export, or export all custom presets you created. Refer to Figure 1-224.

CHAPTER 1   ADJUSTMENT LAYERS, BLENDING MODES WITH MASKS FOR PHOTO RESTORATION: PART 1

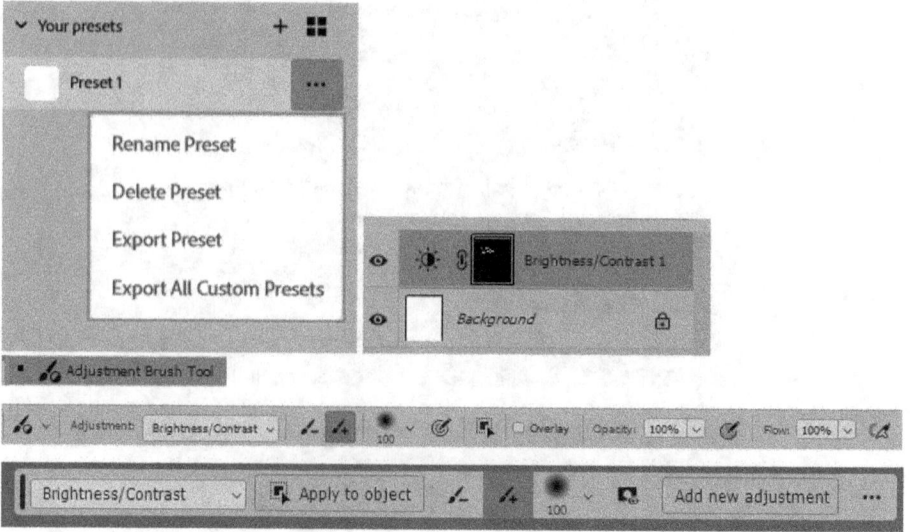

Figure 1-224. *Rename, delete, or export your presets from the Adjustments panel and the Settings in the Options bar panel and contextual task bar for the new Adjustment Brush tool with example on an Adjustment layer.*

Note that all exported presets are saved as PSAP(.psap) files and you can use the panel's menu to import your custom presets in the same file format.

More details on these settings can be found here:

https://helpx.adobe.com/photoshop/using/adjustment-fill-layers.html

https://helpx.adobe.com/photoshop/using/color-adjustments.html

https://helpx.adobe.com/photoshop/using/targeting-images-press.html

CHAPTER 1   ADJUSTMENT LAYERS, BLENDING MODES WITH MASKS FOR PHOTO RESTORATION: PART 1

Important Note: Recently a new brush has been added for working with your Adjustments called the Adjustment Brush tool which is dedicated to working with Adjustment Layers rather than relying on simply your Brush and Eraser tools to edit the layer's Mask. When this tool is selected when you click on the canvas it will automatically add a new adjustment layer with the first brush stroke to a Layer mask and you can continue to paint on it as you would with the other Brush or Eraser tool using the X key toggle. Refer to Figure 1-224. You can use the Options bar panel or Contextual Task bar drop down list to quickly switch the kind of adjustment layers you are using without having to add a new mask. Refer to the Options bar panel and look from left to right at the icon buttons you will notice that like other brushes you can:

- Subtract or Add to the layer mask selection as you paint.

- Change the brush size, hardness, angle, and tilt using the brush preset picker menu.

- Icon: "Always use pressure for size. When off, brush preset controls pressure."

- Choose an object and have the adjustment applied to it this is similar to using the Object selection tool as seen in Volume 1.

- Use the checkbox to turn the overlay on or off quickly to see the affected areas.

- Set the Opacity of the brush stroke (1-100%).

- Icon: "Always use pressure for Opacity. When off, brush preset controls pressure."

CHAPTER 1   ADJUSTMENT LAYERS, BLENDING MODES WITH MASKS FOR PHOTO
             RESTORATION: PART 1

- Set the Flow rate of the brush stroke (1-100%).

- Icon: "Enable airbrush-style build-up of effects."

The contextual task bar will also allow you to add a new adjustment layer if required as you work.

Note that you are not bound to use this tool on your Adjustment layer mask exclusively as you will see in the next chapter, and you can at any time switch to using the Brush tool, Eraser tool or a Selection tool if you feel more comfortable with those options. Note that this tool cannot be used on layer masks applied to Fill Layers, Normal, or Smart Object Layers. More information can be found at the following link: `https://helpx.adobe.com/photoshop/using/adjustment-brush.html`.

Summary

In this chapter we looked at a wide range of adjustment layers and looked a bit at blending, opacity, fills, and layer mask options that can affect the color correction of an image. In the next chapter we will explore more about the Properties panel masks and how colors are further affected by different color blending modes and when colors are considered out of gamut. We will also look at a few more color adjustment options as well as layer styles that you may want to use for specific projects.

CHAPTER 2

Adjustment Layers, Blending Modes with Masks for Photo Restoration: Part 2

In this chapter we will continue to review adjustment layers with the layer mask as it relates to the Properties panel. Then we will look at other mask options that include clipping masks, vector masks, and smart object layer filter masks.

We will look at a few options with the Pen Tool and Paths panel for mask creation.

Then we will explore opacity and other blending mode options and take a brief look at layer styles.

We will also return to the Image ➤ Adjustments panel and work with smart object layers to add another adjustment in a nondestructive way.

Then we will look at a few advanced color blending options, which will include working with HDR image options, and complete the color correction of the army photo project, which was started in Volume 1.

CHAPTER 2   ADJUSTMENT LAYERS, BLENDING MODES WITH MASKS FOR PHOTO
            RESTORATION: PART 2

Note this chapter does contain projects found in the Volume 2 Chapter 2 folder. Some text on selections has been adapted from my book *Accurate Layer Selections Using Photoshop's Selection Tools*.

We will now continue with the review of the Properties panel.

Properties Panel and Adjustment Layer Masks

Each adjustment layer can have its own unique layer mask, and you can copy the mask from one adjustment layer to another by Alt/Option + dragging the mask onto the other layer. The message Replace Layer Mask? will appear, and you can click Yes. Refer to Figure 2-1.

CHAPTER 2 ADJUSTMENT LAYERS, BLENDING MODES WITH MASKS FOR PHOTO RESTORATION: PART 2

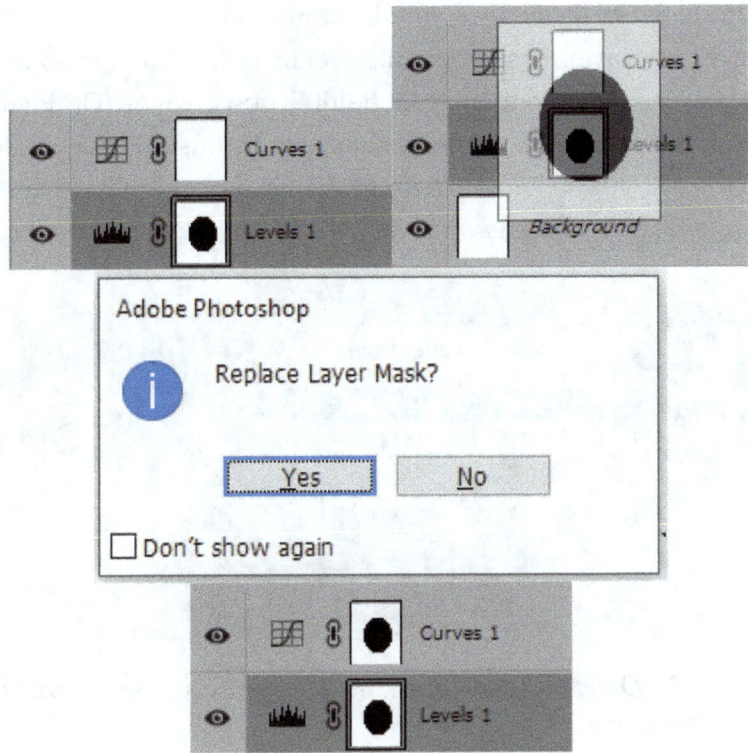

Figure 2-1. Copy one layer mask from one layer to another layer

However, as you update one mask by painting with your Brush Eraser, Adjustment brush tool or using a selection tool, the other will not update. Refer to Figure 2-2.

Figure 2-2. Paint on your layer mask with your Brush tool, Eraser, Adjustment Brush tool use X to switch masking settings

CHAPTER 2 ADJUSTMENT LAYERS, BLENDING MODES WITH MASKS FOR PHOTO
RESTORATION: PART 2

Alternatively, if you need your layer masks to be the same, you can delete the one layer mask from one layer by right-clicking and choosing Delete Layer Mask and then again holding down the Alt/Option key while you drag a copy of the layer mask back to the adjustment layer. Not holding down the Alt/Option key while dragging just moves the layer mask to the adjustment layer, which is what you don't want to do. Refer to Figure 2-3.

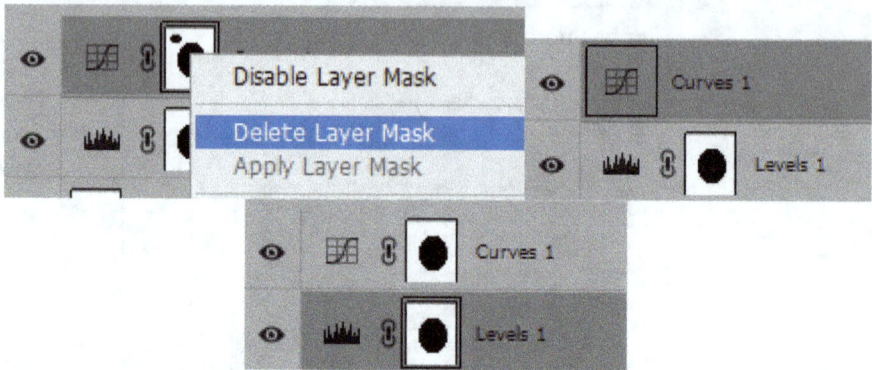

Figure 2-3. Delete a layer mask and copy a layer mask from another adjustment layer

If you want to see how to add several adjustments to one layer mask, refer to the section "Using Smart Filters to Make Certain Color Adjustments Nondestructive" in this chapter.

Removing Gradients from Scan Using Several Layer Masks

Having two of the same kind of adjustment layer, such as Levels or Curves, can be ideal when one masked area requires a slightly different tonal setting than another area that is not quite as faded or damaged.

CHAPTER 2   ADJUSTMENT LAYERS, BLENDING MODES WITH MASKS FOR PHOTO RESTORATION: PART 2

The application of multiple adjustment layers and layer masks with varying settings may be suitable in situations where you scanned a black-and-white photo that was slightly bent in an album and has a gutter highlight or shadow in it. Or it may be because an area of the image faded or something was wrong with the camera that took the image or the film did not develop correctly. This causes a banding-like graduated effect. In Volume 1 using the Clone Stamp tool or one of the healing brushes on a blank layer above the background is not going to fix this.

You can refer to my file **pillars_mulitple_adjustments.psd**. Refer to Figure 2-4.

Figure 2-4. *An image that is very damaged with gradient-like stripes*

Whatever the reason for this color damage, using multiple adjustment layers (Levels and Curves or even Selective Color, Hue/Saturation, or Black & White) of the same kind to feather and blend out in combination with layer masks can assist. Refer to Chapter 1 if you need to review them. Refer to Figure 2-5.

CHAPTER 2   ADJUSTMENT LAYERS, BLENDING MODES WITH MASKS FOR PHOTO RESTORATION: PART 2

Figure 2-5. *Damage can be repaired but only with multiple adjustment layers and masks*

Carefully masking areas and feathering can help certain colors blend together and greatly reduce the banding if not altogether. At the same time some overlaying masks should not blend into each other, creating a color line. Adjustment layer mask order is also very important. Refer to Figure 2-6.

CHAPTER 2 ADJUSTMENT LAYERS, BLENDING MODES WITH MASKS FOR PHOTO RESTORATION: PART 2

Figure 2-6. *Some images will require multiple adjustment layers to repair heavy damage*

CHAPTER 2   ADJUSTMENT LAYERS, BLENDING MODES WITH MASKS FOR PHOTO RESTORATION: PART 2

In other situations, as seen earlier in Chapter 1 when adding Hue/Saturation adjustments, two or more could be useful for some older black-and-white photos or when you want to apply different colorize tints to one or more areas. Refer to Figure 2-7.

Figure 2-7. *Multiple adjustment layers of Hue/Saturation when you want to paint different areas of the image*

We will look at that shortly. However, let's take a moment to review Properties panel layer mask settings as we can use this area to make further adjust adjustments to layer masks on both normal and adjustment layers.

Properties Panel Layer Mask Settings for Normal and Adjustment Layers

To review, as in the example of the tower image that you saw in Volume 1 and recently in this volume's Chapter 1, after you have created a selection on a normal layer (Layer 0) using the Elliptical Marquee Tool or any selection tool, you can then add it to that layer as a layer mask using the Layers panel. To practive refer to **tower_layermask.psd**. Refer to Figure 2-8.

CHAPTER 2 ADJUSTMENT LAYERS, BLENDING MODES WITH MASKS FOR PHOTO RESTORATION: PART 2

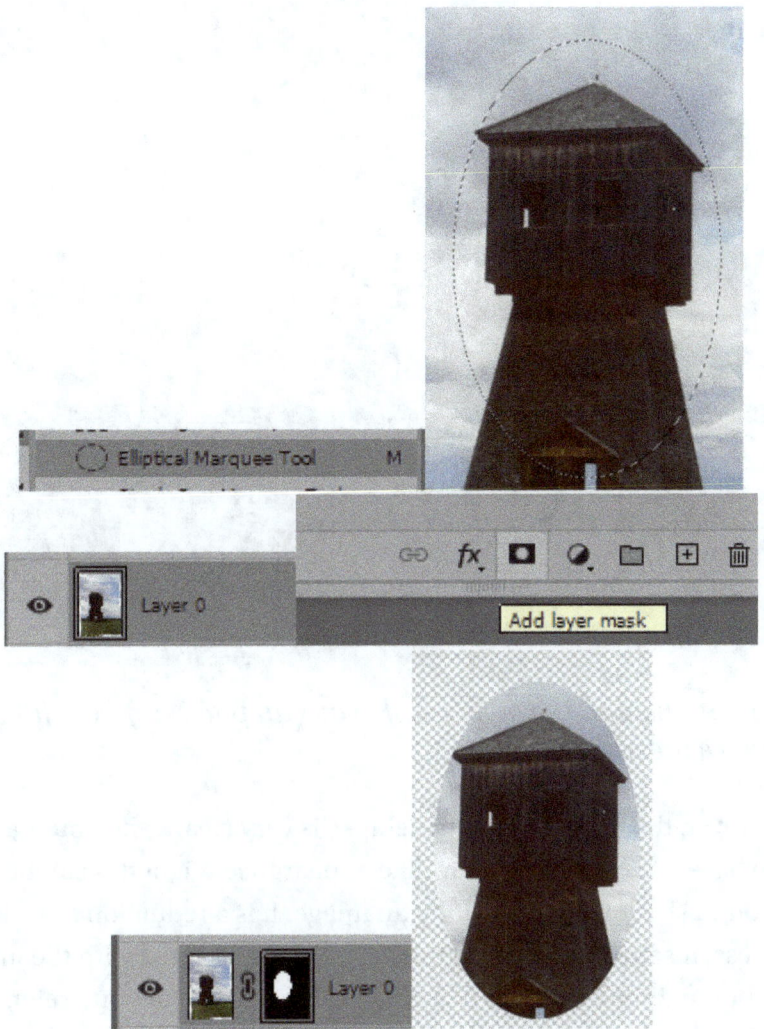

Figure 2-8. *Create and add a selection as a layer mask to an image*

This creates a transparent area behind the layer. However, as you saw in Chapter 1, you could add a solid color or even gradient fill behind the masked layer to give your ellipse a bit of a frame. Refer to Figure 2-9.

CHAPTER 2 ADJUSTMENT LAYERS, BLENDING MODES WITH MASKS FOR PHOTO RESTORATION: PART 2

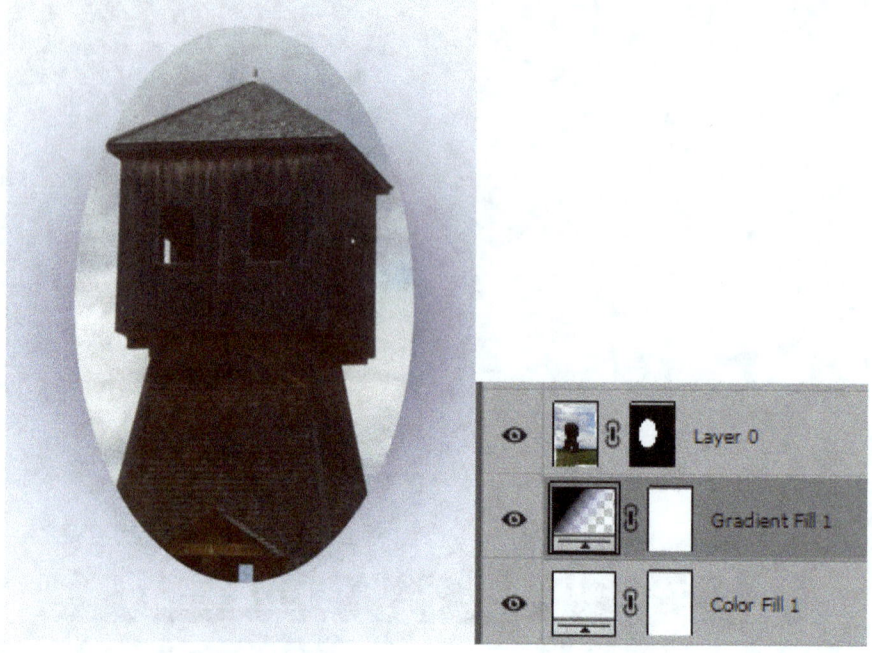

Figure 2-9. *Behind the layer mask, you can place different fill layers to enhance the frame*

However, this edge around the ellipse is very clean, and you may want to have a fuzzier or vignette-like appearance. Vignettes can be dark background shadows surrounding an image. It is a reduction of an image's brightness or saturation toward the periphery compared with the image center, but in Photoshop it can be any background color you prefer.

Rather than edit the layer mask directly on Layer 0 by using a brush or one of the selections options to feather, you can just select the mask and use the Properties panel. Refer to Figure 2-10.

CHAPTER 2 ADJUSTMENT LAYERS, BLENDING MODES WITH MASKS FOR PHOTO RESTORATION: PART 2

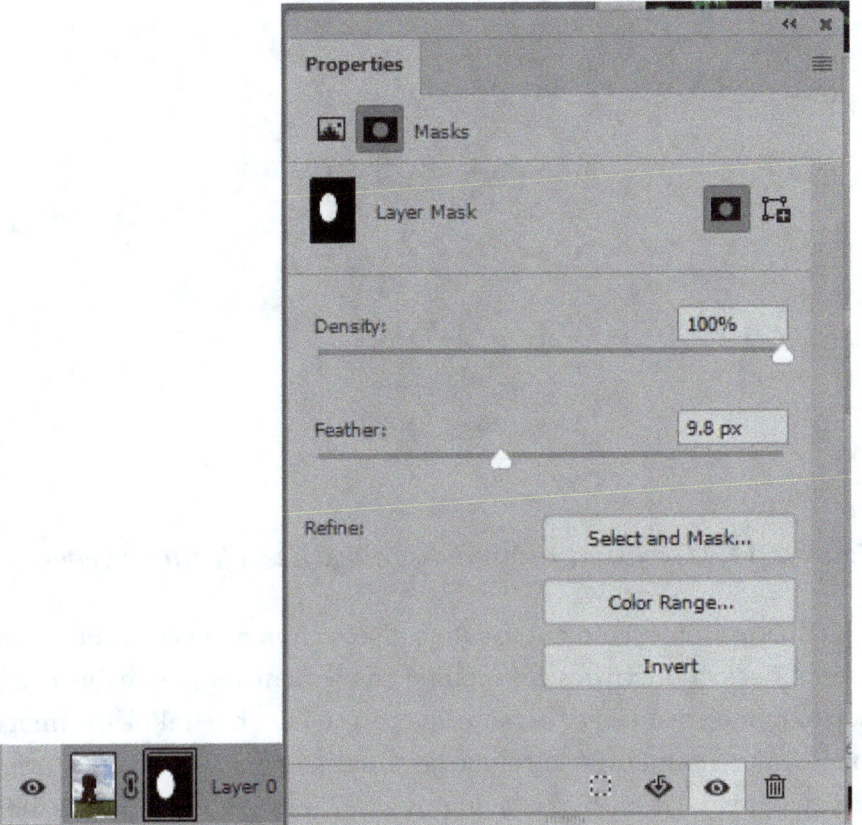

Figure 2-10. *When the layer mask is selected, use the Properties panel to make adjustments*

Clicking the Layer Mask option in the Properties panel then allows you to adjust your Density (0–100%). This is like an opacity but just for the mask. Then adjust the Feather setting (0–1000 px). I put the setting to 9.8 px so that there was still a slight edge and the mask was not overly blurred so that you could still see the ellipse. Refer to Figure 2-11.

CHAPTER 2   ADJUSTMENT LAYERS, BLENDING MODES WITH MASKS FOR PHOTO RESTORATION: PART 2

Figure 2-11. *The frame around the image has a feathered edge*

In this example, I did not use the Refine action of Invert, which would invert the selection. Using this method creates a nice vignette that can be used to frame an object or person. You can at any time unlink the image from the mask. And then select the layer mask or image with the Move tool to align better with the vignette. In this case I moved the mask with the Move tool and then linked it again. Refer to Figure 2-12.

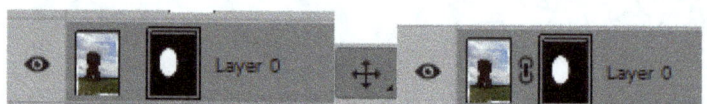

Figure 2-12. *Unlink the layer mask when you need to move with the Move tool and adjust it and link again in the Layers panel*

There is, however, more than one way to create a similar vignette. As I mentioned, layer order is important when working with adjustment and fill layers. Generally, you want the adjustment or fill to be above the background layer as this could make it easier to make certain color adjustments.

CHAPTER 2　ADJUSTMENT LAYERS, BLENDING MODES WITH MASKS FOR PHOTO RESTORATION: PART 2

In this example you could leave the background (Layer 0) without a mask but still create a selection. Refer to Figure 2-13.

Figure 2-13. *The selection does not have to be a mask on the image layer itself*

This time add the fill layer of white, and the selection would be applied to that fill layer. However, in this case the selection may be inverted. Refer to Figure 2-14.

245

CHAPTER 2 ADJUSTMENT LAYERS, BLENDING MODES WITH MASKS FOR PHOTO RESTORATION: PART 2

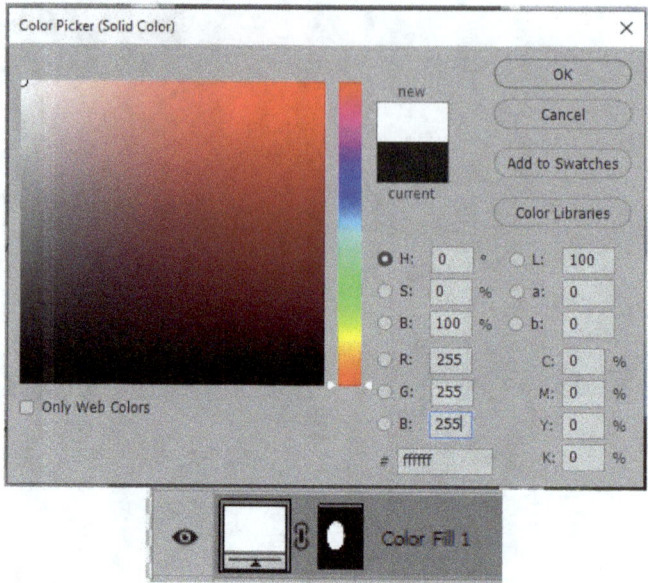

Figure 2-14. *Add the selection to a solid color fill layer*

With the layer mask selected in the Properties panel, you can click the Refine ➤ Invert button to invert the mask. Then again you can adjust the framing of your image and apply the same feather and density settings. Refer to Figures 2-15 and 2-16.

CHAPTER 2 ADJUSTMENT LAYERS, BLENDING MODES WITH MASKS FOR PHOTO RESTORATION: PART 2

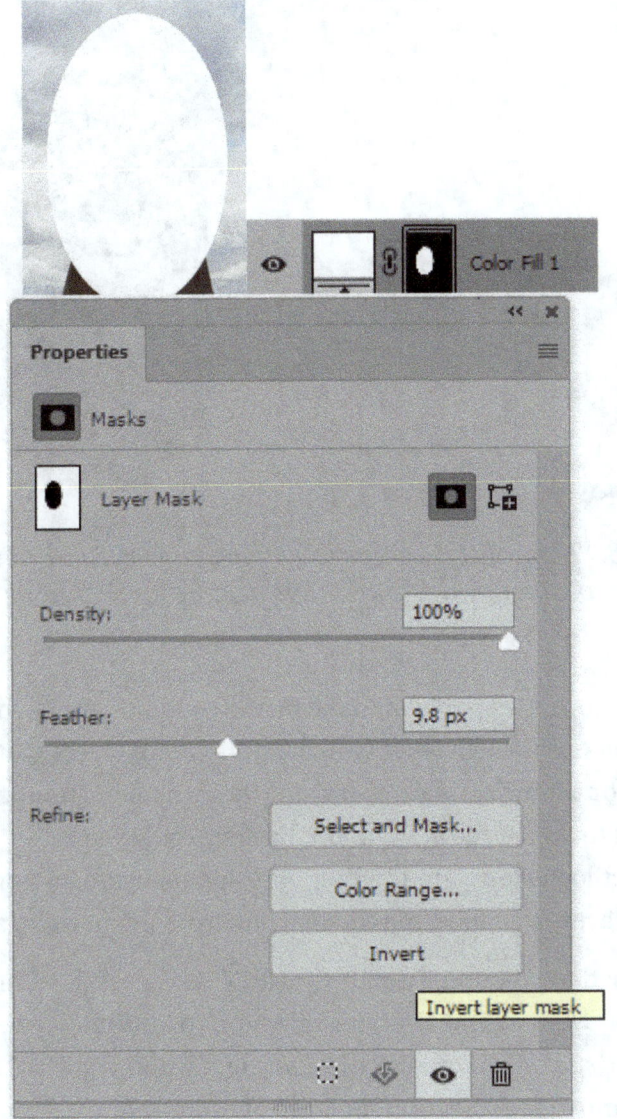

Figure 2-15. *The selection comes in as a solid covering, but you can use the Properties panel to invert the selection*

CHAPTER 2 ADJUSTMENT LAYERS, BLENDING MODES WITH MASKS FOR PHOTO RESTORATION: PART 2

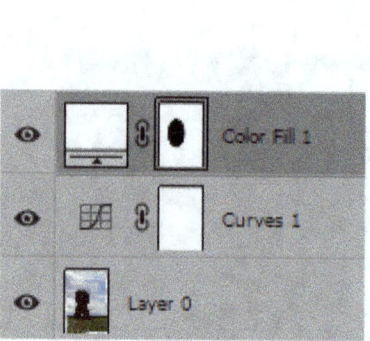

Figure 2-16. *The solid fill color layer can be placed above the image layer to cover and frame areas and be feathered using the Properties panel*

Use the Properties panel to make further adjustment to your layer mask. This technique will work with all adjustment layers that contain layer masks or when you want to hide parts of the adjustment layers that may be used to adjust the color of the background image.

The other icons found in the Properties panel while on normal, fill, or adjustment layers that have masks selected, from left to right, are as follows:

- Load a selection from the mask: This is useful when you want to add a similar selection to another layer. Use Ctrl/CMD + D or Select ➤ Deselect when you want to remove the selection. Refer to Figure 2-17.

- Apply the mask: For normal layers this will apply the mask to the current layer and remove the mask leaving only the selection applied. This option is grayed out for adjustment and fill layers as you want to keep the layer mask applied. Refer to Figure 2-17.

- Enable/disable the mask: Use this to toggle on and off the visibility of the mask. Refer to Figure 2-17.

- Delete the mask: To remove the layer mask. Refer to Figure 2-17.

Figure 2-17. *Visually turn on and off the layer masks using the Properties panel*

Remember Knowing when you are on the adjustment layer or the layer mask itself is important when you switch between layer options using the Properties panel. Refer to Figure 2-18.

Figure 2-18. *Properties panel set to Masks and a layer mask*

We will look at another kind of mask in this section shortly. However, when working in the Properties panel, the options in the lower area change. Refer to Figure 2-19.

CHAPTER 2   ADJUSTMENT LAYERS, BLENDING MODES WITH MASKS FOR PHOTO RESTORATION: PART 2

Figure 2-19. *Use the icons at the bottom of the Properties panel to affect your adjustment layers*

You can now do the following to affect the adjustment layer, looking from left to right. Refer to Figure 2-19.

- Square and arrow icon: This adjustment affects the layers below (click to clip the layer). This creates a clipping mask, which we will look at next.

- Eye with arrow: Click to view the previous state of the adjustment or use the \ key.

- Counterclockwise arrow: Reset the adjustment layer.

- Toggle the layer visibility with the eye.

- Delete the layer using the trash can icon rather than using the Layers panel. Refer to Figure 2-19.

Clipping Masks

While working with normal layers or fill and adjustment layers, there are times when you want to apply select adjustments from another layer to just a layer below. In the case of fill layers such as a gradient and a solid color fill, rather than the gradient covering the whole image, you can Alt/Option + click between two layers to create or remove a clipping mask. The clipping mask has blended the two fill layers together and does not block the mask of the color fill. Refer to Figure 2-20.

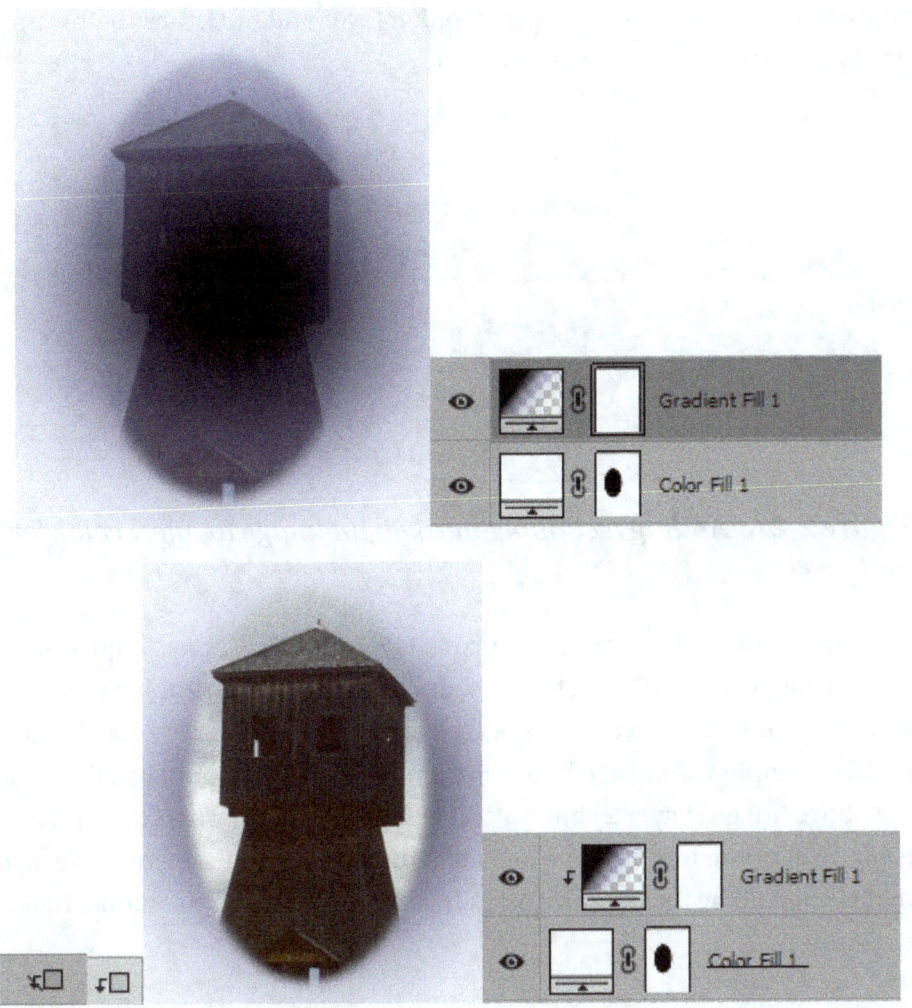

Figure 2-20. *Add a clipping mask to your current layer or adjustment layer*

However, with normal and adjustments layers, you can use the Properties panel. In the Layers panel just select the adjustment layer above the layer you want it to clip to, and from the Properties panel, choose the square and arrow button: "This adjustment clips to the layer." The icon will then change on the layer and in the Properties panel, and now only those

CHAPTER 2   ADJUSTMENT LAYERS, BLENDING MODES WITH MASKS FOR PHOTO RESTORATION: PART 2

adjustment settings will be applied to that layer and not others below it, until you unclip it. Refer to Figure 2-21.

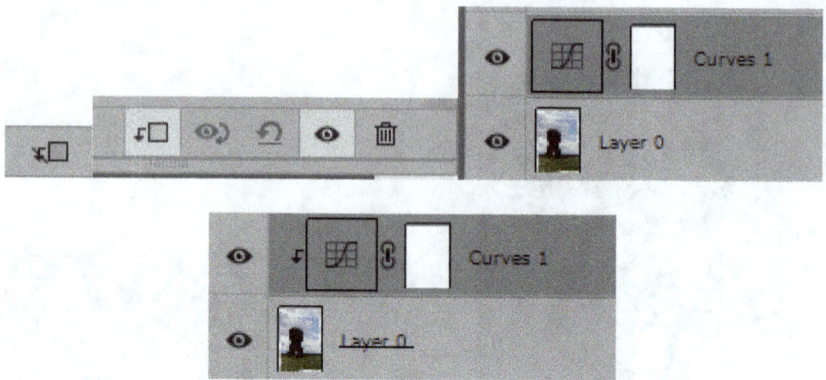

Figure 2-21. *Adding a clipping mask to an image to affect color for that layer*

You can do this for multiple normal layers or, in this case, adjustment layers when you need them to be grouped as part of the clipping mask and you only want those layers to affect the current layer and not others below. In this example we can see how two adjustment layers could be clipped to the above image (Layer 2) but not affect Layer 0 (background layer). This is how a clipping mask can be used to control color adjustments. The layer that is affected by the clipping mask has an underline on the name. Refer to Figure 2-22.

CHAPTER 2   ADJUSTMENT LAYERS, BLENDING MODES WITH MASKS FOR PHOTO RESTORATION: PART 2

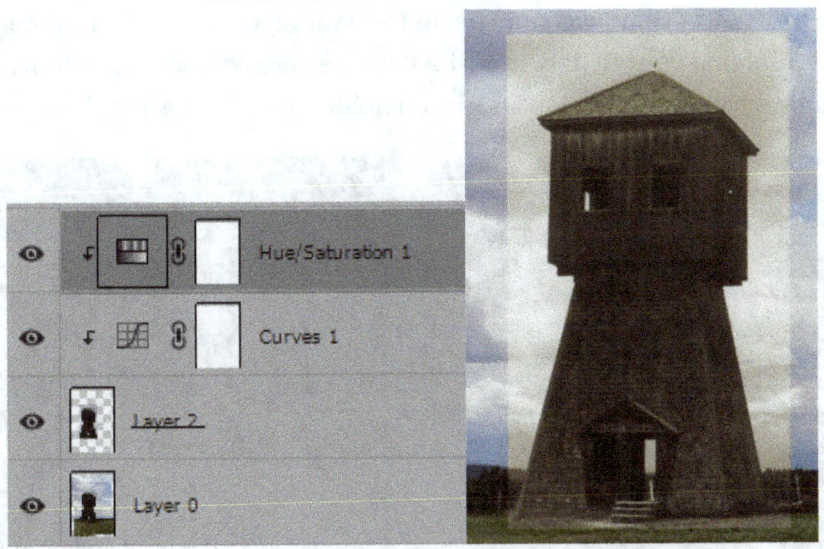

Figure 2-22. *Use the Layers panel to add a clipping mask*

To review this you can view my file **tower_clipping mask_final.psd** or practice on your own file and experiment with layer order of clipping masks.

Applying an Additional Vector Mask with the Properties Panel

Another additional mask that can be applied from the Properties panel to normal layers as well as adjustment layers is the vector mask.

This is more of a clean-edged shape mask, but it still can have feathering and density applied and is good for creating custom geometric framing. If you have already created and saved a selection in your Channels panel, then you can quickly create a vector mask with minimal editing. Refer to the unicorn example we looked at in Volume 1, Chapter 7, which, after being made, was saved through the main menu Select ➤ Save Selection. I have saved a copy of it here in the file **Unicorn_Vector_Mask.psd**, which you can refer to.

CHAPTER 2   ADJUSTMENT LAYERS, BLENDING MODES WITH MASKS FOR PHOTO
             RESTORATION: PART 2

From your Channels panel begin by loading the selection and then make sure that your RGB composite layer is selected and the visibility eye of "unicorn object selection" is turned off. Refer to Figure 2-23.

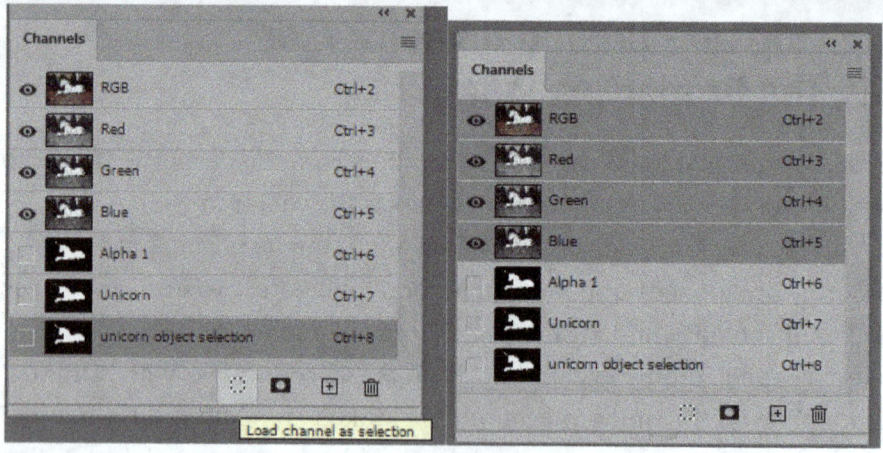

Figure 2-23. *Load a channel as a selection and then make sure you are on the RGB composite in the Channels panel*

CHAPTER 2 ADJUSTMENT LAYERS, BLENDING MODES WITH MASKS FOR PHOTO RESTORATION: PART 2

Then go to the Paths panel and click the lower icon "Make work path from selection." Refer to Figure 2-24.

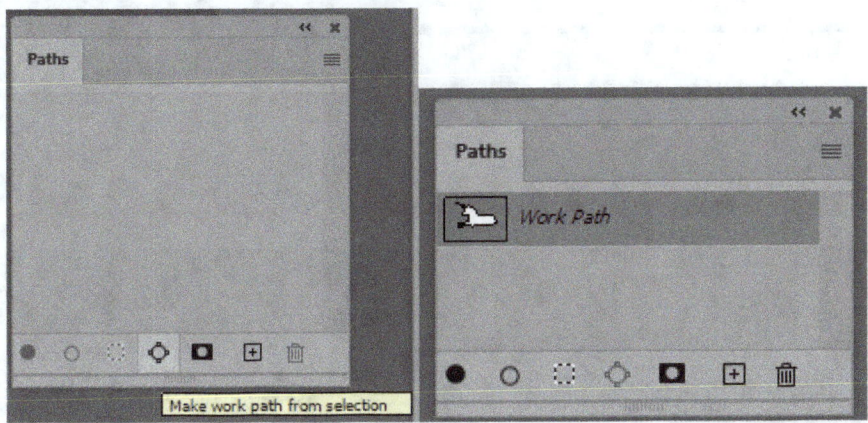

Figure 2-24. *Use the Paths panel to make a work path from the selection*

This adds a temporary work path to the Paths panel where you can then double-click the name and rename the path and view it around the unicorn. This makes the path permanent in the panel. However, it is not a vector mask yet. Refer to Figure 2-25.

CHAPTER 2   ADJUSTMENT LAYERS, BLENDING MODES WITH MASKS FOR PHOTO RESTORATION: PART 2

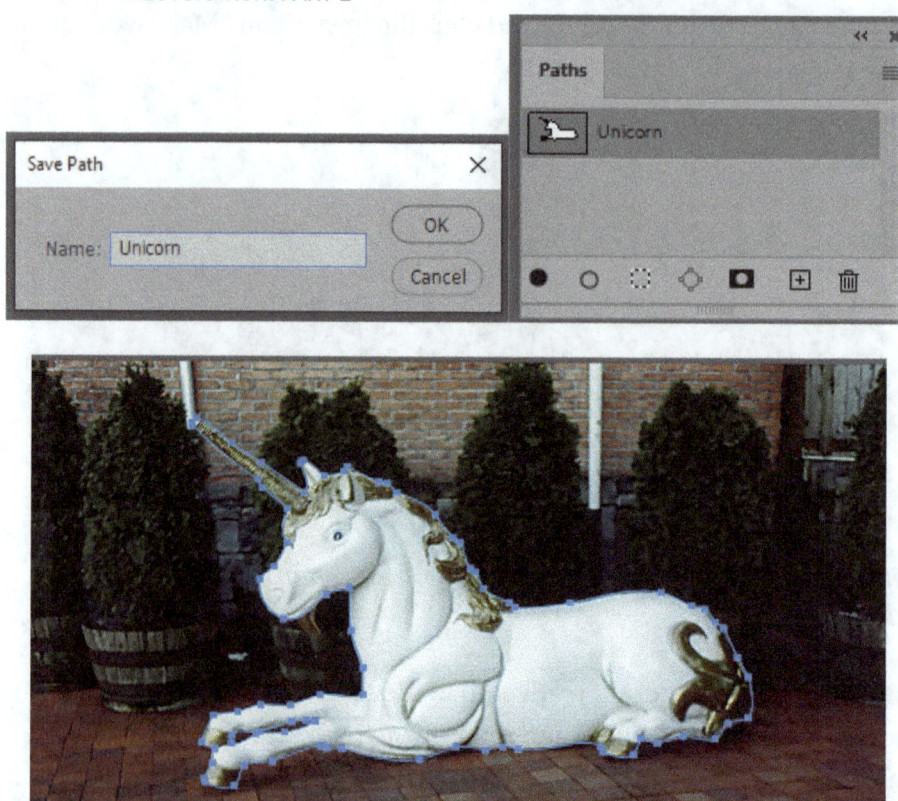

Figure 2-25. *Rename the path to save it in the file*

Now, while the layer is selected in the Layers panel, if a layer mask was already present, you could then click again the mask icon to add the vector mask. You would now have two masks on your layer, but in this case, you only need one. To avoid adding the layer mask, this time when you click the mask button in the Layers panel, hold down the Ctrl/CMD key and click. Refer to Figure 2-26.

CHAPTER 2 ADJUSTMENT LAYERS, BLENDING MODES WITH MASKS FOR PHOTO RESTORATION: PART 2

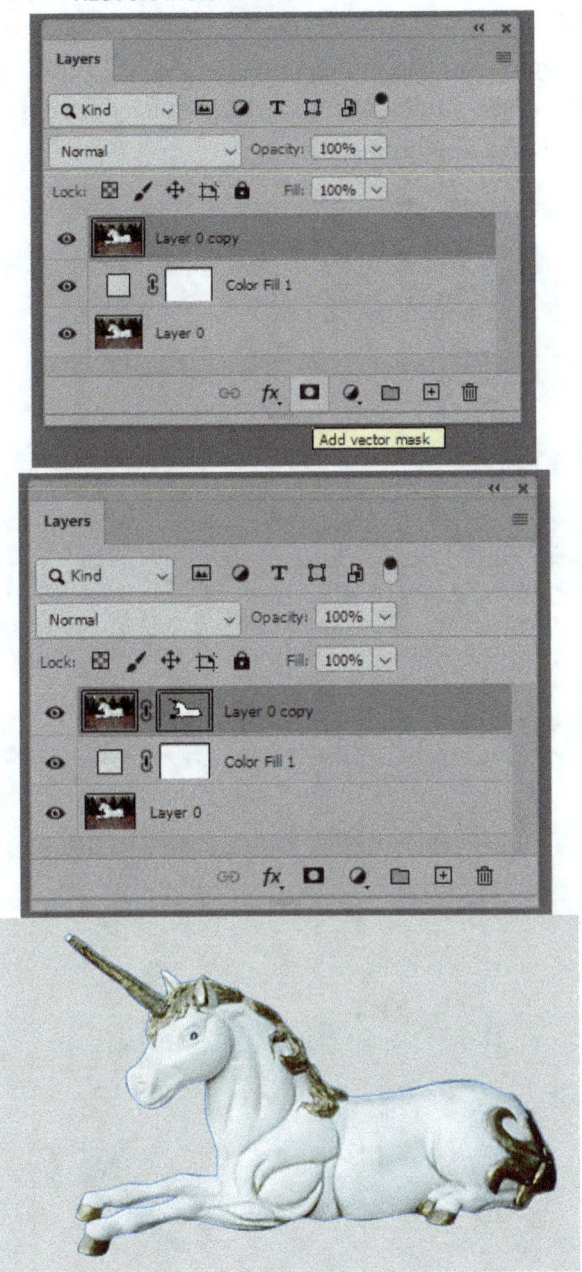

Figure 2-26. *Load the current path as a vector mask*

CHAPTER 2   ADJUSTMENT LAYERS, BLENDING MODES WITH MASKS FOR PHOTO
            RESTORATION: PART 2

In the Properties panel, you would now have a vector mask selected. As with layer masks, you can apply Density (0–100%) and Feather settings (0–1000 px). However, you cannot invert the mask or access anything in the Refine settings. Refer to Figure 2-27.

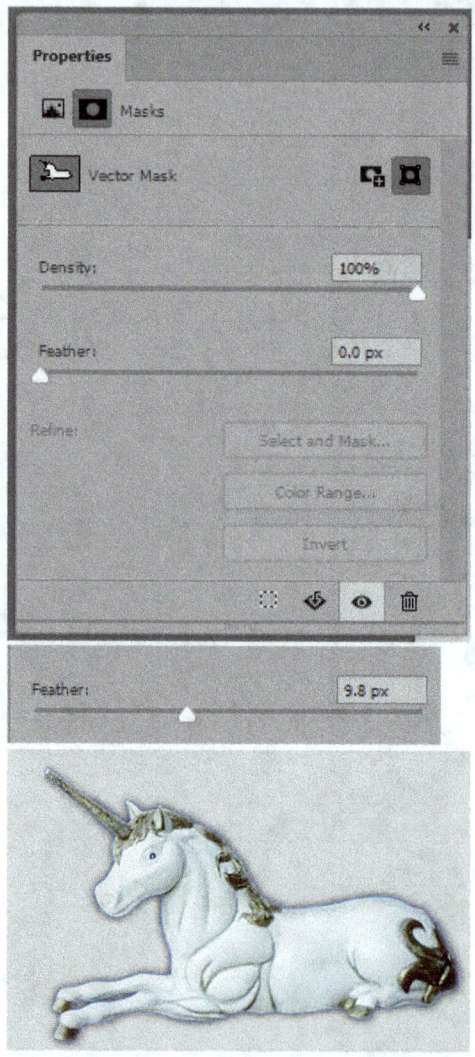

Figure 2-27. *Use the Properties panel to alter your vector mask*

CHAPTER 2 ADJUSTMENT LAYERS, BLENDING MODES WITH MASKS FOR PHOTO RESTORATION: PART 2

Pen Tool and Related Editing and Selection Tools

To create and add this type of mask from scratch, you need to have a bit of knowledge of how to use the Pen Tool in conjunction with the Paths panel and the Path Selection Tool and Direct Selection Tool, before creating a custom vector mask. Refer to Figure 2-28.

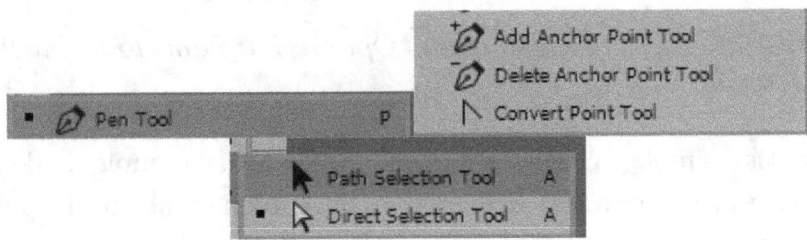

Figure 2-28. *Pen Tool and selection tools used to alter paths and anchor points*

While I will not go into all the features of working with the Pen Tool and its related tools (Add Anchor Point, Delete Anchor Point, and Convert Point Tools), I have provided a link at the end of this section should you want to explore this area on your own. For reference to these tools, refer to Figure 2-28.

I will just give a few tips on how to create simple, smooth, straight and curved vector paths that will appear as work paths in the Paths panel (Figure 2-24). Then while a path is selected, you can then easily add a vector mask by either clicking Ctrl/CMD on the mask icon in the Layers panel or using the Properties panel to add your vector mask to a normal or adjustment layer that may or may not already have a layer mask applied.

Pen Tool Tips

When using the Pen Tool to create a basic mask, follow these next steps. If you need more details on working with the Pen Tool for other projects, you can refer to my book mentioned in the introduction about selections or refer to the link provided at the end of these steps.

CHAPTER 2 ADJUSTMENT LAYERS, BLENDING MODES WITH MASKS FOR PHOTO
           RESTORATION: PART 2

To begin, refer to the Options bar panel for the Pen Tool, not for the other sub-tools as there are no additional settings for them in the Options bar panel. Refer to Figure 2-29.

Figure 2-29. *Use the Pen Tool and Options bar panel to set the Pen to a Path mode*

In this example, I will just show you how to create a simple shaped path. Let's just make a path of the area of the garden framed by the pillars. You can use a copy of my file **Garden_Vector_Path.psd** to practice. Begin by selecting the Pen Tool and then look at the Options bar panel. Refer to Figure 2-29 and Figure 2-30.

Figure 2-30. *You can draw a path and create a framed selection for a vector path*

CHAPTER 2   ADJUSTMENT LAYERS, BLENDING MODES WITH MASKS FOR PHOTO RESTORATION: PART 2

In your Options bar panel, make sure that your Pen Tool mode is set to Path as you will first be creating a path in the Paths panel. It should not be set to Shape or Pixels. Refer to Figure 2-31.

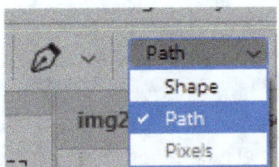

Figure 2-31. *Pen Tool Options bar panel set to Path mode*

The path is not actually visible if printed, just a guide on the screen and is in many ways like when we used the Magnetic Lasso Tool and the Polygonal Lasso Tool in Volume 1, Chapter 6. However, this time, rather than letting the path drag out or just clicking straight angles, you will click out your own set of anchor points where required and be able to accurately curve them at the same time. Refer to Figure 2-32.

Figure 2-32. *Use the Pen Tool to click out a path*

To draw a straight line, click out the points. Note that in the Options bar panel I have Path Operations set to "Exclude Overlapping Shapes" so that I create a distinct mask area and still have gaps, if required, as seen between the legs of the unicorn. Refer to Figure 2-33.

261

CHAPTER 2 ADJUSTMENT LAYERS, BLENDING MODES WITH MASKS FOR PHOTO RESTORATION: PART 2

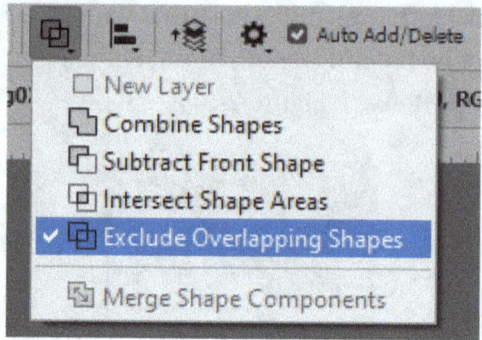

Figure 2-33. *Pen Options bar panel settings should be set to Path Operations ➤ Exclude Overlapping Shapes*

Use the Shift key as you click if you want 45° and 90° angles. If the ground is a bit uneven, then just click without holding the Shift key, and you can, after you finish the path, use the Direct Selection Tool to adjust an anchor point, which I will mention later.

For a curved line, click and then, at the next point, click and drag. Using this technique you can create a curved shape. Dragging in this case to the right causes the curve to bend the left. Refer to Figure 2-34.

Figure 2-34. *Use the Pen Tool to add a curve to the path*

To make the next line in the path straight, you can Alt/Option + click a point again (point 3). Then click to make a point 4 to make the next line straight. Refer to Figure 2-35.

CHAPTER 2   ADJUSTMENT LAYERS, BLENDING MODES WITH MASKS FOR PHOTO RESTORATION: PART 2

Figure 2-35. *Use the Pen Tool to add change from a curve to a straight line*

Continue to create the path using these tips as a guide. Here I have created a basic path for my vector shape, which you can review later in the file **Garden_Vector_Path_final.psd**.

As you work, make sure to use the Ctrl/CMD + + to zoom in and your Hand tool (spacebar) so you do not disrupt the path as you work. Refer to Figure 2-36.

CHAPTER 2   ADJUSTMENT LAYERS, BLENDING MODES WITH MASKS FOR PHOTO RESTORATION: PART 2

Figure 2-36. *Use the Pen Tool to make a complete path*

To close the path, in this case on the lower left, as you saw with the Magnetic Lasso in Volume 1, when you reach the beginning anchor point 1, your cursor will appear with an "O" by the pen. You can click it to close the path. In this case I need to click and drag downward to finish the last curve and have the anchor point's handle appear upward. Refer to Figure 2-37.

CHAPTER 2   ADJUSTMENT LAYERS, BLENDING MODES WITH MASKS FOR PHOTO RESTORATION: PART 2

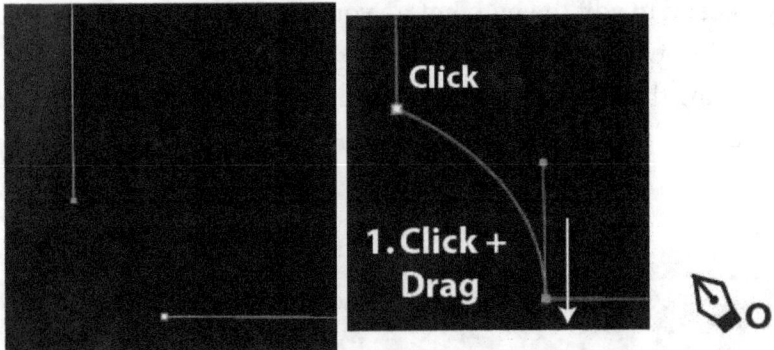

Figure 2-37. *Use the Pen Tool to close the path*

The path is now seen as a work path in the Paths panel. As mentioned earlier you can double-click the name and rename in the dialog box and Click OK so that, like a selection, it is saved and does not get removed by mistake. Refer to Figure 2-38.

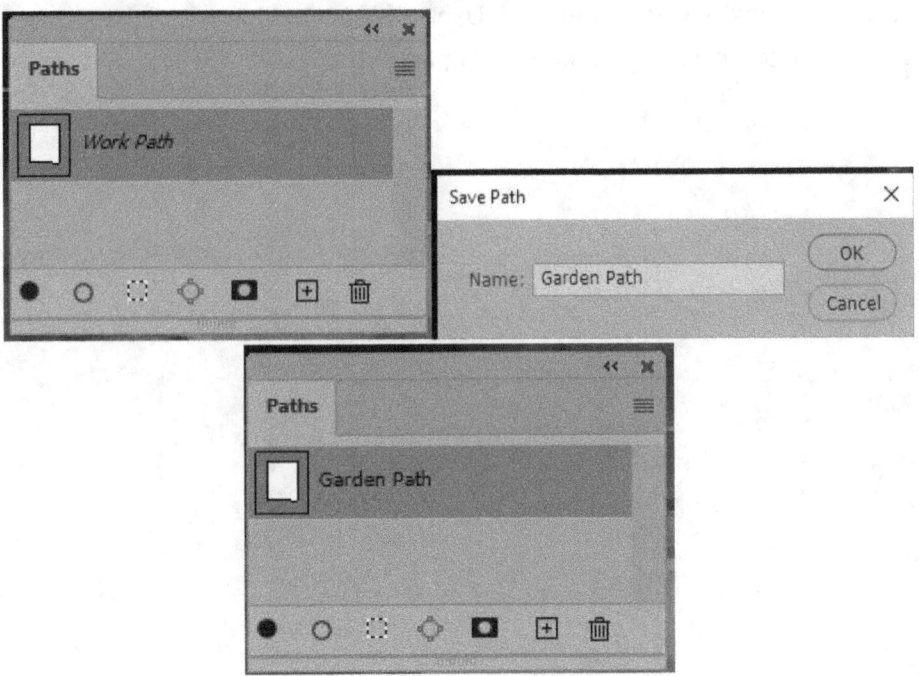

Figure 2-38. *Save the path in the Paths panel*

265

CHAPTER 2 ADJUSTMENT LAYERS, BLENDING MODES WITH MASKS FOR PHOTO RESTORATION: PART 2

If you need to edit the path before you make your final vector mask, you can either use the Add Anchor Point Tool or Delete Anchor Point Tool, or while using the Pen Tool, make sure that the option Auto Add/Delete is enabled in its Options bar panel. Refer to Figure 2-39.

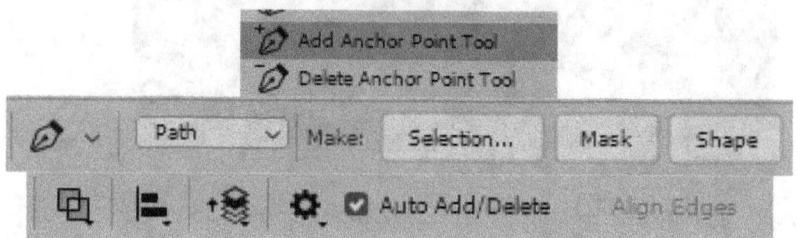

Figure 2-39. *Use the Pen Tool or its related Add and Delete Anchor Point Tools to edit the path or enable the setting in the Options bar panel*

Then click somewhere on a path when you want to add a point or click a point when you want to delete it. Use Ctrl/CMD + Z or your History panel if you need to undo a step. Refer to Figure 2-40.

CHAPTER 2 ADJUSTMENT LAYERS, BLENDING MODES WITH MASKS FOR PHOTO RESTORATION: PART 2

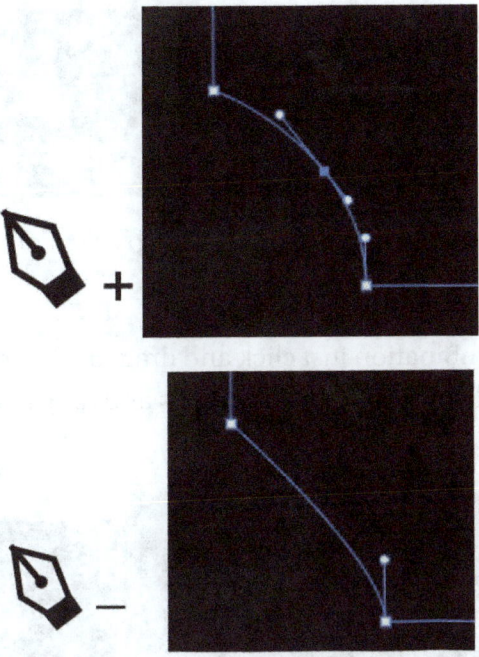

Figure 2-40. *Add or remove points to or from the path using the Pen Tool*

An anchor point can be altered from corner to curved afterward by clicking and dragging on it with the Convert Point Tool. Refer to Figure 2-41.

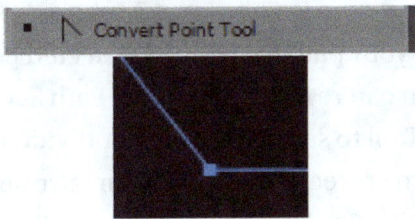

Figure 2-41. *Use the Convert Point Tool to edit paths and points*

Click and drag to create a curved point or click to create a corner point. Refer to Figure 2-42.

CHAPTER 2   ADJUSTMENT LAYERS, BLENDING MODES WITH MASKS FOR PHOTO RESTORATION: PART 2

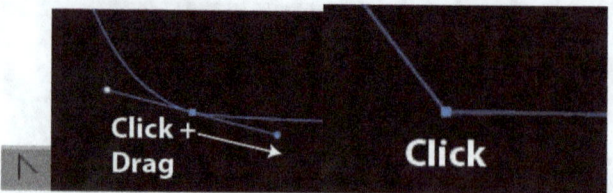

Figure 2-42. *Use the Convert Point Tool to edit paths and points and make them curved or straight*

To create a combination just click and drag to create the curve and then click one of the anchor point's handles and drag it in a new direction. Refer to Figure 2-43.

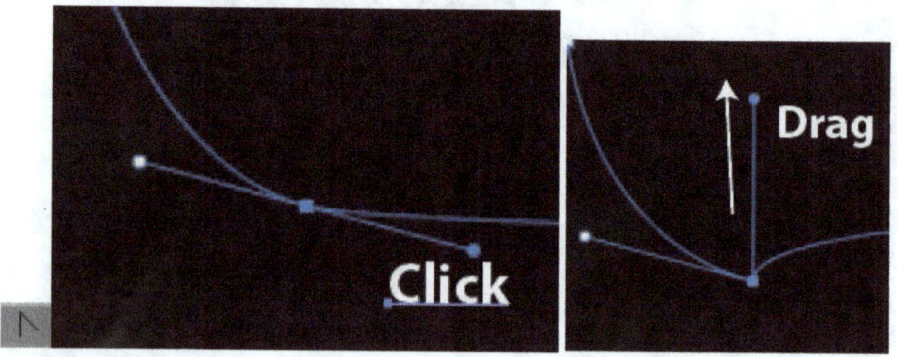

Figure 2-43. *Use the Convert Point Tool to edit points adjusting separate handles*

While working, if your path becomes deselected before you create your vector mask, you can reselect it with the Path Selection Tool or use the Direct Selection Tool to select and move individual anchor points and adjust their handles to correct a curve. You can also select parts of the path with the Direct Selection Tool and drag on it as well. Refer to Figure 2-44.

CHAPTER 2 ADJUSTMENT LAYERS, BLENDING MODES WITH MASKS FOR PHOTO RESTORATION: PART 2

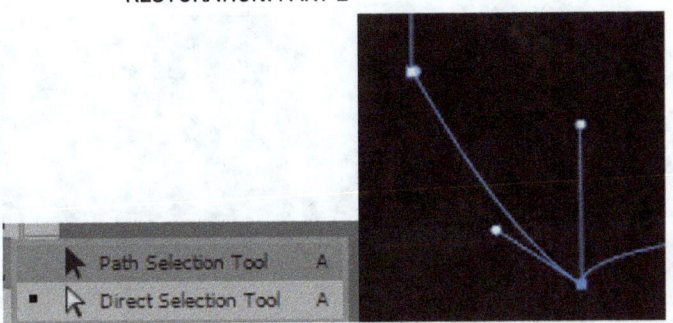

Figure 2-44. *Use the Path Selection Tool to move or select the whole path or Direct Selection Tool to edit an anchor point*

While your entire path is selected, you have two choices. First, you can use the Paths panel to load the path as a selection. This is good if you want to create a layer mask if you click the Add layer mask button right away. Refer to Figure 2-45.

CHAPTER 2　ADJUSTMENT LAYERS, BLENDING MODES WITH MASKS FOR PHOTO RESTORATION: PART 2

Figure 2-45. *Use the path to create a selection for a layer mask*

270

CHAPTER 2 ADJUSTMENT LAYERS, BLENDING MODES WITH MASKS FOR PHOTO RESTORATION: PART 2

Or second, while the path is selected, you can Ctrl/CMD + click the mask icon in the Layers panel to add a vector mask. Refer to Figures 2-46 and 2-47.

Figure 2-46. *Select the path in the Path panel to create a selection for a vector mask*

CHAPTER 2 ADJUSTMENT LAYERS, BLENDING MODES WITH MASKS FOR PHOTO RESTORATION: PART 2

Figure 2-47. *Use the path to create a selection for a vector mask and apply it to the layer*

CHAPTER 2   ADJUSTMENT LAYERS, BLENDING MODES WITH MASKS FOR PHOTO RESTORATION: PART 2

Once you apply your vector mask to your layer, you can continue to edit it with the Path Selection or Direct Selection Tool and related pen tools to apply additional refinement. Likewise, you can use the Properties panel's feathering setting. Refer back to Figures 2-27 and 2-28.

If you ever need to invert a vector mask, since you cannot do it directly with the Properties panel, I recommend loading the selection from the Paths panel as you would for a layer mask. From the Select menu choose Inverse (Shift + Ctrl/CMD + I). Then in the Paths panel, choose "Make work path from selection." Refer to Figure 2-48.

CHAPTER 2 ADJUSTMENT LAYERS, BLENDING MODES WITH MASKS FOR PHOTO RESTORATION: PART 2

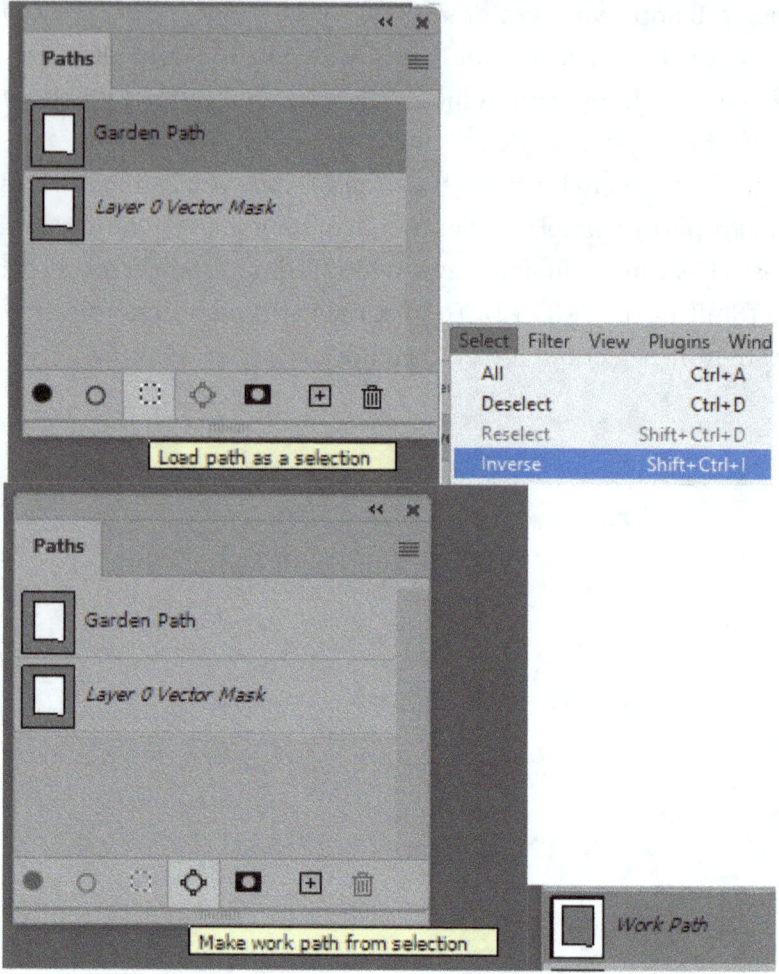

Figure 2-48. *Use the Paths panel and Select menu to assist in inverting a selection*

After you rename the path, you could then select a layer and Ctrl/CMD + click the Layers panel mask button, while a layer or adjustment layer is selected, to create an inverse vector path. Refer to Figure 2-49.

CHAPTER 2　ADJUSTMENT LAYERS, BLENDING MODES WITH MASKS FOR PHOTO RESTORATION: PART 2

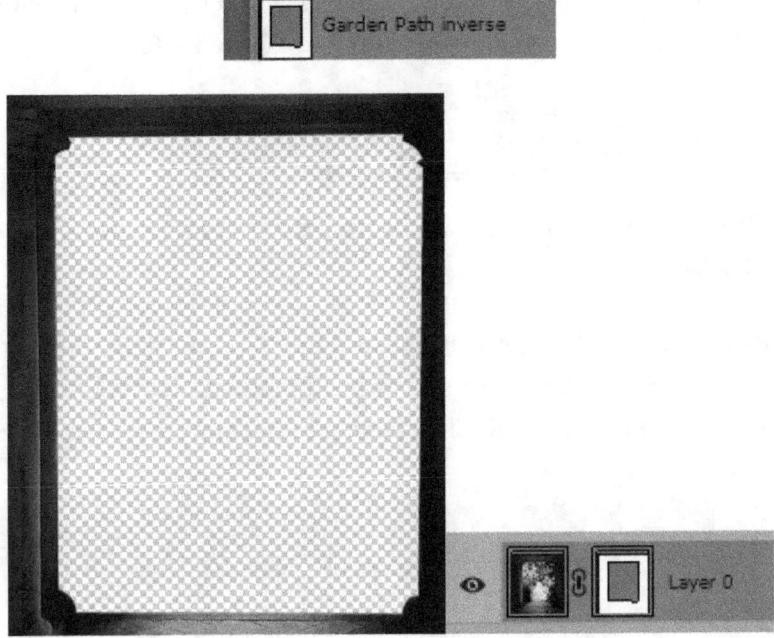

Figure 2-49. *Inverse vector paths can be used for framing an area*

This is a good option for creating a framing effect of another image that you could place behind this layer.

Refer to the following link if you need more details on how to use the Pen Tool and other advanced related pen tools (Freeform pen, Content-Aware Tracing and Curvature Pen) in the set for your own personal projects:

https://helpx.adobe.com/photoshop/using/drawing-pen-tools.html

Multiple Masks

Generally, when I add a mask for digital repair, I will usually just use a layer mask as they are easier to edit and blend with a brush or eraser if you are not yet comfortable with a pen. As was mentioned, you can add both layer

CHAPTER 2 ADJUSTMENT LAYERS, BLENDING MODES WITH MASKS FOR PHOTO
            RESTORATION: PART 2

masks and vector masks separately, which is what I recommend. However, both can be added to the same layer. Refer to Figure 2-50.

Figure 2-50. *Layers can have a combination of layer and vector masks*

If you add one of them by mistake and need to remove it, remember you can easily remove one or the other by dragging that mask to the trash icon in the Layers panel. Click Delete in the alert message. Refer to Figure 2-51.

CHAPTER 2 ADJUSTMENT LAYERS, BLENDING MODES WITH MASKS FOR PHOTO RESTORATION: PART 2

Figure 2-51. *Use the Layers panel to remove a layer or vector mask when you do not require it and use the alert message to delete without applying it*

The layer mask appears as black-and-white, while the vector mask appears gray and white. If you are having difficulty knowing which is a layer or vector, you can use your Layers panel and from the menu's panel options (Layers Panel Options) enable the Show layer mask badges setting. In this book I left this option unchecked/disabled so that you can see the mask clearly. Refer to Figure 2-52.

CHAPTER 2　ADJUSTMENT LAYERS, BLENDING MODES WITH MASKS FOR PHOTO RESTORATION: PART 2

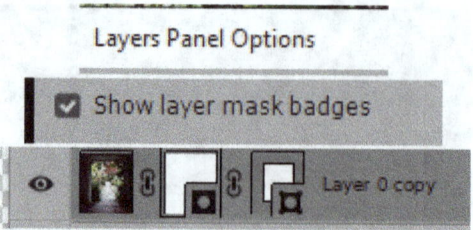

Figure 2-52. Add badges to your masks when you have difficulty identifying them

---

Note　Vector masks can be applied to fill layers, but they will turn the fill thumbnail into a shape layer. Shape layers and shape tools are not a topic of this book and will not be discussed, but they can be used to create vector masks.

Refer to this link should you need more details on shape creation: `https://helpx.adobe.com/photoshop/using/drawing-shapes.html`

For the rest of the book, we will continue to use layer masks and clipping masks.

File ➤ Save any open files you may have at this point.

Working in Combination: Layer Blending Modes and Adjustment Layers

Whether talking about normal layers or adjustment layers, we need to also consider blending modes, which can also be used to alter the overall color of the image or the masked area. While a normal layer or adjustment layer is selected, you can change its blending mode by selecting that option from the list in the Layers panel. Refer to Figure 2-53.

CHAPTER 2   ADJUSTMENT LAYERS, BLENDING MODES WITH MASKS FOR PHOTO RESTORATION: PART 2

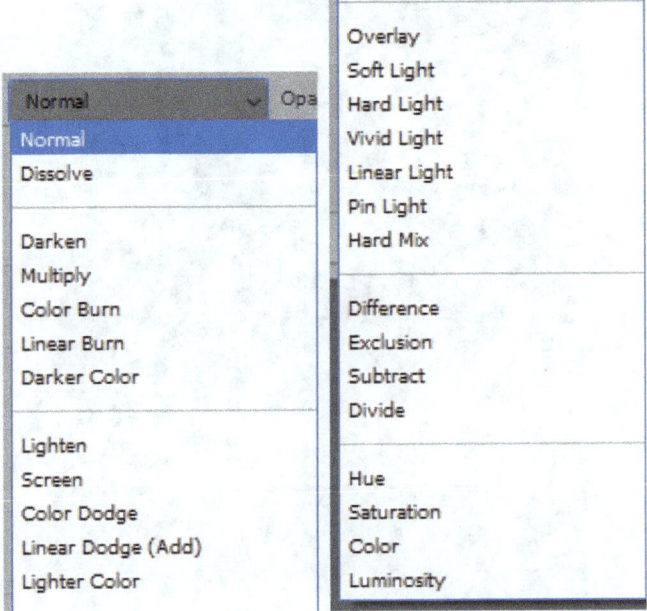

Figure 2-53. *Apply blending modes to a layer*

The blending mode (blend color) chosen will alter the colors of the underlying (base) layer in a variety of ways, creating a resultant color. Different color combinations create different blends. For example, a part of an ancient grinding stone wheel image (**blending_mode_examples.psd**) has been color corrected, and then I've applied a Hue/Saturation adjustment layer with the following settings in the Properties panel – Hue: 22, Saturation: 25, Lightness: 0, and then set to Colorize. Refer to Figure 2-54.

279

CHAPTER 2 ADJUSTMENT LAYERS, BLENDING MODES WITH MASKS FOR PHOTO RESTORATION: PART 2

Figure 2-54. *The image before adjustment and then I add an adjustment layer to an image with settings in the Properties panel*

280

CHAPTER 2 ADJUSTMENT LAYERS, BLENDING MODES WITH MASKS FOR PHOTO RESTORATION: PART 2

By default, this Hue/Saturation adjustment layer is set to Normal. Refer to Figure 2-55.

Figure 2-55. *The adjustment layer is applied with a blending mode of Normal*

CHAPTER 2 ADJUSTMENT LAYERS, BLENDING MODES WITH MASKS FOR PHOTO RESTORATION: PART 2

However, if I use different blending mode options, it will change: Dissolve, Darken, Multiply, Color Burn, Linear Burn, and Darker Color. Except for Dissolve these blends will darken the colors in the image. Refer to Figure 2-56.

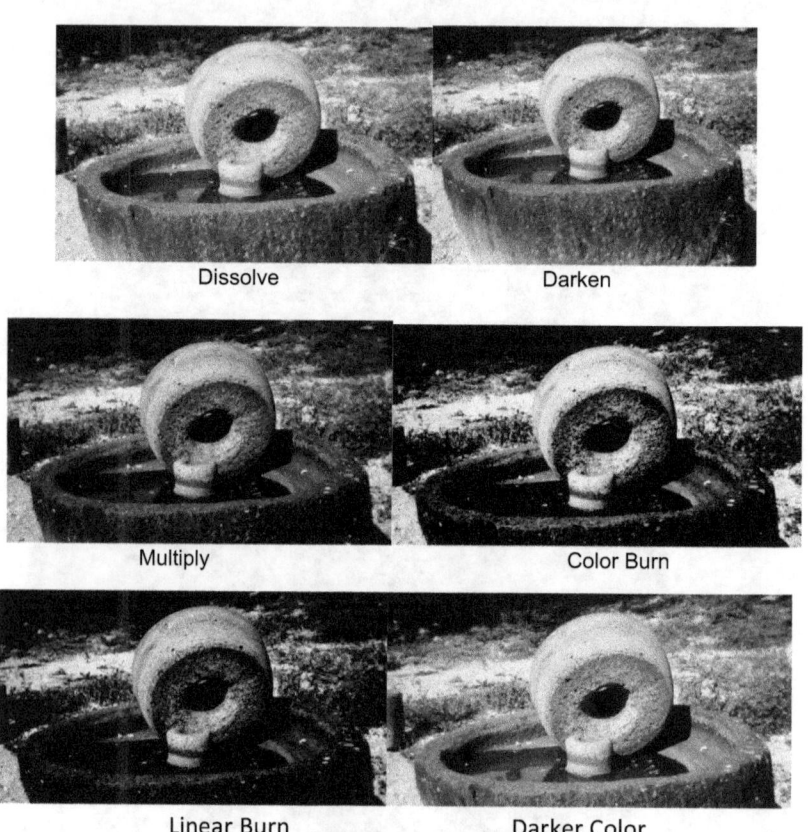

Figure 2-56. *Blending modes altering the color of the adjustment layer above the image: Dissolve, Darken, Multiply, Color Burn, Linear Burn, and Darker Color*

Lighten, Screen, Color Dodge, Linear Dodge (Add), and Lighter Color: These blends will lighten the colors in the image. Refer to Figure 2-57.

CHAPTER 2   ADJUSTMENT LAYERS, BLENDING MODES WITH MASKS FOR PHOTO RESTORATION: PART 2

Figure 2-57. Blending modes altering the color of the adjustment layer above the image: Lighten, Screen, Color Dodge, Linear Dodge (Add), and Lighter Color

Overlay, Soft Light, Hard Light, Vivid Light, Linear Light, Pin Light, Hard Mix, Difference, Exclusion, Subtract, and Divide: Some of these blends will darken some of the colors in the image and others lighten, and at least four cause a type of colorful inverted effect that is hard to view. Refer to Figures 2-58 and 2-59.

CHAPTER 2   ADJUSTMENT LAYERS, BLENDING MODES WITH MASKS FOR PHOTO RESTORATION: PART 2

Figure 2-58. *Blending modes altering the color of the adjustment layer above the image: Overlay, Soft Light, Hard Light, Vivid Light, Linear Light, Pin Light, and Hard Mix*

CHAPTER 2   ADJUSTMENT LAYERS, BLENDING MODES WITH MASKS FOR PHOTO RESTORATION: PART 2

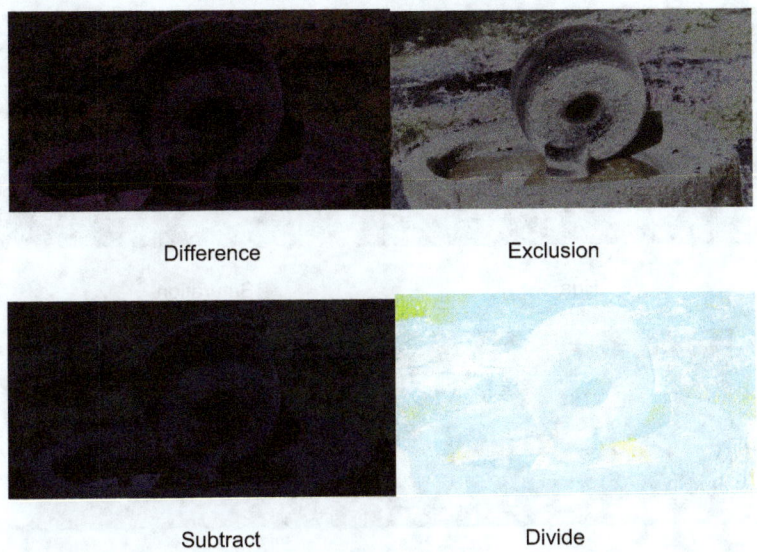

Figure 2-59. *Blending modes altering the color of the adjustment layer above the image: Difference, Exclusion, Subtract, and Divide*

Hue, Saturation, Color, and Luminosity: These blends will alter the colors, hue, saturation, or luminosity in the image. Refer to Figure 2-60.

CHAPTER 2   ADJUSTMENT LAYERS, BLENDING MODES WITH MASKS FOR PHOTO RESTORATION: PART 2

Figure 2-60. *Blending modes altering the color of the adjustment layer above the image: Hue, Saturation, Color, and Luminosity*

When we use these blending modes in combination with fill and adjustment layers, you can see how a variety of color-improving or artistic blends can take place over the background image. Some of these color shifts would be difficult to make quickly by just adjusting the sliders in Hue/Saturation alone. Scrolling though the blending mode options while a layer is selected using the up and down arrow keys can often be best to find a specific blend. And as mentioned each image may require a different blend depending on the colors within the image. Try different blending modes now on one of your own images to compare the similarities and differences to the example presented here.

If you need to know more about a specific blend and its meaning with further examples, you can refer to the following link.

https://helpx.adobe.com/photoshop/using/blending-modes.html

By using blending modes and solid fill, you could do such things as enhance a human's or animal's eye color. See file **cat_eyes.psd**. Refer to Figure 2-61.

CHAPTER 2   ADJUSTMENT LAYERS, BLENDING MODES WITH MASKS FOR PHOTO RESTORATION: PART 2

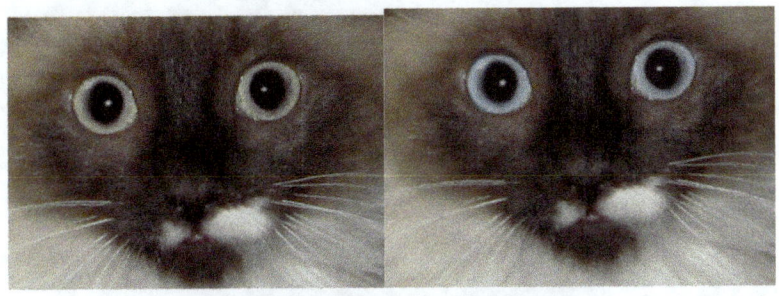

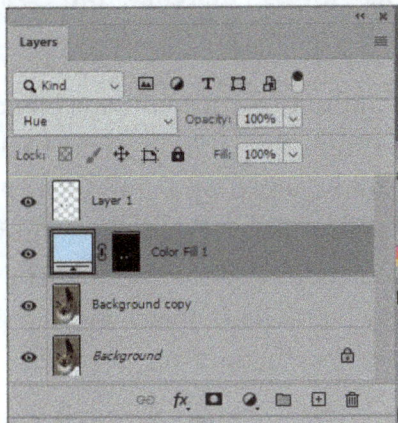

Figure 2-61. *Use blending modes to alter the color of the underlying image when applied to a fill layer*

In this case a blending mode of Hue was added to the Color Fill (R: 158, G: 218, B: 252) layer to enhance the cat's eyes, which under the house lighting were not turning up as blue as they should be.

Blending modes can also be applied to paintbrush mode effects in the Brush tool, Pencil tool, and some healing brushes, including the Clone Stamp tool, as you saw in Volume 1 in Chapters 3 and 4 in the Options bar panel. Refer to Figure 2-62.

CHAPTER 2   ADJUSTMENT LAYERS, BLENDING MODES WITH MASKS FOR PHOTO RESTORATION: PART 2

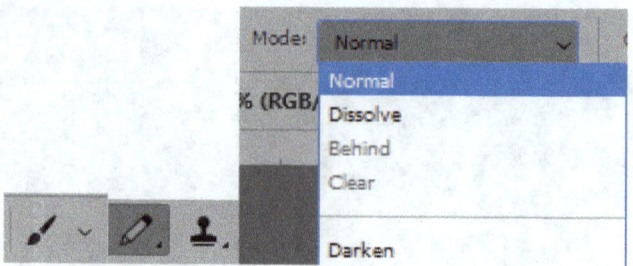

Figure 2-62. *The Brush tool, Pencil tool, and Clone Stamp tool can all have blending mode options for painting*

The brushes will often come with additional blending modes, like Behind and Clear, specifically for painting on the background image. Painting on a normal blank layer in a painting effect blend mode other than Normal will have little effect on those brush strokes until you switch to another painting effect mode or another color. The change is only apparent when there is a buildup of colorful overlapping pixels on the originally blank layer. Refer to Figure 2-63.

CHAPTER 2 ADJUSTMENT LAYERS, BLENDING MODES WITH MASKS FOR PHOTO RESTORATION: PART 2

Figure 2-63. *Painting with blending modes only affects areas with pixels on the current layer*

In no way does this affect the actual layer's blending mode, which can remain at Normal while painting.

However, using the brushes in this manner does not enhance the overall color correction, as I would wish, so this is why I generally leave my brush's painting mode at Normal and rely on a combination of adjustment layers and layer blending modes.

When you want to add the effect overall to several brush stokes that you applied on a blank layer for the purpose of colorizing an image, like what we were doing in Chapter 1 with the **castle_solid_fill_final.psd**, first paint in Normal mode on the new layer. Then select that layer and change the blending mode for that layer. For example, change to Multiply, as I did for the green tree on the left of the image, to complete my painting of some of the leaves in green. Refer to Figure 2-64.

CHAPTER 2   ADJUSTMENT LAYERS, BLENDING MODES WITH MASKS FOR PHOTO RESTORATION: PART 2

Figure 2-64. *When you want to paint on a layer and alter the color overall, then you need to add a blending mode to the layer*

This may be a better option for your work, and in some instances, you may prefer doing this rather than using multiple adjustment layers that may increase the file size. Blending modes like Darken, Multiply, Linear Burn, Darker Color, Hard Light, Linear Light, and Pin Light may all be good blends while retaining the color that you painted with but still showing some of the underlying details.

CHAPTER 2   ADJUSTMENT LAYERS, BLENDING MODES WITH MASKS FOR PHOTO RESTORATION: PART 2

In other situations, as you saw with the Adjustments presets from the Adjustments panel, you may want to keep multiple adjustment layers stored in a group folder. To that folder you may prefer to use a specific blending mode to affect all layers below, which are inside or outside of the folder. In this case a blend mode of Pass Through is used. Group folders can also have a layer and vector mask applied. See the file **forest_blend.psd**. Refer to Figure 2-65.

Figure 2-65. *Blending modes can be added to group folders to affect layers inside or outside of the group folder*

Keep in mind that layer order of the adjustment layers within the folder can affect the final color correction outcome.

Opacity, Fill, and Layer Styles

When working with normal, fill, and adjustment layers with blending modes, you can also adjust the opacity of each layer, and sometimes this can also improve the color correction, making an adjustment layer effect less intense or more transparent and closer to the pre–color corrected file. Refer to file **forest_blend_options.psd**. Refer to Figure 2-66.

292

CHAPTER 2 ADJUSTMENT LAYERS, BLENDING MODES WITH MASKS FOR PHOTO RESTORATION: PART 2

Figure 2-66. *Alter the opacity of an adjustment layer to make the effect less intense*

However, you may notice another type of opacity setting in the Layers panel just below called Fill. Fill (0–100%) and Opacity seem to work the same way, causing the pixels to disappear on the layer if we reduce either of them. So which is correct to use? Refer to Figure 2-67.

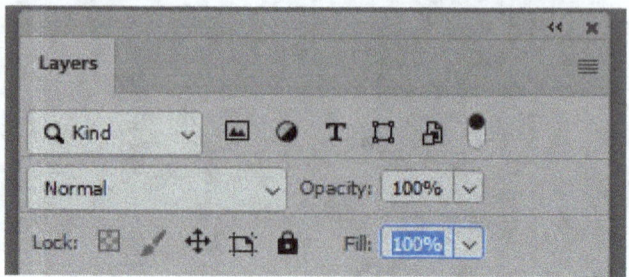

Figure 2-67. *The Layers panel has two kinds of transparency options for layer: Opacity and Fill*

Fill is often used in conjunction with another option in the Layers panel called layer styles. These are applied directly to the normal layer (like Layer 0 or a copy of the layer) itself. The layer style effect is more visible when the layer mask has been altered either with the Eraser tool or a selection like the Rectangular Marquee Tool. Here we can see an example of an altered mask over a white fill layer. Two layer style effects have been applied: one is Drop Shadow and the other is Stroke to make the image stand out. Refer to Figure 2-68.

CHAPTER 2　ADJUSTMENT LAYERS, BLENDING MODES WITH MASKS FOR PHOTO RESTORATION: PART 2

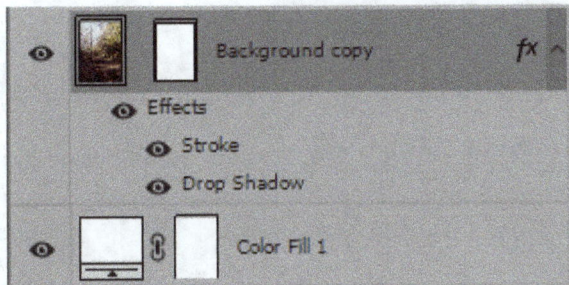

Figure 2-68. *Layer style options including Blending Options can be found in the Layers panel layer style list*

In this example both the opacity and fill are at 100%. However, first, I will reduce the opacity to 27%, return to 100%, and then set the fill to 27% to show you the difference between them. Refer to Figure 2-69.

295

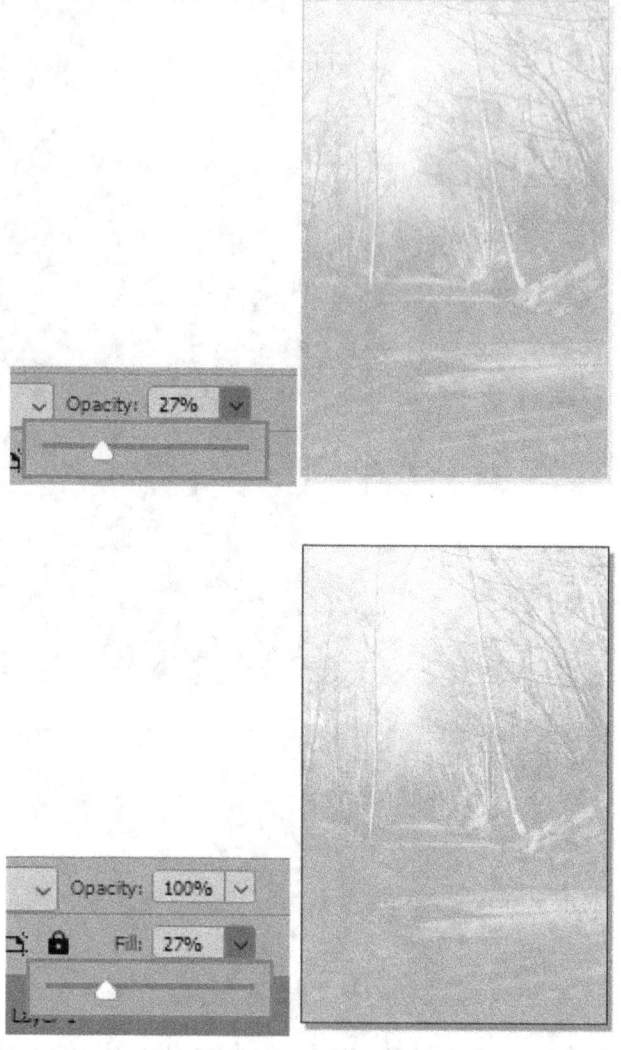

Figure 2-69. *Use Opacity or Fill to affect the layer and its layer style*

It should be noted that Opacity will affect everything on the layer including the layer style. However, Fill will affect only the pixels, but the layer style effect will remain unaffected.

CHAPTER 2 ADJUSTMENT LAYERS, BLENDING MODES WITH MASKS FOR PHOTO RESTORATION: PART 2

Layer Style Blending Options

When you want to affect your blend options in advanced ways on a normal or even a fill or adjustment layer, you would, from the layer style list, choose Blending Options. This will open the Layer Style dialog box to that tab. Make sure to keep Preview selected so you can observe updates on the duplicate image of **forest_blend_options.psd**. Refer to Figure 2-70.

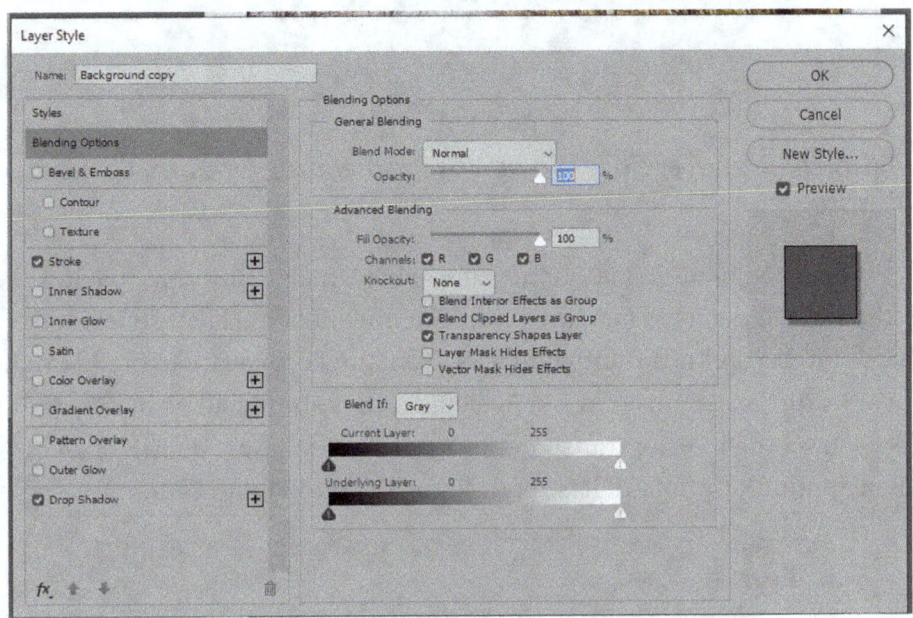

Figure 2-70. *Layer Style dialog box for Blending Options*

I will now just give a quick review of the Blending Options tab and what it includes.

CHAPTER 2 ADJUSTMENT LAYERS, BLENDING MODES WITH MASKS FOR PHOTO
RESTORATION: PART 2

Blending Options in the Layer Style Dialog Box

General blending with the blend mode and opacity is what you have been doing in this chapter and Chapter 1. If you have at some point altered the blend mode or opacity for a layer in the Layers panel, it will show that same change here. Refer to Figure 2-71.

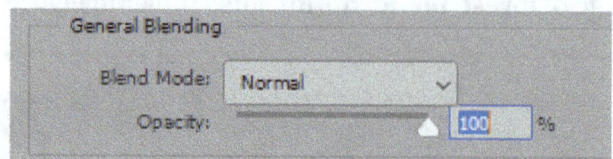

Figure 2-71. *Layer Style dialog box for Blending Options, General Blending*

Advanced blending is where you use Fill Opacity (interior opacity) rather than Opacity to fade the pixels but not affect the layer style. From here you can also affect individual RGB channels you want to blend on the layer by turning them off or on. By default, they should all be on. Knockout lets you set the interior transparency to None, Shallow (Group), or Deep (Background); by default it is set to None. Refer to Figure 2-72.

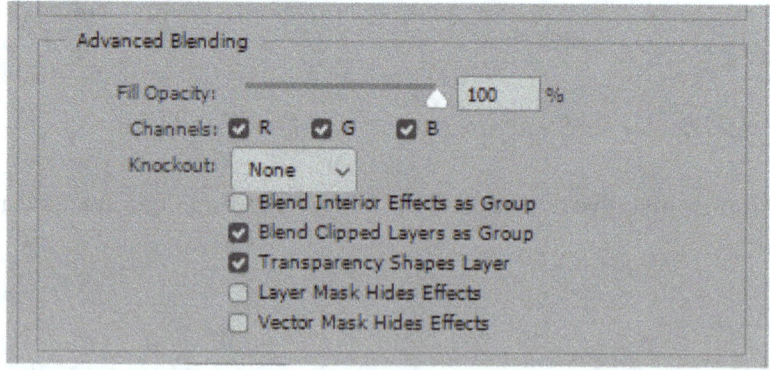

Figure 2-72. *Layer Style dialog box for Blending Options, Advanced Blending*

CHAPTER 2   ADJUSTMENT LAYERS, BLENDING MODES WITH MASKS FOR PHOTO RESTORATION: PART 2

Other options include

- Blend Interior Effects as Group (disabled): If enabled, applies the blending mode of the layer to the layer effects that modify opaque pixels, such as Inner Glow, Satin, Color Overlay, and Gradient Overlay, before affecting the rest of the document. When enabled, this is more apparent when you reduce the fill opacity and have one of the mentioned styles applied.

- Blend Clipped Layers as Group (enabled): Applies the blending mode of the base layer to all layers within the clipping mask group. Deselecting this option, which is enabled by default, then maintains the original blending mode and appearance of each layer in the clipping group.

- Transparency Shapes Layer (enabled): Uses the layer transparency to determine the shape of the interior and the effects. This will restrict layer effects and knockouts to opaque areas of the layer.

- Layer Mask Hides Effects (disabled): If enabled this would use the layer mask to hide the effects rather than shaping the layer and effects. Refer to Figure 2-72.

- Vector Mask Hides Effects (disabled): If enabled this would use the vector mask to hide the effects rather than shaping the layer and effects.

You can then set Blend If to Gray, Red, Green, or Blue. By default, it is set to Gray so that you can specify a blending range for all channels. Use Red, Green, or Blue if you want to blend for that specific channel. Refer to Figure 2-73.

CHAPTER 2   ADJUSTMENT LAYERS, BLENDING MODES WITH MASKS FOR PHOTO
RESTORATION: PART 2

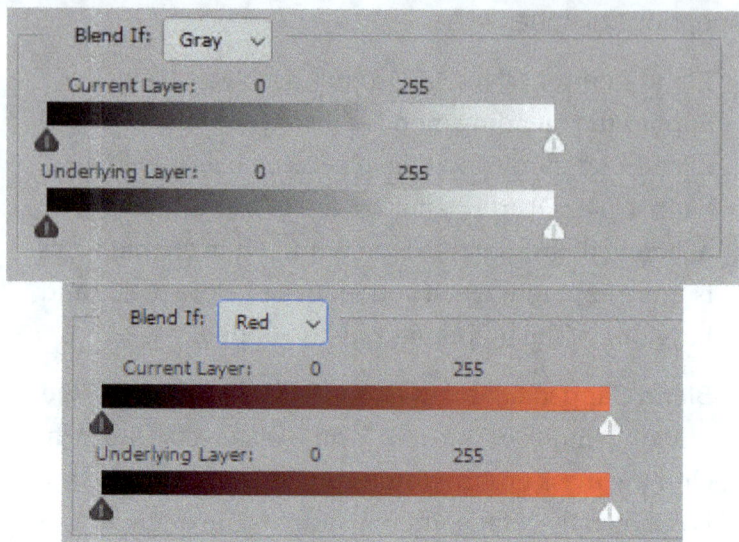

Figure 2-73. *Layer Style Dialog box for Blending Options for Blend If: Gray and Red*

Use the black and white sliders that range from 0 to 255, to either affect the brightness range of the blended pixels for either the current or underlying layer. Moving the sliders can cause certain details on the layer to disappear and show the underlying layer. Refer to Figure 2-74.

CHAPTER 2   ADJUSTMENT LAYERS, BLENDING MODES WITH MASKS FOR PHOTO RESTORATION: PART 2

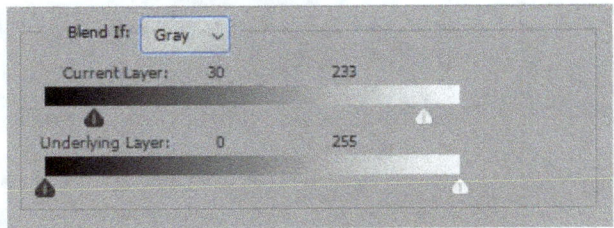

Figure 2-74. *Layer Style dialog box for Blending Options for Blend If: Gray and the result of altering current layer sliders*

Hold down the Alt/Option key on one or both sliders separately to split it and increase the blend. The farther apart the blend when split, the smoother the transition will appear. This creates almost a winter day effect in the scene where the sun is melting the snow. Refer to Figure 2-75.

301

CHAPTER 2   ADJUSTMENT LAYERS, BLENDING MODES WITH MASKS FOR PHOTO RESTORATION: PART 2

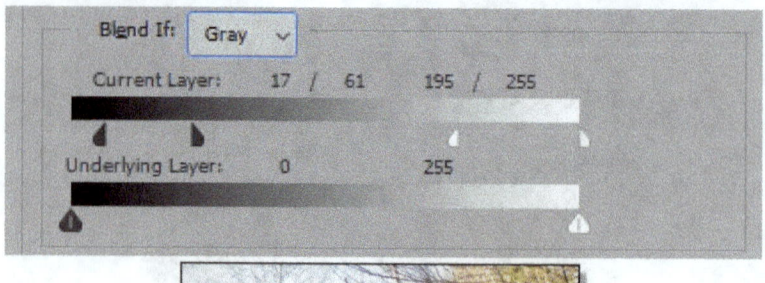

Figure 2-75. *Layer Style dialog box for Blending Options for Blend If: Gray and the result of altering current layer sliders and splitting them*

You can then, on the left of the Blending Options tab, choose various effects such as Bevel & Emboss with Contour and Texture, Stroke, Inner Shadow, Inner Glow, Satin, Color Overlay, Gradient Overlay, Pattern Overlay, Outer Glow, and Drop Shadow. Selecting an effect allows you to review it, edit it, and click OK to add it to your effects applied to a layer. Refer to Figure 2-76.

CHAPTER 2 ADJUSTMENT LAYERS, BLENDING MODES WITH MASKS FOR PHOTO RESTORATION: PART 2

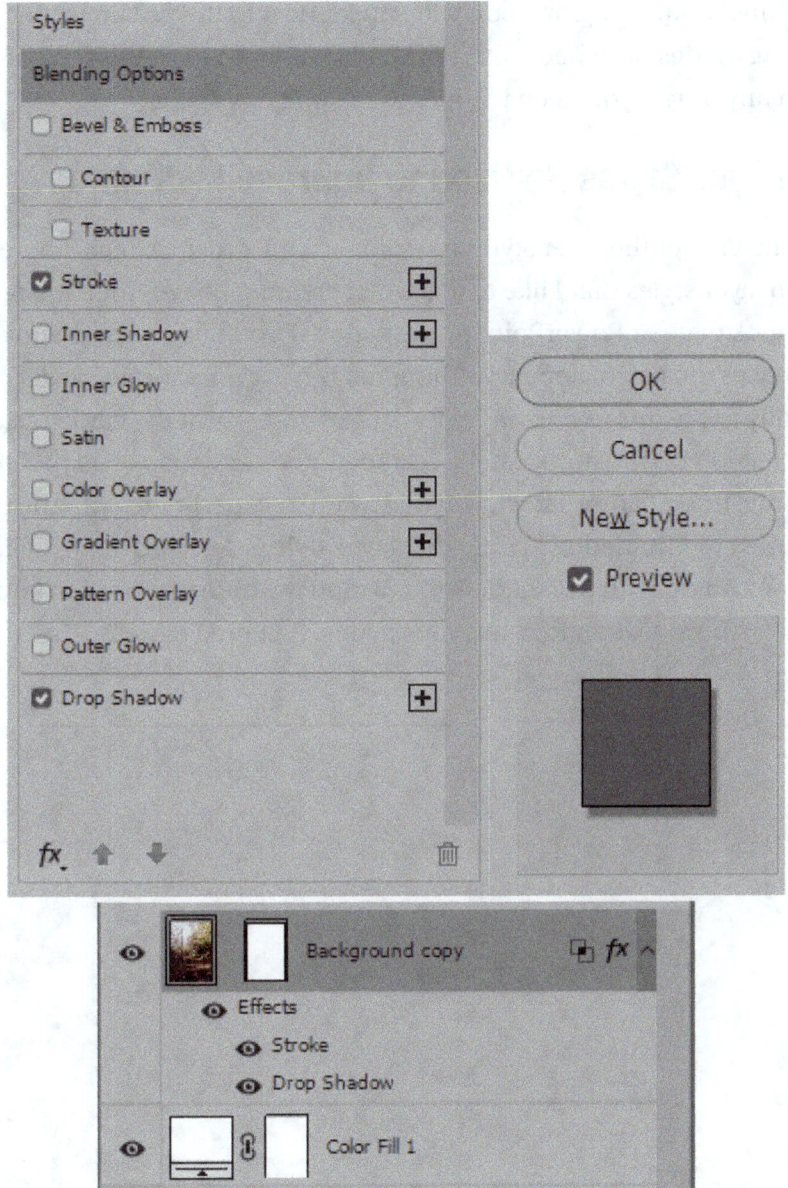

Figure 2-76. *Layer Style dialog box displaying various effects applied while on the Blending Options tab and their appearance in the Layers panel*

CHAPTER 2 ADJUSTMENT LAYERS, BLENDING MODES WITH MASKS FOR PHOTO RESTORATION: PART 2

A small double-square icon will appear next to the *fx* icon when blending modes have been altered. You can double-click this icon or the *fx* icon at any time if you need to enter the dialog box again.

Can Layer Styles Be Used to Improve My Photos?

While I consider the layer styles more for adding artistic effects, there are two layer styles that I like to use when creating images for a digital scrapbook page or PowerPoint presentation: Drop Shadow and Stroke. This makes the photo appear as though it is lying on a surface. I will generally apply this to the masked image as you saw in the earlier example. The selection on the mask can be rectangular or any shape you prefer.

For a Drop Shadow effect, you may want to experiment with the placement of the shadow. While that layer style is selected in the dialog box, you can drag on the shadow to position it where you want to and then use the settings to alter it to suit your needs. Refer to Figure 2-77.

CHAPTER 2 ADJUSTMENT LAYERS, BLENDING MODES WITH MASKS FOR PHOTO RESTORATION: PART 2

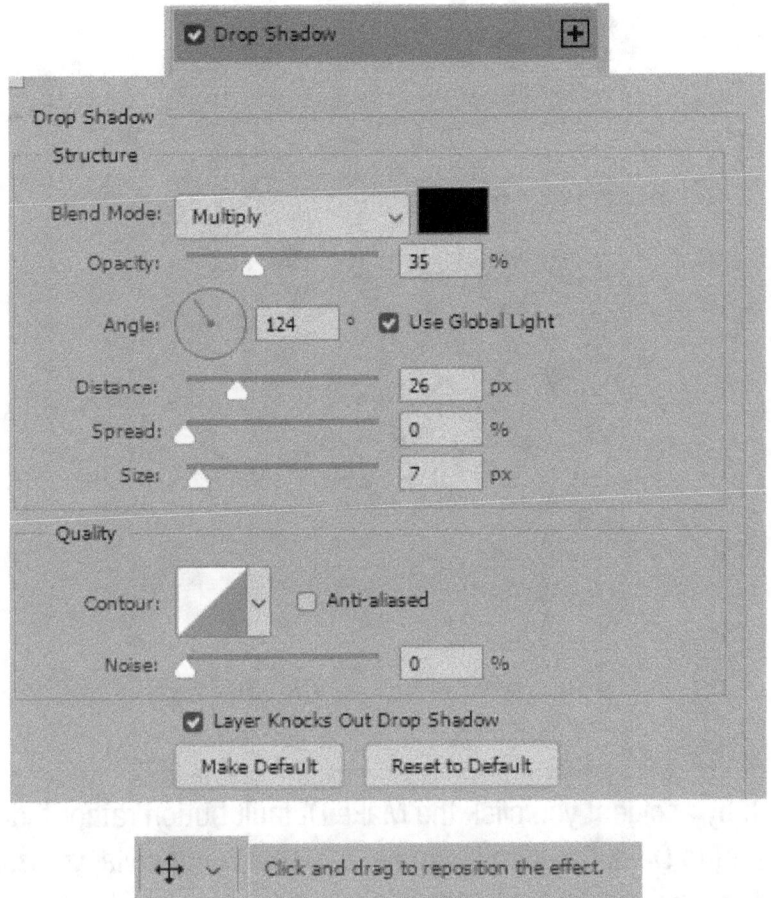

Figure 2-77. Layer Style dialog box for the Drop Shadow style and Move tool to adjust the shadow on the canvas

Settings that I like to alter under Structure are Opacity, Angle, Distance, Spread, and Size. Generally, I will not alter Blend Mode or the Quality settings for contour and noise.

For Stroke, you may want to use a thin or thick stroke and alter Structure's Size, Position, Blend Mode, or Opacity as well as Fill Type's color settings. This is useful if the image has white in some areas near the edge so that it appears rectangular and uniform. Refer to Figure 2-78.

CHAPTER 2   ADJUSTMENT LAYERS, BLENDING MODES WITH MASKS FOR PHOTO RESTORATION: PART 2

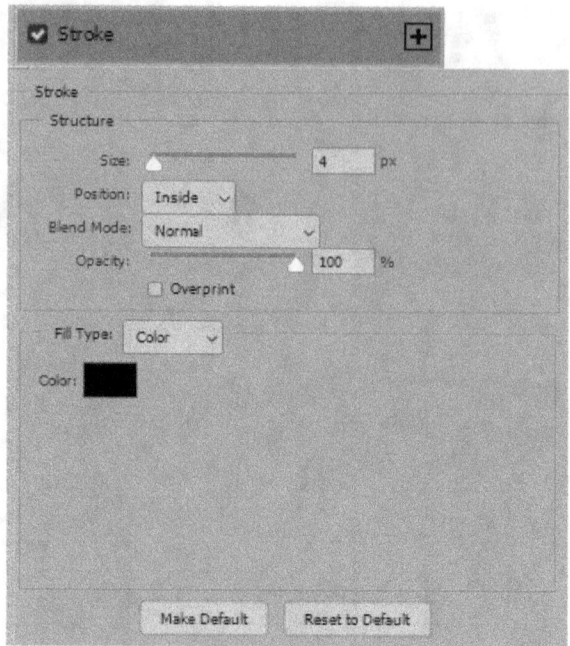

Figure 2-78. Layer Style dialog box for the Stroke style

Tip If by accident you click the Make Default button rather than the Reset to Default button if you need to reset your style, you can reset to the factory default only by, for example, on Windows, going to Edit ➤ Preferences ➤ General and choosing the button Reset Preferences on Quit. But be aware that this may alter some other saved preferences within Photoshop, so you may want to back up any of those settings first. Review this link first if this is something you need to do:

https://helpx.adobe.com/photoshop/using/preferences.html

CHAPTER 2   ADJUSTMENT LAYERS, BLENDING MODES WITH MASKS FOR PHOTO RESTORATION: PART 2

Otherwise, you may just want to create some defaults of your own and make them the new default settings. Whatever settings you choose will be confirmed for that layer when you click OK to exit.

While I will not be going into detail on all layer style options, you can refer to the following links for more details:

https://helpx.adobe.com/photoshop/using/layer-opacity-blending.html

https://helpx.adobe.com/photoshop/using/layer-effects-styles.html

Additional created layer styles are stored in the Window ➤ Styles library. Refer to Figure 2-79.

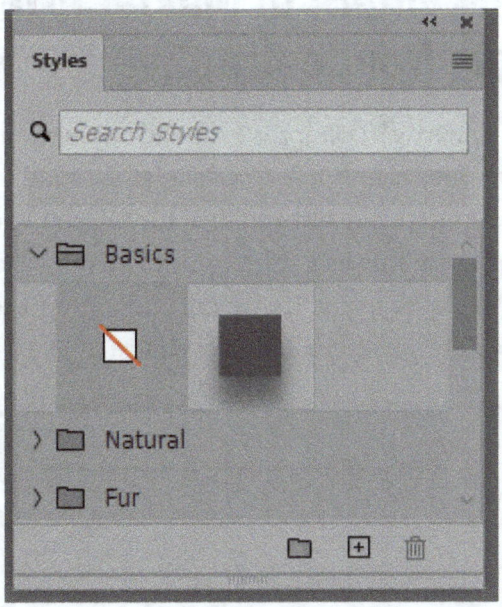

Figure 2-79. *Styles panel for storing and locating styles*

CHAPTER 2　ADJUSTMENT LAYERS, BLENDING MODES WITH MASKS FOR PHOTO RESTORATION: PART 2

Note As mentioned, it is possible to apply a layer style to a fill or adjustment layer. However, for digital photo repair, I do not recommend this as it will not improve the look of the image and some settings may not be obvious unless you paint on the layer mask. I only recommend experimenting with the blending options for adjustment layers.

File ➤ Save any open files at this point.

Using Smart Filters to Make Certain Color Adjustments Nondestructive

Unfortunately, as you saw in Chapter 1, not all adjustment options in the Image ➤ Adjustments menu list are available for adjustment layers. However, there is another way around this, for a certain adjustment command. I will present this as a third option, turning a layer or layers into a single smart object layer using the Layers panel menu, as seen in Volume 1 and as we will review now here. Refer to Figure 2-80.

CHAPTER 2 ADJUSTMENT LAYERS, BLENDING MODES WITH MASKS FOR PHOTO RESTORATION: PART 2

Figure 2-80. *The sunset image can benefit from an adjustment of Shadows/Highlights*

In this example I used my file, from Chapter 1, that I applied Selective Color to. I Shift + clicked these layers and dragged them onto the Create a new layer button to create a copy and, while they were selected from the Layers menu, chose "Convert to Smart Object." Refer to file **sunset_selective_highlight_shadow.psd.** Refer to Figure 2-81.

CHAPTER 2   ADJUSTMENT LAYERS, BLENDING MODES WITH MASKS FOR PHOTO RESTORATION: PART 2

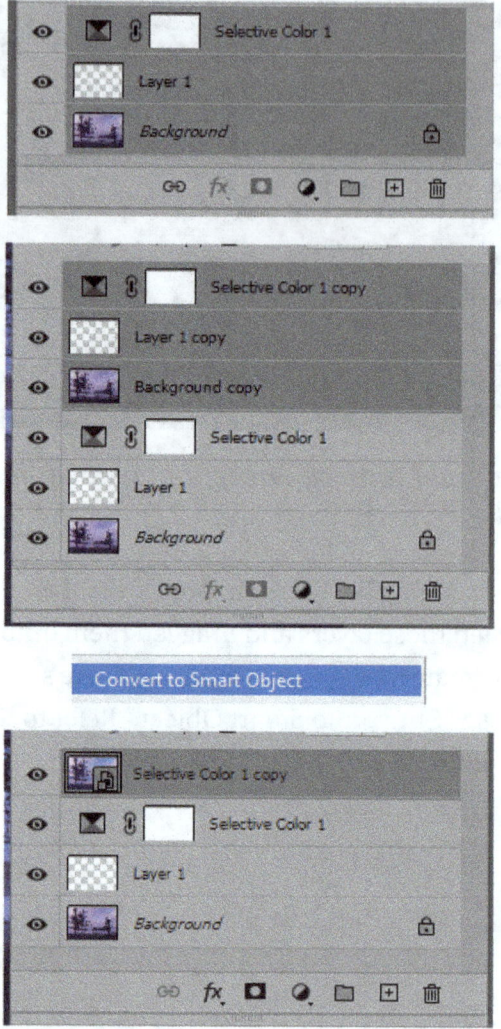

Figure 2-81. Duplicate selected layers and use the Layers panel menu to convert to a smart object

This will allow you to access smart filters, which use the same options found in the Image ➤ Adjustments menu in a nondestructive way, this time with a smart filter mask. Refer to Figure 2-82.

CHAPTER 2   ADJUSTMENT LAYERS, BLENDING MODES WITH MASKS FOR PHOTO RESTORATION: PART 2

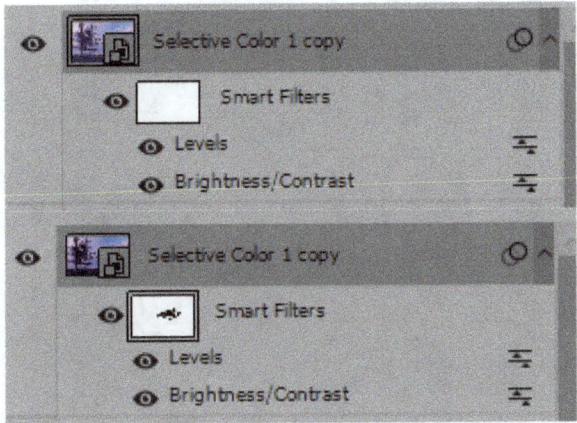

Figure 2-82. *Smart object layers can have multiple adjustments applied to a single smart filter mask*

This allows you to have multiple adjustments that are applied to the same mask rather than having to duplicate the mask each time. You don't have to update the layer mask on each adjustment layer.

This time, rather than using the Properties panel, you will double-click the adjustment word such as Levels in the Layers panel if you need to access the dialog box, to enter the new values. Refer to Figure 2-83.

CHAPTER 2 ADJUSTMENT LAYERS, BLENDING MODES WITH MASKS FOR PHOTO RESTORATION: PART 2

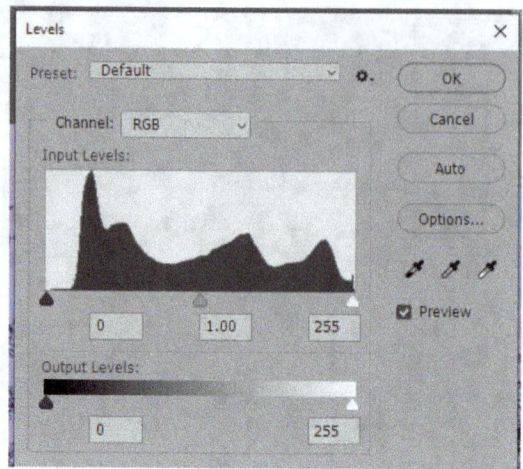

Figure 2-83. *The corresponding adjustment dialog box will open when you double click it in the smart object layer adjustment*

You can, however, still use adjustment layers above a smart object layer if you need every layer mask to be slightly different. Refer to Figure 2-84.

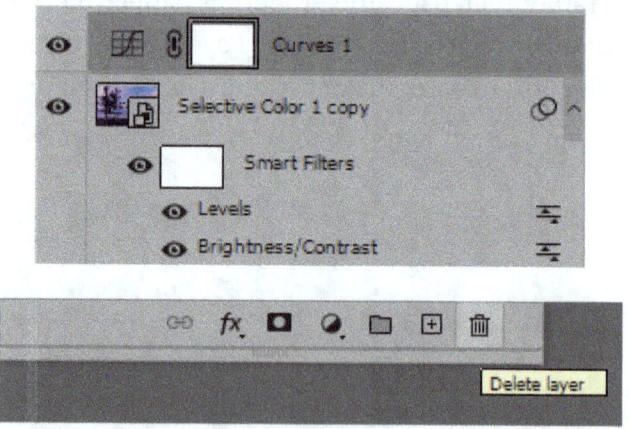

Figure 2-84. *Add additional adjustments above the smart object layer or drag an adjustment to the trash can icon to remove it*

If you do not want any of these adjustments, you can drag them to the trash can icon to remove them.

CHAPTER 2   ADJUSTMENT LAYERS, BLENDING MODES WITH MASKS FOR PHOTO RESTORATION: PART 2

Shadows/Highlights

The other reason that I present this option is that one of the commands, Shadows/Highlights, in the Adjustments menu is not available as a nondestructive adjustment layer. Using this smart object layer, you now have editing access and can adjust any time when you double-click the name. Refer to Figure 2-85.

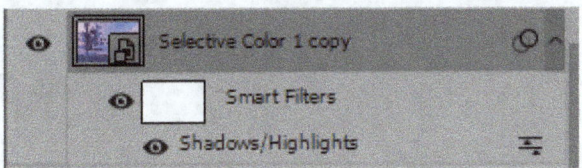

Figure 2-85. *Apply the adjustment of Shadows/Highlights to the smart object layer*

Shadows/Highlights is a good command for correcting photos with silhouetted images due to strong backlight or being underexposed. It can also be used for correcting scenes with items that have been slightly washed out or overexposed. This could be because they were too close to the camera's flash or it was a very bright day. Images that are well lit but still have shadows can also benefit. This command does not do an overall lightening or darkening but rather focuses on the values of surrounding pixels in both the shadows or highlights. As you will see in the dialog box, shadows and highlights are controlled separately, thus providing separate correction, which in some situation is better than just using Levels or Curves. The default settings are meant to correct backlighting issues. Refer to Figure 2-86.

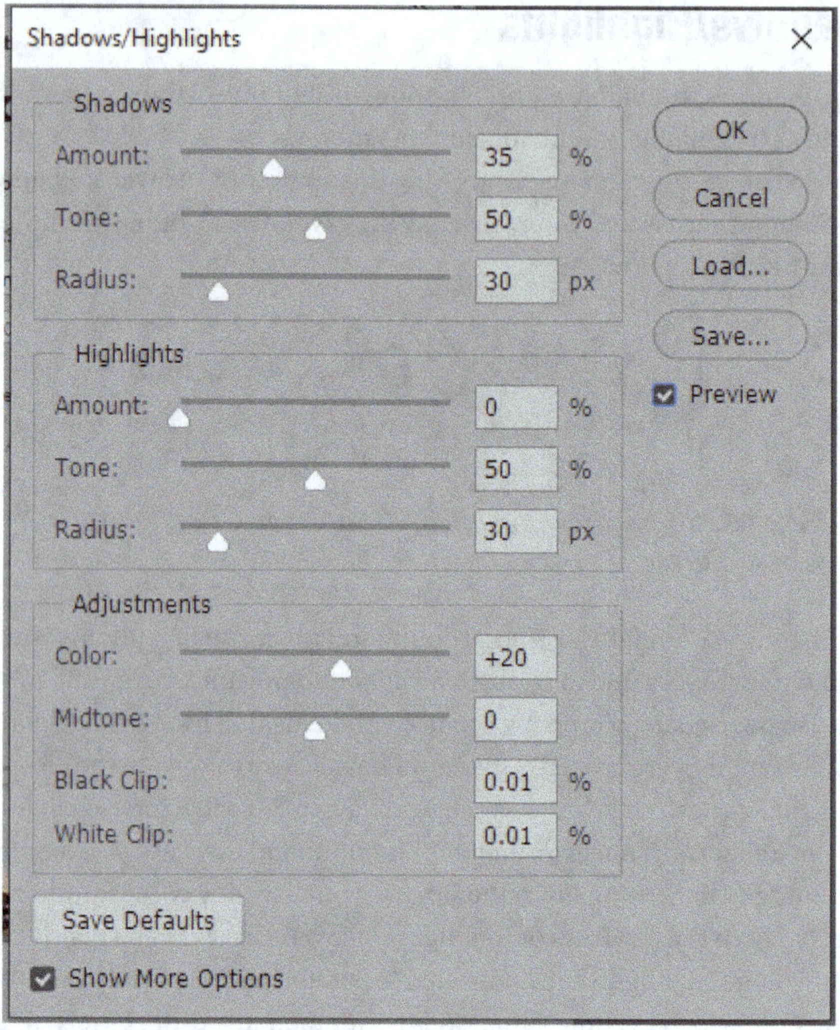

CHAPTER 2 ADJUSTMENT LAYERS, BLENDING MODES WITH MASKS FOR PHOTO RESTORATION: PART 2

Figure 2-86. *Shadows/Highlights dialog box*

The settings in the dialog box are described in the following.

Shadows

Amount (0–100%): Sets the amount of lighting correction. Larger values may provide lightening shadows. In my case I did not want to set beyond 35% as the shadows then became too light and contrast became lost.

Tone (0–100%): Controls the tonal width or range of tones. 0% is considered narrow, restricting you to darker shadow regions, while increasing up to 100% is broad, increasing the range into the midtones, which will become partially affected but not the highlights. By default, it is set to 50%.

Adobe recommends that you experiment with settings in the 0–25% range in both Amount and Tone if the image is otherwise exposed correctly.

Radius (0–2500 px): Enter a radius value to set scale size for corrections or area of localized pixels around what is considered the shadow area. Moving the slider to the left decreases and to the right increases. I left it at a setting of 30 px. Refer to Figure 2-87.

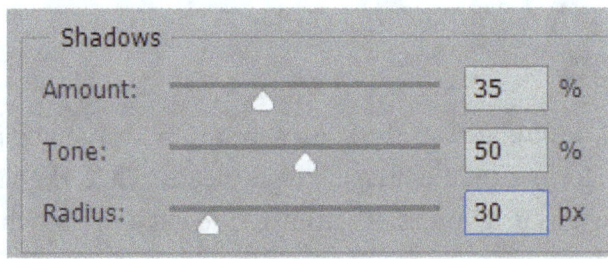

Figure 2-87. Shadows/Highlights dialog box, Shadows sliders

Highlights

Amount (0–100%): Sets the amount of lighting correction. Larger values may provide darkening of highlights, which will become partially affected, but not the shadows. I left the setting at 0% as I did not want to darken the current highlights.

Tone (0–100%): Controls the tonal width or range of tones. 0% is considered narrow, restricting you to lighter highlight regions, while increasing up to 100% is broad, increasing the range into the midtones. By default, it is set to 50%.

Radius (0–2500 px): Enter a radius value to set scale size for corrections or area of localized pixels around what is considered the highlight area. Moving the slider to the left decreases and to the right increases. I left it at a setting of 30 px. Refer to Figure 2-88.

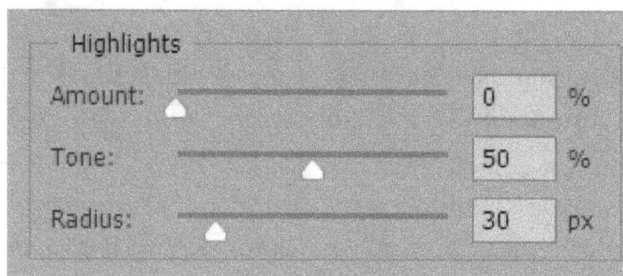

Figure 2-88. Shadows/Highlights dialog box, Highlights sliders

Adjustments

Color (−100, 0, +100): Adjusts the color saturation in changed portions of the image. However, if the image is a grayscale image, then this slider setting is known as Brightness. A setting to the left darkens while a setting to the right brightens the image. By default, it is set to +20.

Midtone (−100, 0, +100): Adjusts the midtone contrast. Moving the slider left will reduce and right will increase contrast. Increasing midtone contrast will create greater contrast in the midtones, while darkening the shadows and lightening the highlights. By default, it is set to 0.

Black Clip and White Clip (0–50%): Enter the values for fraction of whites and blacks to be clipped to the new extreme shadow (black) or highlight (white) colors. Higher values will produce an image with greater contrast. Do not increase clipping values too high, as mentioned when discussing Levels in Chapter 1, as this can reduce detail in the shadows or highlights. Once the intensity values are clipped and rendered, they are considered pure black or pure white. The default for each is 0.01%. Refer to Figure 2-89.

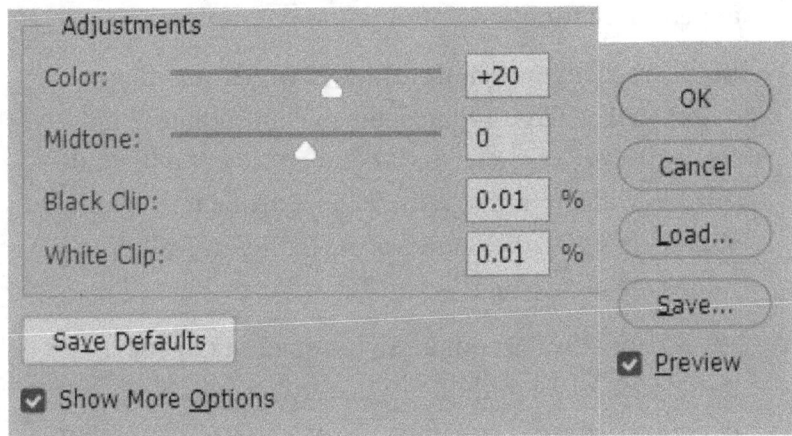

Figure 2-89. *Shadows/Highlights dialog box, Adjustments sliders and Load, Save, and Preview options*

There are also several check boxes and buttons:

Save Defaults: When you want to save the current settings as the new default. Press the Shift key on this button if you need to reset to the factory default.

Check Show More Options if you are not seeing all the available settings.

Additional buttons on the right let you load and save Shadows/Highlights presets as (.SHH) files. Make sure that the Preview check box is enabled so you can see the preview.

Click OK to commit or Cancel if you need to exit without making changes. Hold down the Alt/Option key if you need to change the Cancel button to a Reset button as you work. Refer to Figure 2-89.

CHAPTER 2 ADJUSTMENT LAYERS, BLENDING MODES WITH MASKS FOR PHOTO RESTORATION: PART 2

As you experiment in the dialog box, be aware of the following:

- As you adjust the amounts and various sliders for shadows and highlights, avoid crossing over the setting and suddenly making the shadows too dark so they appear unnatural.

- Be aware that your tonal width will vary from image to image. Too large a tone value may introduce halos around dark or light edges. Keeping at lower or default settings will attempt to reduce these artifacts. Halos can also occur when the Shadows or Highlights Amount values are set too high.

- Try moving the tonal slider in the shadows to affect the shadows and midtones when trying to darken or lighten these areas. You may need to go back and adjust the Amount sliders in both areas.

- The exact setting for Radius can also vary in each image. A large radius may brighten or darken the whole image when what you really want to affect is only the subject of interest. Adjust the Radius settings in the shadows and highlights to obtain the best balance between subject contrast and differential brightening (or darkening) of the subject and then compare this to the appearance of background. However, be aware that too high an adjustment may reduce the contrast in some images.

Tip Use your Histogram panel with this tool if you need to observe changes.

CHAPTER 2   ADJUSTMENT LAYERS, BLENDING MODES WITH MASKS FOR PHOTO RESTORATION: PART 2

In the case of the following image, using Shadows/Highlights did greatly help brighten many of the shadow areas overall. However, the original print suffered with some graininess and noise because the image was shot in low–light level conditions. Refer to Figure 2-90.

Figure 2-90. *The result of adding the Shadows/Highlights adjustments*

Using filters on our smart object, we can minimize some of the noise as we will see in Chapter 3.

Remember that at any time you can double-click the adjustment name to enter the dialog box. Refer to Figure 2-91.

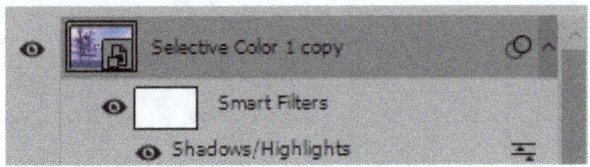

Figure 2-91. *Smart object layers can also be used with other filters*

Additional details about the Shadows/Highlights command can be found here:

https://helpx.adobe.com/photoshop/using/adjust-shadow-highlight-detail.html

Smart Filter Blending Options

The smart adjustment filter also has a separate setting on its right side that you can double-click to set its blending options Mode and Opacity (0–100%). You could use this if you needed to alter or reduce the adjustment slightly. Refer to the section "Working in Combination: Layer Blending Modes and Adjustment Layers" earlier in this chapter if you need to review. Refer to Figure 2-92.

CHAPTER 2   ADJUSTMENT LAYERS, BLENDING MODES WITH MASKS FOR PHOTO RESTORATION: PART 2

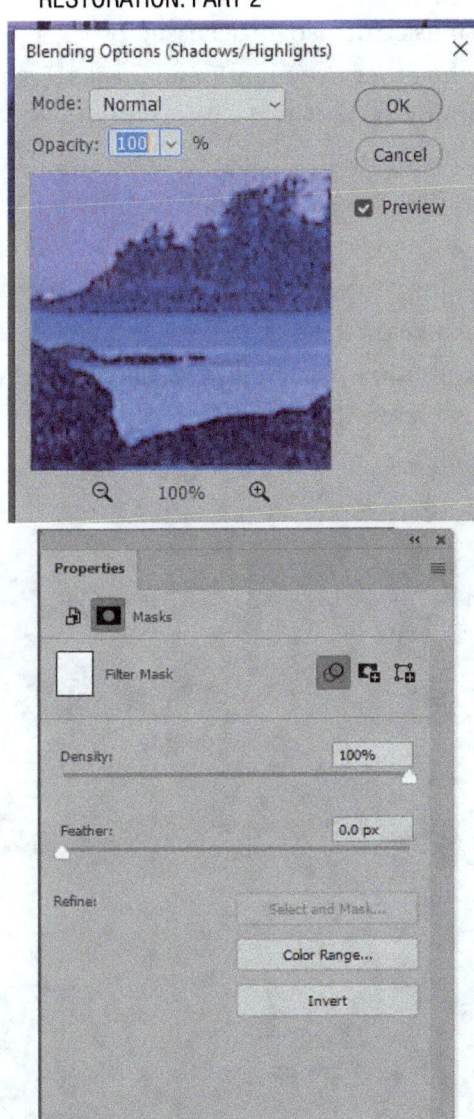

Figure 2-92. *Each adjustment in the smart object layer has its own blending options in the Properties panel*

CHAPTER 2 ADJUSTMENT LAYERS, BLENDING MODES WITH MASKS FOR PHOTO RESTORATION: PART 2

The smart filter mask can also be accessed by the Properties panel while working with the other two mentioned masks (layer and vector). It too has property options of Density, Feather, and Invert, which like the layer mask can be edited with the Brush or Eraser tool. Refer to Figure 2-92. We will look at smart filters again in Chapters 3, 4, and 5, which will include a filter that similarly deals with color, known as Camera Raw.

Shadows/Highlights can work for a variety of outdoor images, so I recommend you practice on a few of your own. Refer to files **sunset_selective_highlight_shadow_final.psd** and **glacier.psd** where I used the exact same settings. Refer to Figure 2-93.

Figure 2-93. *Outdoor images with extreme lighting are great for using Shadows/Highlights adjustments*

CHAPTER 2   ADJUSTMENT LAYERS, BLENDING MODES WITH MASKS FOR PHOTO RESTORATION: PART 2

Advanced Adjustment Settings

While we have looked at many of the image adjustment settings in the previous chapter as they relate to adjustment layers and smart objects in this chapter, I just want to mention a few additional color adjustments that, though more advanced and could be destructive, you should be aware of as they may assist you in completing your particular project. We will look at these options next and then finish the chapter with a photo project that uses some of the settings that were discussed in Chapter 1 and this chapter.

Auto Correction

In the Image menu itself are several quick auto steps that you can use if you feel confident that one could color correct your image. Refer to Figure 2-94.

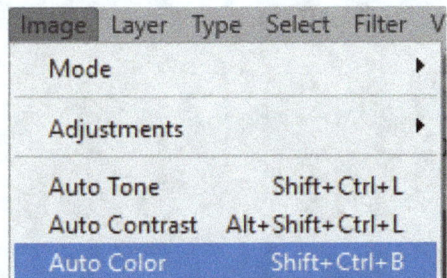

Figure 2-94. *Image menu Auto Color option*

They are Auto Tone, Auto Contrast, and Auto Color. You can apply these directly to a layer. However, keep in mind that unlike the adjustment layers mentioned in Chapter 1, there are no additional dialog boxes or instructions, so you cannot alter these settings once they are made. You can only use the History panel to undo your most recent steps.

CHAPTER 2 ADJUSTMENT LAYERS, BLENDING MODES WITH MASKS FOR PHOTO
           RESTORATION: PART 2

I also do not recommend using these settings with smart object layers. While they do work, if you do click one, in the adjustment filters the setting does not hold and automatically resets itself, as it is not a true filter effect.

For more accurate settings, it is better to just access more options by Alt/Option + clicking the Auto button in either your Levels or Curves dialog box. Refer to Figure 2-95.

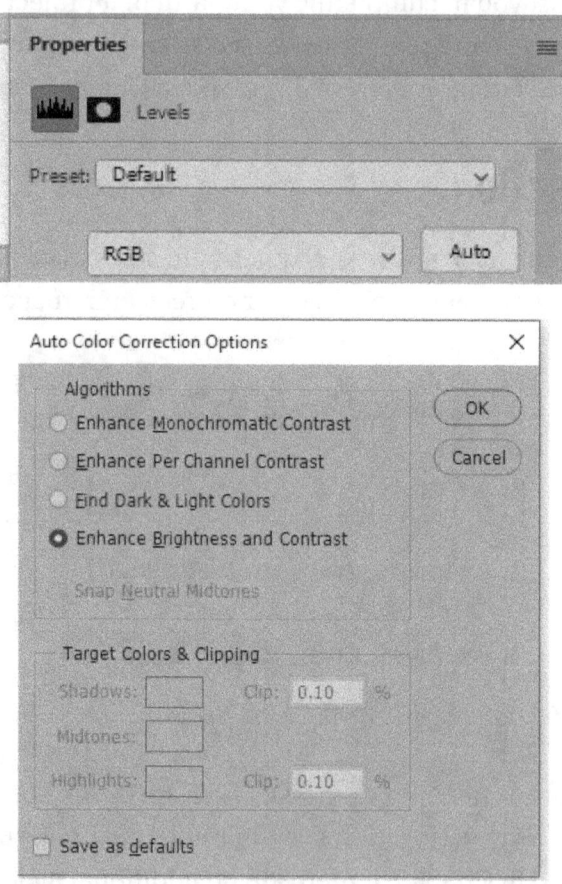

Figure 2-95. *Properties panel for adjustment Levels and the Auto Color Correction Options dialog box*

CHAPTER 2   ADJUSTMENT LAYERS, BLENDING MODES WITH MASKS FOR PHOTO RESTORATION: PART 2

However, these current default settings are globally applied to the auto correction commands. To review some of those details, you can refer to Chapter 1 or refer to this link:

https://helpx.adobe.com/photoshop/using/making-quick-tonal-adjustments.html

Equalize and Desaturate

In the Image ➤ Adjustments menu are two other destructive commands that you can use to quickly adjust your image. I will just mention them here and give some alternative suggestions so you can operate in a less destructive way. Let's look at Equalize and Desaturate.

Equalize: Has no dialog box or additional instructions unless you have created a selection on the background layer first. If no selection is created, it will automatically equalize the entire image. With a selection you can choose to "Equalize selected area only" or "Equalize entire image based on the selected area," which could affect the pixels outside the selection. Refer to Figure 2-96.

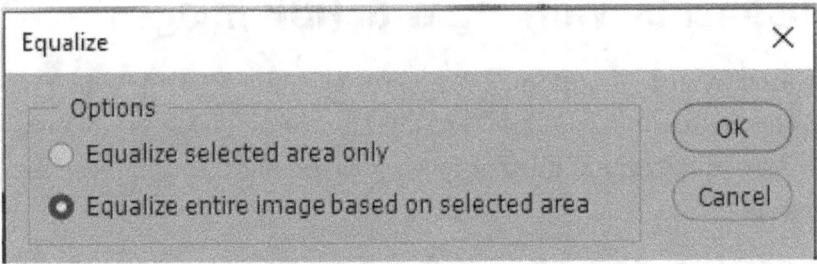

Figure 2-96. *Equalize dialog box with Options settings*

Equalize is meant to balance and redistribute the brightness values of the pixels in an image so that they more evenly represent the entire range of brightness levels. This is similar to what you would do with the Levels adjustment layer with the eyedroppers where you want the brightest value to represent white (highlight) and the darkest value to represents black (shadow) and intermediate values (midtone) are evenly distributed throughout the grayscale. However, the command can also brighten the image too much.

Equalize could be used to correct a scanned image that for some reason appears darker than the original and it requires balanced lightening. You could use Equalize together with your Histogram panel and markers, created with your Color Sampler Tool, to check before and after brightness settings.

Adobe recommends, for similar settings that are nondestructive, to use your adjustment layers or the Camera Raw Filter, which we will look at in Chapter 4.

Desaturate: No dialog box or additional instructions. It just desaturates the current layer of color to a grayscale. For a more accurate desaturation, I recommend using the adjustment layer Hue/Saturation.

Refer to this link for more details:

https://helpx.adobe.com/photoshop/using/applying-special-color-effects-images.html

Adjustments: Working with HDR Images

There are three other options/commands available in the Image ➤ Adjustments menu. I would recommend for these to always work with a duplicate of a document image or a copy of the background layer, as these are destructive.

HDR Toning

This command is specifically for High Dynamic Range (HDR) images. Basically, you need to have three or more identical images taken of a scene, with a tripod for stabilization and minimization of camera shake. They each have slightly different exposure settings to more accurately define light and dark regions, keeping your aperture setting constant.

CHAPTER 2 ADJUSTMENT LAYERS, BLENDING MODES WITH MASKS FOR PHOTO RESTORATION: PART 2

Photoshop has two options for working on these kinds of photos. The first example found in the HDR_folder I will show does not require more than one image, so you can test this on a scan you may already have on hand if you do not have any HDR images. Use the beach example **image_HDR_before.psd**. Refer to Figure 2-97.

Figure 2-97. *An outdoor image of the beach to apply HDR Toning to*

This option only works if you flatten the image first down to one layer. The image will increase in size to a 32-bit HDR image while working in the dialog box. Later, you will need to use the History panel if you need to undo this step. Go to Image ➤ Adjustments ➤ HDR Toning. Click Yes on the alert message if you have multiple layers to flatten them down to one single layer. Refer to Figure 2-98.

CHAPTER 2　ADJUSTMENT LAYERS, BLENDING MODES WITH MASKS FOR PHOTO RESTORATION: PART 2

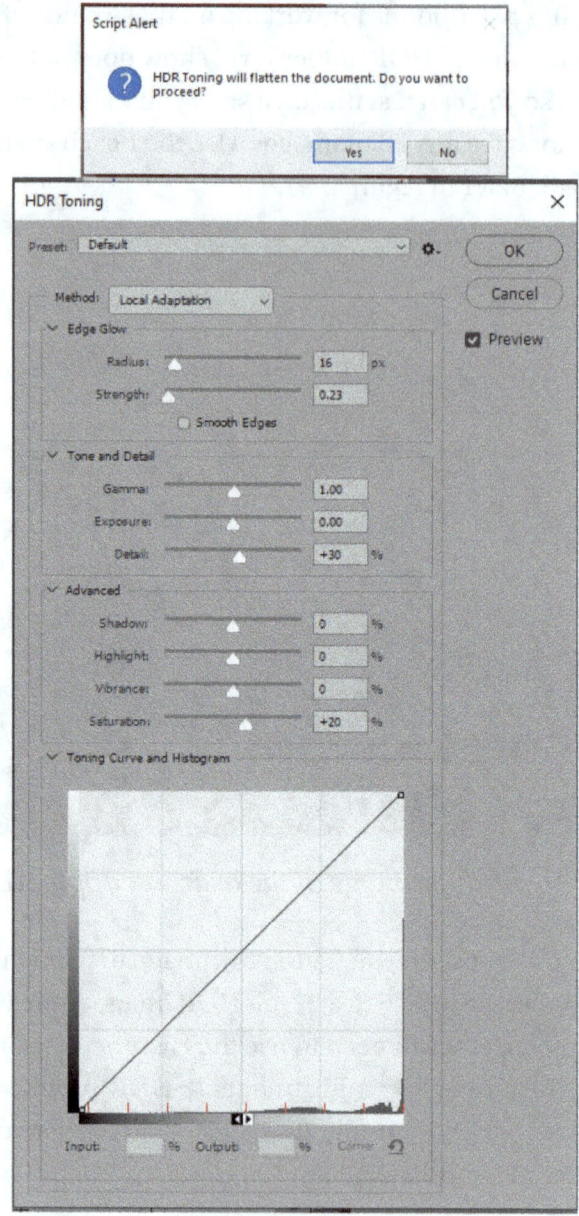

Figure 2-98. *Alert message that may appear when an image has more than one layer and the HDR Toning dialog box*

CHAPTER 2 ADJUSTMENT LAYERS, BLENDING MODES WITH MASKS FOR PHOTO RESTORATION: PART 2

While I will not be going into all the advanced settings of this dialog box, you can refer to the link at the end of this section for more details on HDR.

I will just point out its purpose, which is to use for correction to make your images High Dynamic Range–like. If you have several similar images, you can refer to my second automated option to combine all images into one image. In that example you will be merging them together to create an HDR composite as a single layer. In this case we are just working with one image, the background layer, but once the changes are made, they are permanent. Refer to Figure 2-99.

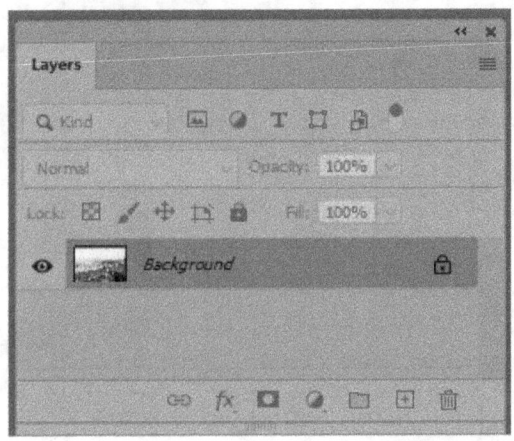

Figure 2-99. *Layers are flattened to a single layer after HDR Toning*

This is why you are working on a duplicate of your file. In Chapter 1, we talked briefly about the image adjustment layer Exposure, which is also good for working with HDR and non-HDR images. Using this command on single non-HDR digital images and scanned images may improve the tonal range and details and give you more options than the adjustment layer does.

CHAPTER 2　ADJUSTMENT LAYERS, BLENDING MODES WITH MASKS FOR PHOTO RESTORATION: PART 2

The dialog box has adjustments for the following.

Preset: This allows you to set a toning preset from the menu list. Note that the gear menu to the right lets you load and save your preset as a 32-bit toning option (.HDT) file. Refer to Figure 2-100.

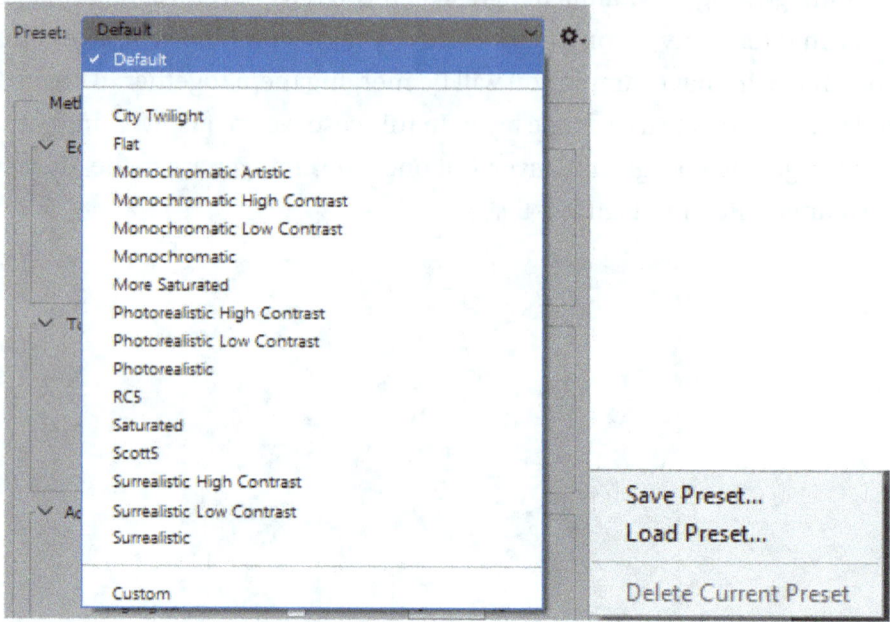

Figure 2-100. *HDR Toning dialog box, presets*

The current default setting was not too bad and did add some tonal range. Other presets like Saturated and Scott5 are interesting as well. Refer to Figure 2-101.

CHAPTER 2   ADJUSTMENT LAYERS, BLENDING MODES WITH MASKS FOR PHOTO RESTORATION: PART 2

Figure 2-101. *Different HDR Toning presets applied to the same image change the color slightly or dramatically*

For now, I will just work with the default setting.

Method: The options for the tone mapping method are Local Adaption, Exposure and Gamma, Highlight Compression, and Equalized Histogram. Currently I am set on Local Adaptation, which has the most options. The method "Exposure and Gamma" only allows you to adjust such options. "Highlight Compression" and "Equalized Histogram" have no options as they are automatic. Refer to Figure 2-102.

CHAPTER 2 ADJUSTMENT LAYERS, BLENDING MODES WITH MASKS FOR PHOTO RESTORATION: PART 2

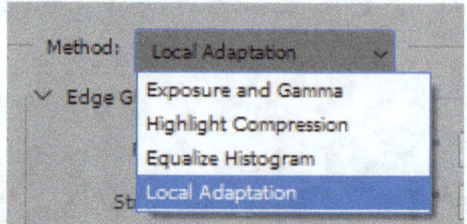

Figure 2-102. HDR Toning dialog box, Method options

Continue to look at the Local Adaption settings as these are used to alter HDR tonality by adjusting local brightness regions throughout the image.

Edge Glow

Radius (1–500 px): Controls the size of the glow effect or brightness regions. The current setting is 79 px. A higher setting makes the images darker.

Strength (0.1–4): Controls the contrast of the glow effect or calculates the distance of two pixels' tonal values before they're no longer part of the same brightness region. The current setting is 0.52. A higher setting adds more shadow or glow back into the image depending on the lighting.

Smooth Edges: Enable this check box to provide edge preserving smoothing while boosting details. In this case I left it disabled. Refer to Figure 2-103.

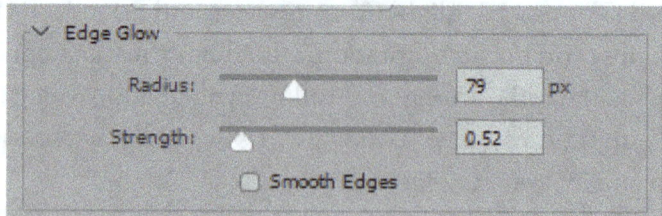

Figure 2-103. HDR Toning dialog box, Edge Glow sliders and Smooth Edges check box

332

CHAPTER 2   ADJUSTMENT LAYERS, BLENDING MODES WITH MASKS FOR PHOTO
RESTORATION: PART 2

Tone and Detail

Gamma (9.99–0.01): Adjust the difference between highlights and shadows. The default setting is 1.00. A lower setting will affect midtones, while higher settings affect highlights and shadows.

Exposure (-5.00, 0, +5.00): Adjust overall image tone. The values reflect the camera's f-stops. Currently I left the exposure at 0. If too low the sky becomes gray and if too high it causes overexposure.

Detail (-100, 0, +300%): Find detail in the image when you drag the slider. To the left you reduce or blur details and to the right you increase or sharpen details. Currently it is set to +30%, but a higher number would bring more detail into the rocks on the beach and the mountains in the background. Refer to Figure 2-104.

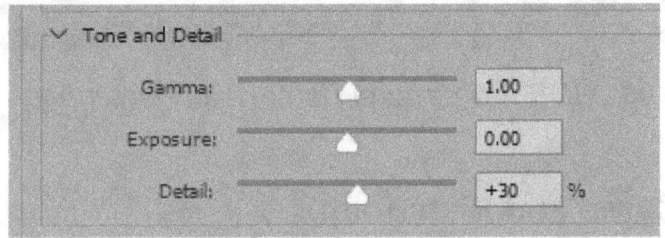

Figure 2-104. HDR Toning dialog box, Tone and Detail sliders

Advanced

Shadow (-100, 0, +100%): Adjust the luminance of the shadow regions. Currently it is set to 0. Lower values increase the shadow. Higher values decrease the shadow.

Highlight (-100, 0, +100%): Adjust the luminance of the highlight regions. Currently it is set to 0. Lower values decrease the highlight. Higher values increase the highlight.

Vibrance (–100, 0, +100%): Adjust the saturation or subtle colors while minimizing clipping of highly saturated colors. Currently it is set to 0. Lower values decrease the vibrance making in grayscale. Higher values increase the vibrance.

Saturation (–100, 0, +100%): Adjust color intensity of all colors. –100 is considered monochrome, while +100 is considered double saturation. Currently it is set to +20. Refer to Figure 2-105.

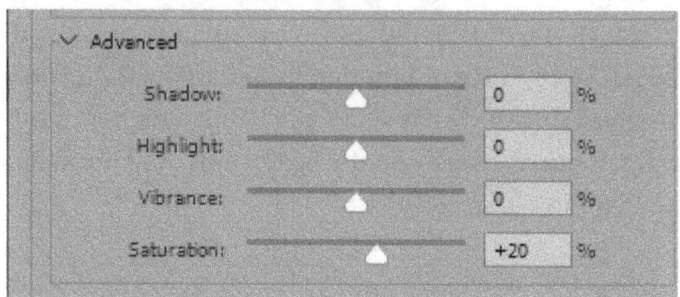

Figure 2-105. *HDR Toning dialog box, Advanced settings*

Toning Curve and Histogram

This area is similar to using the adjustment layer Curves where you can add control points to the curve and observe the histogram in the background, which displays the original luminance values. Refer to Figure 2-106.

CHAPTER 2　ADJUSTMENT LAYERS, BLENDING MODES WITH MASKS FOR PHOTO RESTORATION: PART 2

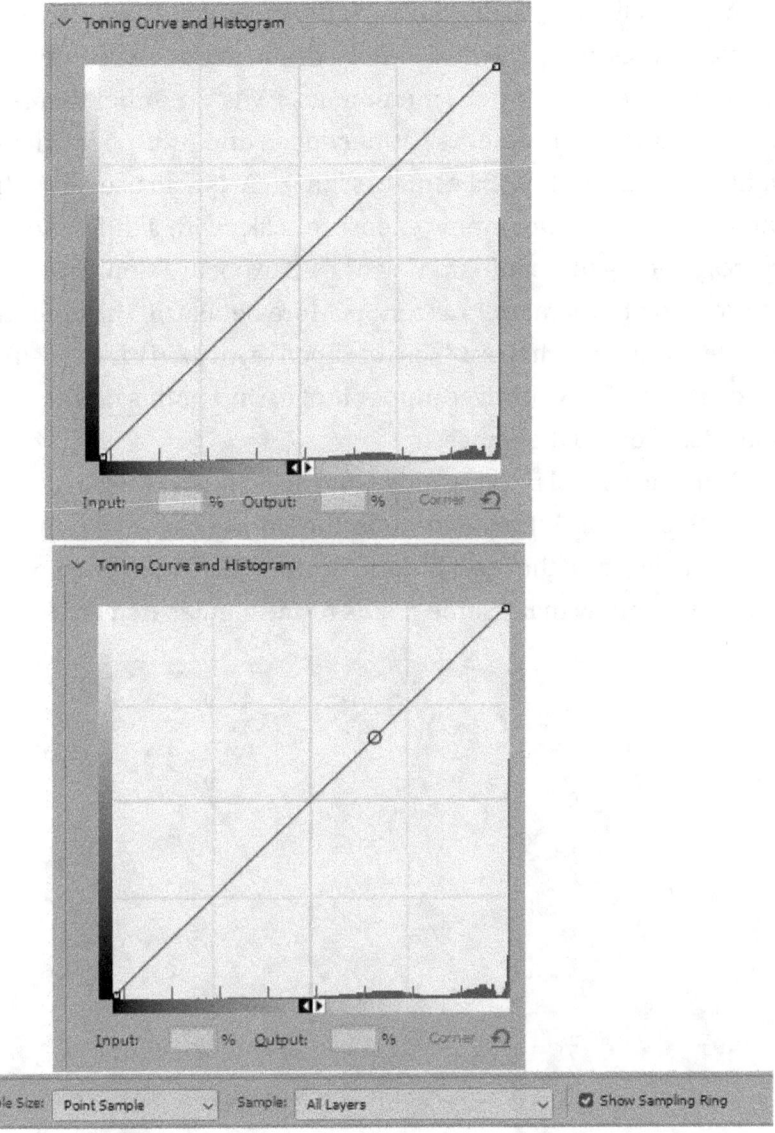

Figure 2-106. *HDR Toning dialog box, Toning Curve and Histogram, with the Eyedropper tool in the Options bar panel*

CHAPTER 2   ADJUSTMENT LAYERS, BLENDING MODES WITH MASKS FOR PHOTO
            RESTORATION: PART 2

You can flip the histogram and curve using the lower arrowheads. The red tick marks along the horizontal axis are in one Exposure Value or EV (approximately one-f-stop) increments. EV is a number that represents a combination of a camera's shutter speed and f-number (measure of light gathering ability of a camera's lens). EV is also used to indicate an interval on the photographic exposure scale, with a difference of 1 EV corresponding to a standard power-of-2 exposure step. This is commonly referred to photographers as a stop. More details on the definition of EV can be found here. https://en.wikipedia.org/wiki/Exposure_value. Next you can use your Eyedropper tool to find points on the curve when you click areas of the image.

When a control point is added and selected, you also have access to the Input % text box, Output % text box, the Corner check box (for more extreme adjustments), and the reset button. Adding more than one point with a corner point may make some points more angular. Refer to Figure 2-107.

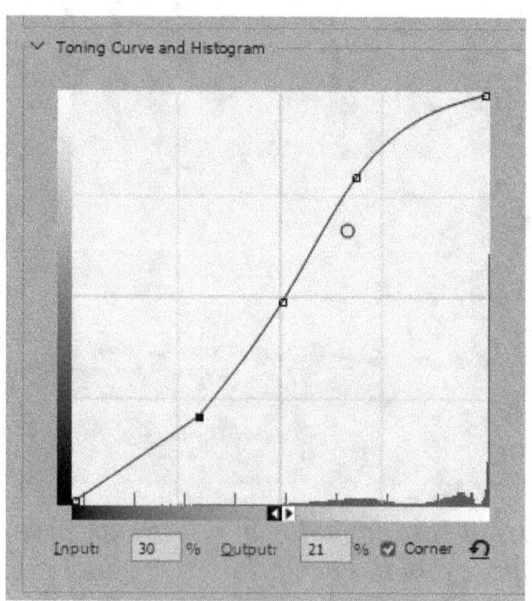

Figure 2-107. HDR Toning dialog box, altering the toning curve with points

CHAPTER 2 ADJUSTMENT LAYERS, BLENDING MODES WITH MASKS FOR PHOTO RESTORATION: PART 2

Click OK to confirm the settings you choose or Cancel to exit without making changes. Use the Alt/Option key to change the Cancel button to a Reset button. In this case I just left the image on the default settings and did not add any points to the curve. Refer to Figure 2-98 and Figure 2-108.

Figure 2-108. *The result of the HDR default toning adjustments*

Refer to **image_HDR_after.psd** for reference.

Note After you have completed working on the file, it will return from 32 bits to a setting of RGB 8 bits. However, if you ever need to reduce the file's bit size manually, remember to go to Image ➤ Mode and select a lower setting such as 8 Bits/Channel. Refer to Figure 2-109.

CHAPTER 2   ADJUSTMENT LAYERS, BLENDING MODES WITH MASKS FOR PHOTO RESTORATION: PART 2

Figure 2-109.   HDR files convert from 32 bit back down to 8 bit once you exit the dialog box

Merge to HDR Pro

The second option if you are working with separate files for HDR is to use the Automation feature File ➤ Automate ➤ Merge to HDR Pro. Browse for the files you want and make sure to enable "Attempt to Automatically Align Source Images" and click OK. You can use the files found in the HDR_ Folder for practice. Refer to Figure 2-110.

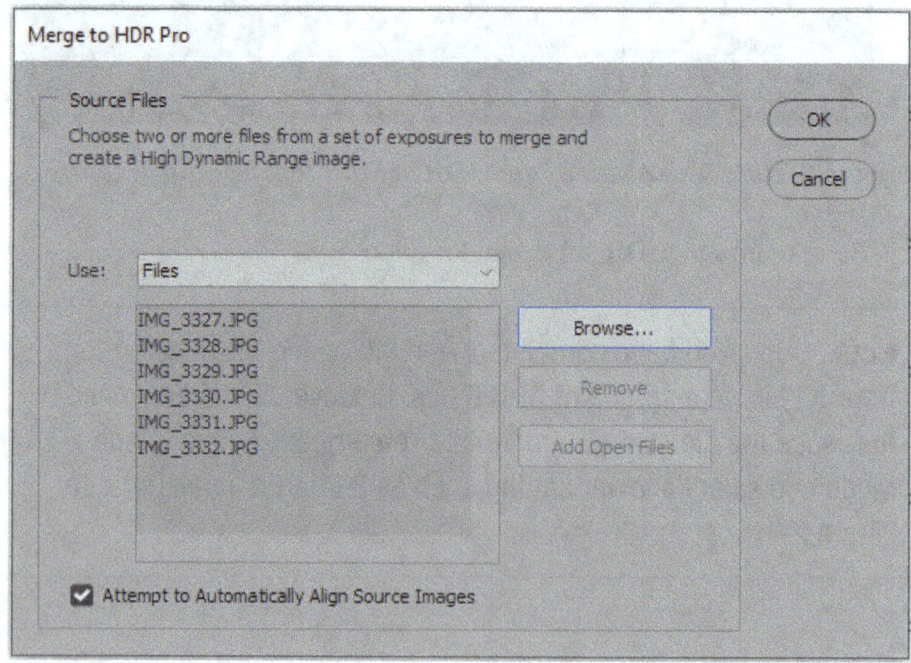

Figure 2-110.   Merge to HDR Pro dialog box for selecting files

CHAPTER 2   ADJUSTMENT LAYERS, BLENDING MODES WITH MASKS FOR PHOTO RESTORATION: PART 2

This time, rather than opening in just a dialog box, you will open all the images in a workspace, with very similar settings. However, this time you will be able to use all your images at once to get the ideal range. I selected the one set to EV 0.00. Refer to Figures 2-111 and 2-112.

Figure 2-111. *HDR Pro workspace options with the ideal photo selected from the list*

CHAPTER 2　ADJUSTMENT LAYERS, BLENDING MODES WITH MASKS FOR PHOTO RESTORATION: PART 2

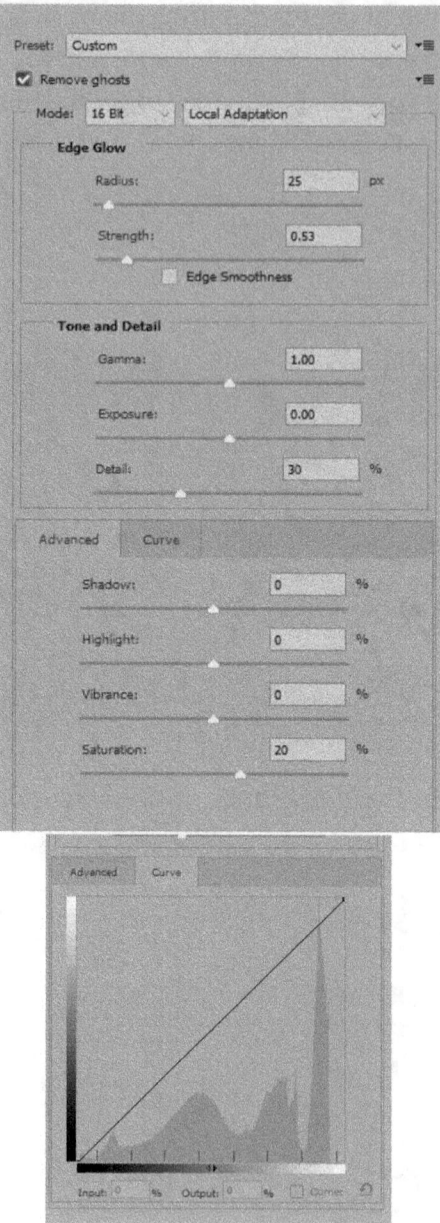

Figure 2-112. *HDR Pro workspace options for the current image collection*

CHAPTER 2   ADJUSTMENT LAYERS, BLENDING MODES WITH MASKS FOR PHOTO RESTORATION: PART 2

Remove ghosts: Removes ghosting shapes that are caused by moving object. In this case I used that setting as I had to deal with the waves and tide as I shot each image one after the other on a different exposure shutter speed. Also, here I can set the output bit mode to whichever I would like, in this case 32 Bit, 16 Bit, or 8 Bit. In this case I set to 16-bit. I set the Edge Glow: 25px and Strength to 0.53 with no edge smoothness. Otherwise, I used the same setting as in the HDR Toning example. Gamma: 1, Exposure: 0, Detail 30%, Shadow, Highlight, and Vibrance 0% and Saturation: 20%. Once you have adjusted your settings as you want, click OK to exit and create the new HDR image. Refer to Figure 2-113.

Figure 2-113. *HDR Pro workspace options to confirm settings*

And then save your file. See **composite_HDR-2.psd** as a final example in the HDR example folder.

Use this link to explore more about HDR and other options that may be available for certain images:

https://helpx.adobe.com/photoshop/using/high-dynamic-range-images.html

Some of these settings you may be able to work with more accurately using Camera Raw, which we will review in Chapter 4.

Advanced Color Adjustments

The next two Image ➤ Adjustments commands are similar to the Color Replacement tool mentioned in Volume 1, Chapter 4.

I will just explain their purpose briefly here along with the basic settings.

CHAPTER 2   ADJUSTMENT LAYERS, BLENDING MODES WITH MASKS FOR PHOTO
          RESTORATION: PART 2

Match Color

This is used to match the color: from one image to another image and from one layer to another layer using a target and a source. This option is used with a selection in an image to another selection in the same image or a different image. This command also adjusts the luminance and color range and neutralizes color casts in an image. You can only work with RGB images.

This dialog box lets you set the following for the destination image.

Destination Image

Target: In this case this is the currently opened document.

Ignore Selection when Applying Adjustment: If no selection is made, then this option is grayed out and disabled. When a selection is active, then this option is available, and you can choose whether to apply the adjustments to the entire image or layer. When no selection is made, then the command matches the overall image statistics between images (Target and Source). Refer to Figure 2-114.

CHAPTER 2　ADJUSTMENT LAYERS, BLENDING MODES WITH MASKS FOR PHOTO RESTORATION: PART 2

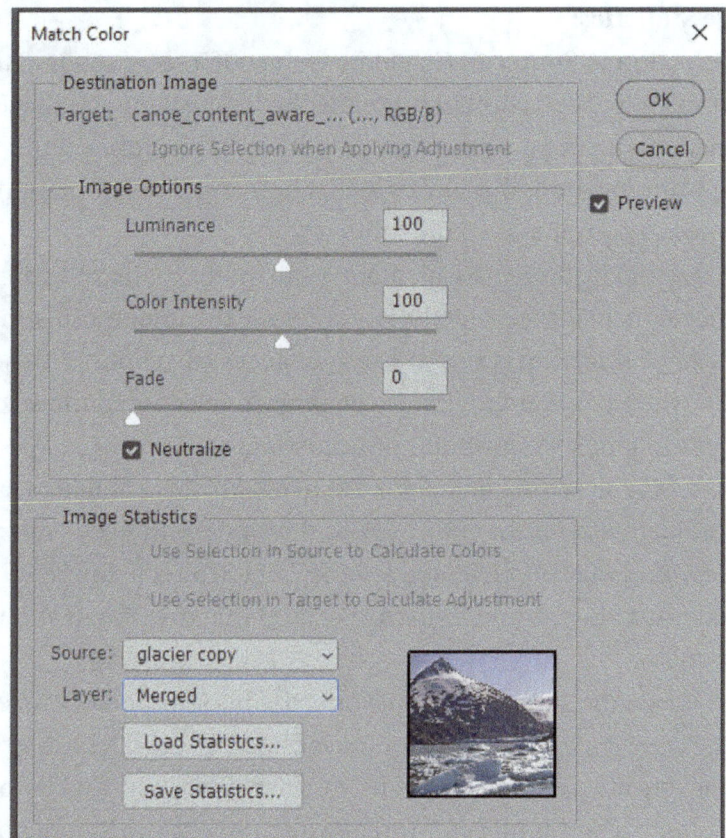

Figure 2-114. *Match Color dialog box*

Image Options:

Luminance (1–200): Allows you to adjust the brightness of the target image. The default is 100.

Color Intensity (1–200): Allows you to adjust the saturation of the target image. The default is 100.

Fade (0–100): Fades the amount of the adjustment in the target image. The default is 0.

Neutralize check box: Enable if you need to neutralize the color casts in the target image.

343

Image Statistics:

Use Selection in Source to Calculate Colors: If a selection is active, use colors in source selection to calculate the image adjustment. Unless a source selection is set, you cannot access this option. Deselect this option when you want to ignore the source's selection and use colors from the entire source to compute the adjustment.

Use Selection in Target to Calculate Adjustment: If the selection is active, use colors in target selection to calculate the image adjustment. Unless a source selection is set, you cannot access this option. Deselect this option when you want to ignore the target's selection and use colors from the entire target to compute the adjustment.

Source: A None setting will not reference a different image to calculate the color adjustment for the match. With the None setting chosen, the target image and the source image are the same. To set a different source image, you must choose one from the list, and that document should be currently open.

Layer: When the source is set to None, the background or current layer is chosen. However, if a different source is chosen, you will have access to whatever layers are available in the list as the new source, and it does not have to be the background layer. You can also choose the Merged option from the menu if you want to match colors from all the layers in the source image. A preview of the current selected layer or layers will display in the square on the right.

Load Statistics and Save Statistics buttons allow you to save the setting as (.STA) files.

Click OK to confirm changes or Cancel without making changes. Make sure the Preview check box is active as you work.

Tip Using the Info panel can help you review the changes as you work.

CHAPTER 2　ADJUSTMENT LAYERS, BLENDING MODES WITH MASKS FOR PHOTO RESTORATION: PART 2

In my example, I used my **canoe_content_aware_photo_filter.psd** image (target) and the **glacier_2.psd** image (source). Make sure that when you use a copy of the canoe file that you use the Layers menu to flatten the image first so that the color is applied overall to the background layer. I experimented with setting the Neutralize check box as this made the image less blue and still retain some of the original colors. However, in some situations I would recommend in this case using Levels or other adjustment layers as that would be less destructive with more natural colors and easier to control. However, use your own images to see what kind of color results you encounter. Try changing the source image or changing the Layer to a setting of Merged. Refer to Figure 2-115.

CHAPTER 2　ADJUSTMENT LAYERS, BLENDING MODES WITH MASKS FOR PHOTO RESTORATION: PART 2

Figure 2-115. *Use Match Color settings to alter the color in another background image*

More details can be found at this link:

CHAPTER 2   ADJUSTMENT LAYERS, BLENDING MODES WITH MASKS FOR PHOTO RESTORATION: PART 2

https://helpx.adobe.com/photoshop/using/matching-replacing-mixing-colors.html

Replace Color

This dialog box shares some similarities to the Select ➤ Color Range dialog box. As we saw with the Color Replacement tool in Volume 1, Chapter 4, this dialog box can be used to replace specified colors in an image with new color values. That can either be controlled using the slider or the color picker within the dialog box. Use the **bird.psd** image in this example again, to test. Refer to Figure 2-116.

Figure 2-116. *Locate an image where you want to replace a selection of color*

Use Image ➤ Adjustments ➤ Replace Color to open the Replace Color dialog box. Refer to Figure 2-117.

CHAPTER 2   ADJUSTMENT LAYERS, BLENDING MODES WITH MASKS FOR PHOTO RESTORATION: PART 2

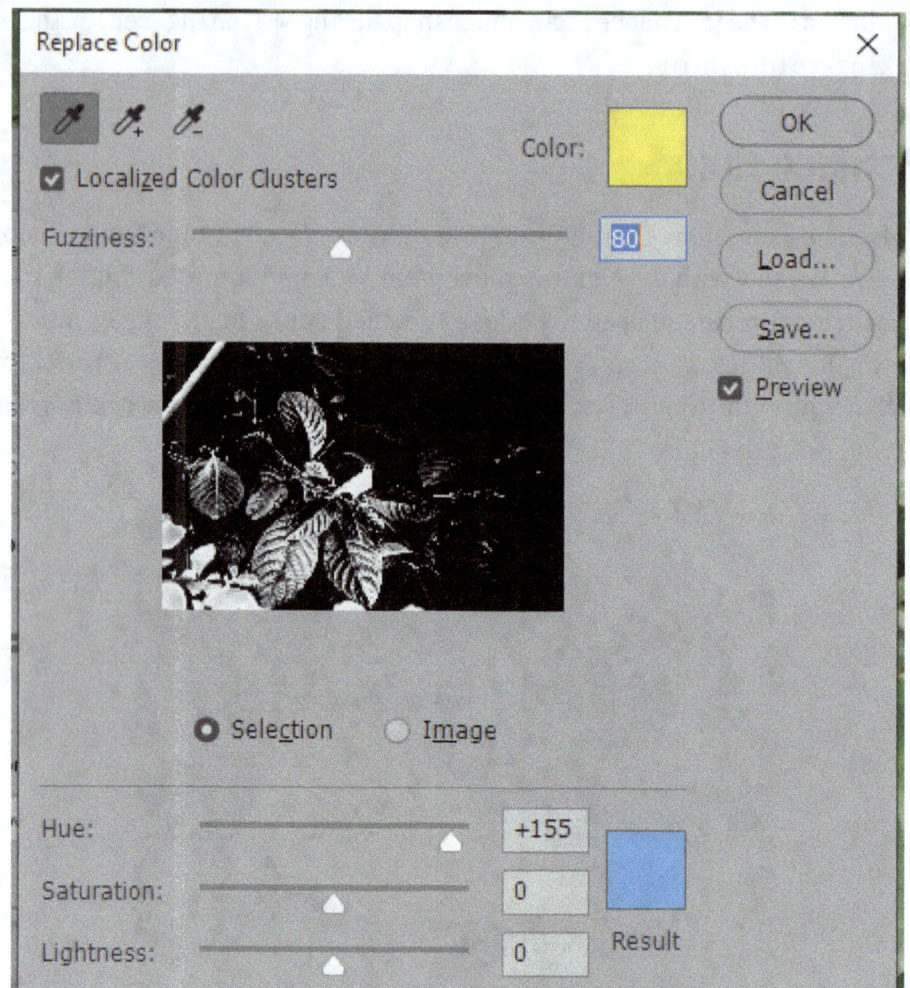

Figure 2-117. *Replace Color dialog box*

The following settings are in reference to Figure 2-117:

Eyedropper, Add to Sample, Subtract from Sample: Use to initially sample from the layer and then use the other eyedroppers to add (Shift + click) or subtract (Alt/Option + click) to or from the sample.

Localize Color Clusters: Enable this setting to make contiguous selections.

CHAPTER 2   ADJUSTMENT LAYERS, BLENDING MODES WITH MASKS FOR PHOTO RESTORATION: PART 2

Color: Click the square swatch to change the selection color using the color picker. You can target the color you want replaced, and this will update in the preview box.

Fuzziness (0–200): Adjust the fall-off beyond the selection boundaries and to what degree related colors are included in the current selection.

Preview box with mask radio buttons: View Selection or Image mask. Black areas of the selection are masked, and white areas are unmasked. The semi-masked area will appear gray. The Image radio button may be helpful if you are currently zoomed into the image.

Sliders – Hue (–180, 0, +180), Saturation (–100, 0, +100), Lightness (–100, 0, +100): Use the slider or enter the numbers in the text boxes.

Result: Click the square to use the color picker to adjust the setting.

Use the button on the right to Load or Save your presets as (.AXT) files.

Click OK to commit changes or Cancel to exit without saving changes and keep Preview enabled as you view the changes on the canvas. Refer to Figure 2-117.

Use the Alt/Option key if you need to change the Cancel button to a Reset button.

Adobe mentions that when using this command you cannot replace pure gray, black, or white with a color. You can change the Lightness setting to affect the color; however, the Hue and Saturation settings are relative to existing color, so those sliders have no effect on those colors. Refer to Figure 2-118.

CHAPTER 2   ADJUSTMENT LAYERS, BLENDING MODES WITH MASKS FOR PHOTO RESTORATION: PART 2

Figure 2-118. *A small area of color can be replaced on the current selected layer*

While this option does replace color in select sections, it can be difficult to control unless you made a prior selection and is not ideal for masking out set areas. It will destroy the color of the background image. For specific color adjustments done nondestructively, the Hue/Saturation adjustment layer mentioned in Chapter 1 may be a better option for your project.

More details can be found at this link:

`https://helpx.adobe.com/photoshop/using/replace-colors.html`

In Chapter 5, we will look at a neural filter called Color Transfer that can perform similar conversions in a nondestructive way.

Advanced Image Adjustment Options

Besides the color adjustments mentioned in this chapter, there are two more advanced options found in the Image menu that you may want to use as you edit photos using the Image menu. Here are some suggestions as to when you may want to use them, as well as some alternative solutions.

CHAPTER 2   ADJUSTMENT LAYERS, BLENDING MODES WITH MASKS FOR PHOTO RESTORATION: PART 2

Apply Image

This is found under Image ➤ Apply Image.

As you saw with the Image ➤ Adjustments ➤ Match Color example, you can use a source file and apply settings to the current open target document. The source file can be the current target file, but it can also be another open document from which you want to apply a specific layer or a group of layers. Note that you can also invert the source file. The source must match the target dimensions. Refer to Figure 2-119.

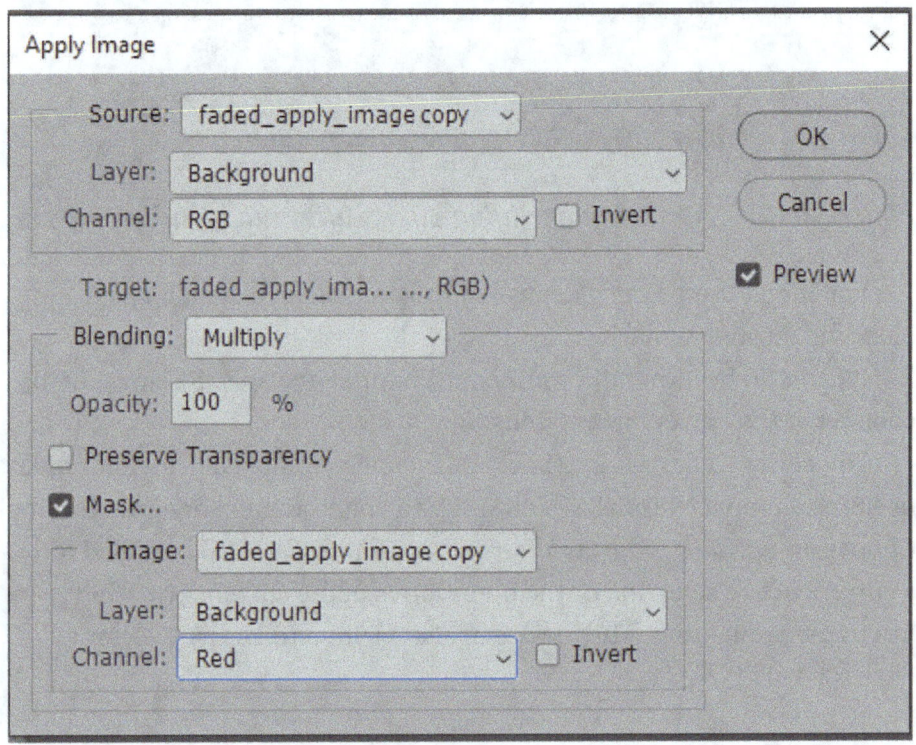

Figure 2-119. *Apply Image dialog box*

The target can then be blended using a blending mode and opacity. You can enable Preserve Transparency if working with multiple layers.

351

CHAPTER 2 ADJUSTMENT LAYERS, BLENDING MODES WITH MASKS FOR PHOTO
          RESTORATION: PART 2

Apply Image and Calculations commands offer two additional blending modes called Add and Subtract, which let you set an offset (–255, 0, 255) and scale setting (1.000–2.000). Altering these settings will lighten or darken the image. Add will add the pixel values in two channels, while Subtract is used to subtract the pixel values in the source channel from the corresponding pixels in the target channel. Refer to the link at the end of the Calculations command if you need more information on this topic. Refer to Figure 2-120.

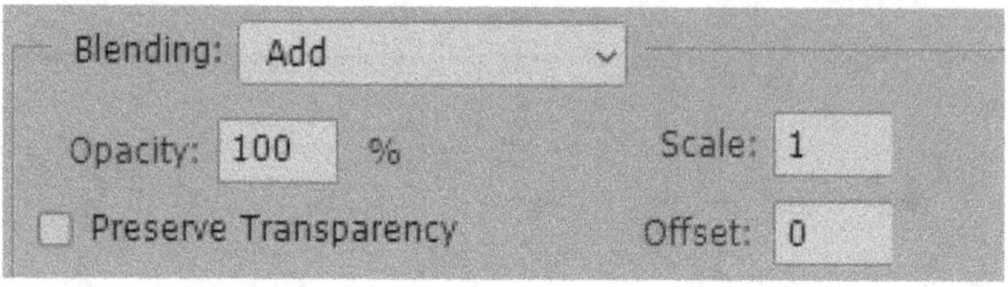

Figure 2-120. *Apply Image dialog box, additional blending modes*

For Target there is also a mask setting in which you can apply a blending through a mask.

It can also be either the composite channel or a specific single RGB channel to the current target image.

You can select an image (Source), then a layer or layers for a merged mask, and then a channel, which will be a color channel or alpha channel. Choose an option of Gray, Red, Green, or Blue. It can also be based on a current active selection or the boundaries of the current layer that has transparent areas. The mask can also be inverted as well. Refer to Figure 2-121.

CHAPTER 2 ADJUSTMENT LAYERS, BLENDING MODES WITH MASKS FOR PHOTO RESTORATION: PART 2

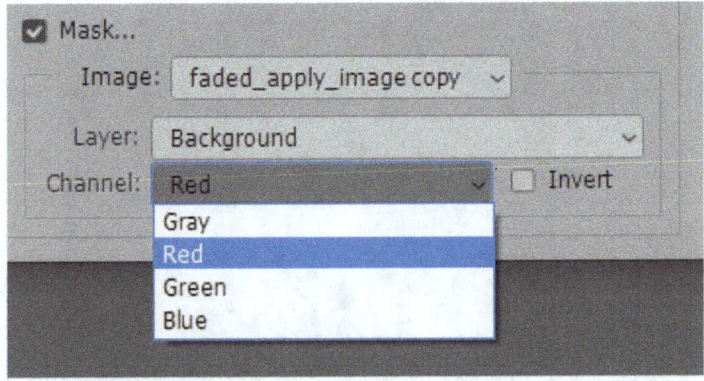

Figure 2-121. *Apply Image dialog box, setting Mask options*

This command can be ideal with faded images where you need to build up more pixels to create a more tonal range. Here is an example of a before and after of a background image. Refer to Figure 2-122.

CHAPTER 2 ADJUSTMENT LAYERS, BLENDING MODES WITH MASKS FOR PHOTO RESTORATION: PART 2

Figure 2-122. *Apply Image can make the current image less overexposed and reduce fading*

CHAPTER 2   ADJUSTMENT LAYERS, BLENDING MODES WITH MASKS FOR PHOTO RESTORATION: PART 2

However, a nondestructive alternative to this is to make a duplicate of your current faded layer and apply a blending mode of Multiply to it over the current background layer. You could reduce the copied layer's opacity if you prefer to 51% and add an adjustment layer over it for color correction, such as Levels. This is also ideal if you need to add a layer for clone stamps to cover any dust and scratches you may discover as you color correct. Refer to Figure 2-123.

CHAPTER 2 ADJUSTMENT LAYERS, BLENDING MODES WITH MASKS FOR PHOTO RESTORATION: PART 2

Figure 2-123. *Use the Layers panel to create a duplicate copy of a layer and apply a blending mode and adjustment layers for an improved effect*

Calculations

The Image ➤ Calculations command is like the Apply Image command but can be used to blend two individual layers or channels from one or two source images. The result in this case will be more monochrome/grayscale in appearance. You can then apply the results to a new (target) image or to a new channel or selection in the active (target) image. You cannot apply the Calculations command to composite channels. Refer to Figure 2-124.

CHAPTER 2 ADJUSTMENT LAYERS, BLENDING MODES WITH MASKS FOR PHOTO RESTORATION: PART 2

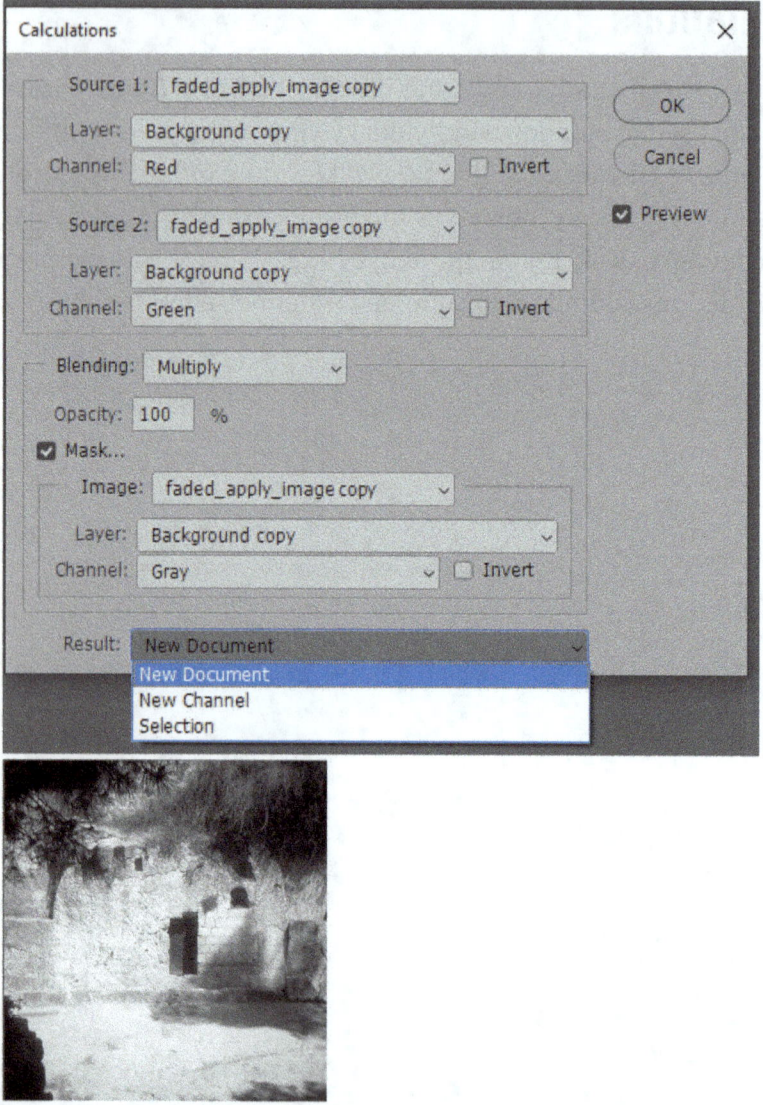

Figure 2-124. *The Calculations dialog box can be used to create a black-and-white image*

CHAPTER 2 ADJUSTMENT LAYERS, BLENDING MODES WITH MASKS FOR PHOTO RESTORATION: PART 2

The result, in this case, can be a new document, a new channel, or a new selection.

You can refer to my file **faded_apply_image.psd** to review the Apply Image example.

A new channel can be useful in situations where there is extreme damage to a specific channel and you need to create a blend to remove the damage. Once the new alpha channel was created, you could then Ctrl/CMD + A to Edit ➤ Copy it and then select the entire damaged channel and Edit ➤ Paste the copied channel into it. However, this is no guarantee that this will also color correct the image, so I recommend first experimenting with one of your adjustment layers, as in Chapter 1, to see if you can retrieve any color or you may just have to settle with a monochrome image or colorize the image yourself.

However, in the case of a new document like Image ➤ Apply Image, you can apply blending modes. Remember that you can experiment with blending modes and opacities on duplicate layers to achieve similar results.

More information on the topic of Apply Image and Calculations can be found here:

https://helpx.adobe.com/photoshop/using/channel-calculations.html

File ➤ Save your open files so far.

Notes on Out-of-Gamut Colors

As you work on various color projects of scanned images, you will be dealing with colors that may be out of viewer range with either your computer screen or printer. In this case Adobe refers to out of gamut when viewing RGB colors that will not match CMYK printing values. Here are some options for viewing your images on screen that you may want to print. I used a copy of the file **sunset_selective_highlight_shadow_gamut.psd**. I used the Layer panel to then flatten the image.

CHAPTER 2   ADJUSTMENT LAYERS, BLENDING MODES WITH MASKS FOR PHOTO
            RESTORATION: PART 2

To detect out-of-gamut colors, you can use the following:

View ➤ Proof Setup: I have this set to Working CMYK so that the colors on the screen emulate CMYK as closely as possible. Refer to Figure 2-125.

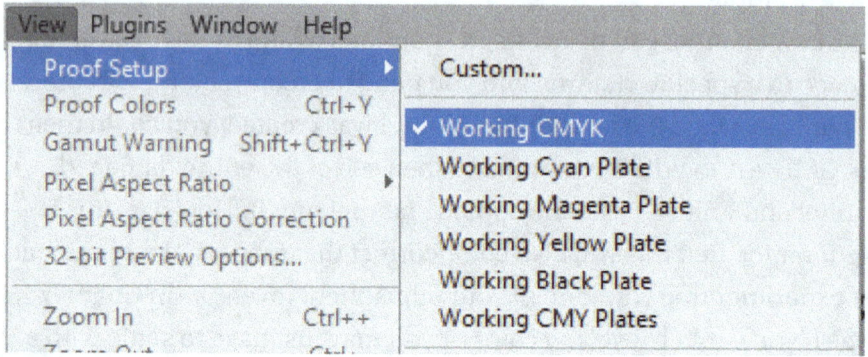

Figure 2-125.   View menu for creating a Proof Setup of Working CMYK

View ➤ Gamut Warning (Shift + Ctrl/CMD + Y): Toggle this on and off to see a preview in gray of what areas may not print as brightly as you hoped. Some of your color-corrected images may have very minimal area, and others may have areas of blue that are difficult for most CMYK printers to achieve and will print less vibrant than as seen on the screen. Refer to Figure 2-126.

CHAPTER 2   ADJUSTMENT LAYERS, BLENDING MODES WITH MASKS FOR PHOTO RESTORATION: PART 2

Figure 2-126. *Previewing out-of-gamut areas on an image*

Tip   You can, while in the Tools panel color picker (double-click), set the View ➤ Gamut Warning on to get a better idea of colors that RGB cannot reproduce as well in CMYK. Just remember to turn the View ➤ Gamut Warning off again so that you can view your screen colors correctly. Refer to Figure 2-127.

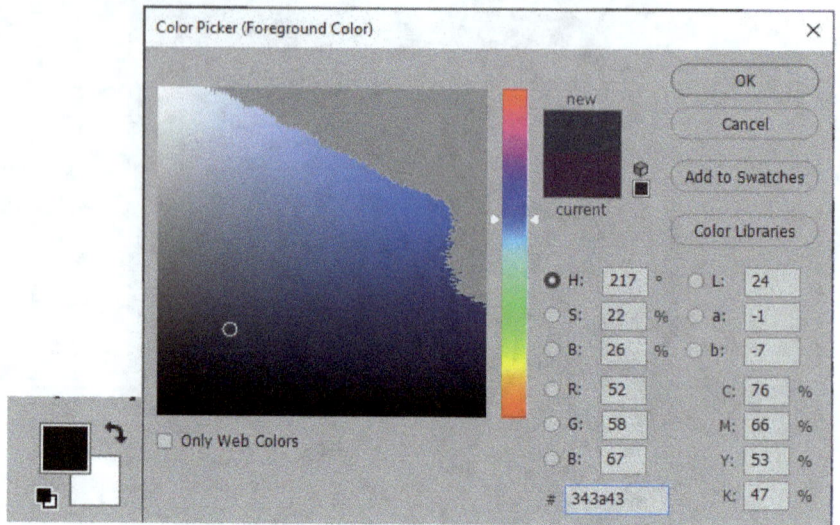

Figure 2-127. *Using the color picker to preview out-of-gamut colors*

In Chapter 4 we will also look at the Camera Raw Filter that can help you visually detect the color highlight and shadow clipping warnings.

Knowing what is out of gamut in your images can help you adjust your setting while using adjustment layers and filters if you plan to print your photos, and we will consider this more in Chapter 7.

However, I will just mention that if you know you have a lot of out-of-gamut colors after you have done a test print, one thing you can try to balance this may be to use your Select ➤ Color Range to identify those areas by selecting the Out of Gamut setting from the list and click OK. Once you have an active selection, you could then use Hue/Saturation or another adjustment layer to create a mask and then balance those areas. Check your out-of-gamut warning and create another test print to see if you like the results. Refer to Figure 2-128.

CHAPTER 2　ADJUSTMENT LAYERS, BLENDING MODES WITH MASKS FOR PHOTO RESTORATION: PART 2

Figure 2-128. *The Color Range dialog box can be used to create out-of-gamut selection, and then you can use an adjustment layer to correct as required and preview the result*

Remember, however, that while traditional CMYK process standard printing may have certain gamut warnings, an inkjet printer may have a wider range of ink colors. This may vary from printer to printer, and likely your inkjet printer will produce better results. So always do a test print to compare. File ➤ Save any changes you made to the copies of your files, and you can see the Hue/Saturation adjustment layer mask I used in the file **sunset_selective_highlight_shadow_gamut.psd**.

Working in Lab vs. RGB Color in Separate Channels

Rather than working in RGB color mode, some professional photographers prefer to work in Lab color mode when adjusting an image. As we saw, however, in Chapter 1, this may limit which adjustment layers you can access. Can working in Lab color mode and with channels improve the color balance of certain photos more than RGB? Yes, in some situations it can. However, it is a more advanced topic, but if it is of interest to you, a book that I recommend is *Photoshop LAB Color: The Canyon Conundrum and Other Adventures in the Most Powerful Colorspace* by Dan Margulis. The second edition was done in 2015. In this book the main adjustment layer is Curves, and he uses it to do many complex adjustments.

Photo Project

From Volume 1, I am now continuing with the army image. Refer to file **army_healing_color_adjustment.psd**. In Volume 1 we corrected the damage of rips and tears as well as the border color. However, here you will see how you could use adjustment layers to improve the overall black-and-white of the photo, removing areas of stains and discoloration, and this may help you discover areas that you still need to use the healing and clone stamping tools on as well as the Eraser tool. As your overall image improves, you can return to a specific layer or create a new one (Layer 2) and continue to correct turning on and off the visibility of the adjustment layer.

Using a layer mask in specific areas can control the stain in selected sections, such as the redness around the man's shoe or elsewhere. In this example Black & White is a good layer adjustment option at the default setting while painting on the layer mask with the Eraser tool. Remember when you first create a Black & White adjustment layer it will be a white mask as it applies the adjustment overall you can then use the Properties panel's Invert button to Invert the mask and then start to paint back the white with the Eraser tool. Overall or selective Hue/Saturation with Colorize enabled may be something you want to add as well. Refer to Figures 2-126, 2-129, 2-130, and 2-131.

CHAPTER 2   ADJUSTMENT LAYERS, BLENDING MODES WITH MASKS FOR PHOTO RESTORATION: PART 2

Figure 2-129. *The color stain around boot is then removed with a select masked adjustment layer, and then a stamp tool can be used on an underlying layer to further correct the damage*

CHAPTER 2 ADJUSTMENT LAYERS, BLENDING MODES WITH MASKS FOR PHOTO RESTORATION: PART 2

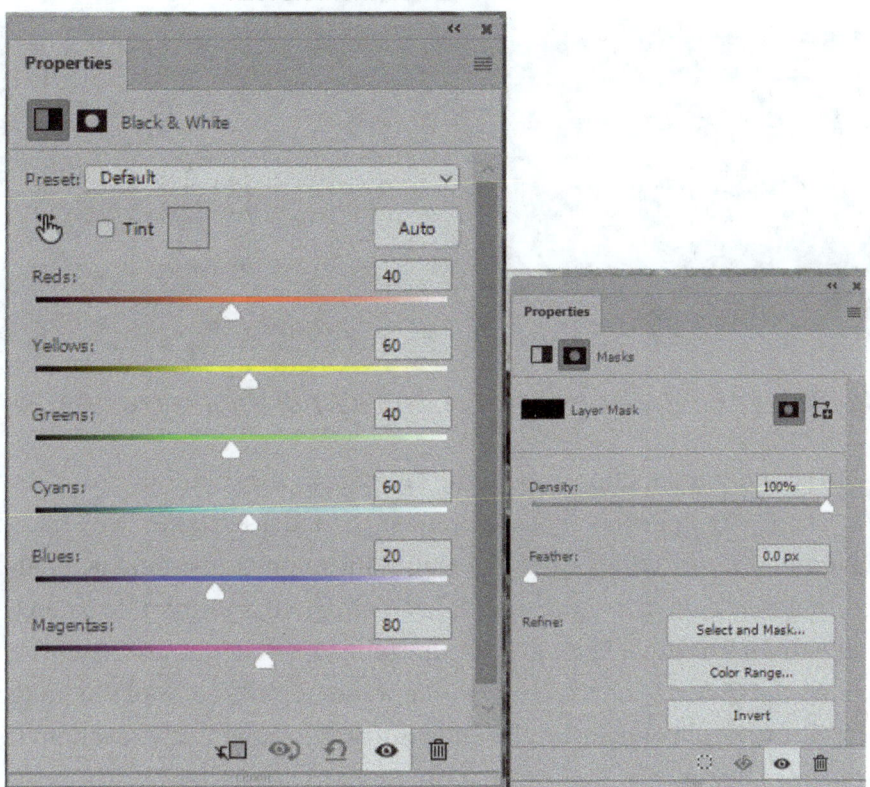

Figure 2-130. *Unusual colors can be corrected with the Black & White adjustment layer as well as masks, and then further corrections can be made to a layer below using the Clone Stamp tool as you work*

CHAPTER 2   ADJUSTMENT LAYERS, BLENDING MODES WITH MASKS FOR PHOTO RESTORATION: PART 2

Figure 2-131. *The current image with overall color correction*

To create the selection area of the layer mask for Hue/Saturation, I then Ctrl/CMD + clicked my Layer 1 mask to load a selection, which is the rectangular frame. I then applied a Hue/Saturation adjustment layer above the other Black & White Adjustment layer and, in the Properties panel, enable Colorize with a Hue: +75, Saturation: +5, and Lightness: 0. I also enabled the Colorize check box. This kept the original color of the image but took out some of the overall yellowing of the paper and prevented the frame from being colorized by mistake. Refer to Figure 2-132.

CHAPTER 2 ADJUSTMENT LAYERS, BLENDING MODES WITH MASKS FOR PHOTO RESTORATION: PART 2

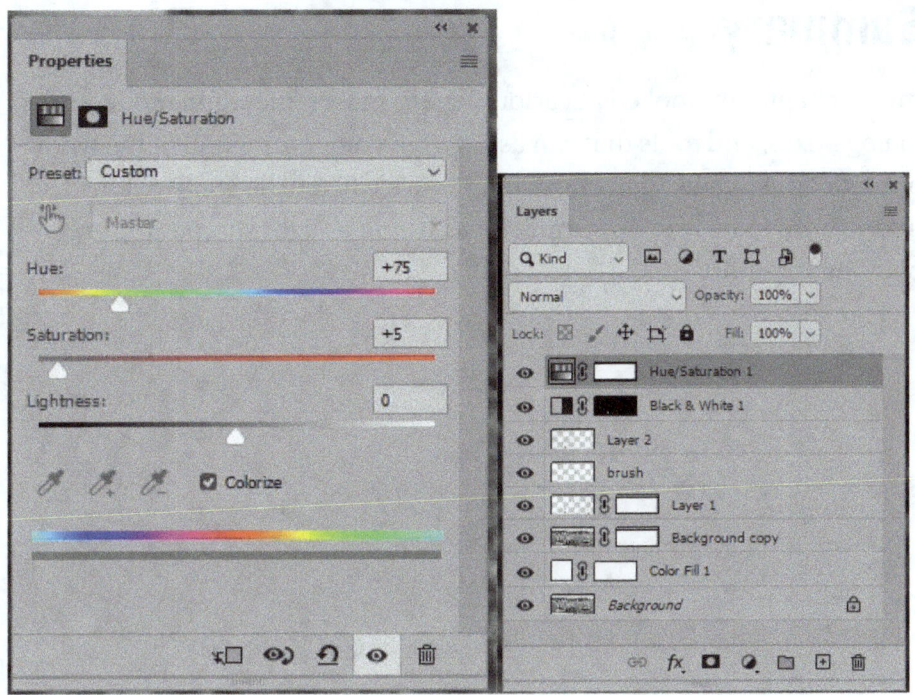

Figure 2-132. *Create a selection from Layer 1 and apply an adjustment of Hue/Saturation to cover the image with a single color*

However, overall, we still must correct for dust or scratches, which we will look at in the next chapter.

On your own projects, try some of the options from Chapter 1 and this chapter on your color images. Begin with an adjustment layer of Levels and then Curves, and then try fine-tuning the color with Hue/Saturation or Brightness/Contrast. Look at your image and decide if an overall color adjustment needs to be made, or does one or more sections of the image require a slightly different tonal adjustment that only can be controlled with a layer mask? And then decide should you use a similar adjustment layer in another selection of the image with different settings and another layer mask?

File ➤ Save any of your open files at this point.

Refer to the **army_healing_color_adjustment_final.psd** for reference.

CHAPTER 2   ADJUSTMENT LAYERS, BLENDING MODES WITH MASKS FOR PHOTO
            RESTORATION: PART 2

Summary

In this chapter we looked at various layers, masks, blending mode, styles, dialog boxes, and tools that can assist us in color correction of the whole or part of the image. In the next chapter we will look at some of the basic filters that can be used to correct areas where a slight sharpening or blurring is required.

CHAPTER 3

Basic Filters for Photo Restoration

As you work through the process of restoring photos, whether it be to repair minor rips and tears, for selective color correction, or to attempt to fill in gaps after straightening the image, you will encounter various additional correction issues. With older photos and slides, there are always situations where you need to deal with multiple scratches and dust particles that are small, but too time consuming to correct one at a time. After cropping and straightening the image, when you begin the process of filling in the gaps in the image using a selection tool like the Magic Wand tool and then the Edit ➤ Content-Aware Fill command and Clone Stamp tool from Volume 1, you may find this to be a fairly easy process. However, the consequence of doing so without adequately cleaning up all the dust particles overall can result in incorporation of more dust added to the newly generated pixels around the border. Refer to Figure 3-1.

CHAPTER 3   BASIC FILTERS FOR PHOTO RESTORATION

Figure 3-1. *Image cropped and rotated and straightened with layers in the Layers panel*

In these situations, you will encounter the need to correct overall or mask large select areas that require blurring, sharpening, or a reduction in noise, like dust, in set increments before you continue adding new parts to the image or using a clone stamp or content-aware fill on separate layers. Refer to Figure 3-2.

CHAPTER 3 BASIC FILTERS FOR PHOTO RESTORATION

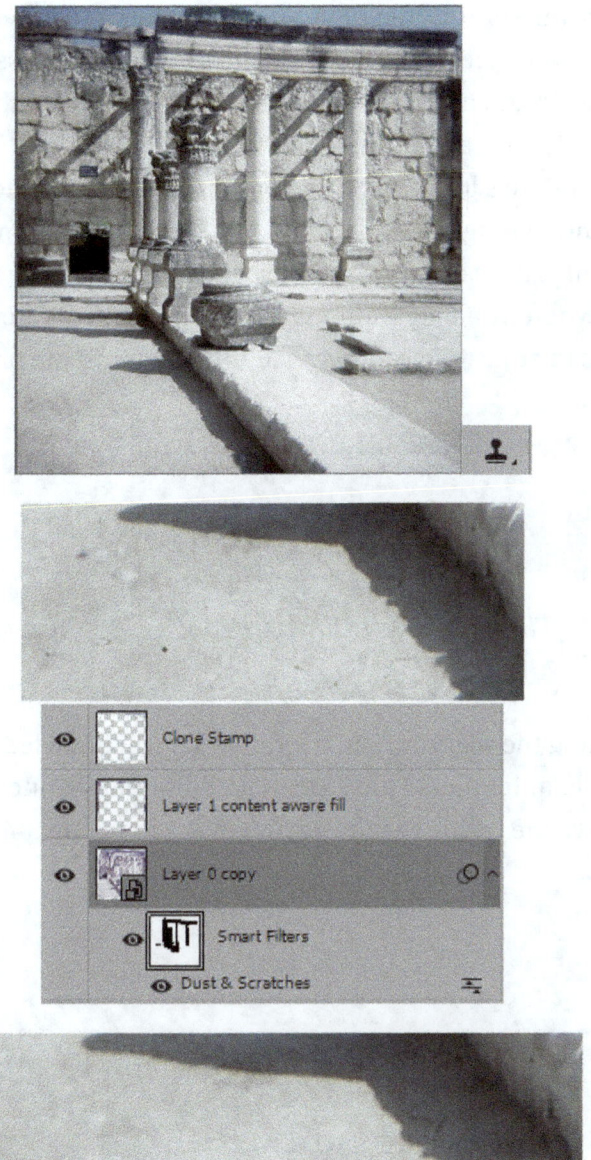

Figure 3-2. *Areas of the image may either require a clone stamp or filter to remove dust and scratches and lessen damage*

CHAPTER 3   BASIC FILTERS FOR PHOTO RESTORATION

Some scanners as noted in Volume 1, Chapter 1, will come with blurring software. However, if during the scanning process the auto software results are not ideal, sometimes you want to do the process yourself and just on a select area of the image.

In Volume 1 we looked at some brush-related tools such as Blur, Sharpen, and Smudge, but while they are helpful with minor areas of correction, it is time consuming to use these brushes overall, and there are situations where you may want to mask some of the blur or sharpening and be able to adjust the setting, as required later in the process. Refer to Figure 3-3.

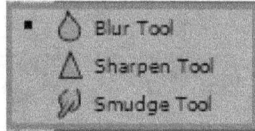

Figure 3-3. *The Blur Tool, Sharpen Tool, and Smudge Tool are found in the Tools panel*

Regarding the scanner, while scanning, I will often leave the scanner settings at default unless I am sure that additional scanner settings will help improve the image repair process. Refer to Figure 3-4.

CHAPTER 3 BASIC FILTERS FOR PHOTO RESTORATION

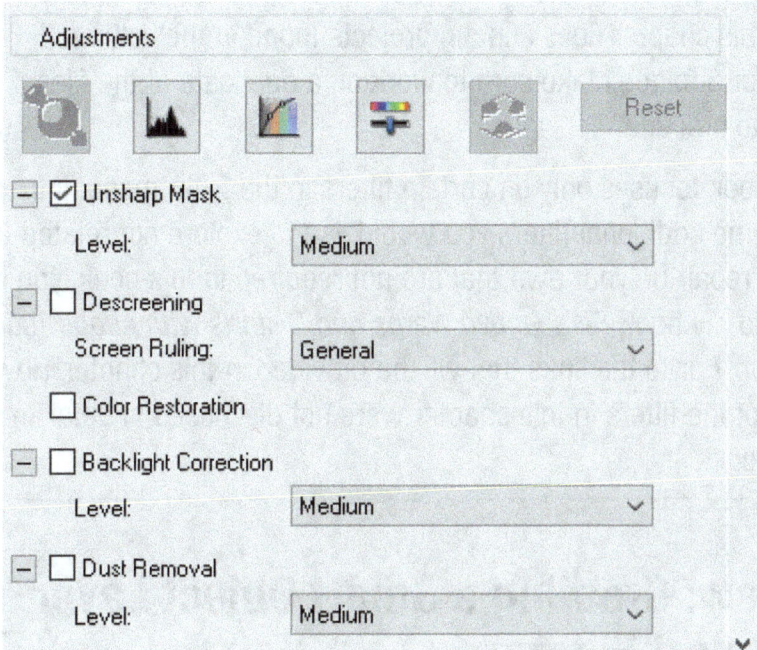

Figure 3-4. *Most scanners will present some adjustment options for color correction and image repair before scanning*

Thankfully, Photoshop has filters that can help us perform many of the same scanner functions of blurring, sharpening, and noise reduction.

In this chapter we will now look at some of Photoshop's basic filters that are found in the Filter menu for blurring, noise reduction, and sharpening and how they can be used on layers in nondestructive ways. We will also discuss how they can be used with layer masks and channels.

Later, I will also discuss a few other basic filters you may want to use to enhance your images, and then we will complete the photo project from the previous chapters.

CHAPTER 3   BASIC FILTERS FOR PHOTO RESTORATION

Note this chapter does contain projects found in the Volume 2 Chapter 3 folder. Make sure to work on a duplicate of the files if you want to practice.

This book focuses only on certain filters in the Filter menu. If there are some additional filters you would like to explore not related to photo repair on your own that are not required in this book, you can refer to my book *Perspective Warps and Distorts with Adobe Tools: Volume 1* or to the links that will be provided in this chapter. However, most of the filters in this chapter were not discussed in detail in that book.

Review: Creating a Smart Object Layer for Smart Filters

As you saw in Chapter 2, you can create smart object layers and apply smart filters to them for the purpose of adjusting color.

However, smart object layers can also be used with the Filter menu so that you can alter most of your basic and advanced filter adjustments at any time. Now we focus on the main filters that can be used for basic digital photo repair. Refer to Figure 3-5.

CHAPTER 3   BASIC FILTERS FOR PHOTO RESTORATION

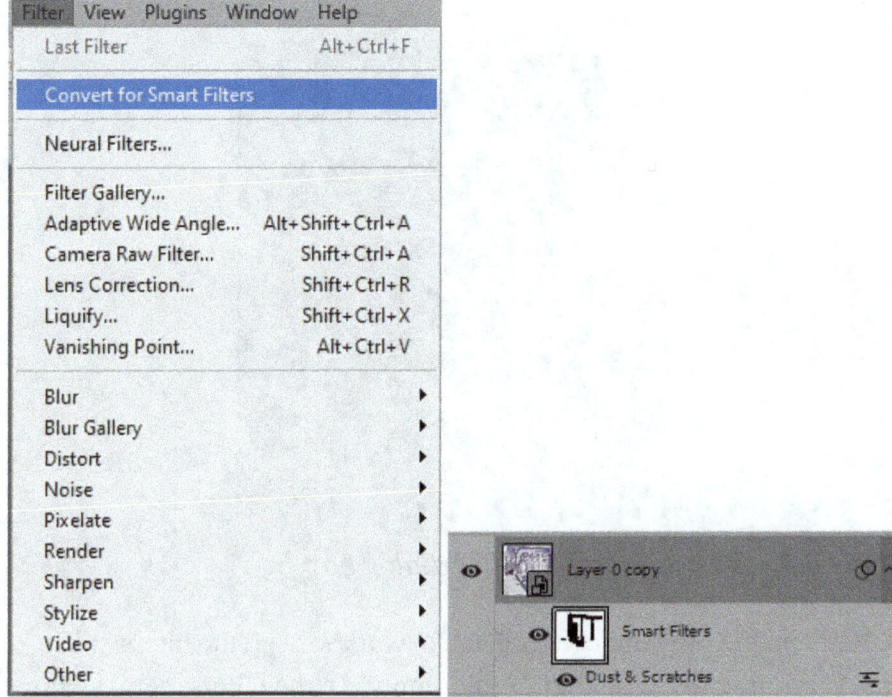

Figure 3-5. *Filter options from the main menu and then filter applied to the layer*

Note that the files I have supplied in the following examples already have the final layers turned into a smart object layer using the Layers panel.

Once a smart filter is applied, you can always return to that filter through the Layers panel by double-clicking the name for additional editing. In the case of the filter Dust & Scratches, we will explore it in more detail later in the chapter. Refer to Figure 3-6.

377

CHAPTER 3　BASIC FILTERS FOR PHOTO RESTORATION

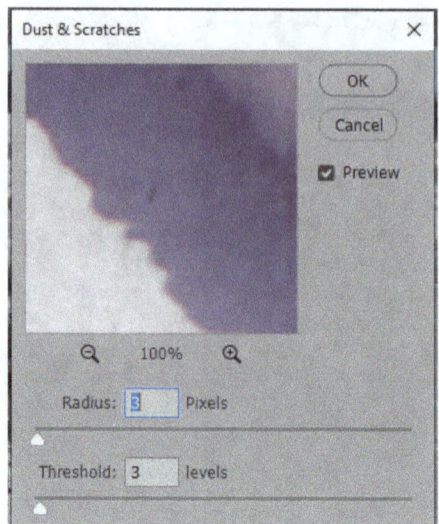

Figure 3-6. *Dust & Scratches filter dialog box*

Remember with your own project, to work with all the filters, make sure that your images are in RGB color mode. In the Filters menu all the filters can work with RGB 8-bit images. However, be aware that some filters may not work in CMYK mode or if the file is set to 16-bit or 32-bit. You can review the link at the end of this chapter if you are working in a color mode other than RGB 8-bit.

Basic Filter Overview Specifically for Photo Correction

In the Filter menu there are four basic sections that I like to use for photo correction. They are the Blur, Blur Gallery, Noise, and Sharpen. We will look at some of the filters within each area, and then later I will mention a few additional helpful filters in other sections, such as Render and Other.

CHAPTER 3 BASIC FILTERS FOR PHOTO RESTORATION

Blur Filters

There are several blur filter options available to you from the Blur filter menu. I have explored quite a number of these in my book *Perspective Warps and Distorts with Adobe Tools: Volume 1*. However, there are a few that were not discussed in detail, and we will focus on five of them in this book as they relate to digital photo repair. Use Filter ➤ Blur to access any of the following I will mention in this section. Refer to Figure 3-7.

Figure 3-7. *Blur filter submenu list*

We will be using the file **deer_blur_image.psd** and **deer_blur_image_final.psd** to review some of these blur filters. Refer to Figure 3-8.

CHAPTER 3 BASIC FILTERS FOR PHOTO RESTORATION

Figure 3-8. *Image of a group of deer on the farm*

While the background is slightly out of focus, you may want to blur the area around the deer more to make it the area of focus. In that case, rather than having a blur overall after you have applied a select blur, you would then paint on the smart filter mask with your Eraser or Brush tool to keep the area of the deer in focus. Using the Options bar panel, I use a variety of round soft and hard brush sizes and make sure to zoom in closely (Ctrl/CMD + +) to get an accurate selection while working on the mask. Switch the default black and white to hide or reveal by pressing D and then press X to toggle between hide/reveal as you paint. Refer to Figure 3-9.

CHAPTER 3 BASIC FILTERS FOR PHOTO RESTORATION

Figure 3-9. *Mask out areas on the smart filter with your Brush tool, Eraser tool, and Tools panel swatches after the filter has been applied*

First, I will note that with filters Average, Blur, and Blur More have no dialog box settings. Testing these on a smart object layer is ideal if you want to use them to compare settings. Average can be used to average all colors, while Blur or Blur More blurs an image. However, when you use them, you can't control how much of a blur occurs, as there is no way to set a precise value. In the case of Average, you will likely end up with a solid color fill, and for photo repair this is not helpful. Refer to Figure 3-10.

CHAPTER 3   BASIC FILTERS FOR PHOTO RESTORATION

Figure 3-10. *Applying the Average filter to the image and how it appears on a smart object layer in the Layers panel*

Blur and Blur More will produce a very subtle blur, but there is no way to increase or adjust the amount. Refer to Figure 3-11.

CHAPTER 3 BASIC FILTERS FOR PHOTO RESTORATION

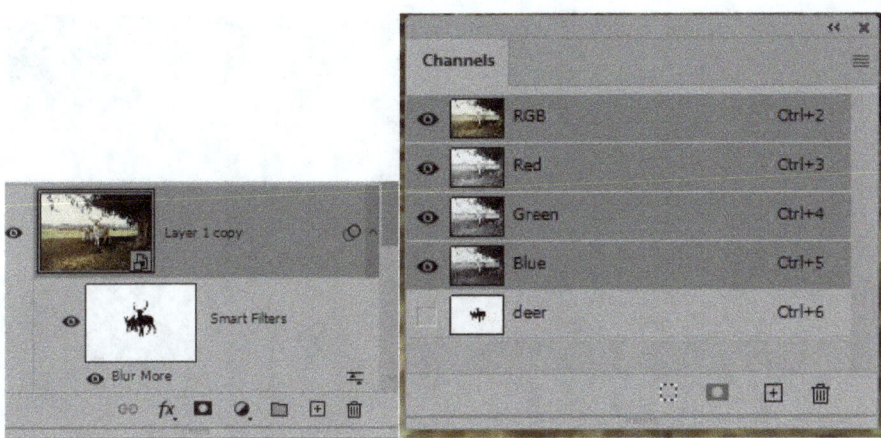

Figure 3-11. *How the Blur More filter appears on the smart object layer in the Layers panel and the mask in the Channels panel*

Tip If you need to remove a filter while you work, drag it to the trash can icon to delete it. However, be aware that if you remove all smart filters, you will also delete your smart filter mask so you may want to save your selection in the Channels panel or as a layer mask on a duplicate layer for backup to avoid having to recreate complex masks. From the Channels panel or the layer mask, you could then load the selection by Ctrl/CMD + clicking the thumbnail before adding the smart filter, and it will add it to the smart filter mask. In my examples I have saved the masks in the Channels panel for you should you want to quickly add them to your smart filters as you work if they are not already present in the Layers panel. Refer to Figure 3-11.

The filters Box Blur, Radial Blur, and Shape Blur are for creating specialized artistic blur effects, such as square, round, twisted, or even a blur based on the selection of a custom shape known as a kernel. Your selection or mask needs to be exact so that it does not appear unevenly blended. Refer to Figures 3-12 and 3-13.

CHAPTER 3   BASIC FILTERS FOR PHOTO RESTORATION

Figure 3-12. *Box Blur and Radial Blur filters applied around the deer*

Figure 3-13. *Shape Blur dialog box and the filter applied to the image of the deer*

CHAPTER 3　BASIC FILTERS FOR PHOTO RESTORATION

However, for photo repair, the five blur filters that I like to use are Gaussian Blur, Lens Blur, Motion Blur, Smart Blur, and Surface Blur.

Gaussian Blur

This is a helpful blur when you want to create an overall blur quickly, or you may create a selection and then layer mask when you want some areas to remain in focus as seen with the deer. The radius of the blur can be set from 0.1 to 1000 px. In this case I used a setting of 1.6 pixels and previewed the image. Refer to Figure 3-14.

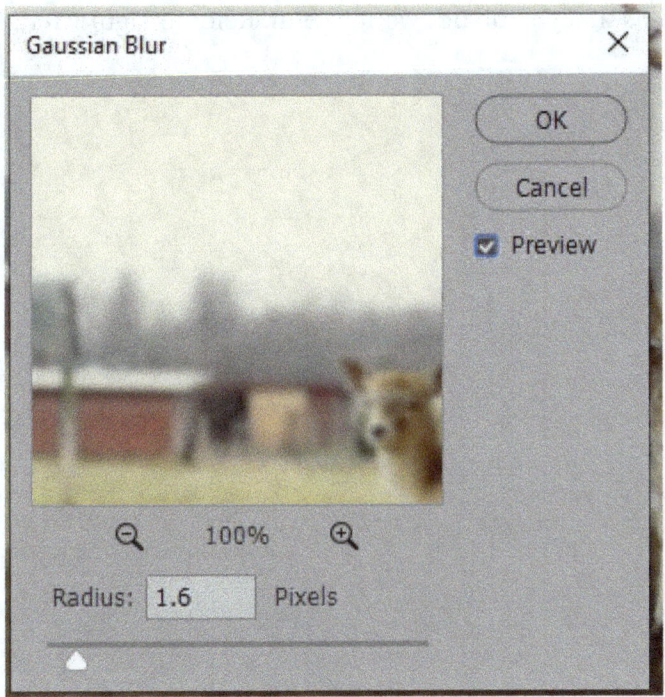

Figure 3-14. Gaussian Blur dialog box

In the dialog box, use the zoom-out (–) and zoom-in (+) magnifying glass icons when you want to zoom in on a section in the preview box to see a blurred area up close and zoom out after. Drag in the preview area

385

when you need to move the image about and compare the blur in certain areas. You can also toggle Preview on and off to compare the settings in the dialog box to the canvas.

Optionally, use the Alt/Option key to change the Cancel button to Reset to reset your original slider settings if you click the button. Holding down the Ctrl/CMD key changes the Cancel button to the Default button. These options can be found for most filters.

Click OK to commit the changes. Refer to Figure 3-14.

Outside the dialog box, at any time, you can use a selected smart filter layer mask and a soft or hard eraser brush to paint back some of the detailed areas that you do not want to blur. Refer to Figure 3-15.

CHAPTER 3   BASIC FILTERS FOR PHOTO RESTORATION

Figure 3-15. *Image of deer with Gaussian Blur applied to the surrounding mask in the Layers panel*

Remember to click back on the smart object thumbnail when you want to apply another filter, or you may apply the filter to the smart filter or a layer mask by mistake.

For an overall Gaussian Blur, consider low-light images where you want to reduce film grain. But care should still be taken that you do not lose important details or shift the colors in the process. In this case I just used a setting of 0.6 pixels as I wanted to keep as much fine detail as possible. See **sunset_gaussian_blur.psd** as a reference. Refer to Figure 3-16.

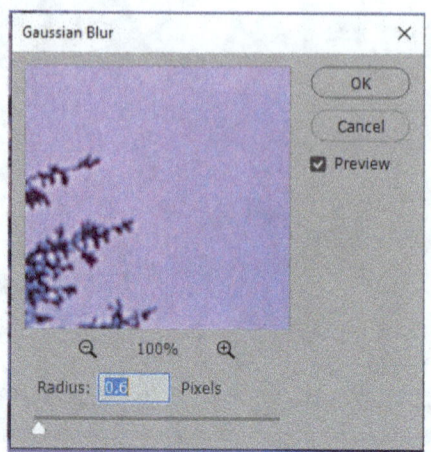

Figure 3-16. *Gaussian Blur dialog box with the blur applied to the smart object layer along with the previous color adjustment in the Layers panel*

CHAPTER 3   BASIC FILTERS FOR PHOTO RESTORATION

Note that ordering your color adjustments and smart filters on a smart object layer can affect how colors would appear. In the earlier example (Figure 3-16), I placed the Gaussian Blur filter above the Shadows/Highlights adjustment. However, if I drag it below this color adjustment, you will notice that the colors in the image will darken, which may not be what you want. Refer to Figure 3-17.

Figure 3-17. *The blur applied to the smart object layer along with the previous color adjustment in the Layers panel with order reversed in the Layers panel*

In this case I left the Gaussian Blur above the Shadows/Highlights adjustment. Refer to Figure 3-16.

389

CHAPTER 3 BASIC FILTERS FOR PHOTO RESTORATION

The word *Gaussian* refers to the bell-shaped curve function calculation (named after the mathematician and scientist Carl Friedrich Gauss). Photoshop uses this function to generate and apply a weighted average to the pixels. By adjusting the slider, the filter produces a low-frequency detail and can produce a hazy or blurred effect in lowered or elevated values. Refer to Figure 3-18.

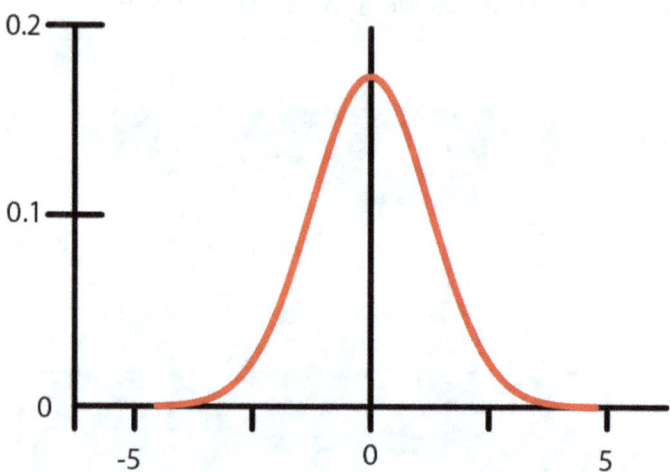

Figure 3-18. Graph of an example of a Gaussian Blur curve

The Gaussian Blur filter, as well as some of the other blur filters like Box, Motion, and Shape, should be observed closely as you apply them as they can sometimes produce some unexpected visual effects near the edges of a selection. You should try to feather your blur on your layer mask with your Eraser or Brush tool if the blur does not blend correctly. Here we see a kind of glow or outline around areas of the deer's antlers. Refer to Figure 3-19.

CHAPTER 3 BASIC FILTERS FOR PHOTO RESTORATION

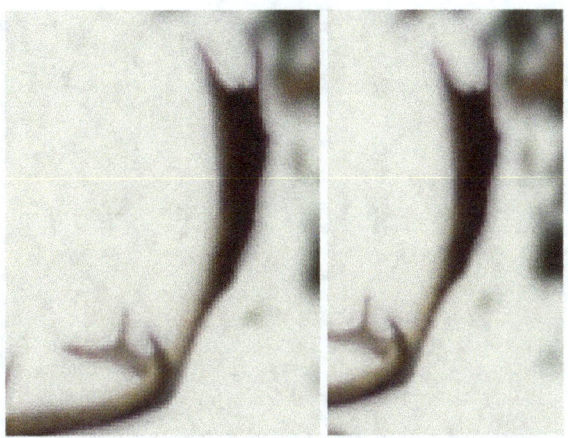

Figure 3-19. *Areas between mask and blur need to feather correctly to avoid unwanted banding around the border of the mask on the antlers*

Reducing the hardness of the brush using the Options bar panel Brush Preset picker can minimize this, causing a better blend.

Alternatively, in a very simple masked area, you may want to use your Properties panel to feather the selection. However, in this complex example I would not recommend doing that as it may affect small areas where you want to retain mask details. Leave the Feather setting at 0 px. Refer to Figure 3-20.

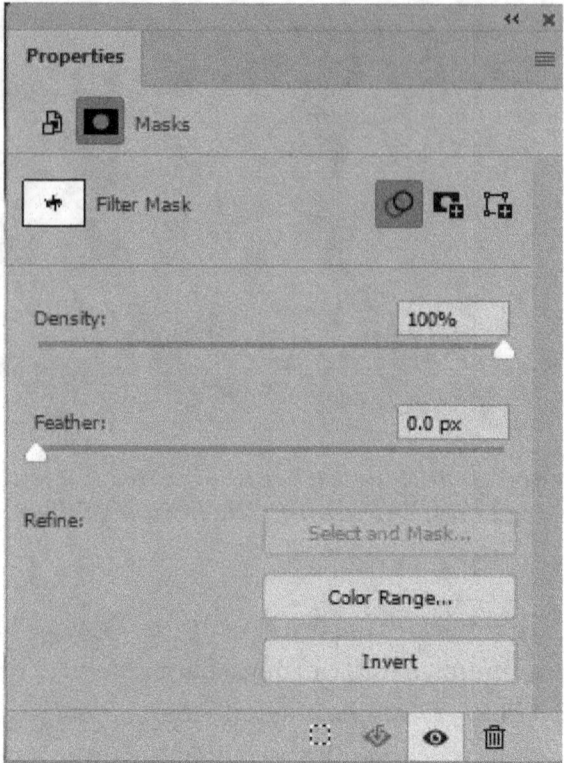

Figure 3-20. Properties panel with Filter Mask active

This uneven blend is more apparent on normal and smart object layers that have a mask painted on, rather than when you are applying the effect to the entire layer. Some blur filters, like Gaussian, use the image data that is outside of the current selection to create the new blurry pixels that will reside inside the selection of blur. Areas that border around the blurred (out-of-focus) selection may be contaminated with colors producing a muddy outline around the area that you want to keep in focus.

To avoid such issues, you will later want to experiment with other blur options like Smart Blur, Lens Blur, or Surface Blur.

File ➤ Save your work on your copy of the image **deer_blur_image.psd**. We will return to this image again later.

Lens Blur

Lens Blur is used to blur an image to give the effect of a narrower depth of field so that some objects in the image stay in focus, while other areas are blurred. While this is a helpful filter, unfortunately, it is one of the few that cannot be used on a smart object layer, and so you must work on a duplicate layer of the image if you don't want to destroy the original. In this case, if you already had a smart object layer, you could duplicate that layer and then, from the Layers panel, choose Rasterize Layer. I will be using the example file **Canoe_lens_blur.psd** in this case. Refer to Figure 3-21.

CHAPTER 3　BASIC FILTERS FOR PHOTO RESTORATION

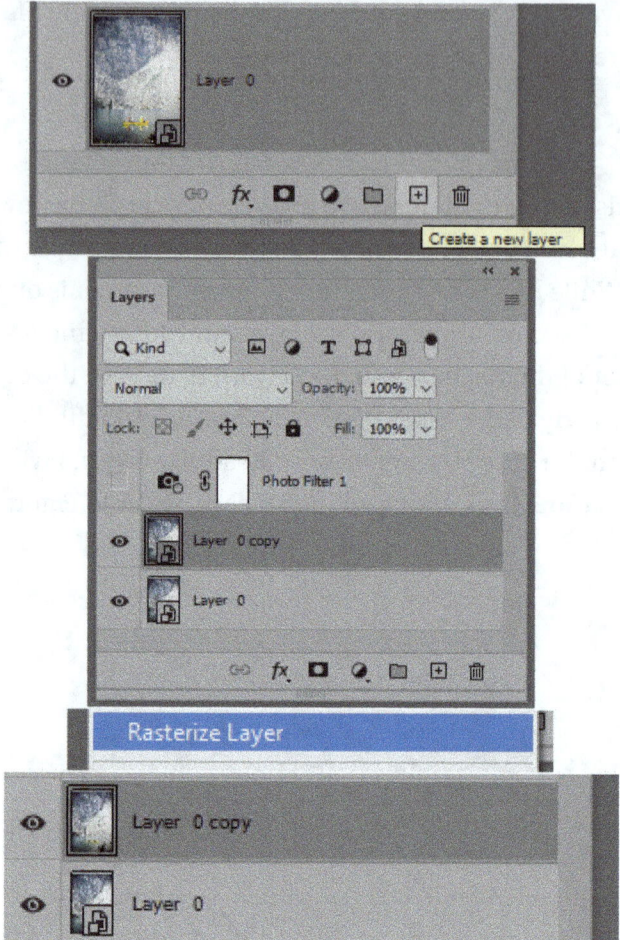

Figure 3-21. *In the Layers panel rasterize a copy of the smart object layer for working with the Lens Blur filter*

In the Lens Blur workspace, we can review the following blur tools and options. Make sure that the Preview check box is enabled. Refer to Figure 3-22.

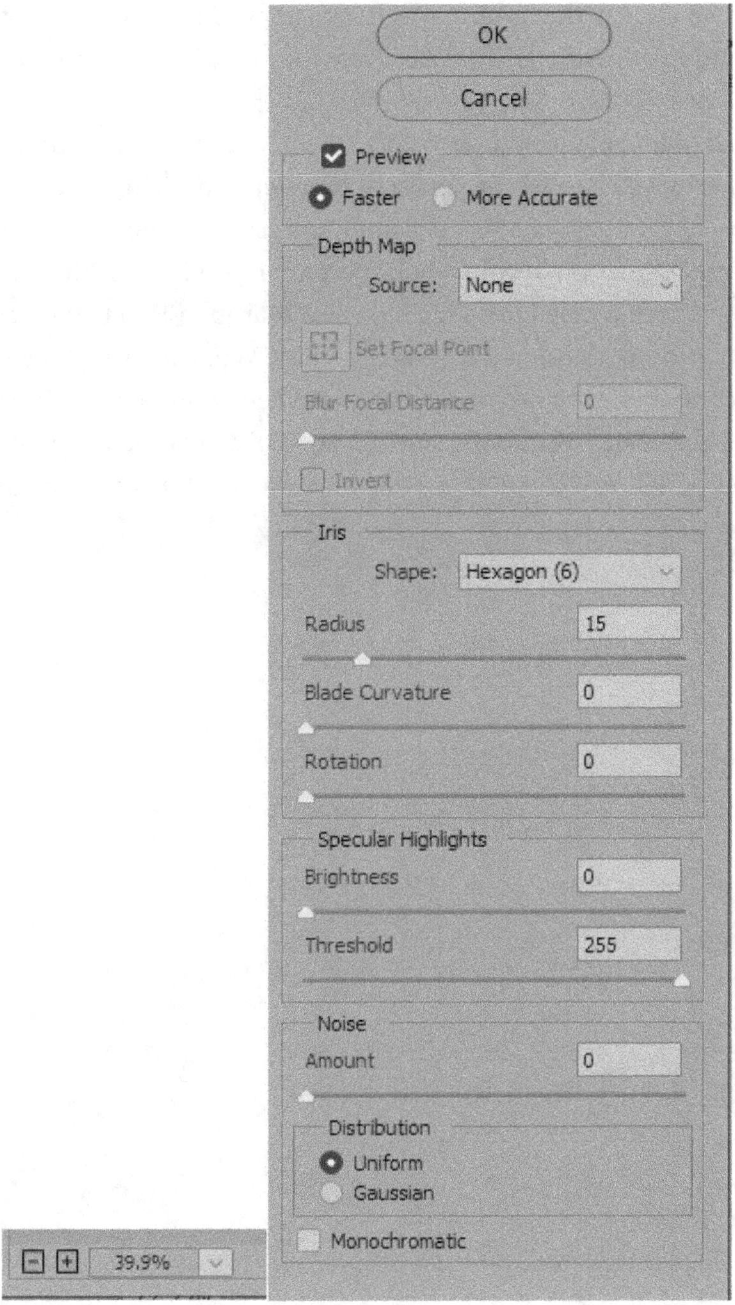

CHAPTER 3 BASIC FILTERS FOR PHOTO RESTORATION

Figure 3-22. *Lens Blur workspace options*

You can choose the option of either Faster or More Accurate. Stay on the setting of Faster as More Accurate may take longer to process. Refer to Figure 3-22.

Depth Map: Set the source to either None, Transparency, or Layer Mask, or select a channel that may contain depth map information. Transparency and Layer Mask will allow access to the next set of options. If you have a selection in your Channels panel, you can use this as your focal point. In this case I used my Elliptical Marquee Tool to create a selection prior to entering the Lens Blur filter. While active, I then saved the selection using the menu Select ➤ Save Selection to open the dialog box, gave the selection a name, and clicked OK so it appeared in the Channels panel. You will find the selection created for you in the file. Refer to Figure 3-23.

CHAPTER 3 BASIC FILTERS FOR PHOTO RESTORATION

Figure 3-23. *Creating and saving a selection for Lens Blur in the Channels panel prior to using Lens Blur*

CHAPTER 3   BASIC FILTERS FOR PHOTO RESTORATION

Then, I went to Filter ➤ Blur ➤ Lens Blur, and in the Depth Map Source list it will appear as one of the Source options and you can select it. Refer to Figure 3-24.

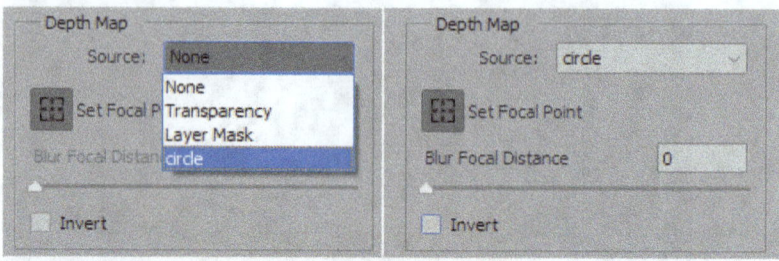

Figure 3-24. *Lens Blur filter Depth Map settings when the saved selection is chosen and how it currently previews*

CHAPTER 3 BASIC FILTERS FOR PHOTO RESTORATION

For the moment that area will appear blurry, which you can correct.

Set Focal Point: Click somewhere in the canvas, in this case in between the two canoeists, to set a focal point. This blurs the surrounding area and leaves the canoe and its occupants in focus. Refer to Figure 3-25.

Figure 3-25. *Applying the selection to the Lens Blur as a focal point*

Use the Blur Focal Distance slider to set a value (0–255). This allows you to select an "in-focus" depth. In this case I left it at 255, so I did not blur the people in the boat. Refer to Figure 3-26.

CHAPTER 3 BASIC FILTERS FOR PHOTO RESTORATION

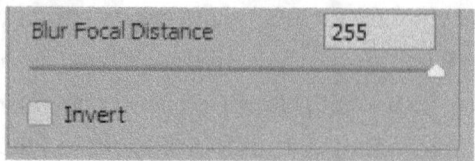

Figure 3-26. Lens Blur workspace setting the Blur Focal Distance

The Invert check box setting, when toggled, allows you to flip close and far depths in the depth map or reverse the blur as you saw earlier. Refer to Figures 3-26 and 3-24.

The Iris settings allow you to adjust the lens shape or, in this case, the surrounding blur around the selection. Refer to Figure 3-27.

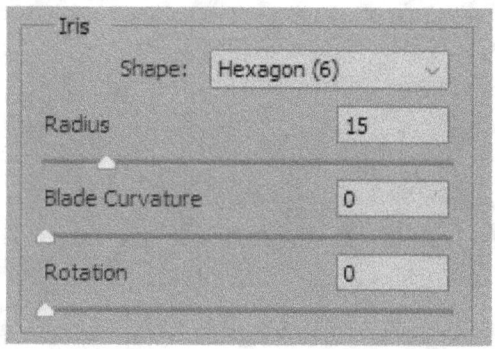

Figure 3-27. Lens Blur Iris settings

You can choose a shape from the list, such as Hexagon (6). The options range from Triangle (3) to Octagon (8), each giving a slightly different blurring result. This will become more apparent as you adjust other settings in this section. For now, remain on Hexagon (6). Refer to Figure 3-28.

CHAPTER 3 BASIC FILTERS FOR PHOTO RESTORATION

Figure 3-28. *Lens Blur Iris settings Shape options of 3, 6, and 8*

Radius: Lets you set the maximum amount of blur (0–100). A setting of 15 makes the transition from blur to in focus subtle, while a setting of 29 makes the selection area more apparent. Refer to Figure 3-29.

CHAPTER 3 BASIC FILTERS FOR PHOTO RESTORATION

Figure 3-29. *Lens Blur Iris Radius adjustments and preview*

Blade Curvature: Sets the roundness of the iris (0–100). If the Iris is already rounder, like a hexagon, it may have little effect. However, if you set the shape to Triangle (3) and move the slider, you may notice a shift in the blur. Refer to Figure 3-30.

CHAPTER 3 BASIC FILTERS FOR PHOTO RESTORATION

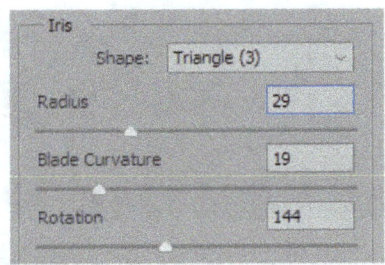

***Figure 3-30.** Lens Blur Iris Blade Curvature adjustments and preview*

Rotation: Sets the amount of iris rotation (0–360). This setting is noticeable when set to Shape: Triangle (3) rather than Hexagon (6) and you move the slider.

Specular highlights, as mentioned in Chapter 1, are often the bright spots you see on shiny objects like fruits or foreheads on very sunny days. For this section you can control the following sliders. Refer to Figure 3-31.

403

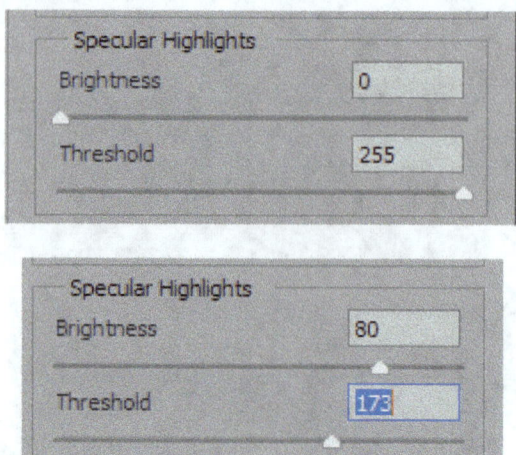

Figure 3-31. *Lens Blur Specular Highlights options*

Brightness: Sets the amount of highlight brightness boost (0–100). By default, it is set to 0, but move the slider to a higher number like 80 to see some of the highlights in the blur more vividly.

Threshold: Selects which pixels to brighten (0–255). By default, it is set to 255, but move it down to 173 to see how it affects the blur area of the image. Refer to Figure 3-32.

CHAPTER 3   BASIC FILTERS FOR PHOTO RESTORATION

Figure 3-32. *Lens Blur preview of current settings with a Triangle shape Iris*

The last section, called Noise, is also common in many of the often used filters to add or remove graininess or pixilation from images. Refer to Figure 3-33.

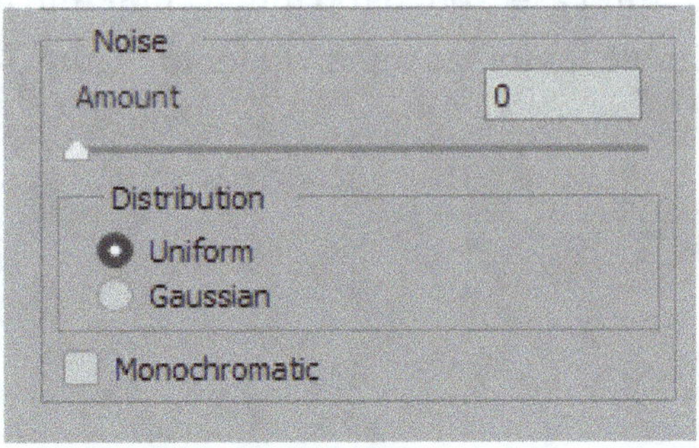

Figure 3-33. *Lens Blur Noise settings*

CHAPTER 3 BASIC FILTERS FOR PHOTO RESTORATION

Amount: Sets the amount of noise to add to each pixel (0–100). By default, it is set to 0, but if you increase it to 4, you will start to notice a noise forming in the blur of the shadows. Refer to Figure 3-34.

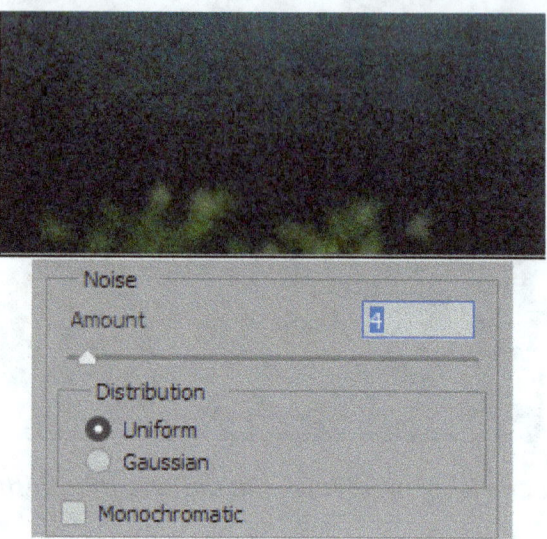

Figure 3-34. Lens Blur Noise settings with resultant Uniform noise added to shadow in preview

Distribution: Can be set to either Uniform (flat) noise or Gaussian noise. Gaussian, in this case, added too much color into the noise, and this would not be desirable for image repair. Refer to Figure 3-35.

CHAPTER 3 BASIC FILTERS FOR PHOTO RESTORATION

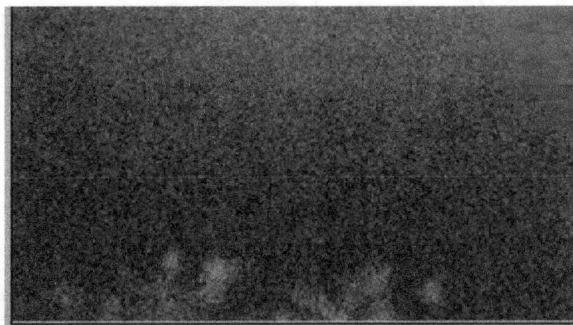

Figure 3-35. *Lens Blur Noise settings with resultant Gaussian noise added to shadow in preview*

Monochromatic: Makes the added noise gray rather than colorful. Some images that are not intended to be full color can benefit from this setting. Refer to Figure 3-36.

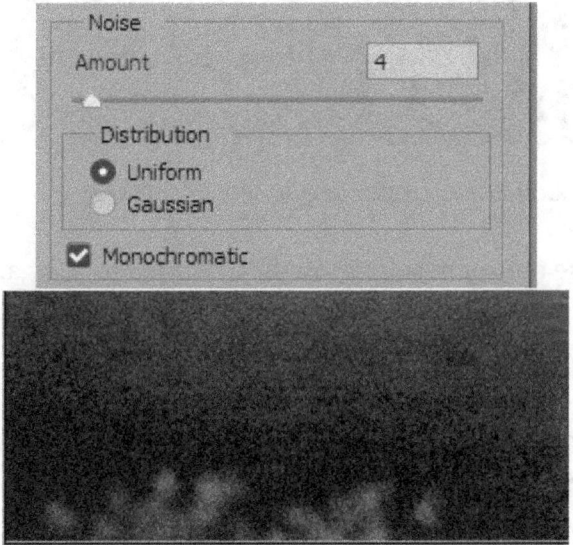

Figure 3-36. *Lens Blur Noise settings with resultant Uniform Monochromatic noise added to shadow in preview*

CHAPTER 3 BASIC FILTERS FOR PHOTO RESTORATION

However, in this case I would recommend keeping your noise amount at 0 and disabling the Monochromatic setting for a smooth blur and keeping at Uniform. Refer to Figures 3-33, 3-34 and 3-37.

Figure 3-37. Lens Blur preview of current settings

You can use the zoom settings in the lower left to navigate or use Ctrl/CMD + + or Ctrl/CMD + – to zoom in and out. Refer to Figure 3-38.

Use Ctrl/CMD + Z to undo or Alt/Option + click the Cancel button to reset.

Holding down the Ctrl/CMD key changes the Cancel button to the Default button.

You can also use the spacebar key if you do need to access your Hand tool.

Once you have adjusted the settings to your preference, click OK to confirm settings. Refer to Figure 3-38.

CHAPTER 3 BASIC FILTERS FOR PHOTO RESTORATION

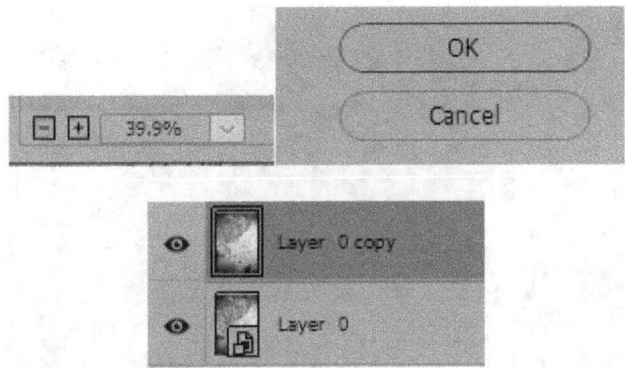

Figure 3-38. *Lens Blur OK and Cancel buttons with result in the Layers panel on the normal layer*

Upon exit the changes will be applied to the layer permanently. If your selection is still active, use Select ➤ Deselect (Ctrl/CMD + D) to deselect on Image.

If you want to work with similar features such as Lens Blur on a smart object layer, you may want to experiment with Blur Gallery later in the chapter.

Further details on Lens Blur can be found at the following link:

https://helpx.adobe.com/photoshop/using/adjusting-image-sharpness-blur.html#add_lens_blur

File ➤ Save your work and refer to my file **Canoe_lens_blur_final.psd**.

Motion Blur

This filter is used to give the effect of movement when taking a picture with a fixed exposure time, such as someone running, a car racing, or an object falling, also known as action shots. If you did not have a fast-enough exposure time or a slow shutter speed like 1/60 and the camera was not mounted on a tripod, as the person, animal, or object moves quickly before the lens, you would have a blur. Refer to Figure 3-39.

CHAPTER 3   BASIC FILTERS FOR PHOTO RESTORATION

Figure 3-39. *Examples of Motion Blur due to a fast-moving cat*

Sometimes, you want to add blur to make it appear like very fast action is happening. But you don't want everything to be entirely out of focus while still capturing the main action. In that case you can set the following settings in the Motion Blur dialog box. In this example of the dog jumping in the water, he was captured clearly because the shutter speed was very quick. Use a copy of the file **dog_motion_blur.psd** and refer to **dog_motion_blur_final.psd**. Refer to Figure 3-40.

Figure 3-40. *Image of dog bounding through the water at the beach*

CHAPTER 3 BASIC FILTERS FOR PHOTO RESTORATION

I used Filter ➤ Blur ➤ Motion Blur and set the following settings:

Angle (-360°, 0°, 360°): Sets a direction of blur to create the effect of movement. If I set the speed of the water, I could leave it level at the angle at 0°. However, because I am trying to show the dog rising quickly out of the water, I will change the angle to -30°.

Distance (1–2000 pixels): This controls the level of the intensity of the blur to the pixels. Large numbers drag the pixels outward giving the impression of speed to an otherwise stationary image. I set it to 141 pixels. Refer to Figure 3-41.

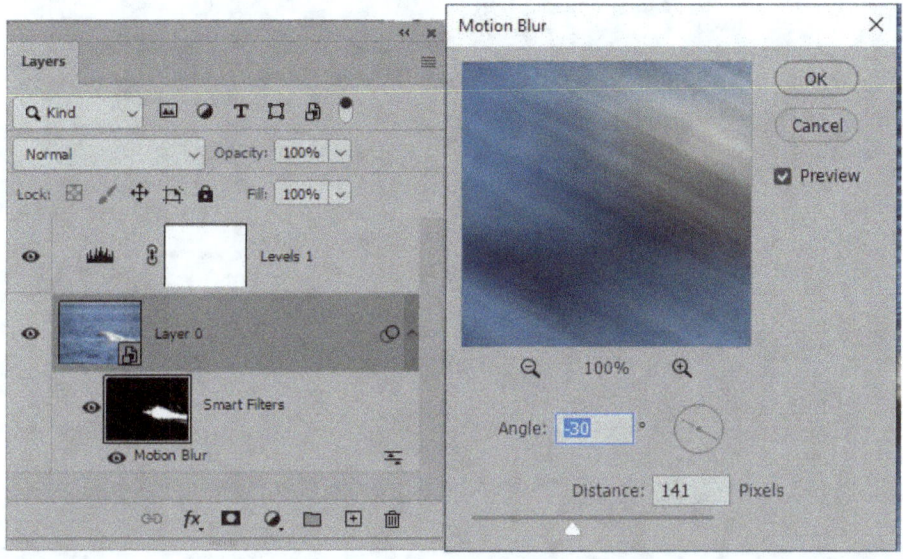

Figure 3-41. *Layers panel with a smart filter mask and Motion Blur applied and settings in the dialog box*

In the dialog box, use the zoom-out (-) and zoom-in (+) magnifying glass icons when you want to zoom in on a section in the preview box to see a blurred area up close and zoom out after. You can move the preview if you need to see another location. You can also toggle Preview on and off to compare the settings in the dialog box to the canvas.

411

Optionally, Use the Alt/Option key to change the Cancel button to Reset to reset your original slider settings, if you click on it. Holding down the Ctrl/CMD key changes the Cancel button to the Default button.

Click OK to commit the changes.

I also painted on the smart filter mask with my Eraser tool and then, using the Properties panel, feathered the smart filter mask so that the dog and some of the water would appear blurred, making it appear like the dog was moving much faster out of the water. I used Feather: 17.1px. Refer to Figure 3-42.

CHAPTER 3 BASIC FILTERS FOR PHOTO RESTORATION

Figure 3-42. *Properties panel with feathering applied to the filter mask altered with the Eraser tool and the resulting image*

Remember as with the Layer mask, if you do not want to see the filter effect until you start to paint on the mask with white you can invert the Filter mask to black and then start to paint the white back with the eraser or brush. File ➤ Save your work for now and refer to **dog_motion_blur_final.psd**. We will return to this image later.

Smart Blur

Smart Blur is considered a more precise blur with additional settings. If you return to the image of the deer (**deer_blur_image.psd** and **deer_blur_image_final.psd**), you can see how this blur compares to the Gaussian Blur in the background. Refer to Figure 3-43.

Figure 3-43. Deer image with a smart filter applied

Go to Filter ➤ Blur ➤ Smart Blur and refer to Figure 3-44.

CHAPTER 3 BASIC FILTERS FOR PHOTO RESTORATION

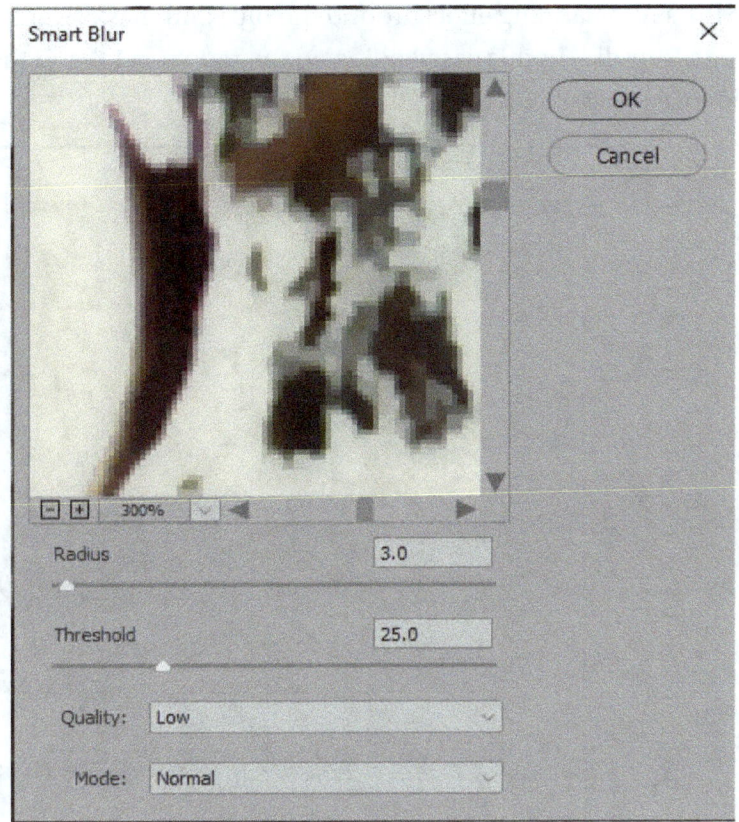

Figure 3-44. *Smart Blur dialog box*

In the dialog box you can set the following settings:

Radius (0.1–100.0): A set value determines the size of the area searched for dissimilar pixels.

Threshold (0.1–100.0): This value determines how dissimilar pixels should be before they are affected. This setting works together with the Radius value.

As you work with these two sliders, be aware, as you blur, not to give your image a blocky or posterized appearance. That can be OK for an artistic effect, but not for photo repair that needs to be smooth. At the current setting (Figure 3-44), we can see however that this blur does

CHAPTER 3   BASIC FILTERS FOR PHOTO RESTORATION

not have the same banding effect around the blur and mask selection as Gaussian Blur did. In this case I adjusted the radius to 1.3 and the threshold to about 8.9. Refer to Figure 3-45.

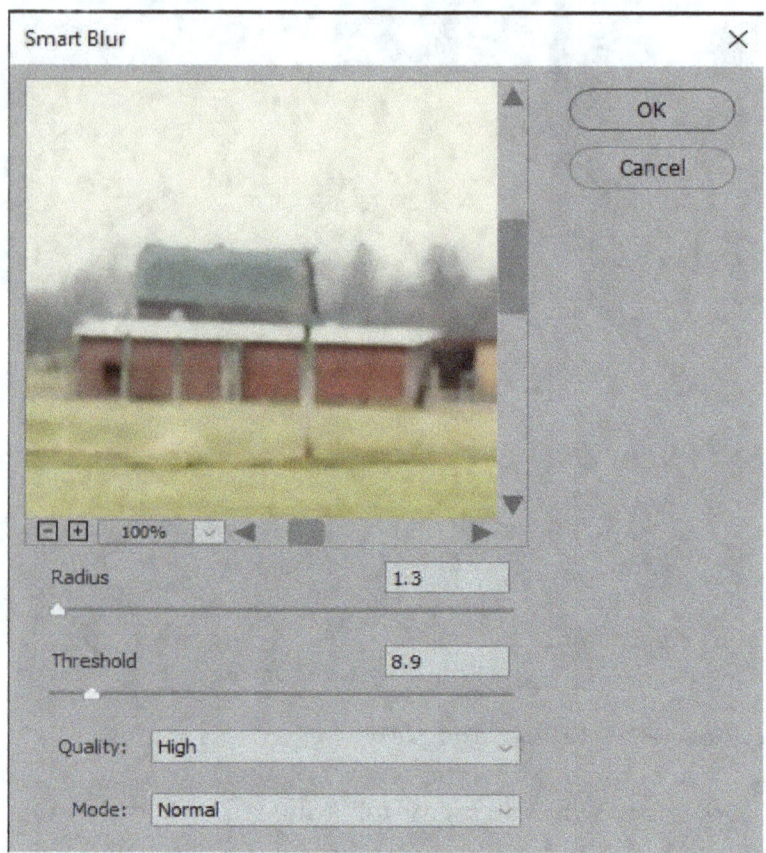

Figure 3-45. *Smart Blur dialog box with adjusted settings*

Quality (Low, Medium, High): Sets the quality of the blur. You may need to zoom in close to areas of the image to see the changes. Use a high blur setting when you want a smoother appearance.

Mode (Normal, Edge Only, Overlay Edge): Normal is the default and is set for the entire selection. However, for artistic effects that alter the edges of color transitions, you can use the other options of Edge Only or Overlay Edge. Refer to Figure 3-46.

CHAPTER 3 BASIC FILTERS FOR PHOTO RESTORATION

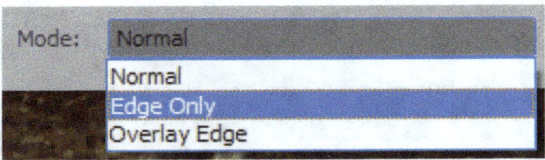

Figure 3-46. *Smart Blur dialog box with adjusted settings in Mode: Edge Only and Overlay Edge*

Adobe mentions that in areas of significant contrast, Edge Only will apply black-and-white edges, and Overlay Edge will apply white, but leave some color visible.

Tip These settings could be used with the layer's Smart Blur filter set to a blending mode option, which would define edges. For example, in the Filter dialog box, if you tried the mode of Edge Only, clicked OK, and then afterward set your blending mode option in that dialog box to Subtract, this could result in the appearance of an illustration-like drawing, but still retains some photographic potential. Refer to Figure 3-47.

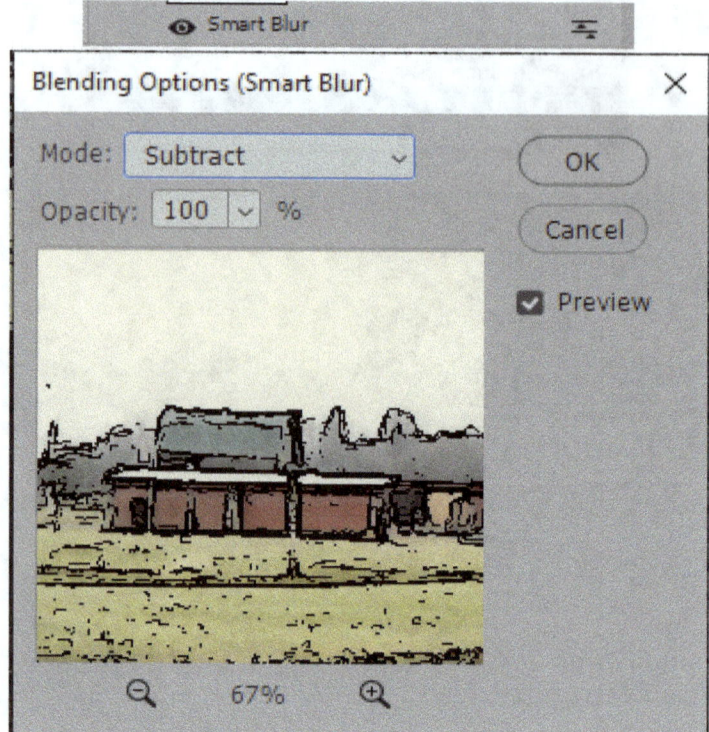

Figure 3-47. *Smart Blur filter Blending Options with a mode of Subtract and opacity of 100%*

In the Smart Blur dialog box, use the zoom-out (-) and zoom-in (+) magnifying glass icons when you want to zoom in on a section in the preview box to see a blurred area up close and zoom out after. You can move the preview around to compare settings on the board to the canvas.

Optionally, use the Alt/Option key to change the Cancel button to Reset to reset your original slider settings. Holding down the Ctrl/CMD key changes the Cancel button to the Default button. Refer to Figures 3-45 and 3-47.

In this case I left the filter's mode on Normal, clicked OK to commit the changes, and left the Blending Options Mode on Normal with Opacity at 100%. The blur is definably more subtle than the Gaussian, but it does create a smooth blend of the colors in areas like the barn and grass. Refer to Figure 3-48.

CHAPTER 3   BASIC FILTERS FOR PHOTO RESTORATION

Figure 3-48. *Smart Blur filter applied to the deer image in Normal mode*

File ➤ Save you work, and you can refer to my file **deer_blur_image_final.psd** if you need a reference to both Gaussian Blur and Smart Blur examples.

Surface Blur

Surface Blur is useful for blurring the image while preserving the edges. It can often be used over skin for an even blur. It is also used to create special effects while removing noise or graininess.

Refer to my images files **falcon_surface_blur.psd** and **falcon_surface_blur_final.psd**. In this example I want to blur the area surrounding the small kestrel bird. Refer to Figure 3-49.

CHAPTER 3   BASIC FILTERS FOR PHOTO RESTORATION

Figure 3-49.   Image of a kestrel resting on a man's hand

You can use the sliders in the dialog box to control the following settings. Refer to Figure 3-50.

CHAPTER 3   BASIC FILTERS FOR PHOTO RESTORATION

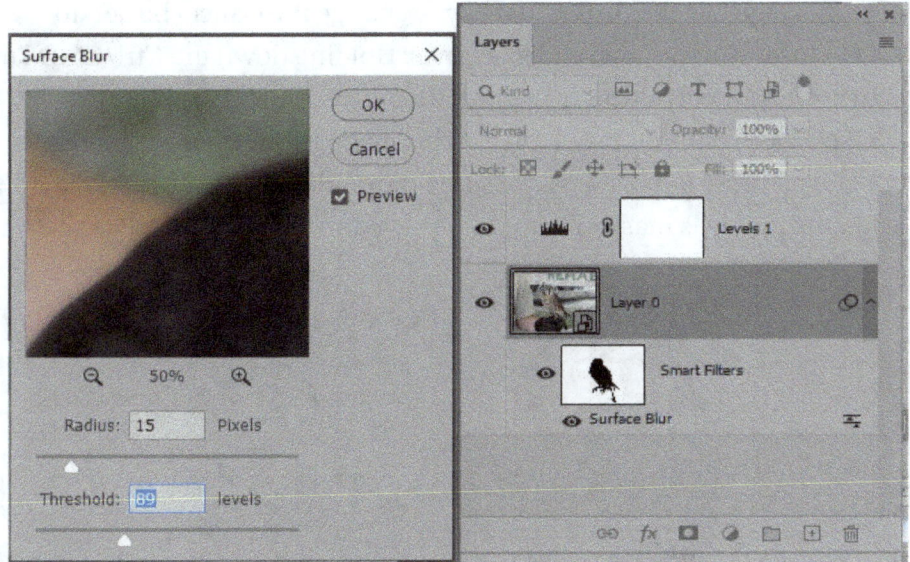

Figure 3-50. *Surface Blur dialog box and Layers panel with a smart filter and filter mask*

Radius (1–100 pixels): This is the size of the area that is sampled for the blur. I set it to 15 pixels.

Threshold (2–255 levels): Controls how much the tonal values of neighboring or adjacent pixels must diverge from the center pixel value before becoming part of the blur. Pixels with tonal value differences less than the threshold level value are excluded from the resulting blur. Radius and Threshold values work together to determine this final blur calculation on the canvas. In this case I set it to 89 levels as I did not want to overblur but blend the image with the area that I wanted to remain in focus, which I later painted out on the smart filter mask with my Eraser tool.

In the dialog box, use the zoom-out (–) and zoom-in (+) magnifying glass icons when you want to zoom in on a section in the preview box to see a blurred area up close and zoom out after. You can move the preview area if you need to compare other areas of the image. You can also toggle Preview on and off to compare settings in the dialog box to the canvas.

421

Optionally, use the Alt/Option key to change the Cancel button to Reset to reset your original slider settings. Holding down the Ctrl/CMD key changes the Cancel button to the Default button.

Click OK to commit the changes. This made the man's arm and glove appear a bit more out of focus, yet some minor details were preserved now so that the bird was masked to make it the main focus. Refer to Figure 3-51.

Figure 3-51. *Surface Blur applied to the area surrounding the kestrel*

Alternatively, you could also experiment with adding a second Surface Blur with different settings like Radius: 44 and Threshold: 91 on a duplicate copy of the image. However, you would have to add a layer mask and paint on that to mask out a separate selection area, as the current smart filter mask affects all filters applied to that specific layer. Refer to Figure 3-52.

CHAPTER 3   BASIC FILTERS FOR PHOTO RESTORATION

Figure 3-52. *Layers panel example of applying two surface blurs to different smart object layers with filter mask and layer mask*

File ➤ Save your work and check out my file **falcon_surface_blur_final.psd** for reference.

Now we will look at the next set of blur filter options.

Blur Gallery Filters

The Blur Gallery (Filter ➤ Blur Gallery) is a type of workspace that has five kinds of blur that you can use with smart object layers. Some of these blurs I have discussed in the book I mentioned in the beginning of this chapter, for the purpose of creating unique warped and artistic effects. However, three, which relate to digital repair or improvement, were not discussed in detail, which we will now focus on in this book. They are Field Blur, Iris Blur, and Tilt-Shift. Refer to Figure 3-53.

423

CHAPTER 3   BASIC FILTERS FOR PHOTO RESTORATION

Figure 3-53.   Filter ➤ Blur Gallery submenu

We will practice with the following **road_image.psd**. Refer to Figure 3-54.

Figure 3-54.   Image looking down at the town, river, and roads from a mountain

Upon opening the workspace, you will find all of these five filters present in the gallery, so you do not have to add them one at a time as you work in a single smart object layer.

If you choose, for example, Filter ➤ Blur Gallery ➤ Field Blur, then this will be currently selected on the right side with a check box enabled,

CHAPTER 3 BASIC FILTERS FOR PHOTO RESTORATION

and the options will be expanded in the Blur Tools panel, while the others that have not been chosen will remain unchecked and collapsed. Refer to Figure 3-55.

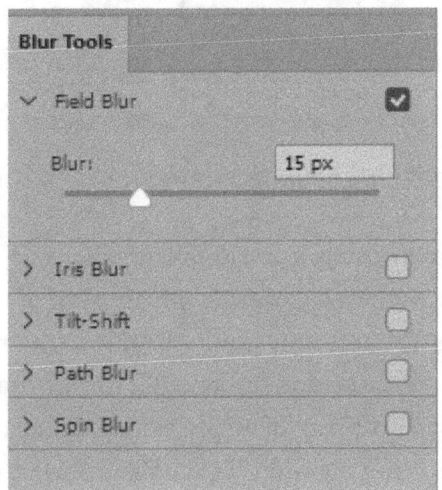

Figure 3-55. *Blur Gallery Blur Tools panel*

You will now focus on the Field Blur, Iris Blur, and Tilt-Shift. As you do that, you will tour the workspace.

On the top is the Options bar panel, which is used by all filters in the Blur Gallery. Refer to Figure 3-56.

Figure 3-56. *Blur Gallery Options bar panel*

It controls the pin options, which will be set on the preview of the canvas for each blur, which can have more than one. Refer to Figure 3-57.

CHAPTER 3　BASIC FILTERS FOR PHOTO RESTORATION

Figure 3-57. *Selected blur pin with ring*

Each blur will have access to various options:

Selection Bleed (0–100%): Controls the amount of blur that filters into the selected regions and how gradually the blurring bleeds to the edge of the selection. This option is available for normal layers but will be unavailable for smart object layers. However, you can still create a selection prior to entering the filter. This will apply the selection to the smart filter mask, which you can later blur or feather on your own using the Properties panel layer mask area, and this was also mentioned with the blur filters in this chapter. Refer to Figures 3-58 and 3-59.

CHAPTER 3 BASIC FILTERS FOR PHOTO RESTORATION

Figure 3-58. *Rectangular Marquee Tool used prior to entering the Blur Gallery*

CHAPTER 3 BASIC FILTERS FOR PHOTO RESTORATION

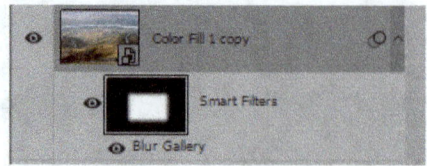

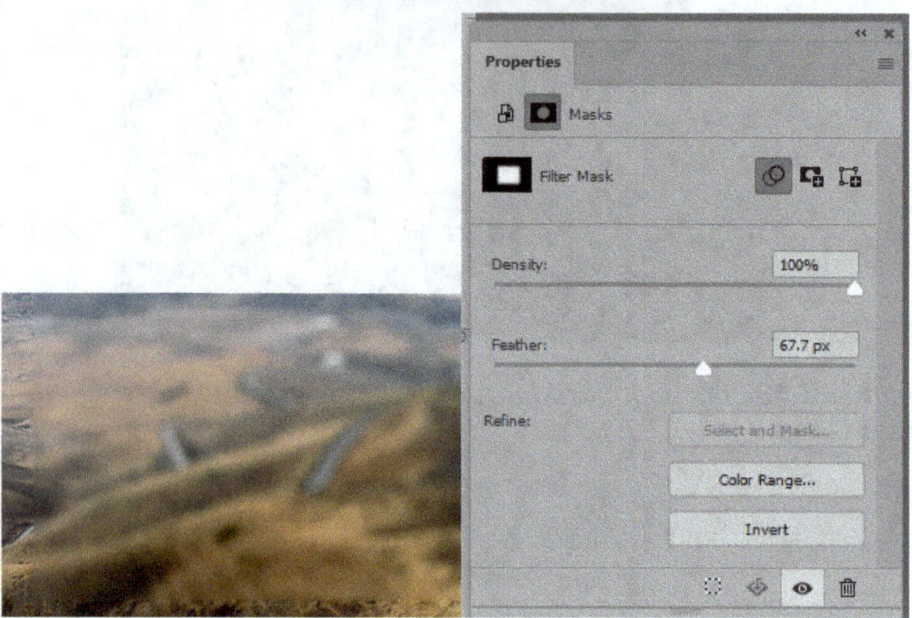

Figure 3-59. *The selection of the blur can be feathered later using the Properties panel after exiting the Blur Gallery*

Focus (0–100%): Controls the amount of blur in a protected region of a pin. This is available for Iris Blur and Tilt-Shift. Refer to Figure 3-60.

Figure 3-60. *Blur Gallery Options bar panel: Focus and other options*

Save Mask to Channels: Saves a copy of the blur mask in the Channels panel after exiting. While in the workspace hold down the M key for a preview. The mask could later be used for other parts of the image or to make a layer mask on an adjustment layer for further color editing. And depending on the blur chosen, some masks may be more visible than others. Refer to Figure 3-61.

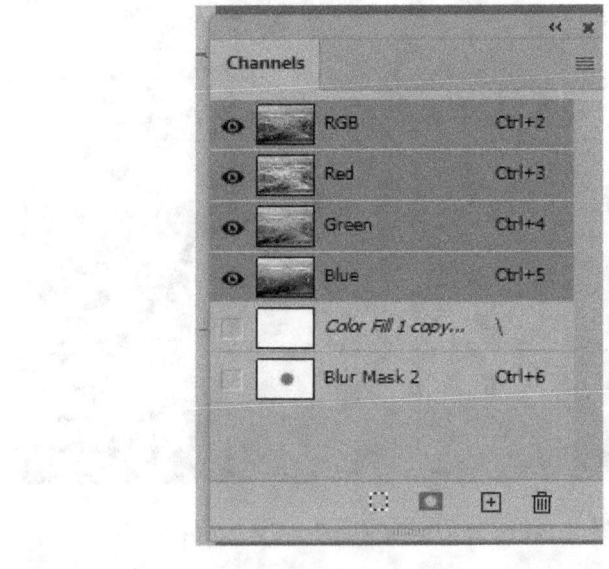

Figure 3-61. *Channels panel and Blur Gallery setting enabled*

High Quality: Enable for a more accurate bokeh (doing so may affect performance and speed). Bokeh is a type of blur with settings found in the Effects panel, which I will mention shortly.

Preview: Turn the blur's preview on and off with the check box.

Reset (counterclockwise arrow): Reset all blurs and remove all the pins. The Alt/Option key in this case cannot change the Cancel button into a Reset button as it is used for other tasks.

OK and Cancel buttons: Use these buttons to exit the workspace after you have made your adjustments, OK to commit and Cancel to exit without saving changes. Refer to Figure 3-61.

For now, you want to remain in the workspace with a single pin. Refer

CHAPTER 3   BASIC FILTERS FOR PHOTO RESTORATION

to Figure 3-62.

Figure 3-62. *Single selected blur in Blur Gallery preview*

Click to add some more pins to the four corners of the image. The entire image is quite blurry, but you will correct that shortly. Refer to Figure 3-63.

CHAPTER 3   BASIC FILTERS FOR PHOTO RESTORATION

Figure 3-63. *Five pins in Blur Gallery preview with the lower right selected*

As you review the preview of each blur pin, note that you can drag on the center and move the pin on the canvas at any time to a new location.

To remove a single selected blur pin, press the Delete/Backspace key. In this case you want to have five pins.

Press H when you need to temporarily hide pins while working.

Unselected pins will appear as a single white dot, while selected pins will often have additional adjustment settings, which include the blur ring. Refer to Figure 3-63.

While in the panel you can zoom in and out using the key commands Ctrl/CMD + +, Ctrl/CMD + – as well as Ctrl/CMD + 0. As you cannot access your History panel, if you need to undo a step, you can use Ctrl/CMD + Z.

Remember to use your (spacebar) Hand tool when you want to navigate on the canvas.

Field Blur

Field Blur builds a gradient of blurs, by defining multiple blur points with different amounts of blur. As multiple pins are added to the canvas, the final result is the combined effect of all pins. Some pins can be placed off the canvas when you want to blur edges or corners. Refer to Figure 3-64.

Figure 3-64. Adjusting a pin for Field Blur slightly off the canvas

When a pin or multiple pins are placed on the canvas, you have access to options in the following panels.

Blur Tools Panel

Use the Blur slider to set a blur size amount of 0–500 pixels. For now, I will have the blur for my four corners each set to 15 px, but the blur in the center of the image I will set to 0 px. Refer to Figure 3-65.

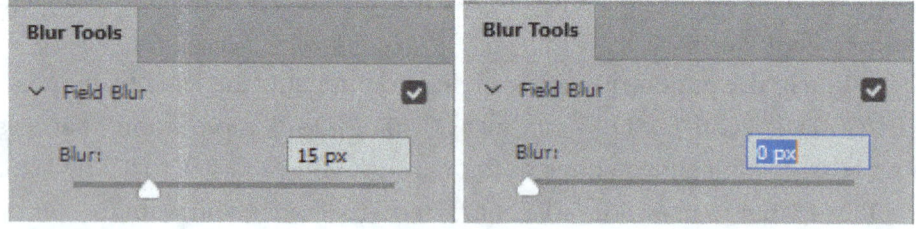

Figure 3-65. Blur Tools panel for Field Blur and adjusted settings

CHAPTER 3   BASIC FILTERS FOR PHOTO RESTORATION

Likewise, while a pin is selected, you can use the ring blur handle on the pin itself to adjust the blur size by dragging on the ring. When setting multiple pins some should be set to 0% to keep some areas in focus as I have done for the center of the image. Refer to Figure 3-66.

Figure 3-66. *Five field blurs on an image with the center field blur selected*

For your own projects, the blur for other areas you may want to set pins to ranges from 15–25 px (low blur) up to 500 px for the highest blur. However, if there is too much blur, you will remove important details. Refer to Figure 3-67.

CHAPTER 3   BASIC FILTERS FOR PHOTO RESTORATION

Figure 3-67. *A corner field blur set to a high number causes too much blur*

Effects Panel

This panel controls overall the blur effect known as Bokeh, and this setting is enabled by default. Toggling the check box on and off allows you to preview the effects. Refer to Figure 3-68.

CHAPTER 3   BASIC FILTERS FOR PHOTO RESTORATION

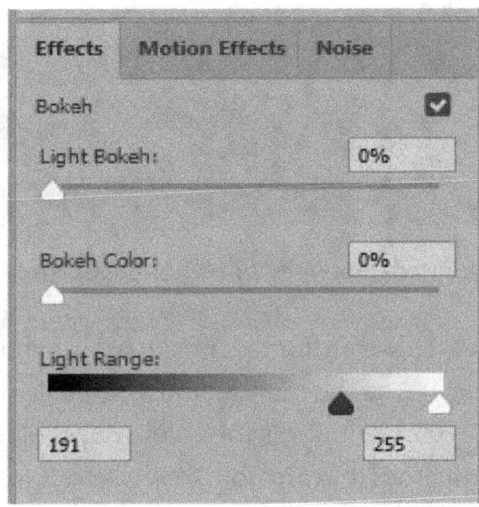

Figure 3-68. *Blur Gallery Effects panel*

Bokeh (pronounced "BOH-kay") is derived from the Japanese word for blur or haze. Blur, depending on its kind, forms a pattern based on the highlights and shadows. The camera lens generally should produce a pleasing or good bokeh or background blur. However, in older types of cameras or ones that may be damaged when the image is taken, there's a possibility of bad bokeh and so Blur Gallery may be able to correct that.

Tips on bokeh and taking pictures with your digital camera can be found here:

www.adobe.com/creativecloud/photography/discover/bokeh-effect.html

The sliders found in Bokeh are used to control the style of the overall blur effect.

Light Bokeh (0–100%): Controls the amount of highlights in the blur. Used to brighten out-of-focus areas. Do not set too high, or you could cause the image to appear overexposed in certain blur areas. Refer to Figure 3-69.

CHAPTER 3　BASIC FILTERS FOR PHOTO RESTORATION

***Figure 3-69.** Preview of changes to the Effects panel Light Bokeh*

This is set at 55%. However, for this image I would not recommend setting it higher than 14% at the most. For now, I will leave at 0%.

Bokeh Color (0–100%): Controls the colorfulness of the bokeh in color areas in the highlight areas that are not 100% white. It works together with Light Bokeh. Again, if Light Bokeh and Color Bokeh are set too high, you will get an odd color shift in the highlight area, which you do not want. Refer to Figure 3-70.

***Figure 3-70.** Effects panel with changes to Bokeh Color*

436

CHAPTER 3 BASIC FILTERS FOR PHOTO RESTORATION

For this example, leave both these settings at 0%. Refer to Figure 3-68.

Light Range (0–255): Use the black and white sliders to control the range of light or tones where the bokeh appears. Be careful as you move the slider to not create an undesirable color effect if you have already adjusted your Light Bokeh and Bokeh Color sliders. In this case I will leave the black slider at 191 and the white slider at 255. Refer to Figure 3-71.

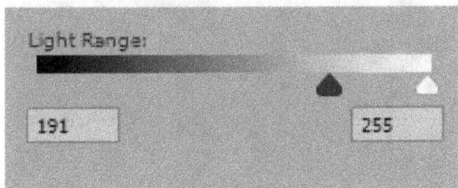

Figure 3-71. Effects panel settings for Light Range

Motion Effects Panel

Field Blur and other blurs in the gallery that I will be discussing in this book do not require this panel, and you can only use it with Path Blur and Spin Blur as they have a blur that affects movement. Refer to Figure 3-72.

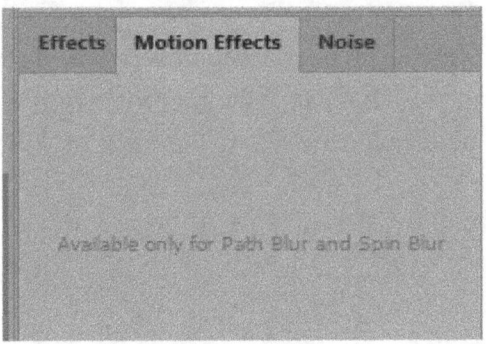

Figure 3-72. Blur Gallery Motion Effects panel with no settings

437

Noise Panel

This panel is used for adding and controlling the level of noise or grain in the blur areas of the image overall. You can use the Noise panel to make your custom adjustments. Refer to Figure 3-73.

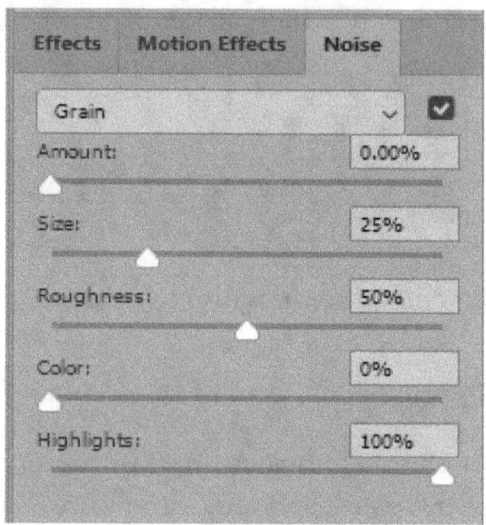

***Figure 3-73.** Blur Gallery Noise panel settings*

Sometimes an image will become too blurred and appear unnatural, and so adding some grain back into the picture may give it a more realistic appearance and a better blend. Refer to Figure 3-74.

CHAPTER 3　BASIC FILTERS FOR PHOTO RESTORATION

Figure 3-74. *Blur Gallery preview with some noise applied to the blur*

This preview setting is enabled by default and set to the Grain option.

In the list you can choose the type of noise you want: Grain, Uniform, or Gaussian. It is set to Grain by default, and this has the most slider options in the panel. However, as you experiment you may prefer one noise pattern over the other. For now, remain on the Grain setting. Refer to Figure 3-75.

CHAPTER 3 BASIC FILTERS FOR PHOTO RESTORATION

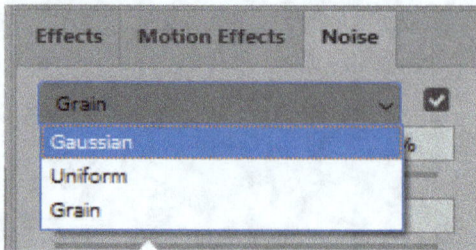

Figure 3-75. Blur Gallery using the Noise panel list to set the type of noise

Amount (0–100%): Sets the amount of noise to add to blurred areas and used to match the noise in non-blurred areas as closely as possible. I found that a setting of around 19% was fairly close to the non-blurry areas. Refer to Figure 3-76.

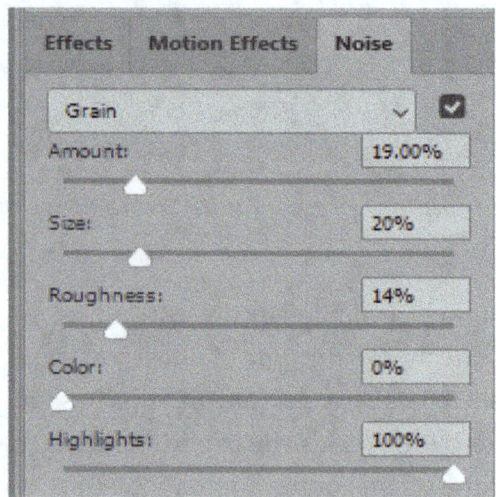

Figure 3-76. Blur Gallery using the Noise panel with adjusted settings

Size (0–100%): Controls the size of the noise grain. The slider is not available for Uniform or Gaussian noise. I set it to a setting of 20% to reduce the grain size.

440

CHAPTER 3 BASIC FILTERS FOR PHOTO RESTORATION

Roughness (0–100%): Controls the coarseness of the grain texture. Under 50% the grain will appear uniform, but over 50% the grain starts to become uneven. The slider is not available for Uniform or Gaussian noise. I set it to about 14% so the grain was not overly visible.

Color (0–100%): Controls the amount of color variation in noise being added to blurred areas. Leaving it at 0% will leave the noise monochromatic or uncolored. I left it at 0% so as not to add extra red dots into the image.

Highlights (0–100%): Used for better shadow/highlight matching. Adjusts and reduces the amount of noise applied to image highlights. In this case I left it at 100%.

Turning the noise preview off and on can help you visualize the effect of the filter. Refer to Figure 3-76.

Preview the result when you zoom in on areas of the image. Refer to Figure 3-77.

Figure 3-77. *Blur Gallery preview of the subtle noise added to the image*

CHAPTER 3 BASIC FILTERS FOR PHOTO RESTORATION

In the Blur Tools panel, you can then either turn off the current blur or leave it on and add then try the next blur in the gallery to the current image. Generally, most blur kinds are used one at a time, but they can be combined.

Expand that area in the panel to see all the options. Refer to Figure 3-78.

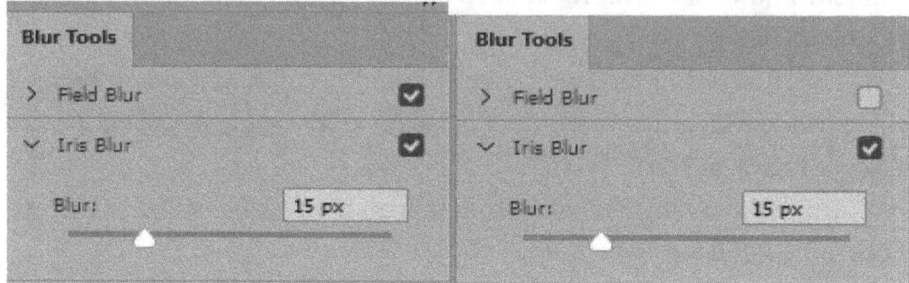

Figure 3-78. *Blur Gallery transitioning from Field Blur to Iris Blur*

In this case I will turn off the Field Blur for now and try the next blur option. Doing this places an Iris Blur in the center of the image.

Iris Blur

The Iris Blur is used to simulate a shallow depth-of-field effect to your picture, regardless of the camera or lens used. This is a similar to the Lens Blur filter we looked at earlier in this chapter but is in this case nondestructive. When a pin or multiple pins are placed on the canvas, you have access to options in the earlier mentioned panels. Refer to Figures 3-78 and 3-79.

CHAPTER 3 BASIC FILTERS FOR PHOTO RESTORATION

Figure 3-79. *Blur Gallery adding an Iris Blur to the preview*

Blur Tools Panel

Use the Blur slider to set a blur size amount of 0–500 pixels. Likewise, you can use the ring on the pin itself to adjust the blur size. I tried a blur of 17 px. Refer to Figure 3-80.

CHAPTER 3 BASIC FILTERS FOR PHOTO RESTORATION

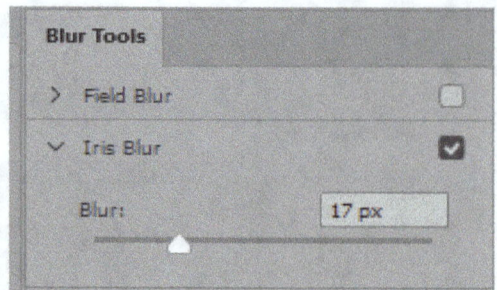

Figure 3-80. *Blur Gallery Blur Tools panel with selected blur in the panel*

Drag on the center of pin to move it to a new location. On the canvas the pin can be further controlled by dragging on the ellipse handles to expand or rotate the blur. Refer to Figure 3-81.

CHAPTER 3 BASIC FILTERS FOR PHOTO RESTORATION

Figure 3-81. *Iris Blur handles for scale/rotation, roundness/squareness, and feathering*

To make the blur less rounded and more of a rounded rectangle, use the square roundness knob. The four inner circular feather handles can also be used to adjust the blur's sharp area and fade area by dragging them in and out. Refer to Figure 3-82.

Figure 3-82. *Blur Gallery previewing the altered Iris Blur*

Tip Holding down the Alt/Option key + dragging will allow you to move each of these four feather handles independently. Refer to Figure 3-83.

CHAPTER 3 BASIC FILTERS FOR PHOTO RESTORATION

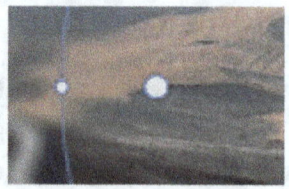

Figure 3-83. *Alter one feather handle independently with the Alt/Option key and drag*

Notice in the Options bar panel you can also set the pin focus within the selected ellipse. Refer to Figure 3-84.

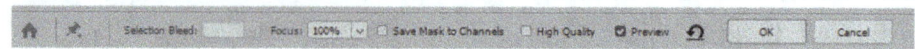

Figure 3-84. *Blur Gallery Options bar panel: pin focus*

Effects Panel and Noise Panel

The same settings are available as those found in Field Blur, and you can refer back to that section for more details on Effects and Noise panels. Note that the Motion Effects panel has no available settings. In the case of the Effects and Noise panels, if you already set some settings from a previous blur, they will be retained here. Refer to Figure 3-85.

CHAPTER 3   BASIC FILTERS FOR PHOTO RESTORATION

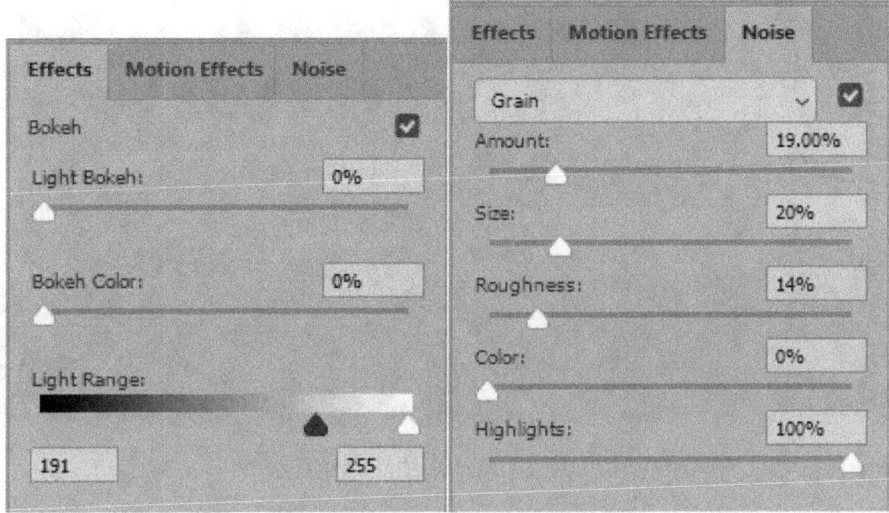

Figure 3-85. *Blur Gallery Effects and Noise panels*

Tilt-Shift

This filter is used to simulate an image taken with a tilt-shift lens. For information on this kind of lens, you can do an online search on "tilt-shift photography." This unique effect blur defines an area of sharpness and then fades to a blur at the edges in straight sections or bands. It is often used to simulate photos by giving them the appearance as if they were miniature objects or landscapes. When a pin or multiple pins are placed on the canvas, you have access to options in the following panels. Refer to Figure 3-86.

CHAPTER 3 BASIC FILTERS FOR PHOTO RESTORATION

Figure 3-86. *Blur Gallery Tilt-Shift blur applied*

Blur Tools Panel

Use the Blur slider to set a blur size amount of 0–500 pixels. This controls the blur and sharpness. In this example I set it to 17 px. Refer to Figure 3-87.

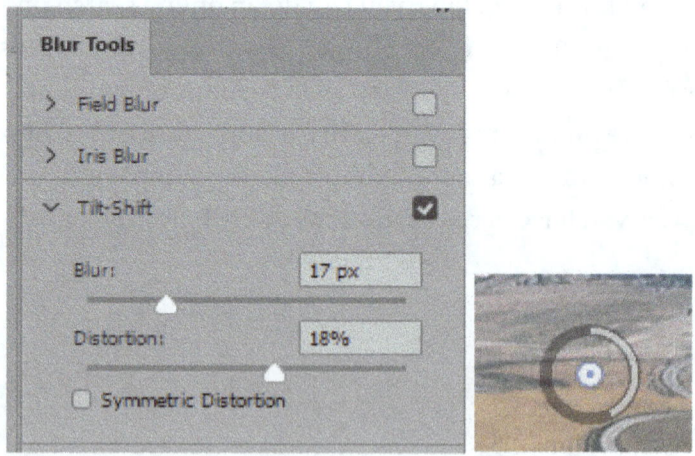

Figure 3-87. *Blur Gallery Blur Tools panel with a selected blur pin*

CHAPTER 3   BASIC FILTERS FOR PHOTO RESTORATION

Likewise, you can use the ring on the pin itself to adjust the blur size.

Distortion (–100, 0, 100%): This slider controls the shape of the blur distortion. I set it to 18%.

Symmetric Distortion: When enabled, applies distortion from both directions. In some cases, the change may be minimal, so I left this option disabled. Refer to Figure 3-87.

Using the round handles on the canvas, you can drag to rotate the blur in negative and positive angle values. Dragging on the inner solid focus lines allows you to control the sharp and fade area boundaries, and dragging on the outer dashed feather lines controls the blur area. Refer to Figure 3-88.

Figure 3-88. *Drag on the handle or solid line to control angle/fade or dashed line to control feather of blur*

You can control each of the four lines separately. Refer to Figure 3-89.

CHAPTER 3   BASIC FILTERS FOR PHOTO RESTORATION

Figure 3-89. Blur Gallery preview of current blur

Notice that like the Iris Blur, in the Options bar panel, you can also set the pin focus between the two feather lines. Refer to Figure 3-90.

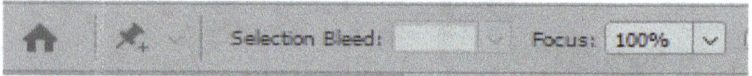

Figure 3-90. Blur Gallery Options Bar panel with a focus setting

Effects Panel and Noise Panel

The same settings are available as found for these panels in the Field Blur, and you can refer back to that section for more details. There are no settings in the Motion Effects panel. For the Noise panel, adjust the noise type as required to affect the overall noise. In this case, if you have already made adjustments to the Effects and Noise panels, those settings will still be present. Refer to Figure 3-91.

CHAPTER 3 BASIC FILTERS FOR PHOTO RESTORATION

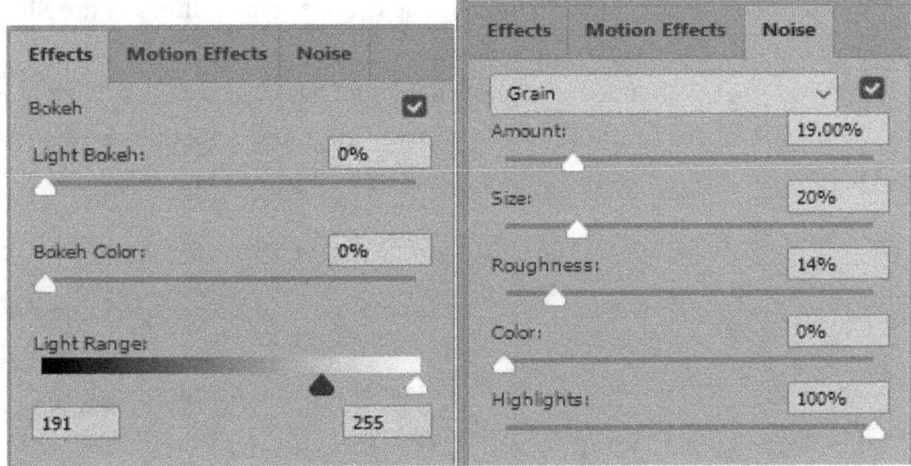

Figure 3-91. Blur Gallery Effects and Noise panel settings

Note Path Blur and Spin Blur are also part of this gallery and can be used for more artistic types of blur. Like the other blurs, you can use them separately or grouped with the other blurs in the gallery when you enable or disable the check boxes. Refer to Figure 3-92.

Figure 3-92. Blur Gallery Blur Tools panel with Path Blur and Spin Blur enabled but not edited in the workspace

Path Blur can be used to create a type of motion blur along a path, while Spin Blur can create a type of rotational motion blur from a center point pin.

CHAPTER 3   BASIC FILTERS FOR PHOTO RESTORATION

If you need more details on how to use these specific filters in the Blur Gallery, you can refer to the following link:

https://helpx.adobe.com/photoshop/using/blur-gallery.html

When you have completed your settings, click OK to exit the workspace and review the results on the smart object layer. Refer to Figure 3-93.

Figure 3-93. Preview of the result of Blur Gallery Tilt-Shift applied to a smart object layer

File ➤ Save your work and refer to my file **road_image_final.psd** if you need a reference.

CHAPTER 3 BASIC FILTERS FOR PHOTO RESTORATION

Noise Correction Filters

Noise correction filters can be used to either add or remove noise to or from an image. Noise can be defined as pixels with randomly distributed color levels. In an image this could be a grain effect, a texture, or unwanted dust and scratches. Noise can also occur in images of low-level light, under exposure, or when scanning some film, as you saw earlier in the sunset image that we applied the Gaussian Blur filter to.

Noise may also appear in a grayscale (luminance) grain or patch or in color with small unwanted color artifacts.

Artifacts will often be more obvious in one or more RGB channels, often the blue channel, especially in digital cameras. However, when you're dealing with a damaged image like a print or slide, noise and dust can be on every channel. Refer to Figure 3-94.

CHAPTER 3 BASIC FILTERS FOR PHOTO RESTORATION

Figure 3-94. Selected blue channel in the Channels panel and looking for potential noise

Refer to the Reduce Noise filter for more details on this particular topic.

Now we will look at five noise filters to either clean up unwanted dust or scratches that are evenly distributed throughout the image or add some noise back into the image. Go to the Filter ➤ Noise submenu to review the following. Refer to Figure 3-95.

CHAPTER 3   BASIC FILTERS FOR PHOTO RESTORATION

Figure 3-95. *Filter ➤ Noise submenu*

Add Noise

This filter adds random pixels to an image, simulating the effect of shooting pictures on high-speed film giving a type of grainy appearance. Adding grain to an image does not necessarily improve the quality of an image you are trying to repair but is considered more of an effect. Refer to Figure 3-96.

However, as you saw with the Blur Gallery, sometimes adding noise back is good. You can use this filter for corrections as well such as

- To reduce banding in feathered selections or graduated fills
- To give a more realistic look to heavily retouched areas that have become blurry due to a healing or clone stamping tool where you need to match the original texture again

In the dialog box you can set the following options.

Create a copy of **dog_motion_blur_final.psd** with the Motion Blur as the example to add some grain back. Refer to Figure 3-96.

CHAPTER 3   BASIC FILTERS FOR PHOTO RESTORATION

Figure 3-96. *Add Noise dialog box with the Layers panel displaying smart filters of Add Noise and Motion Blur*

Amount (0.10–400%): Higher percentage values add more colored pixels to the image. In this case I wanted to be very subtle, so I used a setting of 4.6%.

Distribution: Can be set to either Uniform or Gaussian for noise distribution. Uniform will distribute the noise's color values using random numbers between 0 and plus or minus the specified value. It creates a subtle effect. However, Gaussian, as mentioned with the blurs, distributes the noise's color values along a bell-shaped curve calculation to create a speckle effect.

In this case I use Uniform.

Monochromatic: When enabled, applies this filter to only the tonal elements in the image without altering the colors. The color of the noise is now grayscale and no longer colorful, which is good for images that are black-and-white. In this case there is color in the image so I will leave this setting disabled. Refer to Figure 3-96.

In the dialog box, use the zoom-out (-) and zoom-in (+) magnifying glass icons when you want to zoom in on a section in the preview box to see an affected area up close and zoom out after. You can move the preview area around to see other areas in the image. You can also toggle Preview on and off to compare settings in the dialog box to the canvas.

Optionally, use the Alt/Option key to change the Cancel button to Reset to reset your original slider settings. Holding down the Ctrl/CMD key changes the Cancel button to the Default button.

Click OK to commit the changes and look at the subtle added noise to the blur in the image. Refer to Figures 3-96 and 3-97.

Figure 3-97. Add Noise applied to an image of a dog in a masked area

File ➤ Save your work and check out the file **dog_motion_blur_noise_final.psd** for reference.

Despeckle

While this filter has no dialog box with additional options, it is used to detect the edges in an image. The edges are areas where significant color changes can occur. Then it blurs all of the selection except those edges. The blurring is meant to remove or reduce noise while preserving details.

If you apply this filter to an image use your visibility eye on your smart object layer to turn this setting off and on. In some images the change will be very subtle. Refer to Figure 3-98.

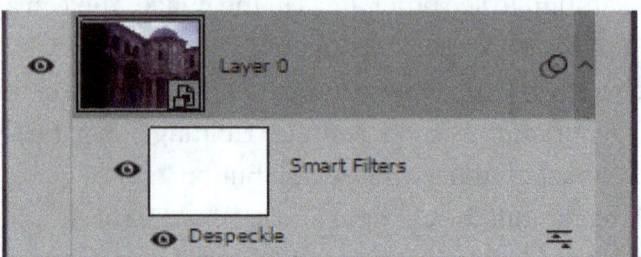

Figure 3-98. *Apply the Despeckle filter as seen in the Layers panel*

From experimenting I found that it only blurs very slightly and does not adequately remove dust and scratches. In this case I recommend using the next filter instead, but you can try Despeckle on one of your own images.

Dust & Scratches

Dust & Scratches is a good filter to experiment with, either overall or as a mask to selected areas when your image has a lot of dust, scratches, and artifacts covering it and it would take too long to clone stamp and cover them. At the beginning of the chapter, I showed an example of a structure of some ancient pillars. The slide had over time acquired dust particles, which were too small to remove easily. So I used Filter ➤ Noise ➤ Dust & Scratches. Check out file **pillar_dust_example.psd** for reference to various layers. Refer to Figure 3-99.

CHAPTER 3 BASIC FILTERS FOR PHOTO RESTORATION

Figure 3-99. *Image of pillars that requires Dust & Scratches to be applied*

In the original image, as mentioned earlier, it had to be rotated and cropped. However, before missing gaps could be filled in with the Edit ➤ Content-Aware Fill workspace, to avoid adding more dust to the image, this filter needs to be used first. See Volume 1 on the topic of using the Content-Aware Fill workspace with selections.

Dust & Scratches can reduce noise by blurring dissimilar pixels. To achieve a balance between sharpening the image and hiding defects, you will need to experiment with various combinations of Radius and Threshold sliders. Here I am showing the settings that I use in masked smart filter areas. Refer to Figure 3-100.

CHAPTER 3   BASIC FILTERS FOR PHOTO RESTORATION

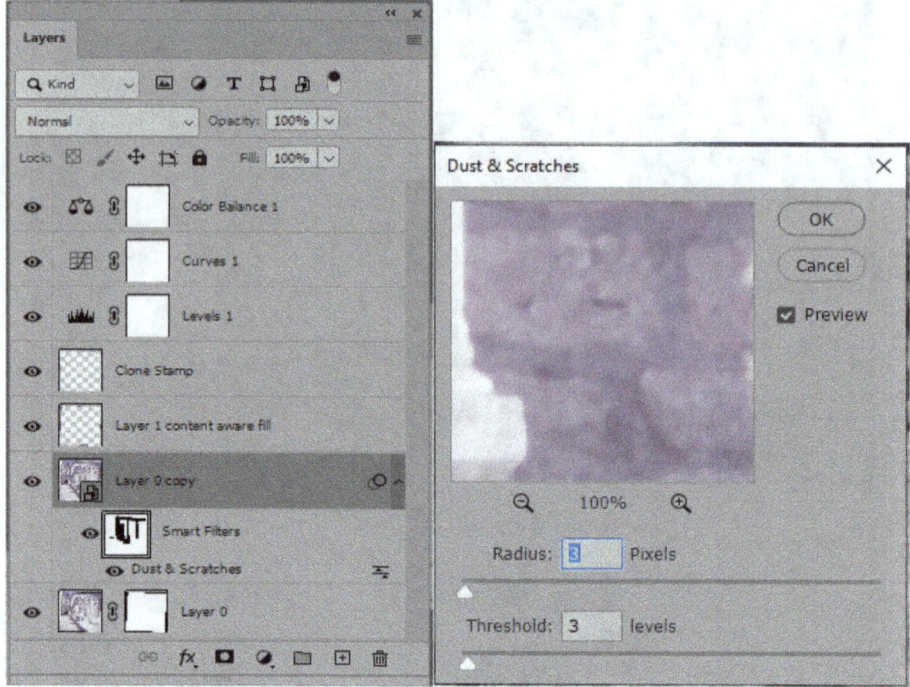

Figure 3-100. *Smart object layer with smart filter Dust & Scratches applied and the dialog box*

Radius (1–500 pixels): Determines the size of the area searched for dissimilar pixels. Try entering values between 1 and 16 to blur the image gradually and then increase or decrease the value as you move the Threshold slider. In this example I used a radius of 3 pixels.

Threshold (0–255 levels): Determines how dissimilar the pixels should be before they are eliminated or blended together. Try experimenting first with values between 0 and 128 and increase if necessary if you need to bring some of the details back. To avoid too much blurring, I left the setting at 3 levels.

CHAPTER 3   BASIC FILTERS FOR PHOTO RESTORATION

In the dialog box, use the zoom-out (–) and zoom-in (+) magnifying glass icons when you want to zoom in on a section in the preview box to see an affected area up close and zoom out after. You can also move the preview around to see another area. You can also toggle Preview on and off to compare settings in the dialog box to the canvas.

Optionally, use the Alt/Option key to change the Cancel button to Reset to reset your original slider settings. Holding down the Ctrl/CMD key changes the Cancel button to the Default button.

Click OK to commit the changes and review the result. Refer to Figure 3-101.

Figure 3-101. *Area of stone without and with the Dust & Scratches filter applied*

Using this filter with a layer mask is helpful when you know that some of the lines or fine details are not scratches and you want to restore them to the image. Refer to Figure 3-102.

461

CHAPTER 3   BASIC FILTERS FOR PHOTO RESTORATION

Figure 3-102. *Dust & Scratches filter enabled in the Layers panel with additional layers later added to fill in gaps*

Using Dust & Scratches will not completely remove every single dust particle as some will be too large. Larger particles will still need to be covered on a separated blank new layer using one of your healing tools such as the Clone Stamp tool, as I demonstrated in Volume 1.

As mentioned, once you have used this filter, you could then add a new blank layer and use your Magic Wand tool in selected areas below the new layer on Layer 0 and then enter the Edit ➤ Content-Aware Fill workspace to fill in the gaps without adding extra dust particles as was demonstrated in Volume 1. In this case it would rely on the detail in the blurred areas of the smart layer (Layer 0 copy). In this example you can see the result of working in that Workspace on "Layer 1 content aware fill" for reference Figure 3-102, and then again, I made a second blank layer, which I named "Clone Stamp", and made adjustments with the Clone Stamp tool in areas such as the sky or near the edges where the newly filled area meets the original image to blend everything together. File ➤ Save your work and refer to the file **pillar_dust_example_final.psd** for reference.

CHAPTER 3 BASIC FILTERS FOR PHOTO RESTORATION

We will return to the Dust & Scratches filter at the end of the chapter to complete the photo project.

Median

This reduces noise in an image by blending the brightness of pixels within a selection and is often used on images with high luster or stipples that appear unsharp or grainy after scanning. You saw some examples in Chapters 1 and 2. This filter can help reduce the appearance of a textured surface and acts similar to the Dust & Scratches filter.

Using the Radius value, it searches the radius of a pixel selection for pixels of similar brightness and then discards pixels that differ too much from adjacent pixels. It then replaces the center pixel with the median brightness value of the searched pixels. Using the image **white_terrace_walls_median.psd**, you can see what occurs when you use Filter ➤ Noise ➤ Median when applied to the smart object layer. Refer to Figure 3-103.

CHAPTER 3 BASIC FILTERS FOR PHOTO RESTORATION

Figure 3-103. *Image that was scanned from a textured print*

Radius (1–500 pixels): A low setting is recommended of 1–2 pixels to improve the overall surface. Otherwise, it may become too blurry. Because the details in this image are so fine, I used 1 px. The filter can also be useful for eliminating or reducing the effect of slight motion on an image. Refer to Figure 3-104.

CHAPTER 3 BASIC FILTERS FOR PHOTO RESTORATION

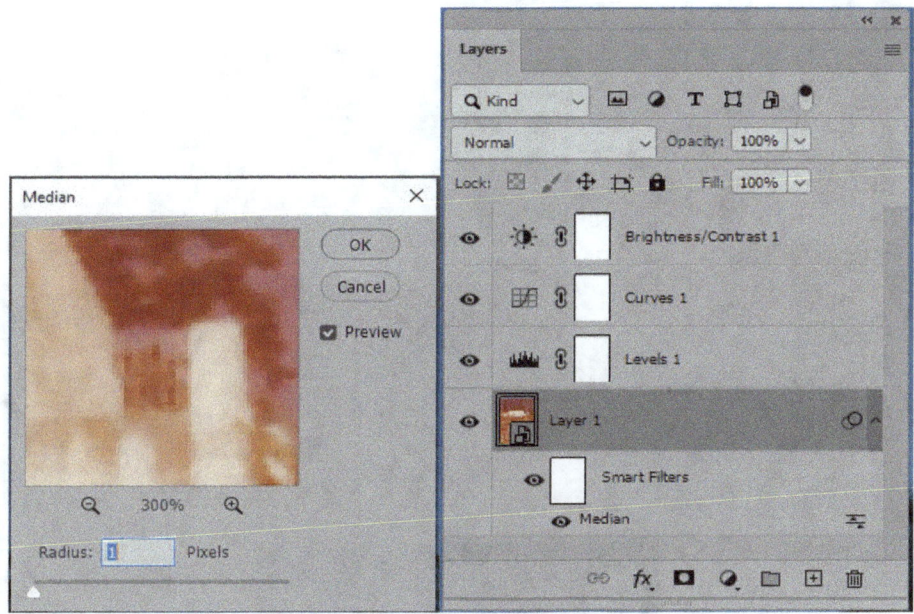

Figure 3-104. *Median dialog box and the filter applied to a smart object layer in the Layers panel*

In the dialog box, use the zoom-out (-) and zoom-in (+) magnifying glass icons when you want to zoom in on a section in the preview box to see an affected area up close and zoom out after. Move the preview area around if you need to see other areas of the image. You can also toggle Preview on and off to compare settings on the dialog box to the canvas.

Optionally, use the Alt/Option key to change the Cancel button to Reset to reset your original slider settings. Holding down the Ctrl/CMD key changes the Cancel button to the Default button.

Click OK to commit the changes. Refer to Figure 3-104.

To keep some details but still blur a bit more, I found that adding Filter ➤ Blur ➤ Surface Blur also improved the image, with a radius of 2 and a threshold of 5. Refer to Figure 3-105.

465

CHAPTER 3 BASIC FILTERS FOR PHOTO RESTORATION

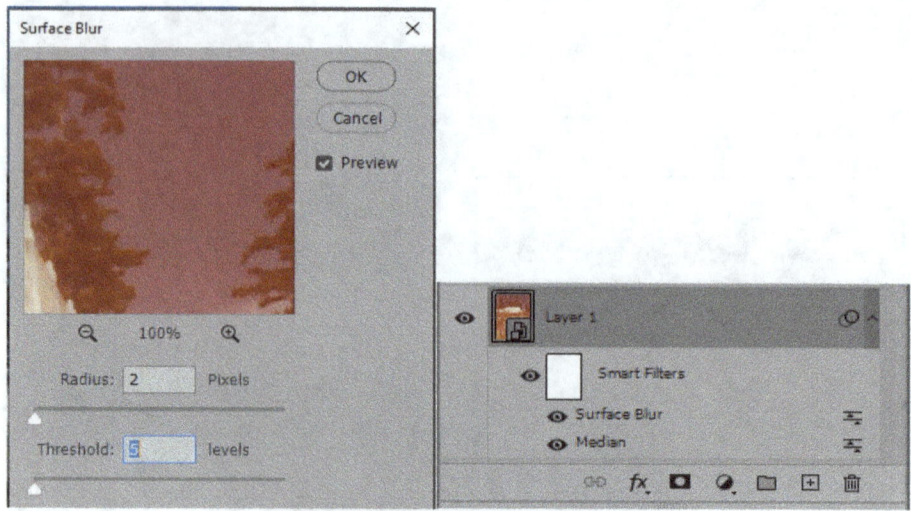

Figure 3-105. Surface Blur dialog box and the filter applied to a smart object layer in the Layers panel and preview

---

Tip Another option you could experiment with is layering duplicate smart object layers with the similar smart filter applied but a different opacity to improve the blend.

File ➤ Save your work so far and refer to my file **white_terrace_walls_median_final.psd**.

Reduce Noise

This filter is used to reduce noise while preserving edges based on user settings. This could affect the overall image or individual channels. As mentioned earlier in this section, some channels, such as the blue channel, can have more noise in them. This may be easier to determine from an image from a digital camera rather than a scanned image. However, you can use this for your scanned digitized image as well. Before you start using this filter, take a moment to examine your Channels panel and see if one of the channels has more noise than the others. Refer to Figure 3-106.

CHAPTER 3 BASIC FILTERS FOR PHOTO RESTORATION

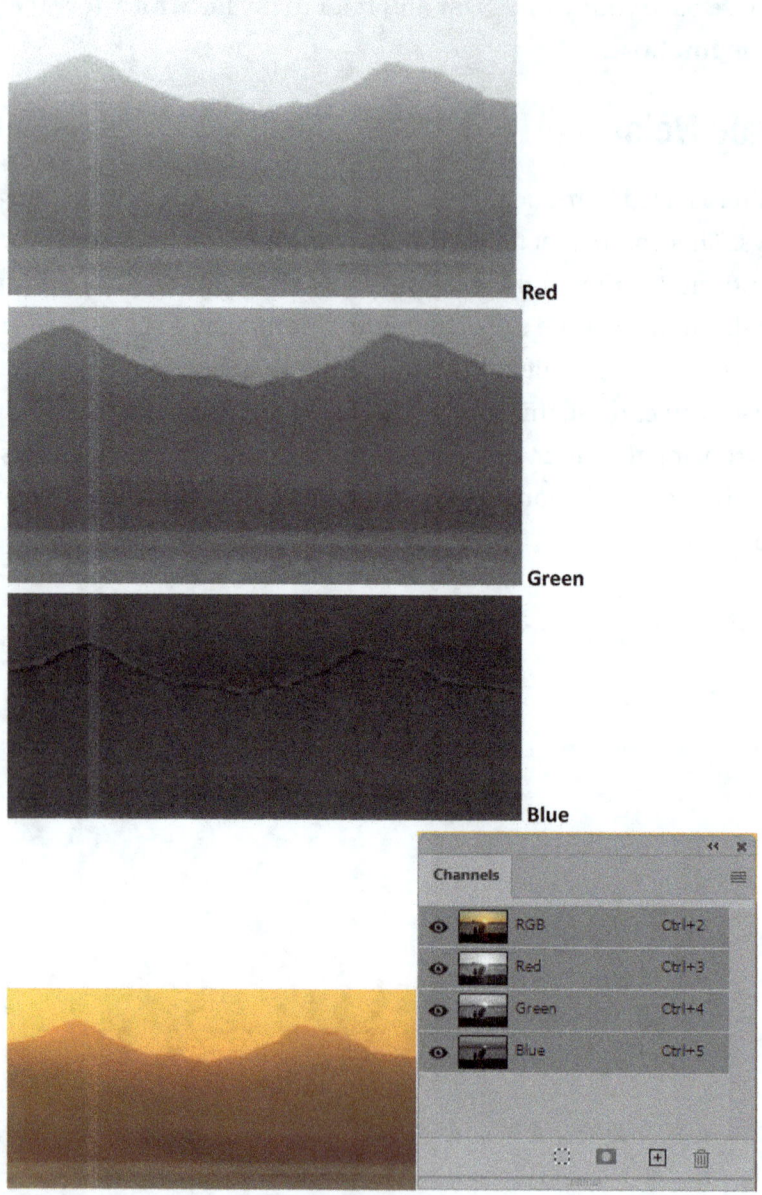

Figure 3-106. *Check the red, green, and blue channels in the Channels panel to determine which has the most noise; in this case, it is the lower blue channel*

CHAPTER 3   BASIC FILTERS FOR PHOTO RESTORATION

In this next dialog box, you can make the following adjustments. Make sure that the Preview check box is enabled as you work. In this case use the file **sunset_reduce_noise.psd**. Go to Filter ➤ Noise ➤ Reduce Noise and refer to Figure 3-107.

Figure 3-107. *Reduce Noise dialog box*

There are two radio button options, Basic and Advanced. For working with your channels, use the Advanced setting.

Settings: The preset settings currently, set to Default, but you can save a copy of the current settings. They will then be stored in the dialog box for another time. Unwanted settings can be selected and removed with the trash can icon.

Overall tab: Many images may need noise reduction overall. The settings for this tab include

Strength (0–10): Enter the strength for reducing luminance noise in all the image's channels. If the setting is 0, then Preserve Details will be unavailable. In this example I used a setting of 6.

Preserve Details (0–100%): Enter the amount of detail to be preserved for the edge and image overall. This could include fine details like hair and textures on objects. 100% preserves all details but may not balance luminance noise overall. Experiment with the Strength and Preserve Details sliders to find an ideal balance in noise reduction. I left it at the default of 60%.

Reduce Color Noise (0–100%): Enter the strength for reducing chromatic noise appearing as random color pixels. Gradually increase the value to reduce the overall noise. As the image had only minor noise issues, I left it at the default setting of 45%.

Sharpen Details (0–100%): Enter the amount of sharpening to be applied to restore minor details. As you remove noise the sharpness of the image is reduced. Setting it too high, however, can produce additional artifacts. Later, outside the dialog box, you can also apply one of the sharpen filters to adjust this setting further and restore some sharpness. I set the slider to a low setting of 25%. Refer to Figure 3-108.

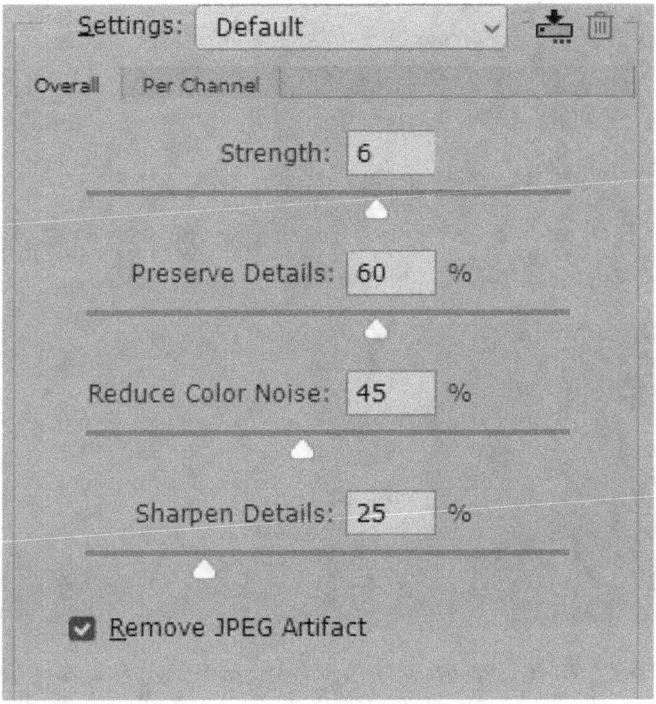

CHAPTER 3   BASIC FILTERS FOR PHOTO RESTORATION

Figure 3-108. *Reduce Noise dialog box: Overall tab*

Remove JPEG Artifact: When enabled, will remove blocky artifacts and halos due to JPEG file compression. This can occur when images like a copy of a copy have been saved multiple times and varying degrees of lower quality have been set. Be aware it is better to always work from your scanned bitmap or TIFF image to keep the highest original quality. With digital camera .jpg images always work on an image duplicate so as not to degrade the original. In this example, it can also smooth out the graininess in some of the low-light areas near the water. However, if you find that with the setting enabled you are losing some shadows or highlights, then disable this setting. Refer to Figure 3-109.

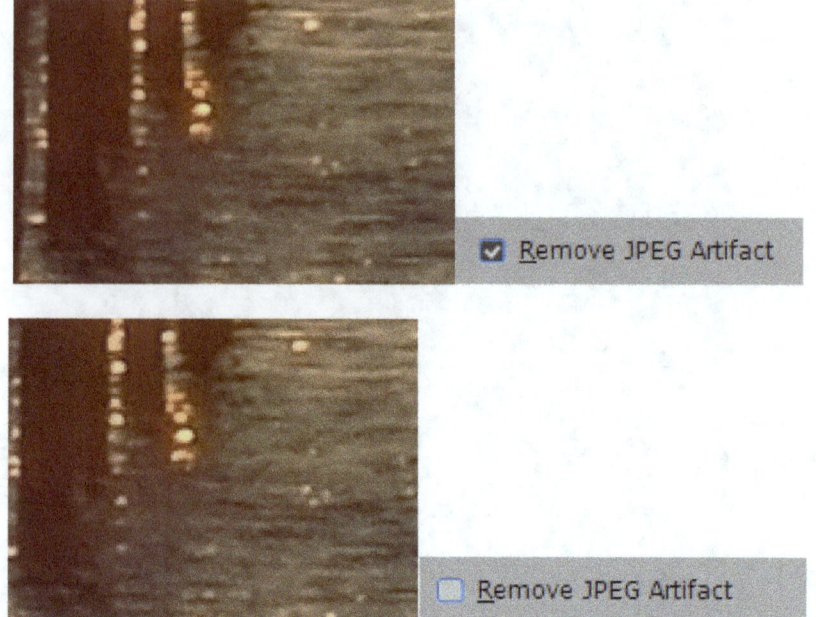

Figure 3-109. *Reduce Noise dialog box preview: by enabling and disabling the Remove JPEG Artifact check box, there can be very subtle color shifts*

Toggle the check box on and off in various close-up areas of the image to see what is affected by the setting of Remove JPEG artifact.

Per Channel tab: Sometimes just correcting the noise on one or two channels can improve the overall image. Refer to Figure 3-110.

CHAPTER 3   BASIC FILTERS FOR PHOTO RESTORATION

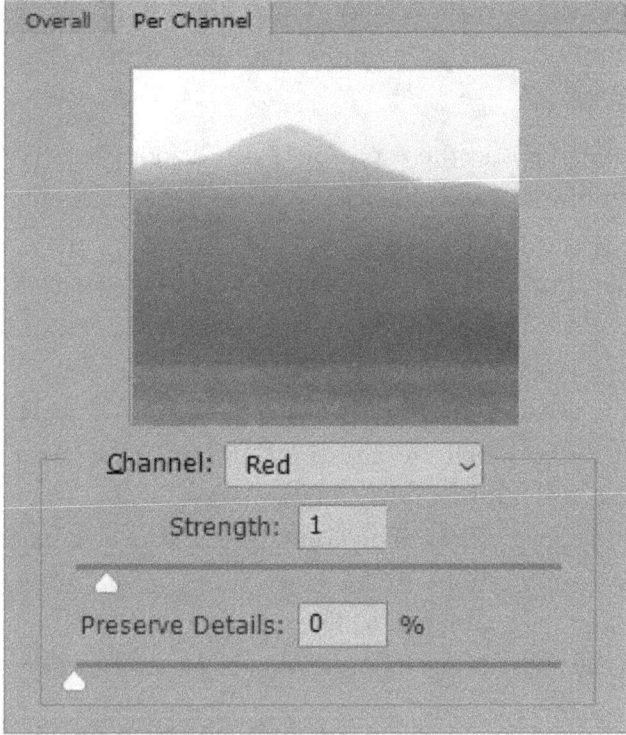

Figure 3-110. *Reduce Noise dialog box: Per Channel tab*

The settings for this tab include

Channel: Preview a channel by choosing Red, Green, or Blue from the list. Then select a channel to reduce the noise.

Strength (0–10): Enter the strength of the noise reduction. If the setting is 0, then Preserve Details will be unavailable.

Preserve Details (0–100%): Enter the amount of detail to be preserved. In this example, for each channel, try the following settings:

- Red: Strength 1, Preserve Details 0%.

- Green: Strength 0, Preserve Details 0%.

CHAPTER 3   BASIC FILTERS FOR PHOTO RESTORATION

- Blue: Strength 10, Preserve Details 60%. I set this one higher because, as mentioned earlier, the blue channel had more noise.

In the dialog box, use the zoom-out (-) and zoom-in (+) magnifying glass icons when you want to zoom in on a section in the preview box to see an affected area up close and zoom out after. You can move in the various preview boxes (overall and per channel). However, you can also zoom in and out on the canvas. You can also toggle Preview on and off to compare the settings in the dialog box to the canvas.

Optionally, use the Alt/Option key to change the Cancel button to Reset to reset your original slider settings. Holding down the Ctrl/CMD key changes the Cancel button to the Default button.

Click OK to commit the changes and review your results. Refer to Figure 3-107.

In the mountain region you will notice a subtle smoothness of the grain noise, especially in the blue channel. Refer to Figures 3-111 and 3-112.

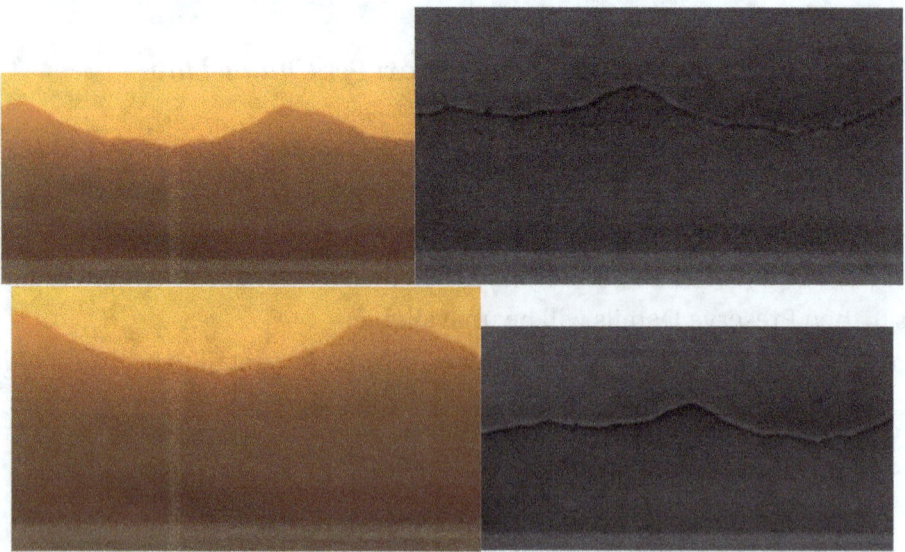

Figure 3-111. Composite RGB and reduced noise in specifically the blue channel

474

CHAPTER 3 BASIC FILTERS FOR PHOTO RESTORATION

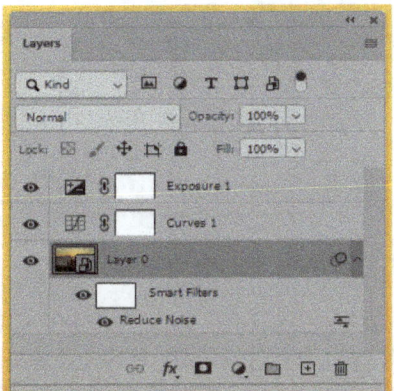

Figure 3-112. *Layers panel and the final image with the Reduce Noise filter applied*

File ➤ Save your work, and you can check out my file **sunset_reduce_noise_final.psd** for reference.

Sharpen Filters

The sharpen filters can be used to do basic corrections to an otherwise blurry image. However, you can oversharpen, but with the filter you can adjust your setting more accurately. Go to Filter ➤ Sharpen to review the five filter options. Refer to Figure 3-113.

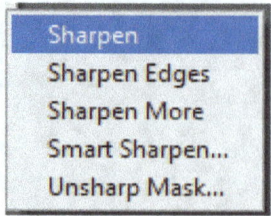

Figure 3-113. *Filter ➤ Sharpen submenu*

Note that the options of Sharpen, Sharpen Edges, and Sharpen More have no dialog box and no additional settings. Sharpen More is, however, a stronger setting than Sharpen, but the changes on some images can be very subtle. So, for better control, we will focus on the main two, Smart Sharpen and Unsharp Mask.

Smart Sharpen

Use this dialog box to set a preset sharpening algorithm or manually control the amount of sharpening that occurs in shadows and highlights. This is ideal to use when you need to experiment with sharpening settings and reduce noise and halo effects. Besides sharpening layers, it can also be used to sharpen individual channels. In this example I used file **Plant_Sharpen.psd**, where I sharpened the layer of the pot and plant in the forefront area, which was out of focus. Refer to the file **Plant_Sharpen_final.psd**. If you would like to apply a filter mask, go to Filter ➤ Sharpen ➤ Smart Sharpen. Refer to Figure 3-114.

CHAPTER 3 BASIC FILTERS FOR PHOTO RESTORATION

Figure 3-114. *Slightly blurry plant image that requires some sharpening*

Once in the dialog box, make sure that the Preview check box is enabled so that you can see changes. Refer to Figure 3-115.

CHAPTER 3　BASIC FILTERS FOR PHOTO RESTORATION

Figure 3-115. *Smart Sharpen dialog box*

Gear settings: This allows you to use the original legacy settings Use Legacy or use More Accurate.

The Use Legacy option is from the older CS6 version and processes the file slowly. You can also enable More Accurate for the removal of blurring. This, however, as you test and preview, can sometimes oversharpen and not smooth areas at the same. Refer to Figure 3-116.

CHAPTER 3　BASIC FILTERS FOR PHOTO RESTORATION

Figure 3-116. *Smart Sharpen dialog box settings: Use Legacy and More Accurate disabled and enabled*

By default, these options are disabled to let Smart Sharpen do its job.

479

CHAPTER 3 BASIC FILTERS FOR PHOTO RESTORATION

The next set of options include

Preset: Use the custom preset settings that you create. Upon entering the dialog box, it will show default settings, but when altered it will reset to custom. From the Preset list files can be saved and loaded as (.SHR) files. Presets can also be deleted. Refer to Figure 3-117.

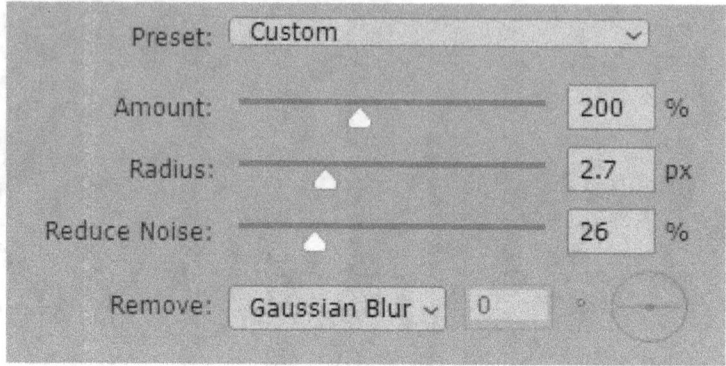

Figure 3-117. Smart Sharpen dialog box settings

Amount (0–500%): Enter the strength of the sharpening applied. Try high values first and then gradually lower the value to see the effect on the image. Higher values increase the contrast between the edge pixels giving the illusion that the image has come into focus. However, if there is dust, scratches, or rough areas, these are enhanced as well. I will use a setting of 200%. Refer to Figure 3-118.

CHAPTER 3 ■ BASIC FILTERS FOR PHOTO RESTORATION

Figure 3-118. *Sharpening can make details including dust more visible*

Radius (0–64 px): Enter the width of the sharpening effect. This determines the number of pixels surrounding a defined edge that will be affected by the sharpening. Higher radius values show wider edge effect, and the sharpening appears more dramatic. First, increase to the point where you see a halo or increased edge effect and then gradually reduce it. Work together with the Amount slider to find a balance. In this case I set the radius to 2.7. Refer to Figure 3-119.

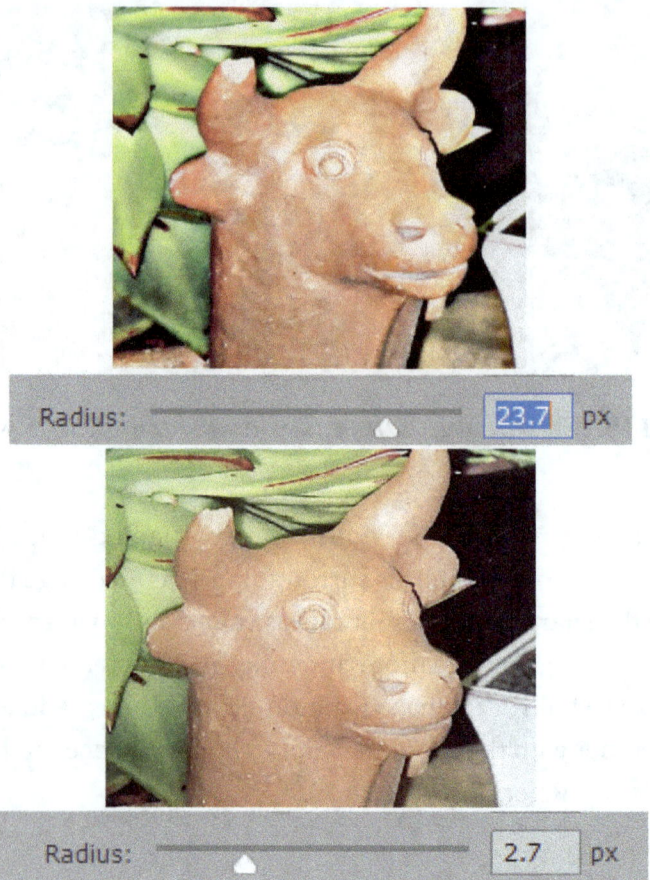

Figure 3-119. *Smart Sharpen dialog box: adjusting the Radius setting*

Reduce Noise (0–100%): Enter the amount of noise reduction. Use this to reduce unwanted noise, but not affect the important edge areas. If prior blurring has been applied to the image, then you may want to add back some noise so that the image does not appear too smooth and plastic-like, which a high setting can create. If the Amount has been set higher, you may need to adjust this slider. In my case I want some texture, so I set the Reduce Noise to 26%. Refer to Figure 3-120.

CHAPTER 3 BASIC FILTERS FOR PHOTO RESTORATION

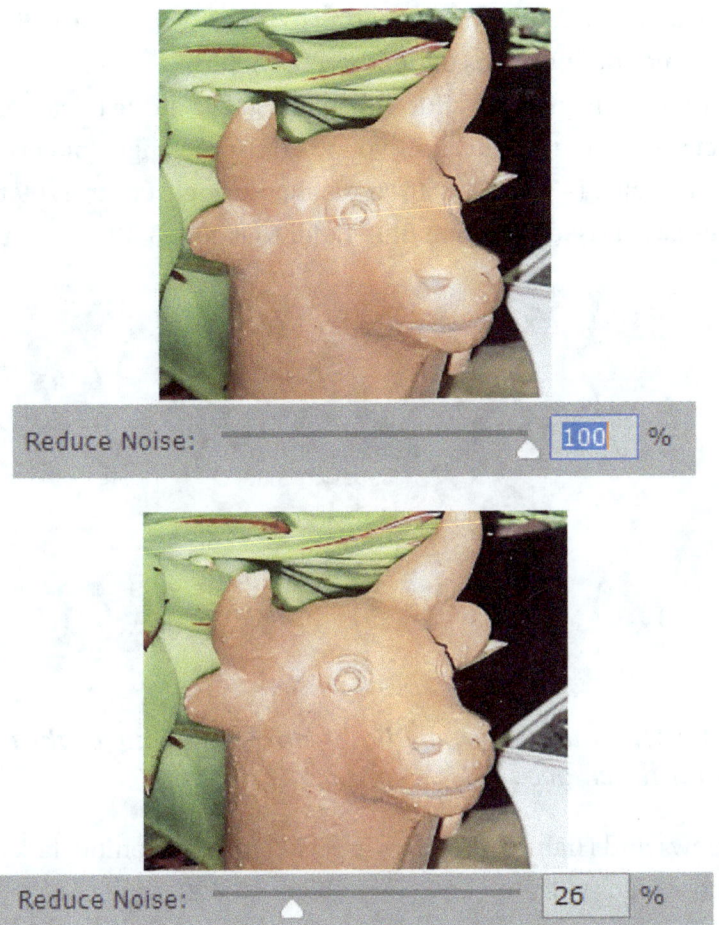

Figure 3-120. *Smart Sharpen dialog box: adjusting the Reduce Noise setting*

Remove: Used to remove a type of blur such as Lens Blur, Gaussian Blur, or Motion Blur.

Lens Blur: Detects the image's edges and details. It is recommended to provide finer sharpening of details and reduce the sharpening of halos.

483

CHAPTER 3 BASIC FILTERS FOR PHOTO RESTORATION

Gaussian Blur: Uses a similar setting to the Unsharp Mask filter and can sometimes define edges better than Lens Blur.

Motion Blur: Is used to reduce the effects of blur due to camera shake or subject movement. It will allow you to adjust the angle for correction by entering the value (–360°, 0°, 360°) or using the angle control rotation icon.

In this case I used Gaussian Blur. Refer to Figure 3-121.

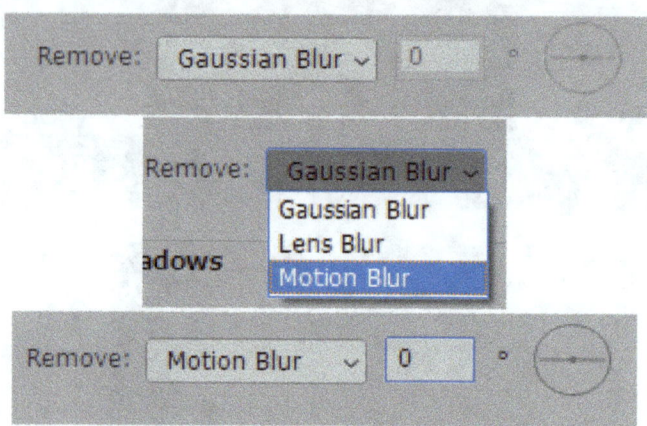

Figure 3-121. *Smart Sharpen dialog box: adjusting for the correct type of blur to remove*

Shadows and Highlights sliders are used for sharpening dark and light areas where halos still appear. Refer to Figure 3-122.

484

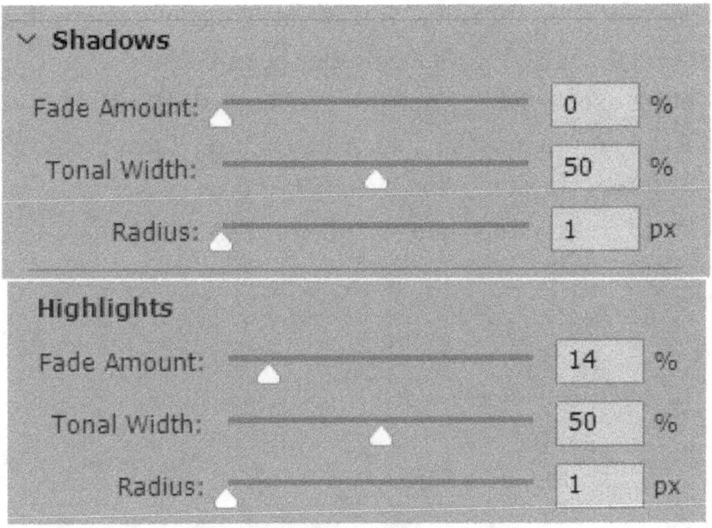

CHAPTER 3   BASIC FILTERS FOR PHOTO RESTORATION

Figure 3-122. Smart Sharpen dialog box: adjusting Shadows and Highlights settings

You can set the following for Shadows and Highlights:

Fade Amount (0-100%): Enter an amount of correction to adjust the amount of sharpening. For Shadows I left the amount at 0%. For Highlights I increased it to 14%, to reduce some of the white highlights on the pot.

Tonal Width (0-100%): Enter a tonal width value to control the range moving the slider left or right. 0 is considered narrow and 100 is considered broad. For both the Shadows and Highlights, I left this setting at 50%.

Radius (1-100 px): Enter a value to set the scale size for corrections. The value controls the size of the area surrounding each pixel. The value is used to determine whether a pixel is in the Shadows or Highlights. Move the slider to the left to set a small area and move it to the right to set a larger area. In this example for Shadows and Highlights, I left the setting at 1 px.

In the dialog box, use the zoom-out (-) and zoom-in (+) magnifying glass icons when you want to zoom in on a section in the preview box to see an affected area up close and zoom out after. Move the image in the

CHAPTER 3　BASIC FILTERS FOR PHOTO RESTORATION

preview area to see another area. You can also toggle Preview on and off to compare the settings on the dialog box to the canvas.

Optionally, use the Alt/Option key to change the Cancel button to Reset to reset your original slider settings. Holding down the Ctrl/CMD key changes the Cancel button to the Default button.

Click OK to commit the changes. Refer to Figure 3-123.

CHAPTER 3　BASIC FILTERS FOR PHOTO RESTORATION

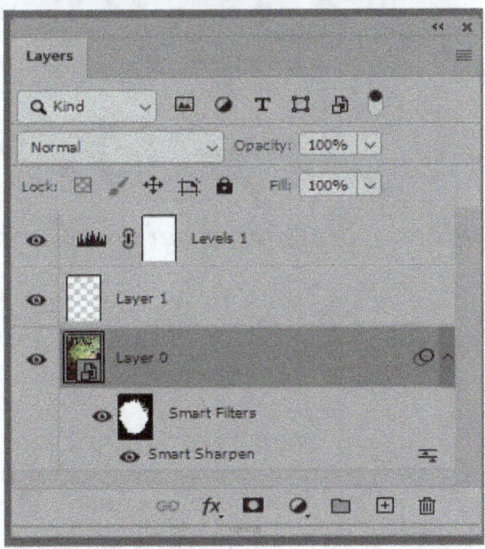

Figure 3-123. *Smart Sharpen filter applied to the smart object layer and a painted mask for the smart filter*

CHAPTER 3 BASIC FILTERS FOR PHOTO RESTORATION

In this example, you can refer to **Plant_Sharpen_final.psd** for the layer's smart filter mask. I also painted with the Eraser tool on the smart filter mask so that only the plant and pot were sharpened and not the background and area below the pot. Additionally, you may also, on a separate layer (Layer 1), want to use the Clone Stamp tool to cover any unwanted dust and scratches that were made visible by the sharpening. In this case using the Options bar panel Brush Preset picker, a small round brush of about 9 px, with a 12% hardness, was good for covering tiny dots. Refer to Figure 3-124.

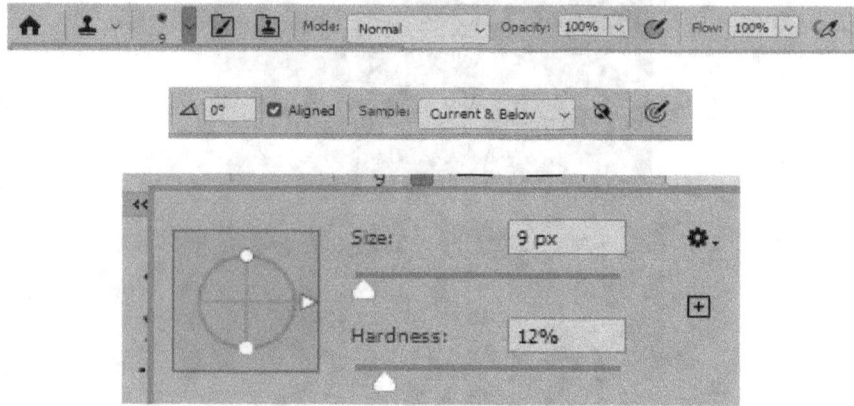

Figure 3-124. *Settings in the Options bar panel for the Clone Stamp tool*

File ➤ Save your work and check out my file **Plant_Sharpen_final.psd** for reference.

Unsharp Mask

While not as complex as Smart Sharpen, you can use this filter to find the areas in the image where significant color changes occur and sharpen them. You can use Unsharp Mask in combination with the Sharpen Edges filter, which sharpens only edges while preserving the overall smoothness of the image. However, that filter does not allow you to specify an amount.

CHAPTER 3 BASIC FILTERS FOR PHOTO RESTORATION

For better color correction control, it is recommended to use the Unsharp Mask filter with a blending mode to adjust the contrast of edge detail and produce a lighter and darker line on each side of the edge.

However, before you apply the blending mode, first use the Filter's dialog box to emphasize the edge detail and create an illusion of a sharper image.

In this example I will just show you how the same plant image could appear using Unsharp Mask, and then you can decide if you prefer it over Smart Sharpen. Refer to the file **Plant_Sharpen_final2.psd**. I have turned the visibility off for Smart Sharpen. Refer to Figure 3-125.

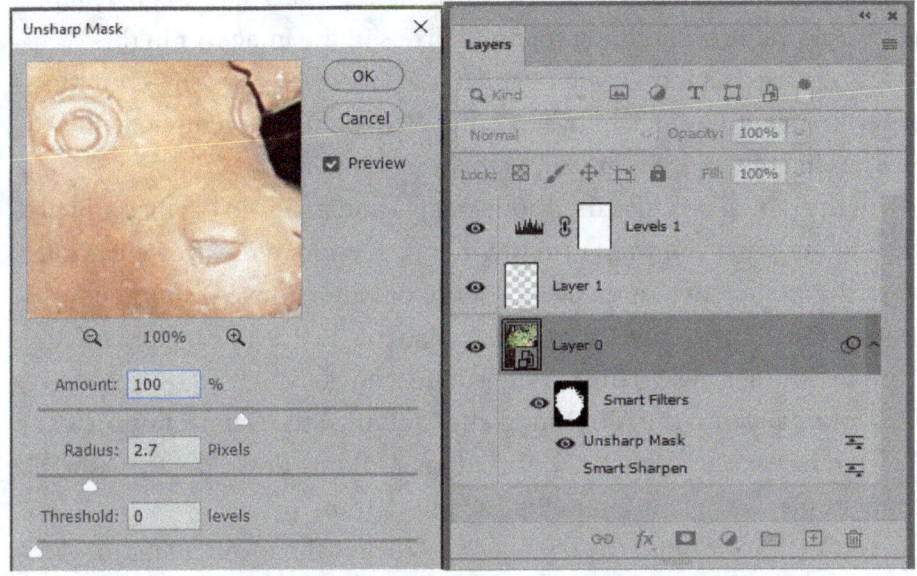

Figure 3-125. *Unsharp Mask dialog box and the Unsharp Mask filter applied to the smart object layer with the Smart Sharpen filter turned off*

The following settings in the dialog box are

Amount (1–500%): Use the slider or enter a value to determine how much to increase the contrast of pixels. Adobe recommends a setting for high-resolution printed images of between 150% and 200%. I found visually a setting of 100% did not oversharpen.

489

Radius (0.1–1000.0 pixels): Enter a value to determine the number of pixels surrounding the edge pixels that will affect the sharpening. High values will cause more dramatic effects, and the sharpening effect will appear more obvious. On screen, the lower settings you choose may look OK. However, keep in mind that if the image will be printed, you may have to increase the radius from 1 to 2 pixels to see improved sharpening in a wider range of pixels. In this case I tried 2.7 pixels.

Threshold (0–255 levels): Enter a value to determine how different the sharpened pixels must be from the surrounding area before they are considered edge pixels, and the sharpening takes place. The default Threshold value is 0; this sharpens all pixels in the image, or in this case, the area that is revealed by the mask. However, you may want to experiment with a value between 2 and 20 depending on how much sharpening the image requires. In this case I left it at 0.

In the dialog box, use the zoom-out (–) and zoom-in (+) magnifying glass icons when you want to zoom in on a section in the preview box to see a sharpened area up close and zoom out after. Move your preview around to see different areas. You can also toggle Preview on and off to compare the settings in the preview to the canvas.

Optionally, use the Alt/Option key to change the Cancel button to Reset to reset your original slider settings. Holding down the Ctrl/CMD key changes the Cancel button to the Default button.

Click OK to commit the changes and review the result. Refer to Figure 3-126.

CHAPTER 3 BASIC FILTERS FOR PHOTO RESTORATION

Figure 3-126. *Unsharp Mask applied to the image*

Each sharpen filter has its own unique sharpen settings. However, I would not recommend using the two together as this could again cause an oversharpening in the highlights. Use these one at a time.

Other things that you can try with the smart filter applied are as follows:

- As noted, use a layer mask or smart filter to avoid sharpening some areas altogether and leave them intentionally blurred. This may avoid adding additional noise or banding to areas that contain skin tones.

- As mentioned, to control color correction, if colors start to appear oversaturated in some areas or desaturated in others, you may want to experiment with the smart filter blending options to fade blend settings and try setting the blending mode to Luminosity as well as fading the opacity. In this example I left the blending mode at Normal and the opacity at 100%. Refer to Figure 3-127.

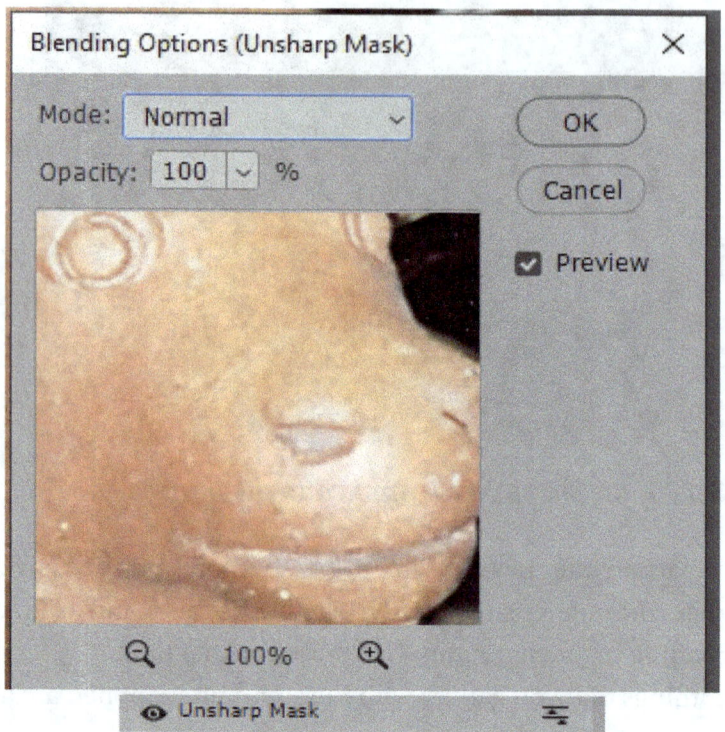

Figure 3-127. *Unsharp Mask blending mode options*

- If you work on a duplicate copy of an image or layer, you can use Unsharp Mask on individual layer masks and channels.

- Creating selections for the Unsharp Mask filter can be found on the following link (see "Sharpen an image using an edge mask"):

  https://helpx.adobe.com/photoshop/using/adjusting-image-sharpness-blur.html

Refer to this example to discover how you can, on a duplicate of one of the channels, create an alpha channel that can later be loaded as a selection for the filter. Besides using Unsharp Mask, you can use additional filters and adjustment layers to complete this process.

Sharpening Low-Resolution Images

Use Unsharp Mask after resampling when creating an enlargement of a low-resolution image such as 72 dpi/ppi to 300 ppi. First, use Image ➤ Image Size to enlarge the image. While it is not possible to recreate pixels that do not exist, after enlargement, adding this Unsharp Mask filter will at least give the appearance of a sharpened image, as after expansion some images can be blurry.

During enlargement, in the Image Size dialog box, use the recommended Resample options (enable check box) of either Preserve Details (enlargement), Preserve Details 2.0, or Bicubic Smoother (enlargement) as other settings may introduce unwanted pixels during scaling or are better suited for reduction. Refer to Figure 3-128.

CHAPTER 3 BASIC FILTERS FOR PHOTO RESTORATION

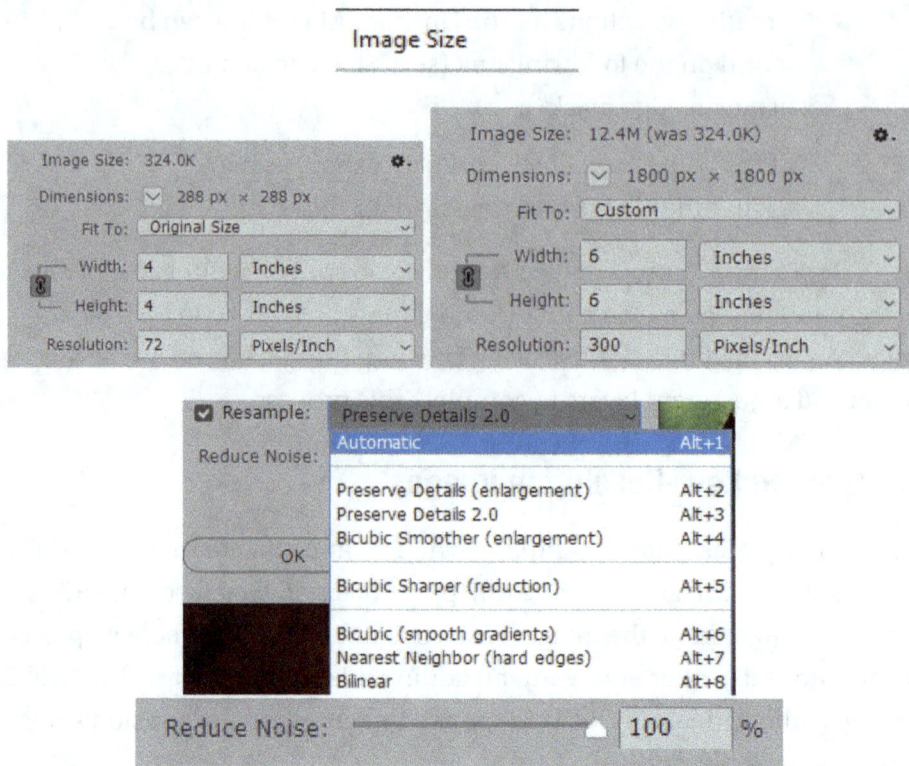

Figure 3-128. *Image Size dialog box and settings*

Then for your project apply the Filter ➤ Sharpen ➤ Unsharp Mask filter with your settings.

However, after any expansion or sharpening adjustments, always do a test print. I find that most images cannot expand with good-quality results beyond 10%–50% of the original scan size. If 100% is the original, then no higher than 150% in width and height is advised. If the original scanned or digital image was presented to you at 4 × 4 inches at 72 dpi and you increase the size to 6 × 6 inches, that might look OK for a basic print or website. But at the same time, you may want to resample it to 300 dpi at the same size 4 × 4 or to 6 × 6 inches at 300 dpi, and this might be OK after sharpening. However, keep in mind, because the resolution is

CHAPTER 3   BASIC FILTERS FOR PHOTO RESTORATION

increasing too, this is actually a scaling of about 417–625% or about 4–6.25 times larger. Any higher an enlargement, unless it is meant to be seen at a distance and not up close, would look very blurry and there would be no sharp details. This is why I recommend scanning your images at at least 300–600 dpi or higher with the scanner or using a digital camera for professional photography with a camera resolution higher than 12 megapixels because you never know when someone might ask for an enlargement.

Later, for sharpening, you may want to experiment with the Camera Raw Filter, which we will look at in Chapter 4.

Render Filters

For artistic work you should, on your own, explore the other filters. However, I will just mention two render filters that I recommend for your digital scrapbook projects. Go to the Filter ➤ Render submenu. Refer to Figure 3-129.

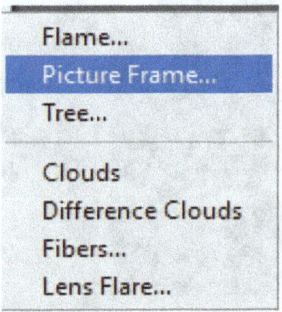

Figure 3-129. *Filter ➤ Render Submenu*

Picture Frame

This filter cannot be used on a smart object layer. However, it does create a nice decorative frame, which you can later use in conjunction with the layer style of Drop Shadow that was mentioned in Chapter 2.

CHAPTER 3   BASIC FILTERS FOR PHOTO RESTORATION

You can use the file **castle_frame.psd**.

Working on a new blank transparent layer in this case is best, as well as leaving a transparent area around the image, which you can always crop around later. Work with a rectangular image and start by creating a selection area with the Rectangular Marquee Tool or just use Select ➤ All. Refer to Figure 3-130.

Figure 3-130. *Use the Rectangular Marquee Tool to create a selection for a frame*

Go to Filter ➤ Render ➤ Picture Frame.

You can use the default setting or create your own preset custom frame; they can be saved as .xml files. Refer to Figure 3-131.

CHAPTER 3   BASIC FILTERS FOR PHOTO RESTORATION

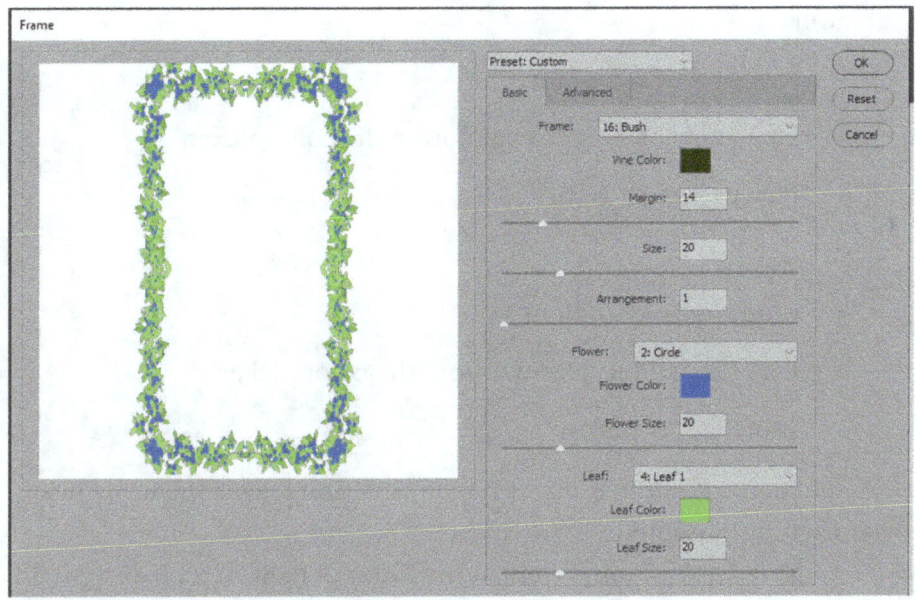

Figure 3-131. *Frame dialog box*

Basic Tab

From the Basic tab, you can choose from at least 47 different kinds of preset frames.

Options that you can choose from are for

Vines

- Vine Color: Select a color from the color picker.
- Margin (1–100).
- Size (1–100).
- Arrangement (1–200).

CHAPTER 3　BASIC FILTERS FOR PHOTO RESTORATION

Flower

- Kinds (over 20 options).
- Flower Color: Select a color from the color picker.
- Flower Size (1–100).

Leaf

- Kinds (over 20 options).
- Leaf Color: Select a color from the color picker.
- Leaf Size (1–100).

Actual frame kinds without vines, flowers, and leaves will have these current settings disabled.

I am using 42: Art Frame with a Vine Color of R: 64, G: 0, B: 0. Refer to Figure 3-132.

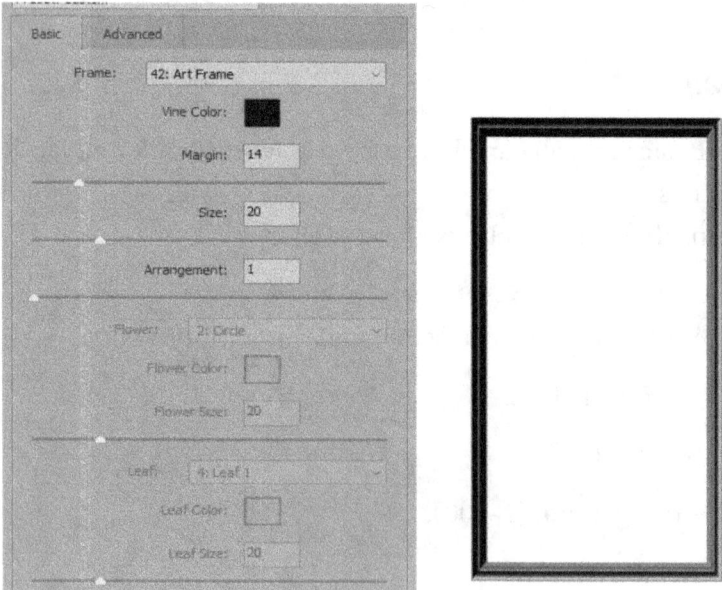

Figure 3-132.　*Frame dialog box: Basic tab*

CHAPTER 3 BASIC FILTERS FOR PHOTO RESTORATION

However, additional settings will be available under the Advanced tab.

Advanced Tab

Use this tab when you are creating non-floral frames. You can also use some floral frames, but not all options will be available for all frames. Refer to Figure 3-133.

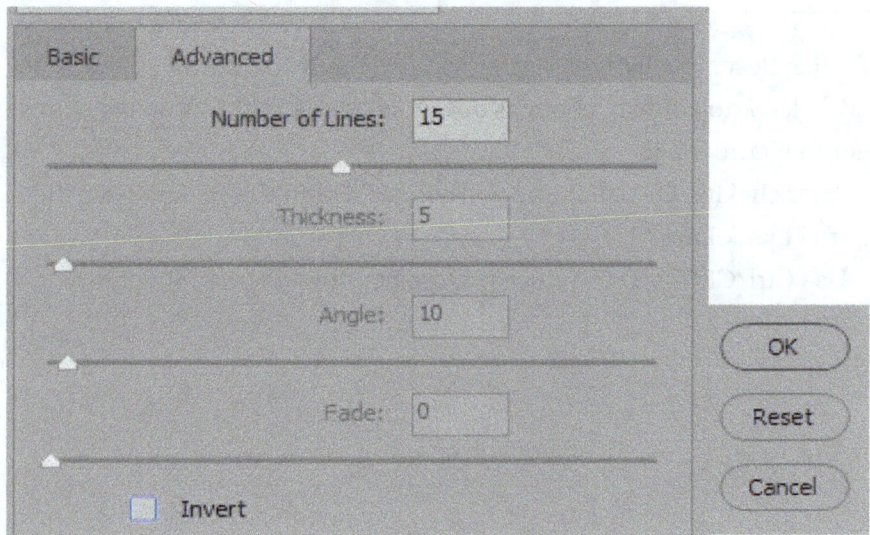

Figure 3-133. Frame dialog box: Advanced tab

The possible options are

- Number of Lines (1–30): Here I set it to 15.
- Thickness (1–200): Sets the line thickness.
- Angle (0–360): Sets the angle of floral design.
- Fade (0–100): Fades the frame.

CHAPTER 3 BASIC FILTERS FOR PHOTO RESTORATION

- Invert: This setting can be used with floral and non-floral frames to invert the color of the embossed appearance.

Note that if you need to change the frame's color, go back to the Basic tab and use the Vine Color option to access your computer's color picker.

Click Reset if you need to reset to the default settings.

Click OK to confirm changes or Cancel to exit without saving changes. Refer to Figure 3-133.

After clicking OK the frame will appear within the selection on the original blank Layer 1.

Use Ctrl/CMD + D to Select ➤ Deselect the selection. Refer to Figure 3-134.

CHAPTER 3 BASIC FILTERS FOR PHOTO RESTORATION

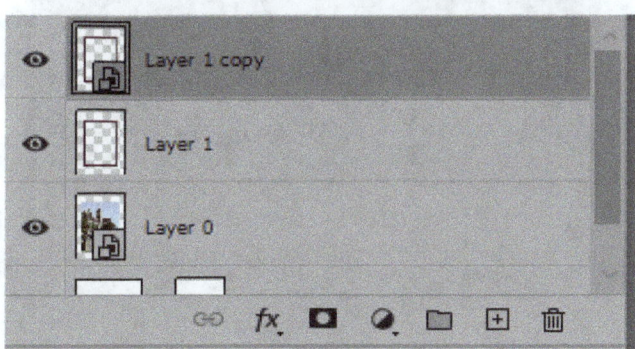

Figure 3-134. *Frame applied to blank Layer 1 and a copy made into a smart object layer*

If you find the frame is too small, you can always, afterward, turn it or a copy (Layer 1 copy) into a smart object layer.

CHAPTER 3 BASIC FILTERS FOR PHOTO RESTORATION

Use Edit ➤ Transform ➤ Scale or Rotate and the bounding box handles with your Options bar panel, as seen in Volume 1, to make further size adjustments. Click the check to confirm, in this case, the scale of 117.58%. Refer to Figure 3-135.

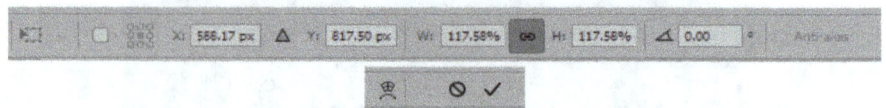

Figure 3-135. *Smart object layer scaled and the settings in the Options bar panel*

Then I apply the Drop Shadow using the Layers panel and the Layer Style dialog box. Refer to notes in Chapter 2.

CHAPTER 3   BASIC FILTERS FOR PHOTO RESTORATION

While in the dialog box drag the Drop Shadow around on the canvas to make the shadow appear inside and outside of the frame in the lower right direction. Set a Structure blend mode to Multiply and the color it black, Opacity:100%, Angle:135º, Distance:15px, Spread:0px, and Size:7px and under Quality a contour:Linear and Noise:0. The anti-aliased checkbox is disable and the Layer Knocks Out Drop shadow is enabled.

File ➤ Save your work and refer to Chapter 2 if you need more details on using Drop Shadow. Refer to **castle_frame_final.psd** if you need to review the effect. Refer to Figure 3-136.

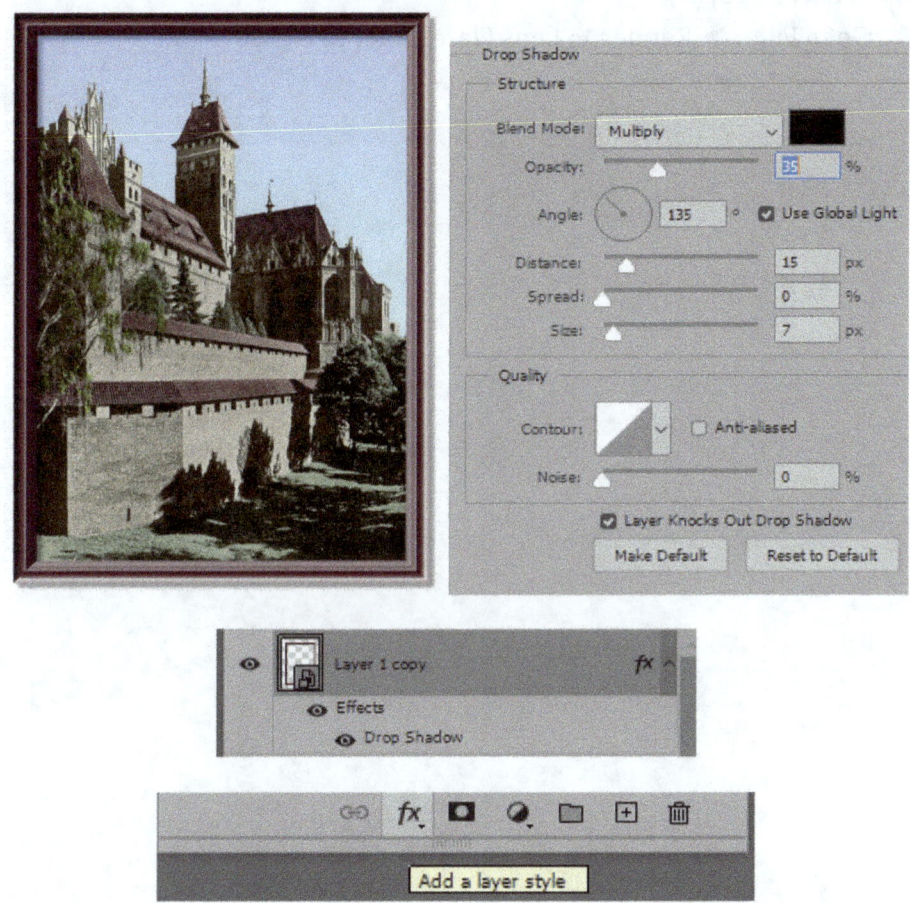

Figure 3-136. *Final frame with a Drop Shadow layer style applied*

Lens Flare

While in most cases you would likely want to reduce lens flare, for artistic effects, you may want to add the lens flare back into the image.

However, be aware that if the layer already has a filter mask, it will then mask certain areas, including parts of the lens flare.

In this case I worked on a duplicate of the layer of the Smart Object that I then rasterized using the Layers menu. This applied the current filter and mask. Check out my example **lighthouse_lens_flare.psd** for reference to the Layer 0 copy.

Go to Filter ➤ Render ➤ Lens Flare. Refer to Figure 3-137.

CHAPTER 3 BASIC FILTERS FOR PHOTO RESTORATION

Figure 3-137. *Lens Flare applied to a layer without a mask and the dialog box*

Drag on the preview to move the point where you want the lens flare to occur. Holding down the Alt/Option key and clicking the flare lets you set a precise flare center for the X: 1146.5 and Y: 886.8 coordinates in pixels. Click OK to commit. Refer to Figure 3-138.

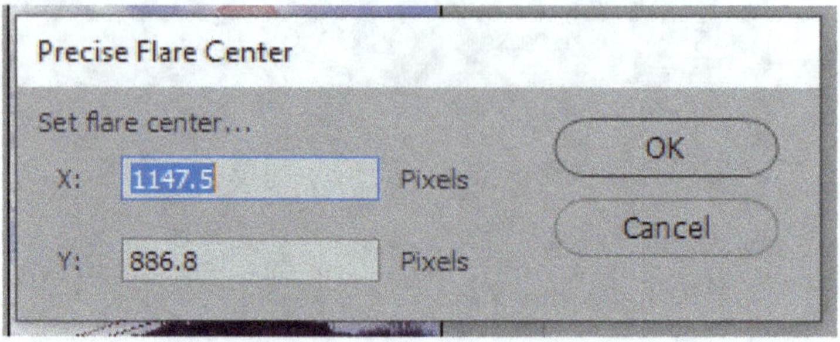

Figure 3-138. Lens Flare Precise Flare Center dialog box

Brightness (10–300%): Sets your brightness level. I set it to 138%. Refer to Figure 3-137.

Lens Type: Choose a type from the four different options: 50-300mm Zoom, 35mm Prime, 105mm Prime, and Movie Prime. Refer to Figure 3-139.

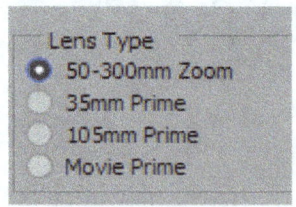

Figure 3-139. Lens Flare dialog box: setting for Lens Type

In this case I used 50-300mm Zoom.

Optionally, use the Alt/Option key to change the Cancel button to Reset to reset your original slider settings. Holding down the Ctrl/CMD key changes the Cancel button to the Default button.

Click OK to commit the changes, in this case the normal rasterized layer. Refer to Figure 3-140.

CHAPTER 3 BASIC FILTERS FOR PHOTO RESTORATION

Figure 3-140. *Image before and image after the Lens Flare filter was applied*

Alternatively, if you just applied the lens flare to a select location, it can also be applied again right away to a new layer with an Edit ➤ Fill of Black for Contents with the Blending set to Mode: Normal and Opacity: 100%. Leave Preserve Transparency unchecked and click OK. Refer to Figure 3-141.

CHAPTER 3 BASIC FILTERS FOR PHOTO RESTORATION

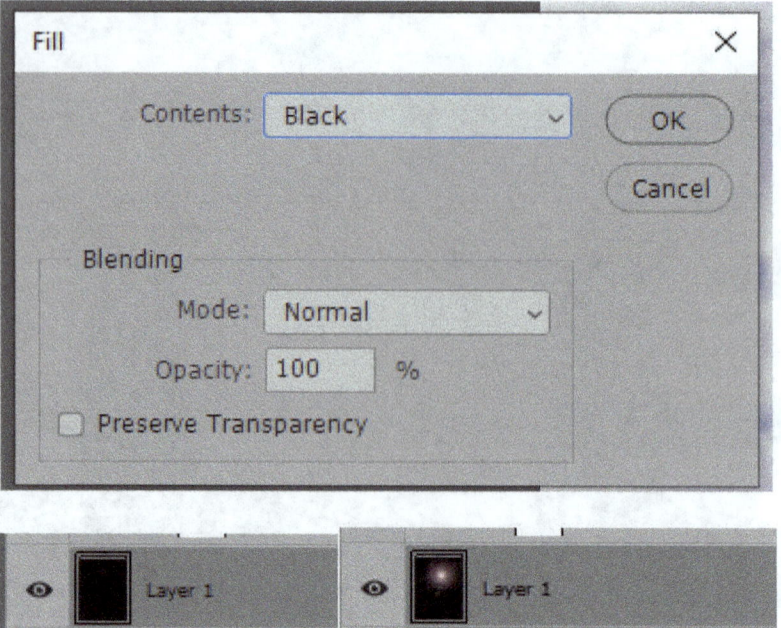

Figure 3-141. *Use the Fill dialog box to make a normal layer filled with black and with a lens flare*

Then apply the same Lens Flare filter again.

Then set the new Layer 1 to a blending mode of Screen and you will get the exact same effect without damaging any layer. You can also adjust that layer's opacity as well as color correct, with additional adjustment layers as required. Refer to Figure 3-142.

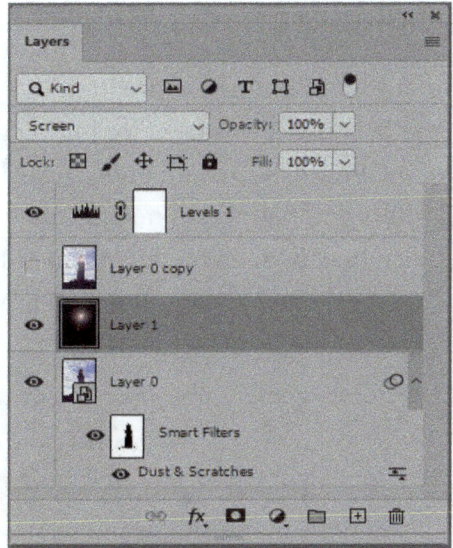

Figure 3-142. *Use the Layers panel to set the new layer to a blending mode of Screen on top of a smart object layer*

File ➤ Save your work and refer to the file **lighthouse_lens_flare_final.psd**.

CHAPTER 3 BASIC FILTERS FOR PHOTO RESTORATION

3D Effects and Lighting Effects Alternatives

Note that in recent versions of Photoshop, the Render ➤ Lighting Effects filter has been removed because it was used for interaction with other 3D effects. The 3D part of the Photoshop main menu has also been removed recently, and any 3D filters and panels are now inactive. 3D effects with basic objects and text can now be recreated in Adobe Illustrator along with some lighting effects, then selected and copied, and then in Photoshop pasted as smart object layers. Refer to Figure 3-143.

Figure 3-143. *Illustrator allows you to select and then paste 3D objects into Photoshop as smart object layers*

CHAPTER 3   BASIC FILTERS FOR PHOTO RESTORATION

Alternatively, you can use the Adobe apps from the 3D Substance collection. Refer to Figure 3-144.

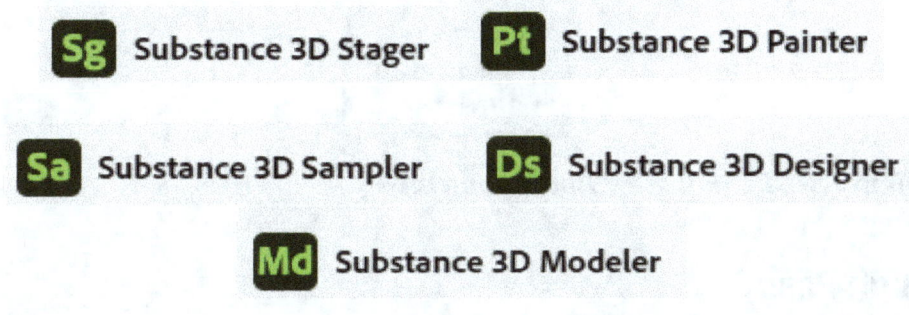

Figure 3-144. *Various applications in the Adobe Substance collection for 3D creation*

More on this topic can be found at the following link:
https://helpx.adobe.com/photoshop/kb/3d-faq.html

3D and Adobe Illustrator are not the topic of this book, but if they are of interest to you, you may want to take a look at my books mentioned in the introduction.

Other Basic Filters to Consider for Image Restoration

We don't use these filters very often when there are called Other filters, but there are a few here that we can use to affect an image. Refer to the Filter ➤ Other submenu. Refer to Figure 3-145.

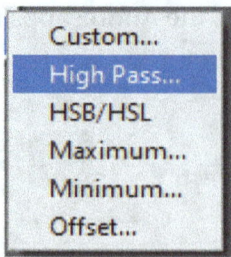

Figure 3-145. *Filter ➤ Other submenu*

High Pass

This filter can be used to retain edge details in the specified radius where sharp color transitions occur and suppresses the rest of the image. This could be images such as a continuous-tone image before applying other commands or adjustments like Threshold. It is mainly used for line art, and on its own it can't be used for image repair. However, if I apply the filter to the duplicate layer and give the entire layer a blending mode of Linear Light, this makes the image appear sharpened.

Radius can be set to a range of 0.1–1000 pixels. A lower setting of 0.1 keeps only the edge pixels. In this case I set it to 10 px. Refer to Figure 3-146.

CHAPTER 3 BASIC FILTERS FOR PHOTO RESTORATION

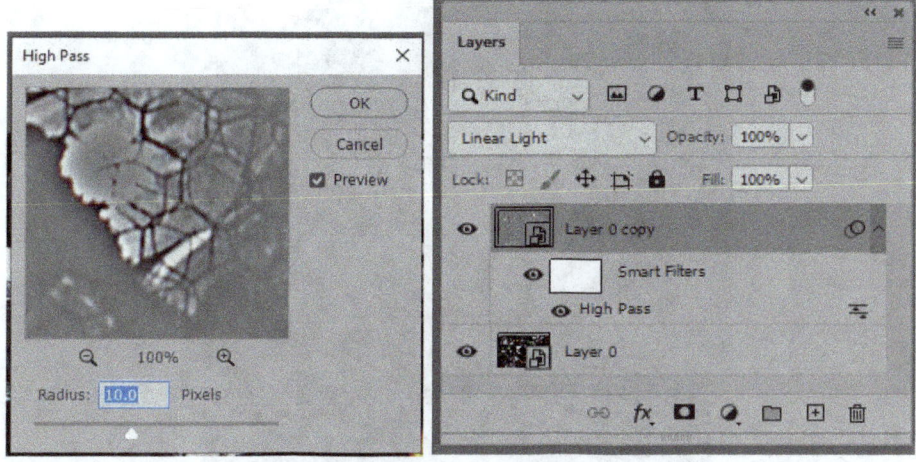

Figure 3-146. *High Pass dialog box and filter applied in the Layers panel*

In the dialog box, use the zoom-out (–) and zoom-in (+) magnifying glass icons when you want to zoom in on a section in the preview box to see an affected area up close and zoom out after. Move the preview to a new location. You can also toggle Preview on and off to compare the settings in the dialog box to the canvas.

Optionally, use the Alt/Option key to change the Cancel button to Reset to reset your original slider settings. Holding down the Ctrl/CMD key changes the Cancel button to the Default button.

Click OK to commit the changes. Refer to Figure 3-146.

After you apply the blending mode of Linear Light, you will see that the originally blurred lines appear more in focus. Refer to Figure 3-147.

Figure 3-147. *High Pass applied to a layer to give the appearance of sharpening*

Refer to my file **High_Pass_example.psd**.

Minimum and Maximum

Along with Gaussian Blur and other blur filters as well as Median, the filters Minimum and Maximum can also be used to assist with creation of blur effects on both layers and masks. For masks Maximum is used to spread out the white areas and decrease black areas. Minimum does the opposite: shrink white areas and increase black areas. Refer to Figure 3-148.

CHAPTER 3   BASIC FILTERS FOR PHOTO RESTORATION

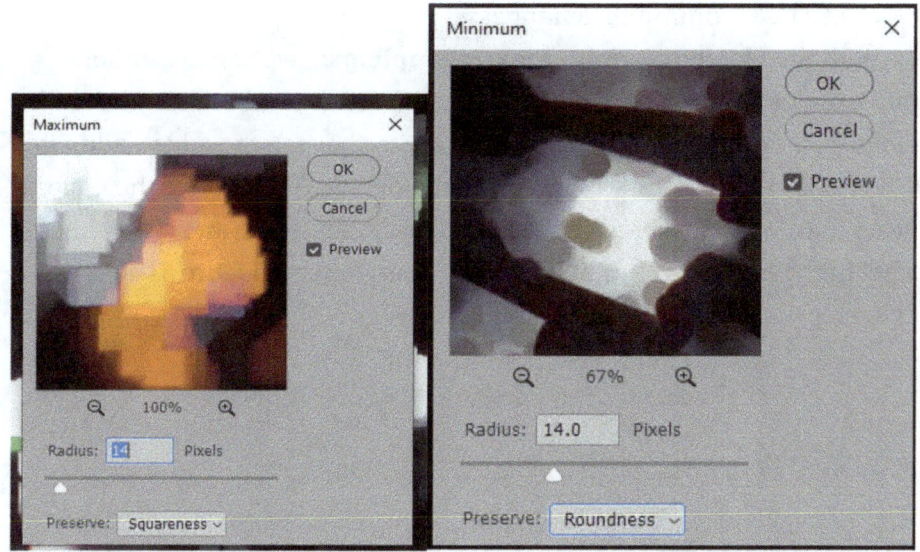

Figure 3-148. *Maximum and Minimum filter dialog boxes*

You can set the following settings for either filter:

Radius (Maximum: 1–500 px, Minimum: 0.2-500 px): Sets a selected pixel range. Replaces the current pixel's brightness value with the highest or lowest brightness value of the surrounding pixels as you move the slider or set a value.

Preserve: If the radius is increased, to promote either corners or curves in the alternation of image contours, you can choose the option of either Squareness or Roundness.

In the dialog box, use the zoom-out (–) and zoom-in (+) magnifying glass icons when you want to zoom in on a section in the preview box to see an affected area up close and zoom out after. Move the preview area to a new location. You can also toggle Preview on and off to compare the settings in the dialog box to the canvas.

Optionally, use the Alt/Option key to change the Cancel button to Reset to reset your original slider settings. Holding down the Ctrl/CMD key changes the Cancel button to the Default button.

515

Click OK to commit the changes.

With the file **bottles_min_max_example.psd**, we can use either Minimum or Maximum on a copy of the image in combination with a blending mode of Multiply. Then as a way to sharpen the edges, add Filter ➤ Stylize ➤ Find Edges, which has no dialog box. To enhance the edge, rather than use a sharpening filter, "Find Edges" creates an interesting effect in the otherwise bright highlight areas. Refer to Figure 3-149.

CHAPTER 3 BASIC FILTERS FOR PHOTO RESTORATION

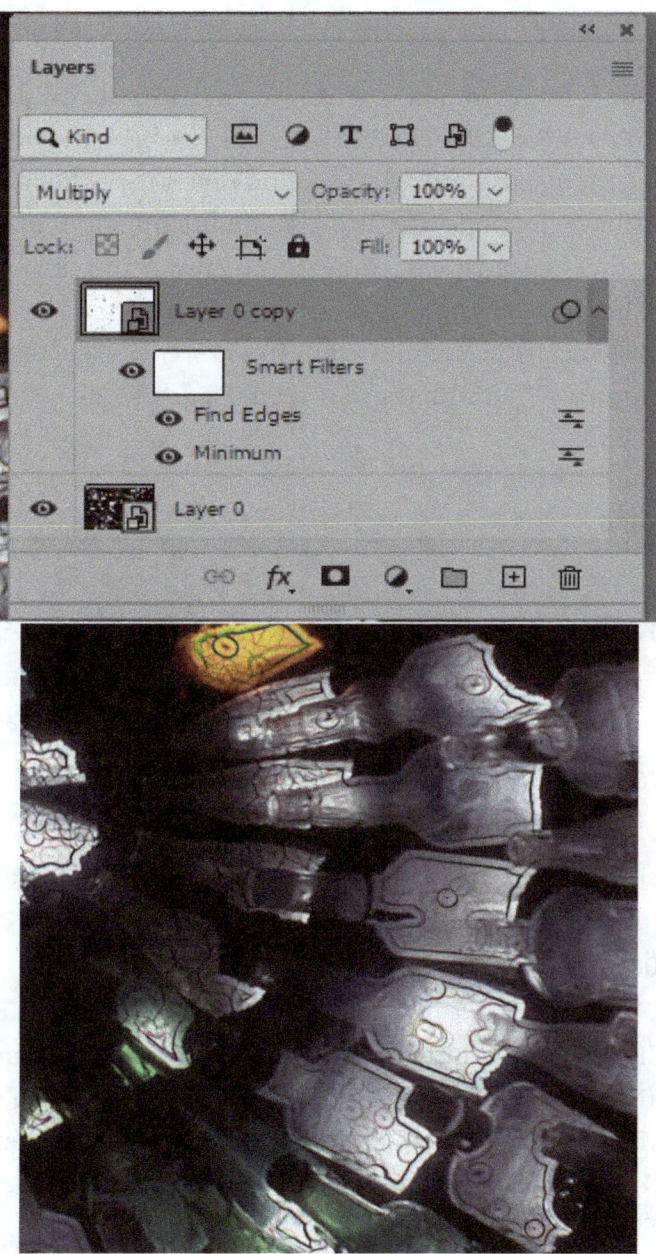

Figure 3-149. *A layer with the filters Minimum and Find Edges applied*

CHAPTER 3 BASIC FILTERS FOR PHOTO RESTORATION

HSB/HSL Filter

HSB stands for Hue, Saturation, and Brightness. HSL stands for Hue, Saturation, and Luminosity. This is a filter that has been in Photoshop for some time though like most filters found under the Other submenu, you probably have not noticed it. It shares some similarities to the Color Lookup filter that I talked about earlier in Chapter 1. You can use it to alter colors in the image by changing the Input Mode and Row Order radio buttons in various artistic combinations (up to six) to make the image appear like as Andy Warhol-like art. Refer to Figure 3-150.

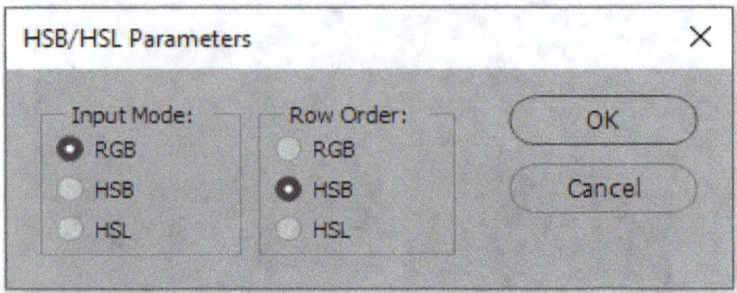

Figure 3-150. *HSB/HSL Parameters dialog box*

Note that if you use the same Input Mode and Row Order, no change will occur, like RGB to RGB. So you need to use, for example, RGB Input Mode with either an HSB or HSL Row Order.

In the dialog box, optionally, use the Alt/Option key to change the Cancel button to Reset to reset your original slider settings. Holding down the Ctrl/CMD key changes the Cancel button to the Default button.

Click OK to commit the changes. Refer to **image statue_filter.psd** for reference. Refer to Figure 3-151.

CHAPTER 3 BASIC FILTERS FOR PHOTO RESTORATION

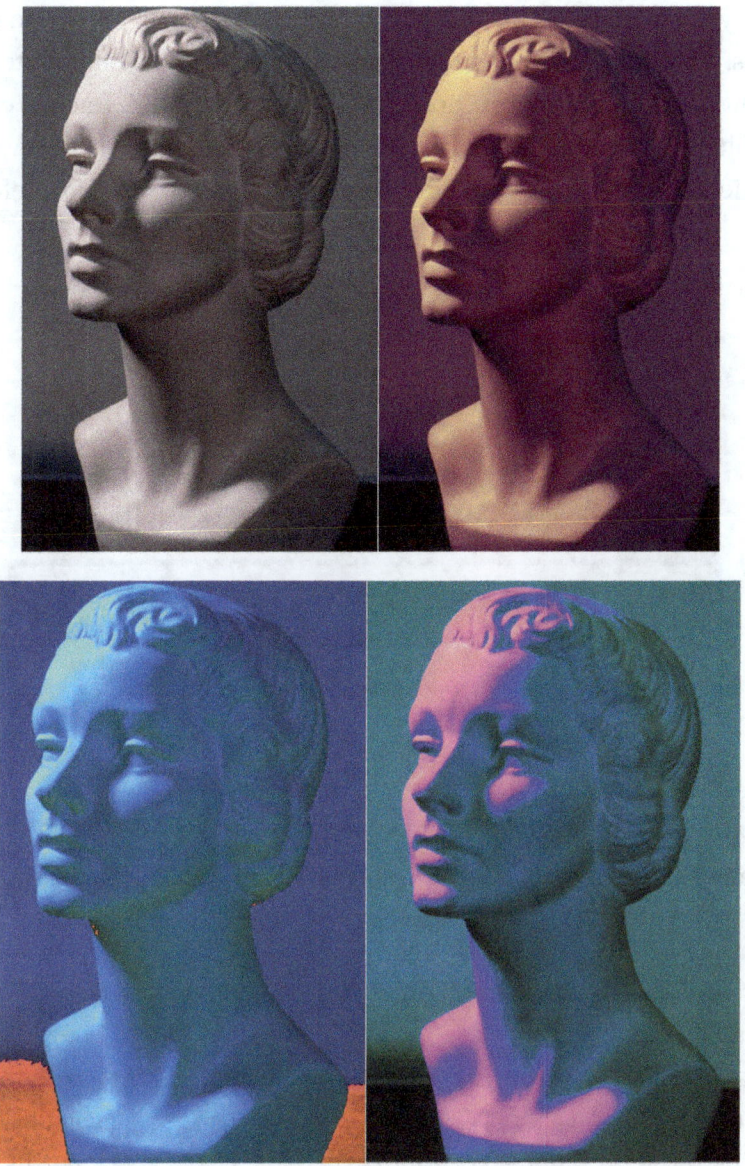

Figure 3-151. *Various HSB/HSL parameters applied to an image*

Use your filter's visibility eye if you need to toggle on and off to see the changes. And double-click the filter name again if you need to enter it and try a new color combination. Note that some smart filters stacked on top of this filter will not preview while the filter is being edited. They will only be applied after you have clicked OK and exited the dialog box. Refer to Figure 3-152.

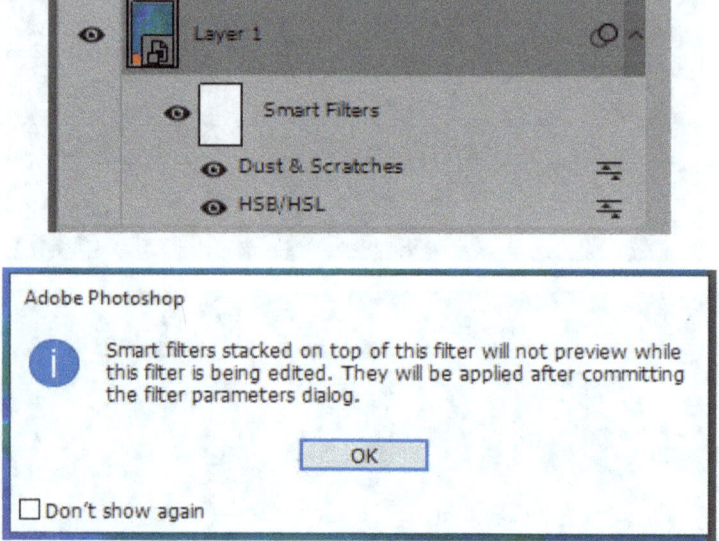

Figure 3-152. *Warning that appears when HSB/HSL parameters are edited when another filter is present*

For additional references to other basic filters, refer to the following links:

https://helpx.adobe.com/photoshop/using/filter-effects-reference.html

https://helpx.adobe.com/photoshop/using/filter-basics.html

https://helpx.adobe.com/photoshop/using/applying-specific-filters.html

https://helpx.adobe.com/photoshop/using/applying-smart-filters.html

CHAPTER 3　BASIC FILTERS FOR PHOTO RESTORATION

Photo Project

To complete the work on the army project, one final thing to do is to clean up the dust and scratches in the background area. In this example I made a duplicate of my file and applied the Filter ➤ Noise ➤ Dust & Scratches overall with a Radius of 3 pixels and a Threshold of 0 levels.

Start with the file **army_filter_example.psd**. Refer to Figure 3-153.

Figure 3-153. *Image with dust and the Dust & Scratches filter applied*

I could then on the smart filter mask paint away areas that I felt were too blurry such as returning details to the men's skin and clothes and the stretchers.

Tip　if you need to load the mask "men" that I used before entering the filter you can find the selection saved in the Channels panel and Ctrl/CMD+click on it load it to continue your work.

Any remaining scratches could be, as before, covered with the Clone Stamp tool on a new layer, if required. Refer to Figure 3-154.

CHAPTER 3 BASIC FILTERS FOR PHOTO RESTORATION

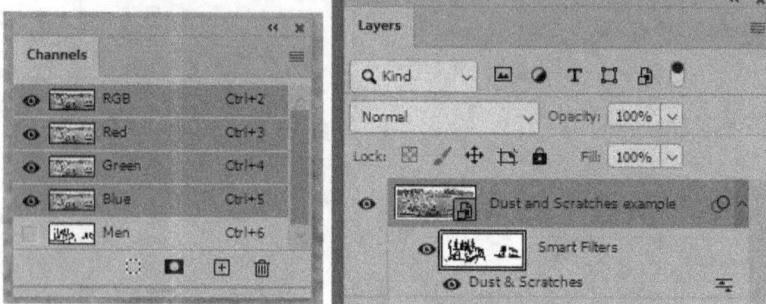

Figure 3-154. Final smart object layer and painted smart mask from the loaded selection in the Channels Panel

File ➤ Save your work. If you need to see the mask that I used, you can find the selection saved in the Channels panel.

Refer to **army_filter_example_final.psd** to examine the settings more closely.

You have completed the restoration project. Note that if you want to print the complete image, make sure, on a duplicate file, to choose Layer ➤ Flatten Image. We will discuss this more in Chapter 7.

On your own, experiment with combinations of filters and layer masks on various layers. Some combinations work well with different blending modes that may improve the overall color of the current images as well. For other projects, you will then want to explore additional filters found in the upper areas of the menu.

Summary

In this chapter we looked at various basic filters that are often used to correct sharpening, blurring, and noise. We also looked at a few additional filters that can enhance your images. In the next chapter we will be looking at some of the newer and advanced filters that you may want to use for more specific kinds of restoration, such as portraits and overall color correction in a single workspace with your smart object layers.

CHAPTER 4

Advanced Filters for Photo Restoration: Part 1

As you have seen in Chapter 3, Photoshop's Filter dropdown menu has a variety of filters for basic correction and artistic effects. However, as you saw with the Blur Gallery filter, some filters are combined into one workspace area. This is true of other advanced filters that we will be looking at in this chapter and later in Chapter 5. Some are specifically for correcting distortion in a photo, and others blur the line between restoration and adding an artistic effect. Many of these filters have been in Photoshop for many years, while others have been recently added or updated. In this chapter we will be taking an overview look at certain advanced filters that would normally be used for restoration and color correction in professional digital photography. However, I will be pointing out sections of these filters that you may want to experiment with on your scanned images as an alternative to the basic filters that were discussed in the previous chapter.

Later I will also mention a new kind of pattern filter that has recently been added to Photoshop.

CHAPTER 4 ADVANCED FILTERS FOR PHOTO RESTORATION: PART 1

Note this chapter does contain projects found in the Volume 2 Chapter 4 folder. Also, some text has been adapted from the book *Perspective Warps and Distorts with Adobe Tools: Volume 1* as well as new information added, specific to photo restoration.

The filters that we will be discussing in this chapter and the next can be found in the upper area of the Filter menu. As before, make sure that the images you work with are in RGB color mode so that you have access to all. Again, we will be working on smart object layers so that you can edit your smart filters at any time during the chapter. Refer to Figure 4-1.

CHAPTER 4 ADVANCED FILTERS FOR PHOTO RESTORATION: PART 1

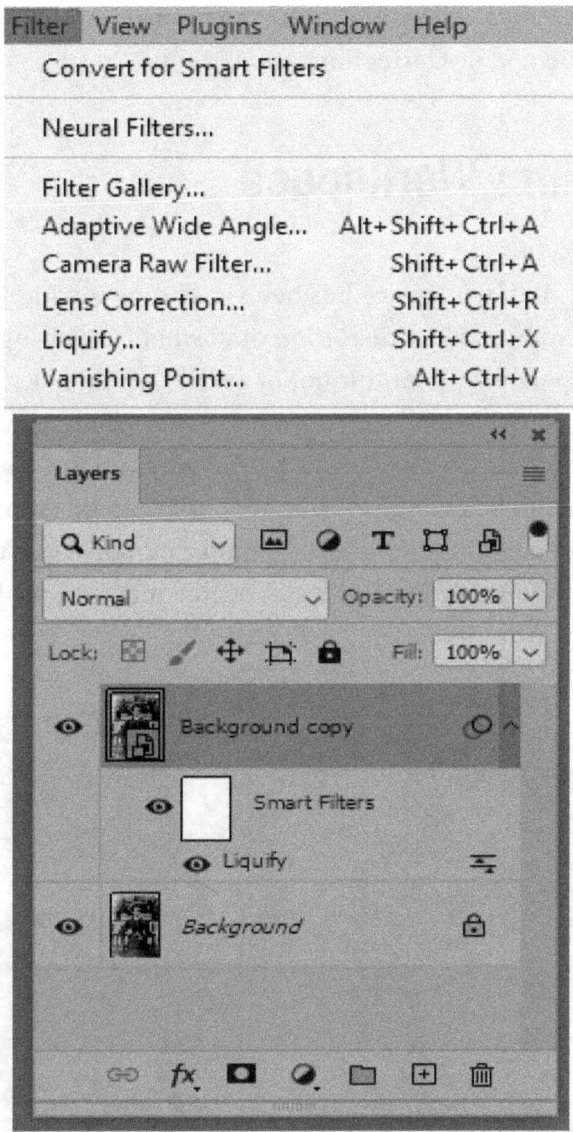

Figure 4-1. *Photoshop advanced filter options and a filter applied to a smart object layer in the Layers panel*

CHAPTER 4　ADVANCED FILTERS FOR PHOTO RESTORATION: PART 1

In this chapter we will be reviewing the filters Adaptive Wide Angle, Camera Raw Filter, Lens Correction, and Liquify.

Liquify Filter Workspace

Go to Filter ➤ Liquify.

The Liquify filter workspace has been in Photoshop for quite a few years. It is generally used for distortion or cosmetic touch-ups such as to make part of a person appear thinner or as they would like to be perceived. However, you can use it to distort objects as well. Whatever your subject you plan to alter, you can use various Liquify tools to mask and do these touch-ups or cosmetic changes to human bodies. In this example we will use first an some mannequin faces and then a person's face that I altered with other mannequin faces. The first example that I supply here, is the file **women_liquify_filter.psd**. Refer to Figure 4-2.

Figure 4-2.　*Mannequin faces to use for practice with the Liquify filter*

CHAPTER 4 ADVANCED FILTERS FOR PHOTO RESTORATION: PART 1

Tools

The tools for cosmetic warping changes include

- Forward Warp Tool (W): For moving pixels, based on the brush size as you drag around on the canvas similar to the Smudge Tool, outside the workspace. Refer to Figure 4-3.

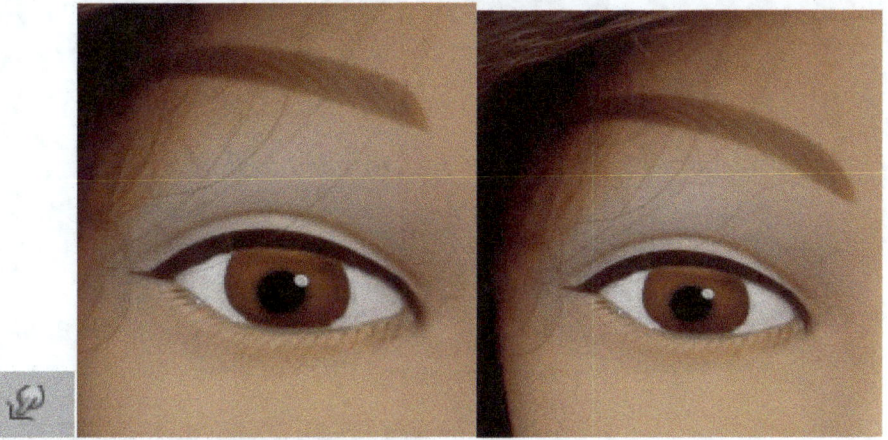

Figure 4-3. *Liquify Forward Warp Tool applied to the eyebrow*

- Reconstruct Tool (R): Does the opposite of the Forward Warp Tool and pushes the pixels back to where they were originally within the current brush size as you drag over the canvas. Refer to Figure 4-4.

529

CHAPTER 4 ADVANCED FILTERS FOR PHOTO RESTORATION: PART 1

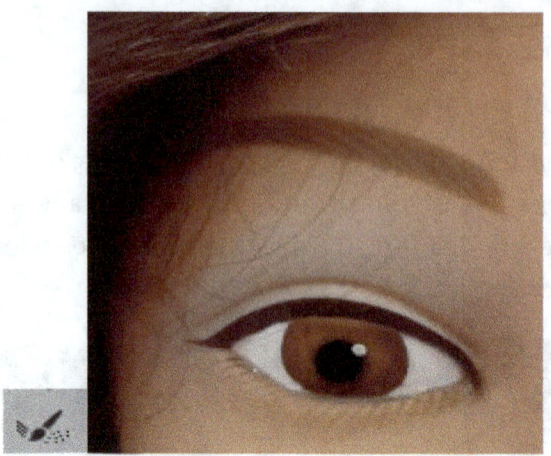

Figure 4-4. *Liquify Reconstruct Tool applied to the eyebrow*

- Smooth Tool (E): Used with the Forward Warp or any of the related Liquify tools to smooth out the distortion making it appear less jagged, within the current brush size as you drag over the canvas. Refer to Figure 4-5.

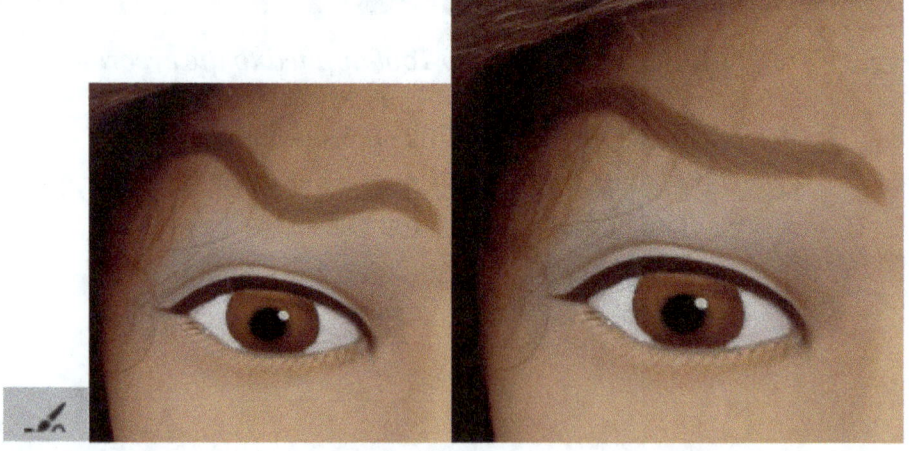

Figure 4-5. *Liquify Smooth Tool applied to the eyebrow*

CHAPTER 4 ADVANCED FILTERS FOR PHOTO RESTORATION: PART 1

- Twirl Clockwise Tool (C): Makes a twirl-like distortion to the affected pixels within the brush. Holding down the Alt/Option key while using the tool allows you to twirl counterclockwise. Refer to Figure 4-6.

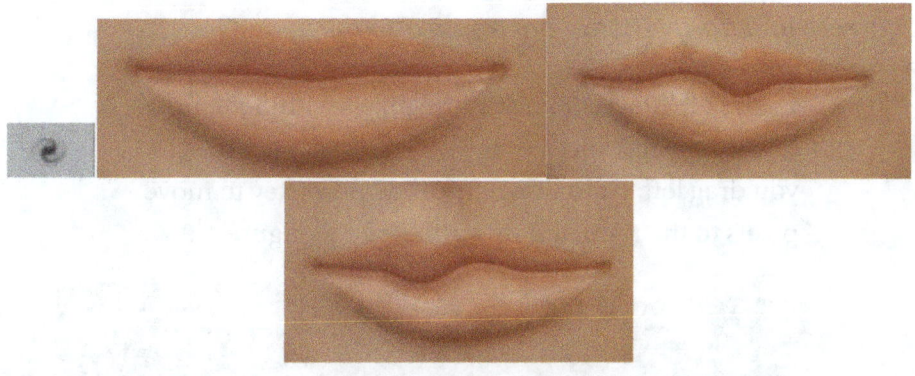

Figure 4-6. *Liquify Twirl Clockwise Tool applied to the lips*

- Pucker Tool (S): Causes the pixels within the brush to move inward and compress within the brush size as you hold the mouse key down in that location. Refer to Figure 4-7.

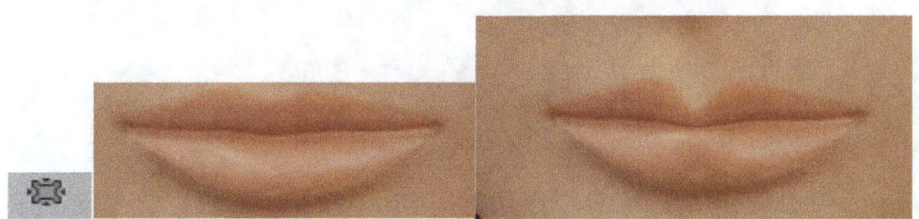

Figure 4-7. *Liquify Pucker Tool applied to the lips*

- Bloat Tool (B): Causes the pixels within the brush to move outward and expand within the brush size as you hold the mouse key down in that location. Refer to Figure 4-8.

531

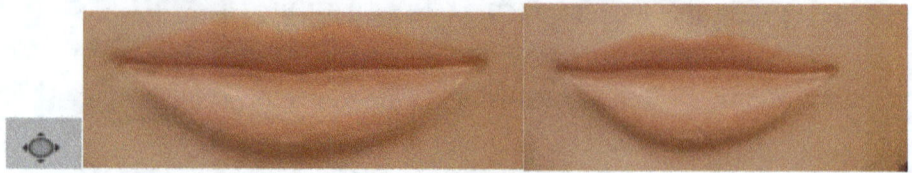

Figure 4-8. *Liquify Bloat Tool applied to the lips*

- Push Left Tool (O): Pushes the pixels within the brush toward the left and downward within the brush size as you drag left. Hold down the Alt/Option key to move pixels to the right and upward. Refer to Figure 4-9.

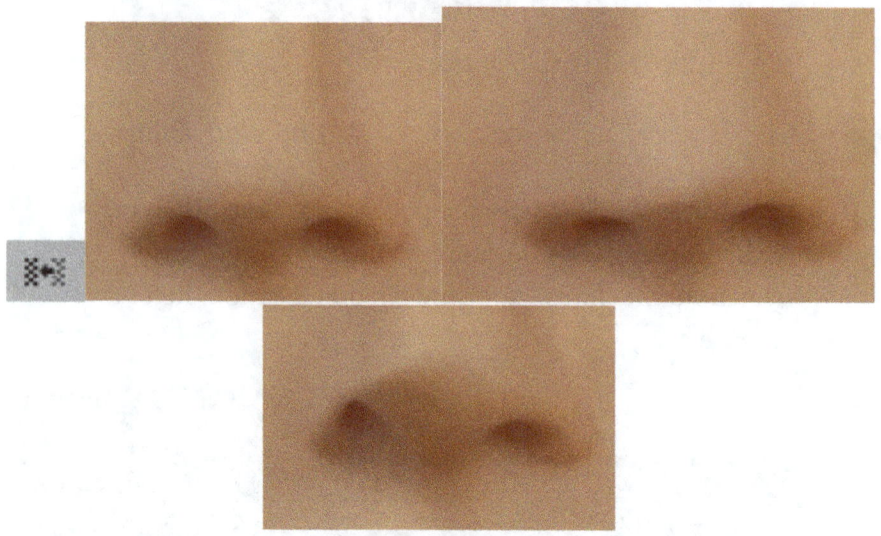

Figure 4-9. *Liquify Push Left Tool applied to the nose*

- Freeze Mask Tool (F): A mask that prevents areas of the image from being altered after it is applied to such areas when you try to paint on the image with various Liquify tools. The area in the mask is not altered. Refer to Figure 4-10.

CHAPTER 4　ADVANCED FILTERS FOR PHOTO RESTORATION: PART 1

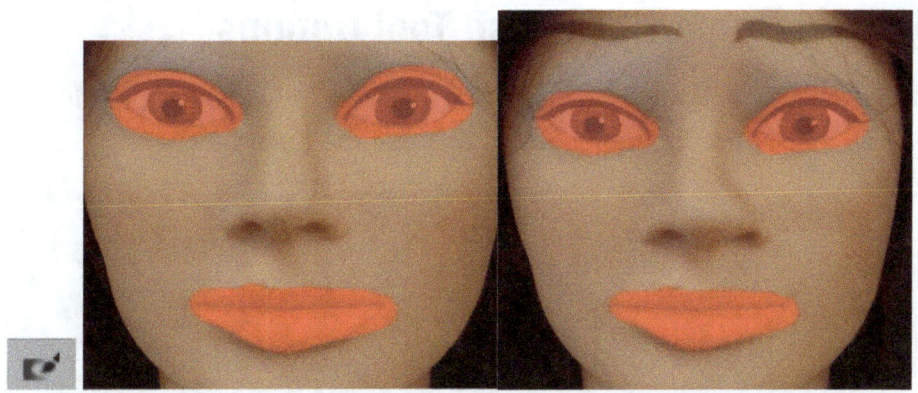

Figure 4-10. *Liquify Freeze Mask Tool applied to parts of the face and then the nose warped with the Forward Warp Tool*

- Thaw Mask Tool (D): Removes the freeze mask and allows you to now alter the area again with one of the other Liquify tools. Refer to Figure 4-11.

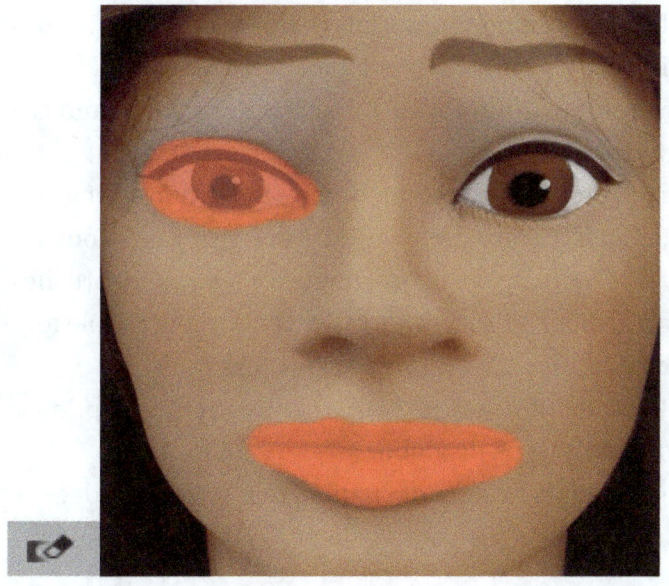

Figure 4-11. *Liquify Thaw Mask Tool used to remove the freeze mask and the Bloat Tool applied to an eye*

CHAPTER 4   ADVANCED FILTERS FOR PHOTO RESTORATION: PART 1

Liquify Properties Brush Tool Options

The provided tools are used together with all or some of the Properties Brush Tool Options found on the right. Refer to Figure 4-12.

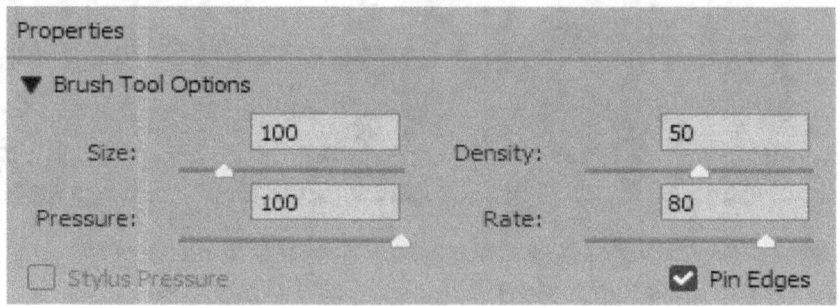

Figure 4-12. Liquify filter Brush Tool Options

Size (1–15000): Controls the size of the brush and is available for all the mentioned Liquify tools. By default, it will be set to 100. Vary the size as you work. I find that sometimes a larger brush is best to cover more area, especially if you are using the Bloat Tool.

Density (0–100): Controls the brush's edge strength and is available for all the mentioned Liquify tools. By default, it set to 50.

Pressure (1–100): Controls the brush's distortion strength. By default, it is set to 100, but is not available for the Pucker or Bloat Tool.

Rate (0–100): Changes the brush rate for stationary brushes. Default settings for brushes can vary. This property is not available for Forward Warp, Push Left, Freeze Mask, and Thaw Mask tools.

Stylus Pressure: If you work with a stylus, then this option will be available; otherwise, it is disabled.

Pin Edges: This is by default enabled to lock image edges so that you do not distort the edges of the canvas. Refer to Figure 4-13.

CHAPTER 4 ADVANCED FILTERS FOR PHOTO RESTORATION: PART 1

Figure 4-13. *Liquify filter Brush Tool Options with Pin Edges enabled and disabled when a brush is applied*

Zoom Tool, Hand Tool, and Undoing steps

The provided tools found on the left side of the workspace can be used in conjunction with the Hand and Zoom tools. Use the Ctrl/CMD + click if you need to access the Zoom tool and zoom in or Ctrl/CMD + Alt/Option + click to zoom out while using another tool as you work. Or hold down the spacebar key to access the Hand tool. Refer to Figure 4-14.

Figure 4-14. *Liquify filter Hand and Zoom tools*

Since you do not have access to the History panel, use Ctrl/CMD + Z to undo any steps.

The Liquify tools can also be used in combination with other properties in the panel on the right, and these are briefly explained here in the following sections.

Load Mesh Options

A mesh helps you see and keep track of distortions; it appears much like a grid. It can be hard to see your mesh if you are not zoomed in. You can choose the size and color of a mesh, in the View Options. Options for the loading of a mesh include Load Mesh, Load Last Mesh, and Save Mesh; you can use a mesh from one image and apply it to other images. The file format is .msh. Refer to Figure 4-15.

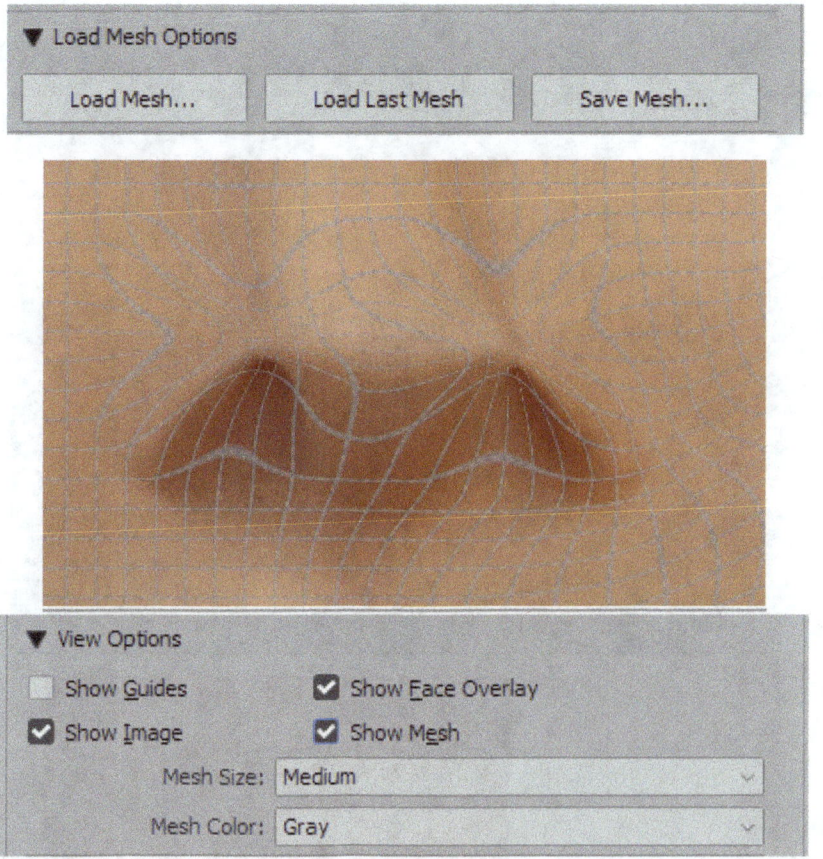

***Figure 4-15.** Liquify filter with Load Mesh Options and View Options settings with Show Mesh applied to preview*

Turn the mesh off in the View Options if you no longer want to see it.

Mask Options

You can create a mask with your Freeze Mask Tool, but you can also create a mask with a saved selection (Alpha 1) from the Channels panel prior to entering the Liquify tool. Refer to Figure 4-16.

CHAPTER 4 ADVANCED FILTERS FOR PHOTO RESTORATION: PART 1

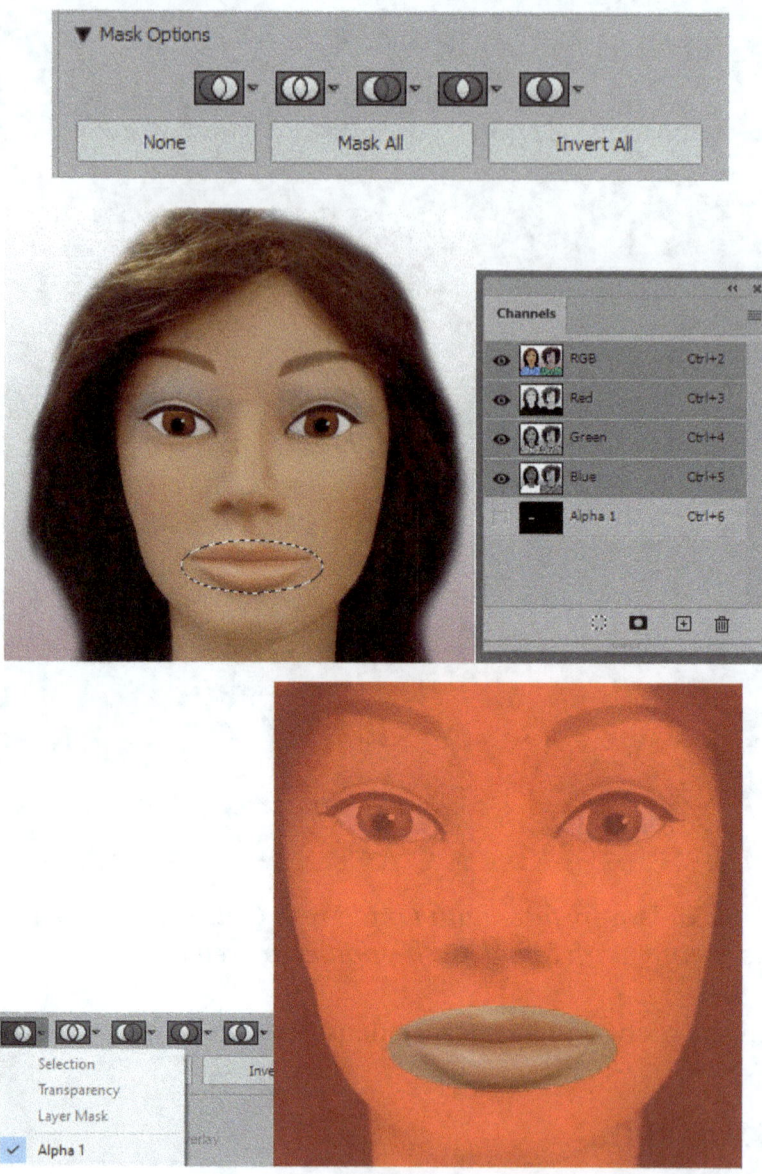

Figure 4-16. *Liquify filter Mask Options settings and a mask previously added to the Channels panel (saved selection) and accessed from the list*

CHAPTER 4   ADVANCED FILTERS FOR PHOTO RESTORATION: PART 1

A mask selection can be Replaced, Added, Subtracted, Intersected, or Inverted. with either a selection, transparency, layer mask or another channel. With the buttons you can also clear the mask (None), Mask All, or Invert All. The View Options also have additional settings for the mask to alter its color. Refer to Figures 4-16, 4-17 and 4-18.

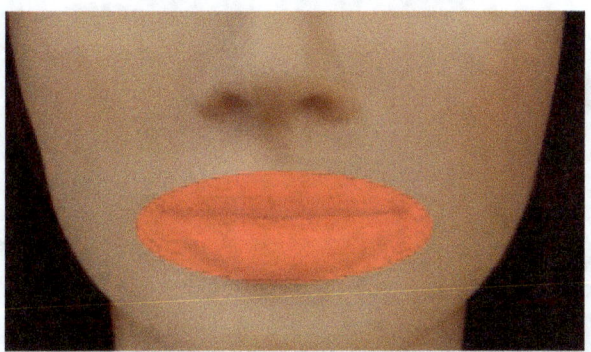

Figure 4-17. *Liquify filter inverted mask*

View Options

These options control how you view the preview and include Show Guides from outside the workspace, Show Face Overlay, Show Image, Show Mesh and its settings, and Show Mask and its settings. Refer to Figure 4-18.

Figure 4-18. *Liquify filter View Options*

Show Backdrop is another view option to let you blend in a backdrop image; by default, it is disabled.

When enabled you can use All or a certain layer and a Mode of In Front, Behind, or Blend and set an Opacity of 0–100 for the backdrop. Refer to Figures 4-19 and 4-20.

Figure 4-19. *Liquify filter Show Backdrop options*

CHAPTER 4 ADVANCED FILTERS FOR PHOTO RESTORATION: PART 1

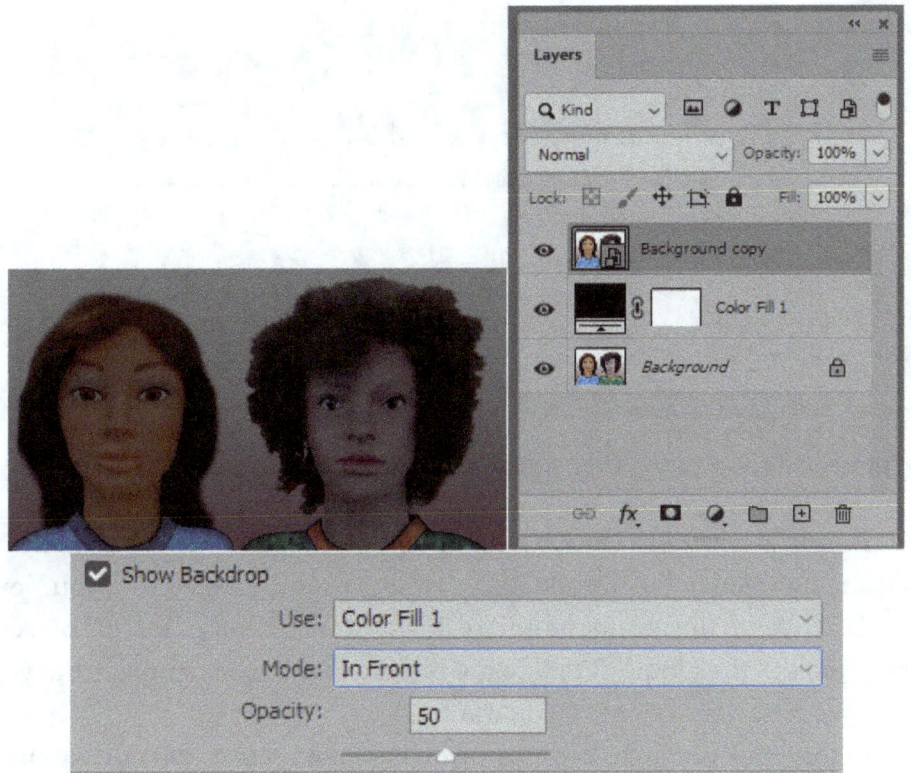

Figure 4-20. *Liquify filter Show Backdrop options and the Layers panel before adding the filter*

By default, I set it back to All Layers and disabled this setting while I worked as in Figure 4-19.

Brush Reconstruct Options

This section is used to alter the settings of the Reconstruct Tool brush. You can reconstruct or set the amount of revert reconstruction for all brushed areas in the range 0–100%. To remove all brushed distortions, use the Restore All button. Refer to Figure 4-21.

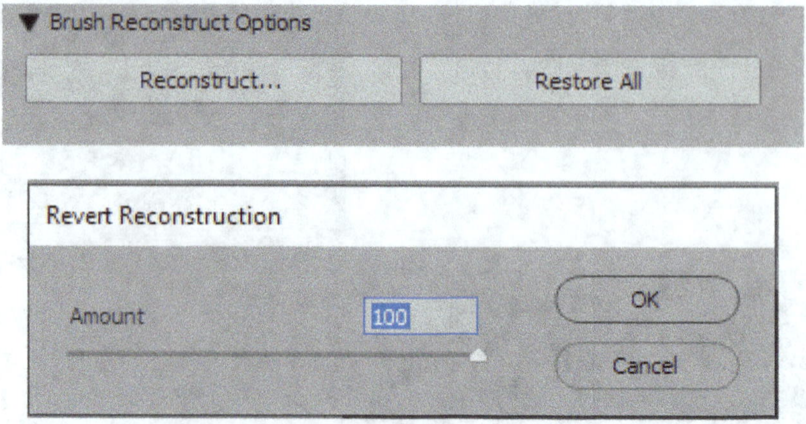

CHAPTER 4   ADVANCED FILTERS FOR PHOTO RESTORATION: PART 1

Figure 4-21. Liquify filter Brush Reconstruct Options

I speak about these Liquify tools and properties in more detail in my book mentioned in the introduction. If this is a topic of interest to you, you can also refer to the link at the end of this section. However, for this book these tools in the Liquify filter are not required for the next project, but you can practice on these faces if you want.

In this book our focus is on doing digital photo repair and not extreme alterations. However, there are times where maybe we would appreciate having a more friendly face rather than a serious-looking face of one of our friends or ancestors. This Liquify filter has a second part to it that you can use to make a few minor facial updates using the Face Tool and its related properties.

Face Tool and Properties

Face Tool (A): Is used for altering single or multiple facial expressions. You can use it in combination with any of the other Liquify tools; however, it will not work if no human face is present or detected in the image. Refer to Figure 4-22.

CHAPTER 4 ADVANCED FILTERS FOR PHOTO RESTORATION: PART 1

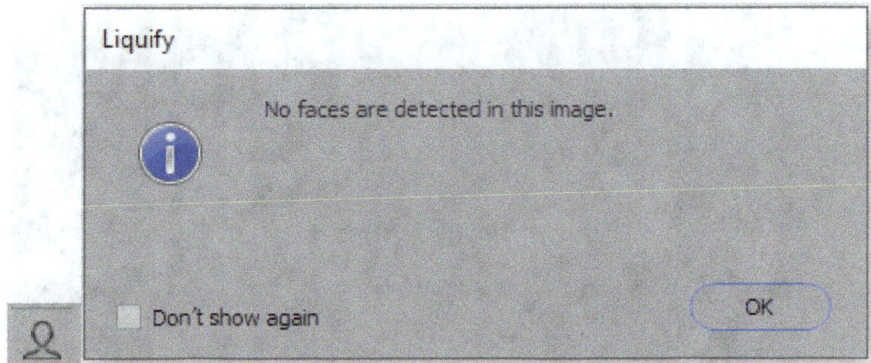

Figure 4-22. *Liquify filter Face Tool and a warning message*

If the face is an animal face or too small or a side view, you will have to rely on your Liquify tools instead to assist. In this case we are using mannequin faces that are realistic enough to detect. You can either continue to use the women's faces or this image of an ancestor, whose face has been modified from the original with a mannequin head. Refer to Figure 4-23.

543

CHAPTER 4   ADVANCED FILTERS FOR PHOTO RESTORATION: PART 1

Figure 4-23. *Old black-and-white family photo restored with various healing tools prior to applying added color*

For interest's sake I will note that on the original I used the Clone Stamp tool and Spot Healing Brush tool to do most of the major repairs on a single Layer 1. This image was also colorized using the Hue/Saturation adjustment layers, which were placed above the layer as I worked. I also used various filters such as Dust & Scatches and Surface Blur to clean up the image further and smooth skin. Refer to Figure 4-24.

CHAPTER 4   ADVANCED FILTERS FOR PHOTO RESTORATION: PART 1

Figure 4-24. *Many Hue/Saturation Adjustment layers were added to the Layers panel to colorize different areas of the image*

In my case I then made an Image ➤ Duplicate of the image and selected all the layers (Shift + click each). I flattened all the layers into one image before I turned that layer into a smart object layer. Here I have made a copy of the layer. In your case you may want to keep all your layers separate. Refer to Figure 4-25.

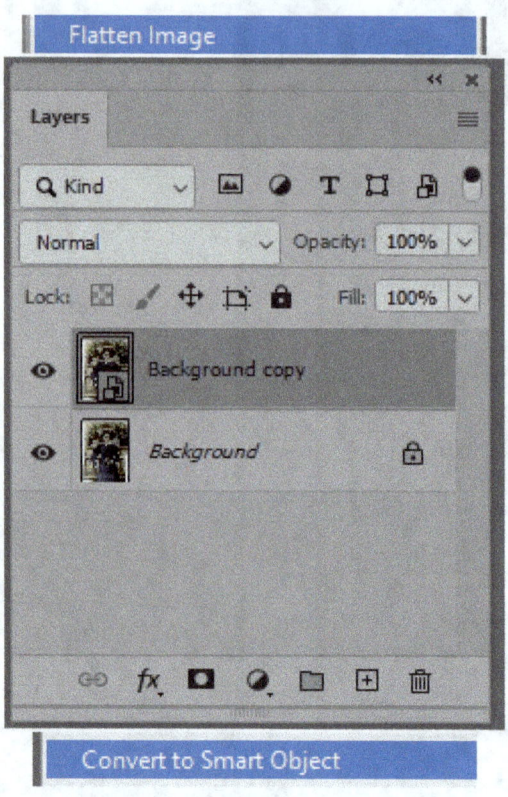

Figure 4-25. *Layers panel: images flattened and a copy of the layer turned into a smart object layer prior to working with the filter*

However, before working with the Liquify filter, always turn the collection of layers into a smart object layer and then apply the Liquify filter to prevent parts of the image from distorting separately or the colors not matching an area afterward.

I have collected some of the Hue/Saturation adjustment layers into a separate file if you want to review them later for reference. See file **woman_smiles.psd**.

Continue to work with the file **woman_smiles_liquify.psd**.

Face-Aware Liquify Properties

Use the properties of Face-Aware Liquify and expand and collapse the triangle options as required to assist you. Refer to Figure 4-26.

Figure 4-26. *Liquify filter Face-Aware Liquify options*

Select Face and Multiple Faces

Choose faces, from the list, you want to alter that have been detected. You can reset your selected face or reset all faces. In this case we will work with just a single face, but if there were more faces, they would be noted in the list. Refer to Figure 4-27.

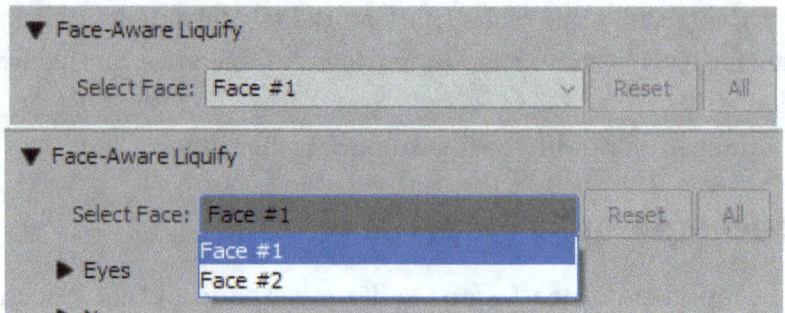

Figure 4-27. *Liquify filter Face-Aware Liquify options for one or more faces*

Note that face detection on various parts of the face will also appear on the preview, which you can use with the following tools as you work. Refer to Figure 4-28.

CHAPTER 4　ADVANCED FILTERS FOR PHOTO RESTORATION: PART 1

Figure 4-28. *Liquify filter View Options*

Also make sure that as you work, in the View Options, Show Face Overlay is on and Show Backdrop settings are disabled.

CHAPTER 4   ADVANCED FILTERS FOR PHOTO RESTORATION: PART 1

Eyes

Alter the eyes on the face by moving the sliders; or, on the preview, use the various points to control each eye. You can manually move each eye. Refer to Figure 4-29.

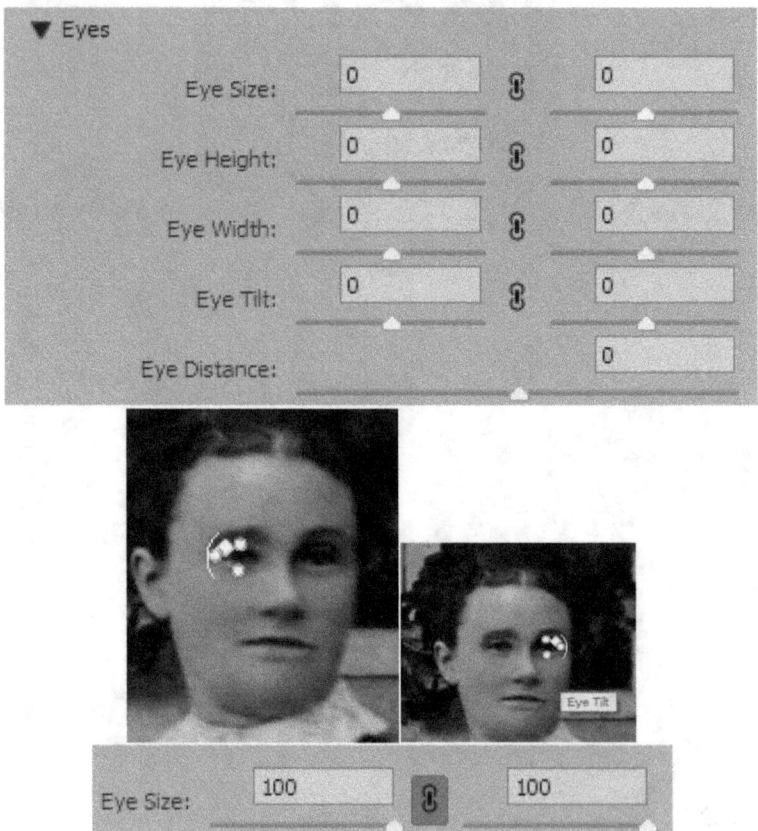

Figure 4-29. *Liquify filter Face-Aware Liquify options for eyes and preview*

CHAPTER 4　ADVANCED FILTERS FOR PHOTO RESTORATION: PART 1

In this case, to avoid distortion use the Properties panel. You can adjust the settings for the right and the left eye together when they are linked (link icon enabled) or when unlinked (link icon disable); separate settings are applied. All settings range from –100 to 100. By default, they are set to 0.

Eye Size: Increase or decrease the eye area. Try a setting of 43 for both eyes.

Eye Height: Expand or contract the eye vertically. Set to 40 for both eyes.

Eye Width: Expand or contract the eye horizontally. Set to 10 for both eyes.

Eye Tilt: Adjust the angle of the eye. Set to 0 for both eyes.

Eye Distance: Expand or contract the amount of space between the eyes. Try a setting of 9 to bring the eyes a bit farther apart.

For both the eyes here are the final settings I used. Notice that the eyes are linked. Refer to Figure 4-30.

CHAPTER 4 ADVANCED FILTERS FOR PHOTO RESTORATION: PART 1

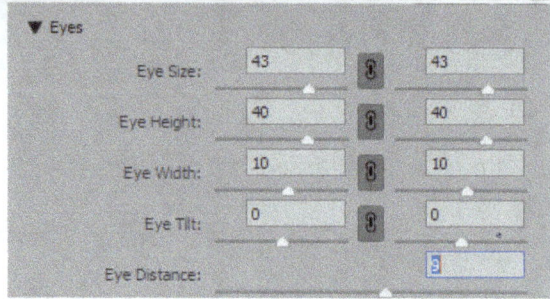

Figure 4-30. *Liquify filter Face-Aware Liquify options for eyes and preview of changes*

Nose

Alter the nose on the face by moving the sliders or work on the preview. On the preview you can manually move the nose. Use the Properties panel. All settings range from –100 to 100. By default, they are set to 0. Refer to Figure 4-31.

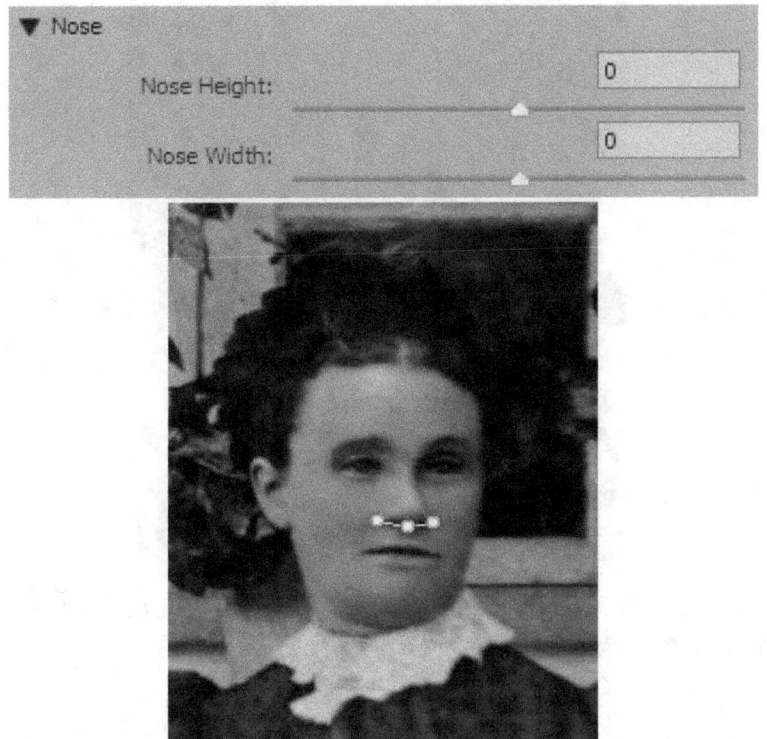

Figure 4-31. Liquify filter Face-Aware Liquify options for nose and preview

Nose Height: Raise or lower the nose. Try a setting of 21.

Nose Width: Expand or contract the nose horizontally. Set to –40. Refer to Figure 4-32.

CHAPTER 4 ADVANCED FILTERS FOR PHOTO RESTORATION: PART 1

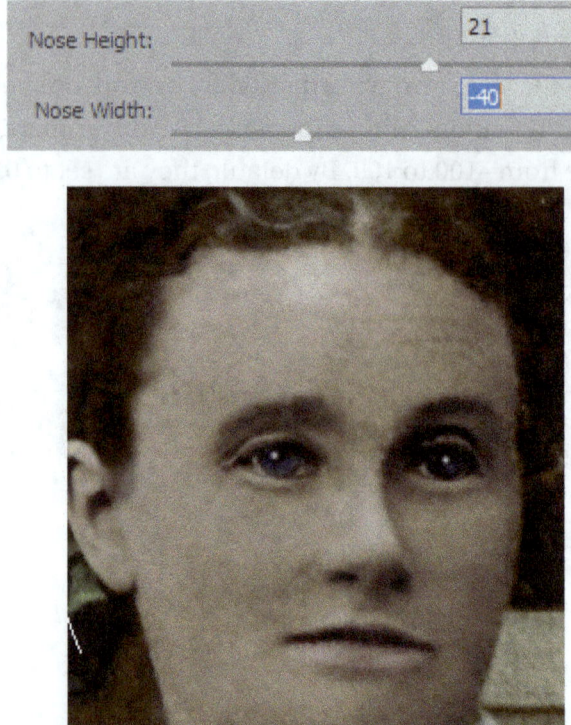

Figure 4-32. *Liquify filter Face-Aware Liquify options for nose and preview of changes*

Mouth

Alter the mouth/lips on the face by moving the sliders or work on the preview. On the preview you can manually move the mouth. Use the Properties panel. All settings range from –100 to 100. By default, they are set to 0. Refer to Figure 4-33.

CHAPTER 4   ADVANCED FILTERS FOR PHOTO RESTORATION: PART 1

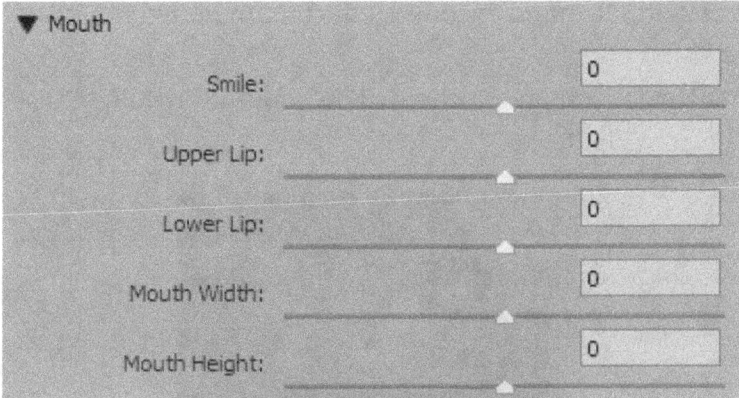

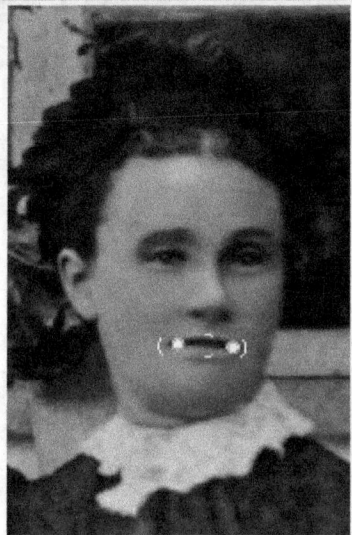

Figure 4-33. *Liquify filter Face-Aware Liquify options for mouth and preview*

Smile: Increase or decrease the curve of the mouth. I use a setting of 77.

Upper Lip: Increase or decrease the thickness of the top lip. Try a setting of 3.

Lower Lip: Increase or decrease the thickness of the bottom lip. Use a setting of 16.

555

CHAPTER 4 ADVANCED FILTERS FOR PHOTO RESTORATION: PART 1

Mouth Width: Expand or contract the mouth horizontally. Use a setting of –33.

Mouth Height: Expand or contract the mouth vertically. Use a setting of –100. Refer to Figure 4-34.

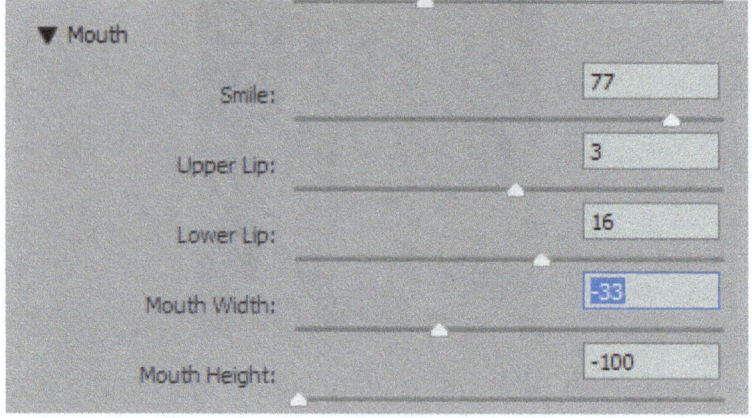

Figure 4-34. *Liquify filter Face-Aware Liquify options for mouth and preview of changes*

The choices that you make for your own projects will vary depending on the face structure. In this case you do not want to overstretch the smile but keep it as natural as possible.

Face Shape

Alter the face shape by moving the sliders or work on the preview. On the preview you can manually move the face shape. Use the Properties panel. All settings range from –100 to 100. By default, they are set to 0. Refer to Figure 4-35.

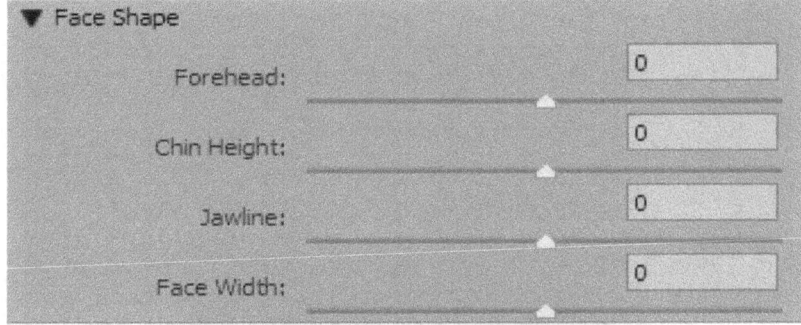

Figure 4-35. *Liquify filter Face-Aware Liquify options for face shape and preview*

Forehead: Expand or contract the forehead vertically. Try a setting of -42

Chin Height: Raise or lower the chin. Try a setting of 100.

Jawline: Expand or contract the jawline. Set to 15.

Face width: Expand or contract the face horizontally. Set to -59. Refer to Figure 4-36.

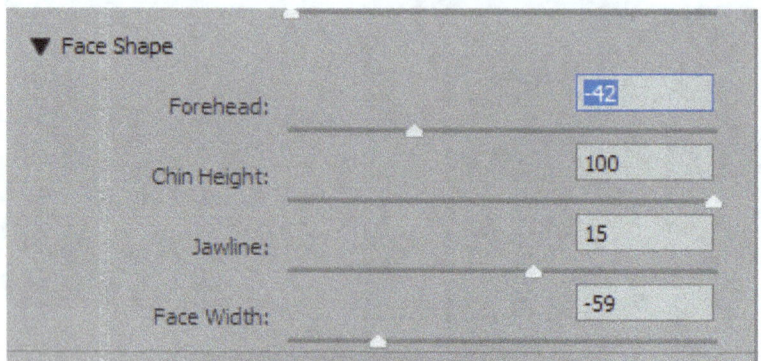

Figure 4-36. *Liquify filter Face-Aware Liquify options for face shape and preview of changes*

Remember to use the view option of Show Face Overlay when you want to display the face's features with overlay in the preview. Disable this setting if you do not require it. Refer back to Figure 4-28.

Committing Changes

Make sure Preview is enabled. You can use Cancel to exit without saving changes or, in this case, use OK to confirm changes. Note that the Alt/Option key will turn the Cancel button into a Reset button to reset certain settings when you click on it and the Ctrl/CMD turns the Cancel button into a Default button. Refer to Figure 4-37.

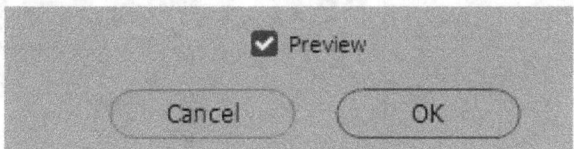

Figure 4-37. *Liquify filter Preview and Cancel and OK buttons*

It nice to see that she is happier now, and I can go back into the Liquify filter at any time if I need to adjust a setting by double-clicking the filter name in the Layers panel. Refer to Figure 4-38.

CHAPTER 4   ADVANCED FILTERS FOR PHOTO RESTORATION: PART 1

Figure 4-38. *Liquify filter final results and Layers panel with the filter applied*

More details on the Liquify filter can be found at the following link:

https://helpx.adobe.com/photoshop/using/liquify-filter.html

File ➤ Save your work and you can refer to my **woman_smiles_liquify_final.psd** for review.

Next, we will look at another advanced filter that can assist you with color correction as well as masking and straightening images.

Camera Raw Filter Workspace

Go to Filter ➤ Camera Raw Filter.

Because some of the settings are more advanced in this area, I will just be giving a basic overview of each section. However, I will also supply links at the end of this section should you need more details on this topic.

CHAPTER 4   ADVANCED FILTERS FOR PHOTO RESTORATION: PART 1

The Camera Raw Filter updates regularly and is often subject to change in its settings. The current version that I am looking at is 16.5. If you are, however, familiar with using Adobe Bridge, then you may have encountered the Camera Raw Filter before for working on projects. In that application you would right-click an image that is selected in the Content panel and open in Camera Raw or, when an image is selected, choose the circular lens icon. If Camera Raw is installed, you will find its icon in the Creative Cloud Desktop as well, but only be able to open this filter either using Bridge or Photoshop. Refer to Figure 4-39.

Figure 4-39. Creative Cloud Bridge and Camera Raw applications and settings

Note that in Bridge not all images will open in Camera Raw, such as bitmap (.bmp). For practice you can try opening a .tif file.

CHAPTER 4   ADVANCED FILTERS FOR PHOTO RESTORATION: PART 1

In Bridge, Camera Raw works in the image's single background layer to make color changes and adjustments to distortions. However, in Photoshop you can apply the filter to a single normal layer or smart object layer while working in your .psd file. There are some other slight differences in Camera Raw for Bridge and in Photoshop.

One is in Photoshop Camera Raw, there is no cropping image option as you are working on a single layer and in multilayer documents you should not crop or rotate the image while inside the workspace. In Photoshop, cropping and rotation should only be done if required after you have exited the Camera Raw workspace, and then you can use the crop tools. For scaling and rotation use Edit ➤ Free Transform or related transform commands as you saw in Volume 1. Refer to Figure 4-40.

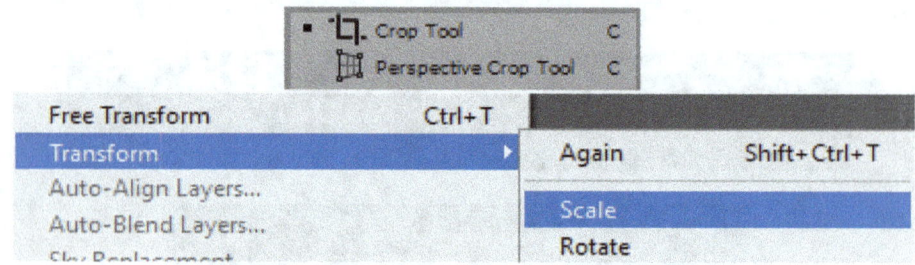

Figure 4-40. *Photoshop Tools panel: crop tools*

Two other main differences are that in Photoshop you only work with one layer at a time, while in Bridge there are options to work with snapshots and film strips for multiple opened images. These settings are not required for this book. The other difference is that lens profile correction in Photoshop is done with a separate filter, which I will point out later as we progress through this chapter.

Camera Raw also shares some similarities with another Adobe application known as Lightroom Classic. However, this application is used mostly for color correction of professional digital photos and not necessarily scanned images. Refer to Figure 4-41.

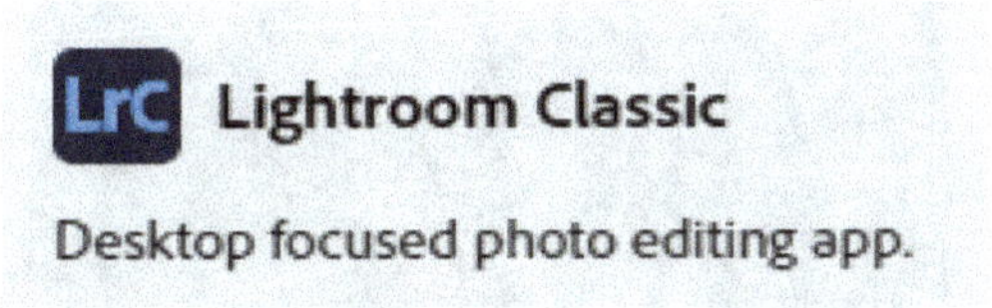

CHAPTER 4   ADVANCED FILTERS FOR PHOTO RESTORATION: PART 1

Lrc Lightroom Classic

Desktop focused photo editing app.

***Figure 4-41.** Creative Cloud Adobe Lightroom Classic application*

As this is not a topic of this book, you can learn more about Lightroom from the following links:

https://helpx.adobe.com/support/lightroom-cc.html
https://helpx.adobe.com/support/lightroom-classic.html

The Camera Raw workspace to a beginner Photoshop learner can be a bit intimidating. While I will not be going into every detail of the workspace, I just want to highlight some of the areas of this filter that you might want to investigate as you enhance your skills in Photoshop and also do some basic digital repair. As you progress you many find that you prefer some of the settings in Camera Raw over filters that you explored previously in the earlier chapters.

I will now use the following file to demonstrate most of the panels and settings. Open image **flower_bed.psd** for practice and create an Image ➤ Duplicate. In the file select the smart object layer before you use the Camera Raw Filter. Refer to Figure 4-42.

CHAPTER 4 ADVANCED FILTERS FOR PHOTO RESTORATION: PART 1

Figure 4-42. *Photo of a flower bed leading to a castle and the Layers panel*

CHAPTER 4 ADVANCED FILTERS FOR PHOTO RESTORATION: PART 1

Workspace Overview

Upon entering the workspace, review the layout and the following options. Refer to Figure 4-43.

Figure 4-43. *Camera Raw workspace*

In the Camera Raw workspace, you will find the preview area on the left and the main navigation on the bottom left and right. The navigation on the lower right allows you to view several view settings of before and after. You can press Q to cycle through these as well as access from the list of the Preview Preferences. Refer to Figures 4-44 and 4-45.

565

CHAPTER 4   ADVANCED FILTERS FOR PHOTO RESTORATION: PART 1

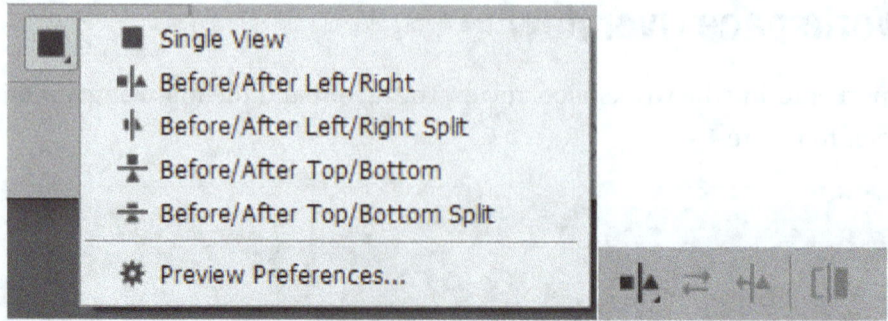

Figure 4-44. Camera Raw Filter settings: before and after viewing options

CHAPTER 4   ADVANCED FILTERS FOR PHOTO RESTORATION: PART 1

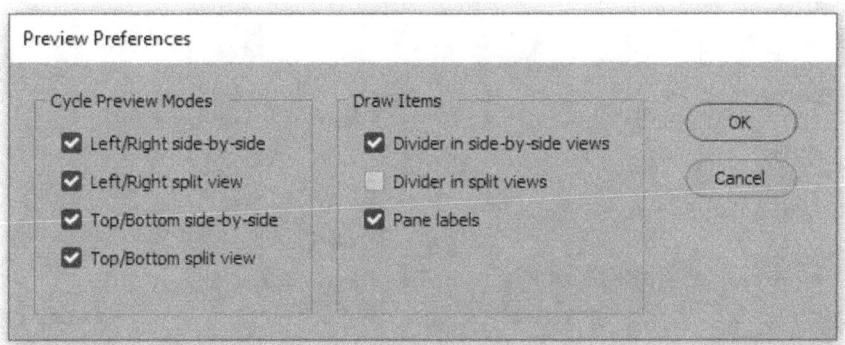

Figure 4-45. *Camera Raw Filter Preview Preferences dialog box*

The other icons, which are currently in gray, allow you to swap before and after settings (P), copy current settings to before (Alt/Option + P), and toggle to default settings (\), but only after you have started to make editing changes. Refer to Figure 4-46.

Figure 4-46. *Camera Raw Filter additional viewing icons*

For now, remain on the viewing setting of Single View. Refer to Figure 4-43.

On the far bottom left of the workspace, you will find your other navigation tools. They allow you to fit in view (Ctrl/CMD+ 0) or to view to a specified level by clicking 100% or choosing another option from the list. Refer to Figure 4-47.

CHAPTER 4 ADVANCED FILTERS FOR PHOTO RESTORATION: PART 1

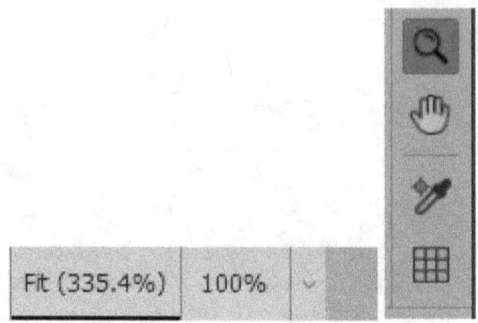

Figure 4-47. *Camera Raw Filter navigation: zoom tool, hand tool, color sampler overlay and grid overlay options*

The navigation tools on the lower right are

Zoom tool (Z): Double-click this icon if you need to fit in view or navigate in the preview. Remember to use Ctrl/CMD + + or Ctrl/CMD + – when you need to zoom in or out. Refer to Figure 4-47.

Hand tool (H): Use to navigate the preview without moving items on it. Use the spacebar key as well and drag the preview around. Refer to Figure 4-47.

Toggle Sampler Overlay (S): Acts as a color sampler eyedropper and lets you select a new sample or reset. This is much like the Color Sampler tool and Info panel outside of the workspace as we saw in Chapters 1 and 2. The additional settings are found above the preview, and you can set up to nine sample points and then observe the changes as you work. Refer to Figure 4-48.

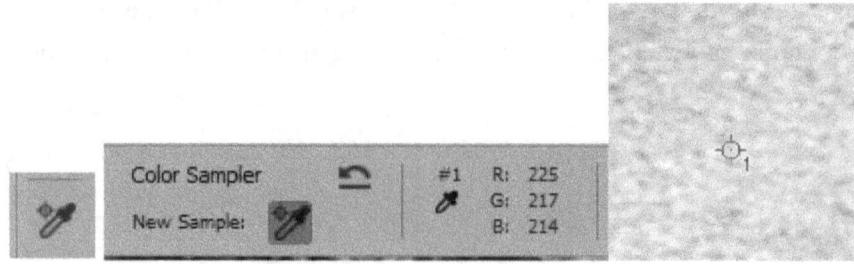

Figure 4-48. *Camera Raw Filter Color Sampler tool and options and a marker placed on the photo*

Toggle Grid Overlay (Ctrl/CMD + Shift + G): Allows you to turn your grid on and off. In the area above the preview, you can set the Grid Size and Opacity using the sliders. By default, the grid is deactivated. Refer to Figure 4-49.

Figure 4-49. *Camera Raw Filter grid overlay tool options*

Since you don't have access to the History panel, remember to use Ctrl/CMD + Z when you need to undo steps quickly.

On the far top right are additional options for

Convert and save image button: This will allow you to access a dialog box so that you can save the same image in various file formats. Settings include setting a destination folder, file naming, format, color space, image sizing, and options for output for sharpening for the screen or glossy and matte paper. Click the downward-pointing arrow in the box icon for this dialog box. Refer to Figure 4-50.

Preferences specifically for Camera Raw for general and performance issues (Ctrl/CMD + K): Click the gear icon to view the dialog box. Refer to Figure 4-50.

Toggle Full-Screen Mode (F): If you need to expand the workspace preview to full screen to cover your current work. Click the diagonal arrows to expand and contract your workspace. Refer to Figure 4-50.

Figure 4-50. *Camera Raw Filter: options for saving, preferences, and full-screen mode*

Now we will look at the various panels and options that are found in the column on the right under various tabs, which I will give a brief overview of next, as well as some tips and thoughts on how they could be used.

Color Adjustments Histogram

Like outside of the Camera Raw workspace, you can work with a ribbon histogram. The Histogram panel was mentioned in Chapter 1 and shows the red, green, and blue channels together. And here you can also set the shadow clipping warning (U) and the highlight clipping warning (O), which will appear as blue for shadow on the preview and red for highlight areas on the preview should colors, while correcting, go beyond these set parameters during your editing. Refer to Figure 4-51.

CHAPTER 4　ADVANCED FILTERS FOR PHOTO RESTORATION: PART 1

Figure 4-51. Camera Raw Filter: working with the histogram to determine areas of color that are clipping

CHAPTER 4   ADVANCED FILTERS FOR PHOTO RESTORATION: PART 1

While there are no out-of-gamut sliders, note that in the workspace you will still have access to arrow buttons that when clicked will show areas of clipped color in red or blue. These can be a good indication of areas that you may be able to adjust in the Camera Raw Filter by correction of color or later with a healing brush either inside or outside of Camera Raw. When colors are OK, the clipping buttons show up as black and the color warnings may disappear. However, if there are areas of concern, they may appear for shadows – either white, yellow, or green – and for highlights, white, red, or yellow, as you work, depending on which channel or channels are affected. Refer to Figure 4-52.

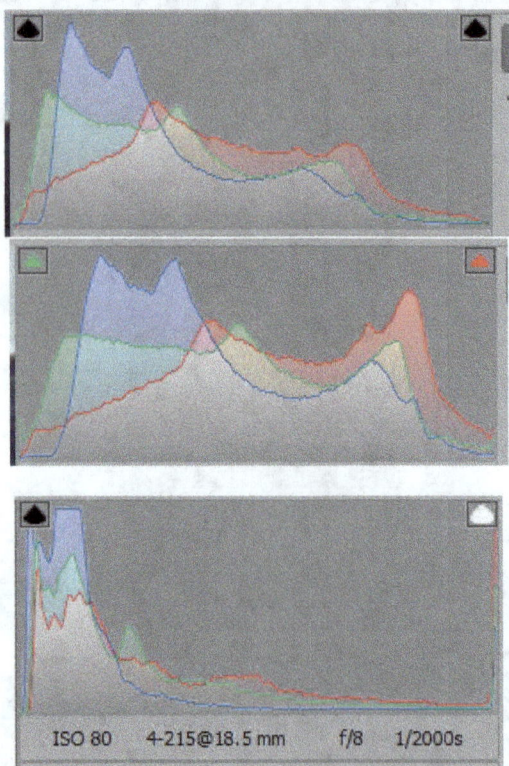

Figure 4-52. *Camera Raw Filter: different images may have different color clipping issues in the highlights and shadows that are revealed in the histogram for scanned and digital camera images (ISO and camera profile) as you work*

CHAPTER 4   ADVANCED FILTERS FOR PHOTO RESTORATION: PART 1

Ultimately, only you can determine this for your image as it will be different for each one, and we will work with the Edit settings next to make adjustments.

Note After you exit Camera Raw, you can then check your View ➤ Gamut Warning if you need to as seen in Chapter 2.

Edit Panel

The Edit panel has many color settings and adjustments, some of which can be viewed by expanding the arrows of each tab. Refer to Figure 4-53.

CHAPTER 4 ADVANCED FILTERS FOR PHOTO RESTORATION: PART 1

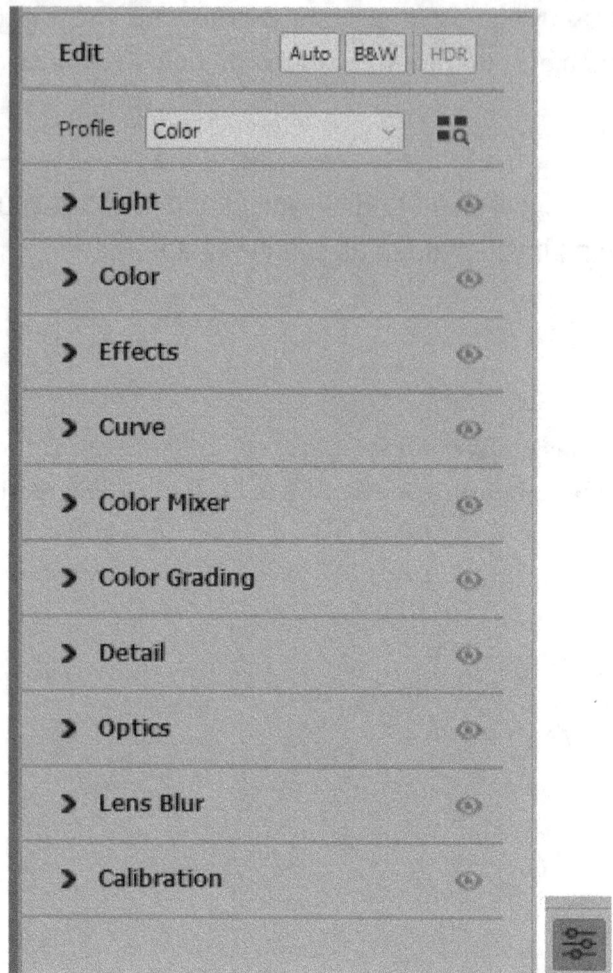

Figure 4-53. Camera Raw Filter options found in the Edit panel

The first area lets you quickly edit your color layer either with the Auto, B&W, or HDR option. Refer to Figure 4-54.

Figure 4-54. Camera Raw Filter basic color settings

In this example we do not have access to the HDR option, not just because our image was a scanned image with no profile, but currently it was not in a format that would accept that option, which is mainly for images taken with a digital camera, and you have to have your display settings for your monitor set correctly.

HDR (Shift + H) or High Dynamic Range allows you to edit, display, and save photos in High Dynamic Range. Depending on the image, you will experience increased depth and realism with brighter highlights, deeper shadows, and improved tonal separation and more vivid colors. Refer to Figure 4-55.

Figure 4-55. *Camera Raw Filter preview of HDR if this setting is available*

In this case we would consider scanned images to be SDR, or Standard Dynamic Range.

For more detailed information on this, you can refer to the following link:

https://helpx.adobe.com/camera-raw/using/hdr-output.html

Note you can still create your HDR images from your digitized photos using the settings mentioned in Chapter 2.

For now, we will continue on with the current scanned photo.

Profile

The current color profile is Color, but you can choose other options from the list, such as Monochrome, which is like the setting B&W. However, if you click the search icon or select Browse from the list, you can look through other profiles, much like using the options in the Adjustments panel to set additional color presets. Refer to Figure 4-56.

Figure 4-56. *Camera Raw Filter basic color settings with basic profile options and the choice to search for more options*

The panel switches to the profile sets you can choose from. They are also found in categories like Basic, Artistic, B&W, Modern, and Vintage. Select one from the list to preview the profile.

Use the ellipsis (…) button when you need to access more profile options. Refer to Figure 4-57.

CHAPTER 4 ADVANCED FILTERS FOR PHOTO RESTORATION: PART 1

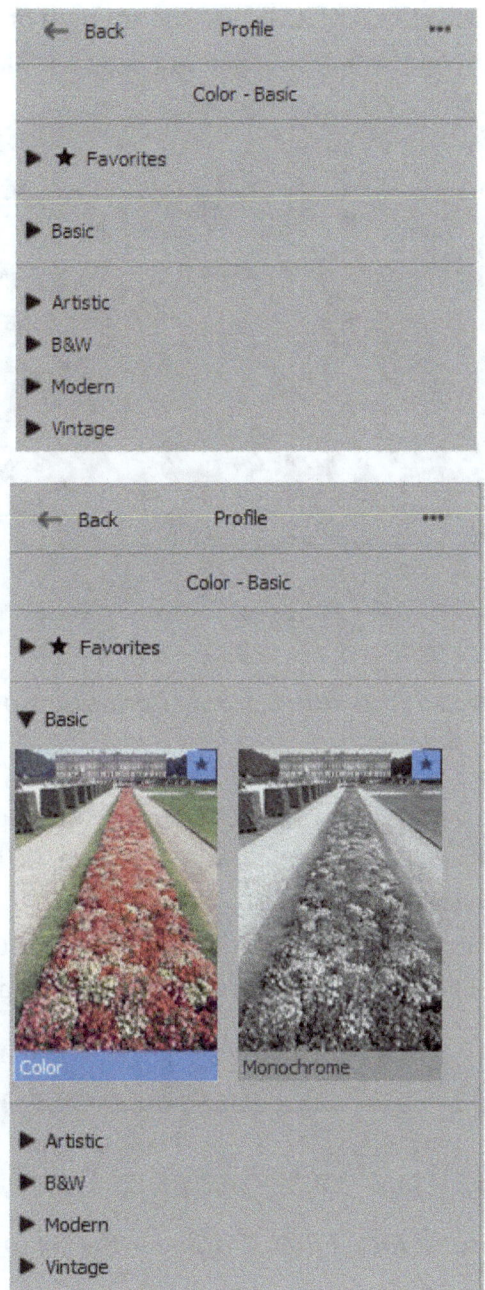

Figure 4-57. *Camera Raw Filter: search for optional profile settings*

Other profiles will allow you to adjust the strength of the setting with a slider (0–200), the default being 100. Refer to Figure 4-58.

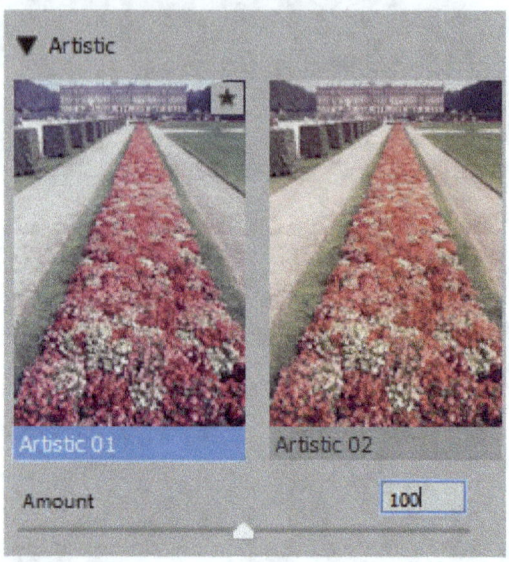

Figure 4-58. *Camera Raw Filter: apply optional profile settings from previews found in the list*

Some of these options may instantly improve the color of your image without having to use all the other settings. However, for this example I am working with the Basic color setting.

Click the back arrow when you need to return to the other Edit settings. Remain on the Profile Color setting for now. Refer to Figure 4-59.

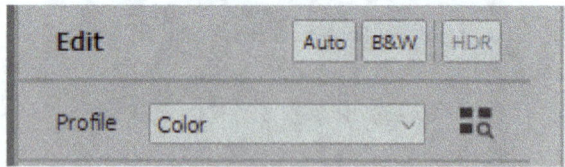

Figure 4-59. *Camera Raw Filter Profile setting set to Color*

Note that when the tabs in the Edit panel are altered, the eye will become active, indicating you made adjustments in these tabs. You can toggle the eye on and off to act as a preview of that adjustment. Also, hover over text if you are not sure what a specific setting does. Refer to Figure 4-60.

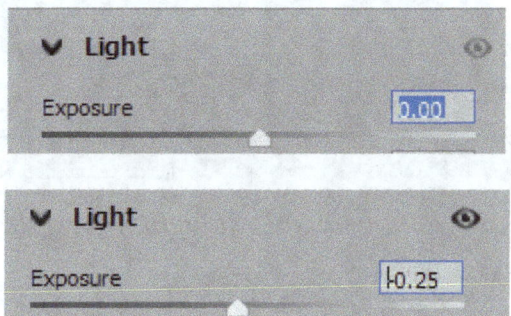

Figure 4-60. Camera Raw Filter: when edits are made to a slider, the visibility eye of that tab appears

Light

The Light tab has the following slider options for light and brightness alterations to colors. Some of these sliders share similarities to the Layer Adjustments that we looked at in Chapter 1. Refer to Figure 4-61.

CHAPTER 4   ADVANCED FILTERS FOR PHOTO RESTORATION: PART 1

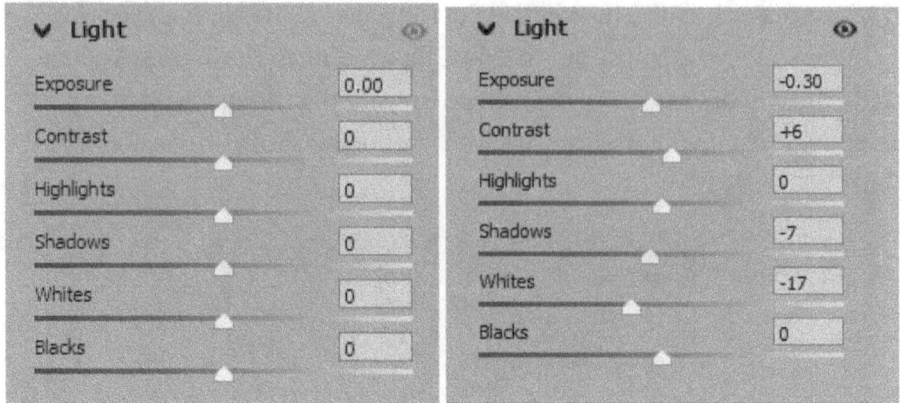

Figure 4-61. *Camera Raw Filter Edit Light tab expanded with sliders adjusted*

Exposure (–5.00, 0, +5.00): Controls the brightness of your photo. Moving the slider left makes the image darker and right lighter. This shares similarities to the adjustment filter Exposure. Try a setting of –0.30. Refer to Figure 4-61.

Contrast (–100, 0, +100): Determines the contrast between your light and dark colors. Move the slider left to flatten or lower the contrast and right to raise or dramatically increase the contrast. This is similar to using your adjustment of Brightness/Contrast. Use a setting of +6.

Highlights (–100, 0, +100): Controls the brightness of the lighter parts of your image. Move the slider left to darken highlights and recover details and right to brighten and reduce details. This and the next slider are similar to using the adjustment of Shadows/Highlights. I did not want to increase the highlights, so I left it at a setting of 0.

Shadows (–100, 0, +100): Controls the brightness of the darker parts of your image. Move the slider left to darken/deepen shadows and right to brighten and recover some details. This is similar to using the adjustment of Shadows/Highlights. Use a setting of –7.

Whites (–100, 0, +100): Sets the white point of the image. Move right to make some colors appear completely white. This is an alternative to using the white point eyedropper as you saw in the adjustments of Levels and Curves. A setting of –17 lessens the histogram warning.

Blacks (–100, 0, +100): Sets the black point of the image and darkens some colors in the process by moving left. This is an alternative to using the black point eyedropper as you saw in the adjustments of Levels and Curves. Refer to Figure 4-61. I left the setting at 0. Refer to Figure 4-62 for before and after.

Figure 4-62. *Camera Raw Filter: viewing subtle color changes as the sliders are adjusted*

In this case, after experimenting with the setting, we can see that this did darken the color slightly and make the image less overexposed, though in this case we cannot completely eliminate all overly white areas, only lessen them.

CHAPTER 4   ADVANCED FILTERS FOR PHOTO RESTORATION: PART 1

Color

The Color tab lets you set the following settings for adjusting your colors overall. These sliders are a bit like using the combination adjustments of Color Balance, Vibrance, and Hue/Saturation from Chapter 1. Refer to Figure 4-63.

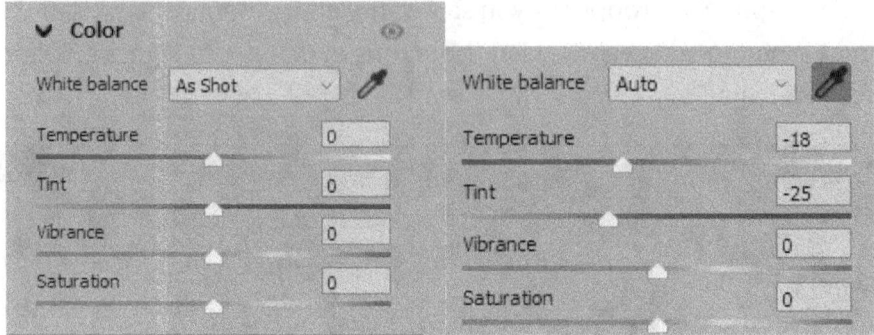
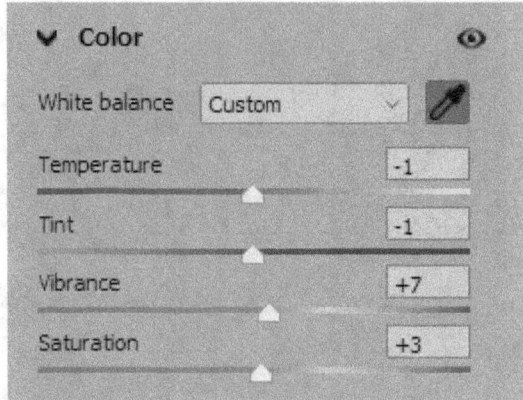

Figure 4-63. *Camera Raw Filter Edit Color tab expanded with sliders adjusted*

CHAPTER 4　ADVANCED FILTERS FOR PHOTO RESTORATION: PART 1

White balance: You can choose the following options from the list: As Shot, Auto, or Custom. Alternatively, by using the eyedropper White Balance tool (I), if you click an area that you deem to be white, the balance changes to Custom. In this case I left the setting on As Shot as I found when I switched to Auto it made the image have a green cast, which I did not like, but for your own project this may be OK. Leave on As Shot for now, and as you move a slider the White balance will change to Custom.

Temperature (-100, 0, +100): Determines how warm or cool the colors appear in your image. Move the slider left if colors are too yellow (adding more blue) and right if colors are too blue (adding more yellow). I liked the current temperature but moved the slider to -1.

Tint (-100, 0, +100): Determines how green or purple the colors are in your image. Move the slider left if colors are too purple (adding more green) and right if colors are too green (adding more purple). In this case I set the slider to -1.

Vibrance (-100, 0, +100): Changes the saturation without causing unpleasant color casts. Move the slider left to decrease and right to increase without causing oversaturation. I used a setting of +7.

Saturation (-100, 0, +100): Controls the saturation of colors equally. Move left to decrease making the photo grayscale and right to increase and give your colors a boost. The photo needed a boost, so I used +3. Refer to Figure 4-64.

CHAPTER 4 ADVANCED FILTERS FOR PHOTO RESTORATION: PART 1

Figure 4-64. *Camera Raw Filter: previewing the image with the colors adjusted after using the sliders*

In this case we are making subtle changes, and we can always go back and alter a slider later if required.

Effects

The Effects tab lets you set the following settings that can clear or add noise to the image. This is an alternative to using some of your basic filters for blur, noise, and sharpening. You may need to zoom in on areas to see the subtle changes. Refer to Figure 4-65.

CHAPTER 4   ADVANCED FILTERS FOR PHOTO RESTORATION: PART 1

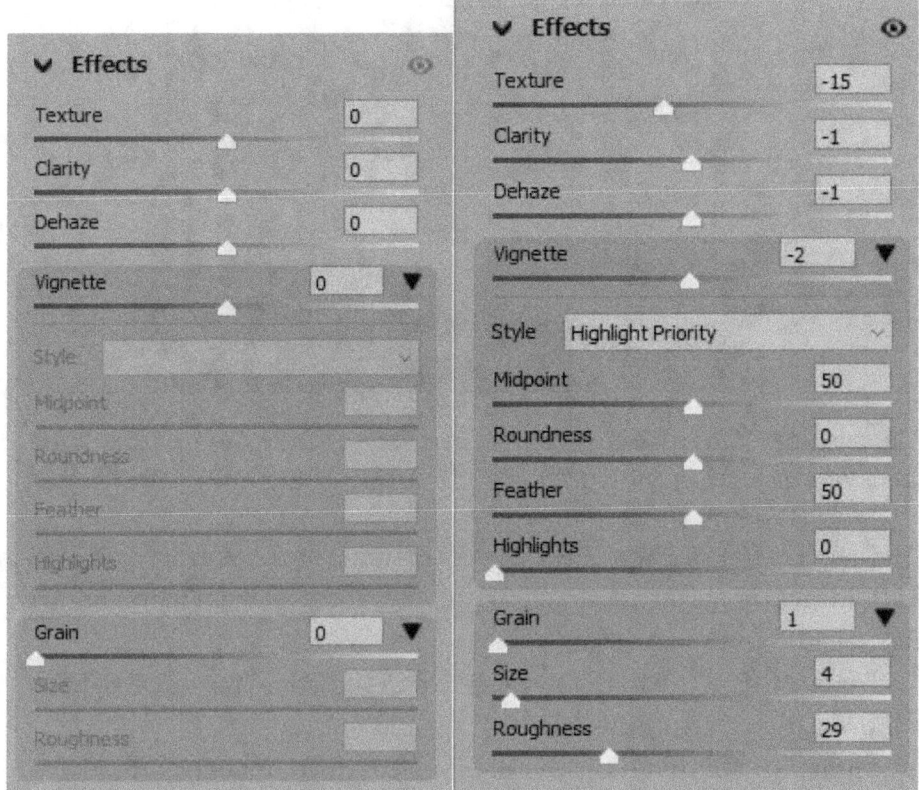

Figure 4-65. *Camera Raw Filter Edit Effects tab expanded with sliders adjusted*

Texture (–100, 0, +100): Enhance or reduce the appearance of texture in your image. Move to the left to soften the effect or to the right to enhance the texture. This filter is good for portraits and landscapes. In this case setting it to –15 reduced some of the noise in the sky but not so much that the finer details became blurry. I still left some noise. Refer to Figure 4-66.

585

CHAPTER 4   ADVANCED FILTERS FOR PHOTO RESTORATION: PART 1

Figure 4-66. *Camera Raw Filter: previewing an area up close to see if nose was altered in the image*

Clarity (–100, 0, +100): Changes the contrast of edges around objects in your images. Move the slider left to soften the edge or right to increase the edge contrast. I used a setting of –1.

Dehaze (–100, 0, +100): Move left to add simulated haze and right to remove. I used a setting of –1.

Vignette (–100, 0, +100): The slider makes the outer edges of the image lighter (right) or darker (left). This is a bit more advanced than using the Properties panel and a color fill to create a vignette. Extreme settings can cause interesting effects similar to the tower image you saw in this volume and Volume 1. Refer to Figure 4-67.

CHAPTER 4 ADVANCED FILTERS FOR PHOTO RESTORATION: PART 1

Figure 4-67. *Camera Raw Filter Edit Effects tab: altering the Vignette setting*

For Vignette try a setting of –2 to slightly darken the edge as seen back in Figure 4-64 and in the settings of Figure 4-68.

587

CHAPTER 4   ADVANCED FILTERS FOR PHOTO RESTORATION: PART 1

Figure 4-68. *Camera Raw Filter Edit Effects tab: altering the Vignette setting to a lower setting*

As the slider is adjusted, you can set additional options that control Style (Highlight Priority, Color Priority, and Paint Overlay), Midpoint (spread) (0–100), Roundness (shape) (–100, 0, +100), Feather (0–100), and Highlights (0–100).

In this case I focused on Highlight Priority, Midpoint: 50, Roundness: 0, Feather: 50, and Highlights: 0. Move the sliders left and right to get a feel of what they actually do and how they affect the vignette.

Grain (0–100): Move the slider to the right to increase the film grain. Then you can set the Size (0–100) and Roughness (0–100). I did not want to add more grain to the image and could have left it on a setting of 0, but for this image set it to 1, with a Size of 4 and Roughness of 29. Refer to Figure 4-69.

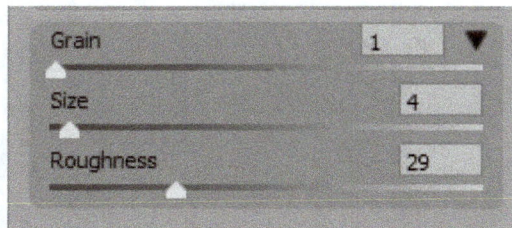

Figure 4-69. *Camera Raw Filter Edit Effects tab: altering the Grain setting to reduced grain setting but still keep some details*

In your own projects you will want to experiment with this panel to get the right balance. In this case the choices I made did not overly shift the color in unexpected ways. Refer to Figure 4-70.

Figure 4-70. *Camera Raw Filter: previewing the effects of adjustments in the upper areas of the image*

Curve

The Curve tab is much like using the adjustment layer of Curves for colors and lets you set the following settings. You can use this section in conjunction with the other previous tabs we discussed here in the workspace or separately to adjust the tonal range and contrast. Refer to Figure 4-71.

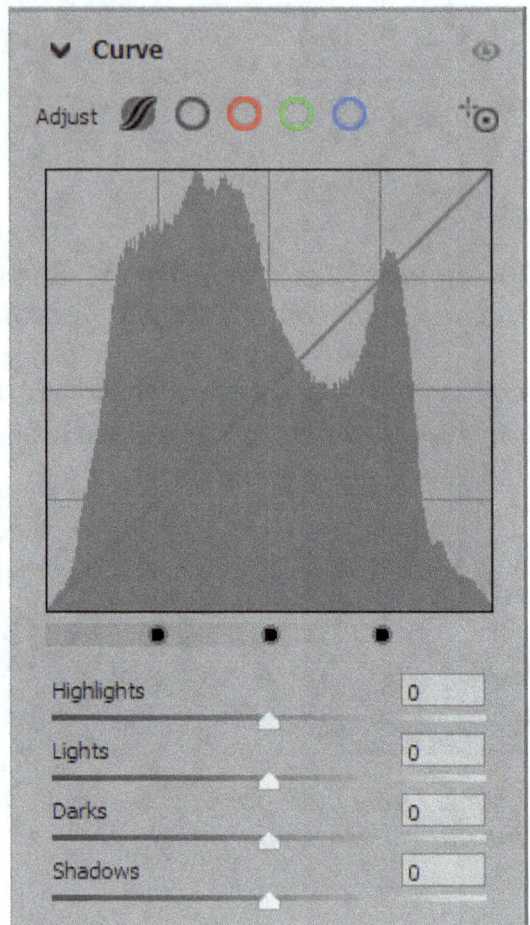

Figure 4-71. *Camera Raw Filter Edit Curve tab expanded*

Adjust options: Allow you to set various curve options. For example, you can click and drag to adjust the Parametric curve and then adjust on the curve manually or use the following sliders:

Highlights, –16; Lights, +18; Darks, +4; and Shadows, 9: The range for each of these is –100, 0, +100. Also, below the curve/ histogram, you can adjust the three circular sliders for shadows, midtones, and highlights. Refer to Figure 4-72.

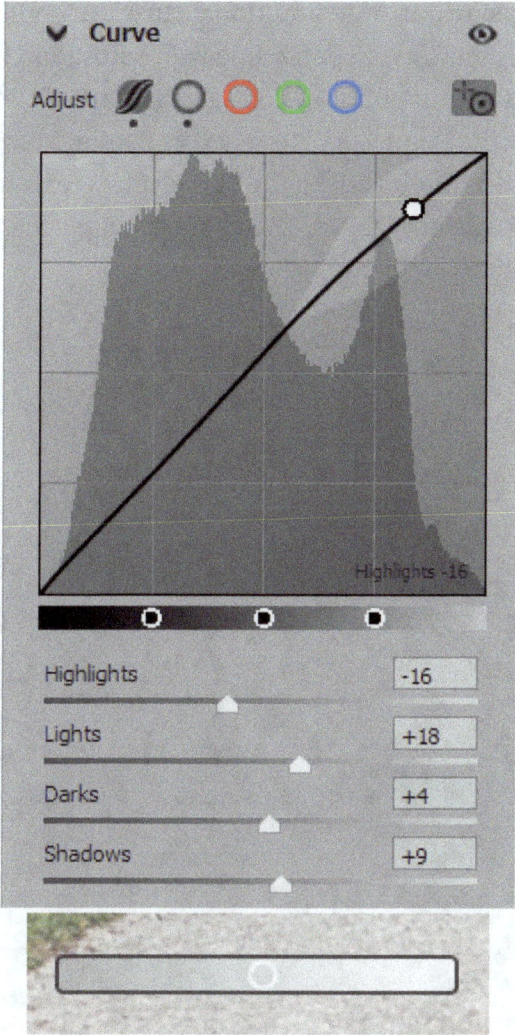

Figure 4-72. *Camera Raw Filter Edit Curve tab expanded with settings altered and the Parametric curve adjusted with the tool on the preview*

When the Parametric Curve Targeted Adjustment Tool is active, you can edit the highlights and shadows on the preview. Refer to Figure 4-72.

CHAPTER 4   ADVANCED FILTERS FOR PHOTO RESTORATION: PART 1

If you prefer using the more traditional curves in combination, use the Click to edit Point Curve. Then refine your saturation (0–100) and set various input and output points as you saw in Chapter 1. You can also use various presets in the Point Curve list such as Linear, Medium Contrast, and Strong Contrast. As you adjust the curve, it will reset to Custom. To remove a point on the curve, Ctrl/CMD + click it. I placed a point at Input 134, Output 121. Refer to Figure 4-73.

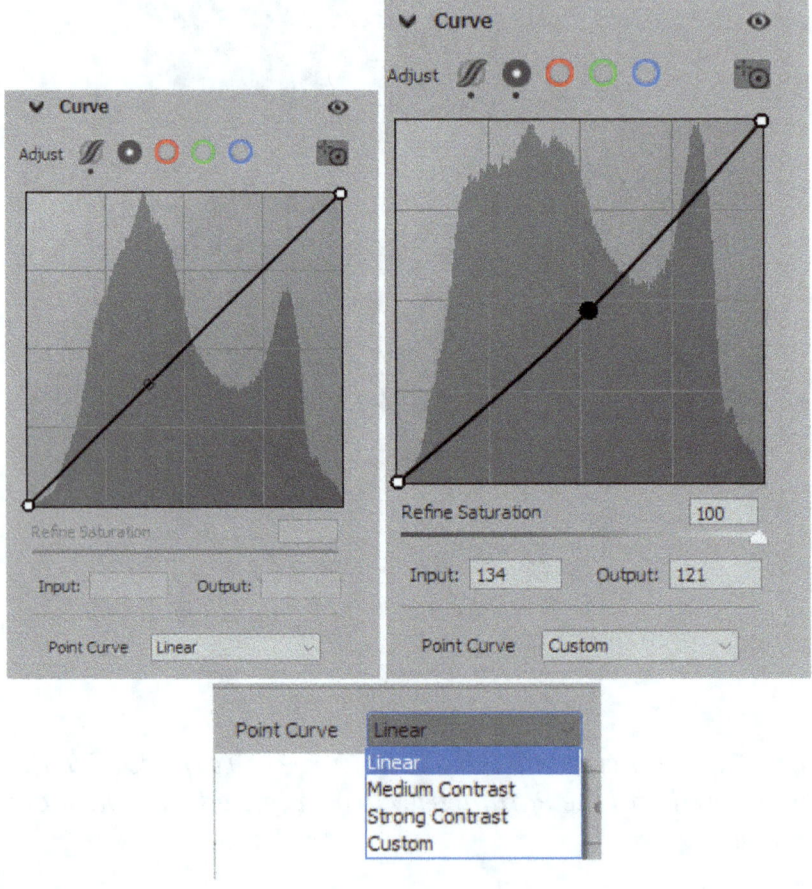

Figure 4-73. Camera Raw Filter Edit Curve tab expanded and using the Point Curve settings

CHAPTER 4   ADVANCED FILTERS FOR PHOTO RESTORATION: PART 1

For Point Curve you can then set the red, green, and blue channels as well, separately. Note that each time you make an adjustment, a dot appears near the altered curve adjustment. In this case I did not alter each channel separately. Refer to Figure 4-74.

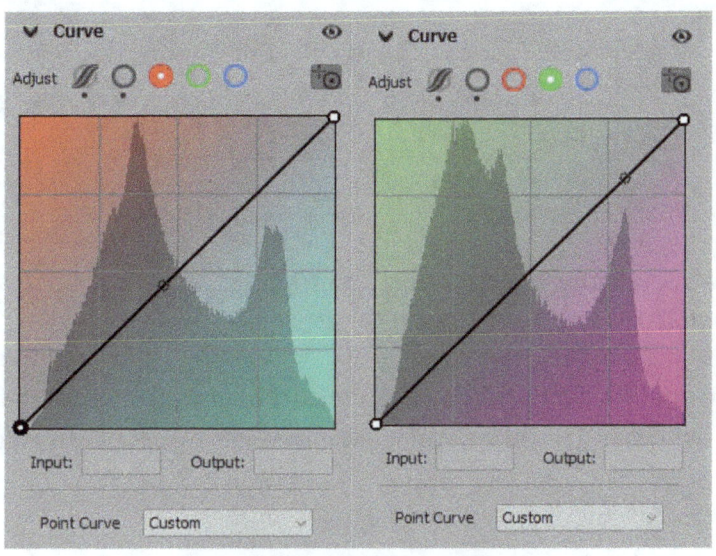

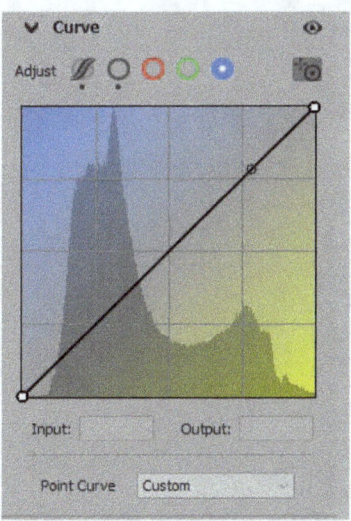

Figure 4-74. *Camera Raw Filter Edit Curve tab expanded and Point Curve to edit each of the RGB channels*

593

CHAPTER 4   ADVANCED FILTERS FOR PHOTO RESTORATION: PART 1

Depending on what type of curve adjustment you are using, the Parametric curve targeted adjustment tool or Point Curve targeted adjustment tool will be available and appear on the preview as well. Refer to Figure 4-75.

Figure 4-75. Camera Raw Filter Parametric curve targeted adjustment tool options used on the preview to edit

When enabled you can use the tone curve setting to adjust your curves on the preview for the current selected curve settings. Refer to Figure 4-76.

CHAPTER 4   ADVANCED FILTERS FOR PHOTO RESTORATION: PART 1

Figure 4-76. *Camera Raw Filter with the Parametric curve targeted adjustment tool displayed on preview*

This tool also can be used to control the Color Mixer, which you will look at next.

595

B&W Mixer/Color Mixer

The Color Mixer tab, or B&W Mixer, when the image appears in grayscale, lets you set the following settings. In this case we are looking at color, and the Color Mixer is divided into two sections: Mixer and Point Color. It shares some similarities with the Hue/Saturation adjustment layer and its Master and selective color settings for color range found in Chapter 1. First, we'll look at the Mixer tab.

Mixer

This section gives you greater control over the individual colors of your image. Use the list to choose an option:

Adjust (HSL): This allows you to adjust your colors with the following tabs of Hue, Saturation, Luminance, and All for your reds, oranges, yellows, greens, aquas, blues, purples, and magentas using the various sliders (HSL sliders). The slider range is -100, 0, +100. The Hue targeted adjustment tool, when enabled, allows you to adjust the color by dragging directly on the image, and you can use the panel as well. You can use it to target Saturation or Luminance by toggling to that option. In the preview it can also be used to toggle back to the curves. Refer to Figure 4-77.

CHAPTER 4　ADVANCED FILTERS FOR PHOTO RESTORATION: PART 1

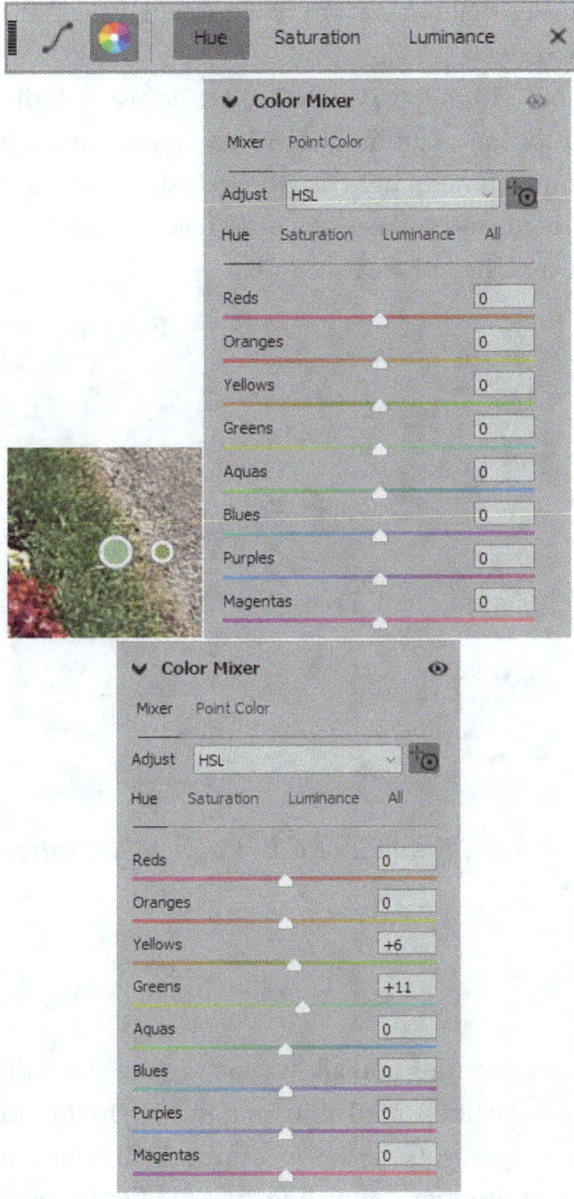

Figure 4-77. *Camera Raw Filter Edit Color Mixer tab expanded with the Parametric Hue targeted adjustment tool on preview*

Here we can see that the grass's color could be altered by adjusting yellows (+6) and greens (+11).

Adjust (Color): This allows you instead to adjust by individual colors the Hue, Saturation, and Luminance. However, you cannot use the Hue targeted adjustment tool. In this case the Hue sliders in the yellows, greens, and All were altered, and you can see a dot below them. Currently the yellows are selected. Refer to Figure 4-78.

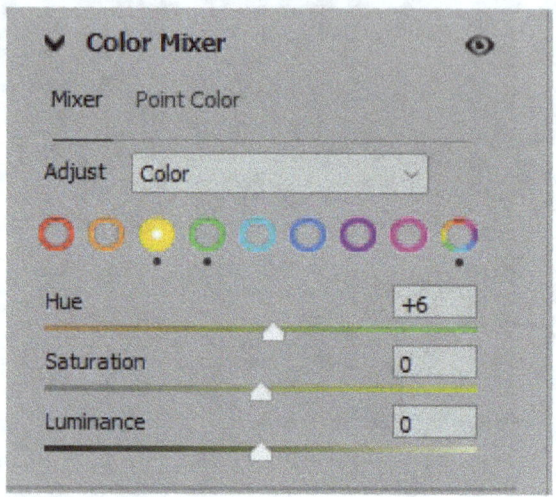

Figure 4-78. Camera Raw Filter Edit Color Mixer tab and Adjust options

Point Color

This is a more recent setting and allows you to select an individual color in your photo and make fine-tuned adjustments to it. In the Hue, Saturation, and Luminance ranges, you can set very fine adjustments for that color. Use the point color dropper somewhere on the photo to add samples. Refer to Figure 4-79.

Figure 4-79. *Camera Raw Filter Edit Color Mixer tab set to Point Color*

CHAPTER 4   ADVANCED FILTERS FOR PHOTO RESTORATION: PART 1

Upon clicking, for instance, a dark-red area of the flower (Figure 4-76), that will then appear as a swatch in the Point Color area. Refer to Figure 4-80.

Figure 4-80. *Camera Raw Filter Edit Color Mixer tab set to Point Color with options and alteration to a swatch*

CHAPTER 4 ADVANCED FILTERS FOR PHOTO RESTORATION: PART 1

Then you can make adjustments to the Hue, Saturation, and Luminance and separately to the range sliders (0–100). Note that you use the eye mask icon by the Range slider to toggle on and off the range overlay to view and highlight selected colors. Refer to Figure 4-80

I moved the Hue to –25 and left Saturation and Luminance at 0. Then I altered the Range to +100 to control the colors that are affected and the Hue Range to 0/28 62/94, Saturation Range 12/67 100/100, and Luminance Range to 9/41 77/100. However, for every image this will be different for each person based on preference. The swatch will alter along with the area above the sliders when changes to colors are made displaying before and after colors. Refer to Figure 4-80. This color change to the swatch is more apparent when drastic changes are made otherwise the changes is subtle.

With the Sample point eyedropper enabled, you can click to add more swatches, like altering the color of the sky with a Hue 0, Saturation +28, and Luminance +17. Range remained at +50 and Hue Range: 0/33 67/100, Saturation Range: 0/0 33/88, and Luminance Range: 10/65 100/100.

As well, you can right-click a swatch and choose to Delete Swatch or Delete All Swatches. Refer to Figure 4-81.

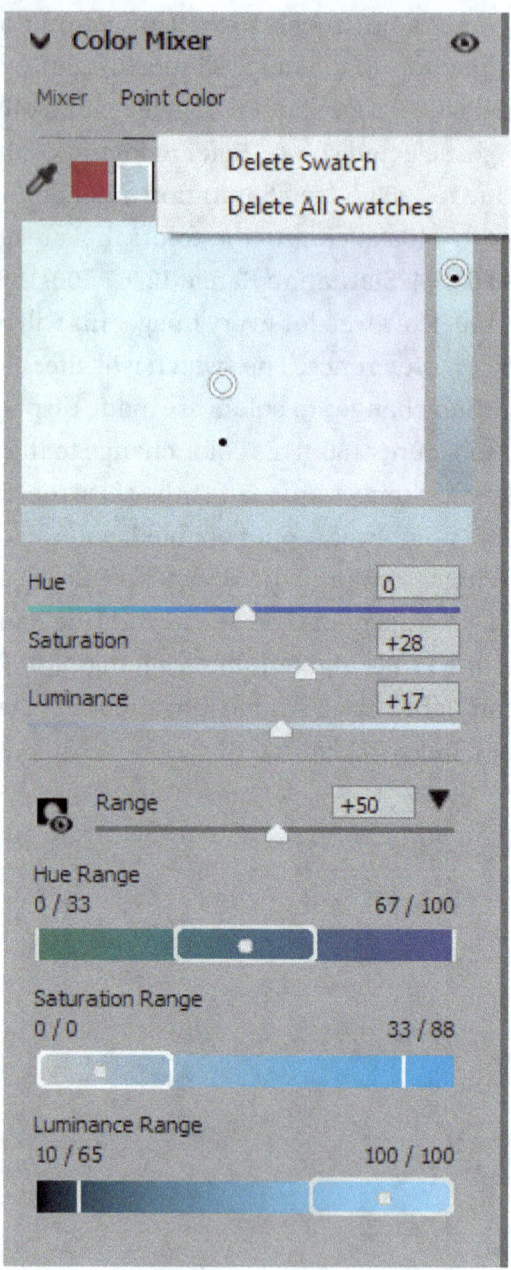

Figure 4-81. *Camera Raw Filter Edit Color Mixer tab set to Point Color with options and alteration to a swatch, which can be deleted*

After making alterations make sure to turn your eye on and off to see changes. Refer to Figure 4-82.

Figure 4-82. *Camera Raw Filter with edits to the Point Color previewing on the photo*

Color Grading

The Color Grading tab lets you set the following settings in regard to stylizing your images by adding color tints to the shadows, midtones, and highlights. Similar to the adjustment layer of Photo Filter in Chapter 1 and a color wheel, you can explore applying complementary colors that are opposite to each other on the wheel, to your shadows and highlights. Try adding a cooler blue to the shadows and warmer yellow to the highlights. Refer to Figure 4-83.

CHAPTER 4   ADVANCED FILTERS FOR PHOTO RESTORATION: PART 1

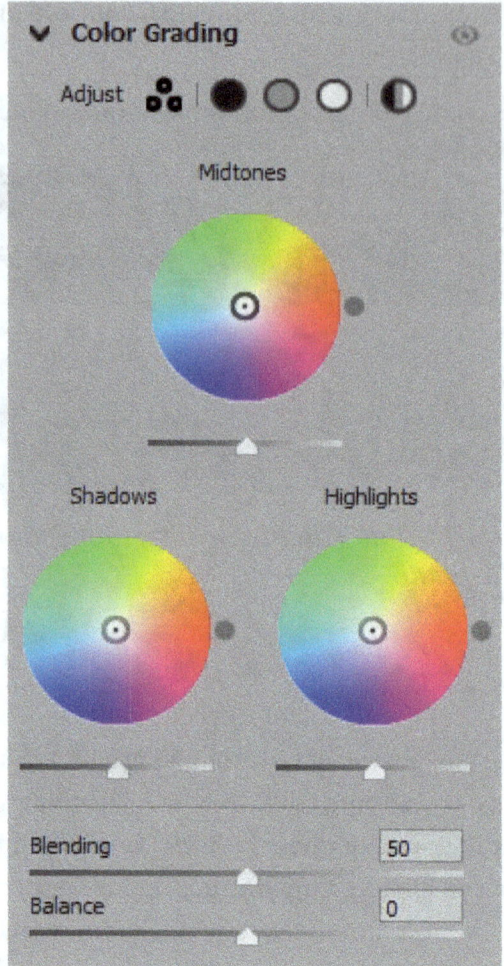

Figure 4-83. *Camera Raw Filter Edit Color Grading tab expanded (three-way)*

Adjustments can be made in all three (three-way) or separately for the shadows, midtones, and highlights, by dragging on the center ring or dot on or near each color wheel to adjust the Hue and Saturation settings or dragging the lower slider to adjust the Luminance. Refer to Figure 4-83.

Alternatively, shadows, midtones, and highlights can be adjusted individually for their sliders Hue (0–360), Saturation (0–100), and Luminance (-100, 0, +100).

Or use the color wheel and the sliders for one single global setting. Refer to Figure 4-84.

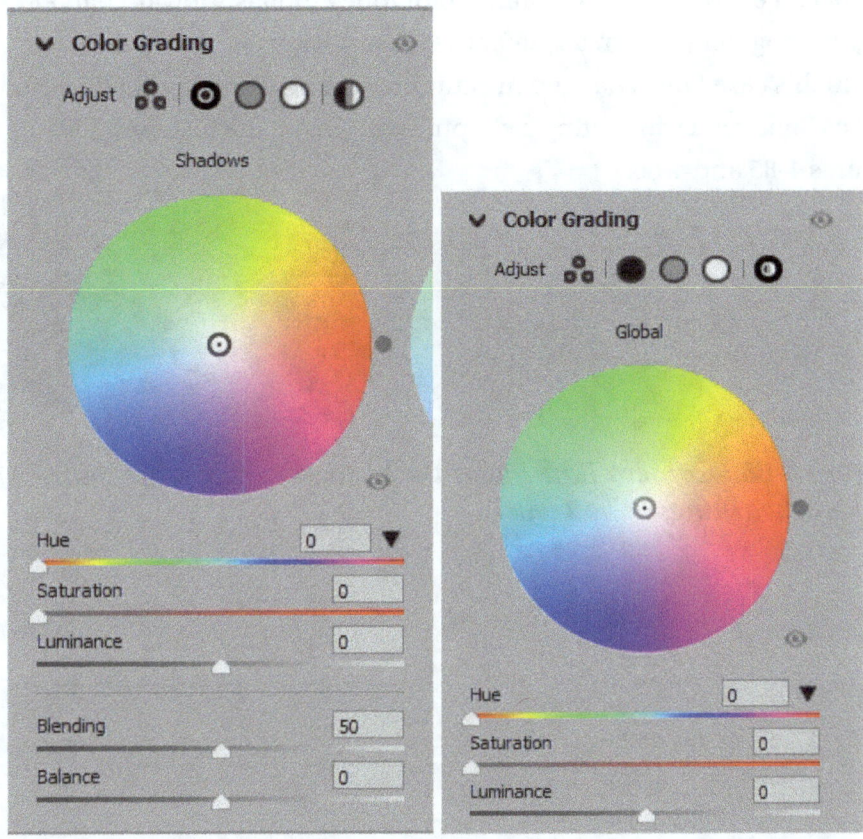

Figure 4-84. *Camera Raw Filter Edit Color Grading tab expanded with Shadows and Global*

CHAPTER 4   ADVANCED FILTERS FOR PHOTO RESTORATION: PART 1

Additional settings for Color Grading include

Blending (0–100): Adjusts the transitions between the shadows, midtones, and highlights. Low blend values will create a more apparent separation between the colors, while higher values create a more subtle gradual transition between colors.

Balance (–100, 0, +100): Shifts color tone emphasis toward darker (right) or lighter (left) areas. Refer to Figure 4-84.

In this case I just changed my Luminance slightly in my shadows to +18 as I noticed I was getting a clipping warning in the histogram. Refer to Figures 4-85 and 4-86.

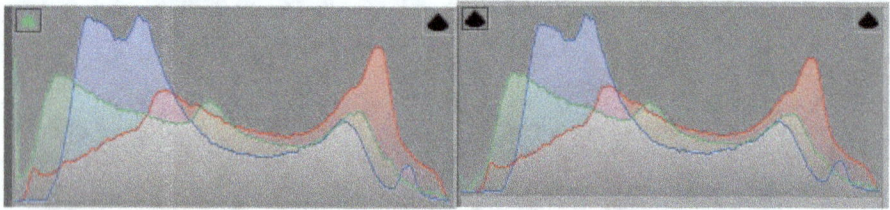

Figure 4-85. *Camera Raw Filter: the histogram may alter with clipping warnings as you work*

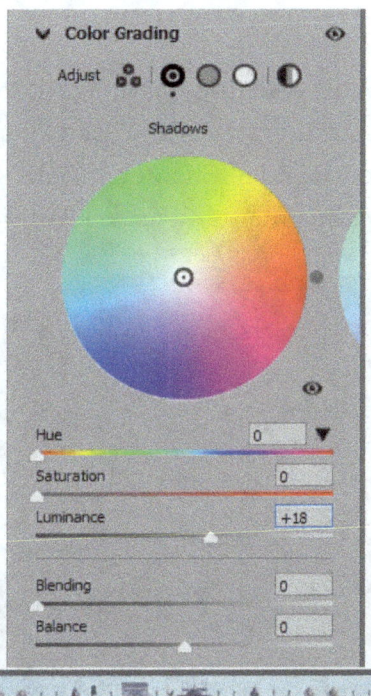

Figure 4-86. *Camera Raw Filter Edit Color Grading tab expanded with changes to shadows and previewing an image*

CHAPTER 4   ADVANCED FILTERS FOR PHOTO RESTORATION: PART 1

Detail

The Detail tab lets you adjust settings for image correction. It also is similar to using some of the basic filters that were used for sharpening and noise reduction that were mentioned in Chapter 3. Make sure to zoom in if you need to make detailed adjustments. Refer to Figure 4-87.

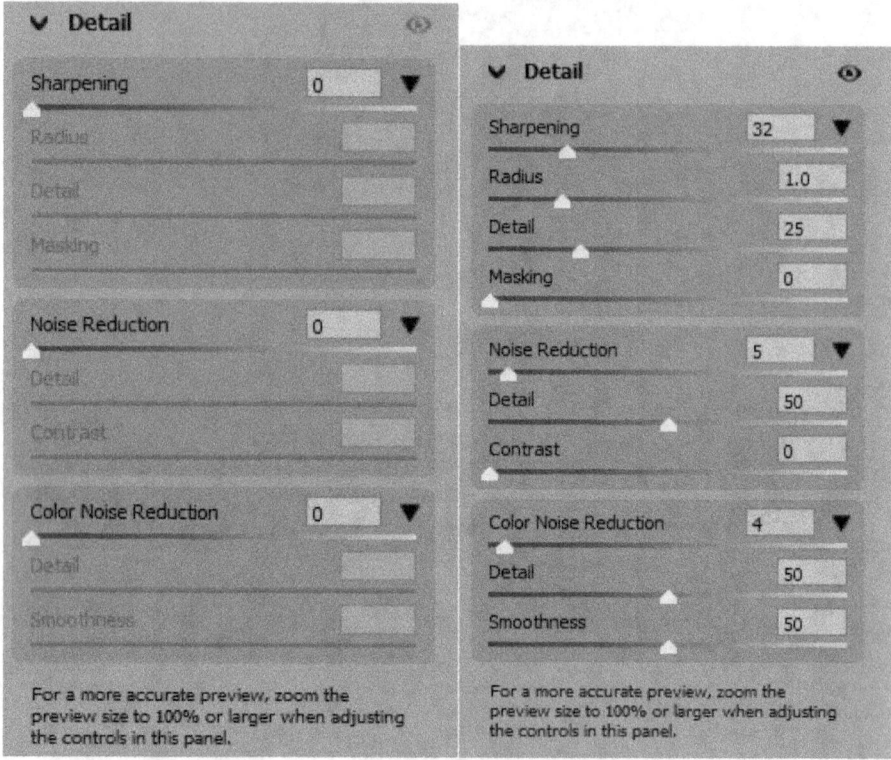

Figure 4-87. Camera Raw Filter Edit Detail tab expanded with changes to sliders

Sharpening (0–150): Allows you to sharpen and brighten details when you move the slider to the right. You can then use the sub-sliders of Radius (0.5–3.0), Detail (0–100), and Masking (0–100) to refine the settings. In this example I did not want to oversharpen so I left the Sharpening at 32, Radius 1.0, Detail 25, and Masking 0.

Noise Reduction (0–100): Move the slider to the right to reduce the luminance noise. You can then use the sub-sliders to adjust the Detail (0–100) and the Contrast (0–100). Noise reduction I set to 5 and Detail 50 and Contrast 0.

Color Noise Reduction (0–100): Move the slider to the right to reduce color noise. You can then use the sub-sliders to adjust the Detail (0–100) and the Smoothness (0–100). I set the Color Noise Reduction to 4 and Detail 50 and Smoothness 50. Refer to Figures 4-87 and 4-88.

CHAPTER 4 ADVANCED FILTERS FOR PHOTO RESTORATION: PART 1

Figure 4-88. *Slight changes are made in the details to sharpen areas of the image up close*

CHAPTER 4 ADVANCED FILTERS FOR PHOTO RESTORATION: PART 1

Optics

The Optics tab lets you set the following settings to control distortion, vignettes, as well as defringe issues. Defringe (chromatic aberration) is the appearance of greenish and red-purple edges that happen in edges of high contrast where a dark silhouette element like a tree or branches are strongly backlit against a bright background like the sky. This can appear with film cameras and be apparent in the print and then be part of the scanned image. In the case of a digital camera and its lens, it can appear when the lens fails to focus on the white light's different wavelengths, which are traveling at different speeds, and combine them into one focal point. None of the filters we have looked at so far deal with defringe. Refer to Figure 4-89.

CHAPTER 4   ADVANCED FILTERS FOR PHOTO RESTORATION: PART 1

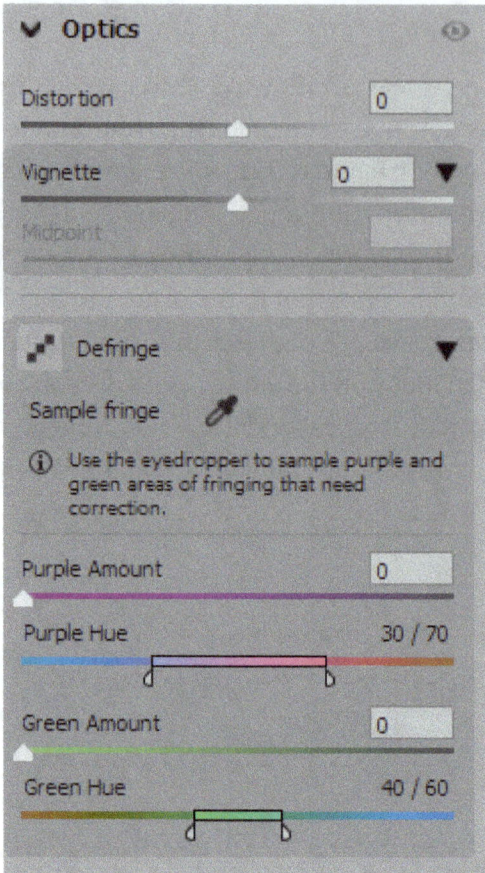

Figure 4-89. *Camera Raw Filter Edit Optics tab expanded*

Distortion (–100, 0, +100): Controls overall pincushion and barrel distortions often caused by the lens. Refer to Figures 4-90 and 4-91.

CHAPTER 4　ADVANCED FILTERS FOR PHOTO RESTORATION: PART 1

Figure 4-90. *Camera Raw Filter Edit Optics tab expanded and Distortion slider moved left*

CHAPTER 4 ADVANCED FILTERS FOR PHOTO RESTORATION: PART 1

Figure 4-91. *Camera Raw Filter Edit Optics tab expanded and Distortion slider moved right*

CHAPTER 4   ADVANCED FILTERS FOR PHOTO RESTORATION: PART 1

The grid becomes active so you can see the distortion more clearly. In the case of the current image we are working on, distortion in this area of the filter setting is too extreme. There is some minor distortion in the upper area of the image we may want to correct. Refer to Figure 4-92.

Figure 4-92. *Camera Raw Filter Edit Optics tab expanded and Distortion slider moved back to 0*

However, I will show you how to deal with that when we look at the Geometry panel. For now, leave the setting at 0.

Vignette (–100, 0, +100): Adjust or add as vignette to the image. Use the sub-slider Midpoint to make further adjustments (0–100) to the spread. Earlier we added a vignette to the edge of the image with the Effects tab to darken the image, so we do not want to remove it. You may prefer, in your own projects, to use this setting to remove a vignette. In this example, I will leave the Vignette at 0, and the Midpoint will not be available. Refer to Figure 4-93.

CHAPTER 4 ADVANCED FILTERS FOR PHOTO RESTORATION: PART 1

Figure 4-93. *Camera Raw Filter Edit Optics tab expanded and Vignette slider moved left and right and then set back to 0*

CHAPTER 4   ADVANCED FILTERS FOR PHOTO RESTORATION: PART 1

Defringe settings can be adjusted using the sample fringe eyedropper to sample purple and green areas of fringing that need correction when you click on those spots in the preview. Then adjust the following sliders:

Purple Amount (0–20).
Purple Hue: Adjust the range of the two sliders 0–100.
Green Amount (0–20).
Green Hue: Adjust the range of the two sliders 0–100.

In our current example there was only a very small amount of chromatic aberration near some of the white area, and it was outside of the color range, so trying to select it was not possible and I got a warning message. Refer to Figures 4-94 and 4-95.

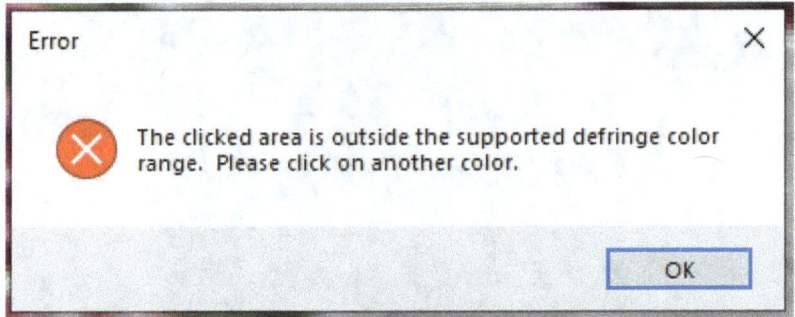

Figure 4-94. *Camera Raw error when defringe is not detected*

In this other example (**fence_defringe.psd**) be aware if you are dealing with areas that contain a lot of green surrounding the aberration. They too could be affected by the eyedropper color ranges and turn colors gray in areas you do not want to alter. Refer to Figure 4-95.

617

CHAPTER 4 ADVANCED FILTERS FOR PHOTO RESTORATION: PART 1

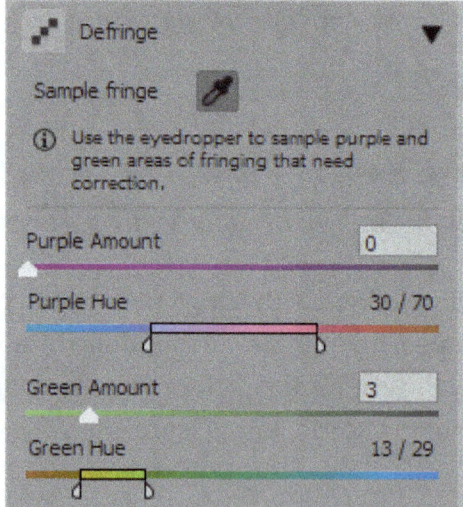

Figure 4-95. *Camera Raw Filter Edit Optics tab: editing an image with the Defringe options*

CHAPTER 4　ADVANCED FILTERS FOR PHOTO RESTORATION: PART 1

Also be aware that some purple aberrations may not be able to be corrected if they fail to fall within the range. One suggestion is to use your layer mask and use an adjustment layer of Hue/Saturation to cover this area with a reduced saturation to about –48 in the master. This is a good alternative to Camera Raw Defringe, if colors are not turning out as you intend and prevent certain greens or purples in select areas from turning gray. Refer to Figure 4-96.

Figure 4-96. *Use the Hue/Saturation adjustment layer and Properties panel and paint on the layer mask when you need to adjust custom areas of chromatic aberration such as along the edge of the post*

CHAPTER 4   ADVANCED FILTERS FOR PHOTO RESTORATION: PART 1

I find with Defringe in Camera Raw, it usually corrects best when it is against a solid background where similar colors are not competing, as when I select the edge of this leaf with a dark wall as a background. Refer to Figure 4-97 and the files **fence_defringe.psd and leaf_defringe.psd** for reference.

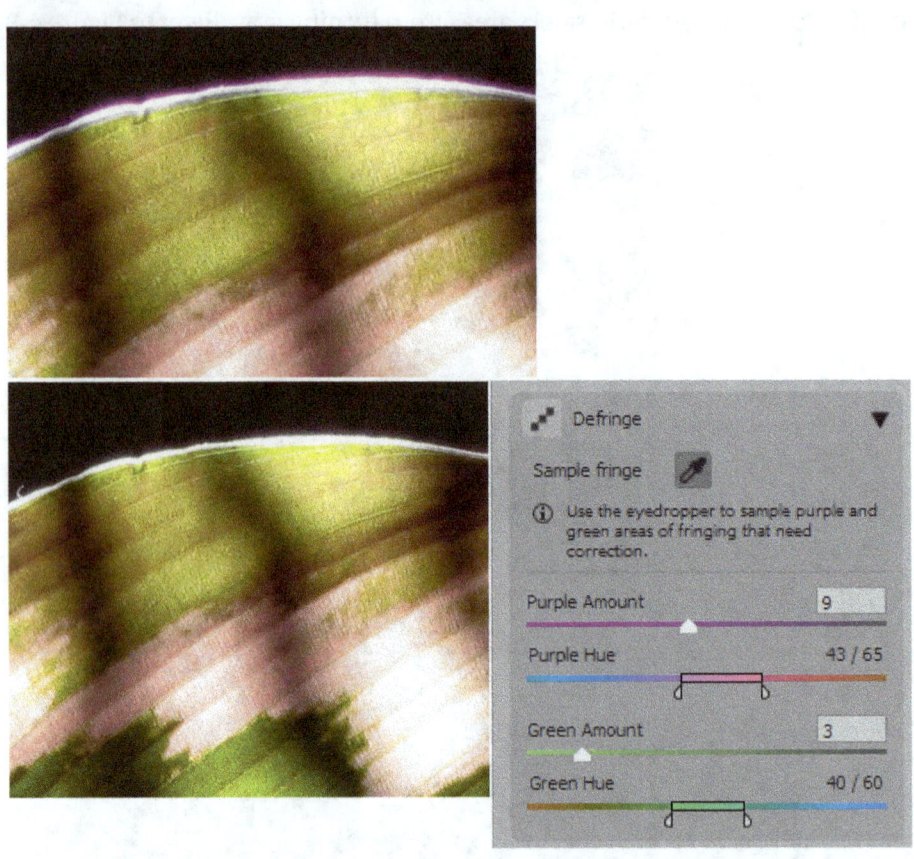

Figure 4-97. *Camera Raw Filter Edit Optics tab: editing an image with the Defringe options with selectable colors*

Here is a link with information on the topic:

www.adobe.com/creativecloud/photography/discover/chromatic-aberration.html

In this case we did not use the Optics tab for the castle flower bed image.

Lens Blur

The Lens Blur tab lets you set some new settings in this version. It is currently set to Early Access and so settings are subject to change. This area is similar to some of the Lens Blur settings that you used in that filter and also in the Blur Gallery. In this case let's see how that looks with the current image that you have been working on. Refer to Figure 4-98.

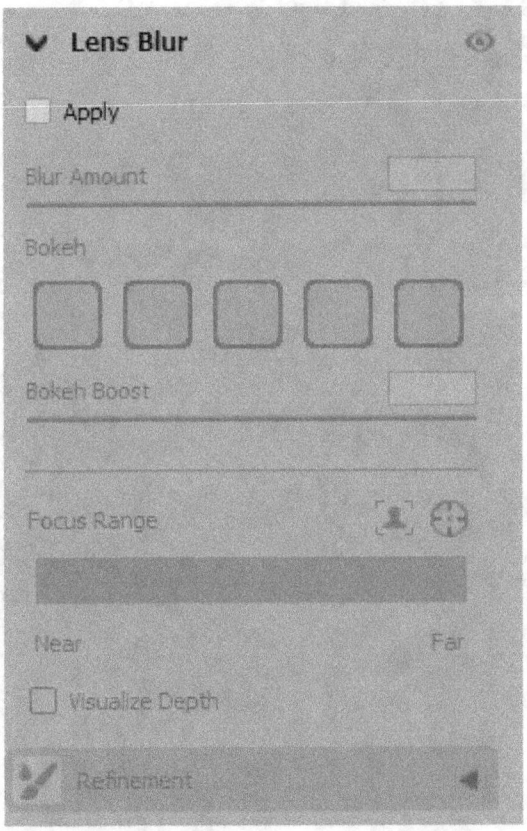

Figure 4-98. Camera Raw Filter Edit Lens Blur tab expanded

CHAPTER 4   ADVANCED FILTERS FOR PHOTO RESTORATION: PART 1

Apply: Enable this check box when you want to access various settings. This may take a few moments, but once it is applied, it will reveal new settings. Currently, however, I think the blur is in the wrong location unless your focus is on the path and not on the building. However, as we progress through the settings, we will alter this. Refer to Figure 4-99.

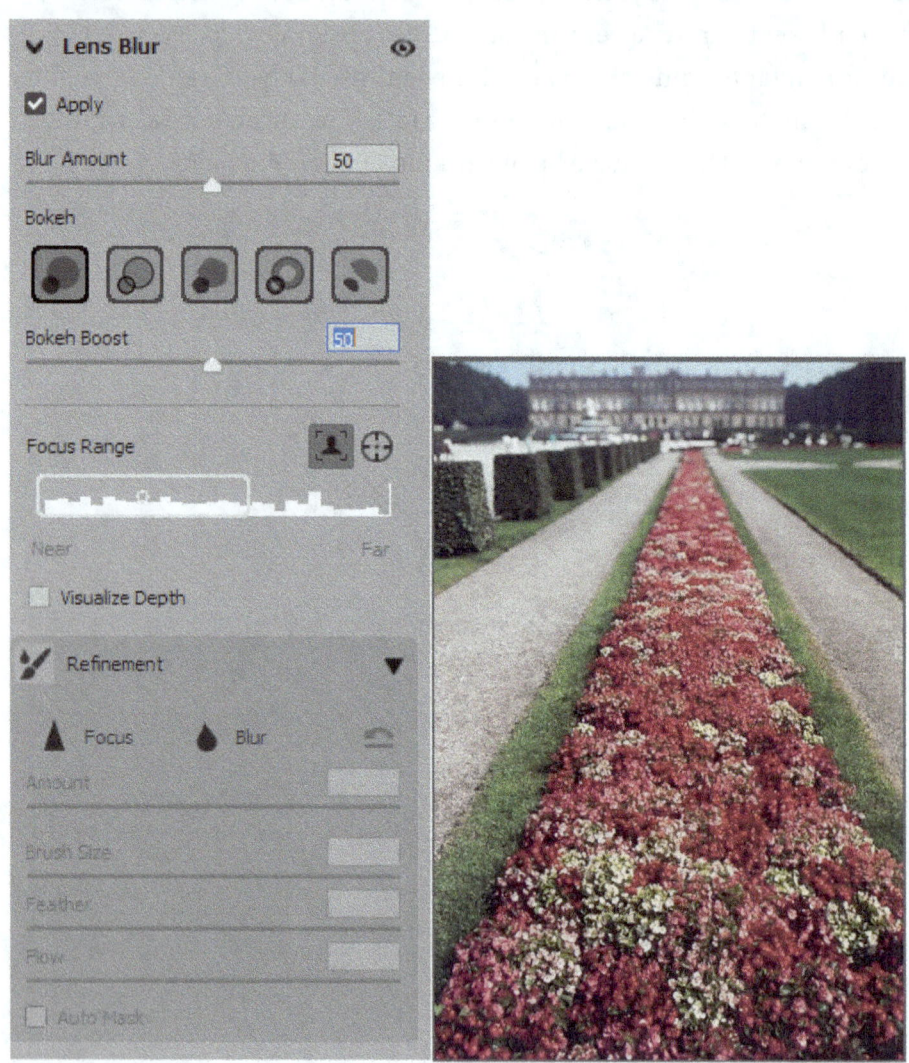

Figure 4-99. *Camera Raw Filter Edit Lens Blur tab expanded and some settings applied and preview of the image*

CHAPTER 4   ADVANCED FILTERS FOR PHOTO RESTORATION: PART 1

Blur Amount (0–100): Adjust the strength of the blur effect. A setting of 0 is no blur, while 100 is an extreme blur. For now, I will leave the setting at 50.

Bokeh: You can click various options, which include Circle, Bubble, 5-Blade, Ring/Doughnut, and Cat-Eye. As you hover over each, more details on each setting are given. Currently, it is set to Circle: Modern circular lens. Refer to Figure 4-100.

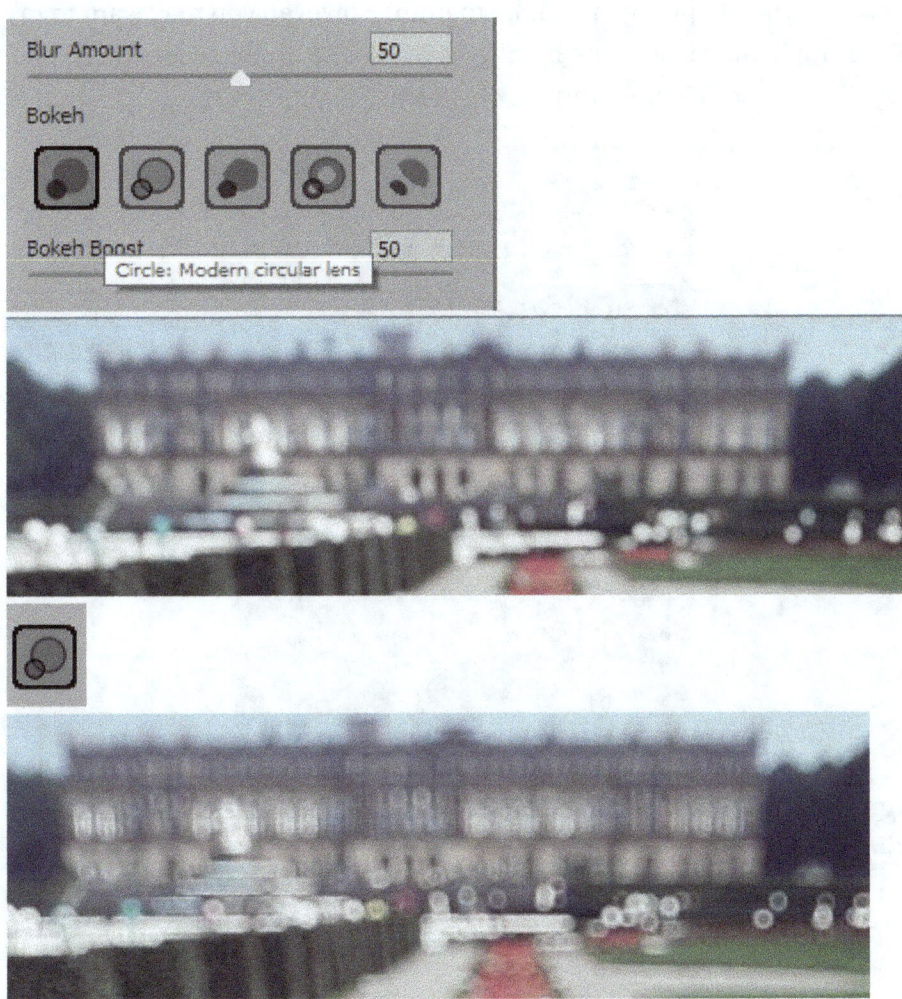

Figure 4-100. *Camera Raw Filter Edit Lens Blur tab expanded and setting blur and bokeh type and then observing change in preview*

623

CHAPTER 4　ADVANCED FILTERS FOR PHOTO RESTORATION: PART 1

As you click another option, like Bubble, notice how the blur changes.

Try each one and then put back on Bokeh Circle for now. Refer to Figure 4-100.

Boost (0–100): Adjust the brightness of out-of-focus light sources. Only highlights in the blur are affected by this slider. Moving to the left darkens and the right lightens. I left at the default of 50. Be aware how even this can affect the white clipping in your histogram. However, you may want to in this example overexpose the highlights in an area. In that case, later, you may want to reduce the setting to 40. Refer to Figure 4-101.

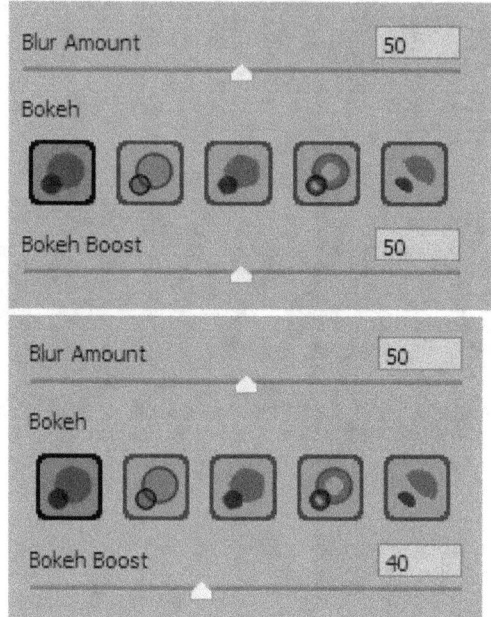

Figure 4-101. *Camera Raw Filter Edit Lens Blur tab expanded and setting Boost*

Next, we will adjust the positioning of the blur and Focus range. Refer to Figure 4-102.

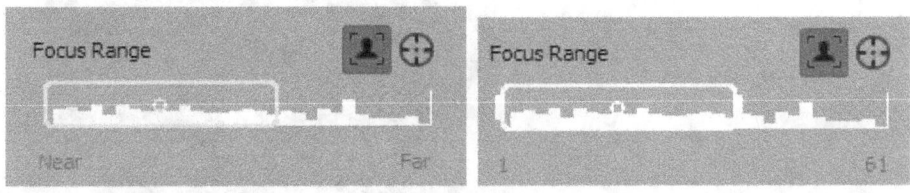

Figure 4-102. *Camera Raw Filter Edit Lens Blur tab expanded and setting Focus Range*

Focus Range: Can be set to Subject focus or Point/Area focus. Currently it is set to Subject and the blur is in the wrong location. Subject will auto-adjust using the Set focal range using AI subject detection and is useful when a person is in a photo. In this case it thinks the subject is the path.

In this case we want to switch to and select Point/Area focus (target). which will allow you to manually click or drag on the image. In this case I dragged the selection from the top downward to the area about a third down as I wanted to have the upper area remain in focus. Refer to Figure 4-103.

CHAPTER 4   ADVANCED FILTERS FOR PHOTO RESTORATION: PART 1

Figure 4-103. *Camera Raw Filter Edit Lens Blur tab expanded and setting Focus Range and making adjustments*

The focus range icon will deselect and for either option you can adjust the range depth values that are in focus using the slider and side handles to get a more custom range and accurate result. Try a setting of 45 and 100.

CHAPTER 4　ADVANCED FILTERS FOR PHOTO RESTORATION: PART 1

The numbers will appear when you move the slider, otherwise it will have the words near and far. Refer to Figure 4-104.

Figure 4-104. *Camera Raw Filter Edit Lens Blur tab expanded and setting Focus Range and making adjustments to the slider*

627

Lastly, we will try to correct the Visualize depth and refine the focus. Refer to Figure 4-105.

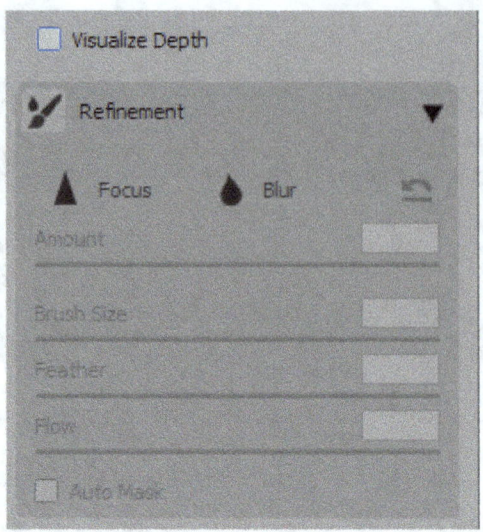

Figure 4-105. *Camera Raw Filter Edit Lens Blur tab expanded to edit depth settings*

Visualize Depth allows you to refine the Lens Blur depth map, and it looks like a rainbow. Enabling this check box shows you what the current map looks like and display colors on the focus range slider which is normally white. Disable so that you can see the current image again. This will then lead to the Refine section. Refer to Figure 4-106.

CHAPTER 4   ADVANCED FILTERS FOR PHOTO RESTORATION: PART 1

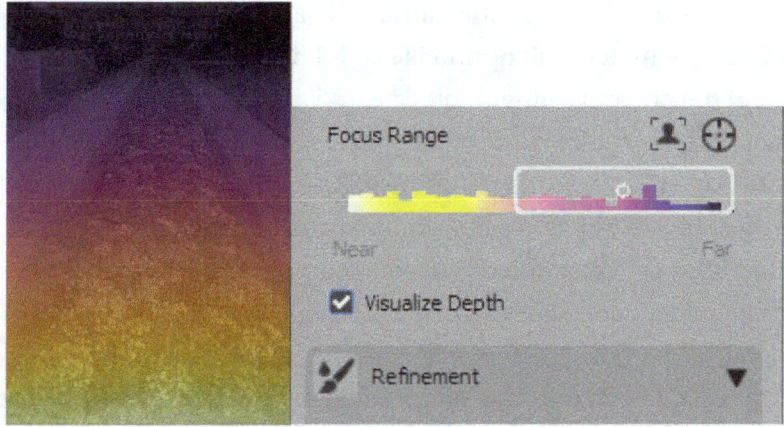

Figure 4-106. *Camera Raw Filter Edit Lens Blur tab expanded to edit depth settings and alter the map*

You can use a brush to add focus or add blur. As you make changes you can start a new refinement with a different blur focus or blur amount or reset. Refer to Figure 4-107.

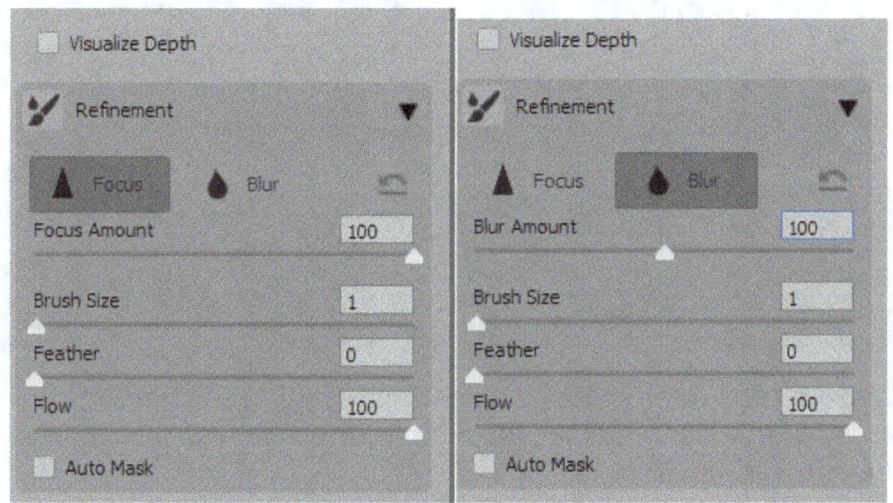

Figure 4-107. *Camera Raw Filter Edit Lens Blur tab expanded to edit depth settings and alter the map with the brush to return focus or add blur*

629

CHAPTER 4   ADVANCED FILTERS FOR PHOTO RESTORATION: PART 1

Focus Amount (0-100)/Blur Amount (0-200): These sliders change depending on which brush option is used. The slider is used to set the strength of the current refinement.

Brush Size (1-100): Size of brush.

Feather (0-100): Size of feathering for the brush.

Flow (1-100): Strength of flow for the brush. By default it is set to 100.

Auto Mask: When enabled is used to combine brush strokes to an area of a similar color. See "Masking Panel Options" later in the chapter for more details.

In this case I want to blur a bit more on my image so that the focus is more on the building than the path. I set the blur amount to 128. I will try a blur brush with a size of 22 and increase the feathering between 84 and 100 and paint over the areas I want to blur more. Refer to Figure 4-108.

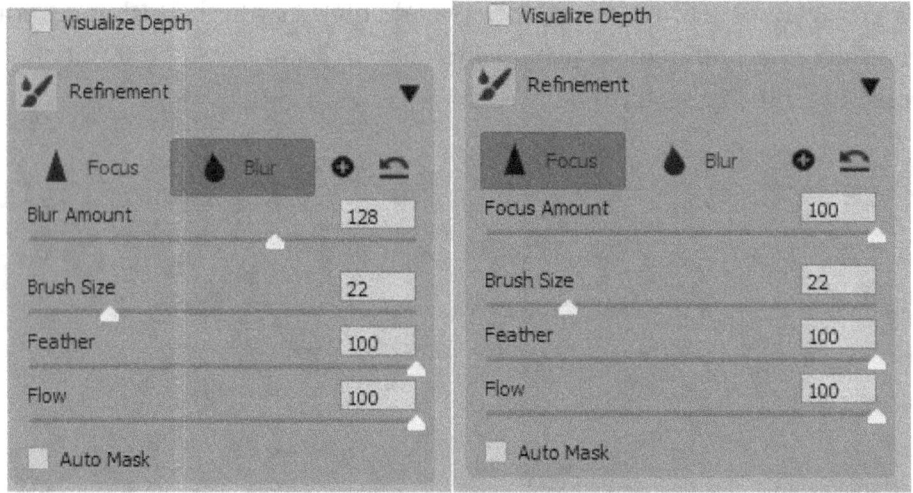

Figure 4-108. *Camera Raw Filter Edit Lens Blur tab expanded to edit depth settings and alter the map with the brush to return focus or add blur with settings adjusted*

630

Note that as you work a new button (+) will be added. It allows you to start a new refinement with a different blur amount; this is similar to using the pins as we saw earlier in the Blur Gallery in Chapter 3. Refer to Figure 4-108.

The blur I create arches upward on each side to a set point.

If, as you work on the Lens Blur, you want to return an area to focus, choose that Focus brush again. The same size setting are retained for the focus and blur brushes except for focus or blur amount and you can paint some areas back in focus. Refer to Figure 4-108

Painting with Visualize Depth on and then off again may help as well. You can see my final results here, but blur as you want to for your own project. Refer to Figure 4-109.

CHAPTER 4   ADVANCED FILTERS FOR PHOTO RESTORATION: PART 1

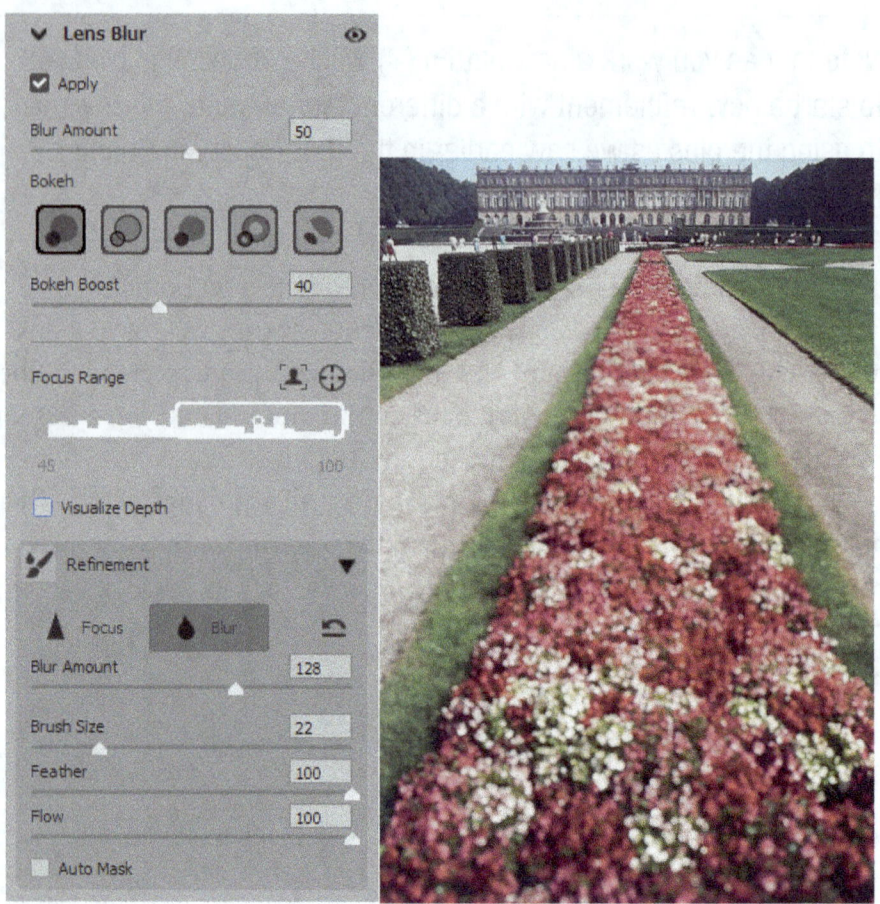

Figure 4-109. Camera Raw Filter Edit Lens Blur tab expanded with changes and preview of the image so far

Calibration

The Calibration tab lets you set the following adjustments if you need to adjust for older versions of Camera Raw. Refer to Figure 4-110.

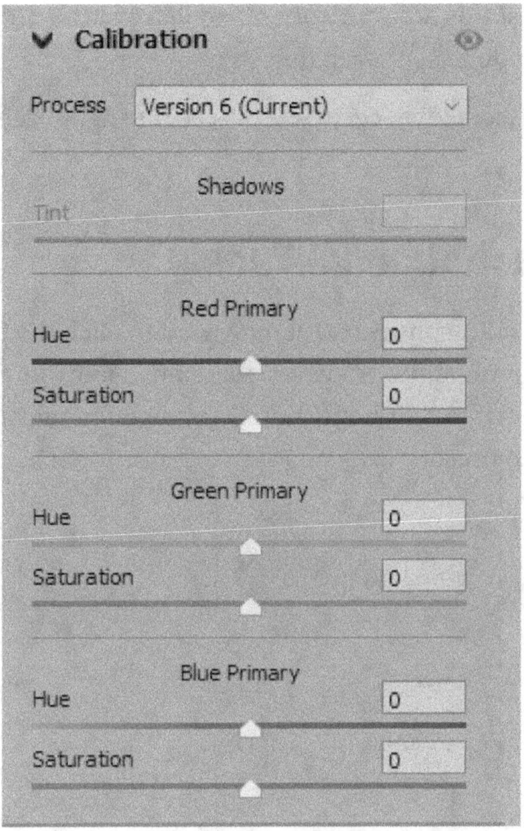

CHAPTER 4   ADVANCED FILTERS FOR PHOTO RESTORATION: PART 1

Figure 4-110. *Camera Raw Filter Edit Calibration tab expanded*

Process: Set a version of process. From the list the current version is 6 or the default setting.

Shadows: Adjust the Tint slider. Currently this settings is disabled.

Red Primary: Adjust the Hue or Saturation slider. Their range is –100, 0, +100.

Green Primary: Adjust the Hue or Saturation slider. Their range is –100, 0, +100.

Blue Primary: Adjust the Hue or Saturation slider. Their range is –100, 0, + 100.

CHAPTER 4 ADVANCED FILTERS FOR PHOTO RESTORATION: PART 1

I do not adjust this area very often and leave at the default settings, but if you need more details, refer to this link:

https://helpx.adobe.com/camera-raw/using/process-versions.html

Workspace Additional Panels

At this point, for many projects you may want to click the OK button to exit and save your changes. However, there are a few more panels on the right that I just want to point out should you need to make a few additional alterations, based on your project. Refer to Figure 4-111.

Figure 4-111. *Other panel options in Camera Raw are found on the right in the workspace*

Geometry Panel

The Geometry panel lets you work with various tools. Set the following settings to straighten photos and correct distortions. Refer to Figure 4-112.

CHAPTER 4   ADVANCED FILTERS FOR PHOTO RESTORATION: PART 1

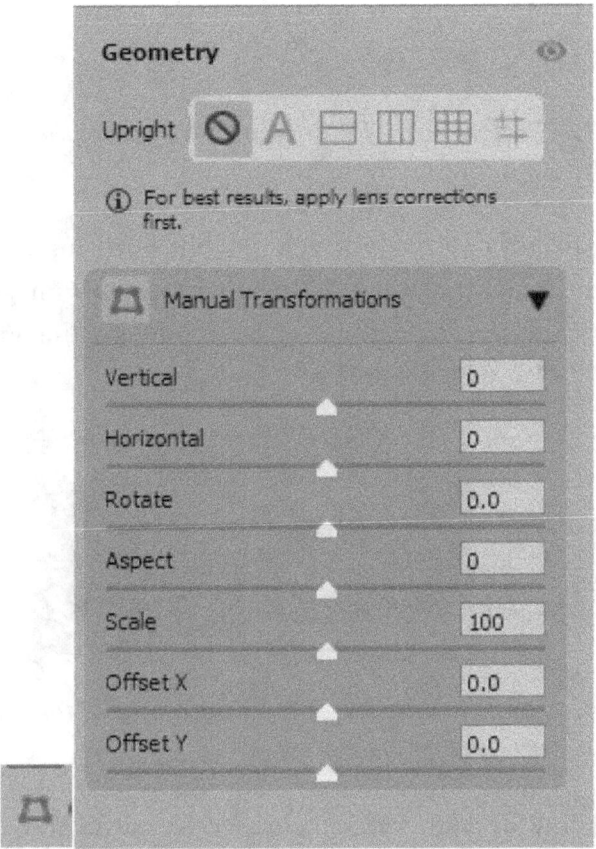

Figure 4-112. *Camera Raw Filter Geometry panel expanded*

Upright: By default, this settings is disabled when there is no distortion to correct. However, you can choose other options to experiment with like

Auto: Apply balanced perspective corrections. However, be aware that this setting may not accurately balance in all situations as you intend, so another Upright setting or manual transformation may be better. Refer to Figure 4-113.

CHAPTER 4 ADVANCED FILTERS FOR PHOTO RESTORATION: PART 1

Figure 4-113. Camera Raw Filter Geometry panel with Upright: Auto

Level: Apply only one level correction in the horizontal. This is a good setting for some images; however, be aware that for this image there is more of a vertical distortion happening on the sides of the building, so this is not helping. Refer to Figure 4-114.

Figure 4-114. Camera Raw Filter Geometry panel with Upright: Level and effect on part of the image

Vertical: Apply level and vertical perspective correction. In this image we are working on, this does correct the structure distortion in the distance but also creates too much distortion in other areas in the image and large blank areas you may not want to alter. Refer to Figure 4-115.

CHAPTER 4　ADVANCED FILTERS FOR PHOTO RESTORATION: PART 1

Figure 4-115. *Camera Raw Filter Geometry panel with Upright: Vertical and effect on part of the image*

Full: Apply level, horizontal, and vertical perspective correction. This can also straighten the structure but again adds some distortion to other areas you may not want to alter, and it leaves larger gaps on the sides. Refer to Figure 4-116.

CHAPTER 4   ADVANCED FILTERS FOR PHOTO RESTORATION: PART 1

Figure 4-116. *Camera Raw Filter Geometry panel with Upright: Full and effect on part of the image*

Guided: Draw two or more guides to customize perspective correction. You can use the Clear Guides button to remove them as you work. Use the Loupe setting when you want to magnify areas and make sure the Show Guides settings is enabled. Guided is a good compromise for this image as I just want to correct the upper area of the building without creating large gaps in the rest of the image. Refer to Figure 4-117.

CHAPTER 4 ADVANCED FILTERS FOR PHOTO RESTORATION: PART 1

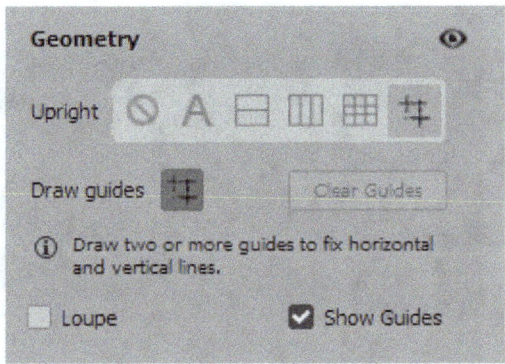

Figure 4-117. *Camera Raw Filter Geometry panel with Upright: Guided selected to apply to part of the image*

Here I dragged two vertical magenta guides on the left and right of the building. If you are using horizontal guides, they will appear green striped. Refer to Figure 4-118.

CHAPTER 4   ADVANCED FILTERS FOR PHOTO RESTORATION: PART 1

Figure 4-118. *Camera Raw Filter vertical magenta guides applied to the right and left of the building*

I then gave the Camara Raw a moment to straighten. Refer to Figure 4-119.

CHAPTER 4   ADVANCED FILTERS FOR PHOTO RESTORATION: PART 1

Figure 4-119. *Draw guides have now straightened the sides of the building.*

You can clear the guides to reset at this point or leave them as I did to show you the result.

Zooming out you can see how this option created a lot less distortion. And outside this workspace you may want to crop the image later or fill in those gaps later using the Edit ➤ Content-Aware Fill workspace that we discussed in detail in Volume 1. Refer to Figure 4-120.

CHAPTER 4　ADVANCED FILTERS FOR PHOTO RESTORATION: PART 1

Figure 4-120. *In Camera Raw you now have an image with gaps, but you may need to use the Content-Aware Fill workspace and other layers to correct this issue for a complete picture*

You can see an example of that in my extra file **flower bed_content-aware.psd**.

However, note that besides Edit ➤ Content-Aware Fill, I also had to make a copy of one of the bushes on the left to make the edge look uniform and then use my imagination with a clone stamp tool to cover or edit gaps that Content-Aware Fill did not edit accurately. Just be aware that if you make color adjustments in Camera Raw afterward, they will appear differently on the Camera Raw, from the newly cloned or content-aware areas outside of the filter, so final touch-ups like this should always be the last steps when working with this filter and distortions. Refer to Figure 4-121. The return to Camera Raw and Geometry.

CHAPTER 4   ADVANCED FILTERS FOR PHOTO RESTORATION: PART 1

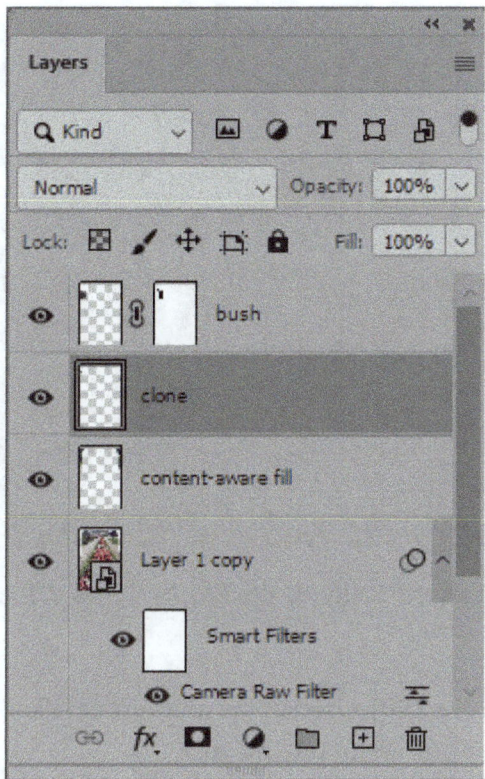

Figure 4-121. *Layers panel with additional layers to cover the gaps left by the adjustments in Camera Raw to correct distortion*

Manual Transformations: Use the sliders to adjust the following distortions manually in your own projects. In this case I left them at the default settings of either 0 or 100. But for your own projects, you can test them if you want to. Refer to Figure 4-122.

CHAPTER 4 ADVANCED FILTERS FOR PHOTO RESTORATION: PART 1

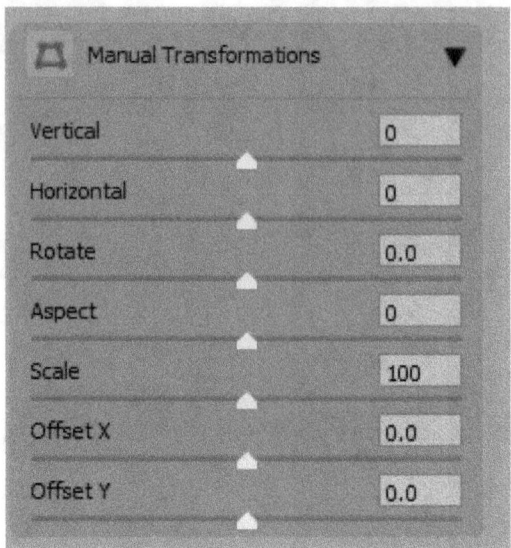

Figure 4-122. Camera Raw Filter Geometry panel Manual Transformations options

Vertical (–100, 0, + 100): Used to correct vertical distortions by adjusting the top or bottom of the image.

Horizontal (–100, 0, + 100): Used to correct horizontal distortions by adjusting the left or right of the image.

Rotate (–10, 0, + 10): Rotates the image, and this can be used to straighten the horizon if required.

Aspect (–100, 0, + 100): Can widen or narrow the image to correct minor aspect ratio issues when the Horizontal or Vertical has been adjusted to an image disproportionately in earlier work.

Scale (50–150): Can be used to expand or contract the image to reduce the amount of cropping required. In this case I left the setting at 100. But for your image, rather than crop, you may want a higher setting for expansion.

Offset X (–100, 0, + 100): Moves the image to the right or left by the set increments.

Offset Y (−100, 0, + 100): Moves the image up or down by the set increments.

Note Further geometry issues can be corrected using the Lens Correction filter, which we will look at briefly, later in the chapter.

Click OK to exit this project. In this case we will look at the other panels using other images. However, make sure to File ➤ Save your work. You can enter the filter any time by double-clicking it. Refer to Figure 4-123.

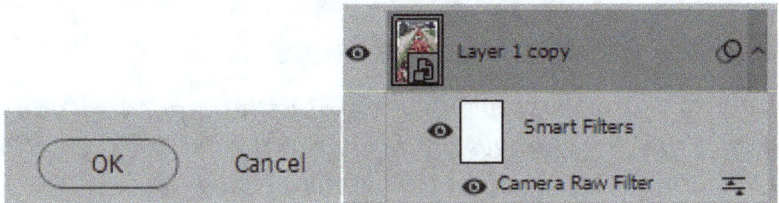

Figure 4-123. *Camera Raw Filter: click OK to exit the panel to see that the filter is applied to the smart object layer file*

Refer to my file **flower_bed_final.psd**.

Saving Changes Options

Remember to click OK or Cancel to exit. Hold down the Alt/Option key if you need to reset the workspace using the Cancel button. Note, if you do click Cancel and have made changes in the workspace, you will get a warning message asking if you want to discard or cancel all changes. If you do, then click Yes to exit or click No and remain in the workspace.

Click OK with your changes confirmed. Refer to Figure 4-124.

CHAPTER 4   ADVANCED FILTERS FOR PHOTO RESTORATION: PART 1

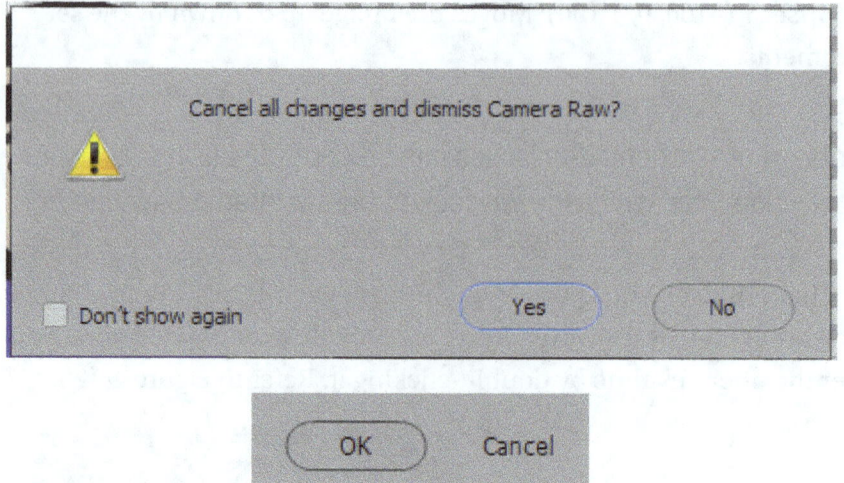

Figure 4-124. Camera Raw Filter warning that appears if you click Cancel after making changes in the filter and you have the option to cancel all changes and dismiss the Camera Raw Filter

Remove Panel

For the next Camera Raw Filter panel, we will use a different image **waterfall_camera_raw.psd**. In this case I have already started to adjust the color on this image in the Edit area for Light, Effects, and Curve to brighten the image of this chaotic waterfall among the cliffs. Refer to Figure 4-125.

CHAPTER 4   ADVANCED FILTERS FOR PHOTO RESTORATION: PART 1

Figure 4-125. *Previewing the color alteration made to the waterfall in the Camera Raw Filter*

It is an interesting image, but there are a few imperfections of dust that need to be covered.

The Remove (B) panel lets you work with various tools and adjust settings on the preview and cover imperfections. This area is similar to working with many of the healing tools mentioned in Volume 1, which include the Spot Healing Brush, Remove, and Clone Stamp tools. Use these tools to remove such things as spots, powerlines, and any other distractions when you paint over the area or click to cover. I find this tool best for files with minor imperfections. When they are more numerous and complex, it may be best to use your healing tools outside this workspace as was demonstrated in Volume 1. Refer to Figure 4-126.

647

CHAPTER 4   ADVANCED FILTERS FOR PHOTO RESTORATION: PART 1

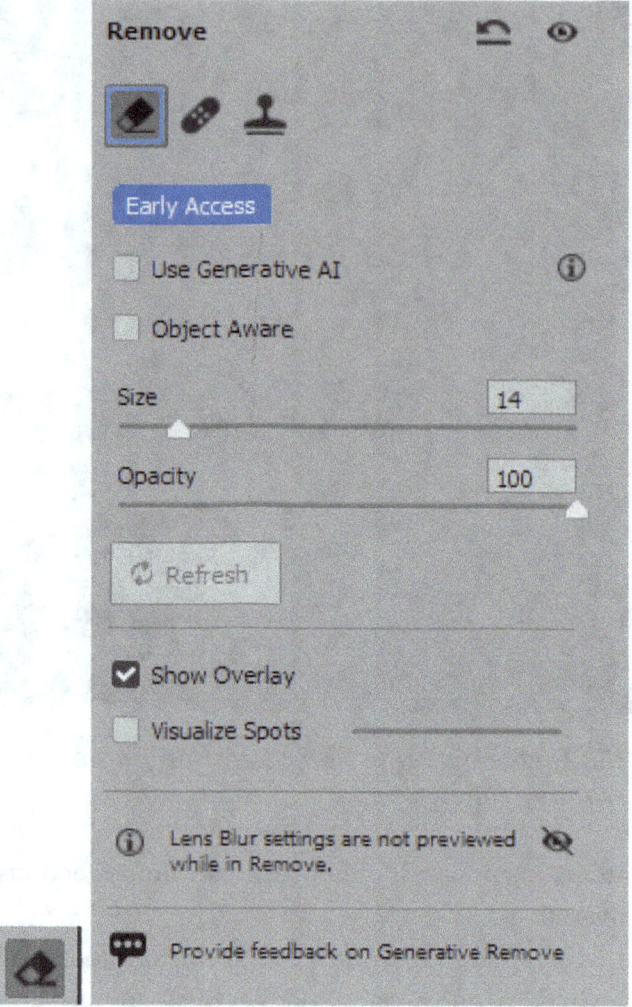

Figure 4-126. *Camera Raw Filter Remove panel*

Remove Tool (Content-Aware): With Early access, new options for Use Generative AI and Object Aware have recently been added. These options however are not available for the next two tools in this panel which we will look at later. For the remove tool use the sliders for the brush settings of Size (1–100) and Opacity (1–100). Click or drag on the board to cover an area, and then later you can move that area to a new location or press

CHAPTER 4 ADVANCED FILTERS FOR PHOTO RESTORATION: PART 1

the Backspace/Delete key to remove the selected area on the preview. Click Refresh to update a selected spot with different content. Refer to Figure 4-126.

In this case there was a small spot in the waterfall that needed to be removed. I used a 14 px brush and set the Opacity to 100 and clicked that location. Refer to Figure 4-127.

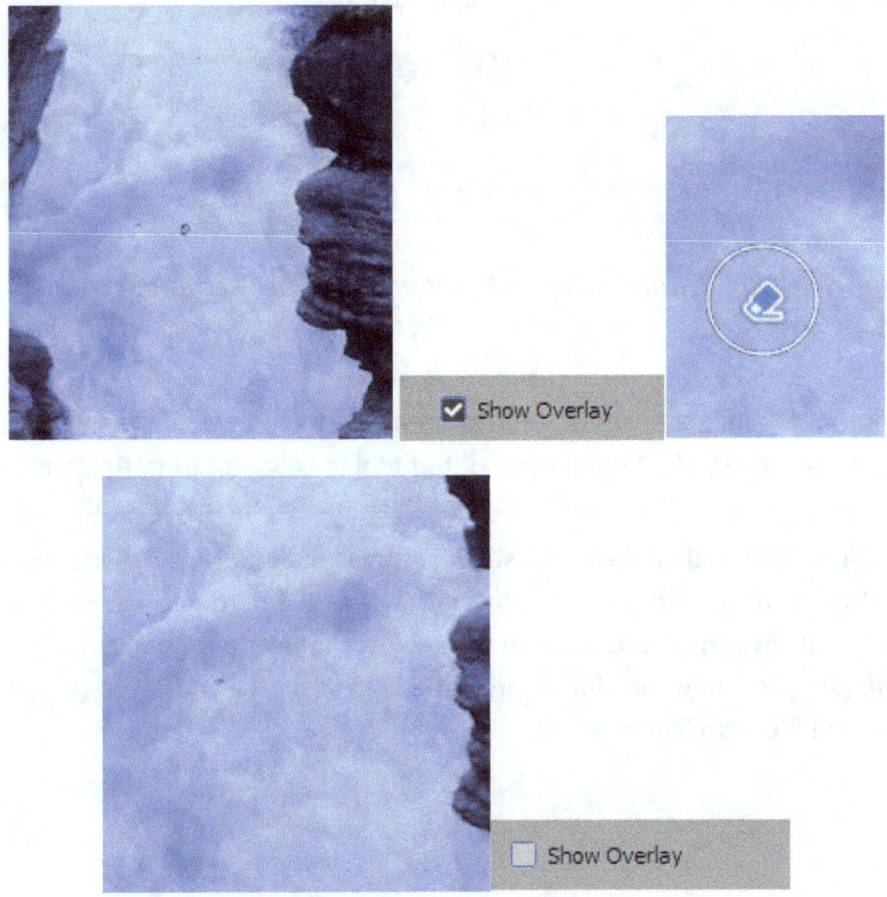

Figure 4-127. *Camera Raw Filter Remove panel with Show Overlay enabled and disabled using the Content-Aware Remove tool*

CHAPTER 4   ADVANCED FILTERS FOR PHOTO RESTORATION: PART 1

Turn off Show Overlay when you need to see the change in the image clearly. The overlay is there to indicate what type of healing tool was used and where.

Continue to remove and cover other spots. You can also Ctrl/CMD + click or drag on the image first to select a custom source before clicking and covering a spot. Then click the Refresh button if you do not like the selected spot's coverage. Refer to Figure 4-128.

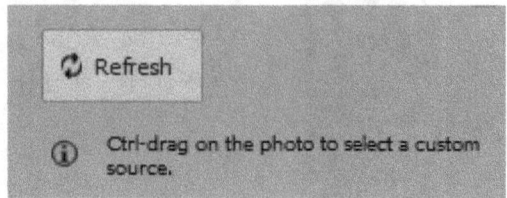

Figure 4-128. Camera Raw Filter Remove panel Refresh button

Note that while a covered remove area is selected, you can change to another healing tool option when that tool is selected from the panel.

Heal Tool: Adjust the brush slider settings for Size (1–100), Feather (0–100), and Opacity (1–100). Click or drag on the board to cover an area, and then later you can move that healed area or just the source area separately to a new location or press the Backspace/Delete key to remove the heal. Refer to Figure 4-129.

CHAPTER 4 ADVANCED FILTERS FOR PHOTO RESTORATION: PART 1

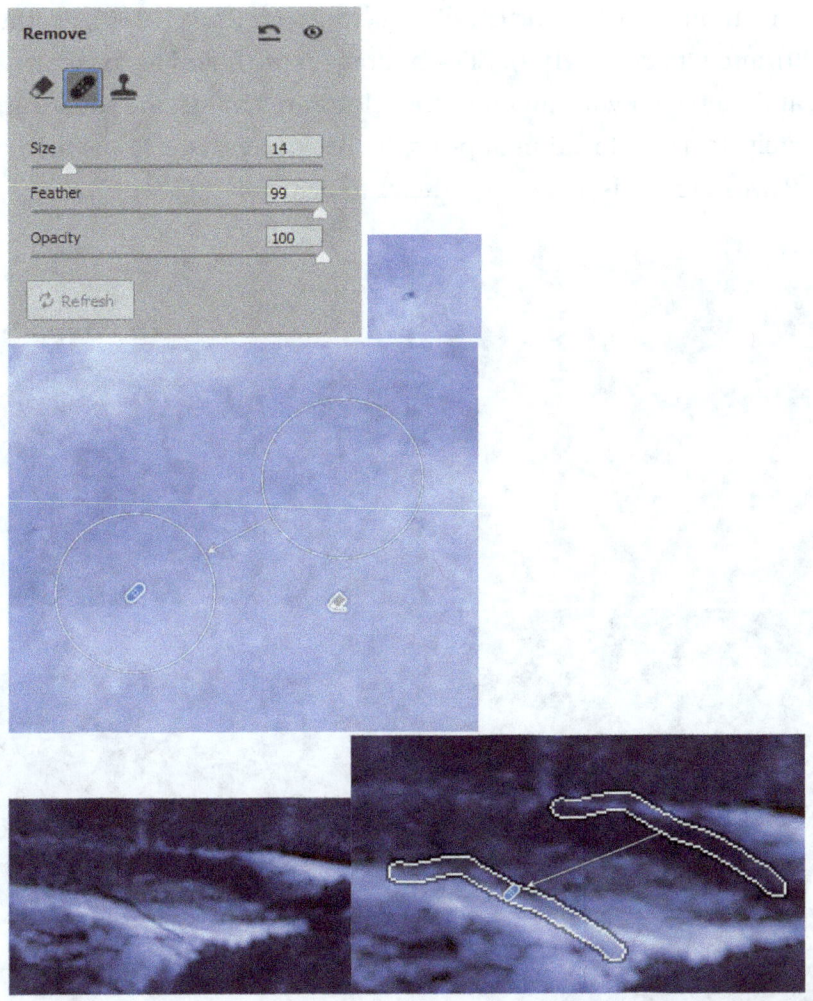

Figure 4-129. *Camera Raw Filter Remove panel: using the Heal Tool*

CHAPTER 4   ADVANCED FILTERS FOR PHOTO RESTORATION: PART 1

Clone tool: Adjust the brush slider settings for Size (1–100), Feather (0–100), and Opacity (1–100). Click or drag on the board to cover an area, and then later you can move that clone area or just the source area, separately, to a new location or press the Backspace/Delete key to remove. Click Refresh to adjust the source. Refer to Figure 4-130.

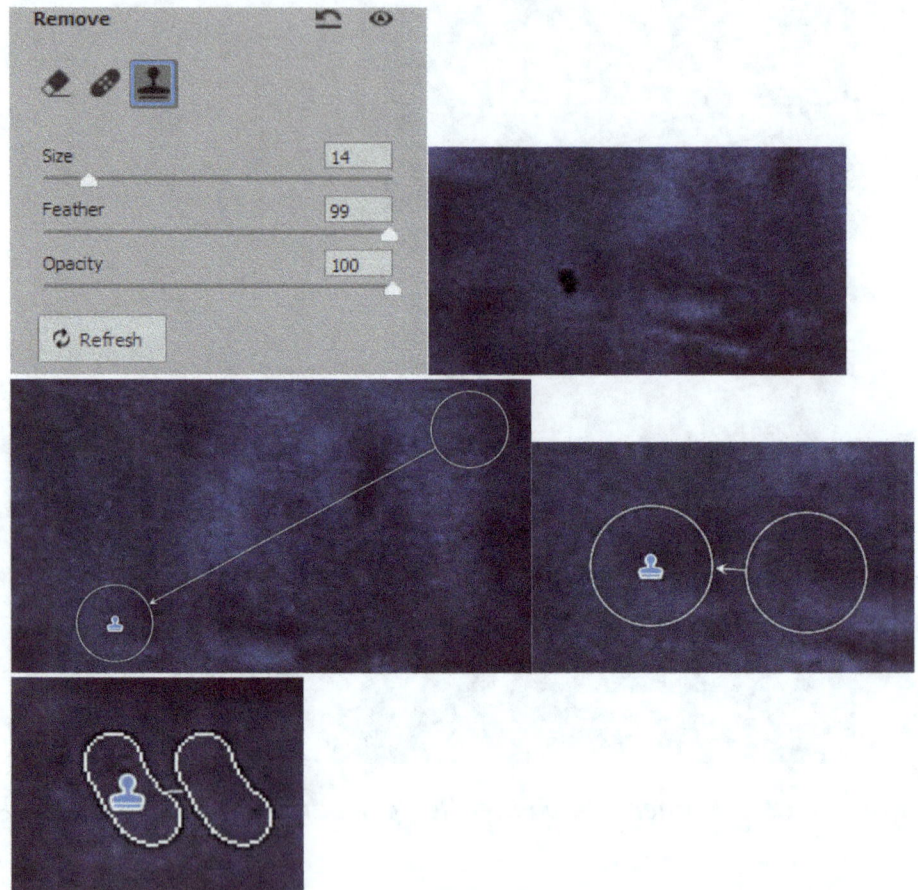

Figure 4-130. *Camera Raw Filter Remove panel: using the Clone tool*

CHAPTER 4   ADVANCED FILTERS FOR PHOTO RESTORATION: PART 1

As mentioned, use the Show Overlay to toggle on and off the visibility of pin and mask overlay.

Use Visualize Spots (Y) check box when enabled to visualize areas of possible spots and toggle the setting on and off to see a black-and-white preview. Adjust the threshold level in the preview using the slider when enabled. Refer to Figure 4-131.

Figure 4-131. *Camera Raw Filter Healing panel: visualizing spots*

Keep this setting disabled while working on the image.

You can keep working on this image or experiment with your own. In this case you can see some of the minor healing areas that I corrected in this image to remove distracting dust particles. Refer to Figure 4-132

CHAPTER 4   ADVANCED FILTERS FOR PHOTO RESTORATION: PART 1

and my file **waterfall_camera_raw_final.psd**. Refer to this link if you need more information https://helpx.adobe.com/camera-raw/using/enhanced-spot-removal-tool-camera-raw.html

Figure 4-132.   Waterfall image with areas of healing and remove applied

Click OK to exit and save changes when you are done.
File ➤ Save your work.

Masking Panel Options

The Masking panel is a more complex masking system of options but does share some similarities with the ones found in the Select and Mask workspace mentioned in Volume 1. It allows you to alter and adjust masks that can be used to adjust the color and effects of selected areas while in the Camera Raw Filter. Note that this mask is internal within the filter and does not appear on the smart filter layer mask in the Layers panel after you exit the filter. In this example, I am not focusing on any one particular image for you to work on but rather to show you which masks to use in certain examples. In this case, you can practice on an image that we have used in past chapters and turn the layer into a smart object layer first and then enter the filter and choose the masking icon. Use my file **tower_camera_raw_mask_test.psd** or another image of your choice. Refer to Figure 4-133.

CHAPTER 4 ADVANCED FILTERS FOR PHOTO RESTORATION: PART 1

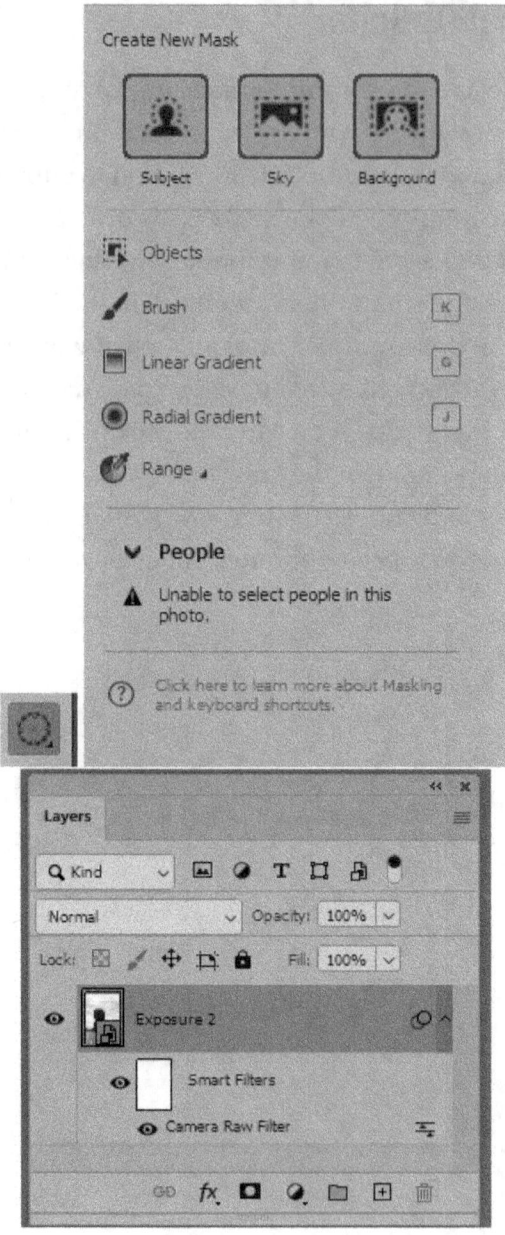

Figure 4-133. *Camera Raw Filter Masking panel and Layers panel with Camera Raw Filter*

CHAPTER 4   ADVANCED FILTERS FOR PHOTO RESTORATION: PART 1

What kind of masking you choose will depend upon the photo and your color correction intentions. Once one of the mask options is chosen, additional options will appear for editing the specific mask or masks.

Some of the more popular masking options are shown at the top of the list.

Create a new mask for the following:

- Subject: Select and mask the prominent parts of the photo quickly. Works well with people, structures, animals, and foreground colors. Refer to Figure 4-134.

Figure 4-134. *Camera Raw Filter Masking panel with a Subject mask applied with options*

CHAPTER 4   ADVANCED FILTERS FOR PHOTO RESTORATION: PART 1

- Sky: Applies the overlay mask to the sky and then you can make adjustment to just the sky area. Refer to Figure 4-135.

Figure 4-135. *Camera Raw Filter Masking panel with a Sky mask applied with options*

CHAPTER 4 ADVANCED FILTERS FOR PHOTO RESTORATION: PART 1

- Background: Automatically selects the background of the photo and applies a mask. Refer to Figure 4-136.

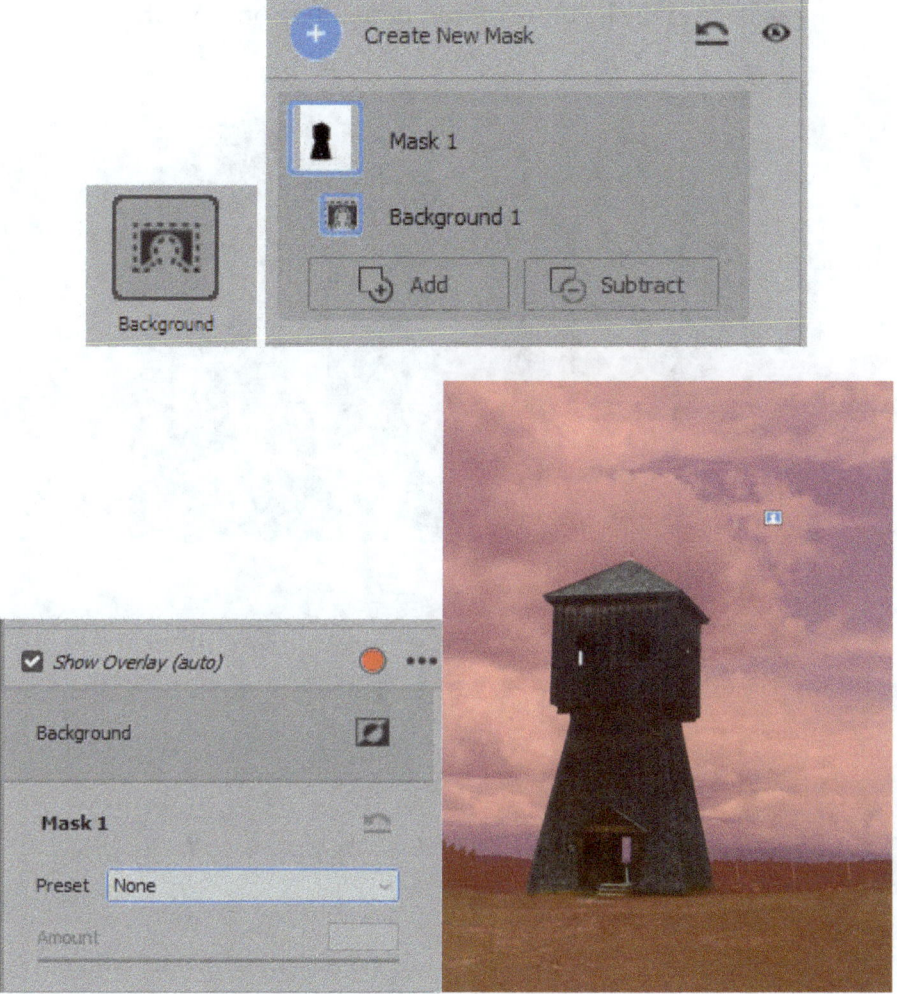

Figure 4-136. *Camera Raw Filter Masking panel with a Background mask applied with options*

Other kinds of mask overlay include

- People: If present and detected, they can be part of the selected mask, and you can apply selected edits to them all or each person selectively. The choices of masking may be more or less, depending on what the filter detects. Refer to Figure 4-137.

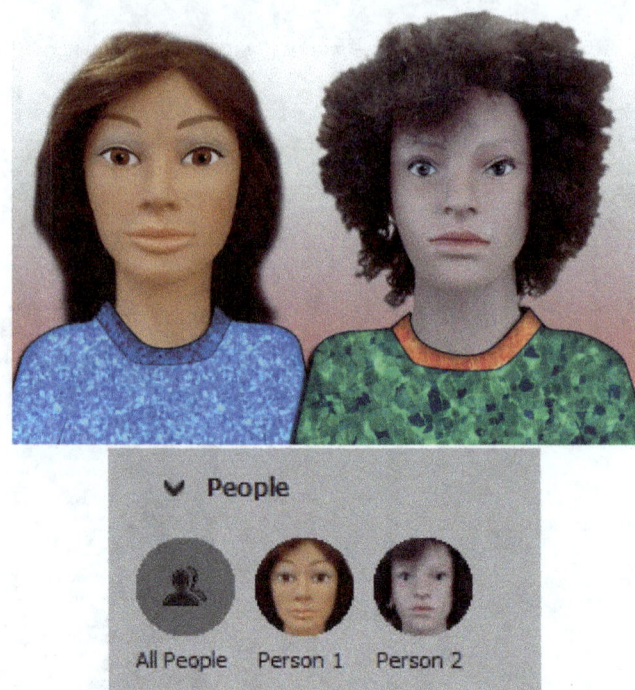

Figure 4-137. *Camera Raw Filter Masking panel with People identification*

Choose an option other than Entire Person, such as Facial Skin or another option like Body Skin, Eyebrows, parts of the eye, Lips, Hair, or Clothes. In some situations, you would also have the option to create separate masks. Click Create. Refer to Figure 4-138.

CHAPTER 4   ADVANCED FILTERS FOR PHOTO RESTORATION: PART 1

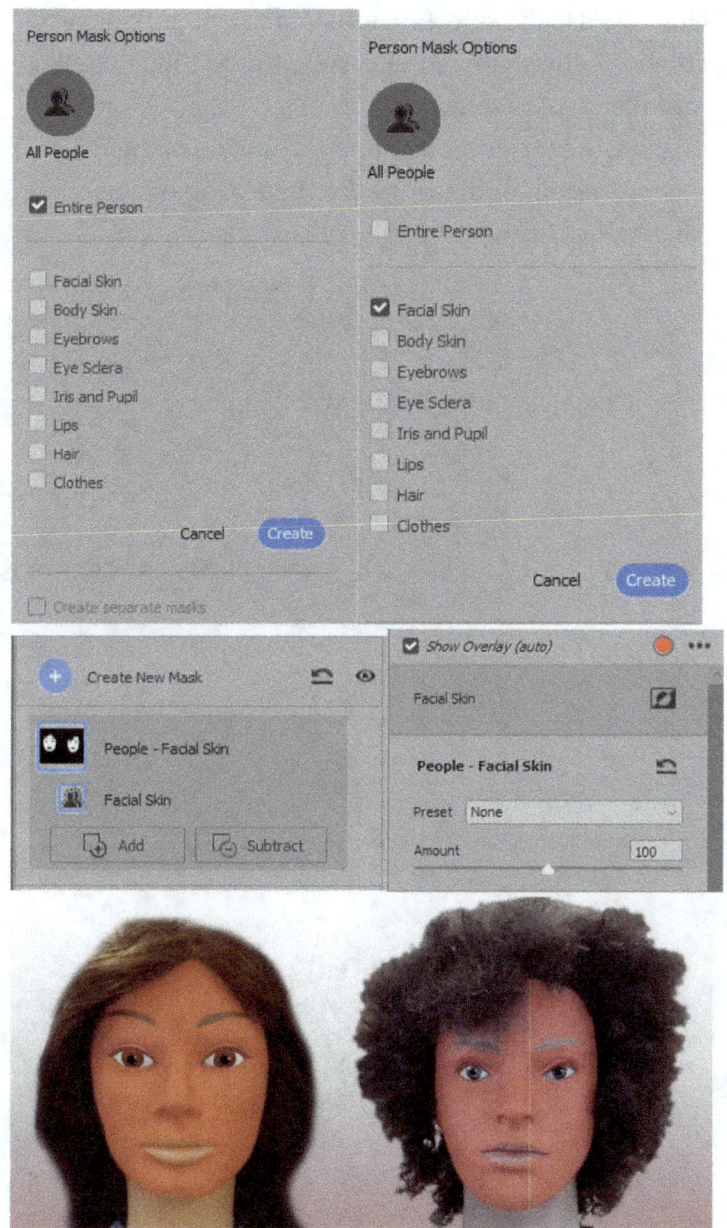

Figure 4-138. *Camera Raw Filter Masking panel with People identification and masking setting applied to select locations*

CHAPTER 4   ADVANCED FILTERS FOR PHOTO RESTORATION: PART 1

- Objects: Use the selection tool to mask objects using either the Brush tool to select areas or the Rectangular Marquee tool to select various objects. This is similar to using the Object Selection tool outside of the filter that on certain photos may do a better job of detection. Refer to Figures 4-139 and 4-140.

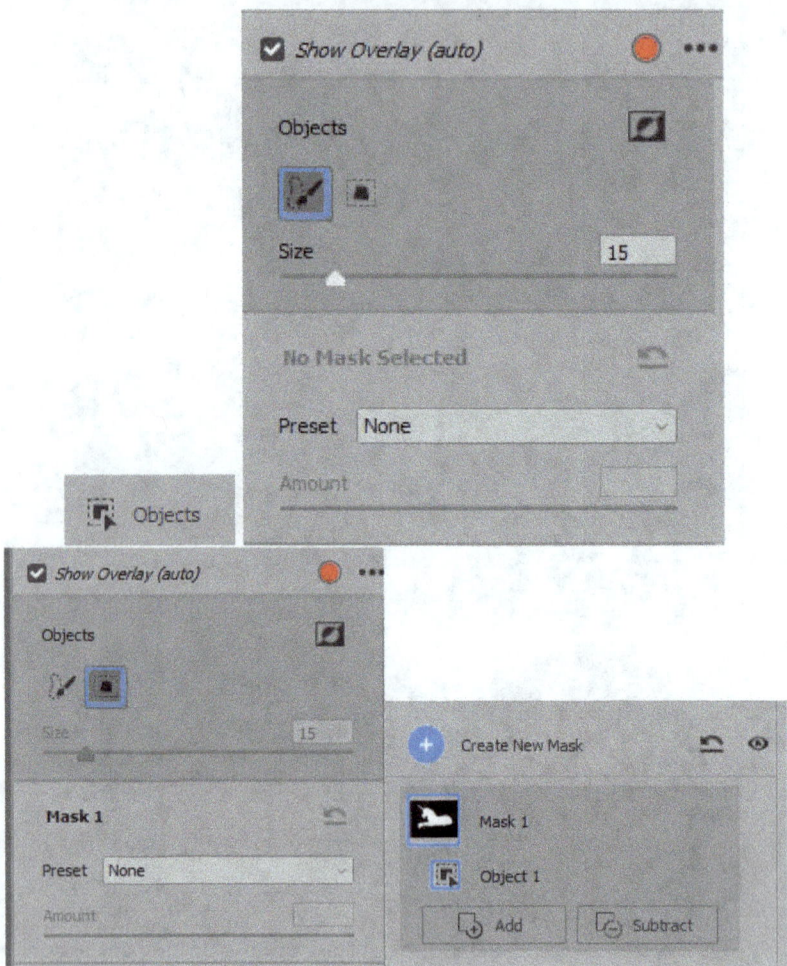

Figure 4-139. *Camera Raw Filter Masking panel with a Objects mask applied with options*

CHAPTER 4   ADVANCED FILTERS FOR PHOTO RESTORATION: PART 1

Figure 4-140. *Subject mask applied to a preview area*

- Brush: Is more of a free-form mask that you can edit as you choose, when you don't have a selection that falls into a set category or when it is hard to mask with the other options. Adjust settings like brush size, feather, flow rate, density, and auto mask sensitivity and then paint or erase over an area you would like to adjust. You can also choose to have separate eraser settings when you choose that option from the ellipsis menu (…). This is much like using a brush or eraser in quick mask mode (Q) or the Select and Mask workspace outside the filter as were discussed in Volume 1. Refer to Figures 4-141 and 4-142.

CHAPTER 4　ADVANCED FILTERS FOR PHOTO RESTORATION: PART 1

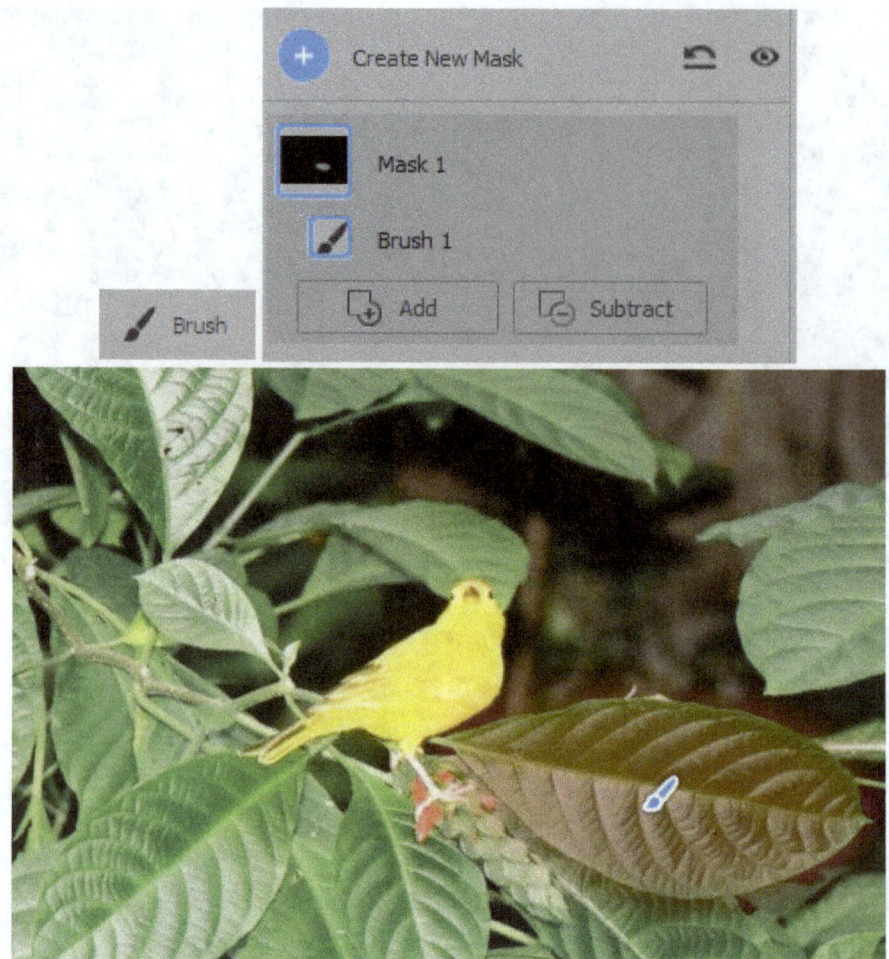

Figure 4-141. *Camera Raw Filter Masking panel with a Brush mask applied with options to a leaf*

664

CHAPTER 4   ADVANCED FILTERS FOR PHOTO RESTORATION: PART 1

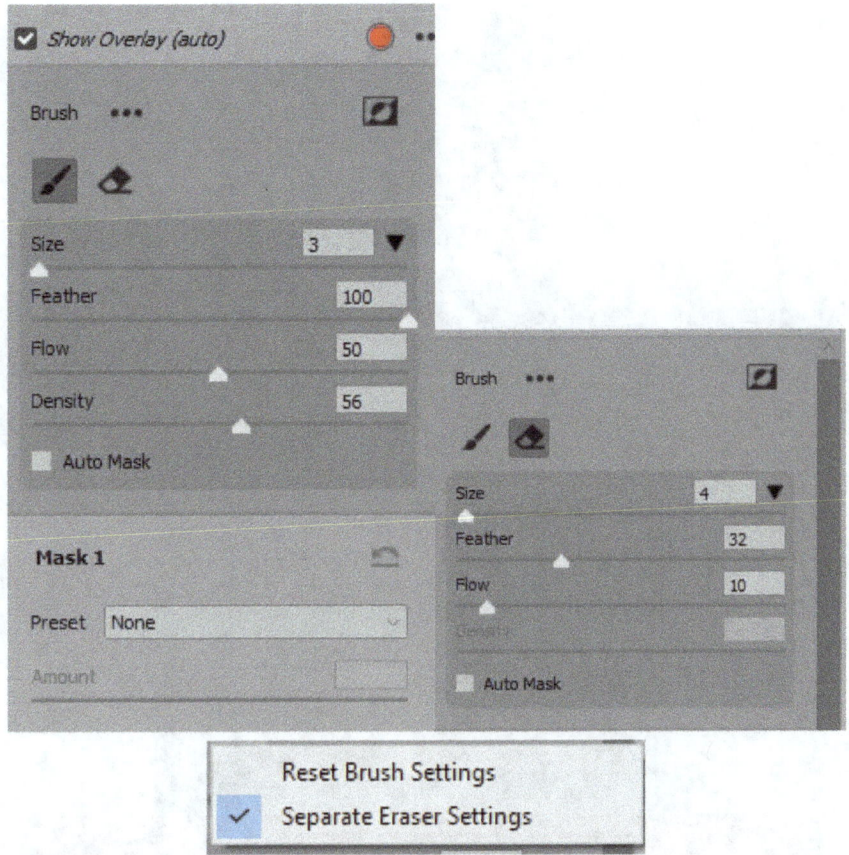

Figure 4-142. *Camera Raw Filter Masking panel with Brush mask options for brush and eraser*

- Linear Gradient: Apply adjustments in a gradually fading pattern that creates soft transitions. It can be used to balance a bright sky with a darker foreground. After the gradient is placed, by dragging on the preview, you can adjust its size and rotation. Refer to Figure 4-143.

CHAPTER 4   ADVANCED FILTERS FOR PHOTO RESTORATION: PART 1

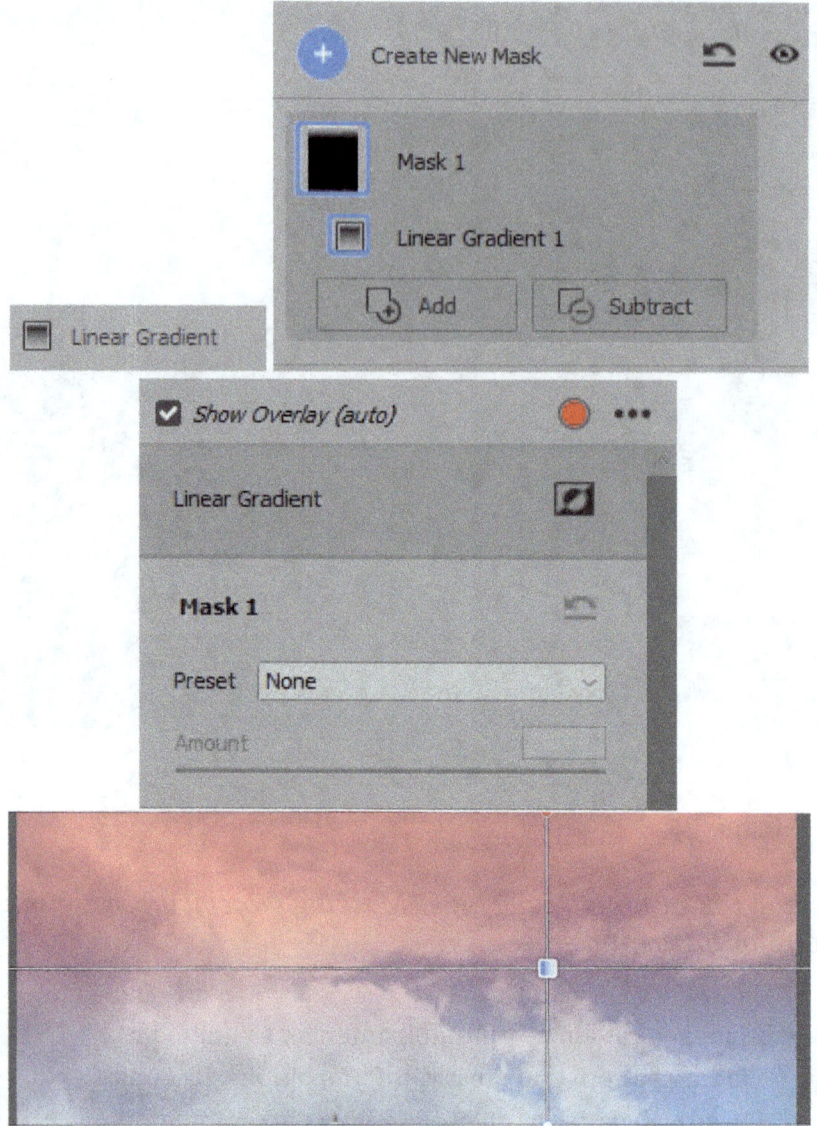

Figure 4-143.* Camera Raw Filter Masking panel with a Linear Gradient mask applied with options*

- Radial Gradient: Applies local adjustments to the inside and outside of an oval gradient that you have dragged onto the preview area. The gradient can be scaled and rotated. For natural-appearing effects, you can also adjust the feathering of the gradient. Refer to Figure 4-144.

CHAPTER 4 ADVANCED FILTERS FOR PHOTO RESTORATION: PART 1

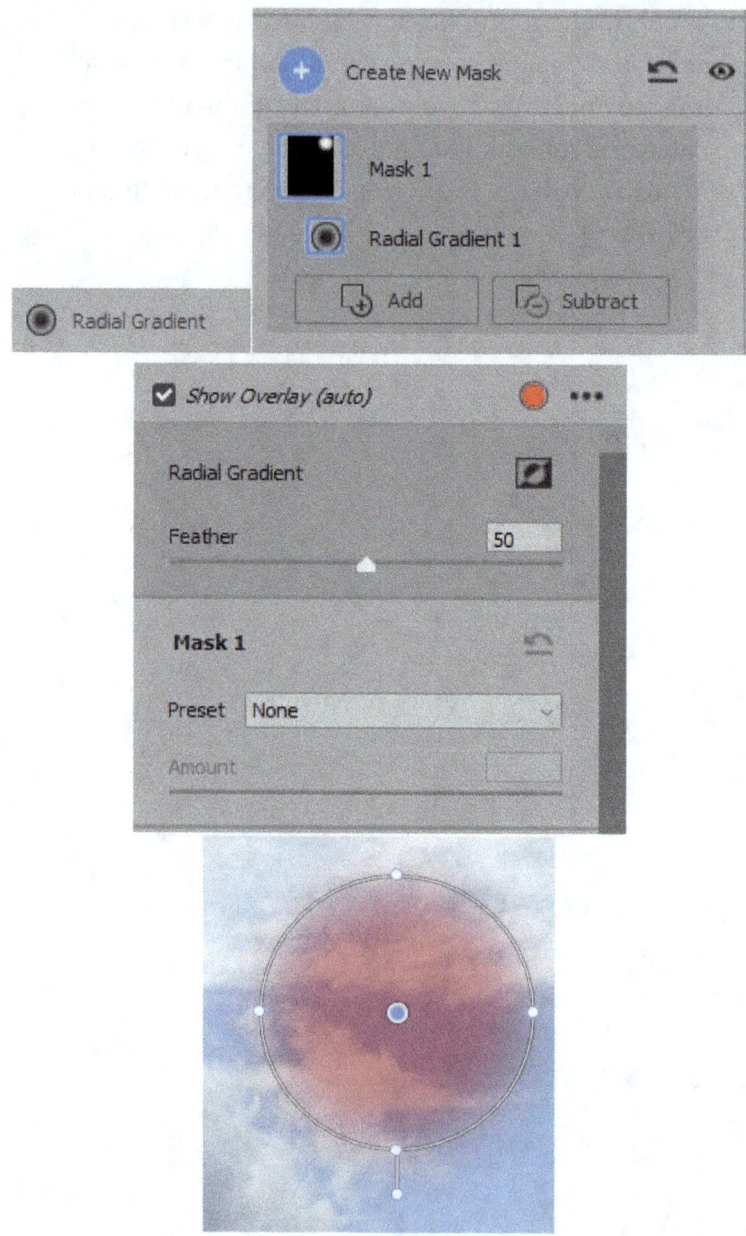

Figure 4-144. Camera Raw Filter Masking panel with a Radial Gradient mask applied with options

- Range: Applies adjustment to certain areas of the photo based on choices from the list of Color Range, Luminance Range, and Depth Range, if available. Color Range, which is similar to Select ➤ Color Range outside the filter, can be adjusted when you click with the eyedropper tool on the photo to sample color. Other options, like click + drag and Shift + click, can also be used to sample color for greater accuracy or add multiple samples. Refer to Figure 4-145.

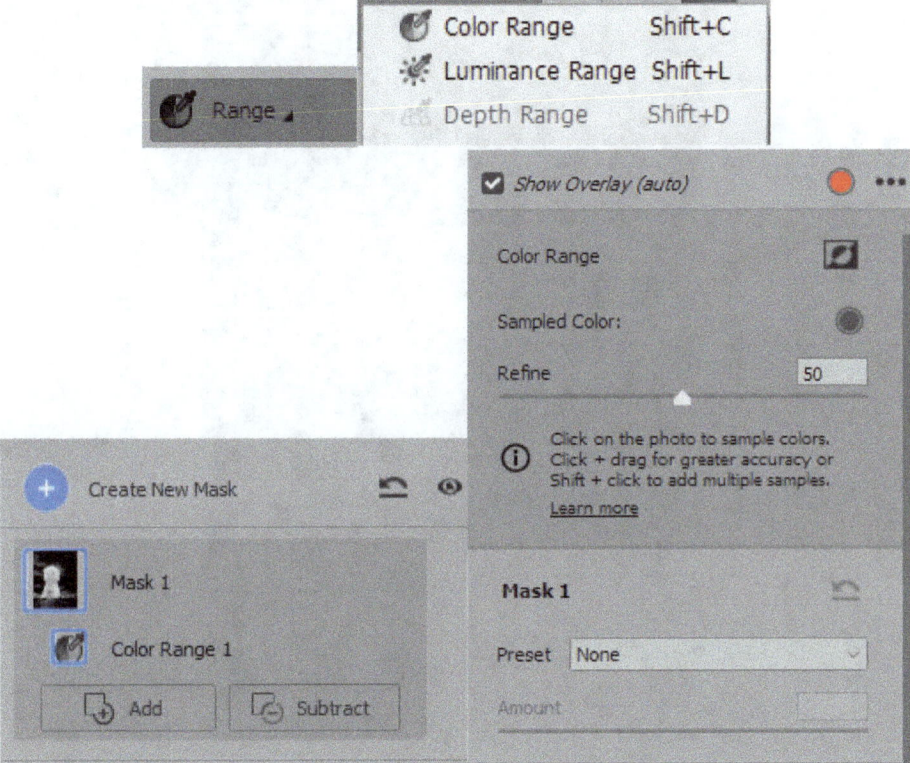

Figure 4-145. *Camera Raw Filter Masking panel Range masks with a Color Range mask applied with options*

CHAPTER 4   ADVANCED FILTERS FOR PHOTO RESTORATION: PART 1

You can also sample Luminance Range with the eyedropper tool in a similar way and edit a luminance map. Refer to Figure 4-146.

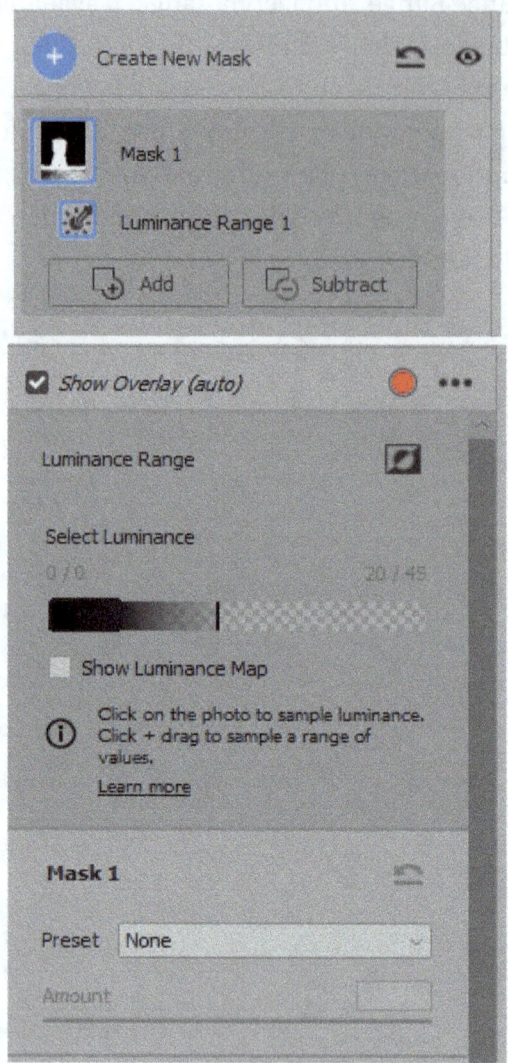

Figure 4-146. *Camera Raw Filter Masking panel with a Luminance Range mask applied with options*

Depth Range is only available for photos that have detectable distance variations or depth information from the camera, which you can then adjust with the depth slider. An example is an iPhone using the HEIC format. In this case we are working with scanned images, so this setting may not be available to you. However, you can learn more about it at the link provided at the end of this section.

Overall Common Mask Settings

Whichever mask you choose, once the mask is added, you can then control the following in the mask area for adding or subtracting to or from the mask using other previous masking options. A mask can also be reset, removed entirely, or renamed when you double-click the name or choose an option from the ellipsis (…) menu. Refer to Figure 4-147.

CHAPTER 4   ADVANCED FILTERS FOR PHOTO RESTORATION: PART 1

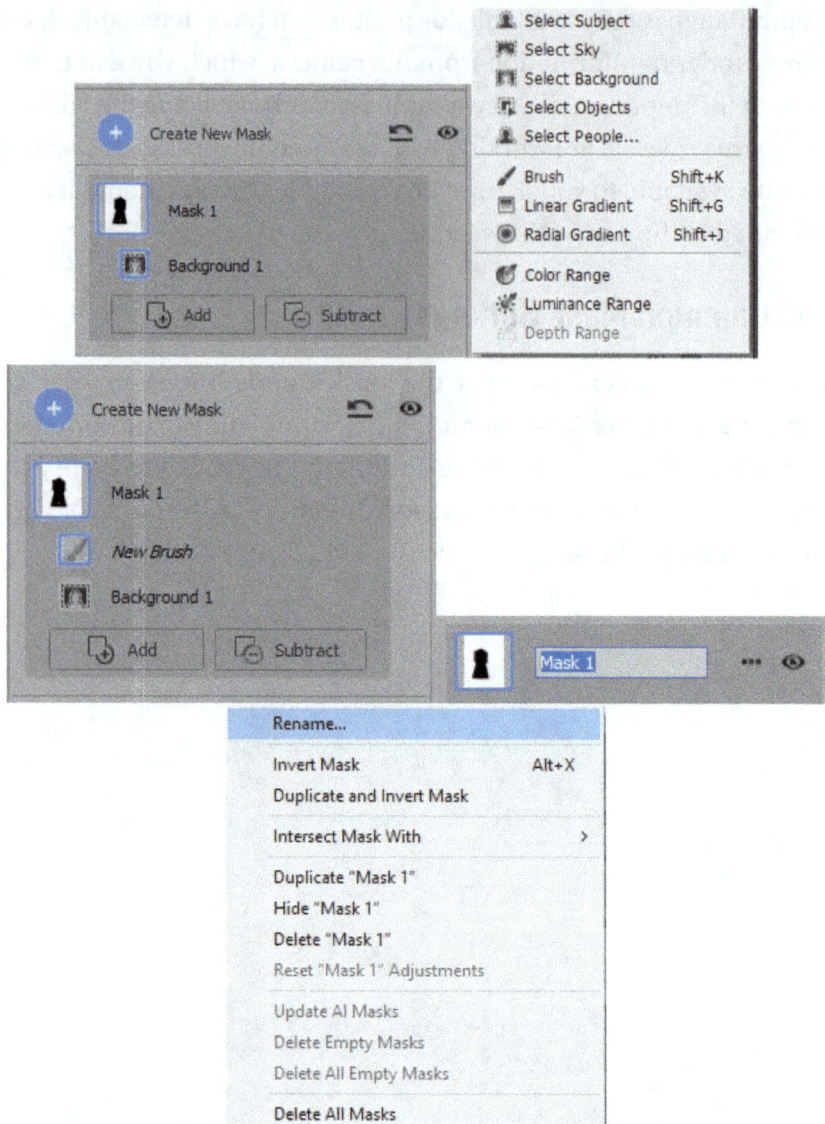

Figure 4-147. *Camera Raw Filter Masking panel with masks applied and various options for mask editing and creation*

As noted, earlier settings for each type of mask will vary with presets and brush options. However, you can hide and show the overlay at any time, change its color, or set additional overlay options, found under the ellipsis (…). You can invert the mask anytime for most masks.

The mask or overlay in this case is the area that is altered by the options that you choose to make additional color adjustments to. The overlay is currently red. On the mask itself it is the white area that is altered.

When a mask is selected, the number of the mask appears here. You can then select a preset adjustment if available. By default it is set to None and, if available, you can adjust the strength amount of a new preset (0–200). Refer to Figure 4-148.

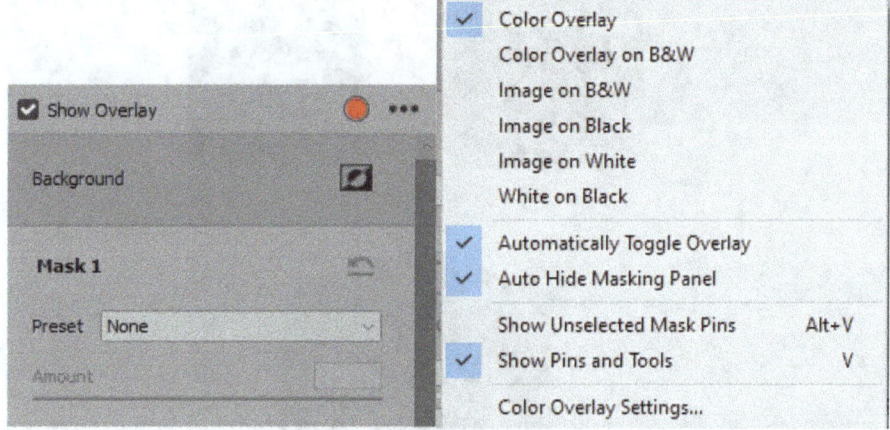

Figure 4-148. *Masking panel overlay options and preset options*

The areas that are covered with the red mask are the areas that are affected. As noted, you can invert the mask if you are not getting the effect on the area you desire or turn off the show overlay to see the effect better, or as you drag the sliders, the masking will disappear temporarily.

Many of these adjustment settings I have already discussed for overall color and sharpening effects in the Edit menu, but now they will apply to masked/overlay areas. When you have the mask to your liking, you can then use various adjustment sliders to modify the overall mask areas further. Refer to Figure 4-149.

CHAPTER 4　ADVANCED FILTERS FOR PHOTO RESTORATION: PART 1

Figure 4-149. *Camera Raw Filter Masking panel with masking color adjustment options and previewing changes of lightening the surrounding sky*

CHAPTER 4 ADVANCED FILTERS FOR PHOTO RESTORATION: PART 1

- Light: Refer to the Light tab for more details on how to set Exposure, Contrast, Highlights, Shadows, Whites, and Blacks.

- Color: Refer to the Color tab and Color Mixer for more details on how to set Temperature, Tint, Hue, Saturation, and Color. Refer to Figure 4-150.

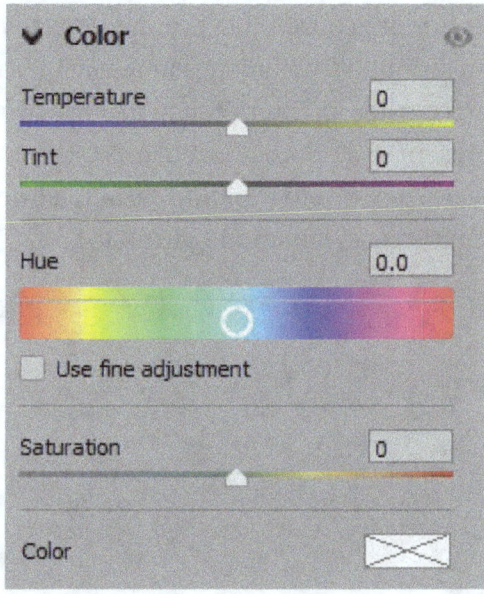

Figure 4-150. Masking color adjustment options for Color

- Point Color: Refer to the Color Mixer tab Point Color for details on how to work with specific Hue, Saturation, and Luminance ranges.

- Effects: Refer to the Effects tab for more details on how to affect Texture, Clarity, Dehaze, and Grain options.

CHAPTER 4 ADVANCED FILTERS FOR PHOTO RESTORATION: PART 1

- Curve: Refer to the Curve tab for details on how to work with Point Curve options for all or separate RGB channels.

- Detail: Refer to the Detail tab and Optics tab for details on how to work with Sharpness, Noise Reduction, and Defringe. Note, however, that neither of these panels has an option for Moire Reduction, which is shown here. This is more common in scanned images that have been scanned from images in magazine, and the dot pattern creates an interference pattern. Moiré can also be present in a photo taken of a TV screen and may also appear when photographing certain fabrics with a rippled tight weave. Refer to Figure 4-151.

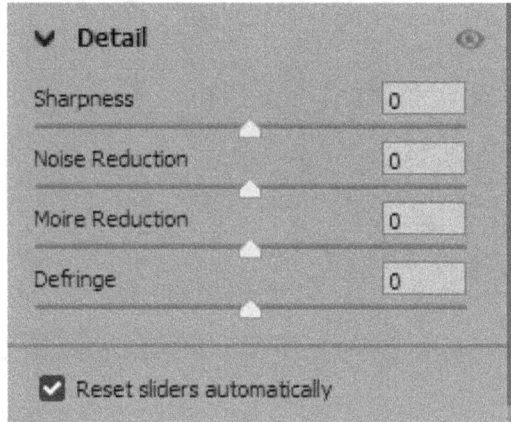

Figure 4-151. *Masking color adjustment options for Detail*

Refer to this link if you want some examples of Moiré:

https://en.wikipedia.org/wiki/Moir%C3%A9_pattern

Reset sliders automatically: When enabled is for switching between photos or creating new masks. Refer to Figure 4-151.

CHAPTER 4 ADVANCED FILTERS FOR PHOTO RESTORATION: PART 1

The masking area gives you key command codes with help and links if you cannot remember a specific setting. Refer to Figure 4-152.

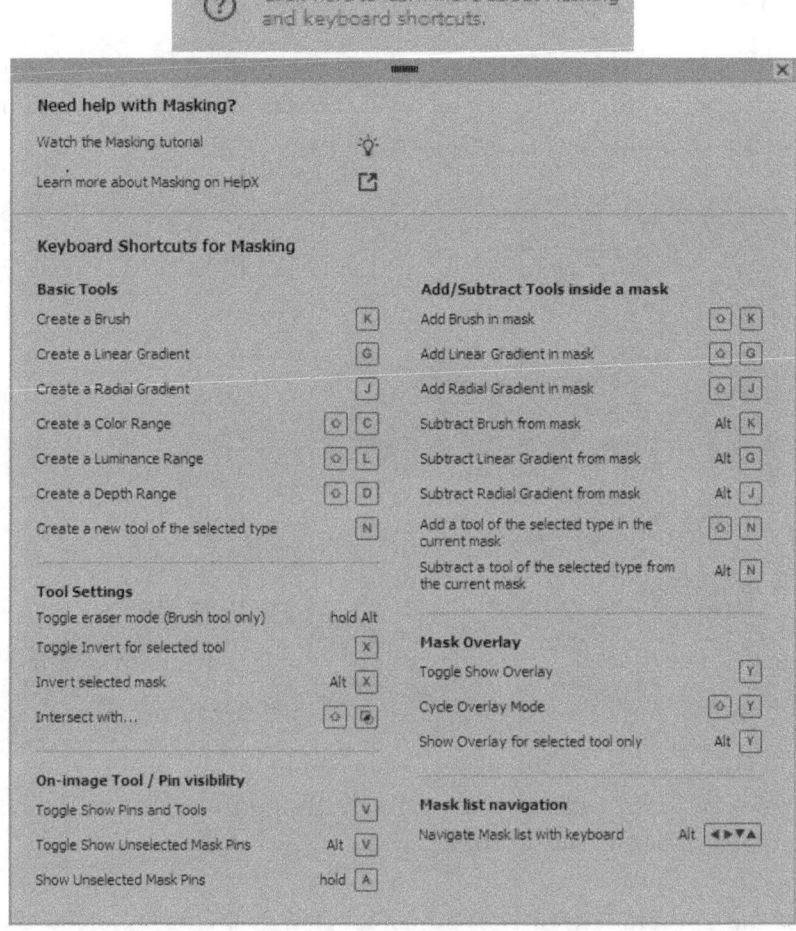

Figure 4-152. Masking options: help chart for shortcuts

To learn more about masking and selective color adjustments, you can refer to the following links:

https://helpx.adobe.com/camera-raw/using/masking.html

CHAPTER 4 ADVANCED FILTERS FOR PHOTO RESTORATION: PART 1

    https://helpx.adobe.com/camera-raw/using/make-local-
adjustments-camera-raw.html

Red Eye (Pet Eye) Panel

The Red Eye panel is used to remove unwanted pupil reflections from people and pets. I am using the **red_eye_camera_raw.psd** file and have selected the smart object layer. Refer to Figure 4-153.

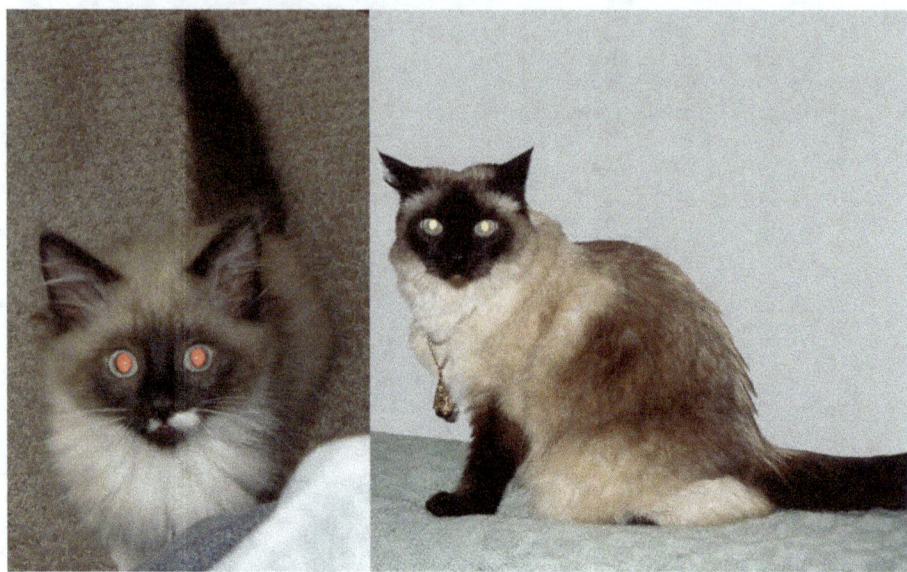

Figure 4-153. *Our pets can have red eye or golden eye that needs color correction in Camera Raw*

Use the Camera Raw filter to adjust for Red Eye. This panel lets you set the following settings based on Type chosen. This is similar to working with the Red Eye tool mentioned in Volume 1; however, now you can also work with pets. Use the cursor to drag a box around the eye or eyes that need correction. Refer to Figure 4-154.

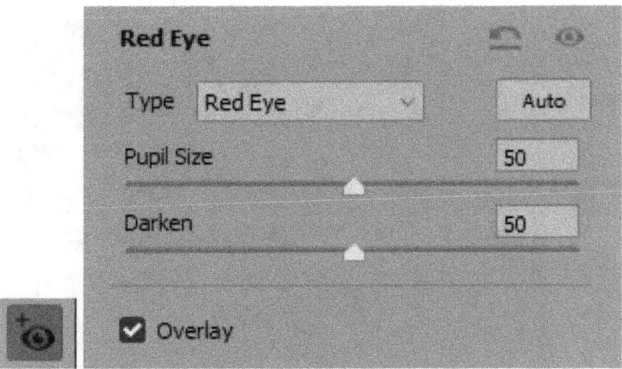

Figure 4-154. *Camera Raw Filter Red Eye panel and options*

Red Eye: Drag over the entire eye to make sure you cover the area. You can always, on the preview, adjust the sizing if it does not fit. In this case, using Auto did not detect the eyes. In the panel you can adjust Pupil Size (0–100) and Darken (0–100) and turn Overlay off and on. Try a setting of Pupil Size: 50 and Darken: 89. Refer to Figure 4-155.

CHAPTER 4 ADVANCED FILTERS FOR PHOTO RESTORATION: PART 1

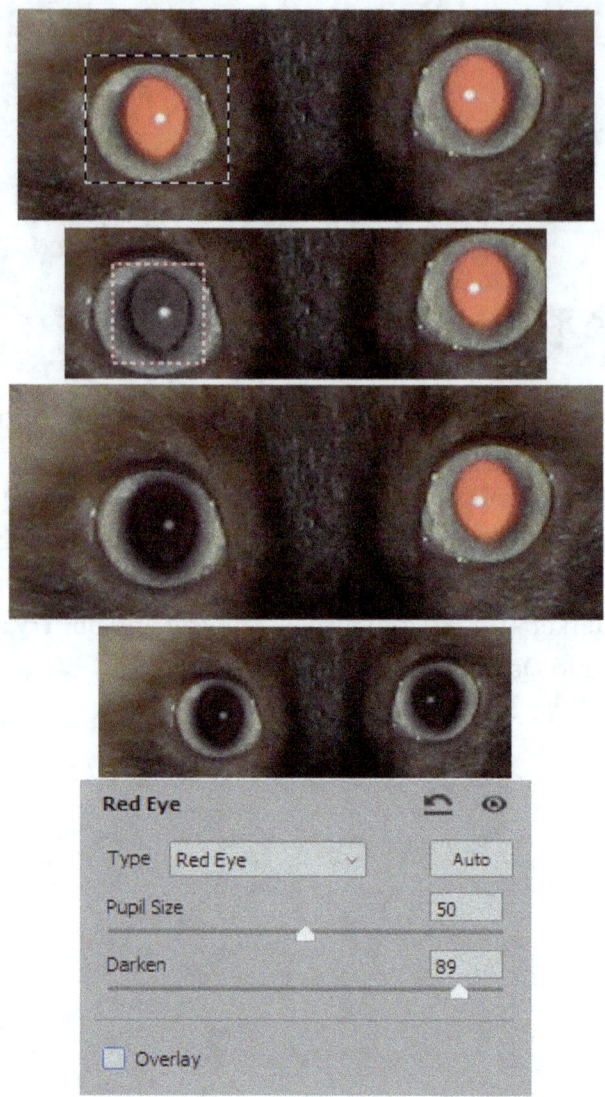

Figure 4-155. *Camera Raw Filter Red Eye panel and options: correction of each eye*

CHAPTER 4　ADVANCED FILTERS FOR PHOTO RESTORATION: PART 1

Repeat the steps on the other eye.

Pet Eye: Good for golden eyes. Drag over each eye, then move, and resize the overlay. In the panel, you can adjust the pupil size (0–100) to 50. Turn on Add Catchlight (specular highlight) and adjust its placement on the preview. Turn Overlay off and to review. Refer to Figure 4-156.

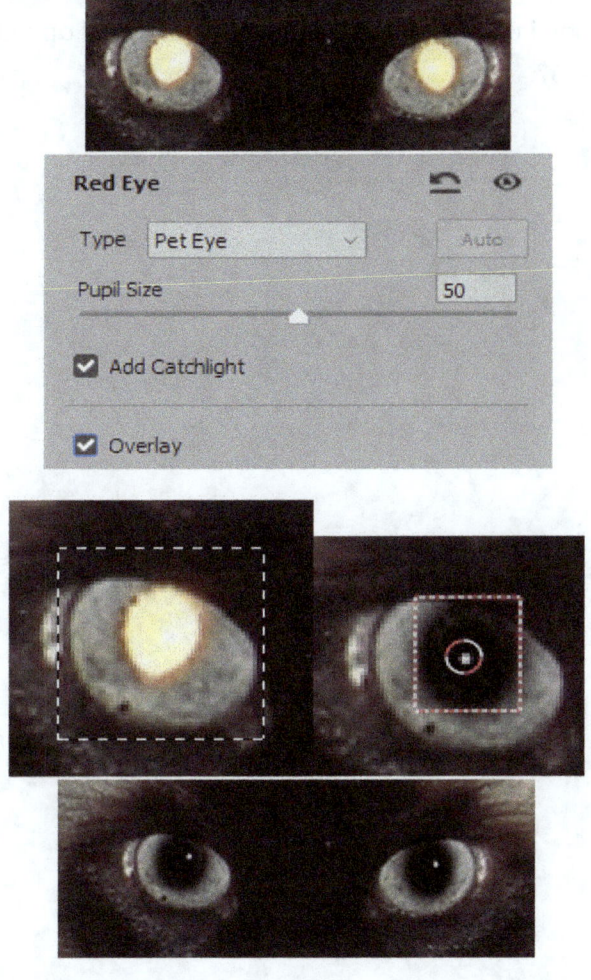

Figure 4-156. Camera Raw Filter Red Eye panel and options: correcting each golden eye with a catchlight

CHAPTER 4 ADVANCED FILTERS FOR PHOTO RESTORATION: PART 1

Use the Reset button to undo steps if required, as well as Ctrl/CMD + Z. Use the Delete/Backspace key if you need to remove a selected overlay.

Click OK to exit and then File ➤ Save your changes.

Later outside of the Camera Raw Filter, to enhance the eyes, you can always add an additional blue color fill of blue: R: 180, G: 229, B: 255. Above the smart object layer and on the layer mask painted over the eyes with the Eraser tool, I used a blending mode of Color and opacity of 28%. Refer to Figure 4-157.

CHAPTER 4   ADVANCED FILTERS FOR PHOTO RESTORATION: PART 1

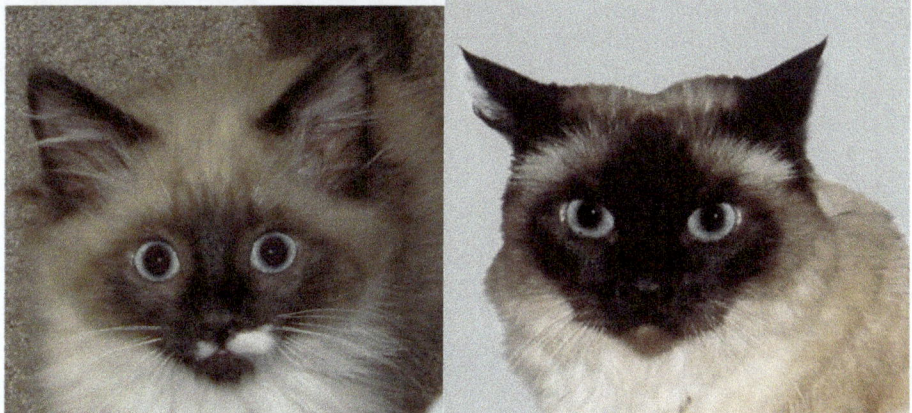

Figure 4-157. *After exiting the Camera Raw Filter, you can enhance your cat's eyes further with a Color Fill layer*

File ➤ Save you work so far.

You can review my file **red_eye_camera_raw_final.psd**.

Presets Panel

When you want to do other fast color adjustments besides the profiles found in the Edit tab, you can use Camera Raw presets, which will affect the panels and options we have just reviewed.

Choose or hover over an item from the list and click the text to test and then move the slider to adjust the strength of that applied preset. By default, this area is set to None; you can reset this if you click the Adobe Default setting in the list. Refer to Figure 4-158.

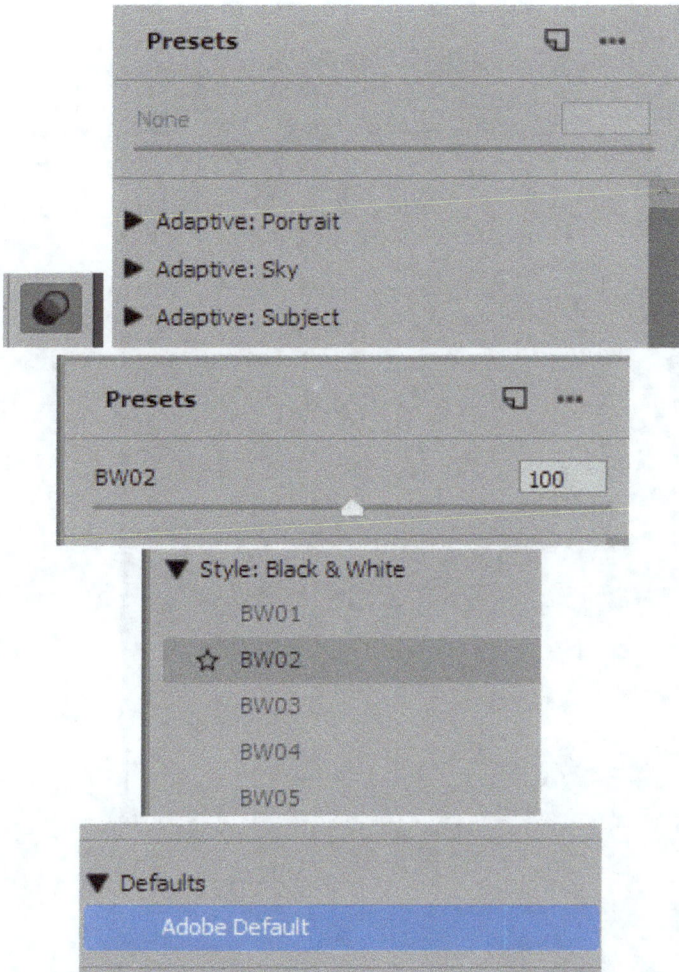

Figure 4-158. *Camera Raw Filter Presets panel and options*

This area also allows you to create your own preset using the button on the left to access a dialog box and under the ellipsis (…). There you have access to more preset options for viewing or managing the presets. Refer to Figures 4-159 and 4-160.

CHAPTER 4   ADVANCED FILTERS FOR PHOTO RESTORATION: PART 1

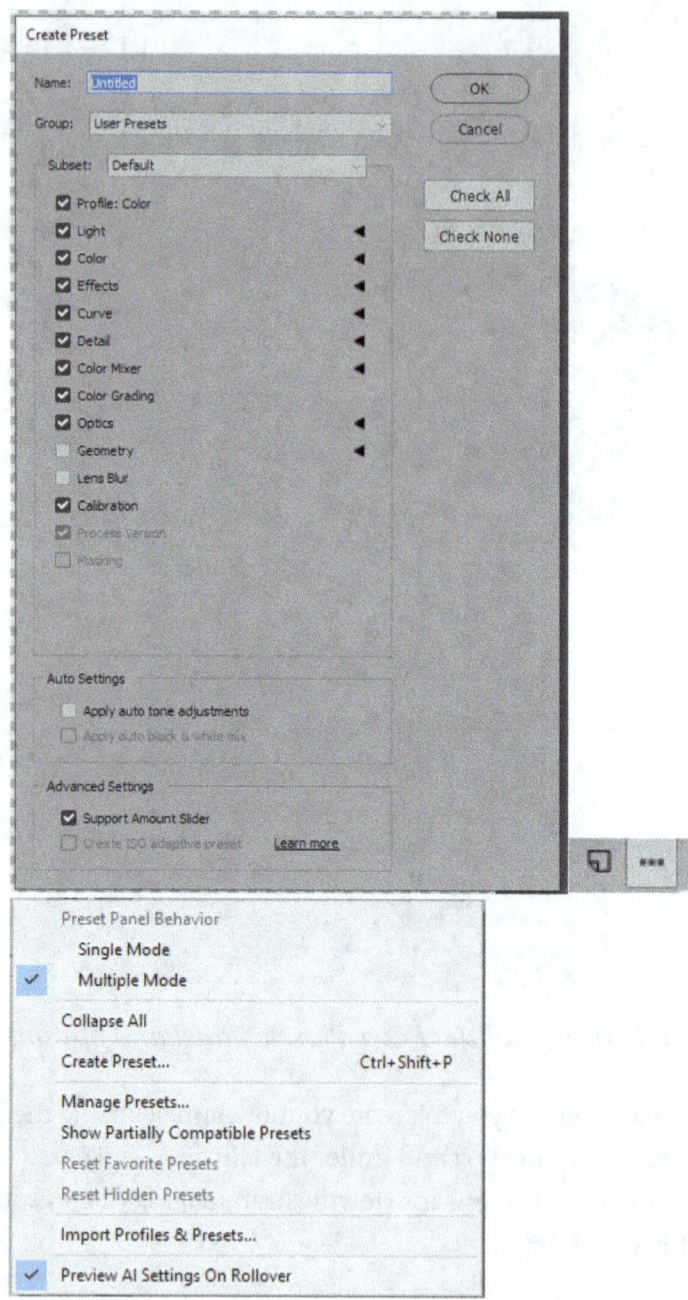

Figure 4-159. *Camera Raw Create Preset dialog box and additional settings*

CHAPTER 4   ADVANCED FILTERS FOR PHOTO RESTORATION: PART 1

Figure 4-160. *Applying a preset to an image using the Camera Raw Filter*

More Image Settings Options

Additional options for saving and loading settings can be found under the ellipsis (…) on the far right. Refer to Figure 4-161.

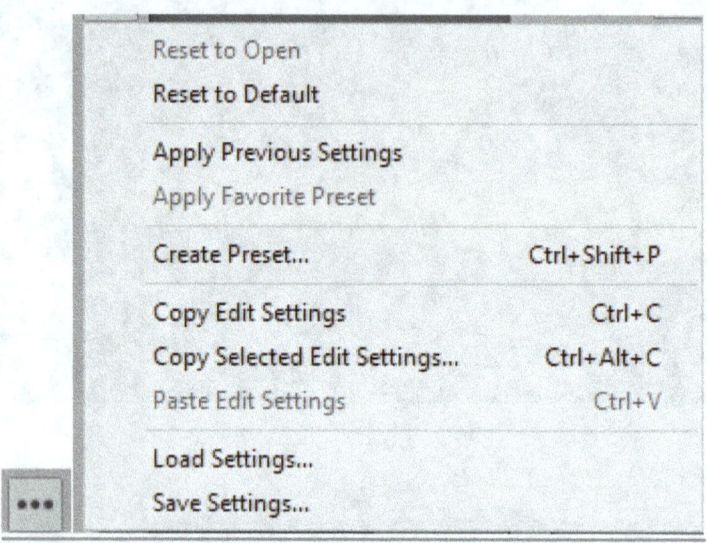

Figure 4-161.   Additional settings in the Camera Raw Filter

Click OK with your changes confirmed. Refer to Figure 4-162.

Figure 4-162.   Click OK in the Camera Raw Filter and save changes

More details or additional information on Camera Raw can be found here:

```
https://helpx.adobe.com/camera-raw/using/introduction-camera-raw.html
```

Other Advanced Filters to Consider Using with Camera Raw

While working with Camera Raw and entering and exiting the filter, here are two filters you may want to consider using in conjunction with it when correcting for distortion, should that be an issue. They are Lens Correction and Adaptive Wide Angle. Either can be added afterward to the smart filter layer. Refer to Figure 4-163.

Figure 4-163. *Other filters can be applied in conjunction with your Camera Raw Filter*

Their use is more common with digital images than images taken with a film camera and later scanned, because for automatic correction they rely on camera type or lens profile detection. However, some of these filters' properties can still be used with scanned images with no profile.

Lens Correction Filter

This allows you to do auto and custom correction. In Photoshop, Adobe recommends, in the Geometry panel, that you use this filter first with the Camera Raw Filter if you need to add additional correction to a photo with distortion to correct pincushion and barrel distortion created by the camera's lens. It is optional to use however, if the image has no noticeable distortions and you feel you have adequately corrected using Camera Raw. Refer to Figure 4-164 and you can use my file **wooden_church.psd**.

CHAPTER 4　ADVANCED FILTERS FOR PHOTO RESTORATION: PART 1

Figure 4-164. *An image of an old wooden church, with some lens distortion*

Go to Filter ➤ Lens Correction to view the workspace of the filter. Refer to Figure 4-165.

CHAPTER 4   ADVANCED FILTERS FOR PHOTO RESTORATION: PART 1

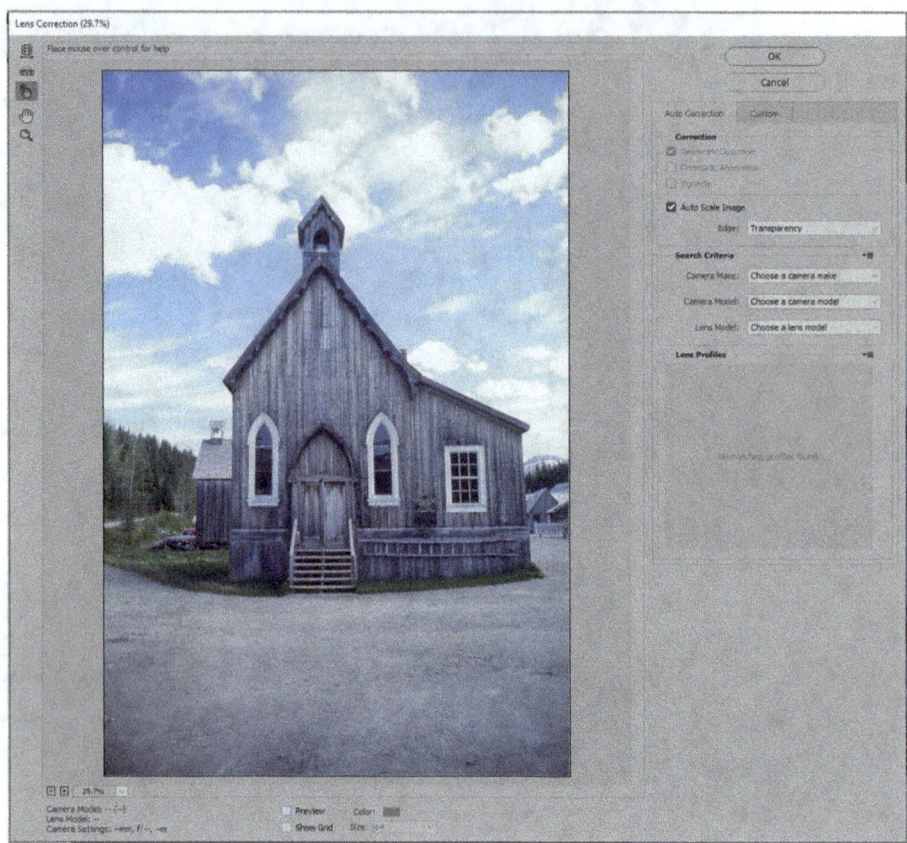

Figure 4-165. *Lens Correction filter workspace*

With digital photos directly from your camera or smartphone, you can work with lens profiles for automatic correction. However, in the book I am just focusing on scanned images, so some of the options may be limited.

Here are the following settings you can use for images that have no lens profile.

Use the following tools on the left. Refer to Figure 4-166.

CHAPTER 4 ADVANCED FILTERS FOR PHOTO RESTORATION: PART 1

Figure 4-166. *Lens Correction filter tools with the Remove Distortion Tool used*

CHAPTER 4 ADVANCED FILTERS FOR PHOTO RESTORATION: PART 1

Remove Distortion Tool (D): On the preview, drag toward or away from the center to correct distortion. Refer to the top icon in Figure 4-166.

Straighten Tool (A): As in the Camera Raw Geometry panel, you can draw a line to straighten the image to a new horizontal or vertical axis. Refer to Figure 4-167.

Figure 4-167. *Use the Straighten Tool to straighten the edge of an image*

Move Grid (M): Drag to move the alignment gird. In this case make sure that the Show Grid preview is on to accomplish this. Refer to Figure 4-168.

CHAPTER 4   ADVANCED FILTERS FOR PHOTO RESTORATION: PART 1

Figure 4-168. *Lens Correction filter with the Move Grid tool and grid applied*

Hand tool (H): Drag to move the image in the window without affecting the settings. Refer to Figure 4-169.

Figure 4-169. *Lens Correction filter Hand and Zoom tools*

Zoom tool (Z): Click or drag over the area you want to enlarge. Alt/Option + click to zoom out. Use the + and − buttons for additional navigation in the lower-left corner.

In the lower area you can turn the preview on and off, show/hide the grid, and set its color and size. Refer to Figures 4-168 and 4-169.

In this case, because the scanned image has no camera model, lens model, or camera settings, these are not indicated on the lower left.

On the right side you will then have limited access to features in the following tabs for Auto Correction and Custom. Refer to Figure 4-170.

695

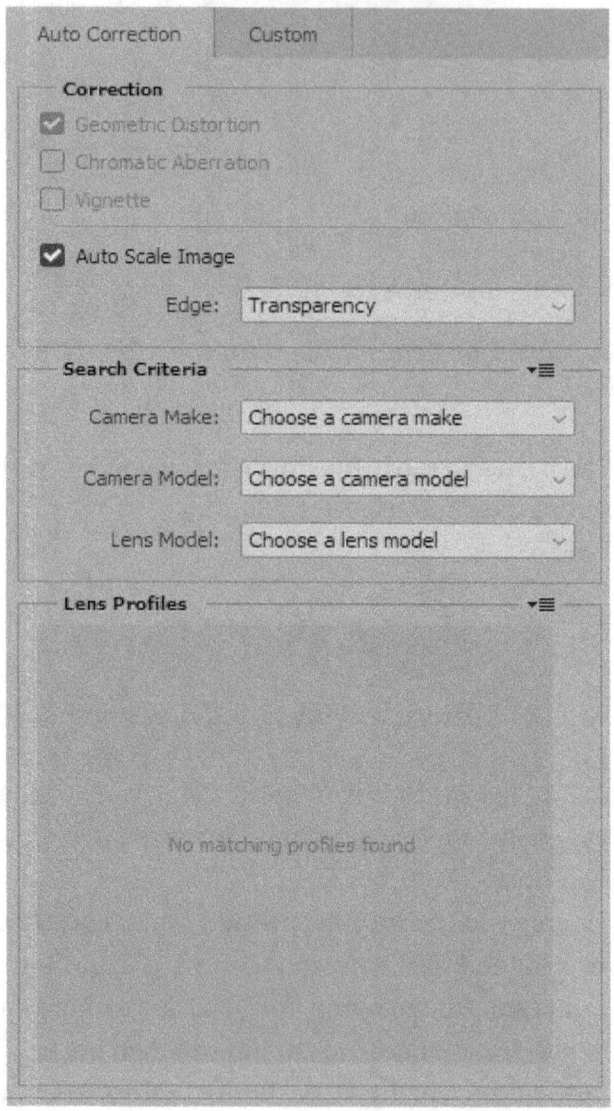

Figure 4-170. *No camera or lens model is identified in the Auto Correction tab*

CHAPTER 4　ADVANCED FILTERS FOR PHOTO RESTORATION: PART 1

Auto Correction Tab

The tab controls settings of the lens profile if present and accessible. The Correction area will be unavailable unless you can set a matching camera model, but the setting of Geometric Distortion will be automatically enabled, while Chromatic Aberration (Defringe) and Vignette will not be available and you will need to set these in the Custom tab manually or the Camera Raw Filter, as seen earlier. You do not need to alter these settings in both filters, only one.

Auto Scale Image: Enable automatic image scaling when correcting distortions.

Select what will fill the edge when the distortion is made. You can set to extend the edge or fill with transparency, black, or white fill. Transparency is best if you plan to alter your image later with the Edit ➤ Content-Aware Fill workspace as mentioned in Volume 1, to fill in the gaps, and was seen after using the Geometry panel with Camera Raw Filter. Refer to Figure 4-170.

In some cases, you may know the camera model or even want to try a model to see if it will correct the distortion. You can then select a camera make from the list. Then narrow down the camera model and lens model, and choose a lens model profile from the list if available. In this example we will leave this area blank. Refer to Figure 4-171.

CHAPTER 4　ADVANCED FILTERS FOR PHOTO RESTORATION: PART 1

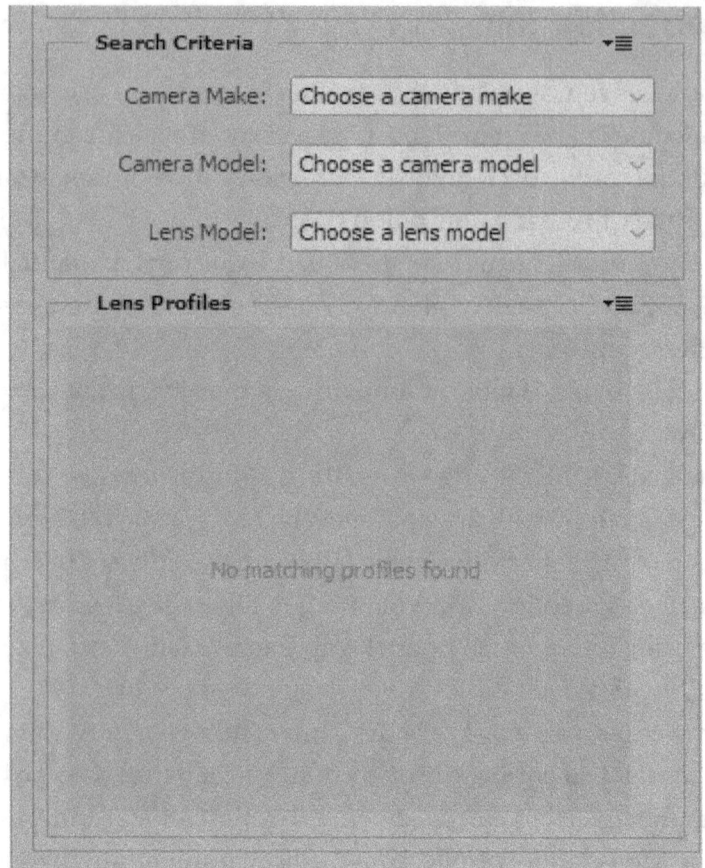

Figure 4-171. Search Criteria in the Auto Correction tab

With scanned images, when you do not know these settings, choose the Custom tab.

Custom Tab

The Custom tab has many of the same settings found in the Camera Raw Edit Optics panel and Geometry panel. So, if you have already set those settings, you do not have to set them again. Refer to Figure 4-172.

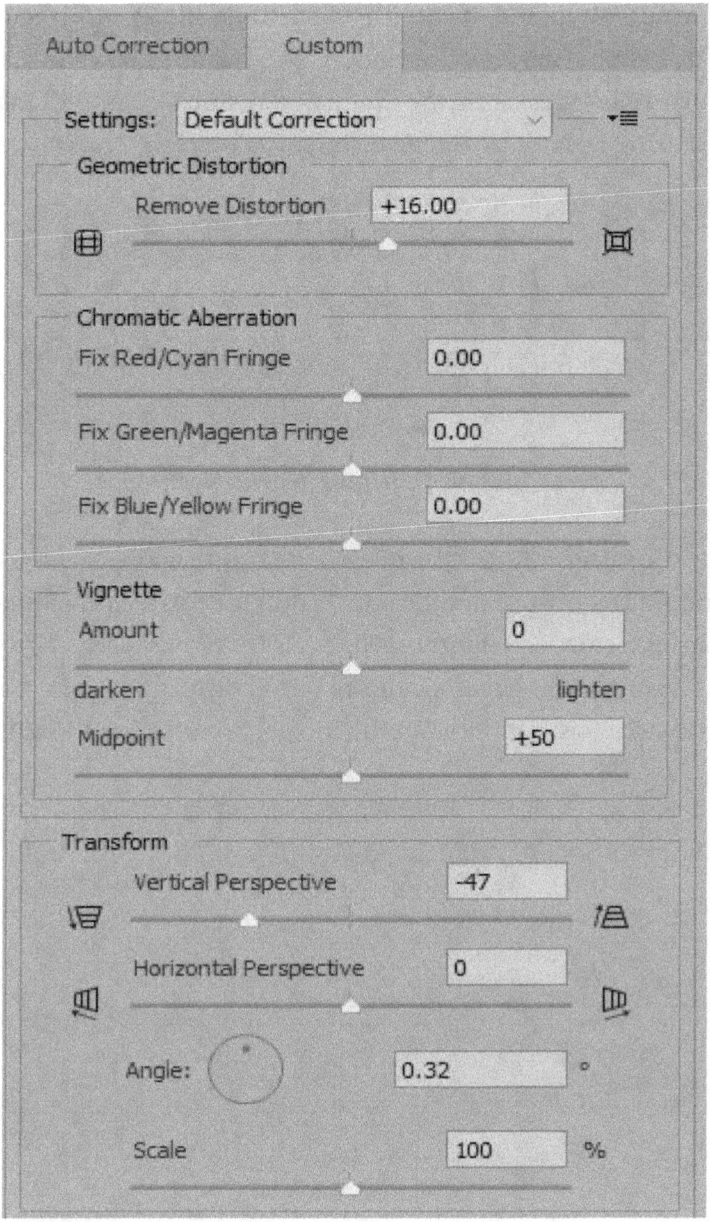

CHAPTER 4   ADVANCED FILTERS FOR PHOTO RESTORATION: PART 1

Figure 4-172. *Lens Correction filter Custom tab*

CHAPTER 4 ADVANCED FILTERS FOR PHOTO RESTORATION: PART 1

I will just point out that it can use the settings of Lens Correction, Default Correction, Previous Correction, and Custom. You can also load or save settings as .lcs files using the menu and delete if required. In this case we are just using Default Correction. Refer to Figure 4-173.

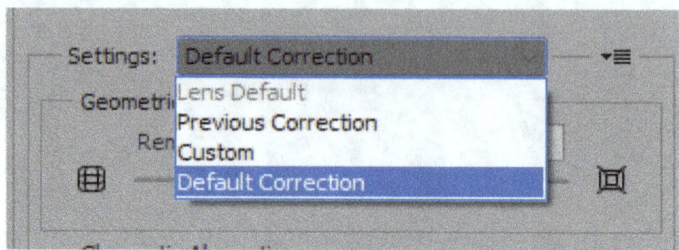

Figure 4-173. *Lens Correction filter Custom settings*

The next section controls the overall distortion caused by the lens.

Geometric Distortion: Remove distortion for correction of pincushion (left) or barrel distortion (right) (–100, 0, +100).

In this example there was a definite barrel distortion, so I moved my slider to the right to straighten out the image, to a setting of 16. Refer to Figure 4-174.

CHAPTER 4　ADVANCED FILTERS FOR PHOTO RESTORATION: PART 1

Figure 4-174. *Lens Correction filter Custom Geometric Distortion setting*

Chromatic Aberration (Defringe): Correct the following colors around edge details, by moving the following sliders left or right) (–100, 0, +100):

- Fix Red/Cyan Fringe
- Fix Green/Magenta Fringe
- Fix Blue/Yellow Fringe

I could alter this area here, or as mentioned in the Camera Raw Filter under the Optics tab, in this case I will leave at the default settings. Refer to Figure 4-175.

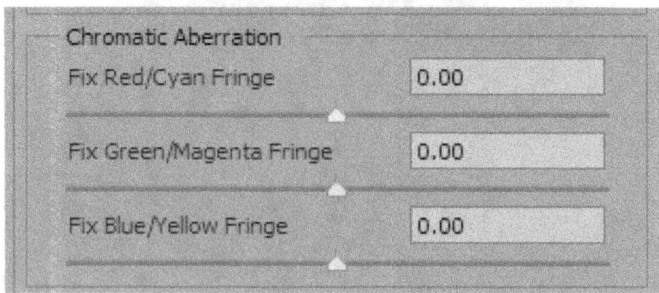

Figure 4-175. *Lens Correction filter Custom Chromatic Aberration settings*

Vignette affects the area around the borders of the image darkening or lightening them. In this case it was already adjusted using the Camera Raw Filter, so I will leave at the default settings.

Amount: Adjust the amount around the edge of the image; left will darken and right will lighten (–100, 0, +100).

Midpoint: Modify to affect the spread for the vignette correction (0–100). Set to +50. Refer to Figure 4-176.

CHAPTER 4 ADVANCED FILTERS FOR PHOTO RESTORATION: PART 1

Figure 4-176. *Lens Correction filter Custom Vignette settings*

Transform: This area will adjust the perspective distortion further using the following options. Refer to Figure 4-177.

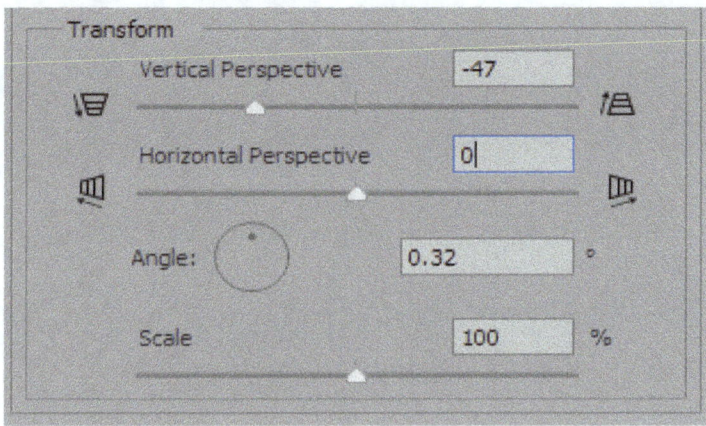

Figure 4-177. *Lens Correction filter Custom Transform settings*

Vertical Perspective (–100, 0, +100): Modify the vertical perspective and the top or bottom of the image. I set it to –47.

Horizontal Perspective (–100, 0, +100): Modify the horizontal perspective and the left or right side of the image. In this case I left it at 0.

Angle (0–360°): Setting the angle of rotation for the image, which may also be set by the Straighten Tool. When using this tool, it sets the angle to 0.32°.

703

Scale (50–150%): Scaling the image after correction, this does not affect the document size. I left it at the default size of 100% as this causes very little cutoff. Refer to Figure 4-177.

Click OK to commit changes or Cancel to exit without saving changes. Optionally, use the Alt/Option key to change the Cancel button to a Reset button and then click. In this case we can see the overall distortion of the structure has been reduced with this Lens Correction filter. Click OK and File ➤ Save your work, and you can check out my file **wooden_church_final.psd** for reference. Refer to Figure 4-178.

CHAPTER 4 ADVANCED FILTERS FOR PHOTO RESTORATION: PART 1

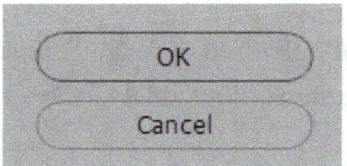

Figure 4-178. Final image with Lens Correction applied

> **Tip** If in situations you need to do a batch lens correction of several files taken with the same settings, use File ➤ Automate ➤ Lens Correction.

Adaptive Wide Angle

Use Filter ➤ Adaptive Wide Angle.

This is the second optional choice that you can also use with Camera Raw, if Lens Correction did not achieve your goal or you want to control the perspective settings more accurately. This filter works best with images that do have a camera and lens model, but you can still use it on scanned images as well. Use the file **adaptive_wide_angle.psd** for practice. Refer to Figure 4-179.

CHAPTER 4 ADVANCED FILTERS FOR PHOTO RESTORATION: PART 1

Figure 4-179. *Apply the Adaptive Wide Angle filter with Camera Raw to adjust an image's distortions*

Here are the following settings you can use for images that have no lens profile. Refer to Figure 4-180.

CHAPTER 4   ADVANCED FILTERS FOR PHOTO RESTORATION: PART 1

Figure 4-180. *Adaptive Wide Angle filter tools*

Constrain Tool (C): Add or edit a constraint by clicking the image or by dragging at an endpoint. Shift + click or drag adding a horizontal or vertical constraint. Alt/Option + click the selected line to delete. Right-click them to choose an orientation from the menu, and this will straighten the image further. By default, they are set to Unfixed, which is OK for diagonal lines. But in other cases, you want them to be Vertical, Horizontal, or Arbitrary. Refer to Figure 4-181.

CHAPTER 4 ADVANCED FILTERS FOR PHOTO RESTORATION: PART 1

Figure 4-181. *Adaptive Wide Angle filter with the Constrain Tool and Polygon Constrain Tool applied*

CHAPTER 4   ADVANCED FILTERS FOR PHOTO RESTORATION: PART 1

Polygon Constrain Tool (Y): Add or edit a polygon constraint by clicking the image or by dragging at an endpoint at least four points. Click the initial starting point to end. Alt/Option + click the polygon to delete. In my case I created a constraint of this kind on the floor area. Refer to Figure 4-181.

Move Tool (M): Drag to move the content in the canvas. Refer to Figure 4-180.

Hand tool (H): Drag to move the image in the preview without affecting the settings.

Zoom tool (Z): Click or drag over the area you want to enlarge. Refer to Figure 4-180. Alt/Option + click to zoom out. Use the + and − buttons for additional navigation, in the lower-left corner.

On the lower left the camera or lens model would display if available. Refer to Figure 4-182.

Figure 4-182. *Adaptive Wide Angle filter additional settings for navigation and previews*

Check Preview to view the before and after.

Enable/disable Show Constraints to show and hide them in the preview.

Enable/disable Show Mesh to show and hide it above the preview as a warped grid; by default it is disabled.

Here we can see an example of several constraint lines and a polygon constraint that was used to correct perspective, in this image that I dragged out and edited. We can clearly see that there was some distortion in this image as now the edge has altered slightly on all sides leaving transparent gap areas. Refer to Figure 4-183.

710

CHAPTER 4 ADVANCED FILTERS FOR PHOTO RESTORATION: PART 1

Figure 4-183. *Adaptive Wide Angle filter: when all the constraints are applied, we can see distortion along the edges*

Alternately, on the left you can set the type of correction (projection model) you want to use on the right. The current settings are available from the list (Fisheye, Perspective, Auto, and Full Spherical). Refer to Figure 4-184.

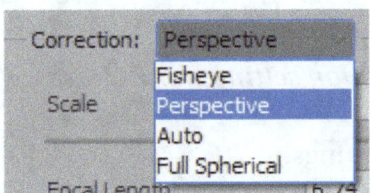

Figure 4-184. *Find your ideal projection or correction model*

Fisheye: For correction of the extreme curvature caused by the fisheye lens. Refer to Figure 4-185.

711

CHAPTER 4   ADVANCED FILTERS FOR PHOTO RESTORATION: PART 1

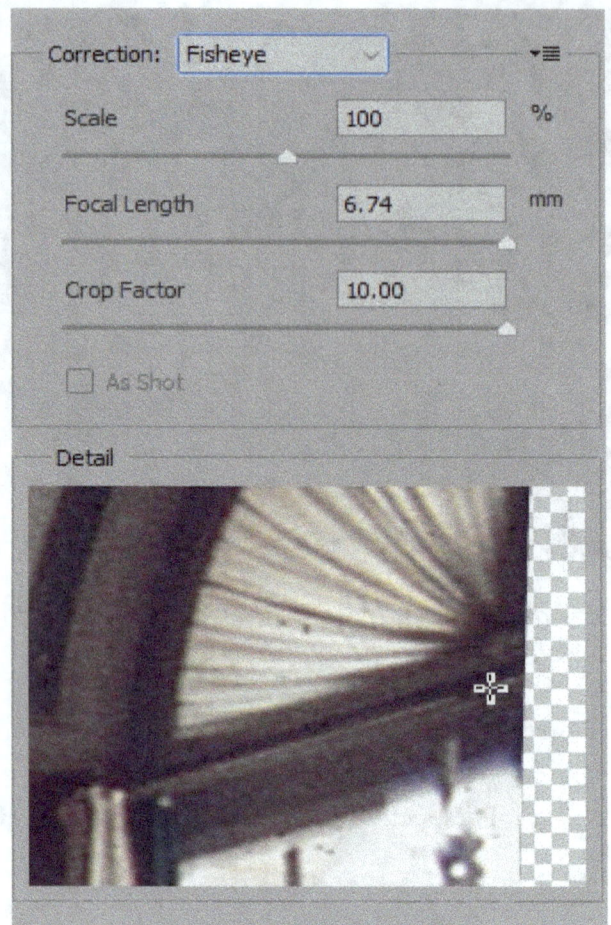

Figure 4-185. *Correction settings for Fisheye*

Set the following settings:

Scale (after correction) (50–150 %): Set a new value to minimize the blank areas that are introduced after applying the projection model.

Focal Length (2.18–65.5 mm). In this case you will have to set it manually as no lens information is found. This setting can vary in different images.

CHAPTER 4　ADVANCED FILTERS FOR PHOTO RESTORATION: PART 1

Crop Factor (0.10–10.00): Set a value to determine how the final image is cropped. Use this number in combination with the Scale value to correct for any blank areas that are introduced while applying the projection model. Dragging to the right will enlarge the image covering the crop but dragging to the left can also further distort if the image is not scaled correctly.

As Shot is enabled to the values as defined in the lens profile if the file were from a digital camera. However, when no lens profile is found, the option is disabled. Refer to Figure 4-185.

Perspective: This has the same settings as Fisheye and is used to correct converging lines caused by angle of view as well as camera tilt. This is the setting that I used for this image with the constraint lines. In this case Scale is set to 100%. Focal Length may be slightly different (0.28–8.49 mm); it is set to 6.74. Crop Factor is 10.00 so I did not distort the image. Refer to Figure 4-186.

CHAPTER 4 ADVANCED FILTERS FOR PHOTO RESTORATION: PART 1

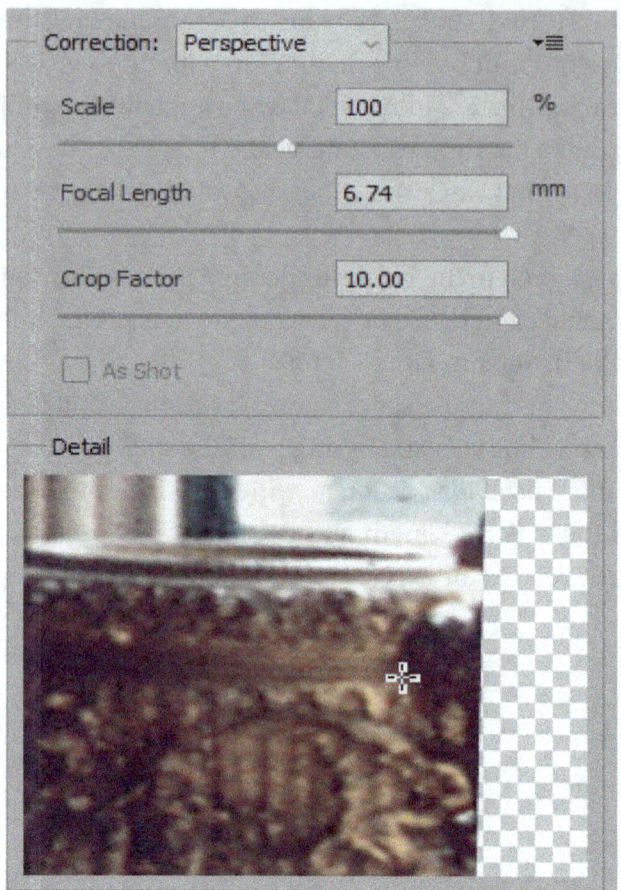

Figure 4-186. *Correction settings for Perspective*

Auto: Detects the appropriate correction, but this setting is not available unless the filter can detect the camera and lens model profile. Click OK to exit the warning. Refer to Figure 4-187.

CHAPTER 4 ADVANCED FILTERS FOR PHOTO RESTORATION: PART 1

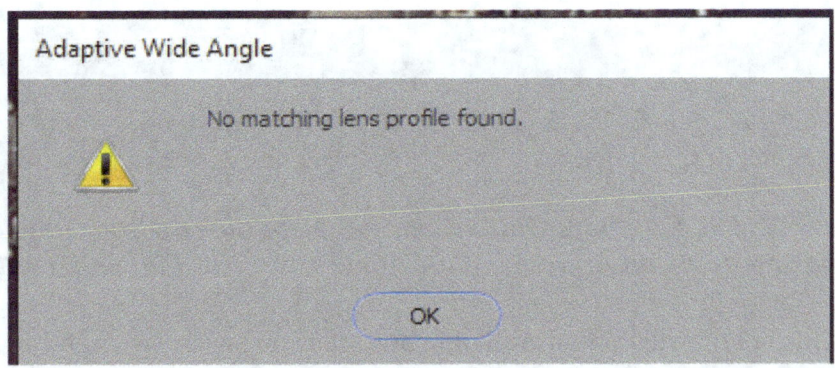

Figure 4-187. *Warning when the Auto setting is not available*

Full Spherical: Corrects 360-degree panoramas and then allows for scaling. Refer to Figure 4-188.

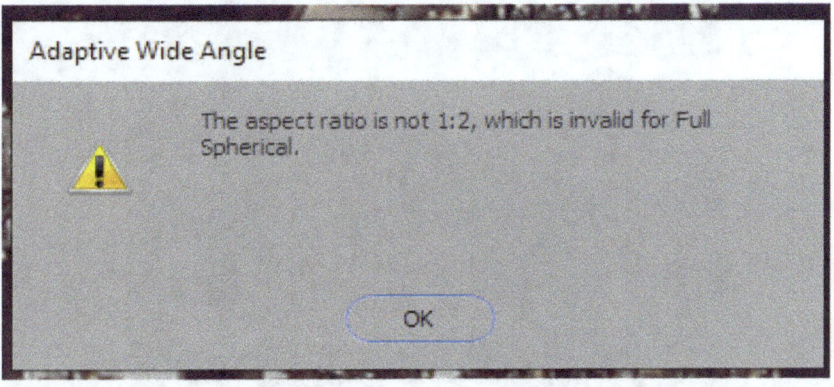

Figure 4-188. *Warning when the Full Spherical setting is not available*

It will not be available unless the image is a certain aspect ratio of 2:1, not 1:2, as it says in the warning. In this case, click OK to exit the warning.

If you want to use this option, use your Crop tool first on your file if you need to set a ratio size for this before changing to a smart object layer and adding the filter. Refer to Figure 4-189.

715

CHAPTER 4   ADVANCED FILTERS FOR PHOTO RESTORATION: PART 1

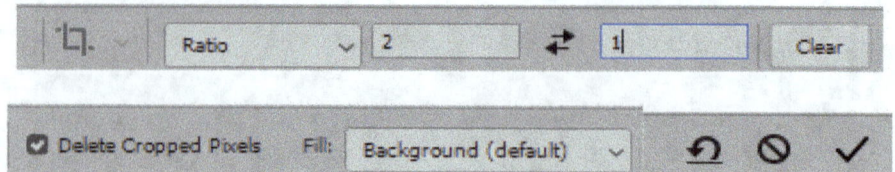

Figure 4-189. *Crop tool Options bar panel for altering your image before you apply an Adaptive Wide Angle setting for Full Spherical*

This option will then be available but will create a very rounded distortion, which you can scale 50–150%. Refer to Figure 4-190.

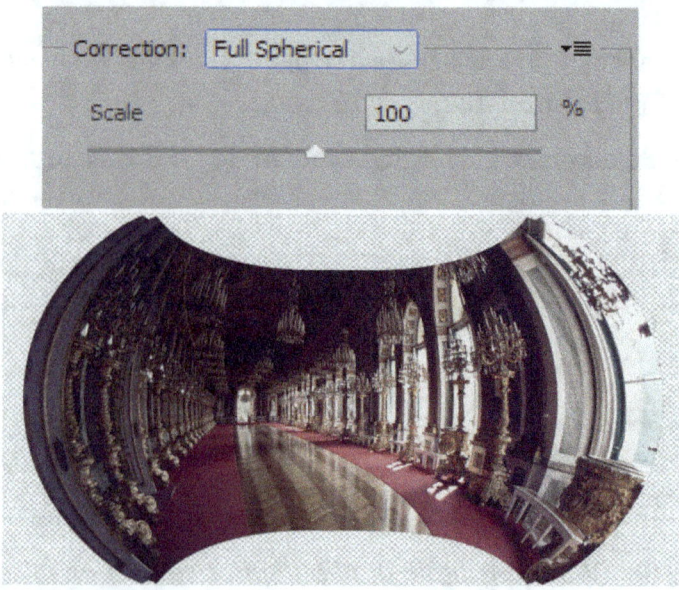

Figure 4-190. *Correction settings for Full Spherical*

Note some photos may also allow for another separate projection model called Panorama after you have used File ➤ Automate ➤ Photomerge, which was mentioned in Volume 1.

CHAPTER 4 ADVANCED FILTERS FOR PHOTO RESTORATION: PART 1

Look at the details in the lower preview area as you hover over areas in the preview. Refer to Figure 4-191.

Figure 4-191. *Adaptive Wide Angle filter details*

Note you can also adjust your preferences from the menu for the constraint settings, as well as save and load constraints that are saved as .wac files. Refer to Figure 4-192.

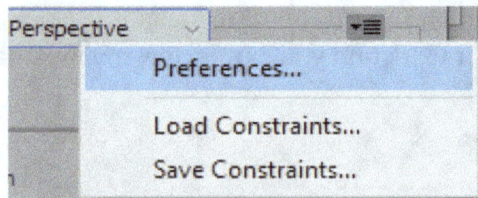

Figure 4-192. *Adaptive Wide Angle filter: additional options menu*

Click OK to commit changes or Cancel to exit without saving changes. Optionally, use the Alt/Option key to change the Cancel button to a Reset button and then click. Use the Ctrl/CMD key to change the Cancel button to a Default button. Click OK to exit. Refer to Figure 4-193.

CHAPTER 4   ADVANCED FILTERS FOR PHOTO RESTORATION: PART 1

Figure 4-193. *Click OK to exit the Adaptive Wide Angle filter and save changes*

File ➤ Save your work and you can review my file **adaptive_wide_angle_final.psd**.

CHAPTER 4　ADVANCED FILTERS FOR PHOTO RESTORATION: PART 1

Note if you are interested in the topic of distortion with images that have lens profiles, which are not required for this book, you can see some examples in my book that I mentioned at the beginning of the chapter or refer to the following links for more details on the topic:

https://helpx.adobe.com/photoshop/using/correcting-image-distortion-noise.html

https://helpx.adobe.com/photoshop/using/adaptive-wide-angle-filter.html

What Are the Materials Parametric Filters?

As mentioned in Chapter 3, in recent years Adobe has moved many of its 3D features out of Photoshop and into Adobe Illustrator or into a group of 3D applications known as the Substance collection. Refer to Figure 4-194.

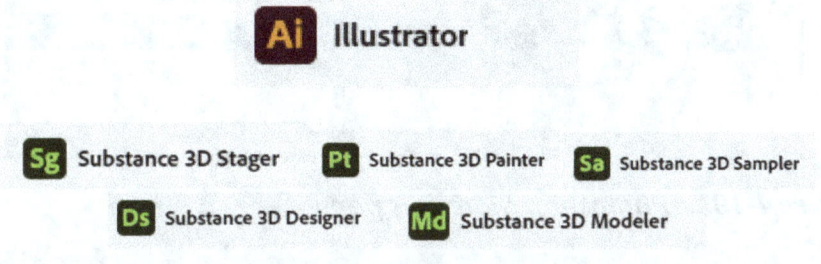

Figure 4-194. Adobe Illustrator and the Substance collection apps now have a number of 3D features

While the focus of this book is not about working in 3D, I will point out that Adobe has continued to save many of these previous 3D Substance materials that are now part of the Substance collection within Photoshop as parametric filters. They are very similar to patterns and can be placed on their own layers. You can access these 3D materials under Window ➤

Materials and review the panel. You can add your own Substance materials that were created in a program like Substance 3D Designer or work with the many Adobe Substance materials supplied in the panel. These filters work best in RGB mode. Refer to Figure 4-195.

Figure 4-195. *Photoshop Materials panel*

When you click a choice from the panel, you add a material layer to the Layers panel. It appears similar to a smart object layer with a smart filter and adds a new parametric filter with blending options. Refer to Figure 4-196.

CHAPTER 4　ADVANCED FILTERS FOR PHOTO RESTORATION: PART 1

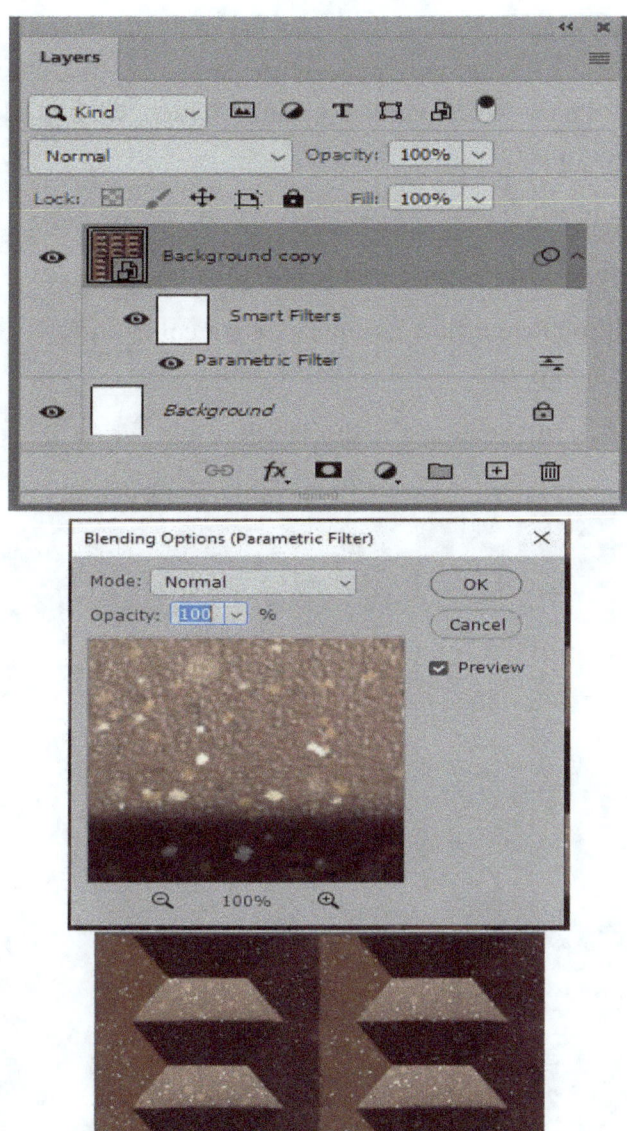

Figure 4-196.*　Photoshop Layers panel with a parametric filter applied*

CHAPTER 4　ADVANCED FILTERS FOR PHOTO RESTORATION: PART 1

To edit the parametric filter using the Parametric Properties panel, either double-click the name or access the panel from the Materials list. Different materials will have varying options, which will include the following. Refer to Figure 4-197.

- Resolution
- Properties: For color, sizing, and texture
- Lighting Properties: Rotation, height color, and displacement
- Transform: Scaling and duplication
- Technical Parameters: Effect color and appearance

CHAPTER 4   ADVANCED FILTERS FOR PHOTO RESTORATION: PART 1

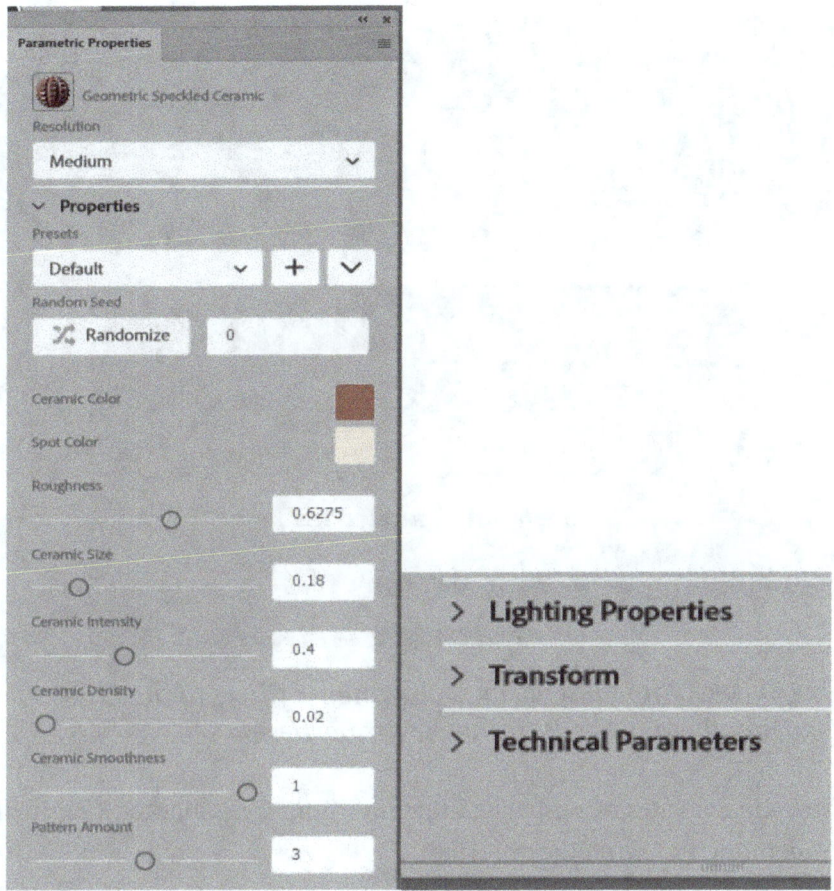

Figure 4-197. *Parametric Properties panel*

These filters offer a wider range of options for each material to customize it by adjusting various list properties and sliders and create your own repeating background patterns. Like other smart filters you can edit the filter mask.

Hold down the Alt/Option key if you want to add a second parametric filter to your layer when you click one from the Materials panel. Use your Blending Options dialog box to adjust blend modes and opacity if you need to blend both patterns together, and you can use the Parametric Properties panel to switch between materials. Refer to Figure 4-198.

723

CHAPTER 4 ADVANCED FILTERS FOR PHOTO RESTORATION: PART 1

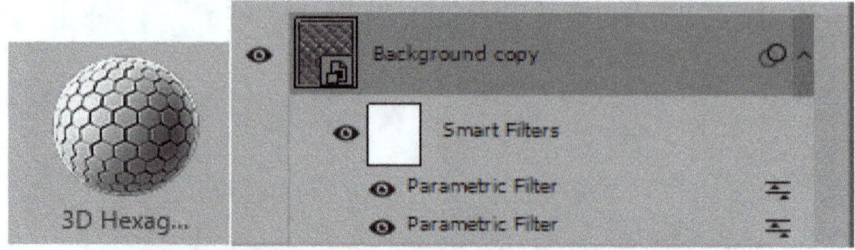

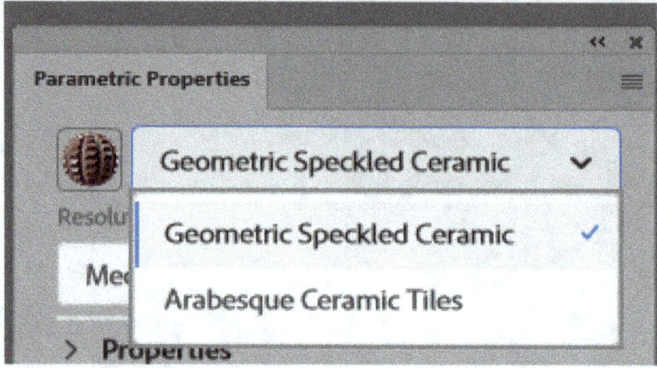

Figure 4-198. *Applying various parametric filters to the Layers panel and editing them in the Parametric Properties panel*

You can also add other basic filters mentioned in Chapter 3 for further enhancement. Refer to Figure 4-199.

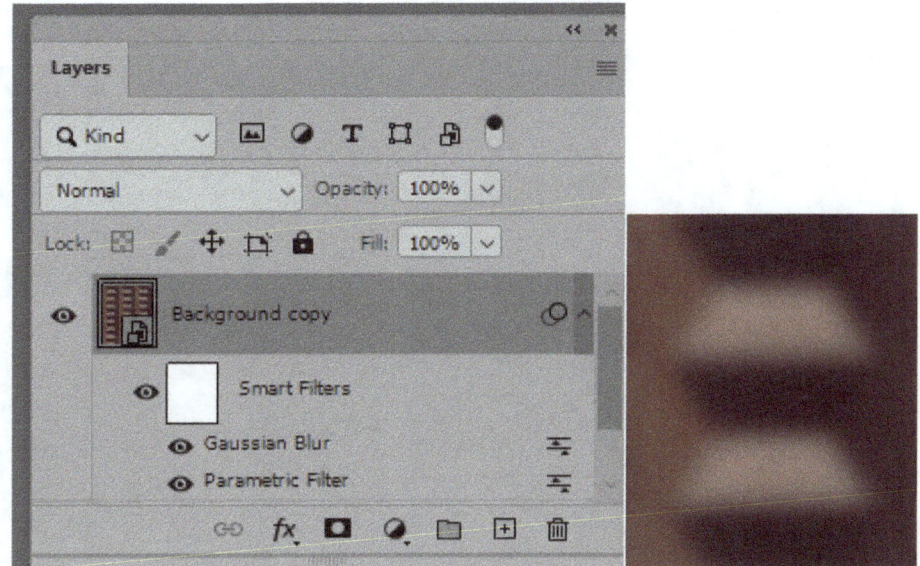

Figure 4-199. *Applying other filters in combination with the parametric filter*

Parametric filters are not the same as the neural filters collection, and Adobe at some point will likely add more parametric filters to this collection after newer filters move out of Photoshop (Beta) development likely replacing some of its older filters for color, noise, grain, blur, and various artistic stylized effects in the future.

However, the neural filter workspace is becoming more popular, and we will look at some of those filters in Chapter 5.

Summary

In this chapter we reviewed the filters of Liquify, Camera Raw, Lens Correction, and Adaptive Wide Angle. Then we briefly looked at the new parametric filters. In the next chapter we will look at the final set of filters that that can be used with smart object layers.

CHAPTER 5

Advanced Filters for Photo Restoration: Part 2

Over the years, Photoshop has added more filters to its collection. In recent years, we have seen some new developments in the neural filters. You may have noticed this name in the list but not had an opportunity to experiment with these new filters. In this chapter, we will explore several of them and consider how they could be applied to a specific project while working in that workspace. Refer to Figure 5-1.

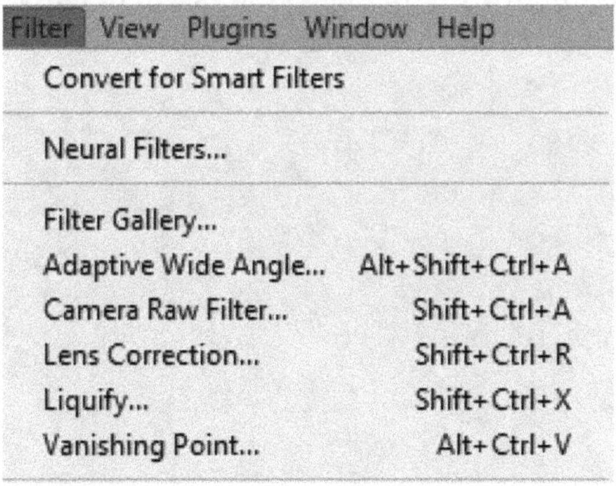

Figure 5-1. *Filter menu for access to neural filters*

J. Harder, *A Beginner's Guide to Digital Image Repair in Photoshop: Volume 2*, https://doi.org/10.1007/979-8-8688-0763-3_5

CHAPTER 5 ADVANCED FILTERS FOR PHOTO RESTORATION: PART 2

Later we will also look at where you can acquire other filters and plug-ins via the Creative Cloud Desktop.

Note this chapter does contain projects found in the Volume 2 Chapter 5 folder. Also, some text has been adapted from the book *Perspective Warps and Distorts with Adobe Tools: Volume 1,* as well as new information added, specific to Photo Restoration.

Neural Filters

The neural filter workspace contains many new filters that you may want to test, some of which may have already been downloaded and others you can download now from the Creative Cloud, which it uses to do calculations with the filters. I will just briefly describe the download process, and then we will look more in depth of at least five filters and briefly mention a few others. I will also provide links in this chapter to more information.

Using a file that has a Smart Object layer as you did with past filters, we will now experiment with this set of filters. Go to Filter ➤ Neural filters. Refer to Figure 5-2.

CHAPTER 5   ADVANCED FILTERS FOR PHOTO RESTORATION: PART 2

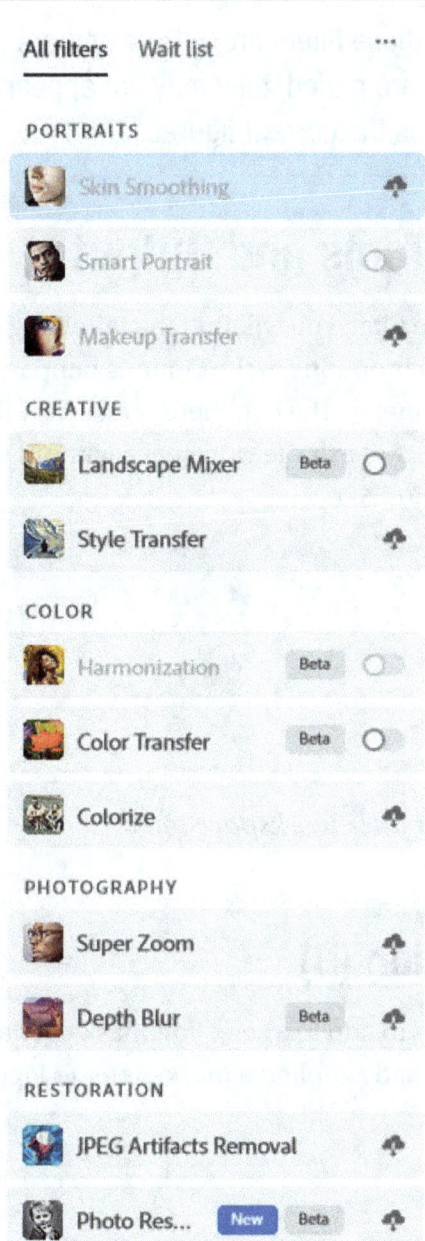

Figure 5-2.   *In neural filter workspace list of current filters available to access and download*

CHAPTER 5   ADVANCED FILTERS FOR PHOTO RESTORATION: PART 2

Note that some of these filters are in Beta and are subject to changes and, as new filters are added, they may not appear in the exact same location in the list as the current figure.

Workspace Tools and Output

On the left side of the filter, you will find the following tools. As you click each you will find their options in the Options bar panel earlier. Note that in the Options bar panel on the left, there is an arrow that will allow you to cancel any operation and exit the workspace without saving changes. Refer to Figure 5-3 and Figure 5-4.

Figure 5-3. Neural filter workspace tools

Add to Selection (B)

This tool can be used to add to a selection mask overlay on your preview image if you have already applied a mask. Refer to Figure 5-4.

CHAPTER 5   ADVANCED FILTERS FOR PHOTO RESTORATION: PART 2

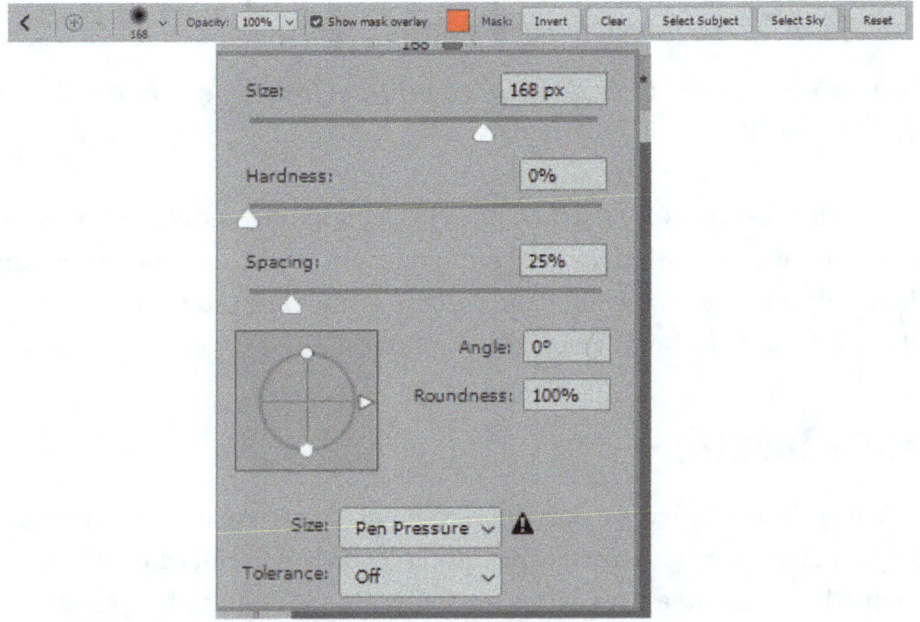

Figure 5-4. *Neural filter workspace Add to Selection tool brush options and Options bar panel*

As with brushes outside of the neural filter workspace, you can control the brush's Size (1–5000px), Hardness (0–100%), Spacing (1–1000%), Angle (-180, 0, 180°), and Roundness (0–100%). Additional settings allow you to set dynamic control for size if you plan to use a pen or stylus wheel and set level of tolerance when using the stylus. Other settings in the Options bar panel include Opacity (1–100%). Hide/Show mask overlay, color of mask, and other mask control buttons which include Invert, Clear, Select Subject, Select Sky, and Reset.

Subtract from Selection (E)

This tool can be used to subtract from a selection mask overlay on your preview image if you have already applied a mask. Its settings are the same as the Add to Selection tool. Refer to Figure 5-5.

CHAPTER 5   ADVANCED FILTERS FOR PHOTO RESTORATION: PART 2

Figure 5-5. *Neural filter workspace subtract from selection tool brush Options bar panel*

While these tools are useful, not all projects in the neural filters require that you use them and so they are optional, as in most cases you are editing the whole image with the filter and you can always later edit your smart filter mask outside the workspace, if required.

Hand Tool (H)

As seen outside the workspace, the Hand tool allows you to move around on your canvas without disrupting settings, which is useful when you are zoomed in on an area. The following options in the Options bar panel include Scroll All Windows, Zoom 100%, Fit Screen, and Fill Screen. Alternatively, you can also use your Spacebar key if you are using another tool. By default when the this filter's workspace is opened it is set to this tool. Refer to Figure 5-6.

Figure 5-6. *Neural filter workspace Hand tool Options bar panel*

Zoom Tool (Z)

The Zoom tool has the same options as seen outside the workspace and in other past workspaces we have looked at in Volume 1 and this volume. Use the Zoom tool to get closer to the subject or zoom out. The other options include Resize Windows to Fit, Zoom All Windows, and Scrubby Zoom as well as the same buttons found in the Hand tool. Refer to Figure 5-7.

CHAPTER 5   ADVANCED FILTERS FOR PHOTO RESTORATION: PART 2

Figure 5-7. *Neural filter workspace Zoom tool Options bar panel*

In the workspace, you can also use the key commands of Ctrl/CMD++ and Ctrl/CMD+-.

If you need to undo a step, since you do not have access to the History panel, remember to use Ctrl/CMD+Z to undo your last action, if required.

Before we work with the filters, I will just point out that while working with your preview you may want to, as you saw in Camera Raw, see a before and after. In this case, the preview button is located in the lower area of the workspace. Refer to Figure 5-8.

Figure 5-8. *Neural filter workspace Preview Navigation and Output Options*

Click to Preview changes or show original artwork. Refer to Figure 5-9.

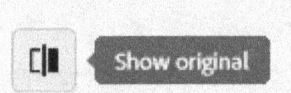

Figure 5-9. *Neural filter workspace Preview Navigation Options before/after*

Other settings in this area include the following:

Layer Preview which allows you to Show all layers or Show selected layer. Refer to Figure 5-10.

733

CHAPTER 5   ADVANCED FILTERS FOR PHOTO RESTORATION: PART 2

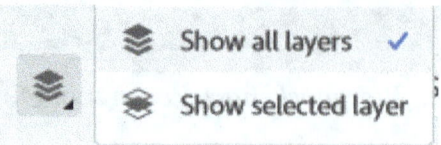

Figure 5-10. *Neural filter workspace Preview Navigation Options viewing layers*

Output options in this case are set to Smart filter when working on a smart object layer, but in other situations as you will see later, you may prefer to output to a New layer, New layer masked, or a New document. Refer to Figure 5-11.

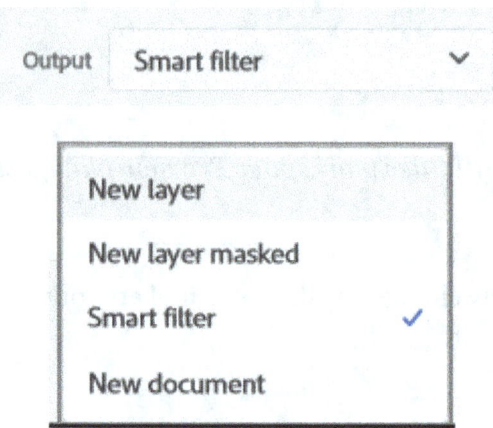

Figure 5-11. *Neural filter workspace output options and list*

After working on the layer with a filter, the OK button will be active, but, if you need to exit before or after making changes without confirming them, you can click the Cancel button. OK will apply the filter settings to the Smart Object layer. Refer to Figure 5-12.

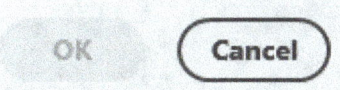

Figure 5-12. *Neural filter workspace OK and Cancel button before changes area made*

In this case, remain in the neural filter workspace.

If you have or have not used some of the filters, they may or may not be downloaded from the All filters list which currently runs on my graphics processor (GPU); this info is found under the ellipsis menu (…). Refer to Figure 5-13.

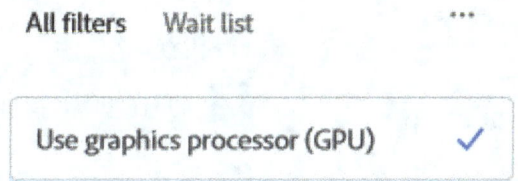

Figure 5-13. *Neural filter workspace enables graphics processor settings*

Those that are downloaded appear with a Toggle button beside them to activate them. However, if in the image something like a face is not detected in the photo, then those that apply to that topic will be inactive, as seen here with Smart Portrait which I will mention later in the chapter. Refer to Figure 5-14.

CHAPTER 5   ADVANCED FILTERS FOR PHOTO RESTORATION: PART 2

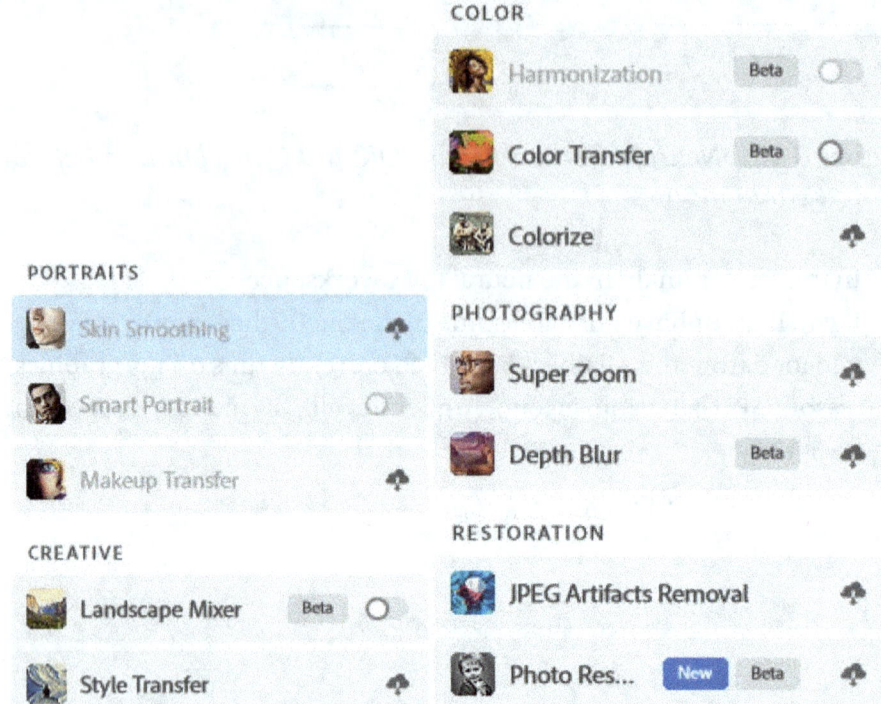

Figure 5-14. Neural filter workspace filters are divided into various categories

Those that are not downloaded yet will have a cloud with a down arrow beside them. Before you decide to download or use the available filters, you can hover over each one and learn more about what they can do and then decide if they will be right for your current project or one you plan to work on. Refer to Figure 5-15.

CHAPTER 5   ADVANCED FILTERS FOR PHOTO RESTORATION: PART 2

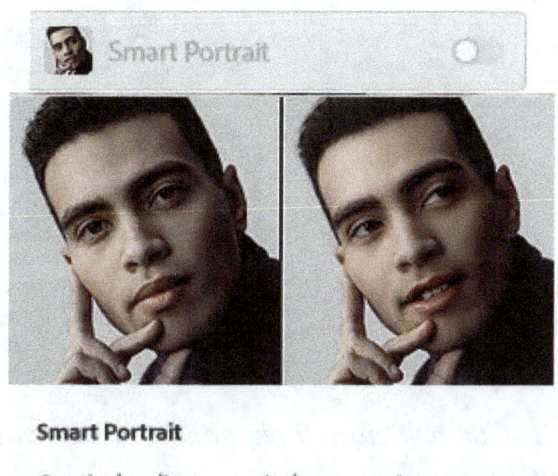

Figure 5-15. *Some filters are not active if people are not in the image, but you can still review what the filter does*

Adding a New Filter

When you want to download a new filter to your collection, here are some steps you can follow.

For example, let's add the colorize filter, which is currently found in the color section of the list and has a cloud symbol beside it. In this case, the other two are already downloaded and available to me. Refer to Figure 5-16.

737

CHAPTER 5　ADVANCED FILTERS FOR PHOTO RESTORATION: PART 2

Figure 5-16. *Review the neural filter, and choose one that you would like to download*

Hover over the filter first to determine what it is for. It looks like it is for colorizing a black-and-white image.

Now click the filter to reveal the download information on the right side of the panel. Refer to Figure 5-17.

CHAPTER 5   ADVANCED FILTERS FOR PHOTO RESTORATION: PART 2

Figure 5-17. *Click the download button to download and install the filter*

If you want to use this filter now or in the future for a project, click the download button to let Photoshop install the filter. This may take a few moments. Refer to Figure 5-18.

CHAPTER 5   ADVANCED FILTERS FOR PHOTO RESTORATION: PART 2

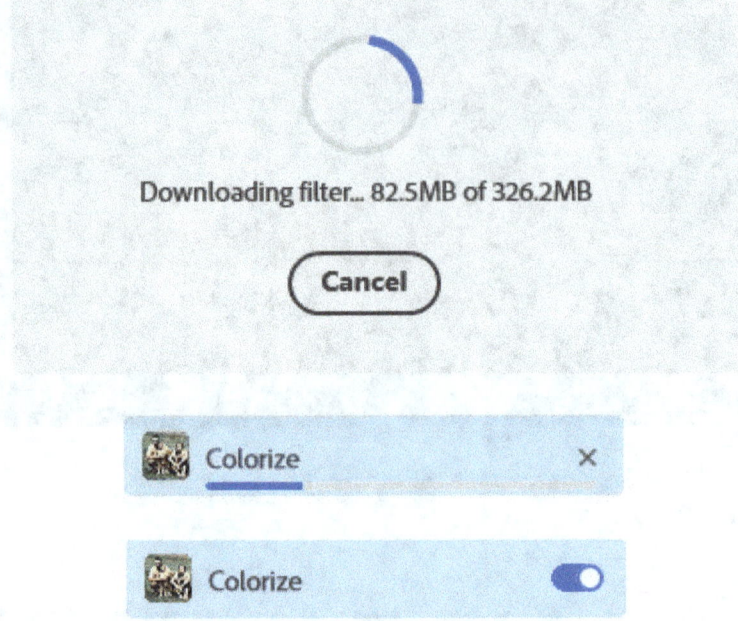

Figure 5-18. *Wait for the installation to complete, and then the new filter will be active or ready to toggle on*

If the filter can be used with your current photo, it will then be toggled on and active. At this point, download any other filters that you might be interested in.

If you don't plan to use the filter now, you can click the Cancel button, but it will still be available when you enter the Workspace for the next project, and you do not have to download it again. Refer to Figure 5-19.

Figure 5-19. *Click OK or Cancel after you have downloaded and used the filter to exit the workspace*

Note if the filter is in Beta you may get updates every time Adobe updates the Photoshop software, so some settings may be altered and not remain the same from filter to filter as seen in the current notes. You can always refer to the links at the end of this chapter if you need some current information.

Now let's start to work with each filter. I will give you a few highlights next, under the various selection.

Color

Alter colors quickly with the following filters found in this section.

Colorize

Along with three other filters, it is found in this section. The filter helps with the re-colorization of black-and-white photos. In Chapter 1, we looked at ways to colorize photos using a variety of fill layers and adjustment layers, such as Hue/Saturation with the colorize settings or painting on a Normal blank layer and then adjusting the Layers blending mode. In this example, we can use a filter to do some of the work. Use the following file. In this example, I spent some time cleaning up some of the more obvious scratches from an older photo and then, while it was black-and-white, used the black-and-white adjustment layer as well so that there were no visible stains and discoloration before I started working on it. I then turned the copy of those layers into a Smart Object layer. Use the file **village_scene_colorize.psd.** Refer to Figure 5-20.

CHAPTER 5　ADVANCED FILTERS FOR PHOTO RESTORATION: PART 2

Figure 5-20. *Select the Smart Object layer that you want to apply a neural filter to*

Select the Layer in in this case called Black & White 1 copy.

Go to Filter ➤ Neural filter if you do not already have the image open, and toggle on the colorize filter as you review it in the preview. Refer to Figure 5-21.

Figure 5-21. *Colorize neural filter activated*

CHAPTER 5   ADVANCED FILTERS FOR PHOTO RESTORATION: PART 2

From the initial preview, we can see that the filter does recognize areas of the sky as being blue, colorizes the people and trees, and does recognize other areas as being gray or brown, but AI on its own does not colorize everything as I would like it to. Refer to Figure 5-22.

Figure 5-22. *Colorize filter applies color automatically*

We need remove some of the green in the lower road area so I will use the setting on the right side of the preview to improve this. Refer to Figure 5-23.

CHAPTER 5   ADVANCED FILTERS FOR PHOTO RESTORATION: PART 2

Figure 5-23. *Colorize filter settings*

CHAPTER 5   ADVANCED FILTERS FOR PHOTO RESTORATION: PART 2

Note   Use the backward pointing underlined arrow in this upper area near the name of the filter if you need to reset your parameters at any time. This is the same for all filters I will mention in this chapter. Refer to Figure 5-23.

To adjust some of the colors in the preview image, use the Focal Points preview to click in areas that you want to add a new color to in the lower area on the street. Refer to Figure 5-24.

Figure 5-24.   *Colorize filter allows you to manually color the image using the Focal Points preview*

On the Preview on the left, click the eyedropper tool and this brings up the color picker (Focus Point Color) so that you can choose a more natural gray brown color R:175, G:167, B:161 and click OK. Refer to Figure 5-25.

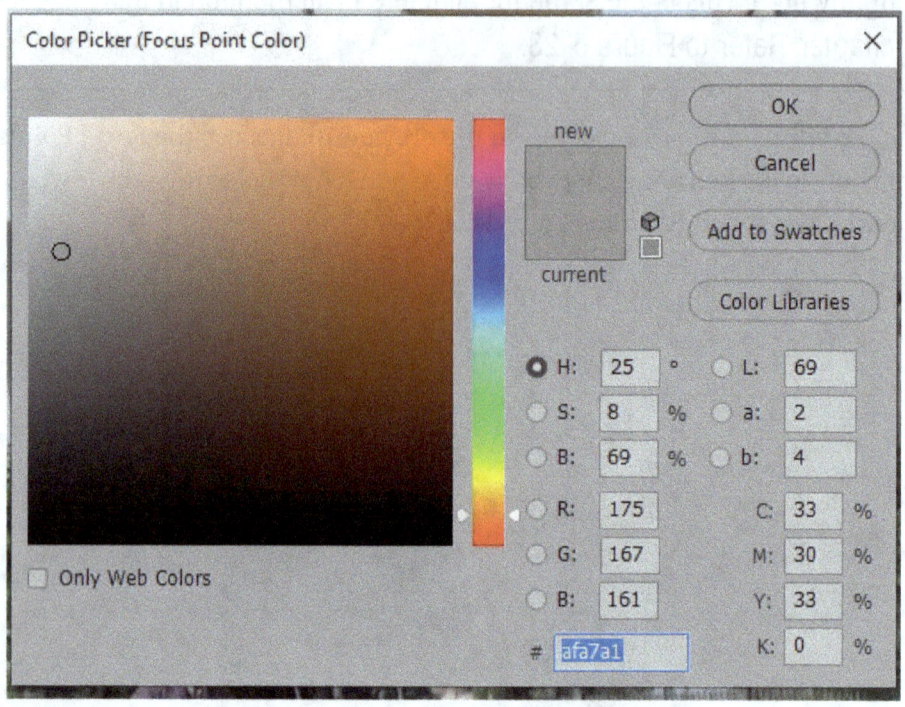

Figure 5-25. *Use the color picker dialog box to set and choose a Focus Point color*

This will now add that color to the general preview area, and then you can adjust the strength or swatch color further. Selected focal points can also be removed as well by clicking that button. Refer to Figure 5-26 and Figure 5-27.

CHAPTER 5   ADVANCED FILTERS FOR PHOTO RESTORATION: PART 2

Figure 5-26. *Focal point and color applied*

CHAPTER 5   ADVANCED FILTERS FOR PHOTO RESTORATION: PART 2

Figure 5-27. *Preview of image with another color focal point added*

In this case, Auto color Image is enabled, but you may still have to click in other areas of the ground or elsewhere to continue to colorize to suit your requirements and alter the colors of the focal points accordingly. Refer to Figure 5-28 and Figure 5-29.

CHAPTER 5 ADVANCED FILTERS FOR PHOTO RESTORATION: PART 2

Figure 5-28. *Preview of image with multiple color focal points added*

CHAPTER 5   ADVANCED FILTERS FOR PHOTO RESTORATION: PART 2

Figure 5-29. *Preview of color focal points in filter*

As you add the various color focal points, you can always go back and select them and then edit the color of that point.

Further adjustments can then be made. Refer to Figure 5-30.

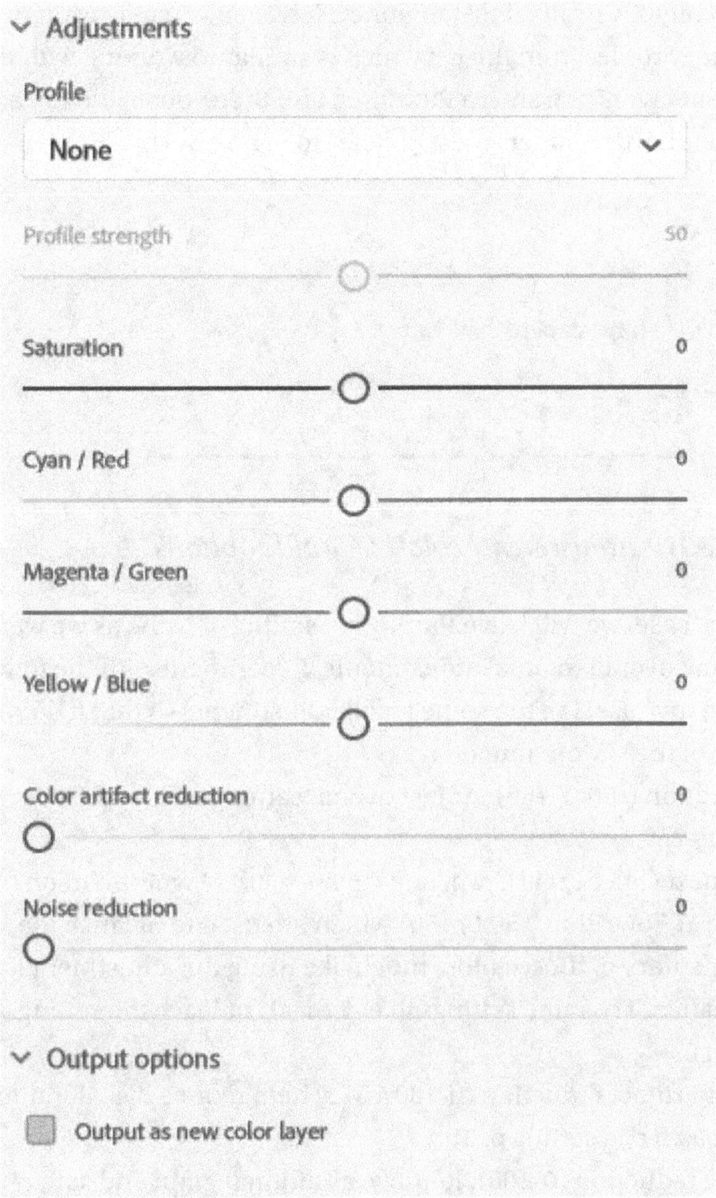

Figure 5-30. Additional adjustments colorize filter options that you can use to alter the overall image

Currently the profile is set to none. However, you may want to test other color profiles from the list which is similar to working with the adjustment layers or Camera Raw filter, and then you would have access to the profile strength slider (0–100). Refer to Figure 5-31.

Figure 5-31. Adjustments colorize profile options

In this case, we will leave Profile at a setting of None as we want to make some overall manual adjustments. Experiment with the following sliders; in my case, I made some small adjustments so that it did not alter the color of the sky too much.

Saturation (-50,0, +50): Adjust overall saturation levels. Try a setting of +2.

The next slider set is Cyan/Red (-50,0, +50), Magenta/Green (-50,0, +50), and Yellow/Blue (-50,0, +50) which are used to balance the complementary of those colors much like using the adjustment layers of color balance. Try some settings like -1 or +1, or leave the settings at the default of 0.

Color artifact reduction (0-100): May help reduce discoloration in select areas. Try a setting of 15.

Noise reduction (0-100): Remove additional grain and soften the image overall; try a setting of 10 or higher. Refer to Figure 5-32.

CHAPTER 5   ADVANCED FILTERS FOR PHOTO RESTORATION: PART 2

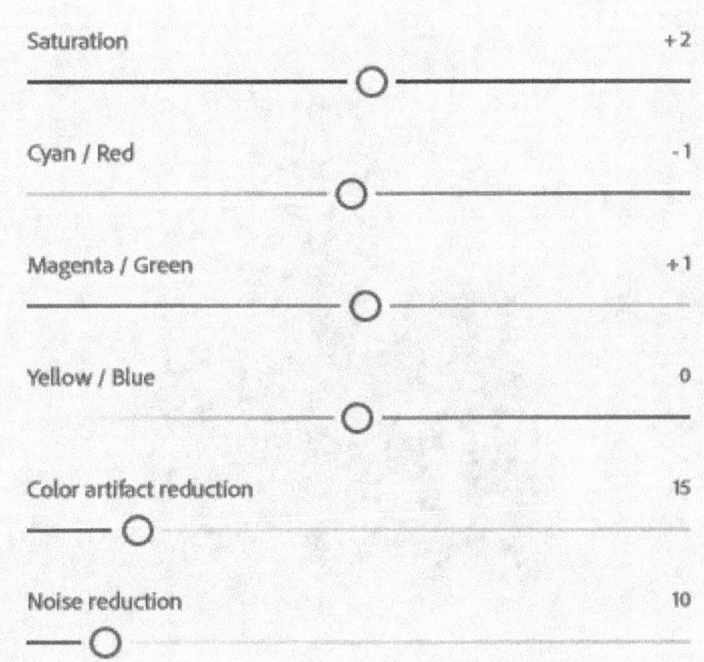

Figure 5-32. *Adjustments colorize slider options*

Keep in mind that as you adjust colors, the filter appears to work in small patches, so you may have to update areas manually of color focal points on your preview. Refer to Figure 5-33.

CHAPTER 5   ADVANCED FILTERS FOR PHOTO RESTORATION: PART 2

Figure 5-33. *Colorize focal points and the final colorized image with the sky adjusted*

CHAPTER 5 ADVANCED FILTERS FOR PHOTO RESTORATION: PART 2

I do like this filter; I would recommend it for simple colorizing projects. However, for more complex ones, using some Hue/Saturation adjustment layers would be best for smaller details to control exact color placement. The control is more exact when you can paint on an individual adjustment layer's layer mask as seen in Chapter 1 and in the example in Chapter 4 of the woman's portrait. Nevertheless it is definitely a good starting point for colorization.

The last setting allows you to output as a new color layer with or without a mask. The output would appear as a normal layer (Layer 2) set to a blending mode of Color with pixel paint applied above the current Smart Object layer. Refer to Figure 5-34.

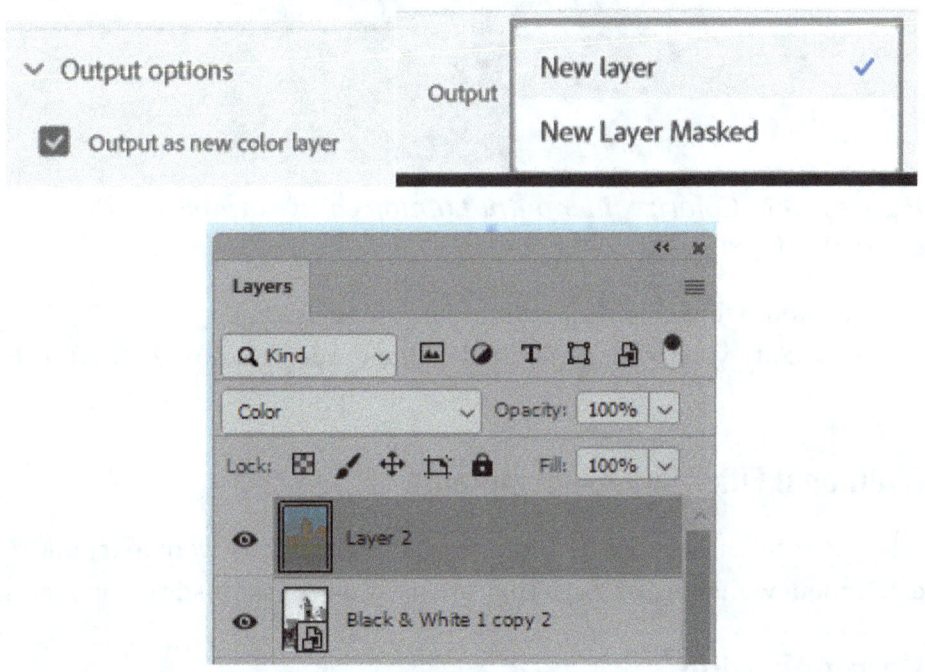

Figure 5-34. Colorize filter output options and example of color layer in the Layers panel

CHAPTER 5   ADVANCED FILTERS FOR PHOTO RESTORATION: PART 2

However, keep this output setting disabled if you want to retain your settings within the smart object output and the color applied to the filter and then click OK. Refer to Figure 5-35.

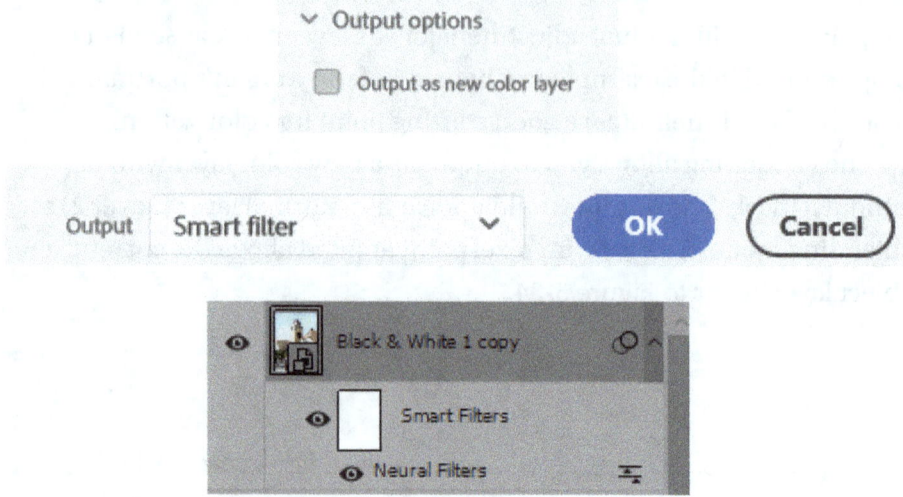

Figure 5-35. Colorize filter output options and example of filter applied to layer in the Layers panel

This would then allow for additional editing later.

File ➤ Save your work. Refer to file **village_scene_colorize_final.psd** for reference.

Additional Filter Color Adjustments

The color section also has two additional filters you may want to try and experiment with on your own. They are used more for artistic color effects.

Harmonization

This filter can be used to harmonize the color and luminosity of one layer to another layer to make a flawless composite. This filter requires a layer with a mask or transparency. In this case, I am just using some normal

CHAPTER 5   ADVANCED FILTERS FOR PHOTO RESTORATION: PART 2

layers that have been named correction and source that I place side by side for comparison. I have selected my layer that I labeled correction before entering the Filter ➤ Neural filter workspace. Refer to Figure 5-36.

Figure 5-36. *Harmonization filter Layers panel and two images side by side for working on*

While this filter is currently in Beta, I can see how it is good for working with making adjustments to similar images that you may have taken on the same day of a particular scene. It can also be for correction of a collection

757

of images that may all be part of a panorama scene. The purpose is so that the overall tone is adjusted and similar. In this case, I selected from the reference image layer called source. Refer to Figure 5-37.

Figure 5-37. *Harmonization filter – choose a reference image*

Further adjustments may still have to be made to the sliders to get a more balanced look. Refer to Figure 5-38.

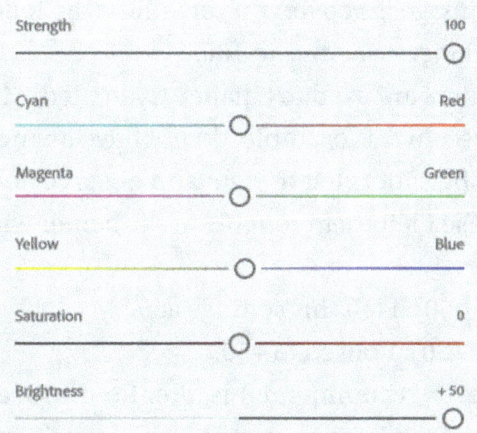

Figure 5-38. *Harmonization filter – adjust the settings to correct the colors in the image*

While the source image is active, you can adjust the following sliders:

Strength (0–100): I increased this to 100.

The next set of sliders are used to balance Cyan/Red, Magenta/Green, and Yellow/Blue. These, in this example, do not have an increment range, so you need to move the sliders left or right and observe how they adjust the preview. In this case I left them roughly in the center with Yellow/Blue moved slightly to the right.

Saturation (-50,0, +50): I left this settings at 0.

Brightness (-50,0, +50): I raised to +50.

I would not, however, recommend this filter for drastically different color shifts or scenes, as the filter currently does have difficultly referencing some color shifts and making it as accurate as I would expect it to be. It is not for black and white images.

In this case, you could output your changes as a smart filter, should you want to reference your changes later for comparison. Then click OK. Refer to Figure 5-39.

CHAPTER 5   ADVANCED FILTERS FOR PHOTO RESTORATION: PART 2

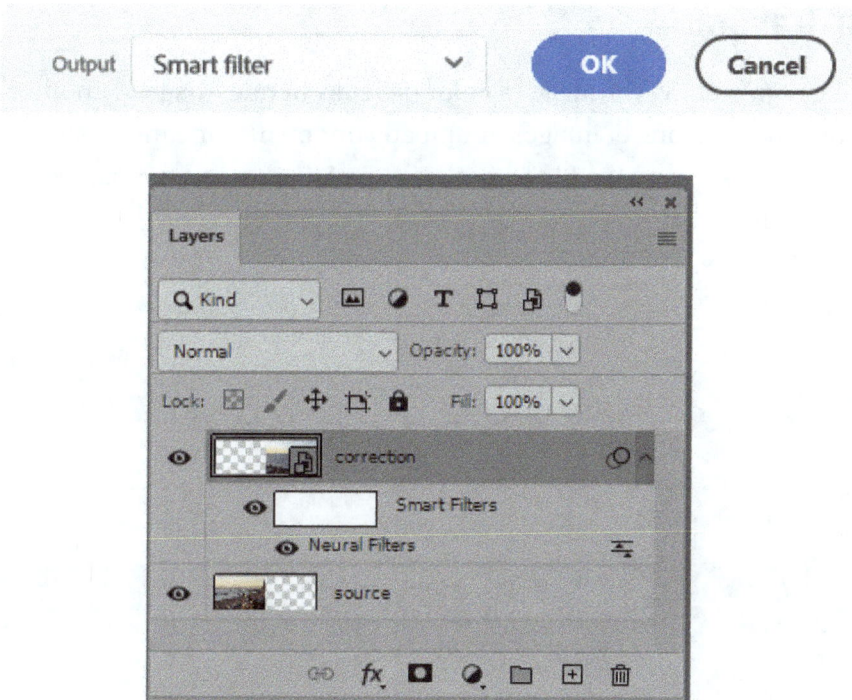

Figure 5-39. *Harmonization filter output to Smart Object layer in the Layers panel and the final result*

Refer to **beach_harmonization.psd** for reference.

CHAPTER 5   ADVANCED FILTERS FOR PHOTO RESTORATION: PART 2

Color Transfer

This filter can creatively transfer a color pallet from one image to another. You can either use preset images or upload your own, using the Custom tab. See and use a copy the file **forest_path.psd** if you want to practice. Refer to Figure 5-40.

Figure 5-40. *Neutral Filter Color Transfer*

While working in the presets, you could select an image to alter the overall color, similar to working with adjustment layers or Profiles in Camera Raw. I used the green leaves to test. Refer to Figure 5-41.

Figure 5-41. *Color Transfer filter with preset applied to image*

Then choose a color space of Lab or RGB; note how the preview alters when the color space change is made. Refer to Figure 5-42 for options from the list.

CHAPTER 5   ADVANCED FILTERS FOR PHOTO RESTORATION: PART 2

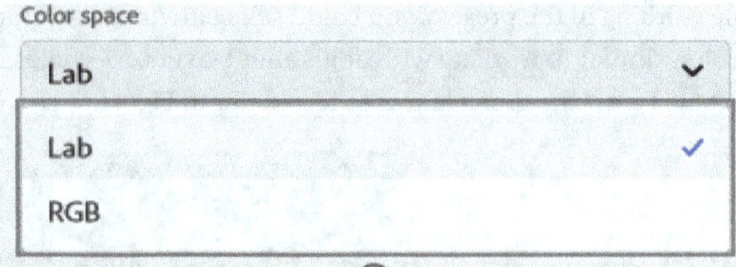

Figure 5-42. Color Transfer filter settings Lab or RGB color space

Work with the Lab color space.

Then adjust the sliders for the following. Refer to Figure 5-43.

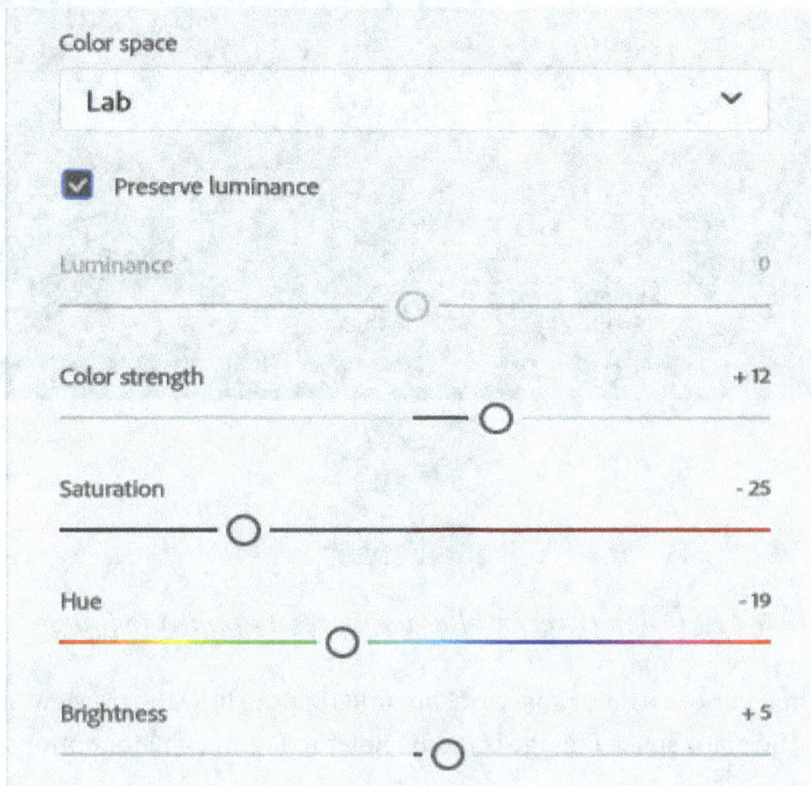

Figure 5-43. Color Transfer filter settings Lab color space options

Preserve Luminance: When enabled, keep the lightness of the image; however, the Luminance slider will not be available. Refer to Figure 5-44.

Figure 5-44. *Color Transfer adding Preserve Luminance to the image*

Luminance (-50, 0, +50): Currently, it is set to 0 as I have enabled the Preserve Luminance slider. However, a setting of -50 can yield a more monochrome result. Refer to Figure 5-45.

CHAPTER 5   ADVANCED FILTERS FOR PHOTO RESTORATION: PART 2

Figure 5-45. *Color Transfer adjusting the Luminance slider on the image and then with Preserve Luminance check box is disabled and then enabled*

Color strength (-50, 0, +50): I set to +12.

Saturation (-50, 0, +50): Try a setting of -25.

Hue (-90, 0, +90): Set to -19.

Brightness (-50, 0, +50): Set to +5. Refer to Figure 5-46.

CHAPTER 5   ADVANCED FILTERS FOR PHOTO RESTORATION: PART 2

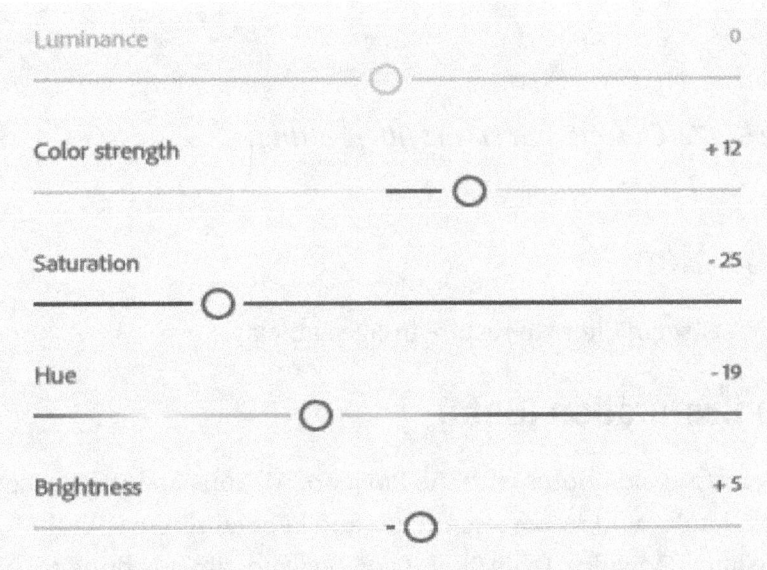

Figure 5-46. *Color Transfer filter settings*

Note that the RGB color space only uses the slider of Saturation, Hue, and Brightness. Refer to Figure 5-42 and Figure 5-46.

Unlike with the Hue/Saturation adjustment layer mentioned in Chapter 1, in this Color Transfer filter, you are a bit more bound by the colors that are used from the reference image. This actually is much like using the Color Lookup adjustment layer from Chapter 1. However, in this filter, the sliders do give a broader range of options which the Color Lookup adjustment layer does not possess.

You can then output as a smart filter and click OK. Refer to Figure 5-47. Refer to **forest_path_color_transfer.psd** as a reference.

CHAPTER 5   ADVANCED FILTERS FOR PHOTO RESTORATION: PART 2

Figure 5-47. *Output as a smart filter settings*

Restoration

Use the next set of filters to restore images quickly.

Photo Restoration (Beta)

Quickly restore old photos with the Power of AI. You can improve contrast, enhance details, and remove scratches and later combine with the colorize filter. Download this filter if you have not already done so, but keep in mind this filter is currently in Beta, so it is subject to changes. Note that afterward, the word new may be removed from the filter. Refer to Figure 5-48.

Figure 5-48. *Neural filter Photo Restoration*

    Can this filter do a better job of restoration than you? You can certainly find out when you apply the filter to the original damaged image or a Smart Object layer and compare. In this case, I think, based on my settings, I was able to eliminate at least 85% of many of the dust particles and scratches in this earlier black-and-white image which I could now go back and colorize again if I wanted to. You can refer to my file **village_restoration.psd**. Refer to Figure 5-49.

CHAPTER 5   ADVANCED FILTERS FOR PHOTO RESTORATION: PART 2

Figure 5-49. *Neural filter Photo Restoration before and after once settings were applied*

CHAPTER 5 ADVANCED FILTERS FOR PHOTO RESTORATION: PART 2

Every image will be different, but you can certainly try the following settings. Refer to Figure 5-50.

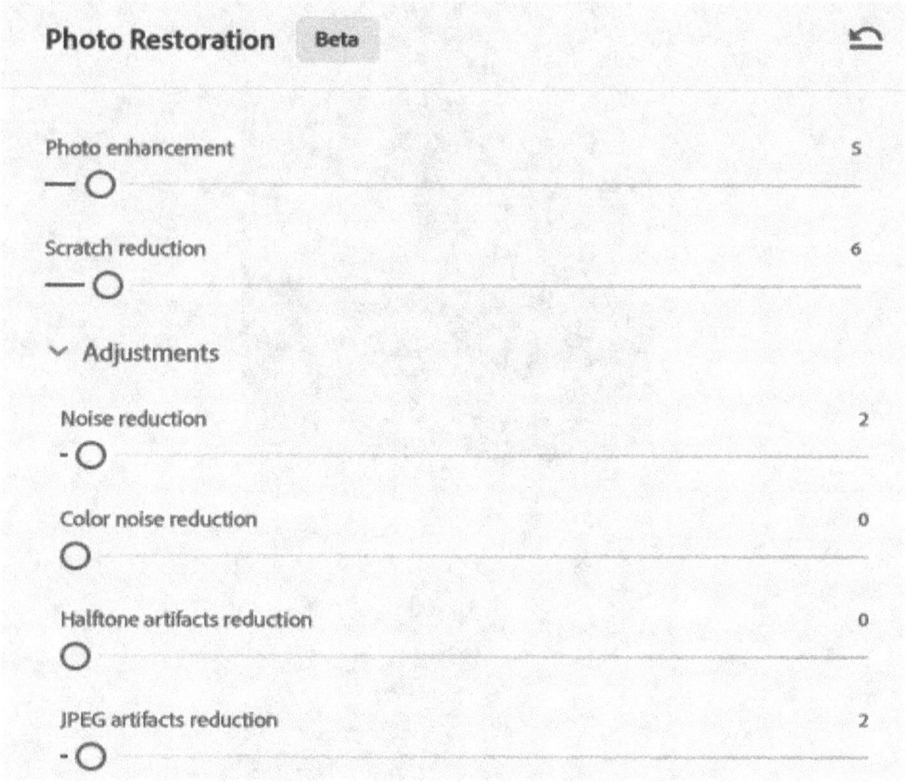

Figure 5-50. *Photo Restoration filter settings*

Photo enhancement (0–100): Move the slider; in this case, I used 5 as I found too high a setting created some unwanted spots or some details were lost.

Enhance face (0–100): This is an optional setting that appears only if a face is visible and present. If there are no recognizable faces in the photo, this option is not present. Refer to Figure 5-51.

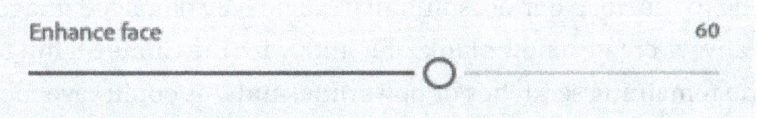

Figure 5-51. *Photo Restoration filter settings for faces*

Scratch reduction (0–100): I set this to 6 so as not to lose important details. However, for your image, you may want a higher setting. Refer to Figure 5-50.

Adjustments can also be for

Noise reduction (0–100): Removes some noise from the image. I set this setting to 2.

Color noise reduction (0–100): Removes some colored spots from the image which would not be present in a black-and-white image. I would try between a range of 0–2. I left at 0.

Halftone artifact reduction (0–100): Some prints that are from a magazine may have visible halftone dots that appear in the scan; this can help eliminate them. Likewise, you could see if this option would improve issues with the Moiré effect. In this case, I left the setting at 0.

JPEG artifact reduction (0–100): Often more common on digital photos, this could be used to clean up any unwanted color artifacts, as was mentioned in Chapter 3 with the Reduce Noise filter. I used a settings of 2.

You can then output to the smart filter and click OK. Refer to Figure 5-52.

Figure 5-52. *Output as a smart filter setting*

While this is not a perfect solution to all heavily damaged images, later I could always create a new blank later and, with the Clone Stamp tool, cover the remaining scratches or powerline, and this could save me some time. And you can paint with the Eraser tool on the smart filter mask to add back any details you did not intend to remove. Refer to Figure 5-53.

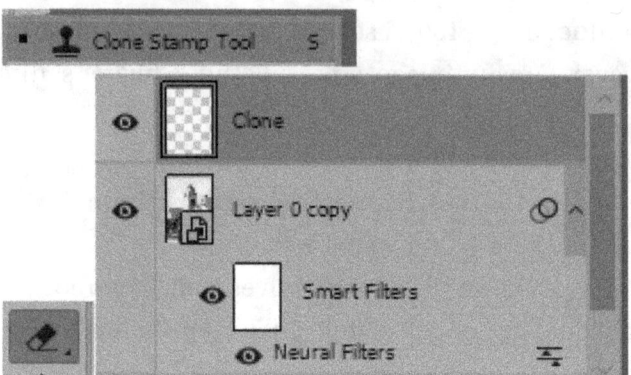

Figure 5-53. Clone Stamp tool and Additional layer in Layers panel for additional touch-ups of file if required

Likewise, you could test this as an alternative to the dust and scratches filter in other images like the Army Photo in Chapter 3 to see if it would be an improvement to that filter. If you do so, work on an Image ➤ Duplicate of the file.

This filter can also work with damaged color images as well and may be able to repair areas that are damaged in some RGB channels as well while working on the composite. So, I do recommend experimenting with this filter.

An additional related Photo Restoration filter that you may want to use for other specific digital projects is also available in this section.

CHAPTER 5 ADVANCED FILTERS FOR PHOTO RESTORATION: PART 2

JPEG Artifacts Removal

Used for removing artifacts resulting from JPEG compression. The following settings are only for Strength: Low, Medium, and High. We saw an example of this in the Reduce Noise filter in Chapter 3. Refer to Figure 5-54.

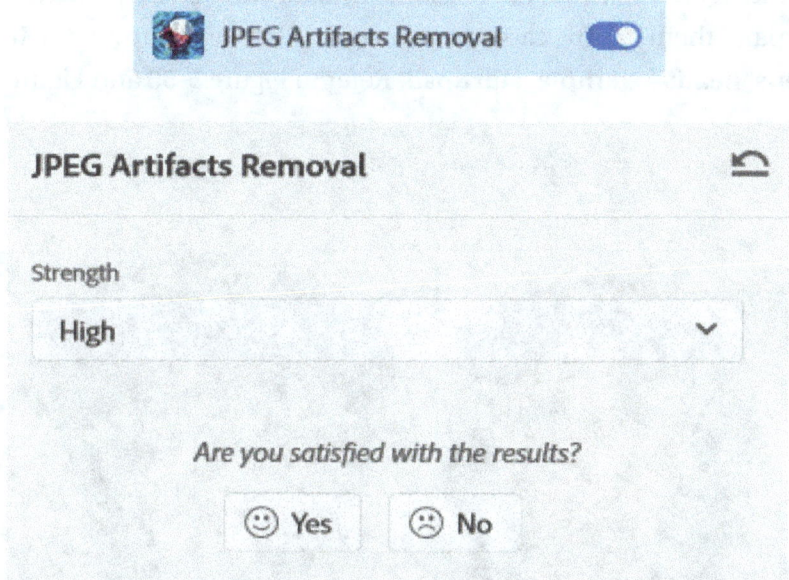

Figure 5-54. Neural filter JPEG Artifacts Removal filter

Just make sure to do a before and after comparison if you are concerned about losing fine details in your image.

Portrait (Facial Adjustments)

There are three filters in this section that you may want to experiment with. As an alternative to Liquify filter from Chapter 4 for faces in this workspace, try **Smart Portrait**. If the filter can detect a face, then it will be active for you to toggle on.

773

CHAPTER 5   ADVANCED FILTERS FOR PHOTO RESTORATION: PART 2

Smart Portrait

I have used this filter in my book, mentioned earlier, which can do many of the similar settings by adjusting the sliders and adding a more realistic smile. You can adjust each face one at a time as you select it from the list.

Some of the key settings in this filter you may want to experiment with are found in the Featured, Expressions, Global, and Setting tabs when you expand them. In this case, you can again work on a copy of the file **womens_heads_example_start.psd**. Refer to Figure 5-55 and Figure 5-56.

Figure 5-55. *Neural filter Smart Portrait filter and preview*

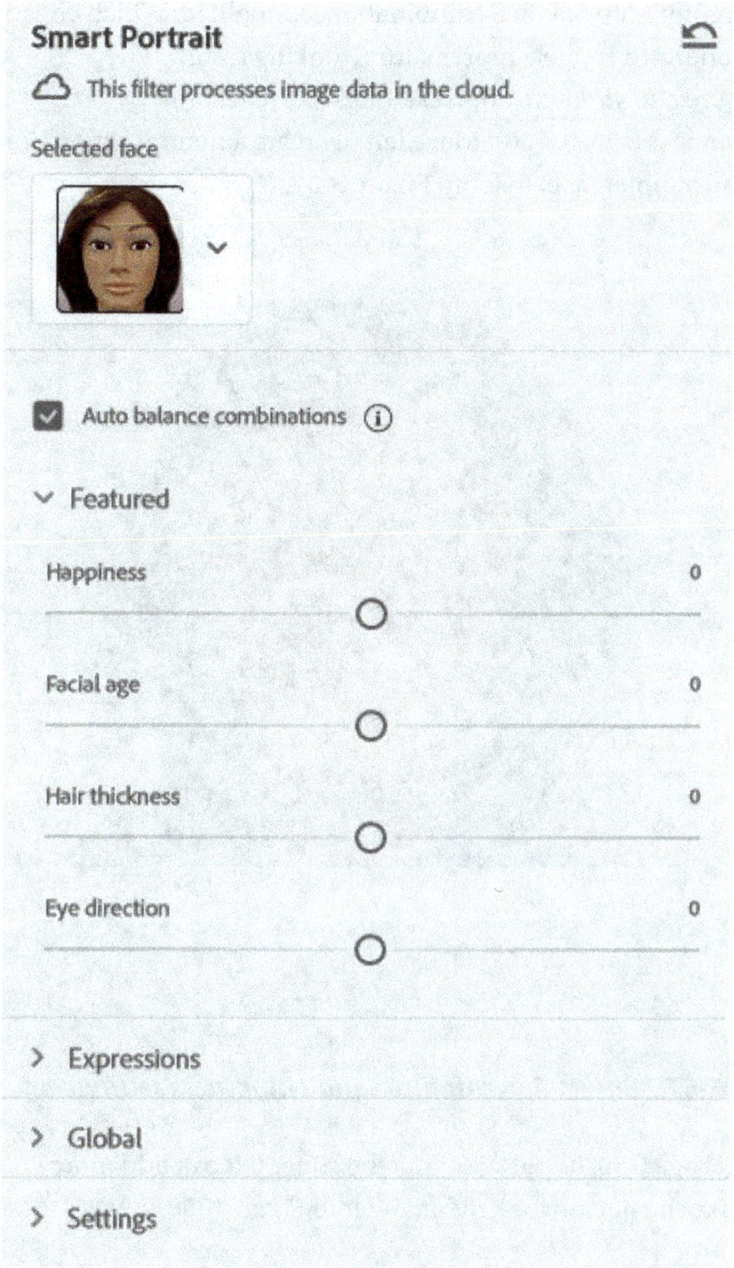

Figure 5-56. Neural filter Smart Portrait filter and settings

CHAPTER 5 ADVANCED FILTERS FOR PHOTO RESTORATION: PART 2

Currently Auto balance combinations is enabled. Which constrains combinations to create a more natural looking result.

Feature allows you to adjust settings like level of

Happiness (-50, 0, +50): Move left to create a neutral expression and right for a happier face. Refer to Figure 5-57.

Figure 5-57. *Smart Portrait filter and Happiness settings*

Facial age (-50, 0, +50): Moving the slider left can add more youth and right make the person look older. Refer to Figure 5-58.

CHAPTER 5   ADVANCED FILTERS FOR PHOTO RESTORATION: PART 2

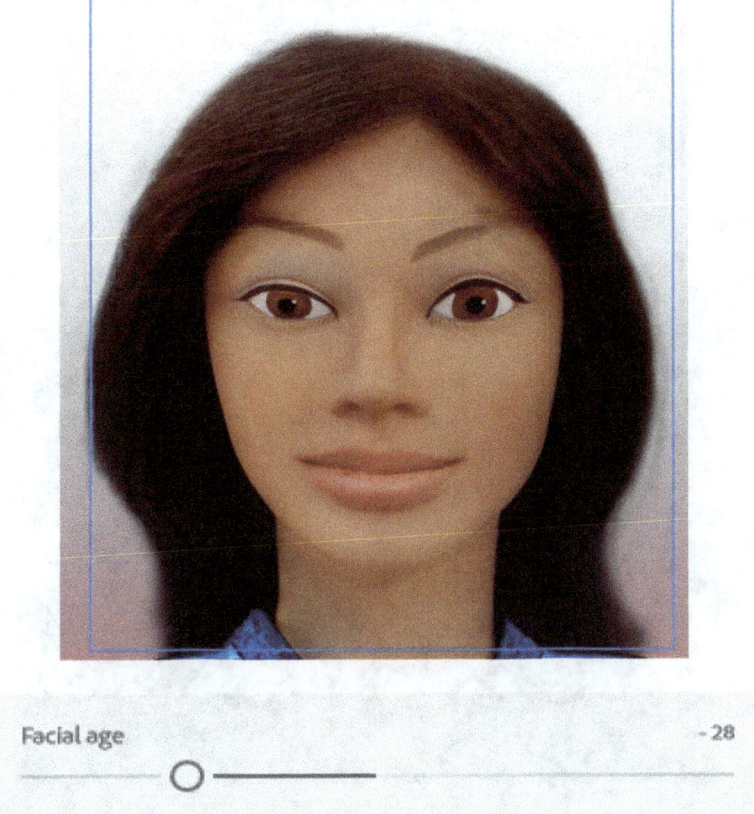

Figure 5-58. *Smart Portrait filter and Facial age reduction*

Hair thickness (-50, 0, +50): For people with thinning hair, this can be a useful setting. This can also correct some gaps that may appear around the head as you adjust other sliders. Refer to Figure 5-59.

777

CHAPTER 5   ADVANCED FILTERS FOR PHOTO RESTORATION: PART 2

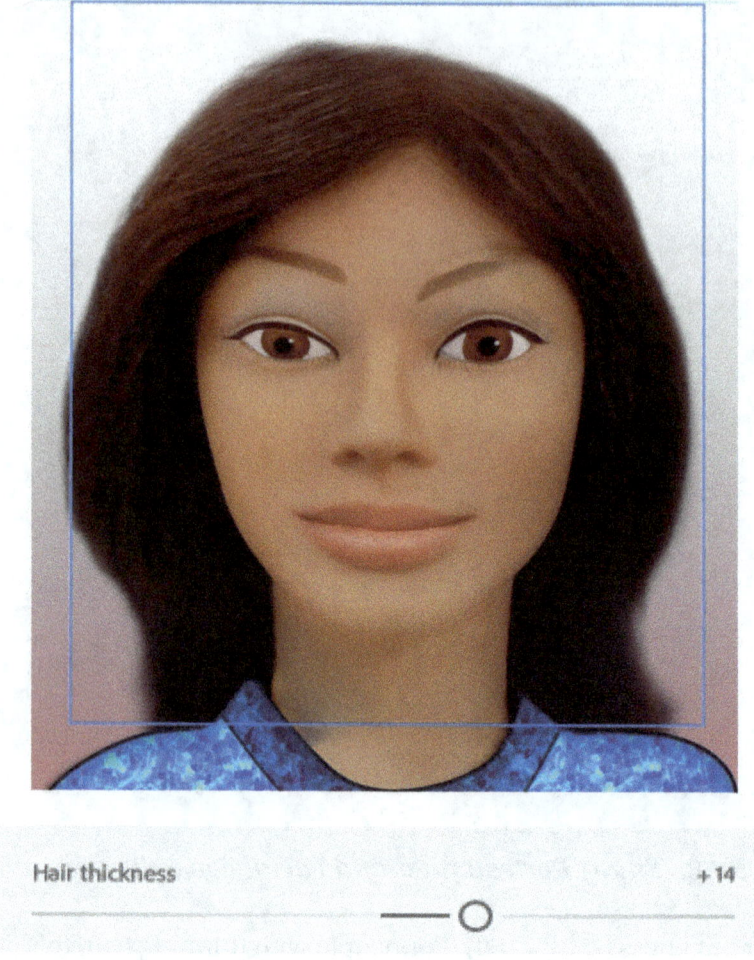

Figure 5-59. *Smart Portrait filter and Hair thickness increase*

Eye direction (-50, 0, +50): This setting can shift the eyes slightly to the left or right. Refer to Figure 5-60.

CHAPTER 5   ADVANCED FILTERS FOR PHOTO RESTORATION: PART 2

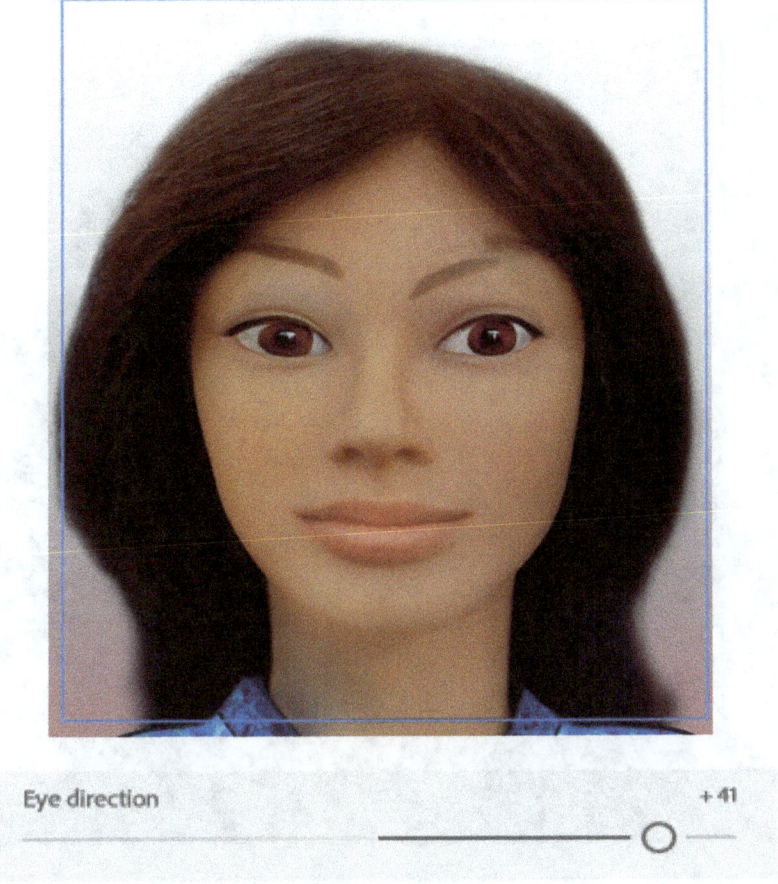

Figure 5-60. Smart Portrait filter and Eye direction moved right

Be aware, as you work with these settings, that areas like the eyebrow or around the neck may be altered in unexpected ways. I will talk about that at the end of this filter section.

Expressions control facial reactions like Surprise (-50, 0, +50) and Anger (-50, 0, +50). Refer to Figure 5-61.

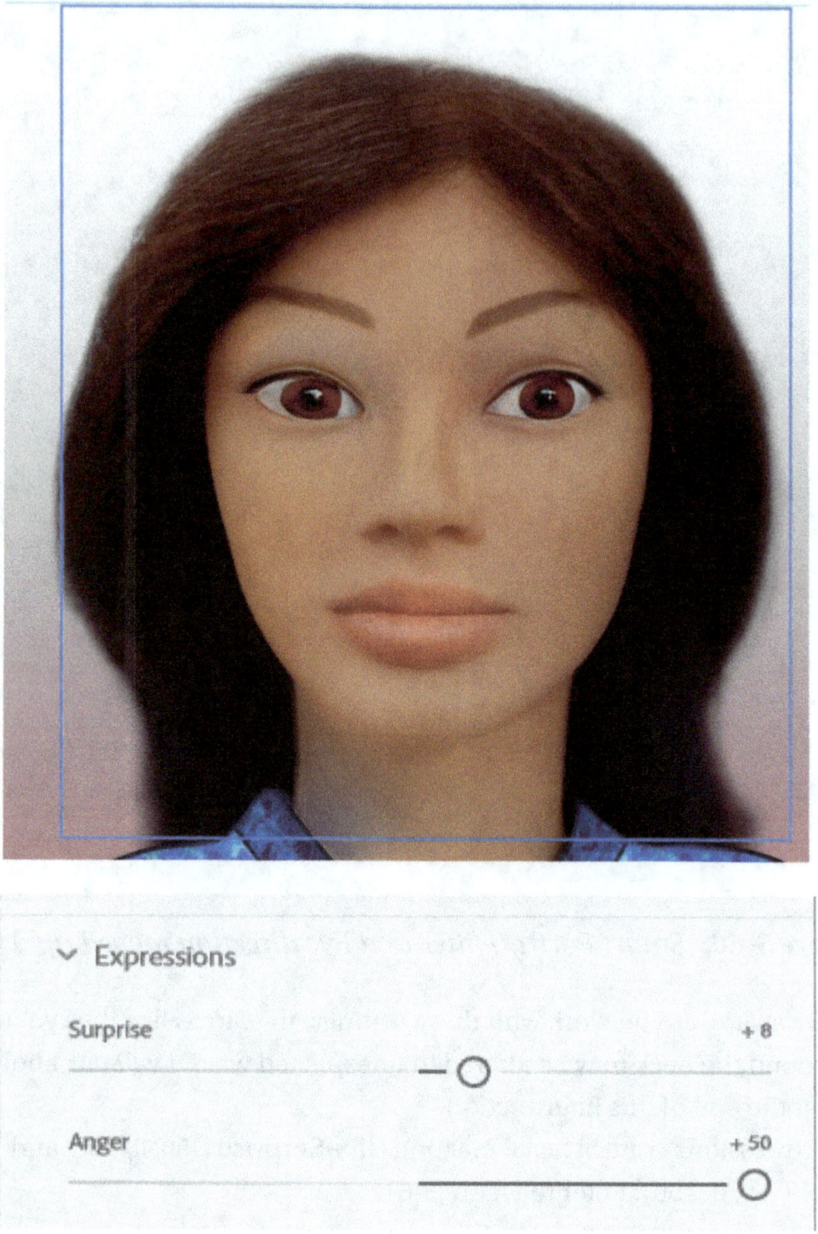

CHAPTER 5   ADVANCED FILTERS FOR PHOTO RESTORATION: PART 2

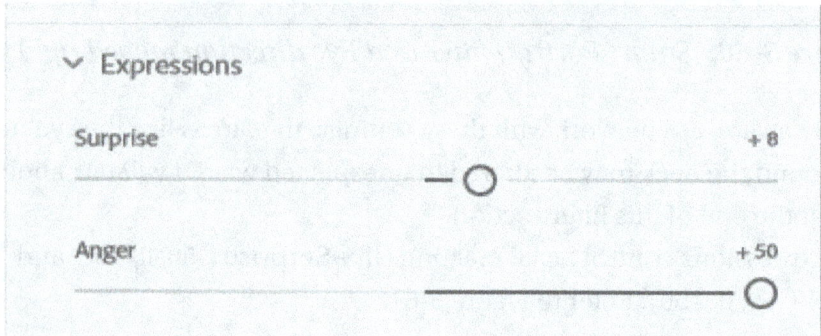

Figure 5-61. Smart Portrait filter and adjustment to expression

Global controls have three main sliders which are for the movement of the Head direction left or right, Fix head alignment if head shifts incorrectly, and Lighting direction. Each has a slider range of (-50, 0, +50). Move the sliders to try different settings and refer to Figure 5-62.

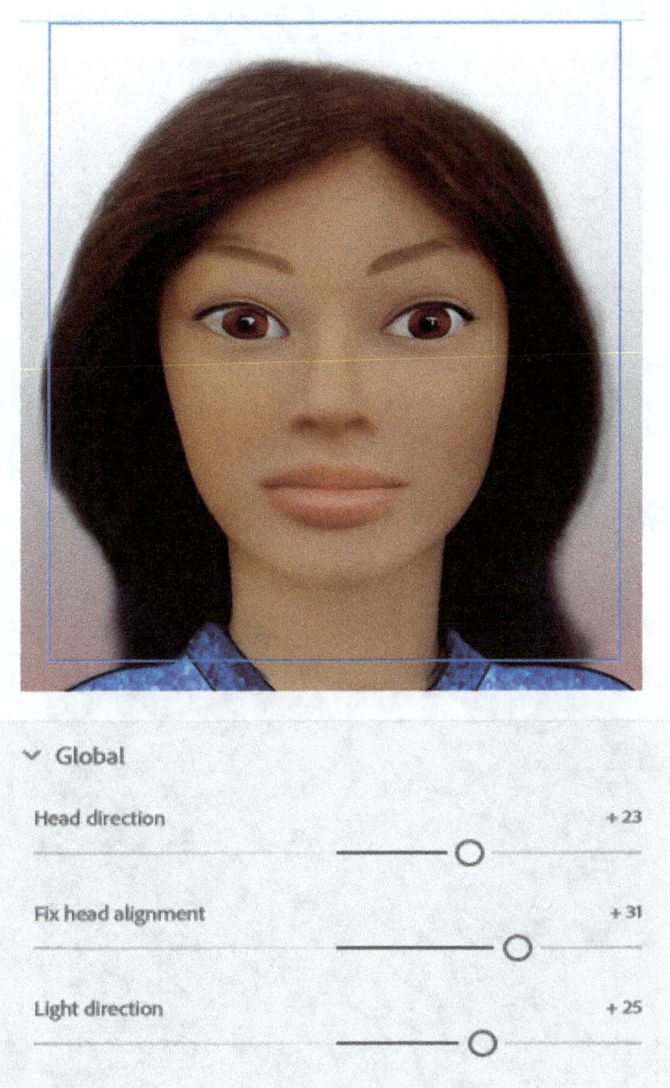

Figure 5-62. *Smart Portrait filter and adjustment to Global direction of the head*

CHAPTER 5　ADVANCED FILTERS FOR PHOTO RESTORATION: PART 2

Settings can be adjusted to control and retain unique details (0–100) in the face as well as mask with feathering (0–100). I found that lowering the retain unique details to 5 and raising the Mask feathering to 85 did eliminate some of the broken areas around the hair eyebrows and neck. Refer to Figure 5-63.

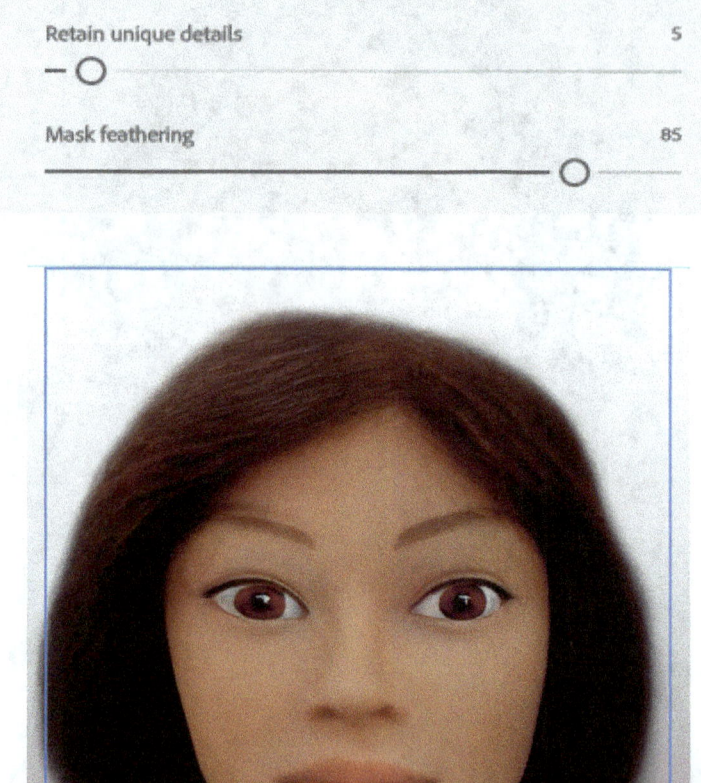

Figure 5-63. *Smart Portrait filter and adjustment to settings options*

CHAPTER 5   ADVANCED FILTERS FOR PHOTO RESTORATION: PART 2

To create a happier face, you may want to go back and set the Expression settings back to 0, and in the retain unique details, set this to 0. Refer to Figure 5-64.

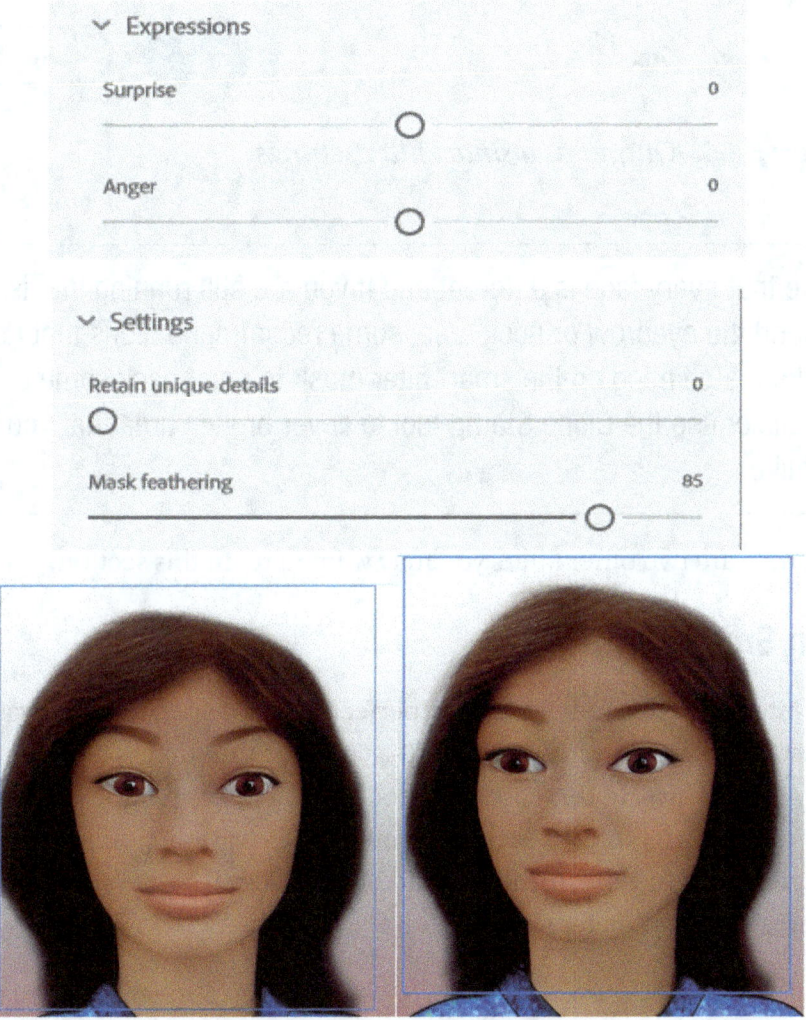

Figure 5-64. *Smart Portrait filter and adjustment to Expressions and Settings options and then try alternative alignments*

For practice, go back and alter the angle of the head in another orientation you want using the sliders.

Then output to smart filter. Refer to Figure 5-65.

Figure 5-65. *Output as a smart filter settings*

Note that every face is different and if you are still running into issues around the eyebrow or neck area, some recommendations that I can make are painting on the smart filter mask to paint back some of the details or use the Clone Stamp tool to cover broken area that you do not like.

There are two other filters you may want to try in this section.

Skin Smoothing

This filter is used to remove skin imperfections and acne from portraits. Adjust additional settings like Blur (0–100) and Smoothness (-50, 0, +50) on a selected face. In this case, our models already have smooth faces, but on your own project, you may want to try these settings to soften their features and skin glare further as I did on the second model's face around the eyes and nose. Refer to Figure 5-66.

CHAPTER 5   ADVANCED FILTERS FOR PHOTO RESTORATION: PART 2

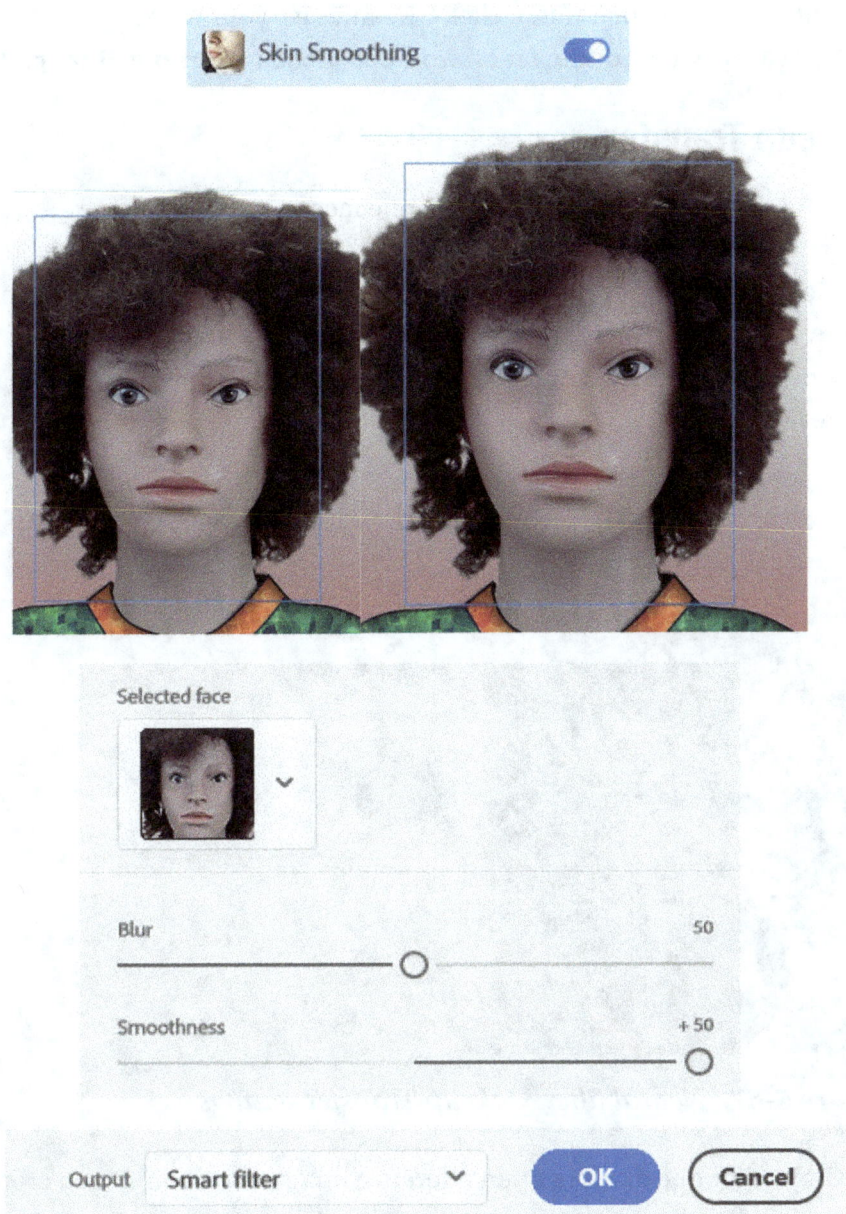

Figure 5-66. *Neural filter Skin Smoothing settings and output as a smart filter settings*

CHAPTER 5   ADVANCED FILTERS FOR PHOTO RESTORATION: PART 2

Output to your smart filter, click OK, and save your work.

You can see the work so far on **womens_heads_example_final.psd**.

Makeup Transfer

This filter is used to move colors from one face to another using a reference image which could be a currently open image. As with the other mentioned filter, you would then select a face in your current image. This filter works best when there is only one person in the image as two or more people seem to throw an error when attempting the transfer. Refer to Figure 5-67.

Figure 5-67. *Neural filter Makeup Transfer settings*

Browse for one or more open reference images. You could then crop the area in the reference image to the targeted areas. Refer to Figure 5-67 and Figure 5-68.

CHAPTER 5   ADVANCED FILTERS FOR PHOTO RESTORATION: PART 2

Figure 5-68. *Neural filter Makeup Transfer settings applied to select face preview*

Then transfer that information onto your selected face.

Beware, however, that if your selected face to add the filter to already has makeup present, this filter may not work as intended. It could also interpret someone with a different skin tone in the reference image and look at areas where there is no makeup present such as around areas above the eye or around the cheeks, and apply that skin tone instead to the selected face which may not be intended. Working with someone of a similar skin tone or cropping the reference image may improve the result.

For more information on this topic, you can refer to the following links at the end of this section.

Refer to my two files in the Makeup Transfer Test folder (**woman_reference.psd** and **woman_subject_selected.psd**) if you need to review.

CHAPTER 5   ADVANCED FILTERS FOR PHOTO RESTORATION: PART 2

Photography

In Chapters 3 and 4, we looked at various filters for sharpening and blurring. Here are two other alternatives you may want to explore. Make sure to download them if you have not already done so.

Super Zoom

Use this filter to get a closer crop to an image, and then let Photoshop add in details to compensate for the loss of resolution. Its main settings let you

Drag to reframe image.

Enhance image details using the magnifying icons and the check box. Then Zoom in 2 or more times.

Remove JPEG artifacts from digital photos.

Noise reduction (0–30): Reduce noise grain in the image.

Sharpen (0–30): Increase to sharpen the image, as when it enlarges it may blur.

Enhance face details when faces are detected. Refer to Figure 5-69.

CHAPTER 5 ADVANCED FILTERS FOR PHOTO RESTORATION: PART 2

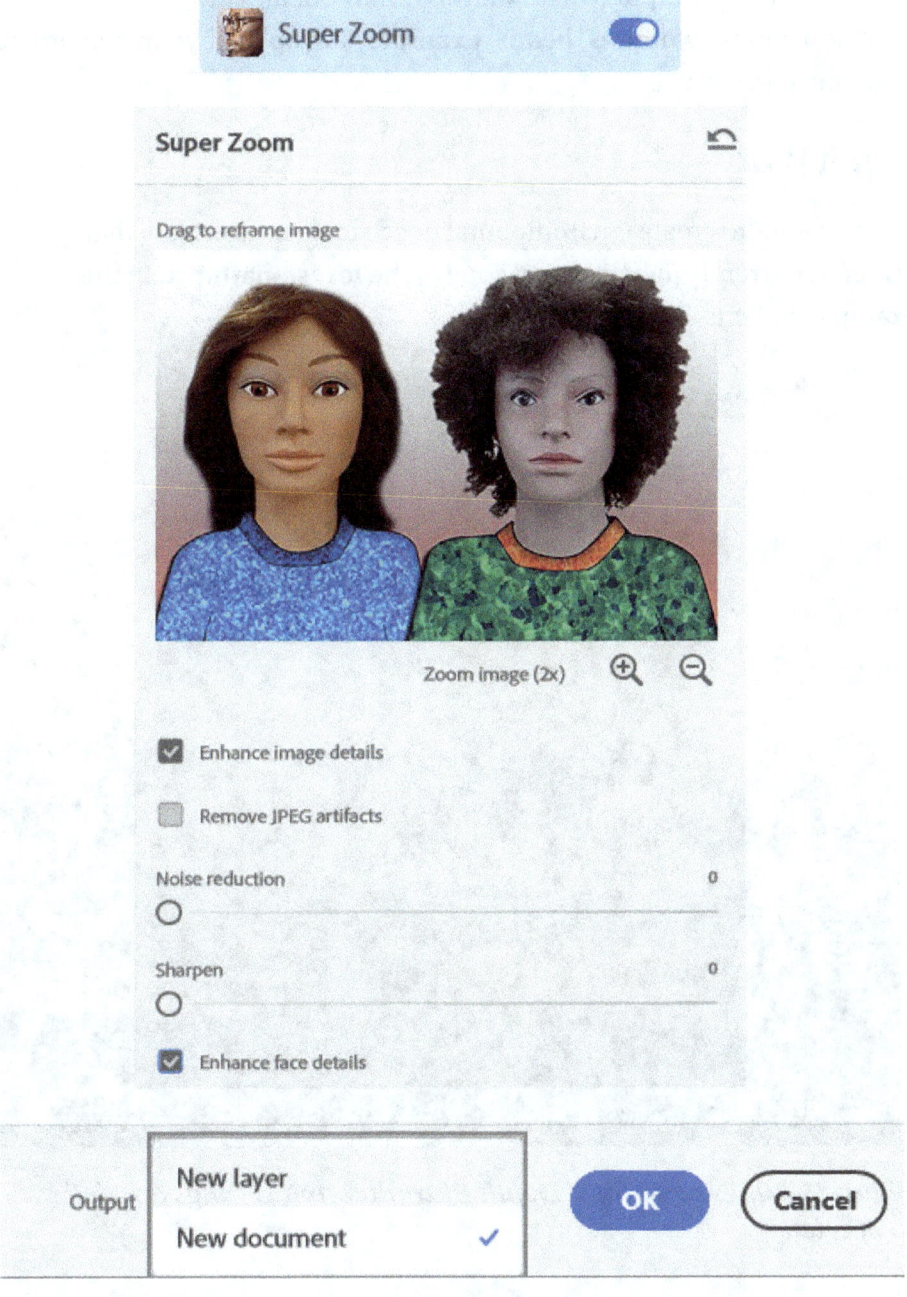

Figure 5-69. *Neural filter Super Zoom settings and Output settings*

You can then output to a new layer or new document.

Use a copy of **womens_heads_example_start.psd** or your own project if you need to test this.

Depth Blur

Use this filter to create environmental depth to an image. Note that this option is currently in beta. Use a copy of the **forest_path.psd** in this example. Refer to Figure 5-70.

Figure 5-70. *Neural filter Depth Blur filter and settings applied to preview*

The initial blur will come in reverse. You can then reset this using the settings on the right to edit the focal point. Click to edit the focal point on the focal point preview. Then drag to a new focal point position. Or remove the focal point. Refer to Figure 5-71.

Figure 5-71. *Neural filter Depth Blur filter setting a focal point*

If no focal point is preset, you can set a focal distance (0–100). I used a setting of 100. Refer to Figure 5-72.

Figure 5-72. *Neural filter Depth Blur filter and filter settings applied to preview*

Focal range (0–100): Use a setting of 47.

Focus subject: Keep this setting disabled if you add a focal point later. Refer to Figure 5-72.

Other settings include

Blur strength (0–100): Decrease or increase the blur. The default is set to 50.

Haze (0–100): Adds a type of mist or atmosphere to the image; by default, it is set to 0.

Temp (temperature) (-50,0, +50): Add more blue or yellow to the image; by default, it is set to 0.

Tint (-150,0, +150): Add more green or magenta to the image; by default, it is set to 0.

Saturation (-50,0, +50): Decrease or increase the saturation; by default, it is set to 0.

Brightness (-50,0, +50): Decrease or increase the brightness; by default, it is set to 0.

Grain (0–100): Increase the noise or grain in the image; currently, it is set to 0. Refer to Figure 5-73.

CHAPTER 5　ADVANCED FILTERS FOR PHOTO RESTORATION: PART 2

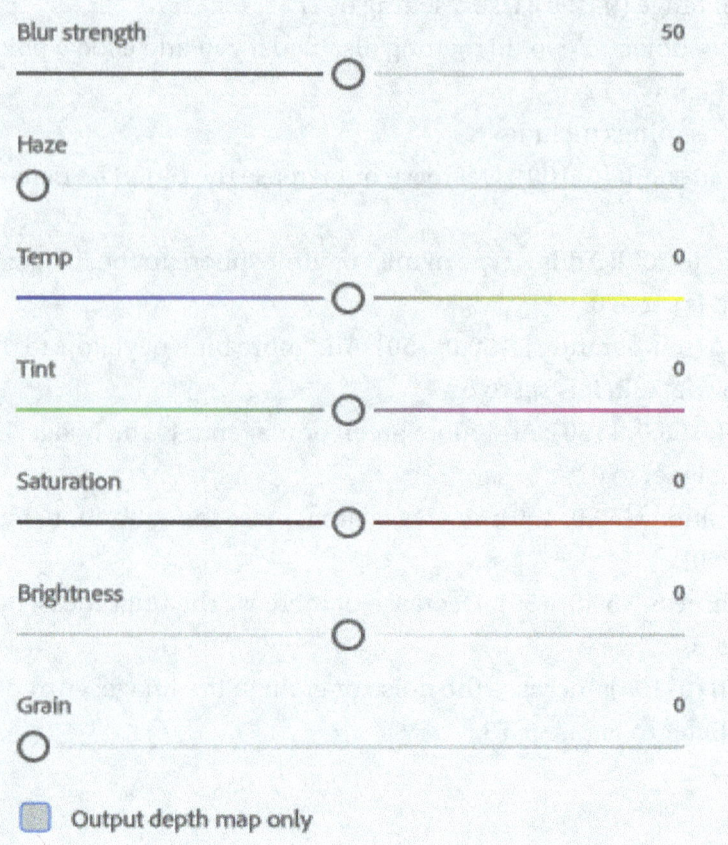

Figure 5-73. *Neural filter Depth Blur filter and filter settings to adjust the blur*

If you need to output depth map only (to a new layer or masked new layer), you can enable this setting. It will also allow you to preview the current gradient depth maps as well.

In this case, I have disabled that setting and want to output to my Smart Object layer filter. Refer to Figures 5-73 and 5-74.

CHAPTER 5　ADVANCED FILTERS FOR PHOTO RESTORATION: PART 2

Figure 5-74. *Neural filter Output settings*

This is a good option for basic blurs. Alternatively, you may prefer to use the Blur Gallery (Chapter 3) or the Camera Raw Lens Blur (Chapter 4) options.

See file **forest_path_depth blur.psd** for reference.

Creative (Filters for Artistic Work) Landscape Mixer and Style Transfer

For more artistic work, I recommend **Landscape Mixer (Beta)**. This can certainly enhance an otherwise dull photo or add more to the scene, by mixing with another image or landscape by changing attributes like time of day or season from a reference image or one you upload. You can continue with the **forest_path.psd** image if you want to continue to test this and setting of the final filter. In this case, I am just using one filter at a time, so I am working with a copy. Refer to Figure 5-75.

Figure 5-75. *Neural Filter Landscape Mixer tool activated*

However, you can create a wide range of scene variations with the presets. Refer to Figure 5-76 and Figure 5-77.

Figure 5-76. *Current image in preview and then a Landscape Mixer preset applied*

CHAPTER 5　ADVANCED FILTERS FOR PHOTO RESTORATION: PART 2

Figure 5-77. *Experiments with other presets in the Landscape Mixer filter*

If you like the idea of an overgrown landscape or a fantasy world, you can certainly experiment with the filter.

The following sliders are available Presets, or upload your own Custom landscape style images using that tab. Refer to Figure 5-78.

CHAPTER 5   ADVANCED FILTERS FOR PHOTO RESTORATION: PART 2

Figure 5-78. *Landscape Mixer filter preset*

Note that some presets lend themselves better to one image over another. I find that forest scenes work best. They can, however, contain features like streams and waterfalls or mountains. Use the preset images to guide you, and then use the sliders to adjust the following.

Strength (0–100): Set the amount of preset that is applied.

Set a time of Day (0–100), Night (0–100), or Sunset (0–100).

Set a season Spring (0–100), Summer (0–100), Autumn (0–100), and Winter (0–100).

Try them in any combination that you want to create a unique image. Refer to Figure 5-79 and Figure 5-80.

Figure 5-79. *Landscape Mixer filter preset applied*

CHAPTER 5   ADVANCED FILTERS FOR PHOTO RESTORATION: PART 2

Figure 5-80. Landscape Mixer filter settings

Other options you can enable are

Preserve Subject: This will allow you to enable the Harmonize Subject check box.

Currently, I disabled these settings, and in some images, the effects may be more visible than others.

You can then output to your smart filter. Click OK. Refer to Figure 5-81.

Figure 5-81. *Neural filter Output settings*

Style Transfer

Another artistic filter found in this section is **Style Transfer** which can transfer texture, color, and style from a reference image or apply a style of a specific artist. This is much like using the Filter Gallery, and you can choose various artist or image styles. It comes with a few preset but you can also download more from the Cloud if you want to. Or upload your own custom reference image artwork using the Custom tab. Refer to Figure 5-82 and Figure 5-83.

CHAPTER 5   ADVANCED FILTERS FOR PHOTO RESTORATION: PART 2

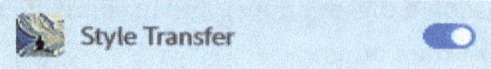

Figure 5-82. *Neural filter Style Transfer using artist styles and preview*

CHAPTER 5   ADVANCED FILTERS FOR PHOTO RESTORATION: PART 2

Figure 5-83. *Neural filter Style Transfer using image styles and preview*

Some of your photos will lend themselves better to one artwork than another, so take time to experiment.

Once you select an image from the menu, you can adjust sliders for the following. Here I left them at the default settings. Refer to Figure 5-84.

803

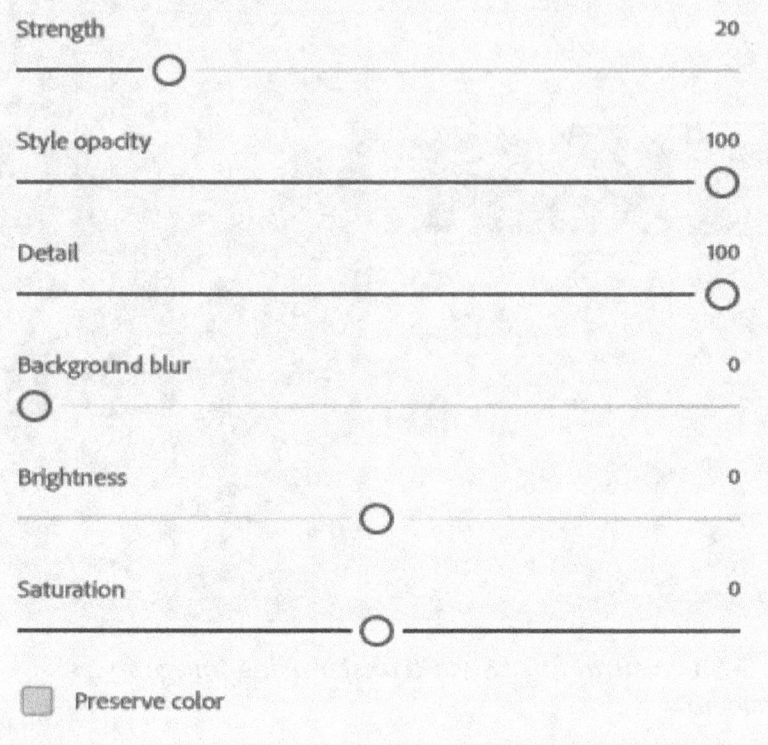

Figure 5-84. *Neural filter Style Transfer options*

Strength (0–100): I left it at the setting of 20.

Style opacity (0–100): Determines how the style covers the artwork. I left this at 100.

Detail (0–100): I left this at the setting of 100 for full artwork details.

Background blur (0–100): Blurs the image. I left it at 0.

Brightness (-50, 0, +50): Decrease or increase the brightness. I left it at 0.

Saturation (-50, 0, +50): Decrease or increase the saturation. I left it at 0.

Preserve color: Enabled when you want to keep some of the color from the original image. Refer to Figure 5-85.

CHAPTER 5　ADVANCED FILTERS FOR PHOTO RESTORATION: PART 2

Figure 5-85. *Neural filter Style Transfer options for preserve color and preview*

You can then output to your Smart Object filter. Refer to Figure 5-86.

Figure 5-86. *Neural filter Output settings*

Refer to my file **forest_path_landscape.psd** and **forest_path_styleT.psd** for reference.

Filters to Come in the Future

Adobe, at some point, will add more filters, and you can preview some possible upcoming ones under the Wait List. For me, Shadow Regenerator would be a nice addition to my digital repair tools. But other ones you may be interested in could be Portrait Generator, Water Long Exposer, and Noise Reduction. Additionally, it would be interesting to see a new Shake Reduction filter added to this list as well, for images with extreme motion blur. Or what about an Urban Landscape Mixer? Refer to Figure 5-87.

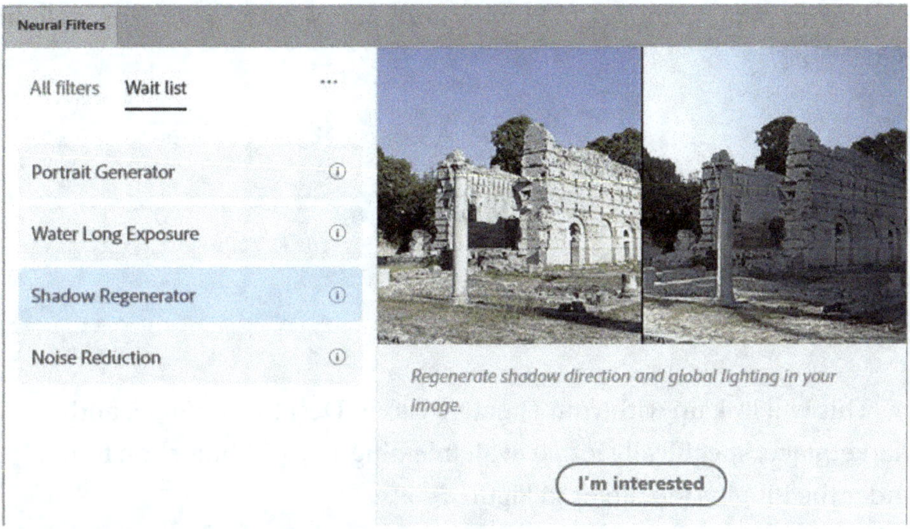

CHAPTER 5   ADVANCED FILTERS FOR PHOTO RESTORATION: PART 2

Figure 5-87. *Neural filter Wait List options*

Click OK to apply any of the chosen filters to your Smart Object layers, and exit the workspace.

File ➤ Save your work so far.

More details on the current filters can be found in the following:

https://helpx.adobe.com/photoshop/using/neural-filters.html

https://helpx.adobe.com/photoshop/using/neural-filters-list-and-faq.html

https://helpx.adobe.com/photoshop/using/neural-filters-feedback.html

Acquiring Other Filter Plug-Ins Through Adobe Creative Cloud

If you want to add additional filters or plug-ins to Photoshop from the Adobe Creative Cloud Stock and Marketplace, here are some steps you can take.

CHAPTER 5   ADVANCED FILTERS FOR PHOTO RESTORATION: PART 2

In your main menu, go to Plugins and Choose Browse Plugins. Refer to Figure 5-88.

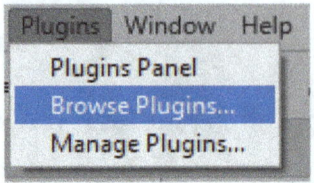

Figure 5-88. *Photoshop Plugin menu*

This will link up with your Creative Cloud Desktop for Stock and Marketplace, specifically for all available plug-ins for Photoshop found under the Plugins tab. Refer to Figure 5-89.

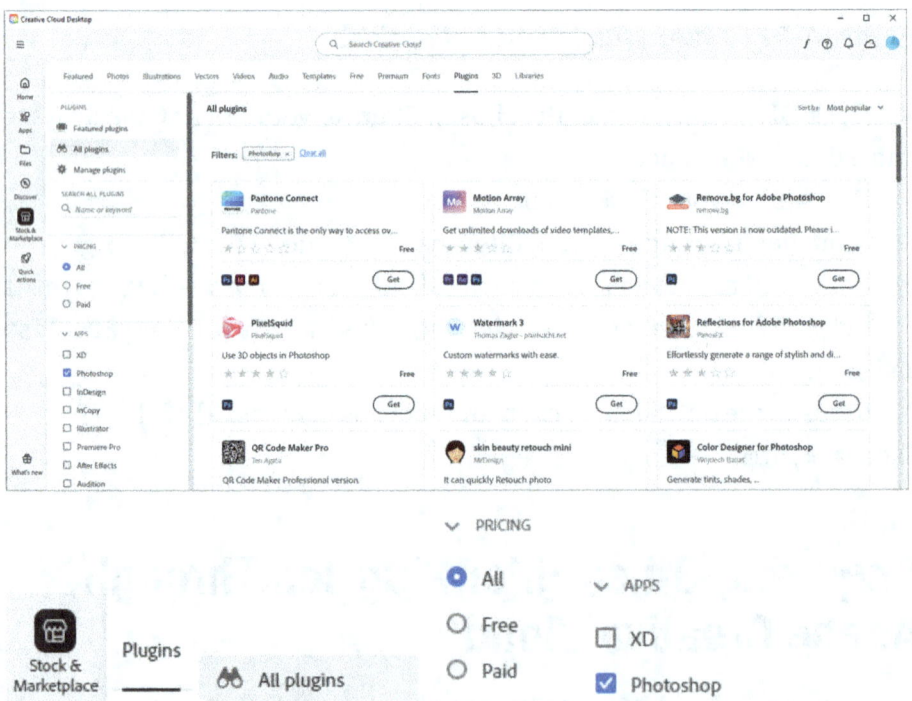

Figure 5-89. *Adobe Creative Cloud Desktop look for Stock and Marketplace plug-ins options*

CHAPTER 5 ADVANCED FILTERS FOR PHOTO RESTORATION: PART 2

You can then see which ones are free or paid for and search by key words such as the word "filter" or "motion blur" to narrow down your search. Press the Enter key to confirm the search word. Refer to Figure 5-90.

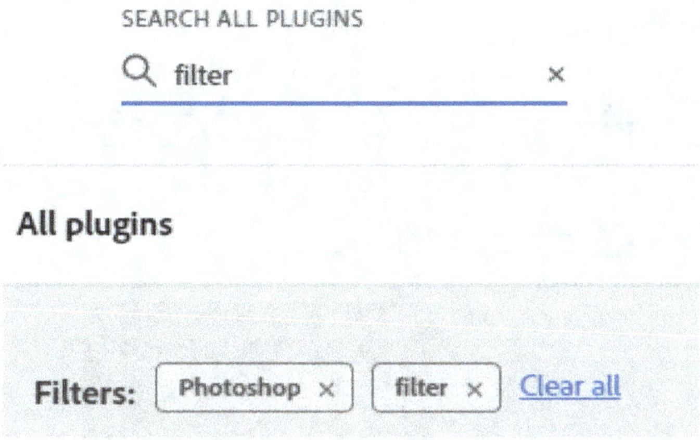

Figure 5-90. *Seach and filter topics with Adobe Creative Cloud Desktop*

Whether it is a free or paid plug-in, click the name of the item so that you can review it's details, and reviews. Before you buy or download and make sure that it is the same version compatibility as the current application. Refer to Figure 5-91.

CHAPTER 5   ADVANCED FILTERS FOR PHOTO RESTORATION: PART 2

Figure 5-91. Locate filters you are interested in and then view details about them

CHAPTER 5 ADVANCED FILTERS FOR PHOTO RESTORATION: PART 2

As mentioned in Chapter 1, Adobe Stock and Marketplace is also a good place to find items such as color LUTs, but you can also look for plug-ins for your other Adobe applications.

The Plugins menu in Photoshop also allows you to view plug-ins in its panel and Manage Plugins. Refer to Figure 5-92.

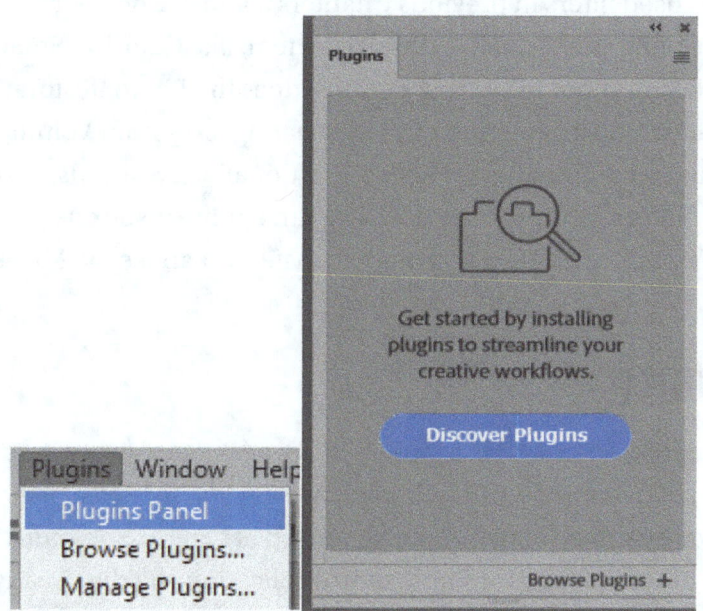

Figure 5-92. Photoshop Plugin menu and Plugins panel

Note Keep in mind that you can also purchase plug-ins and filters outside of Stock and Marketplace. However, if they have not been approved by Adobe or have not been recently updated, they may not work with your latest applications.

811

Photo Project

Now that you have learned about neural filters, you could apply some to your past projects.

In this case, take time to review some of your past image projects where you used filters in previous Chapters 3 and 4. Consider which neural filters you could use instead, to improve them, like Colorize, Smart Portrait, or Photo Restoration. In some situations, does the Photo Restoration filter or another one do a better job than the healing tools from Volume 1, or is it better to use a combination of both? Additionally, try various combination of neural filters together to see how you can apply artistic effects with a portrait or outdoor scene using Style Transfer or Landscape Mixer.

Summary

In this chapter, we looked at a variety of advanced and new filters that have been added to Photoshop in recent years and looked at how they can improve various images. We also looked at where to acquire filters currently not found in your Photoshop application, via the Creative Cloud. In the next chapter, we will look at how you can add interest to your Photo Restoration project and make your static image more dynamic, with basic animation.

CHAPTER 6

Creating a Parallax: Bring Your Vintage or Historical Photos to Life

Static digital photos, while they can be fun to restore using various Photoshop tools, can be made even more interesting for a presentation, if they are turned into a type of basic slideshow or video animation.

One of the easiest animations that you can create is a GIF Photo Gallery, using the Timeline panel frame animation option, if you plan to post a small collection of two or three images on your website that will fade and appear in a timed setting. However, the Timeline panel has even more advanced options with the video timeline, which can be used in combination with an old photo, to create a parallax effect as though we are zooming into or out of the image. This gives the appearance of an almost 3D lifelike effect as in a movie or historical film. That is why it is also known as 2.5D. We will look at what kind of photos work best for this type of animation. Later, you will also look at how to render the animation and what settings to use to complete the rendering, using the application Adobe Media Encoder.

CHAPTER 6   CREATING A PARALLAX: BRING YOUR VINTAGE OR HISTORICAL PHOTOS TO LIFE

Note that this chapter does contain projects found in the Volume 2 Chapter 6 folder. Some of the information in this chapter has been adapted from my book *Graphics and Multimedia for the Web with Adobe Creative Cloud*. However, our focus is working with photographs and not actual video footage which is not required for this chapter.

For this chapter, make sure to download your application Adobe Media Encoder if you have not already done so, from the Adobe Creative Cloud Desktop console. If you have already done so, the word Install will be replaced by the word Open. Media Encoder is an ideal and easy to learn application which is suitable for beginners who are not familiar with the more advanced applications like Premiere Pro and After Effects but just want to quickly render some videos to an .mp4 file. Refer to Figure 6-1.

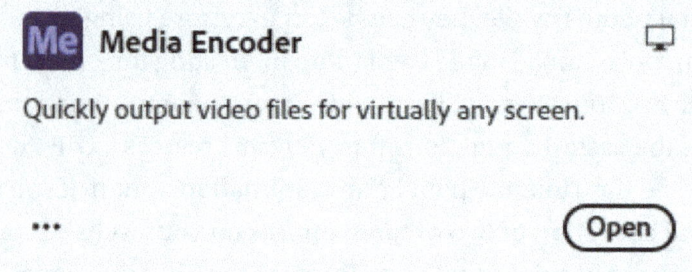

Figure 6-1. *Creative Cloud Adobe Media Encoder*

Overview of the Timeline Panel

Back in Photoshop, let's now explore how to use the Timeline panel. The Window ➤ Timeline panel is for beginner artists and is a very helpful panel if you are interested in both digitized photos, film restoration, and animation. Refer to Figure 6-2.

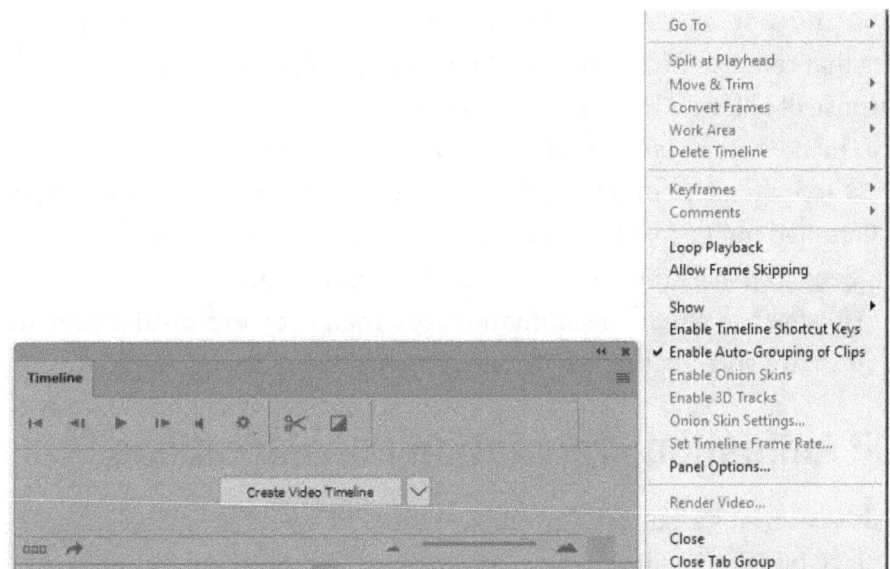

Figure 6-2. Photoshop Timeline panel and its menu

In my book, *Graphics and Multimedia for the Web with Adobe Creative Cloud*, I talk a bit about using video you shot with your digital camera, working with actual film clips and tracks. However, here our focus is on animation of still photos. Learning how to do this is ideal when actual historical footage is nonexistent, but you still want to tell your story.

Nevertheless, before you start to create any animation, there are some things to consider.

Animations (And Preparation)

Before creation of any animation, it is important, as you have seen in Volume 1 and this volume, to make sure that the image that you plan to use is fully restored.

Remember, you can do that using your various healing tools such as the Clone stamp tool found in the Tools panel.

CHAPTER 6 CREATING A PARALLAX: BRING YOUR VINTAGE OR HISTORICAL PHOTOS TO LIFE

In the process, you would also create selections for masking an area that requires healing or use the masks on adjustment layers for the purpose of color correcting your images.

The next step may be adding various filters as required.

Once you have completed this work, you will want to keep the original unflattened image (.psd) with all the layers visible and available, should you need to make adjustments for another project later on.

However, to create the animation, you then need to consider what to do next. Are you creating a GIF animation gallery or a video animation?

GIF Animation Preparation Considerations

In this case, let's assume that you have three images that you want to place into your gallery. These could be on any topic (e.g., family, pets, landscapes, travel). Once you know your theme, here are some considerations to take.

1. Create a copy of each of these photos and flatten the image. If you have been following my recommendations throughout Volume 1 and this volume, currently these photos will likely be at a resolution of 300ppi and in the color mode of RGB. The color mode of RGB (profile sRGB) is good for animations as they will likely appear on a website; however, the resolution for the animation is too high.

2. You could, at this point, lower the resolution of the image using Image ➤ Image Size to 72ppi. We will look at each example on how to reduce the resolution to 72ppi for both the animations shortly and take into consideration scaling as well. However, before you do that to each image, you need to consider what will be the dimensions of the GIF animation width and height overall.

3. GIF animations can be in a variety of sizes and be square or rectangular, but this can all depend on the area you plan to fill on your web/social media site with your gallery image. A size like 720px X 480px @ 72ppi might be a good size to experiment with, but you can always make the size custom if this is too large for the area you plan to fill, or it may be viewed on a mobile phone. Make sure to determine this size first and then go back to your gallery images to see if they will fit or require some scaling, as we will see shortly.

4. Make sure that the images you plan to use are also the orientation of all landscape or all portrait as this will make it much easier to scale them later on.

Video Parallax Animation Preparation Considerations

Much of what I have described in the previous section also applies to your video animation as well, in regard to resolution, which will need to be altered from 300ppi to 72ppi at some point. You also want to make sure the color mode remains in RGB.

However, if you plan to create a video timeline which would be an .mp4 file that might appear on your web site, part of a slideshow presentation, or on the YouTube site, then you need to consider a larger dimension size like HDTV 1920 px X 1080px @72ppi which would be a better option. But keep in mind that this is also dependent on the size and quality of the source images you are working with so you may have to work with a smaller sized file. In this situation, a landscape orientation is best. However, unlike the GIF animation, each of your initial separate overlay images does not need to be any particular orientation, as we will see shortly, because some may include layer masks and selections that will be covering certain areas.

Additional Considerations for Choosing Parallax Images

For the Video Parallax Project, in order to create a short animation, we will need to consider what kinds of photos work best for parallax. Doing this research now can save you time later, so you don't waste time experimenting with photographs that may not allow you to achieve your desired outcome.

Some things to look for in photos that can be used for potential parallaxes are

- For the video animation, you can use single image to create an expansion, but if you have multiple images of the same scene, that will work as well. This is helpful when you need to capture details of the background that in some images may be blocked by a person or object. I will discuss that more as we work through the project and the output render options when we get to that section in the chapter.

- Look for unique historical content or landscape scenes that are not overly cluttered with people or items that are blocking the main content or background.

- A large scene, either square or in landscape view, is the best kind of dimension to work with. Narrow portrait images are not ideal unless you can build more background around the image using Edit ➤ Content-Aware Fill workspace or using the steps in Volume 1 to create a Panorama.

- The image contains various areas of depth that can be used as transition points that can be separated later into sections such as foreground, midground, background, or even sky. Note that while most images can be scaled large or small as one unit, the point of the parallax is to be able to define sections that move at slightly different scales or rotation so that the animation appears similar to how a camera would move or pan across a scene.

- If there are people or objects in the forefront, they should be easily selected with the selection tool and masked so that they can be moved as part of the animation, on a separate layer, such as moving closer or farther away or to the left or the right of the image. If parts of the person or object are missing, then it is more difficult to create an animation with a natural movement throughout the scene, should they need to expand or shrink at some point. If you plan to add a new person to that scene, be mindful of that person's standing perspective, scaling, and eye orientation in the scene. Viewers of the video will notice that something is out of place if the person or even a new object is out of perspective in the scene, if they were not part of the original image.

- In the case of keeping the original person in the image, you will want to select them and place them on their own layer. However, the area behind the person or object that you selected should also be easy to add information back into whether it be with the Clone Stamp tool, Remove tool, or Edit ➤ Content-Aware Fill workspace as seen in Volume 1. Photos where you must guess what might be behind the object may be tricky to figure out, but you don't want areas of the scene to be missing or not evenly blended, especially where movement is happening. Ideally, if you can use additional images of the same scene, this could be helpful to fill in missing gaps. However, with older black-and-white photos, the chances of that are not as common. With color images, if possible, incorporate images with similar colors and perspectives so that the scene looks natural. Also, be aware of the areas of the photo that are in and out of focus. Later, when creating the animation, you can add areas that are, for a time, out of focus but come back into focus as you move in the scene.

- Areas that might be easy to fill in missing details could be water, areas with a lot of trees or sky, and areas of repeating patterns like walls, floors, or solid fabrics. However, in areas where there are crowds of people covering the main structure, this may not work as well.

Don't be discouraged if some images you have don't lend themselves to complex parallax animations. Every project to build a parallax animation will be different, and so you should take time to review your images and practice with a variety of examples.

Creating a New File for the Animation

When you need to create a new file to hold the layers of the animation, go to File ➤ New.

When creating a New Document, rather than choosing the Print Tab for document presets, this time choose a preset from the Film and Video Tab. Adjust the settings slightly and then click Create. Refer to Figure 6-3.

CHAPTER 6   CREATING A PARALLAX: BRING YOUR VINTAGE OR HISTORICAL PHOTOS TO LIFE

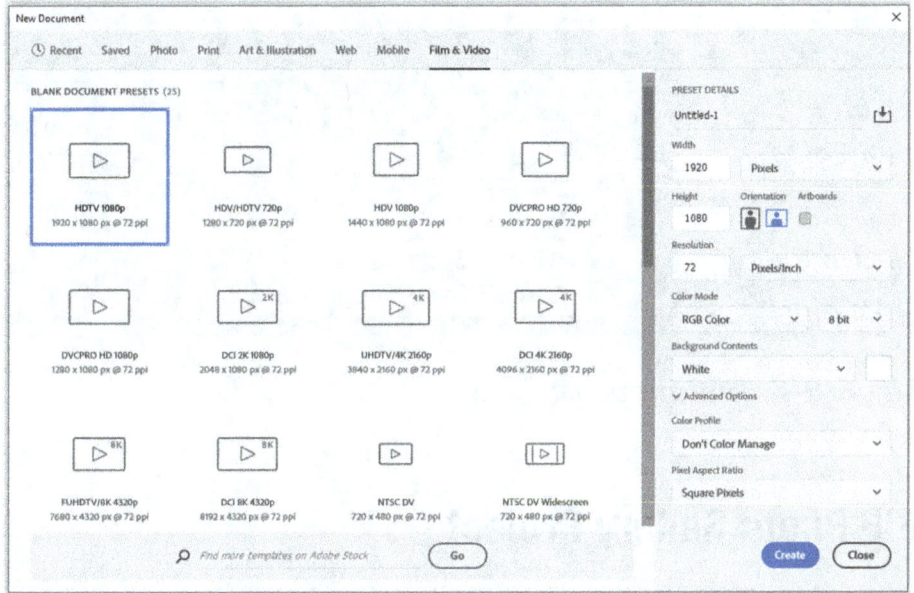

Figure 6-3. *New Document dialog box*

We will look at some specific options and layouts for each project, in a moment.

Timeline Panel and Considerations

Coming back to the Photoshop Timeline panel, there are two kinds of animations to consider when working in Photoshop with your scanned images: GIF animation and video animation.

We can use the button list in the center of Timeline panel to set either one. Refer to Figure 6-4.

CHAPTER 6 CREATING A PARALLAX: BRING YOUR VINTAGE OR HISTORICAL PHOTOS TO LIFE

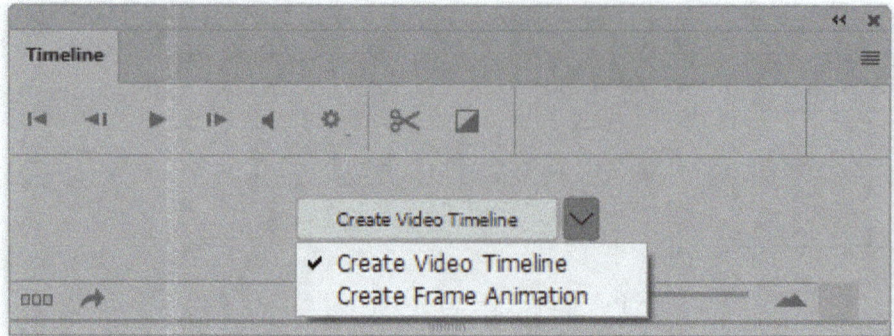

Figure 6-4. Timeline panel

GIF Photo Gallery Project

As noted for the Gallery project, we will work with three images that are each on their own layer in the file and make them fade from one to the next. Then, from the Timeline panel, we will choose the Create Frame Animation to start the process. Refer to Figure 6-5.

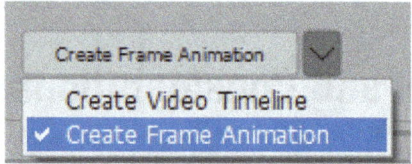

Figure 6-5. Timeline panel settings button to create a Frame Animation

To begin, let's look at the file in the folder called **Gallery**. In this folder are three photos that have been color corrected, and then each image was flattened. In this case, I left them at 300 ppi but as mentioned I could scale them to 72ppi using the Image ➤ Image Size dialog box with resample unchecked and then checked to adjust for pixel with height and resolution. However, in this case, I will not, because, while the images are

CHAPTER 6 CREATING A PARALLAX: BRING YOUR VINTAGE OR HISTORICAL PHOTOS TO LIFE

all landscape, I may want to scale them initially in the new GIF animation file to fit and move them around if they require some centering. Refer to Figure 6-6.

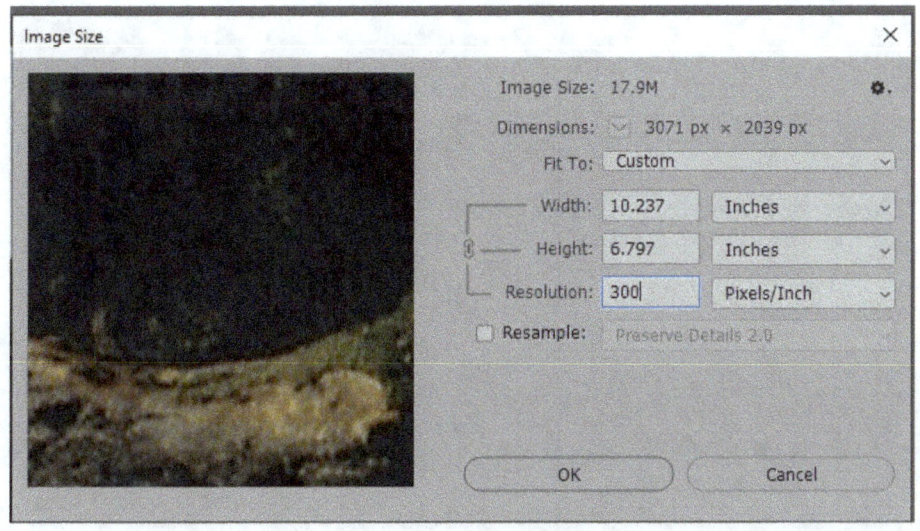

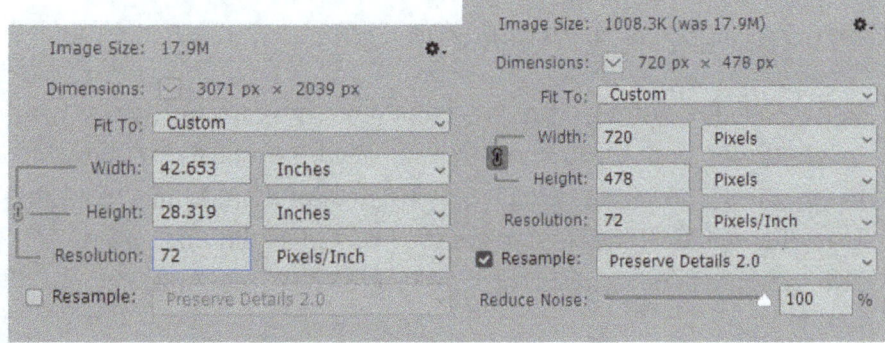

Figure 6-6. Image Size Dialog box settings

Create a New Document

Now using File ➤ New, create a new document from the Film and Video tab that I chose, for this example NTSC DV 720px X 480px@72ppi. Refer to Figure 6-7.

CHAPTER 6   CREATING A PARALLAX: BRING YOUR VINTAGE OR HISTORICAL PHOTOS TO LIFE

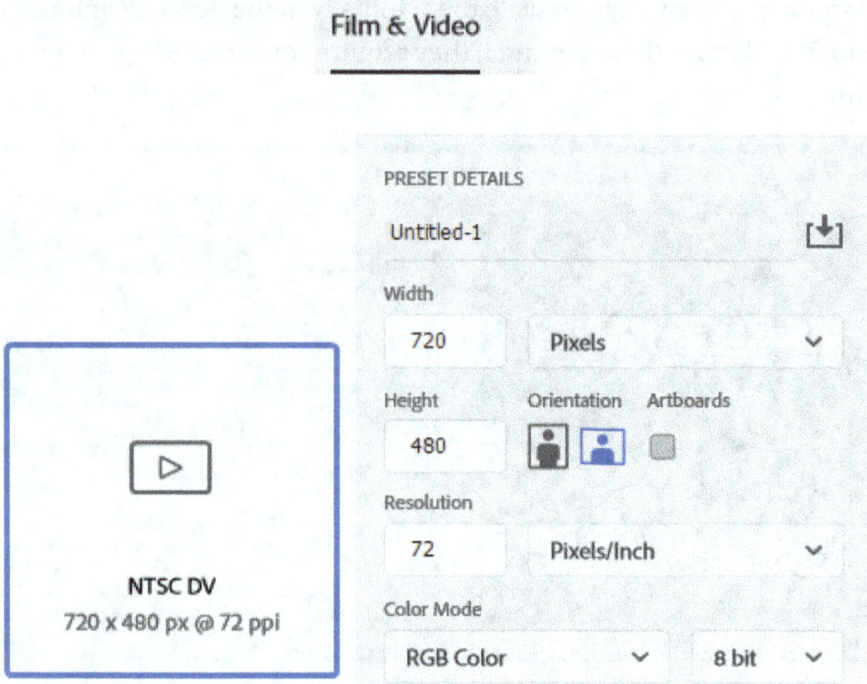

Figure 6-7. New Document dialog box settings

Remember, for your own project, you do not have to choose this width and height dimension. If you know the size of your project, put that width and height dimension in instead; it may be smaller than mine. Figure this out with your web designer first to get the exact pixel dimensions.

Orientation will be landscape, color mode RGB Color 8bit. Refer to Figure 6-7.

Background contents: White. However, now I will modify the preset settings because it was going to be for the Web, not actually film. I set the Color Profile to Working sRGB as I did in the past and set the Pixel Aspect Ratio back to Square Pixels. I then clicked the Create button. Refer to Figure 6-8.

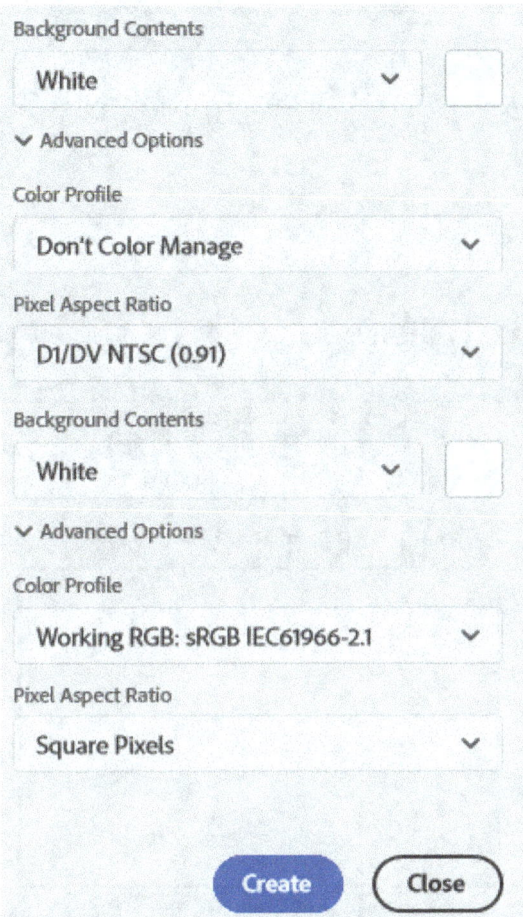

Figure 6-8. *New Document dialog box original Advanced Option settings now modified to custom settings*

Note that this file may appear with guides which can be helpful if you plan to incorporate text and need guidance for placement within select boundaries so that text is orientated correctly. However, we will just View ➤ Guides ➤ Clear the guides to remove them in this example as text is not a focus of this book. Refer to Figure 6-9.

CHAPTER 6 CREATING A PARALLAX: BRING YOUR VINTAGE OR HISTORICAL PHOTOS TO LIFE

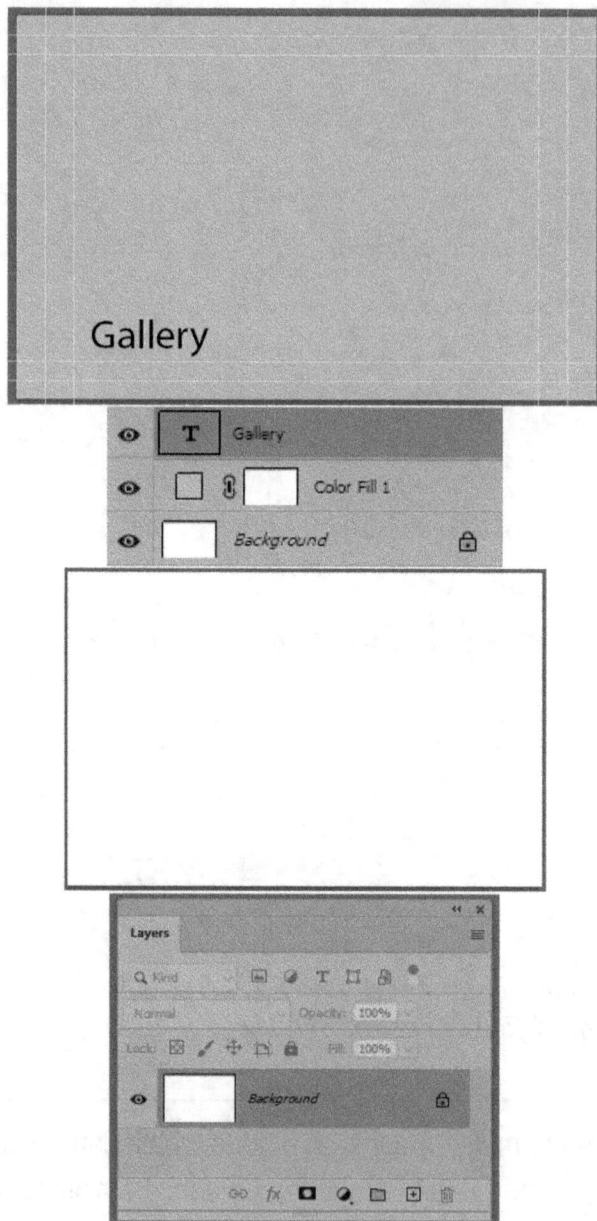

Figure 6-9. *New Document with and without guides and the Layers panel*

You can save this file as a .psd as your work, but you can also start with an Image ➤ Duplicate of my file **animation_gallery_start.psd** if you need a reference point.

In the Gallery folder, File ➤ Open each of my three images so that they are available to you as you work. These have been named **image_1.psd**, **image_2.psd**, and **image_3.psd**. You do not have to number them as I did, but this can help when you want to figure out the order of the sequence you want. Refer to Figure 6-10.

CHAPTER 6　CREATING A PARALLAX: BRING YOUR VINTAGE OR HISTORICAL PHOTOS TO LIFE

Figure 6-10. *Images to use as part of the gallery*

I will then copy each background layer into the New file. Remember to copy a single background layer from each file by choosing Select ➤ All or Ctrl/CMD+A. Then Edit ➤ Copy (Ctrl/CMD+C). Then go to the new gallery animation file and choose Edit ➤ Paste or (Ctrl/CMD +V). This pastes the image on top of the background layer. Refer to Figure 6-11.

CHAPTER 6   CREATING A PARALLAX: BRING YOUR VINTAGE OR HISTORICAL PHOTOS TO LIFE

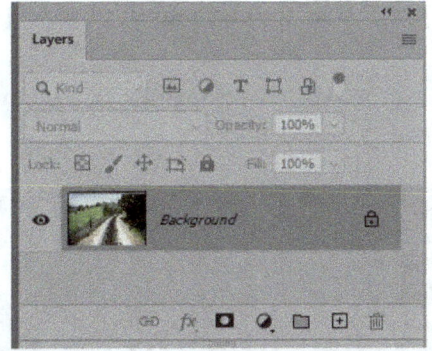

Figure 6-11. *Adding Images to the Layer panel*

CHAPTER 6   CREATING A PARALLAX: BRING YOUR VINTAGE OR HISTORICAL PHOTOS TO LIFE

I started with image 1 and then repeated these steps with image 2 and then image 3.

I should, excluding the white background, now have three layers. Refer to Figure 6-12.

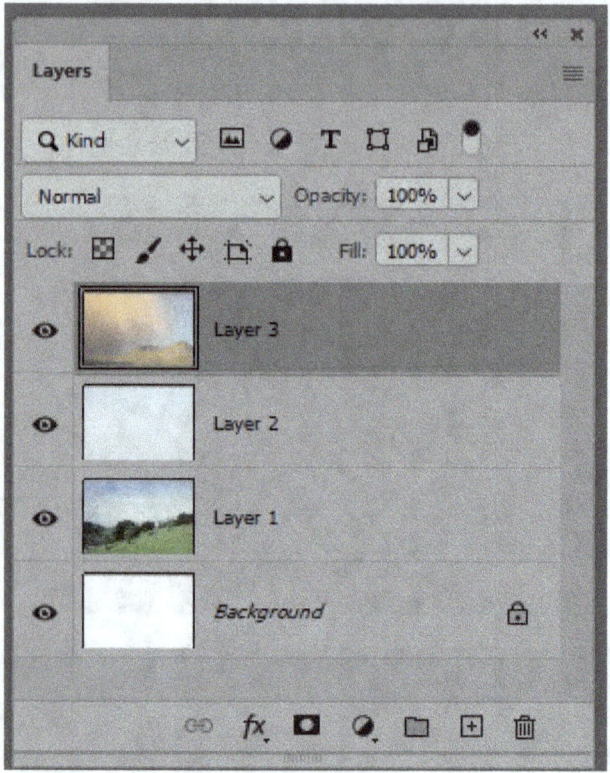

Figure 6-12. *Adding All the images to the Layers panel*

You can, at this point, close the gallery images as you do not need them anymore, but keep the copy of your **animation_gallery_start.psd** file open and File ➤ Save, as you proceed to the next step.

In your case, you can always drag the images up and down in the Layers panel if you need to reorder as I have done here, putting Layer 1 at the top, next Layer 2, and then Layer 3 below. Keep the Background as the lowest level. Refer to Figure 6-13.

830

CHAPTER 6   CREATING A PARALLAX: BRING YOUR VINTAGE OR HISTORICAL PHOTOS TO LIFE

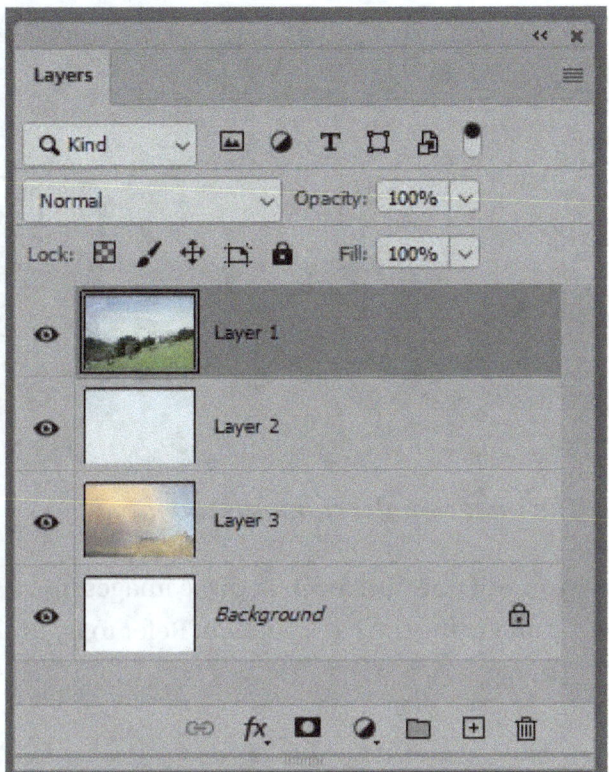

Figure 6-13. *Reordering the Layers in the Layers panel*

Note that at this moment the images are oversized because they came from a file that was 300ppi and while they are 72ppi in this new document, they are too large for the current dimensions. Now you are sizing them down to match the new canvas width and height. Refer to Figure 6-14.

CHAPTER 6 CREATING A PARALLAX: BRING YOUR VINTAGE OR HISTORICAL PHOTOS TO LIFE

Figure 6-14. *The image on the canvas is too large*

In this case, you will now turn each of these images into a smart object Layer by selecting and using the Layers menu. Refer to Figure 6-15.

CHAPTER 6   CREATING A PARALLAX: BRING YOUR VINTAGE OR HISTORICAL PHOTOS TO LIFE

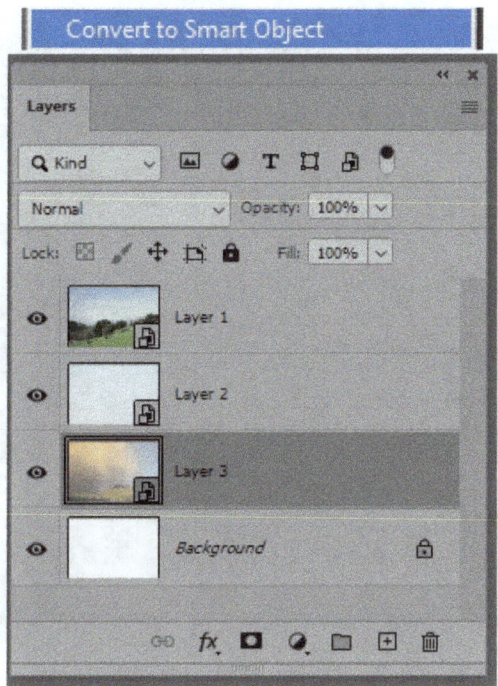

Figure 6-15. *Converting Layers to Smart Object Layers*

Now you will scale them. Start with selecting Layer 1, and then you can repeat these steps for Layer 2 and Layer 3.

Select each one at a time and Edit ➤ Free Transform (Ctrl/CMD+T), and then, using the bounding box handles, scale the images so that they fit the area of the canvas. I use the lower right handle to drag and scale my first image layer to about 41.08% for width and height maintaining aspect ratio link. Refer to Figure 6-16.

CHAPTER 6   CREATING A PARALLAX: BRING YOUR VINTAGE OR HISTORICAL PHOTOS TO LIFE

Figure 6-16. Scaling Gallery Images using Free Transform

If some of the image overlaps off the canvas, that is OK as we will adjust placement later. Click the Check on the Options bar panel to commit your scale settings. Refer to Figure 6-17.

CHAPTER 6   CREATING A PARALLAX: BRING YOUR VINTAGE OR HISTORICAL PHOTOS TO LIFE

Figure 6-17. *Confirming the scale of the gallery image and the result on the layer*

Now repeat those steps with Layer 2 and Layer 3. You can first temporarily turn off the previous layers' visibility if you find it easier to scale, and then Edit ➤ Free Transform. Refer to Figure 6-18.

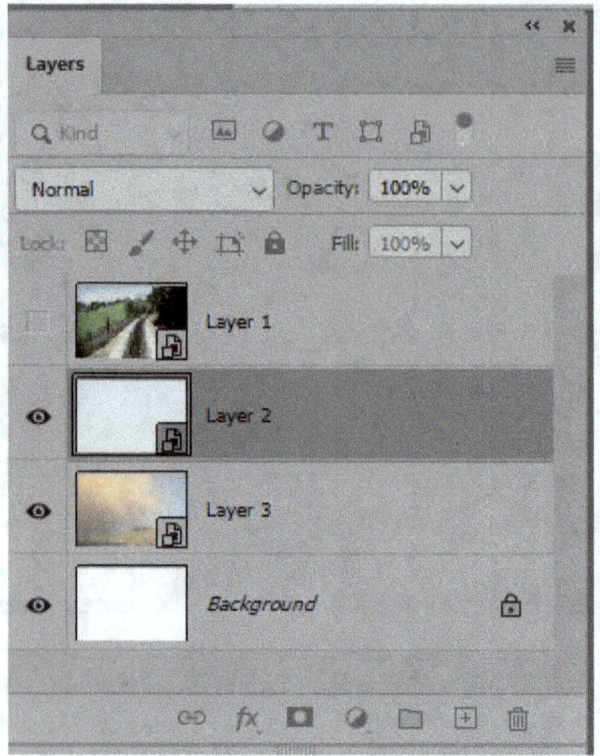

Figure 6-18. *Selecting the next layer to Free Transform*

Layer 2 was scaled to 23.67% for width and height. Refer to Figure 6-19.

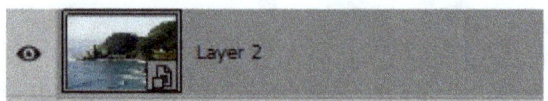

Figure 6-19. *Layer with scaling adjusted*

Layer 3 was scaled to 41.05% for width and height. Refer to Figure 6-20.

Check the Confirm in the Options bar panel after each scale. Refer back to Figure 6-17.

CHAPTER 6   CREATING A PARALLAX: BRING YOUR VINTAGE OR HISTORICAL PHOTOS TO LIFE

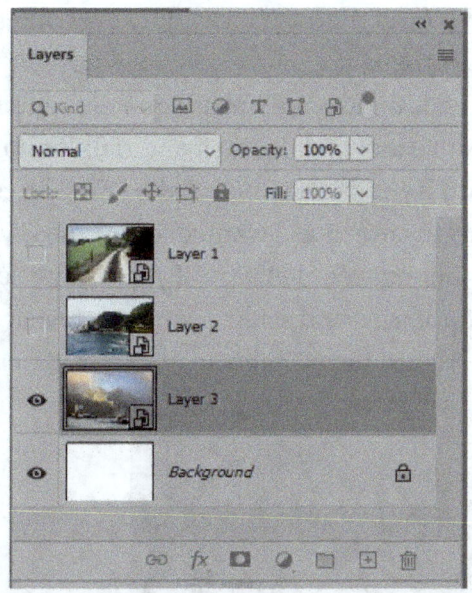

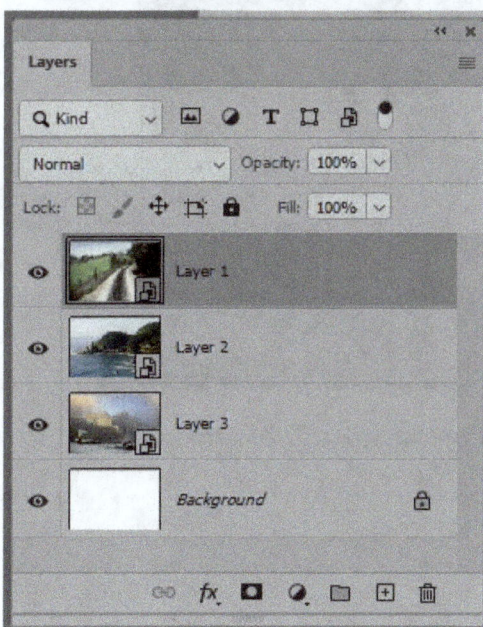

Figure 6-20. *Layer with scaling adjusted and then visibility returned to all layers*

CHAPTER 6   CREATING A PARALLAX: BRING YOUR VINTAGE OR HISTORICAL PHOTOS TO LIFE

Once done, turn on all the layers' visibility eyes and select Layer 1 again. Refer to Figure 6-20.

If you find that your images are not adequately centered, you can afterward use the Move tool and your left and right or up and down arrow keys on the keyboard if you need to nudge the image to center or adjust the placement. I did this to Layer 1 as I wanted less of the sky and more of the rail track, but the other images I left as is. If you cannot see those layers, turn off the visibility temporarily, and select each layer one at a time to nudge it into place and then return the visibility to all layers. Refer to Figure 6-21.

Figure 6-21. *Using the Move Tool and keyboard to nudge images into the correct locations*

838

Once you have centered all three images, you can start to create the animation with the Timeline panel.

Note that if you need to at some point turn your image into a normal layer, select it and choose Rasterize Layer from the Layers menu, but for this example, you can leave each layer as a Smart Object layer. Refer to Figure 6-22.

Figure 6-22. Layers panel menu Rasterize Layer command

Creating the GIF Animation with the Timeline Panel

In this example, you would now select, from the Timeline panel, the Create a Frame Animation option.

You will start with a default single frame; in this case all the Layers in the Layers panel are visible. Click the button to confirm and view the new frame. Refer to Figure 6-23.

CHAPTER 6   CREATING A PARALLAX: BRING YOUR VINTAGE OR HISTORICAL PHOTOS TO LIFE

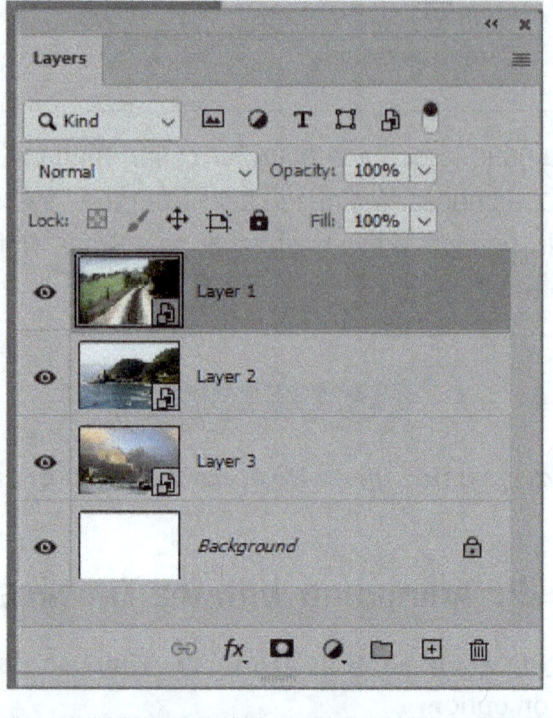

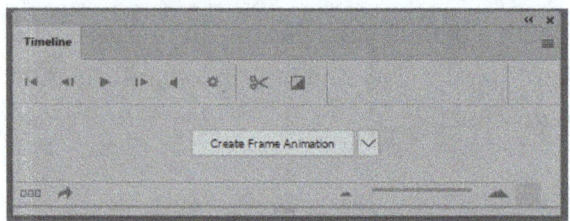

Figure 6-23. *Layers panel with frame animation set in the Timeline panel*

CHAPTER 6   CREATING A PARALLAX: BRING YOUR VINTAGE OR HISTORICAL PHOTOS TO LIFE

Next, you want to create a new identical frame; this will be Frame 2 where the second image will appear. To do that, click the new frame (Duplicates selected frames) button. Refer to Figure 6-24.

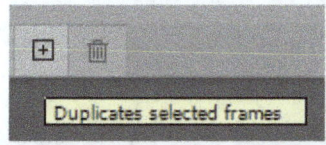

Figure 6-24. Timeline panel duplicating selected frames

With this new Frame 2 selected, in the Layers panel, now turn off the visibility of Layer 1. Refer to Figure 6-25.

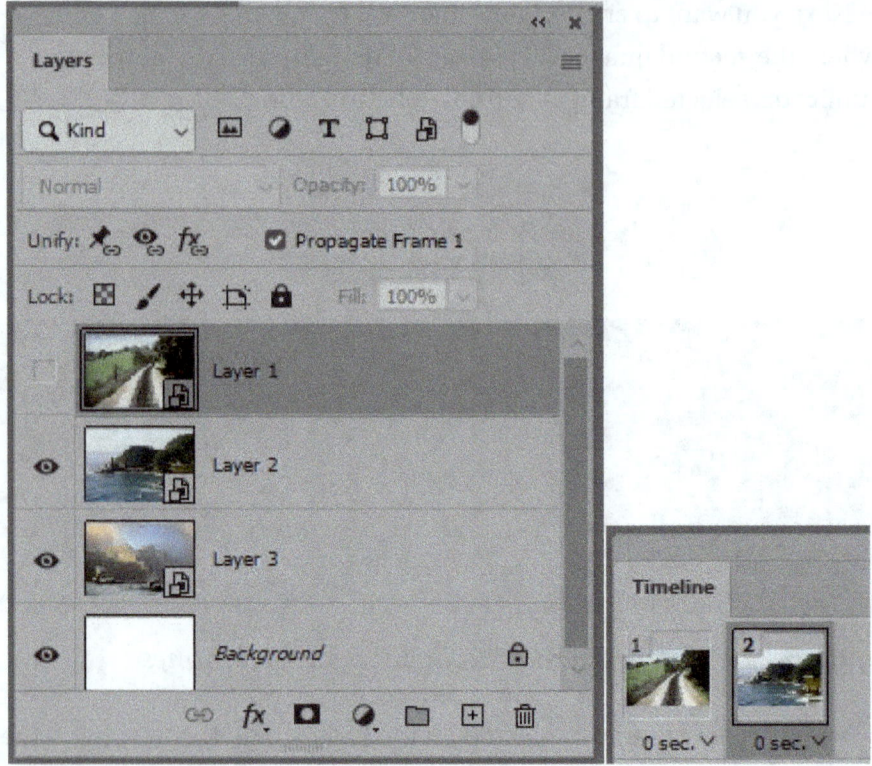

Figure 6-25. *Layers panel hiding layer and Timeline panel with changes*

This creates a frame transition.

Now with Frame 2 selected, create another frame, this time turning off Layer 2 in the Layers panel. Refer to Figure 6-26.

CHAPTER 6 CREATING A PARALLAX: BRING YOUR VINTAGE OR HISTORICAL PHOTOS TO LIFE

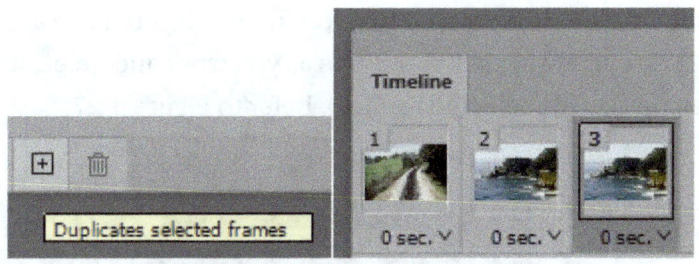

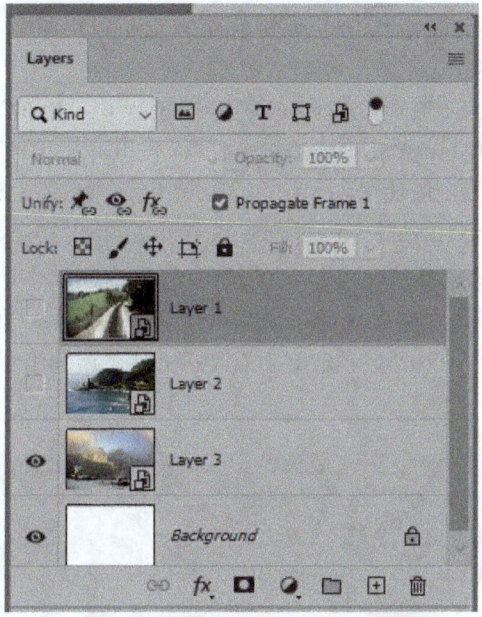

Figure 6-26. *Timeline and Layers panel with changes and three frames*

You should now have three transition frames. If you make a mistake as you work, you can always select a frame as you work and delete, using the trash can icon (Delete selected frames). Refer to Figure 6-27.

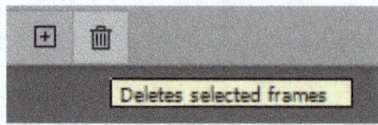

Figure 6-27. *Timeline panel delete selected frames*

Or you can click each frame and observe which layers have been turned off or on and adjust the visibility accordingly. In this case, make sure you have the same three frames. Refer to Figure 6-26.

In this case, the three images can be previewed quickly using the play button and then stop using the stop button. You can also use the addition buttons to select the first frame, previous frame, or next frame as you test. Hover over the icon if you need to refer to a specific button. Refer to Figure 6-28.

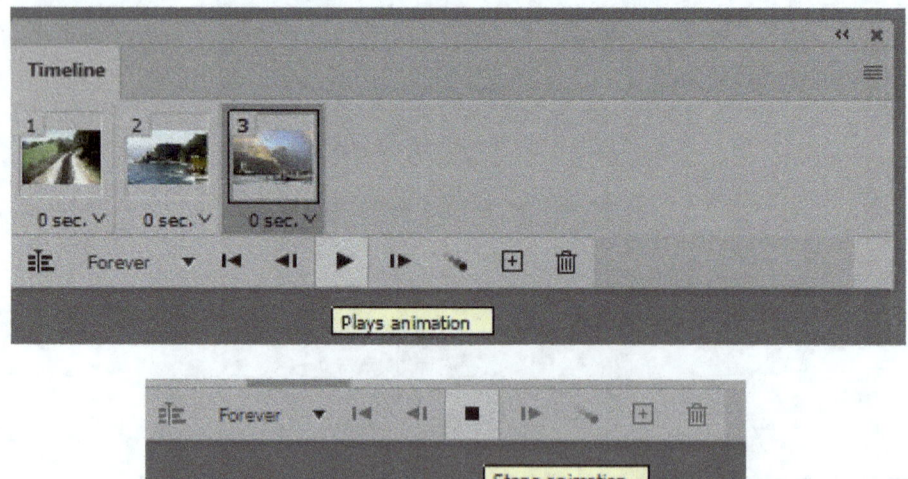

Figure 6-28. *Timeline panel stopping and starting the animation*

CHAPTER 6   CREATING A PARALLAX: BRING YOUR VINTAGE OR HISTORICAL PHOTOS TO LIFE

If you plan to make a cycling animation as we are doing here, then create one more frame at the end with all the layers on again. Refer to Figure 6-29.

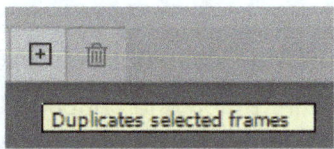

Figure 6-29. *Timeline panel adding a frame and adjusting the layer visibility in the Layers panel*

Another way you can do that is by selecting the first frame, duplicating the selected frame, and then selecting and dragging it to the last frame. Now you will have a total of four frames.

Tip In situations where you need to reverse frames, you can Shift select several or all frames and choose that option from the Timeline menu. Additional settings can always be found in the Timeline menu. Refer to Figure 6-30.

CHAPTER 6 CREATING A PARALLAX: BRING YOUR VINTAGE OR HISTORICAL PHOTOS TO LIFE

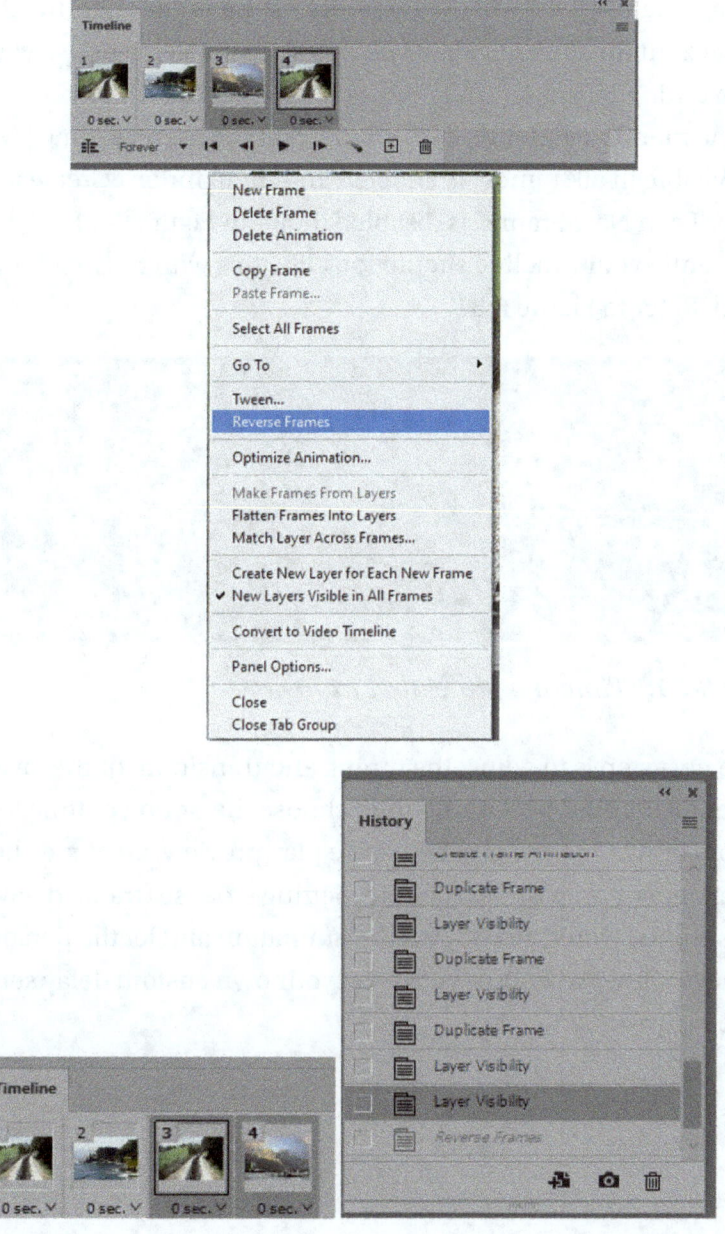

Figure 6-30. *Timeline panel and menu and adjustments with the History panel*

CHAPTER 6　CREATING A PARALLAX: BRING YOUR VINTAGE OR HISTORICAL PHOTOS TO LIFE

In this example, we will not be reversing the order. Click the Reverse Frames text in the menu again if you made that mistake or use your History panel to undo that step.

In the menu, make sure, in this case, that the menu setting "New Layers Visible in all frames" is enabled and then option "Create a New Layer for Each New Frame" is disabled. Refer to Figure 6-30.

Currently your timeline should look like this with the first frame selected. Refer to Figure 6-31.

Figure 6-31. *Timeline panel first frame*

The next step is to adjust the timing and transition for the layer images.

To adjust timing, you would then choose the option of time for when the photo moves to the next. This, if we play preview, creates a short pause and then moves onto the next photo. Setting a pause (frame delay) of at least 2 seconds would slow down the animation and let the person see the next image. Other will allow you to set your own custom delay settings. Refer to Figure 6-32.

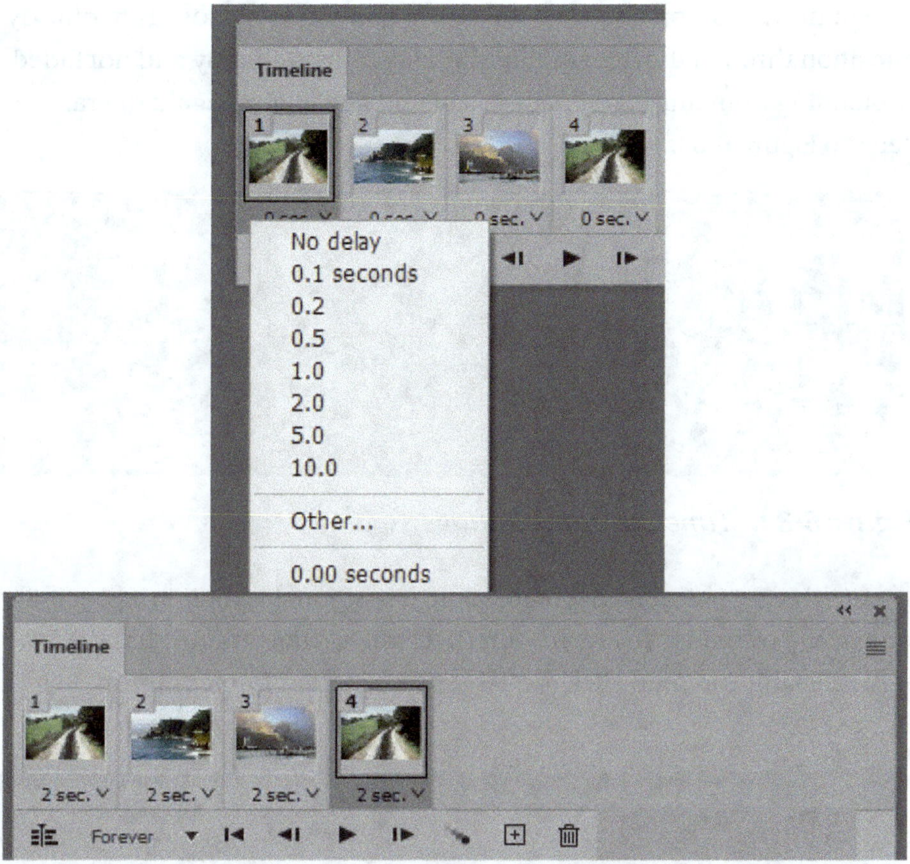

CHAPTER 6   CREATING A PARALLAX: BRING YOUR VINTAGE OR HISTORICAL PHOTOS TO LIFE

Figure 6-32. *Timeline panel adjusting timing*

The Looping Option (Loop count) is set to Forever, but you can set the cycle to other options like once, three times, or other as an amount of your choosing. Refer to Figure 6-33.

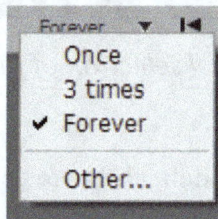

Figure 6-33. *Timeline panel adjusting looping*

For now, leave on a setting of Forever, and this will allow us to quickly transition through the images, but the transition is choppy and not faded or blending from image to image as I would like. Return again to Frame 1. Refer to Figure 6-34.

Figure 6-34. Timeline panel settings

In this case, we need to create some transitional frames in a process known as Tweening. To create your first tween, select frames 1 and 2 by Shift+clicking and then click the Tweens animation frames button. Refer to Figure 6-35.

Figure 6-35. Timeline panel selection of two frames and the tween button

The dialog box will now open, and here you will set how many frames you want in between the two frames and what you expect them to do. Refer to Figure 6-36.

CHAPTER 6   CREATING A PARALLAX: BRING YOUR VINTAGE OR HISTORICAL PHOTOS TO LIFE

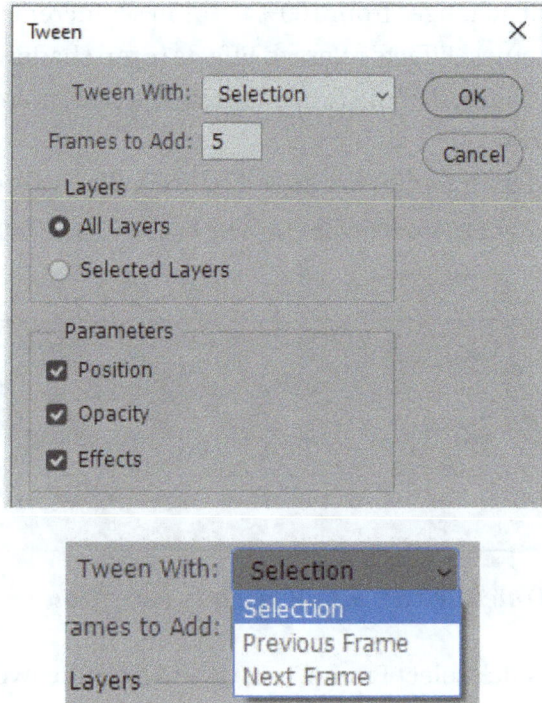

Figure 6-36. *Tween dialog box and settings*

The tween dialog box lets you tween with the selection, previous frame or next frame. Use Selection.

You can then add how many frames you want; between 5 and 8 will make a fairly smooth transition – the range is 1–999. I will try 5 to keep the file size small but you may prefer 8 or more.

This is not the same as frame rate in Video, as we will look at later.

Choose Layers in this case as we are working with "All layers" and not the "Selected Layers" option. Refer to Figure 6-36

Then choose the Parameters. In this case we are allowing such things as position, opacity, and effects to be altered as we transition from one frame to the next. Position would refer to the layers up, down, left, or right movements but not rotation. Opacity for the fade is the most important.

CHAPTER 6 CREATING A PARALLAX: BRING YOUR VINTAGE OR HISTORICAL PHOTOS TO LIFE

The layer's opacity changes from 100% to 0% in set increments based on the number of frames. Effects refers to Effects (drop shadow) applied to the layer that may be altered in the transition. In this case, there are no effects applied to any layer.

Click OK and then frames are added between the two current frames; in this case, between Frame 1 and Frame 7 are five new frames. Refer to Figure 6-37.

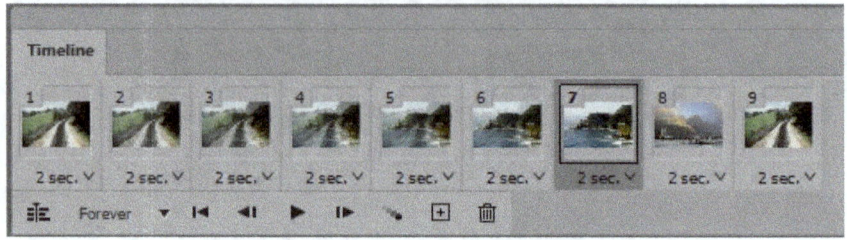

Figure 6-37. *Timeline panel and extra tween frames*

Then Shift + click select Frame 7 and 8 and click the tween button again using the same settings. Click OK. Refer to Figure 6-36 and Figure 6-38.

Figure 6-38. *Timeline panel and frames selected*

CHAPTER 6   CREATING A PARALLAX: BRING YOUR VINTAGE OR HISTORICAL PHOTOS TO LIFE

And repeat these steps with now Frames 13 and 14, and you should have a total of 19 frames. Refer to Figure 6-39.

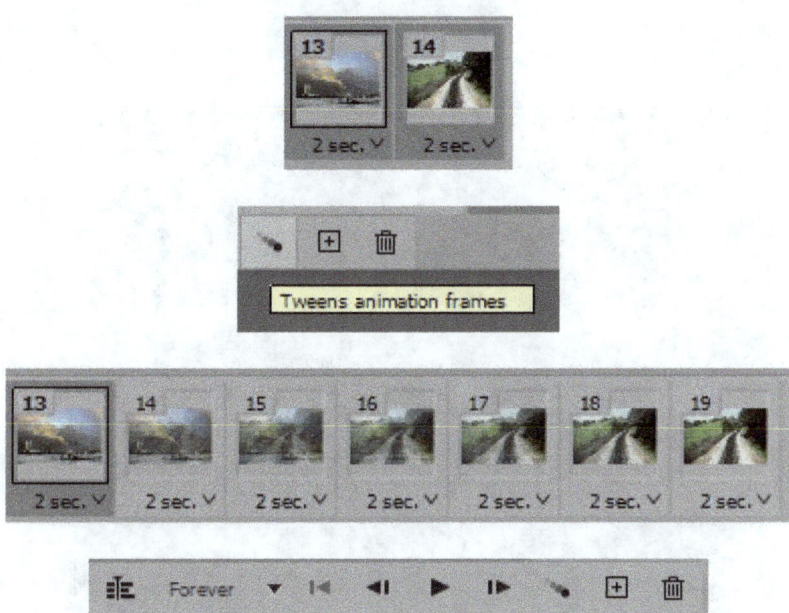

Figure 6-39. *Timeline panel and frames selected and new tween created*

You do not need to add any more tweens as you will be cycling back to the first images. To test, press Play and preview your animation. Click stop.

In this case, the 2 seconds between each tween image is too slow.

Set the timing for those frames back to 0 or no delay. These would be Frames 2–6, 8–12, and 14–18. You can also set 19 to no delay as we are repeating the cycle forever. If you were cycling once, you may just leave it on 2 seconds along with Frames 1, 7, and 13. Refer to Figure 6-40.

CHAPTER 6   CREATING A PARALLAX: BRING YOUR VINTAGE OR HISTORICAL PHOTOS TO LIFE

Figure 6-40. *Timeline panel with time settings and final frame*

Press Play and Stop again. If you are happy with the result, you can continue on to the next section or use your History panel if you need to undo any steps. Refer to Figure 6-41.

Figure 6-41. *Timeline panel play animation*

CHAPTER 6   CREATING A PARALLAX: BRING YOUR VINTAGE OR HISTORICAL PHOTOS TO LIFE

Note: Use your menu to check that your Timeline menu Optimize Animation dialog box settings are set to Bounding Box and Redundant Pixel Removal. This will not affect the current file, but later when you create the final GIF animation. Refer to Figure 6-42.

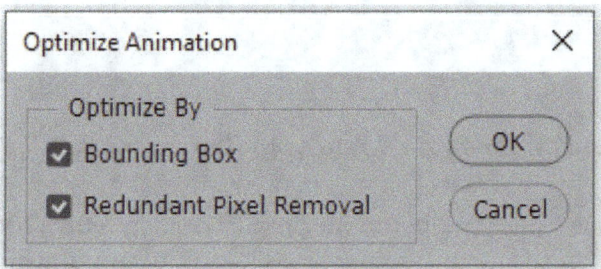

Figure 6-42. *Optimize Animation dialog box*

Another setting that you may want to check is when you right-click each frame, they are set to Automatic. Other options in this area are Do Not dispose and Dispose, as they can affect how the animation renders and plays if it contains transparent areas. For these examples, leave on Automatic as we are only affecting the layers' overall opacity in the transition and there are no solidly transparent areas. Refer to Figure 6-43.

Figure 6-43. *Timeline panel additional frame settings*

Click back Frame 1. Refer to Figure 6-44.

855

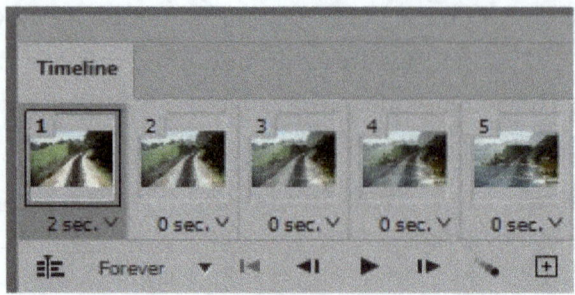

Figure 6-44. *Timeline panel return to first frame*

Then File ➤ Save the document (.psd). You can return to this file at any time if you need to edit the gallery. You can look at my file **animation_gallery_final.psd** if you need a reference.

Make sure your Timeline panel remains visible.

Save for Web the GIF Animation

You will now complete the saving of the GIF animation using the File ➤ Export ➤ Save for Web (Legacy) dialog box. Alt/Option +Shift +Ctrl/CMD +S.

This is the only way to save the GIF animation as the option File ➤ Export ➤ Export As only saves static GIF files and will not create an animation, and we will look at in Chapter 7. Now refer to Figure 6-45.

CHAPTER 6 CREATING A PARALLAX: BRING YOUR VINTAGE OR HISTORICAL PHOTOS TO LIFE

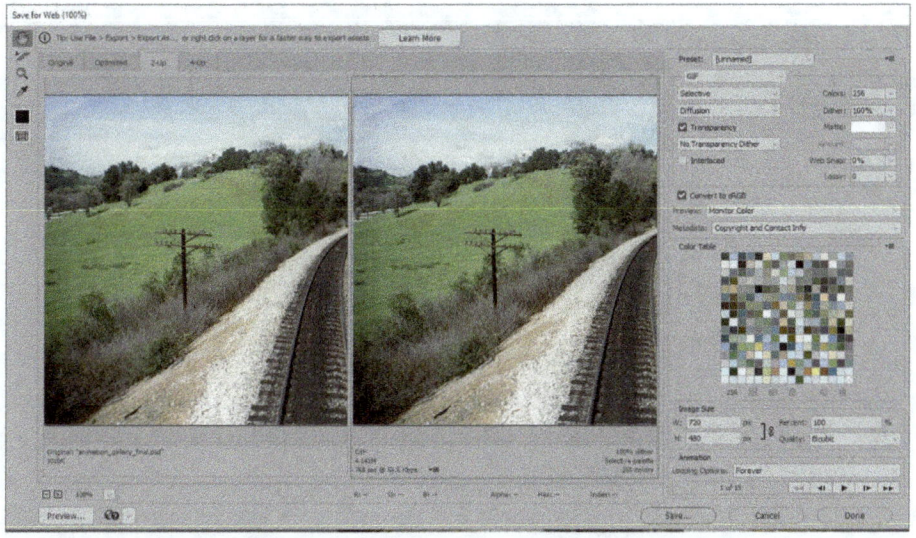

Figure 6-45. *Save for Web dialog box overview*

Once you have entered the dialog box, I will now briefly go over the settings I would use for this animation, but you may need to adjust your settings based on your project and the level of image quality you require.

In all cases on the right, ensure that you have the Optimize file format set to GIF so that you have the animation option. Refer to Figure 6-46.

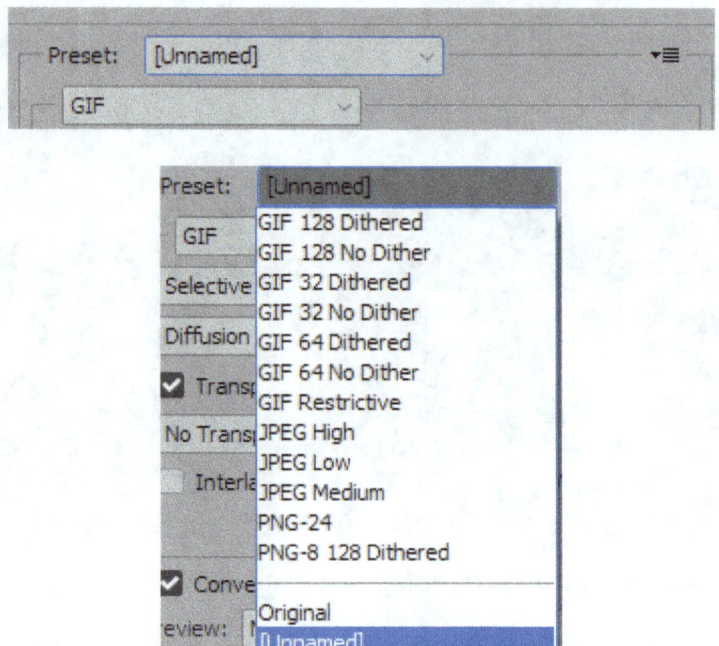

Figure 6-46. Save for Web dialog box Preset settings

Leave the preset [Unnamed] (this is the same as default), but you can choose other GIF options from this list as you would any other presets in this chapter.

You do not need to access anything from the Optimize menu. However, you can use this area to save settings later if you have a preference. Edit Output Settings is more appropriate for building a web page which in this case we are not doing. Refer to Figure 6-47.

CHAPTER 6 CREATING A PARALLAX: BRING YOUR VINTAGE OR HISTORICAL PHOTOS TO LIFE

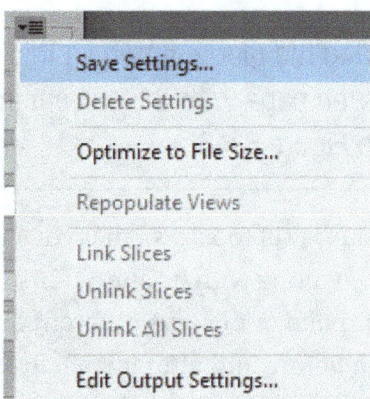

Figure 6-47. *Save for Web dialog box Menu settings*

In this case, you do not need to use any of the tools on the right hand side other than the Zoom tool (Z) and Hand tool (H), if you need to navigate around the image to compare. For the Zoom tool, hold down the Alt/Option key when you need to zoom out. Likewise, you can use the navigation buttons in the lower left. The other tools Slice Select tool, Eyedropper tool, Eyedropper color, and Toggle Slices Visibility are not required for this book and are mainly used for website design. Refer to Figure 6-48.

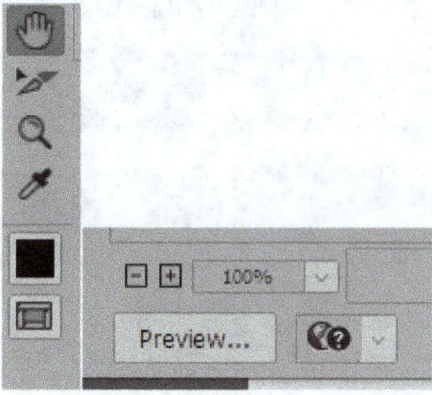

Figure 6-48. *Save for Web dialog box tools and navigation*

859

CHAPTER 6 CREATING A PARALLAX: BRING YOUR VINTAGE OR HISTORICAL PHOTOS TO LIFE

Note The preview and the globe button, in this case, are only used if you are building a web page with the current image, so you can ignore these. Refer to Figure 6-48.

In this case, the image is set to 2up so that you can view the original image and the Optimized along with its alterations. You can have up to four images (4up) if you need to observe different quality settings. But for now, 2up is best to see a before and after image. Refer to Figure 6-49.

Figure 6-49. Save for Web dialog box preview original and optimize setting summary

860

CHAPTER 6   CREATING A PARALLAX: BRING YOUR VINTAGE OR HISTORICAL PHOTOS TO LIFE

Note that because this is a GIF animation, colors will be limited as these types of animation cannot hold the same level of quality as a JPEG or PNG image. These settings are optimized to keep the animation to a small file size, so do not expect the same range of quality colors as you would with a video animation as we will look at later.

Here are the settings. I used on the right image. Refer to Figure 6-50.

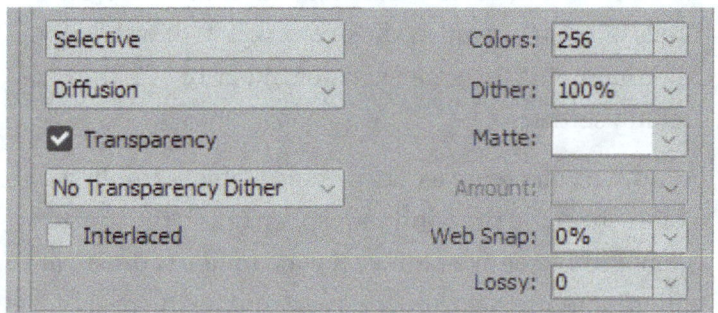

Figure 6-50. *Save for Web dialog box GIF animation settings*

Color reduction algorithm: From the list, you can set the following options: Perceptual, Selective, Adaptive, Restrictive, Custom, Black-White, Grayscale, Mac OS, and Windows. Refer to Figure 6-51.

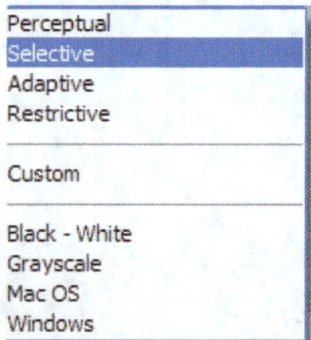

Figure 6-51. *Save for Web dialog box Color reduction algorithm options*

CHAPTER 6   CREATING A PARALLAX: BRING YOUR VINTAGE OR HISTORICAL PHOTOS TO LIFE

For color Photos, using a setting of either Perceptual, Selective, or Adaptive will produce the best results. You may need to zoom in though to see which is giving you the best color distribution.

- Perceptual gives priority to colors for which the human eye has greater sensitivity.

- Selective is similar to Perceptual but favors broader areas of color as well as the preservation of web colors and maintains the greatest color integrity. It is the default setting.

- Adaptive will create a custom color table, sampling colors from the predominant spectrum in the image, such as the greens or blues. If each image is drastically different in its spectrum, this may not be the best solution.

You can try the other options as well, but note how the quality of the image degrades for options like Restrictive in comparison with Selective. Refer to Figure 6-52.

Figure 6-52. *Save for Web dialog box Color reduction algorithm Selective (left) and (right) Restrictive*

CHAPTER 6   CREATING A PARALLAX: BRING YOUR VINTAGE OR HISTORICAL PHOTOS TO LIFE

In this case, I chose the option of Selective. However, if you are making a black-and-white animation, then maybe try the setting of Grayscale. Refer to Figure 6-53.

Figure 6-53. *Save for Web dialog box Color reduction algorithm Selective (left) and (right) Grayscale*

Note that Black-White, Mac OS, and Windows will also limit your color options as well.

Colors (2-256): By default, if you chose Selective, this is set to 256. You can use the menu to set lower options, but this will degrade the image's color. Refer to Figure 6-54.

863

CHAPTER 6 CREATING A PARALLAX: BRING YOUR VINTAGE OR HISTORICAL PHOTOS TO LIFE

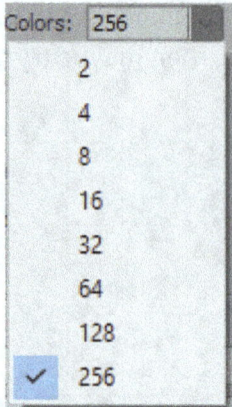

Figure 6-54. *Save for Web dialog box color reduction options*

Dither algorithm: The following options are No Dither, Diffusion, Pattern, and Noise. In this case, this type of grain or noise tricks the eye into believing there are more colors in the image than there actually are. Test each one; in my case, I found that Diffusion displaced the color fairly well randomly and prevented noticeable banding, but in other situations, you may prefer Noise. Refer to Figure 6-55 and Figure 6-56.

CHAPTER 6 CREATING A PARALLAX: BRING YOUR VINTAGE OR HISTORICAL PHOTOS TO LIFE

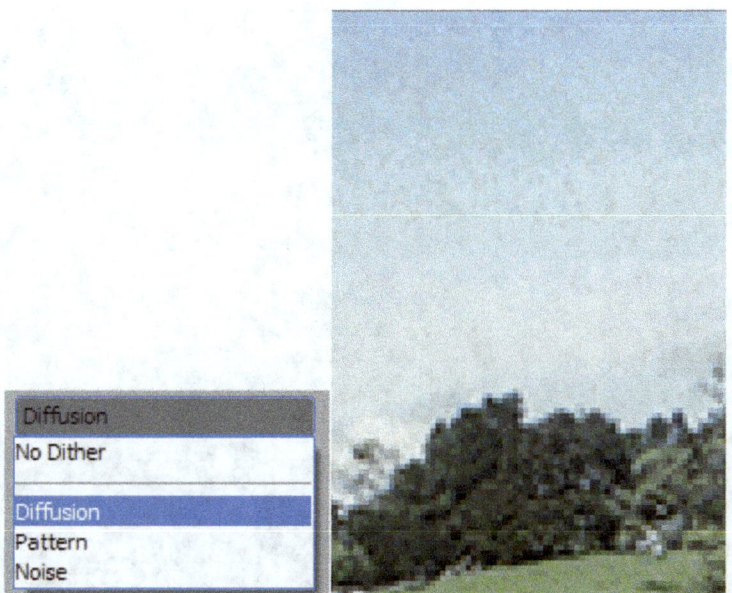

Figure 6-55. *Save for Web dialog box Dither Algorithm set to No Dither*

CHAPTER 6 CREATING A PARALLAX: BRING YOUR VINTAGE OR HISTORICAL PHOTOS TO LIFE

Figure 6-56. *Save for Web dialog box Dither Algorithm set to Diffusion, Pattern, and Noise*

Dither (0–100%): By default, set to 100%. In this case, a lower setting gives the appearance of banding and posterization. This setting is only available for Diffusion. Refer to Figure 6-57.

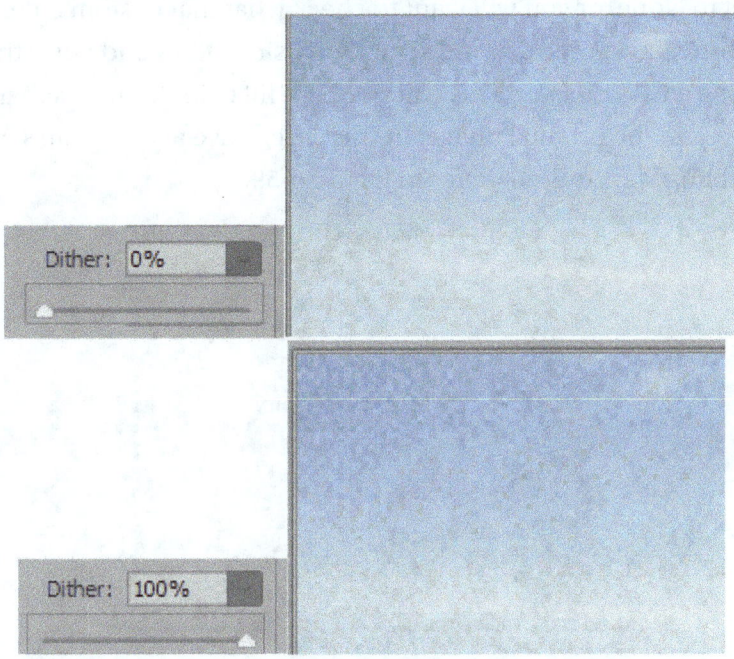

Figure 6-57. *Save for Web dialog box Dither present*

Transparency: If the animation contains actual areas of transparency, enable this setting. If not, it can be disabled, but I leave it on by default. GIF animations can have transparent areas, but they do need direction as to what colors they can blend into if on a website with a custom background. Refer to Figure 6-58.

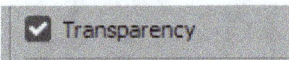

Figure 6-58. *Save for Web dialog box Transparency enabled*

CHAPTER 6   CREATING A PARALLAX: BRING YOUR VINTAGE OR HISTORICAL PHOTOS TO LIFE

Matte: Defines background color to blend transparent pixels against. In this case, it is set to the default of white which is the same as the background layer. If your GIF animation did have transparent areas, you could set to None, or you will want to check what that custom color of your website background is and set it here using Other and enter that HEX color using a Color Picker. This will specify a fill color for pixels that were transparent in the original image. In this case, leave at the white setting and no change is required. Refer to Figure 6-59.

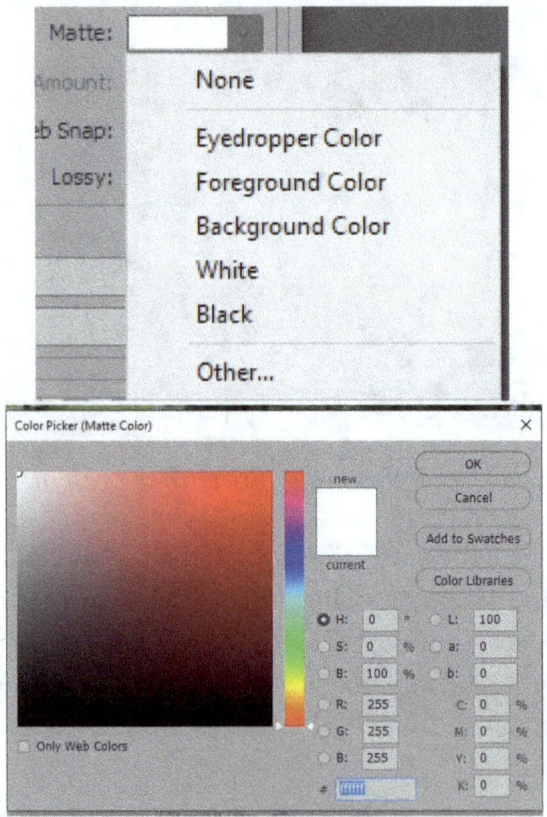

Figure 6-59. Save for Web dialog box Matte setting

Specify transparency dither algorithm: The options are No Transparency Dither, Diffusion Transparency Dither, Pattern Transparency Dither, and Noise Transparency Dither. This is similar to the dithering we saw earlier but specifically for transparent areas. In this example, the images are solid, so No Transparency Dither is set, and the Amount is disabled. Refer to Figure 6-60.

Figure 6-60. *Save for Web dialog box transparency dither algorithm*

Amount (0–100%): This option is for transparency, if preset, or if you have chosen the transparency dither algorithm Diffusion Transparency Dither. Leave this setting disabled for this example. Refer to Figure 6-60.

Interlaced: Download multiple passes first displaying a low-resolution image. This can ensure the viewer that the image is gradually appearing and downloading. However, doing so can increase the file size. By default, it is disabled. Refer to Figure 6-61.

Figure 6-61. *Save for Web dialog box Interlaced, Web Snap, and Lossy options*

Web Snap (0–100%): Snaps close colors to web palette, based on tolerance. By default, I leave this setting at 0% as I find that higher settings can alter the color of the image and limit colors. Refer to Figure 6-61 and Figure 6-62.

CHAPTER 6 CREATING A PARALLAX: BRING YOUR VINTAGE OR HISTORICAL PHOTOS TO LIFE

Figure 6-62. Save for Web dialog box web snap at 0 and altered to 100%

Lossy (0–100): Controls amount of lossiness allowed in GIF compression. By default, it is set to 0, and higher settings can lower the quality of the image. Refer to Figure 6-61 and Figure 6-63.

CHAPTER 6　CREATING A PARALLAX: BRING YOUR VINTAGE OR HISTORICAL PHOTOS TO LIFE

Figure 6-63. *Save for Web dialog box Lossy at 0 and altered to 100%*

Convert to sRGB: Check box to convert image colors to sRGB color space if you have not already done so. In this case, we already have set up this color profile when we built the image, but check this setting anyway. Refer to Figure 6-64.

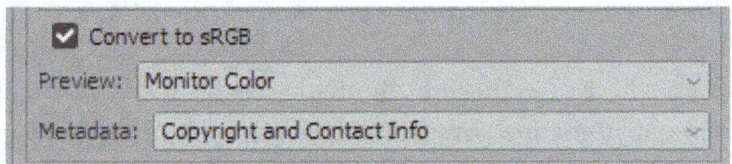

Figure 6-64. *Save for Web dialog box convert to sRGB options*

Preview: Choose how the image display colors in the preview. There are various options that you can view under this setting, but I leave the default on Monitor Color. Refer to Figure 6-65.

CHAPTER 6   CREATING A PARALLAX: BRING YOUR VINTAGE OR HISTORICAL PHOTOS TO LIFE

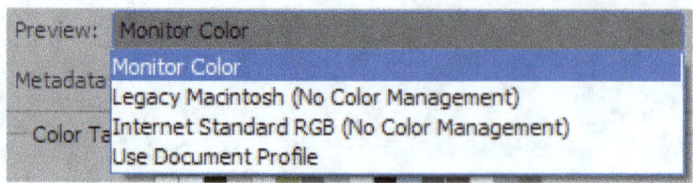

Figure 6-65. Save for Web dialog box preview options

Metadata: Select kind of metadata to include in output images. In this case, it is set to Copyright and Contact Info which is information you may want to include to prevent others from using your animation without permission and you don't get the credit. Alternatively, you can set to None, Copyright, All Except Camera Info, or All. Refer to Figure 6-66.

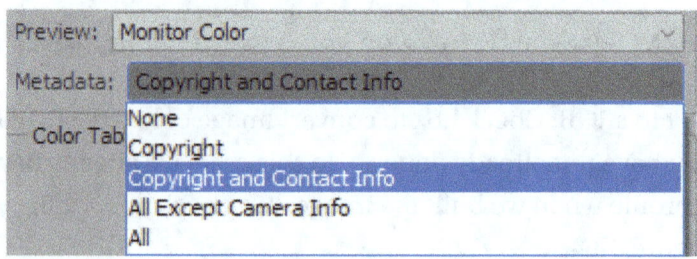

Figure 6-66. Save for Web dialog box metadata options

However, where does this information come from? If you are not sure if you set your copyright and contact information, then before you enter the Save for Web dialog box area, make sure to set it under

File ➤ File Info Basic. Currently this area is blank, but you can, for your own projects, enter your information here in the Basic tab. Refer to Figure 6-67.

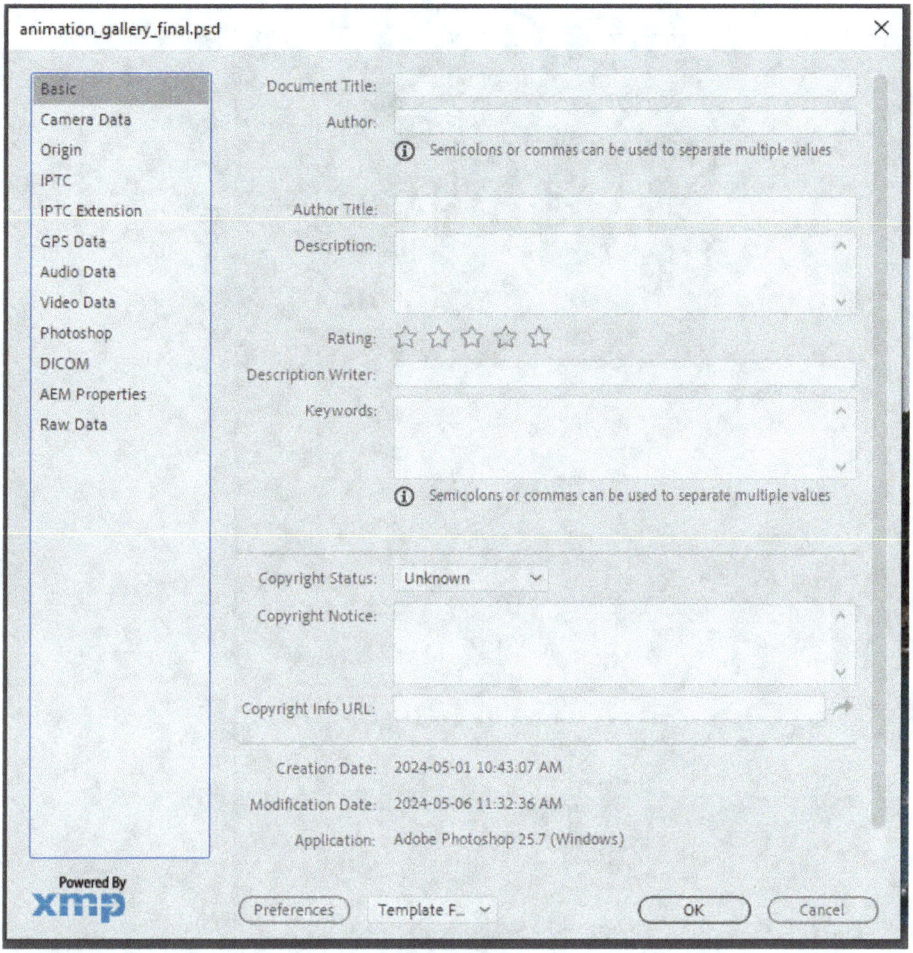

CHAPTER 6 CREATING A PARALLAX: BRING YOUR VINTAGE OR HISTORICAL PHOTOS TO LIFE

Figure 6-67. File Info Dialog box

Back in the Save for Web dialog box Color Table and its menu is a more advanced area; essentially, its purpose is to display all the colors that are present in the image as 256, including the option of transparency. This area will vary in color swatches depending on quality and Color reduction algorithm you choose. Refer to Figure 6-68.

CHAPTER 6 CREATING A PARALLAX: BRING YOUR VINTAGE OR HISTORICAL PHOTOS TO LIFE

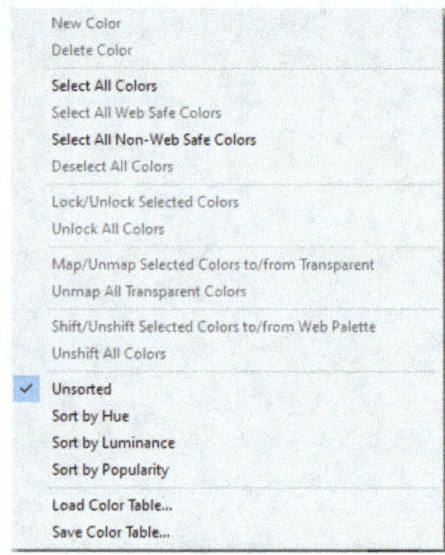

Figure 6-68. *Save for Web dialog box color table and menu*

Or create your own custom colors when selected and alter such things with the icons below the color table

- Map selected colors to be transparent.
- Shift/unshift selected colors to the web palette.
- Lock selected colors to prohibit being dropped.

CHAPTER 6　CREATING A PARALLAX: BRING YOUR VINTAGE OR HISTORICAL PHOTOS TO LIFE

- Add a new color or delete a selected color.
- In this case, when working with photographs, I usually leave this area alone as I am working with the current images. Refer to Figure 6-68.

Image size: Width (W), height (H); currently is set to W:720px and H:480px as the current output size. You can use this area to scale your image, though I would only recommend downscaling and not upscaling as this may not produce quality results. You can scale disproportionately if you unlink, but in this case, I recommend keeping linked to maintain image proportions. Refer to Figure 6-69.

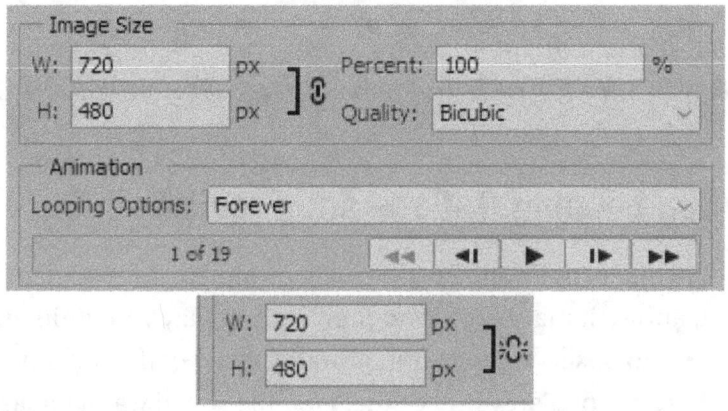

Figure 6-69. *Save for Web dialog box linked and unlinked width and height Image Options*

Note that the current image size is about 4.14MB which should be OK for most websites today, but if the file was smaller in dimensions, this would reduce the file size as well, just like more frames would increase the file size. These are just things to consider if you plan to build more than one animation size from the same .psd file.

CHAPTER 6   CREATING A PARALLAX: BRING YOUR VINTAGE OR HISTORICAL PHOTOS TO LIFE

Percent: You can also scale by percentage. By default, it is set to 100%, but for your project, you may want to scale to 75% or 50% if your animation needs to fill a set area. Leave at 100%. Refer to Figure 6-69.

Quality: Nearest Neighbor, Bilinear, Bicubic, Bicubic Smoother, Bicubic Sharper. By default, it is set to Bicubic, but you may prefer another setting for your image. No change is noticed in this case because you are leaving the animation at the original size. Refer to Figure 6-70.

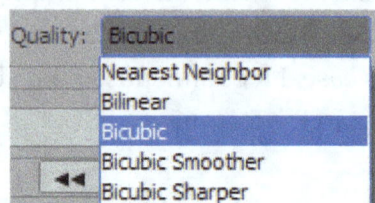

Figure 6-70. *Save for Web dialog box Image Options Quality settings*

Animation Looping Options and Preview

The Timeline panel in Photoshop can be a bit slower than working in the dialog box, and so it may be good to preview and play your animation here, not only to observe quality but also the speed of the transitions. After playing it here on the Forever Looping, I felt the speed was a bit fast. Here you can also go to first, previous, play/stop, next, and last frame. Press the play/stop button to stop the preview. Refer to Figure 6-71.

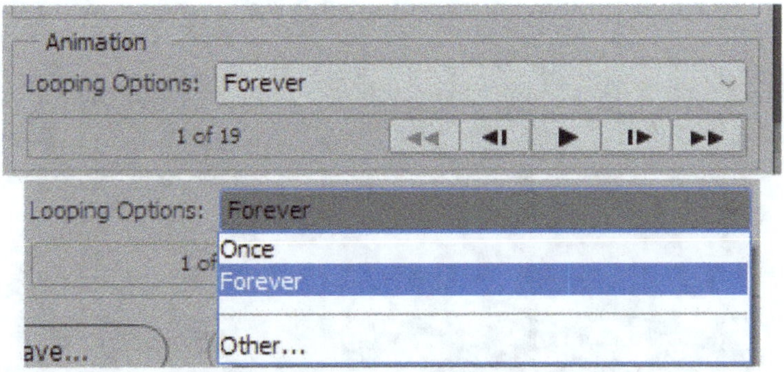

CHAPTER 6   CREATING A PARALLAX: BRING YOUR VINTAGE OR HISTORICAL PHOTOS TO LIFE

Figure 6-71. *Save for Web dialog box Animation options*

To keep my settings so far, I clicked the Done button to briefly exit but save my current settings and then returned to my Timeline panel and edit the timing in my Timeline panel. Refer to Figure 6-72.

Figure 6-72. *Save for Web dialog box option buttons*

I set Frames 1, 7, and 13 to a time of 5 seconds with slides 2–6, 8–12, and 14–19. I set to 0.2 seconds each. Refer to Figure 6-73.

CHAPTER 6 CREATING A PARALLAX: BRING YOUR VINTAGE OR HISTORICAL PHOTOS TO LIFE

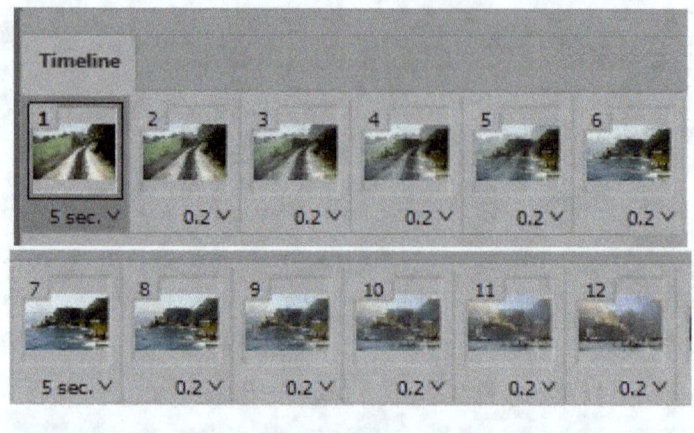

Figure 6-73. Timeline panel adjust time settings for each frame

File ➤ Save and then return to the File ➤ Export ➤ Save for Web (Legacy). Your prior settings should still be there. Test play again and the speed should now be slowed down. Refer to Figure 6-74.

Figure 6-74. Save for Web dialog box Animation preview settings

Click the Save button and save using the next dialog box Save Optimized As in a location of your choice.

Set a file name. In this case, set the Format to Images Only as you only want the GIF animation. Refer to Figure 6-75.

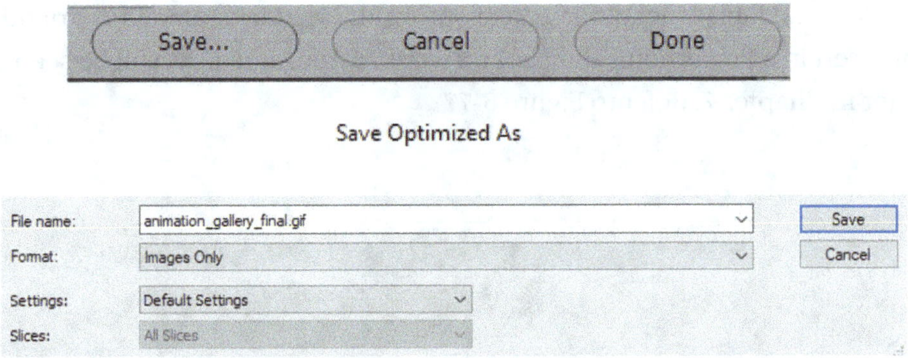

CHAPTER 6 CREATING A PARALLAX: BRING YOUR VINTAGE OR HISTORICAL PHOTOS TO LIFE

Figure 6-75. Save for Web dialog box click save to and enter Save Optimized As and click Save

Leave the settings at the Default settings and Leave All Slices disabled. Navigate to where you want to save the file and Click the Save button. You will then exit the dialog box.

File ➤ Save your .psd file to retain the changes, and close this file as well.

Now that the .gif animation (see file **animation_gallery_final.gif**) is created, you can preview in your computer's Photos application or in your browser. Refer to Figure 6-76.

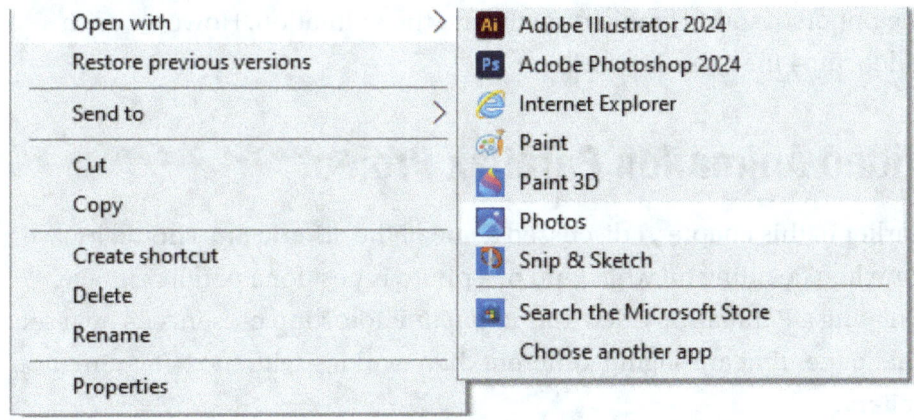

Figure 6-76. Find a viewer to watch your saved GIF file

CHAPTER 6   CREATING A PARALLAX: BRING YOUR VINTAGE OR HISTORICAL PHOTOS TO LIFE

You can later upload this image onto your website or email to a friend or insert in a PowerPoint slide as you would a .jpeg image as will be seen later in Chapter 7. Refer to Figure 6-77.

Figure 6-77. *Final GIF animation file*

For more details on GIF animations settings specifically for website, you can refer to the following link which is both for GIF animations in Photoshop and Adobe Animate which uses a similar dialog box and settings:

`https://helpx.adobe.com/animate/using/optimization-options-for-images-and-animated-gifs.html`

I will talk more about Animate briefly in Chapter 7.

While GIF animations are useful, they are limited in their ability when it comes to movement, scaling, and rotation. You also cannot incorporate the option of sound/audio directly into the animation. However, with video .mp4 files, this is possible.

Video Animation Parallax Project

Earlier in this chapter, I discussed some of the criteria one should look for when deciding on what kind of a photo is best for a parallax image. Creating a Parallax or video animation in Photoshop presents its own set of challenges that are slightly different than working with the GIF animation gallery.

As with the GIF animation gallery for the background, at least you want to make sure that you have a fairly high resolution image that can be scaled up or down should the plan be that you want to create a zooming in and zooming out effect.

In this case, I chose such images and made sure to scan the originals at 300–600dpi/ppi or higher to get the most information out of them as possible before they go into my video file that will be 72ppi.

Also, if I am planning to add anything additional to the image, I will want to scan it as well at a similar resolution so that it can be scaled as well.

In this case, the images that I worked with were originally in black-and-white. To add interest, I colorized them and also altered the woman's face to make it more in focus and protect her original identity. Refer to Figure 6-78.

CHAPTER 6   CREATING A PARALLAX: BRING YOUR VINTAGE OR HISTORICAL PHOTOS TO LIFE

Figure 6-78. *Main images that will be used in the Parallax animation*

These final images, in this case, have already been created for you and flattened using the Layers panel menu, ready for use before I started to create the actual animation file, which I will explain more about shortly. Refer to files **girl_final.psd** and **landscape_final.psd** in the chapters Parallax folder.

However, I will just mention, for your own projects, that to add more interest to your vintage photos, remember to try, as you saw in previous chapters, to add multiple hue/saturation adjustment layers and try various blending modes and opacities. Here is an example of layers that were used on the girl file and with the background landscape scene. Notice how many adjustment layers there are, some with a blending mode of normal and others using Linear Light, Darker Color, Color Burn, and Darken. The opacity of some of the layers was also altered. There are also separate layers for healing with the clone stamp, a sky replacement group folder was required, and various layer masks to show and hide details. You do not need to do this work for these examples as the focus in this chapter is on the animation itself. You can see, however, that each project is unique and has its own set of preparation challenges. Refer to Figure 6-79 and Figure 6-80.

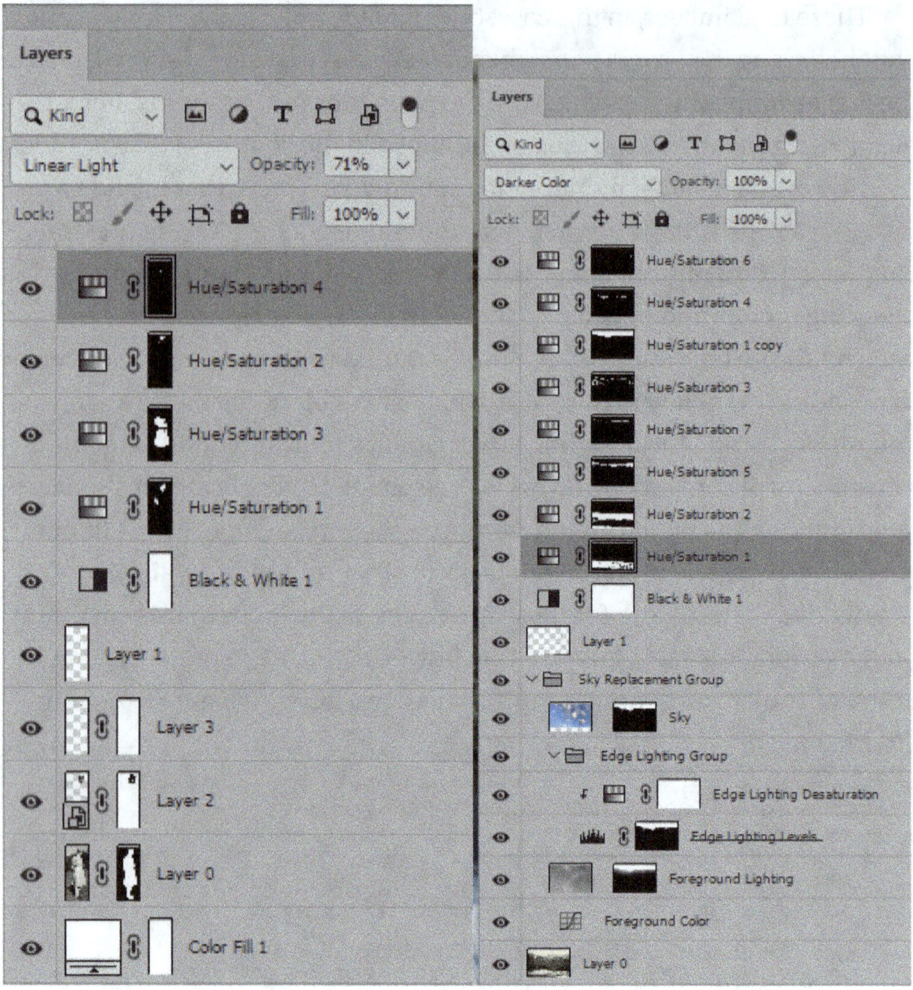

CHAPTER 6   CREATING A PARALLAX: BRING YOUR VINTAGE OR HISTORICAL PHOTOS TO LIFE

Figure 6-79. Layer panel with separate layers

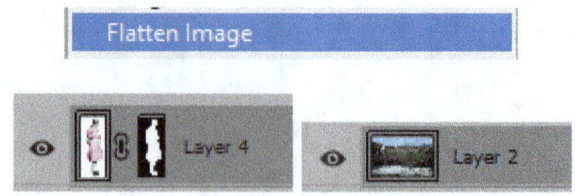

Figure 6-80. Each of the layers has been flattened for the project

CHAPTER 6   CREATING A PARALLAX: BRING YOUR VINTAGE OR HISTORICAL PHOTOS TO LIFE

As you will see shortly, some additional layers and further adjustments were later created within the parallax itself.

I will mention some other additional options while studying a second example of a parallax.

Create a New Document for Your Parallax Video Animation

Creating a new document for your video animation is similar to creating it for the GIF Animation. In this example, we are creating a larger file. For my project, I have already created the file for you. However, should you want to create your own project, I will just review those steps with some slight differences here.

In Photoshop, go to File ➤ New, to enter the New Document dialog box. From the Film & Video tab, this time, choose HDTV 1080p 1920 X 1080 px. @72 ppi. Refer to Figure 6-81.

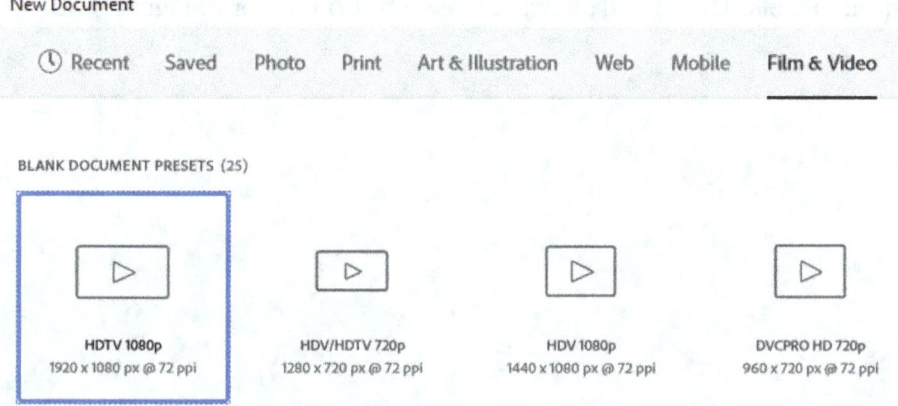

Figure 6-81. *New Document dialog box settings*

There are many other presets in this area, but we will practice with this one because we do not have any actual footage but still want high quality images for the video parallax. This size is also known by the ratio of 16:9 (16x120 = 1920 and 9x120=1080) and is a common size found on YouTube. In your own projects or depending where your video will be posted if not on your own website, you may want to use a different preset. Do your research first to discover what that correct dimensions should be.

Now we'll review the preset options again.

The width and height are 1920 x 1080 pixels. The orientation is landscape which is ideal for video. The resolution is 72 pixels/inch and the color mode is RGB color, 8 bit, and Background Contents: White.

Note, with the Color Profile, we will leave at Don't Color Manage rather than sRGB because it may be used for other purposes other than a website, and we should not alter the color profile too much at this time, as the Rendering process will deal with this. The Pixel Aspect Ratio will remain at Square Pixels. Then I will click the Create button. Refer to Figure 6-82.

CHAPTER 6   CREATING A PARALLAX: BRING YOUR VINTAGE OR HISTORICAL PHOTOS TO LIFE

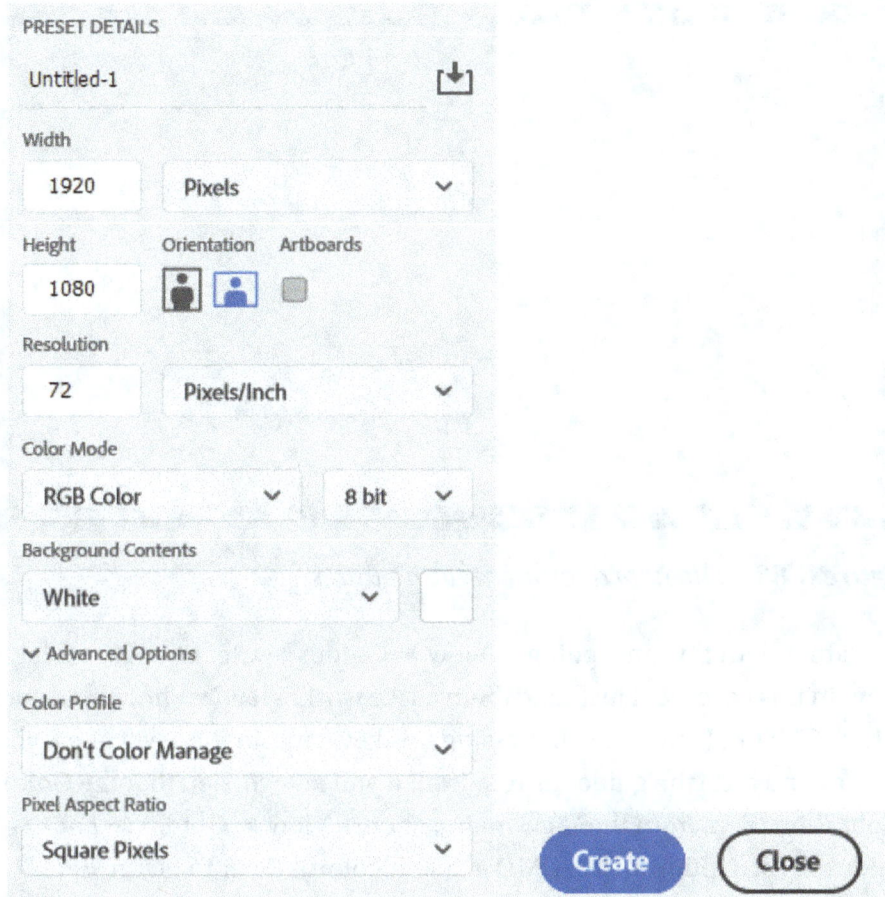

Figure 6-82. *New Document dialog box settings preset settings and Create button*

Again, in this case, the file will come in with guides displayed, and this is ideal should you want to incorporate type and do not want to go beyond the canvas bounds. In this example, we will not be using any Type as we are just focusing on the animation. Refer to Figure 6-83.

CHAPTER 6   CREATING A PARALLAX: BRING YOUR VINTAGE OR HISTORICAL PHOTOS TO LIFE

Figure 6-83. *The new document with guides*

Rather than this time going to View ➤ Guides ➤ Clear Guides to delete them, in this case we'll just hide them as we work. View ➤ Show ➤ Guides or Ctrl/CMD + ; (semicolon). Pressing this key combination will allow you to show and hide the guides as required. If you are worried that the Guides might shift, then, from the View menu, choose View ➤ Guides ➤ Lock Guides or Alt/Option + Ctrl/CMD + ; (semicolon). Refer to Figure 6-84.

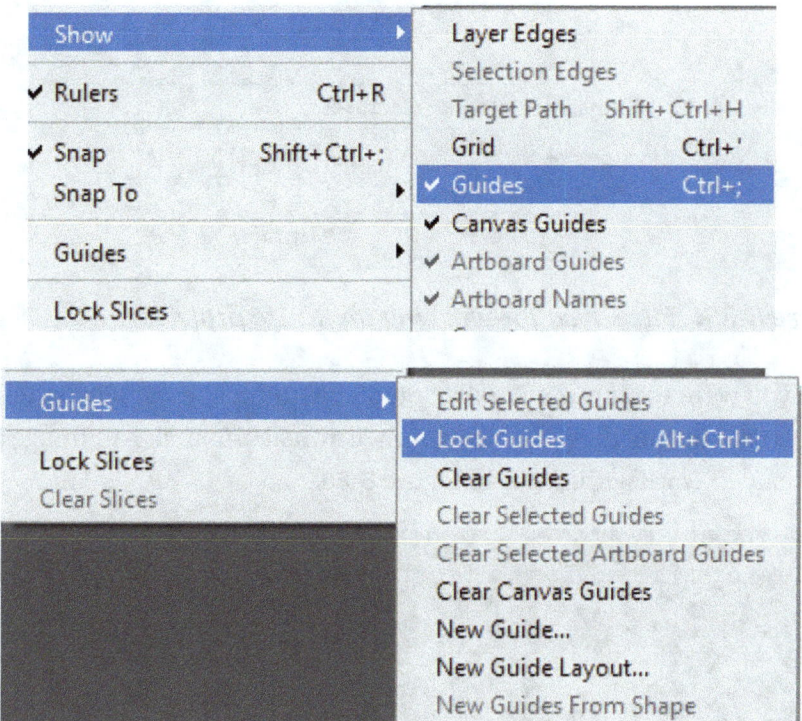

Figure 6-84. *Hiding and Locking guides if required*

If you do need to show or unlock guides, return to these areas of the View menu again.

File ➤ Save your file as before as a .psd file. In this case, you can refer to my file **parallax_start.psd** to begin your own Parallax project. Refer to Figure 6-85.

CHAPTER 6   CREATING A PARALLAX: BRING YOUR VINTAGE OR HISTORICAL PHOTOS TO LIFE

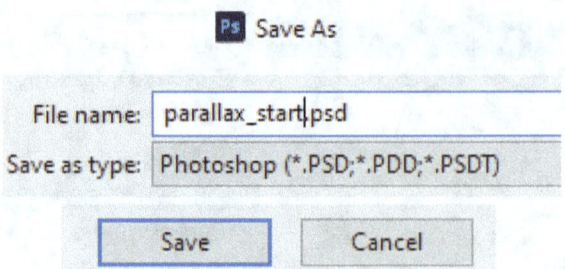

Figure 6-85. File saved for working on future projects

If you want to start the Parallax project with my files, you can then refer to the starting file **parallax_zoom_out.psd** and make an Image ➤ Duplicate to work with. Refer to Figure 6-86.

Figure 6-86. Image of girl placed over blurred background

First let's look at this file and the additional layers that were then added to it. I turned off the guides in my file. Refer to Figure 6-87.

CHAPTER 6   CREATING A PARALLAX: BRING YOUR VINTAGE OR HISTORICAL PHOTOS TO LIFE

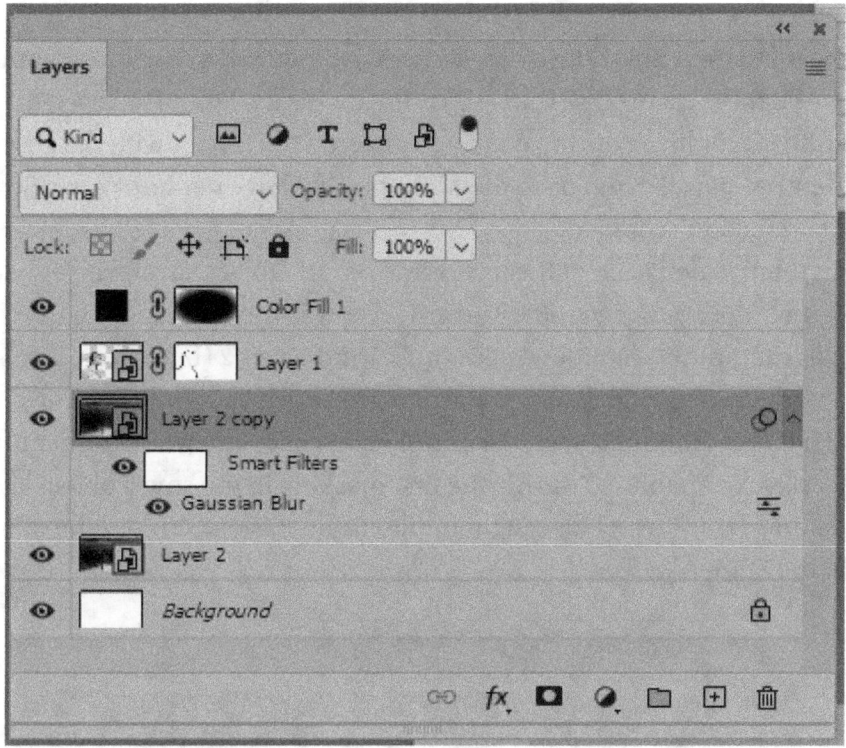

Figure 6-87. *Layers panel for parallax animation*

As with the GIF animation, after all adjustments were complete, the layers from the mentioned files **girl_final.psd** and **landscape_final.psd** were made into an Image ➤ Duplicate file and the Layers were flattened. And saved in the folder Parallax. The girl, in this case, had a mask around her so that I could separate parts of her from the white background to avoid it appearing in the animation. Refer to Figure 6-88.

Figure 6-88. *Layers that were added from other files*

I then copied each Image, such as the background Ctrl/CMD+A to Select ➤ All then Edit Copy (Ctrl/CMD+C). I then went to my new Parallax file and Edit ➤ Paste (Ctrl/CMD+V) onto a separate layer. However, to retain the layer mask during copying I dragged the layer 4 with the girl into the new parallax file and used the Move tool to move her into place. Some layers were later renamed.

In then turned each of the layers into Smart Object Layers. Refer back to Figures 6-86, 6-87 and 6-89. The girl layer was then renamed to Layer 1.

For example, we can see Layer 1 (girl) and Layer 2 (background).

I then used my Move tool to Position these selected layers. Layer 1 (girl) has an additional layer mask applied to cover any white border that might have been missed during the first masking in the smart object layer. Sometimes, this cannot be caught until one layer is placed over the other. Refer to Figure 6-89.

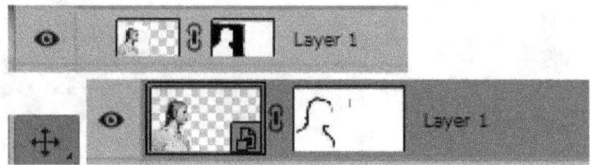

Figure 6-89. Layer renamed

An additional layer, Color Fill 1, is black (R:0, G:0, B:0) and was placed above all the layers. On the layer mask, I used an elliptical marquee to create a selection that went slightly beyond the boundaries of the canvas creating a frame.

I made sure that white was the foreground color in the Tools bar and pressed the Delete/Backspace key to cut out the selection. Then I used Select ➤ Deselect (Ctrl/CMD+D).

The opacity of that layer was left at 100%. However, in the Properties panel, the feathering of the layer mask was altered to 138.0px. It gave a vignette-like appearance that you might see in old vintage photos and film. Refer to Figure 6-90.

CHAPTER 6   CREATING A PARALLAX: BRING YOUR VINTAGE OR HISTORICAL PHOTOS TO LIFE

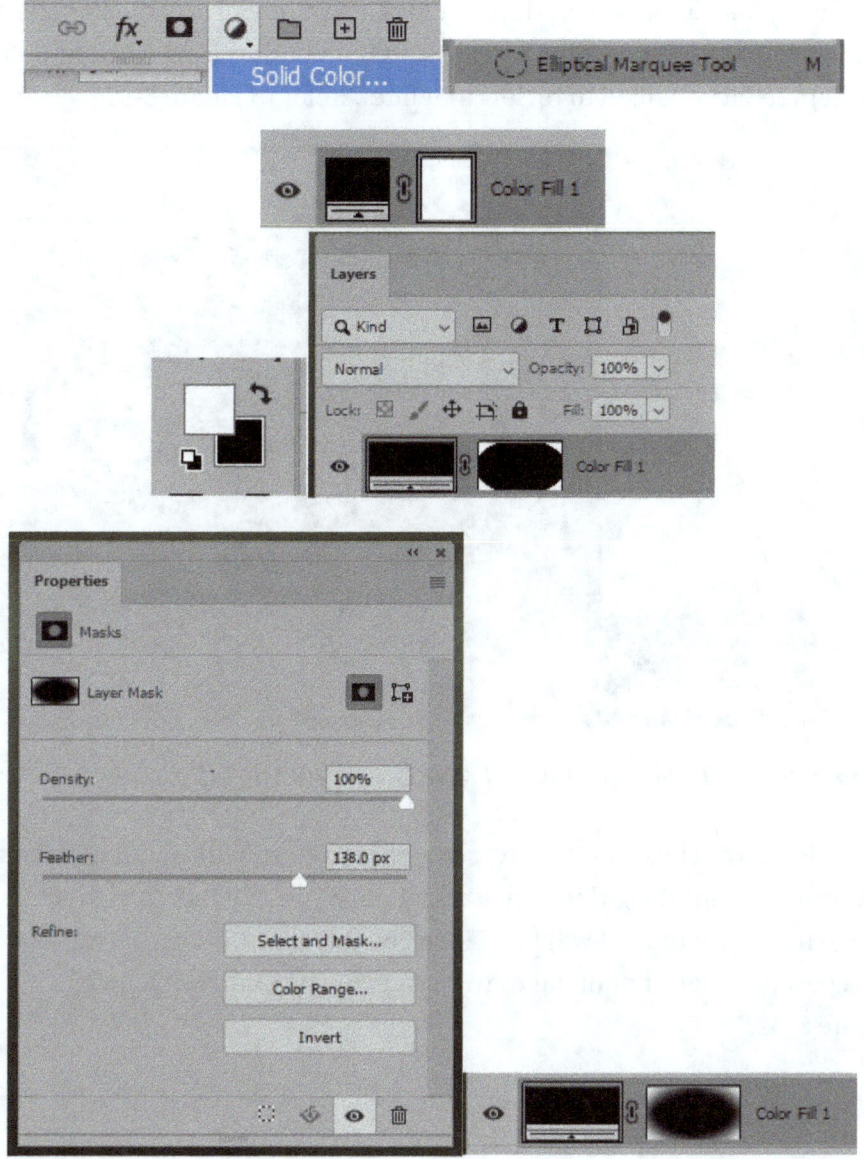

Figure 6-90. *Elliptical Marquee Tool and Tools, Layer and Properties panel Panels used to add a Vignette ellipse*

Layer 2 background was duplicated (Layer Copy 2) and then applied as a Smart filter of Filter ➤ Blur ➤ Gaussian Blur. Radius is 23.5 pixels. Refer to Chapter 3 if you need to review that filter. Refer to Figure 6-91.

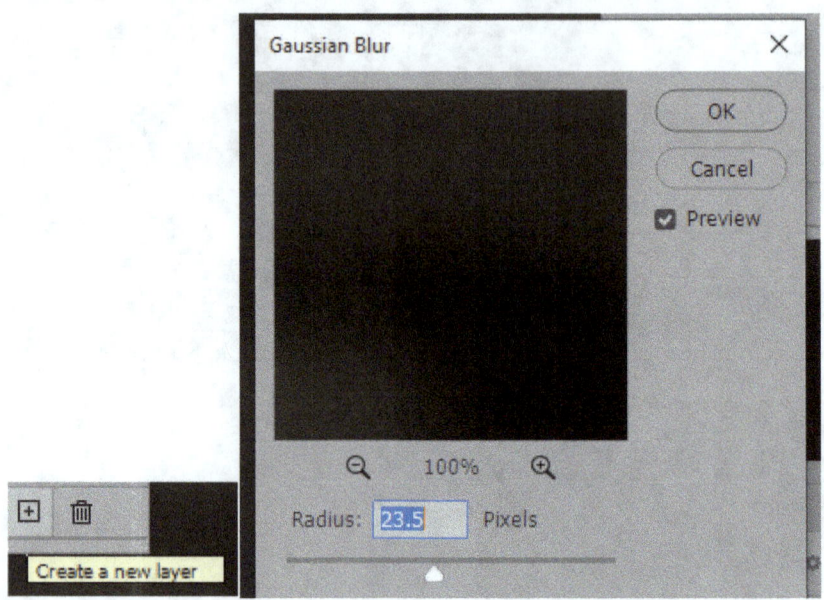

Figure 6-91. *Layer duplicated and Gaussian Blur dialog box*

I did this because on this layer, we want to start with an out of focus background with the girl in focus, and then, as we expand, the whole image including the girl will be in focus by the time we see Layer 2. This part of the animation takes two layers to work correctly. Refer to Figure 6-92.

CHAPTER 6 CREATING A PARALLAX: BRING YOUR VINTAGE OR HISTORICAL PHOTOS TO LIFE

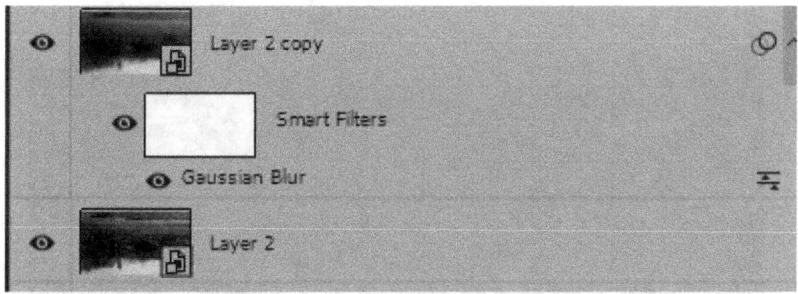

Figure 6-92. *Layers panel with duplicate layer and Gaussian blur applied*

The intent is to have the girl then appear like she is standing by the bank of the river. In this case, I luckily had two similar images as reference: the scene I colorized and also an additional black-and-white image, both which can help me figure out the final perspective and scaling. Refer to Figure 6-93.

CHAPTER 6   CREATING A PARALLAX: BRING YOUR VINTAGE OR HISTORICAL PHOTOS TO LIFE

Figure 6-93. *Reference images as to where the girl should be placed*

CHAPTER 6   CREATING A PARALLAX: BRING YOUR VINTAGE OR HISTORICAL PHOTOS TO LIFE

The girl in that image was not in focus enough to use for my final animation, but as mentioned, it's good to have multiple images of the same scene as you work, to determine how it can be animated.

In this case, I was able to find a similar perspective of the same girl in another old family photo that was more in focus. She too is standing at roughly the same perspective from a larger photo. So now the original photo can assist me to know how much to scale the new girl so that she does not look out of proportion to the scene. Refer to Figure 6-94.

Figure 6-94. *Colorized image of girl to be added to the image and scaled*

This is an ideal scene as I do not have to worry about covering any missing details and cutting the girl out of the background. In your own projects, however, you may have to figure out how to fill in missing details that surround or are behind a person in an image. I had to do this with a completely different image, of a solider, that I wanted to separate from the surrounding castle as he was all part of one image. Some healing and corrections were required as well. Refer to Figure 6-95.

CHAPTER 6　CREATING A PARALLAX: BRING YOUR VINTAGE OR HISTORICAL PHOTOS TO LIFE

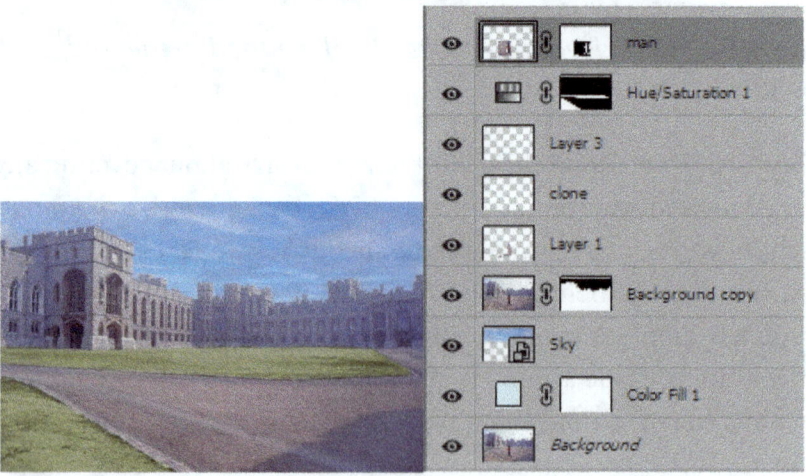

Figure 6-95. *Removing figures from an image*

CHAPTER 6 CREATING A PARALLAX: BRING YOUR VINTAGE OR HISTORICAL PHOTOS TO LIFE

Tools and workspaces that you should use in such examples are the Clone Stamp Tool, Remove tool, and Edit ➤ Content-Aware Fill workspace prior to creating your animations, as were discussed in Volume 1. However, if you want to use the soldier or alter the sky in the animation, these would all need to be grouped as separate smart object layers and created in a new file prior to creating the parallax animation file. Refer to Figure 6-96.

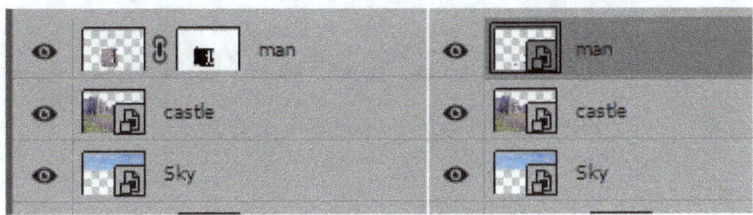

Figure 6-96. *Organizing layers for parallax*

You can review these layers later in the files **castle_sky.psd** and **castle_sky_part2.psd**. I will talk about the file actual animation file **castle_sky_paralax.psd** later.

Returning to the Girl and Landscape example, we will work with these layers in the timeline scaling and adding keyframes.

Then, from the Timeline panel, we will choose the Create Video Timeline to start the process and click the button. Refer to your copy of the file **parallax_zoom_out.psd** and later to the file **parallax_zoom_out_final.psd** if you need a reference as you work. Refer to Figure 6-97.

CHAPTER 6   CREATING A PARALLAX: BRING YOUR VINTAGE OR HISTORICAL PHOTOS TO LIFE

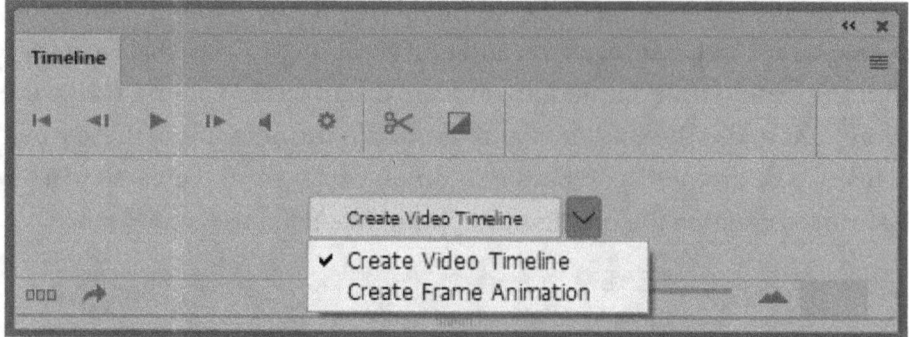

Figure 6-97. *Timeline panel set to Create Video Timeline*

Working with the Timeline Panel with the Layers Panel

The video timeline panel layout is rather different than the Create Frame Animation, and, if you are not used to working with video, it can be a bit overwhelming to a beginner. However, keep in mind that, like the Frame Animation, the Timeline panel works together with the Layers panel. Refer to Figure 6-98.

CHAPTER 6   CREATING A PARALLAX: BRING YOUR VINTAGE OR HISTORICAL PHOTOS TO LIFE

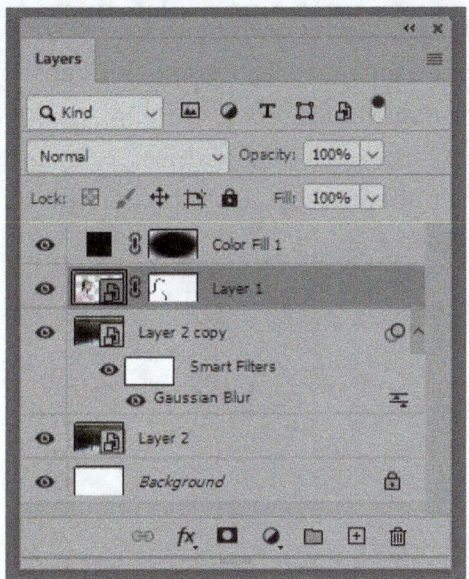

Figure 6-98.   Timeline Track added and Layer panel

Adding Your Layer Tracks

In this case, we start by adding our layers or tracks to the Timeline panel when we click the button. The timeline adds any active layers automatically, as seen in purple. Normally, if we were working with actual video clips, these would be added here as well. These would be the imported video layers. However, in this case, these are just smart object layers and a color fill layer.

The Layers panel currently contains four layers that I will use to create my animation. The background, which is locked and stationary, in this case is not included. For your own projects, as you add more layers to the Layers panel, they are added to the timeline as well as separate tracks. Likewise, you can also use the (+) at the end of each track if you need to add some media to that track line like additional video footage or another file. Refer to Figure 6-98.

The blue playback slider and red line can be moved along the timeline, currently for a duration of 4.29 seconds or about 5 seconds which is a default as you can see no movements or transitions are added and so all the layers currently remain stationary.

Note a .5 second is always left off and this is as far as the playhead can move. This is a type of buffer though the full animation at this point will be 5 seconds. Refer to Figure 6-99.

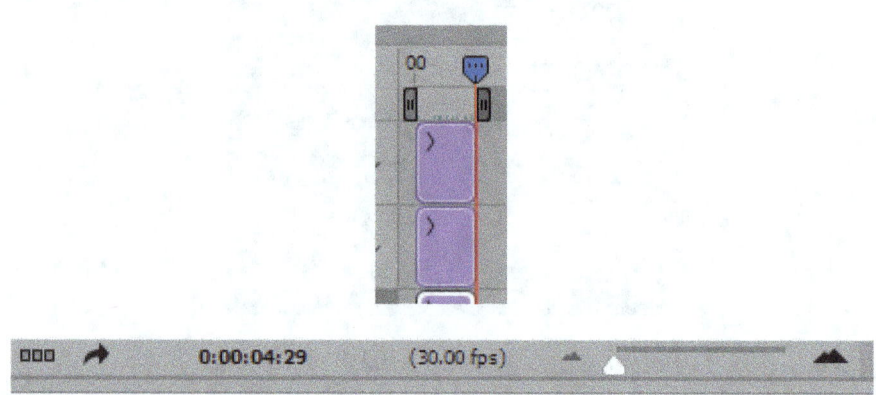

Figure 6-99. Timeline panel with Blue playhead and settings in the lower area of the panel for the location

The two sliders below the blue playback slider are the "Set Start of Work Area" (left) and "Set End of Work area" (right). You can move the "Set Start of Work Area" slider to the right if you need to hide or clip some of the initial animation and the "Set End of Work Area" to the left to clip some of

CHAPTER 6   CREATING A PARALLAX: BRING YOUR VINTAGE OR HISTORICAL PHOTOS TO LIFE

the ending animation. The "Set End of Work Area" slider cannot be moved right to extend the timeline. You will need to extend individual tracks to do this. For now, keep these sliders spread apart so that you do not hide any part of the animation by mistake. Refer to Figure 6-100.

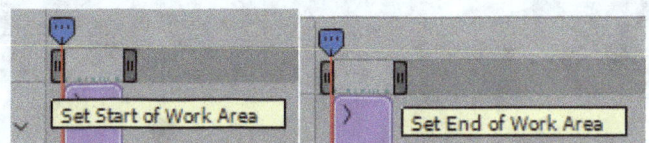

Figure 6-100. *Set Start and End of Work area*

We will explore this section more in a moment.

Now that the layers are added as tracks. Let's consider what is going to happen.

As you plan any video, you need to have a vision. Consider the canvas as your camera lens. What are you planning to do? Pan across the scene left, right, up, or down? Zoom in or out? What else might be taking place while this is happening? A rotation or other objects moving in or out of the scene? Because we are working with static photographic images, we are limited by what kinds of animation objects or people can do. However, basic motion can be used cleverly, and remember to also consider your filters for blurring and your layers for altering opacity. This can all be useful in adding to the animation.

In this case, I would like to focus on the girl's face and then zoom out and focus on the scene beyond. In the process of doing that, the background behind her is currently blurred, but as the scene expands, everything comes into focus. Then the animation stops. Refer to Figure 6-101.

CHAPTER 6 CREATING A PARALLAX: BRING YOUR VINTAGE OR HISTORICAL PHOTOS TO LIFE

Figure 6-101. *Current Starting image*

Some layers will move, and some will remain stationary throughout the animation. In this case, the vignette layer will not move, as it is just an overlay, but the girl and the background do need to contract from the expanded state so that they appear framed in the scene. To these layers, we will need to add some form of transitions and keyframes.

Adding Motions and Keyframes to Your Tracks

We will start by making sure that we are at the beginning of the track. So that we can focus one part of the animation at a time, you will turn off the layer visibility of the color fill vignette, the girl Layer 1, and then turn off just the Smart filter that is currently on Layer 2 copy but keep both Layer 2's visible as I begin my scaling of the layers. Refer to Figure 6-102.

CHAPTER 6   CREATING A PARALLAX: BRING YOUR VINTAGE OR HISTORICAL PHOTOS TO LIFE

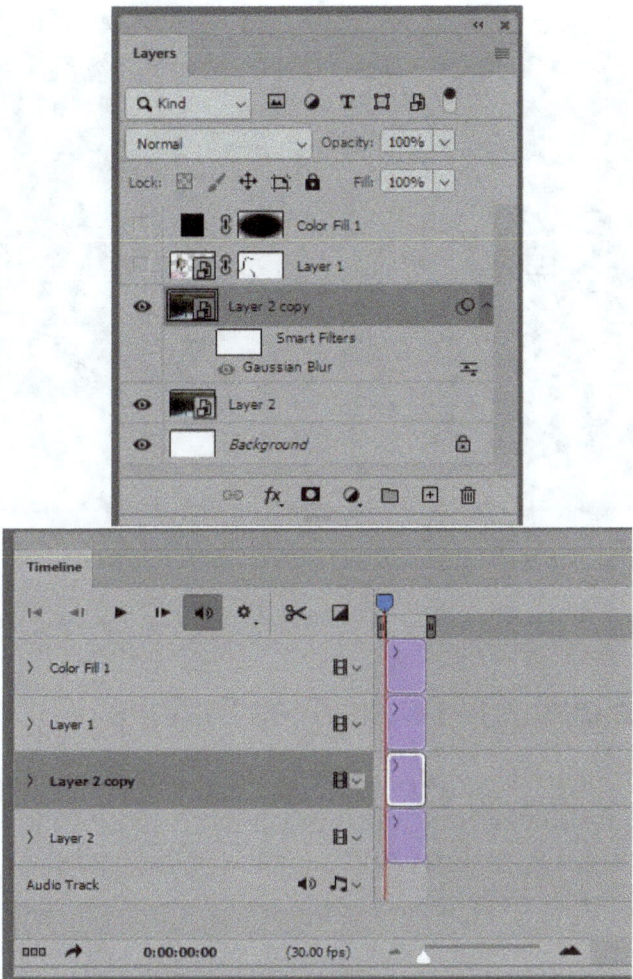

Figure 6-102. *Active Layers in the Layers panel and Timeline panel*

The scene should currently look something like this. Refer to Figure 6-103.

CHAPTER 6   CREATING A PARALLAX: BRING YOUR VINTAGE OR HISTORICAL PHOTOS TO LIFE

Figure 6-103. *Canvas with some layer and the filter visibility turned off*

Track Removal and Other Video Options

Tracks can be deleted as well, if you click the little film strip on the track and choose that option. However, that will also delete the layer as well. Use Edit ➤ Undo (Ctrl/CMD+Z) if you remove a track by mistake, or your History panel. Refer to Figure 6-104.

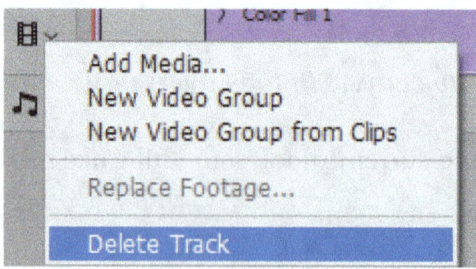

Figure 6-104. *Option menu for each track*

CHAPTER 6　CREATING A PARALLAX: BRING YOUR VINTAGE OR HISTORICAL PHOTOS TO LIFE

This drop-down menu also provides other options used when working with video such as Add Media, New Video Group, New Video Group from Clips, and Replace footage. However, those options are not required for this book.

Increasing Each Track Duration

Now I need to Shift+Click to select all the Layers (visible and hidden) except the Background layer and adjust the duration. Refer to Figure 6-105.

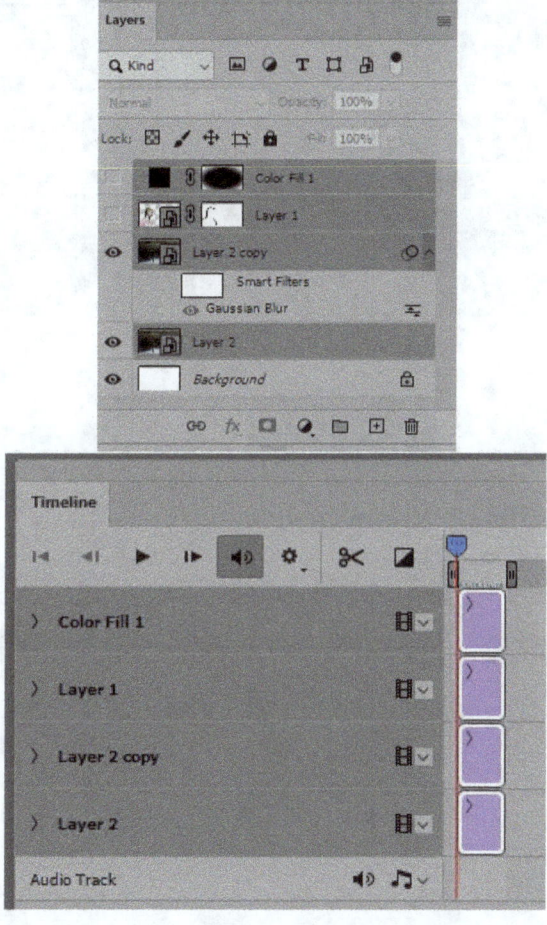

Figure 6-105. *Layers panel and Timeline panel with all layers' tracks selected*

CHAPTER 6 CREATING A PARALLAX: BRING YOUR VINTAGE OR HISTORICAL PHOTOS TO LIFE

Select the end of one of the tracks, and when the mouse pointer changes to the three prong arrow, drag on the end to extend the duration to about 10 seconds. Refer to Figure 6-106 as seen with Color Fill 1.

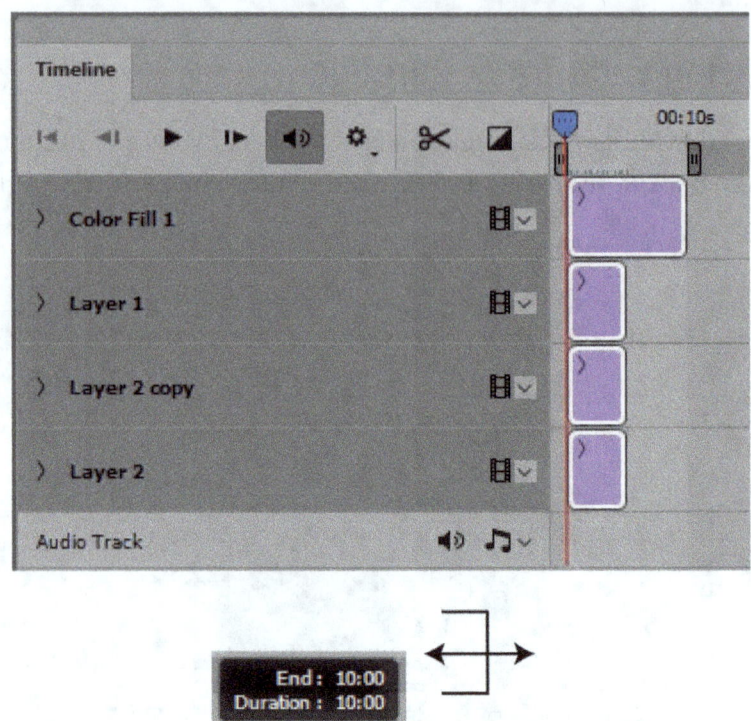

Figure 6-106. Timeline panel lengthening a track

If all the tracks do not stretch at the same time, then drag them one at time so they reach the 10 second duration. Refer to Figure 6-107.

CHAPTER 6   CREATING A PARALLAX: BRING YOUR VINTAGE OR HISTORICAL PHOTOS TO LIFE

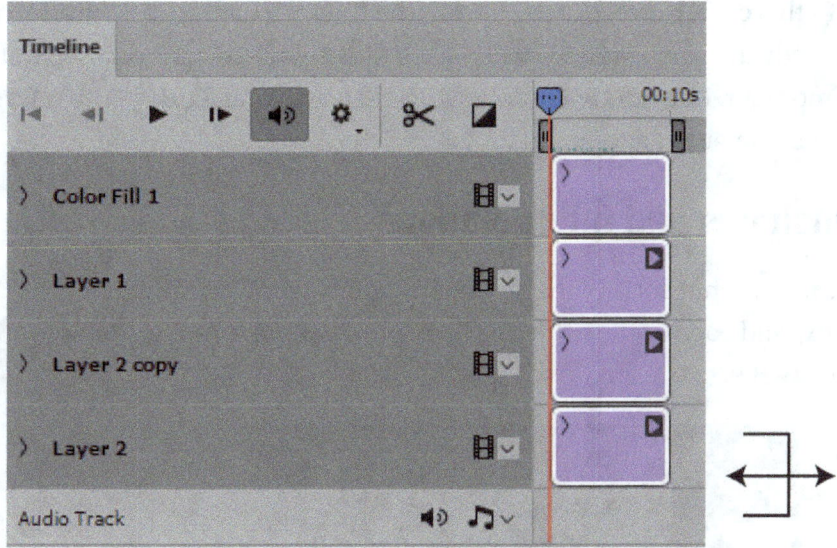

Figure 6-107. *Timeline panel lengthening all tracks*

Generally, even with video, you should scale and move your tracks one at time, and you can even shift their position if required so that they don't all line up in a column. This can be good for a gallery when you do picture changes. Refer to Figure 6-108.

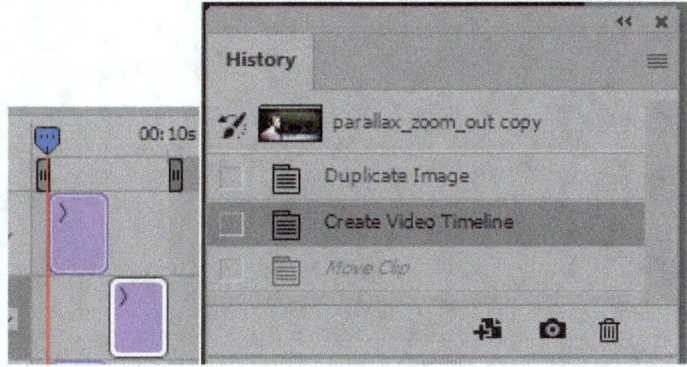

Figure 6-108. *Timeline panel moving a track*

909

CHAPTER 6   CREATING A PARALLAX: BRING YOUR VINTAGE OR HISTORICAL PHOTOS TO LIFE

In this case, however, we do want the track's location and duration to be exactly the same, and we will make adjustments to each one separately in a moment. Use Edit ➤ Undo or your History panel if one of the tracks has become out of alignment.

Transitions and Interpolations

We can see what sorts of things you can affect with keyframes when you expand each area beside the layer name in the timeline. Refer to Figure 6-109.

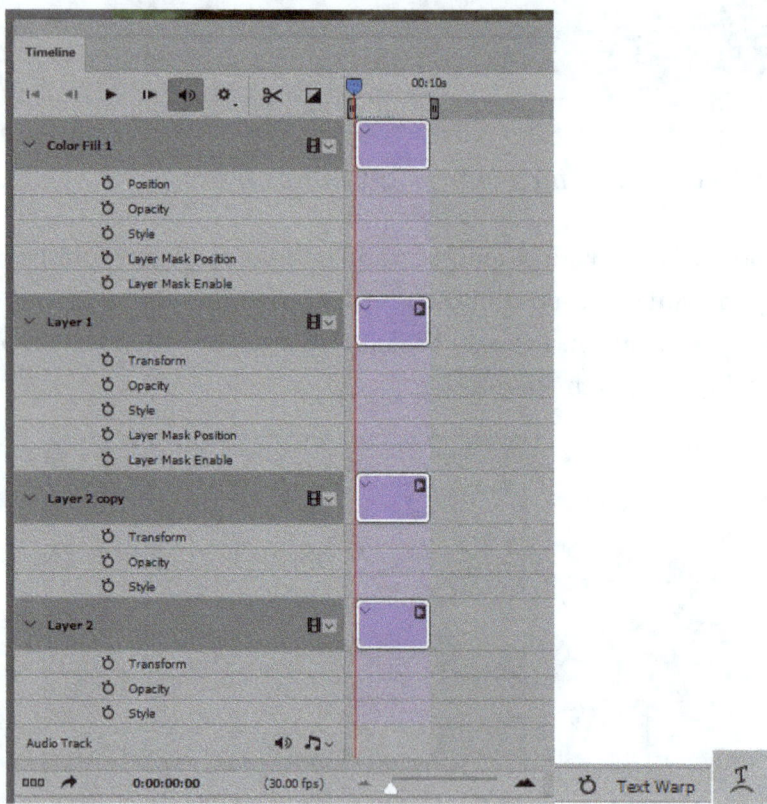

Figure 6-109. *Timeline panel looking at keyframe options*

CHAPTER 6   CREATING A PARALLAX: BRING YOUR VINTAGE OR HISTORICAL PHOTOS TO LIFE

Different kinds of layer tracks contain similar and different keyframe options that you can alter.

For Fill/Adjustment Layers, Normal Layers, Smart Object Layers, and Type Layers, which are optional, you can alter the following.

- Position: For Fill/Adjustment Layers and Normal Layers, this allows you to adjust the placement of the layer at set keyframes.

- Transform: For Smart Object Layers and Type Layers, it allows you to adjust the placement of layers but also do advanced scaling, panning, and rotations.

- Opacity: Adjust the level of opacity for all layers.

- Style: If layer style effects *fx* (drop shadow) have been added in the Layers panel, these can be altered at each keyframe. This could be a hiding or showing of the visibility of the effect or a Fill opacity change.

- Layer Mask Position (optional): This option will only be available to alter the layer mask placement if the layer contains a layer mask. However, it cannot be used to control scaling, which I will explain in more detail as we progress through the project. If a vector mask is present, then the other option will be Vector Mask Position.

- Layer Mask Enable (optional): This option will only be available to Enable or Disable the layer mask when enabled if the layer contains a layer mask. If a vector mask is present, then the other option will be Vector Mask Enable.

- Text Warp (optional): Only available for type layers if present, used to control add warp effects. Refer to Figure 6-109.

- For information on additional kinds of keyframes for layers and lighting, refer to link at end of section.

Preset Motions

We will look at the actual keyframes in a moment. However, note that for Smart Object Layers and Type layers, you will have, on the track, itself a right pointing arrow with some preset motion options that you can use to Adjust your Transform keyframe options, if you do not want to do custom work. Normal Layers and Color Fill Layers and Adjustment layers do not have this option icon. However, normal layers will have this icon and if you use it, they will be automatically converted to smart object layers. Refer to Figure 6-110.

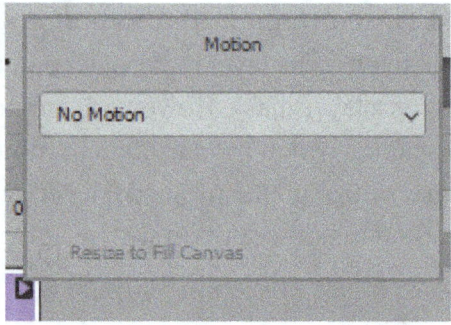

Figure 6-110. Timeline panel preset motions

Currently all Smart Object tracks are set to No Motion which is currently what we want. I will just use Layer 2, in this case, to demonstrate other options.

However, from the motion option menu, you can choose five other options. Refer to Figure 6-111.

CHAPTER 6   CREATING A PARALLAX: BRING YOUR VINTAGE OR HISTORICAL PHOTOS TO LIFE

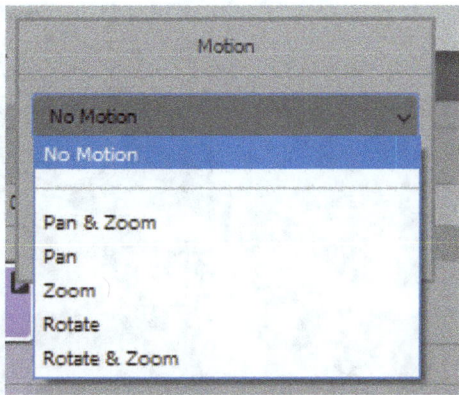

Figure 6-111. *Timeline panel preset motions options from the list*

- Pan and Zoom: Allows you to pan or move across a set area at an angle (-360,0,360°) while either zooming in or zooming out. You can also enable Resize to Fill Canvas before you begin. In this case, I am panning horizontally. If you need to revert back to the original state on No Motion, use Edit ➤ Undo or the History panel. Using only the Motion panel will not undo the change automatically. Note: The Resize to Fill Canvas option is available for all motions to resize the graphic. Refer to Figure 6-112.

CHAPTER 6   CREATING A PARALLAX: BRING YOUR VINTAGE OR HISTORICAL PHOTOS TO LIFE

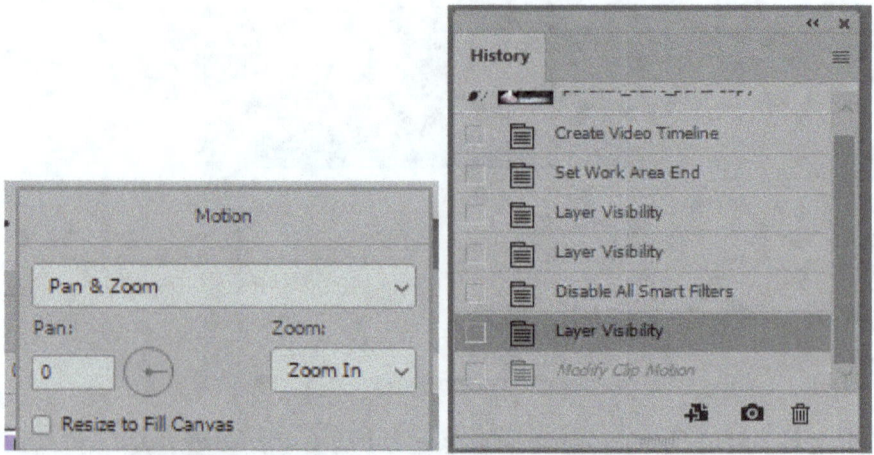

Figure 6-112. *Timeline panel preset motions for Pan and Zoom, the History panel, and motion applied to a layer*

914

CHAPTER 6　CREATING A PARALLAX: BRING YOUR VINTAGE OR HISTORICAL PHOTOS TO LIFE

- Pan: Only allows you to Pan at a set angle (-360,0,360°) and Resize to fill Canvas. In this case with a setting of 0 °, I would be panning in a horizontal movement. To pan vertical, I would adjust my angle to 90 ° first. Refer to Figure 6-113.

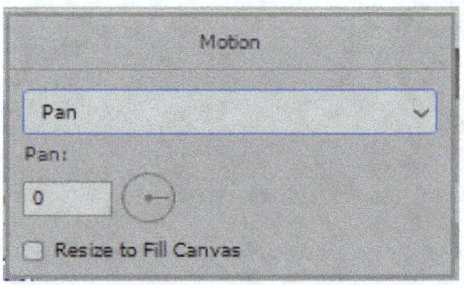

Figure 6-113. *Timeline panel preset motions for Pan and motion applied to a layer*

CHAPTER 6 CREATING A PARALLAX: BRING YOUR VINTAGE OR HISTORICAL PHOTOS TO LIFE

- Zoom: Zoom in or zoom out from a set location that you mark using your reference point location in this case from the center of the layer. Refer to Figure 6-114.

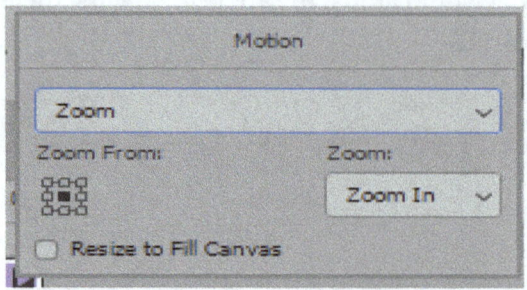

Figure 6-114. *Timeline panel preset motions for Zoom and motion applied to a layer*

CHAPTER 6   CREATING A PARALLAX: BRING YOUR VINTAGE OR HISTORICAL PHOTOS TO LIFE

- Rotate: Used to rotate the layer clockwise or counterclockwise. Refer to Figure 6-115.

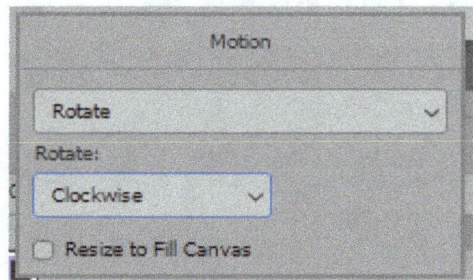

Figure 6-115. Timeline panel preset motions for Rotate and motion applied to a layer

You cannot, however, set the angle to stop or create a complete rotation. That would be something you would have to adjust with your Edit ➤ Free Transform options as a custom setting with additional and custom keyframes which I will mention later.

917

- Rotate and Zoom: Used to rotate the layer clockwise or counterclockwise and zoom in or zoom out at the same time. Refer to Figure 6-116.

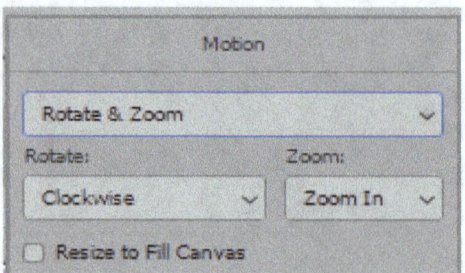

Figure 6-116. *Timeline panel preset motions for Rotate and Zoom and motion applied to a layer*

When any motion is added and the motion menu is collapsed, this automatically sets the keyframes. The motion is applied to the layer for the Transform. These diamond keyframes are called Linear Interpolation keyframes. Interpolation is much like tweening in that we are trying to fill in the parts of the animation that are missing or unknown, between the known values.

Initially, when the motion is applied, they will appear as red diamonds with a red bar. However, when you right-click them individually and move or adjust them they will appear yellow (selected), or gray (unselected). Refer to Figure 6-117.

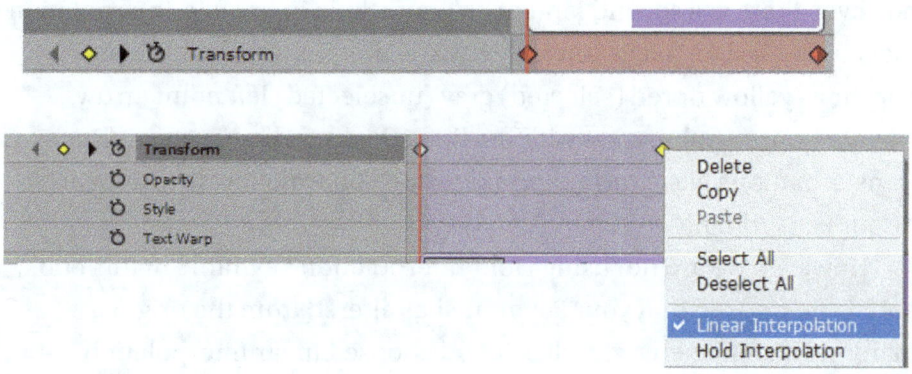

Figure 6-117. *Timeline panel added keyframes for Transform and you can alter the keyframe settings*

Keyframes can also be moved in unison if shift clicked. Also, you can use the pop-up menu when you need to delete, copy, and paste changes to a single keyframe in the same track.

As you move the keyframe, the motion will then change to custom. Refer to Figure 6-118.

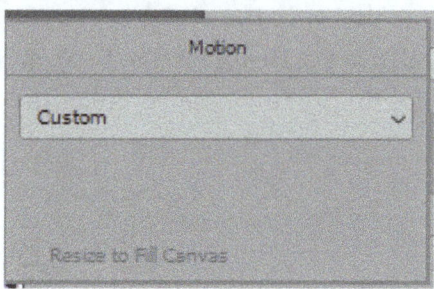

Figure 6-118. *Altered keyframes sets the motion preset to custom*

Note: Linear Interpolation keyframes appear as yellow or gray diamonds which may appear two toned beginning and ending key frames or a solid color if in between or only one keyframe is present. But for Masks options, the Linear Interpolation keyframes will appear as yellow or gray squares as the enabling and disabling of the mask are considered abrupt states.

In other situations, like when working with Transform Transitions, however, there is a second kind of keyframe known as Hold Interpolation that also looks like the yellow gray square. In other situations, it may appear as yellow or red (selected) gray (unselected) left point arrow when used in combination with the linear diamond keyframe during transformations like strobe effects or when you want layers to appear or disappear suddenly.

However, we are not using Hold Interpolation keyframe in this book, and if you noticed that your keyframe has altered from the original diamond shape, then right-click it and choose Linear Interpolation instead. Refer to Figures 6-117 and 6-119.

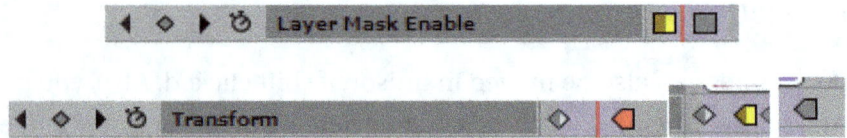

Figure 6-119. *Examples of Linear and Hold Interpolation Keyframes on the Timeline*

For now, make sure that your transform keyframes are set to No Motion. As mentioned, use the History panel to revert if you have tried any of my motion examples on your own. Refer to Figure 6-120.

CHAPTER 6   CREATING A PARALLAX: BRING YOUR VINTAGE OR HISTORICAL PHOTOS TO LIFE

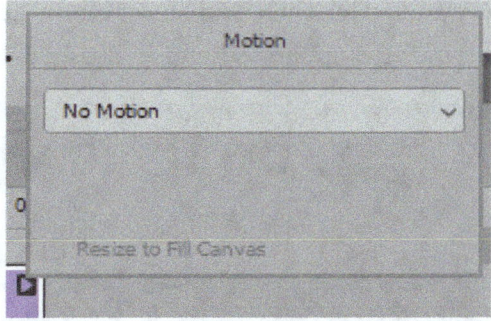

***Figure 6-120.** Timeline panel preset motions set to No Motion*

In this case, I want to start with a custom Zoom for the two Layers. Click Select Layer 2 Copy in the Layers panel. Refer to Figure 6-121.

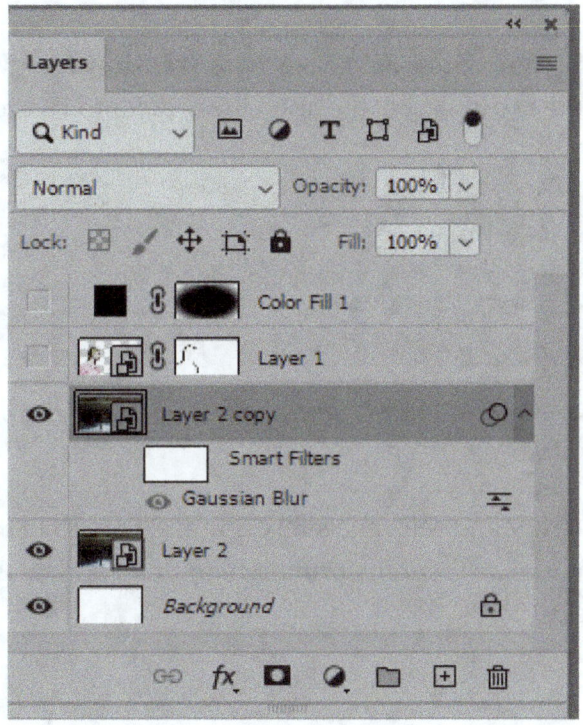

***Figure 6-121.** Layers panel with single layer selected*

In the Timeline panel, click each Transform stopwatch Icon to set a keyframe at the start of the animation. Refer to Figure 6-122.

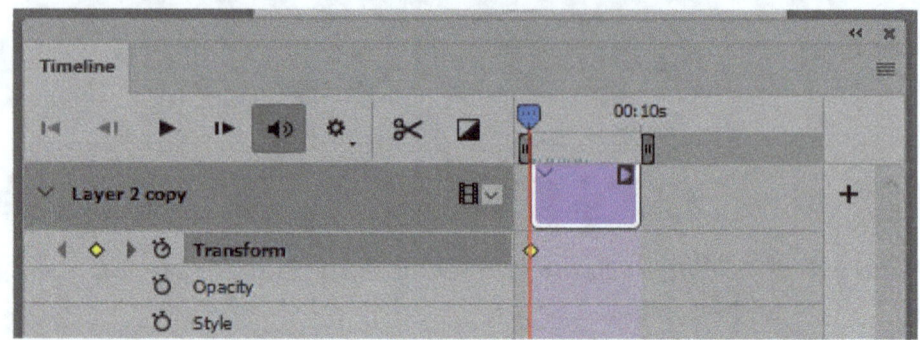

Figure 6-122. *Timeline panel settings a starting keyframe for Transform for one layer*

Then do the same for Layer 2. Select the Transform stopwatch, and apply a keyframe at the start of the animation. Refer to Figure 6-123.

Figure 6-123. *Timeline panel settings a starting keyframe for transform for another layer*

Now Shift+Click and select Layer 2 Copy and Layer 2 in the Layers panel as we want to do the transformation for them both at the same time. Refer to Figure 6-124.

CHAPTER 6 CREATING A PARALLAX: BRING YOUR VINTAGE OR HISTORICAL PHOTOS TO LIFE

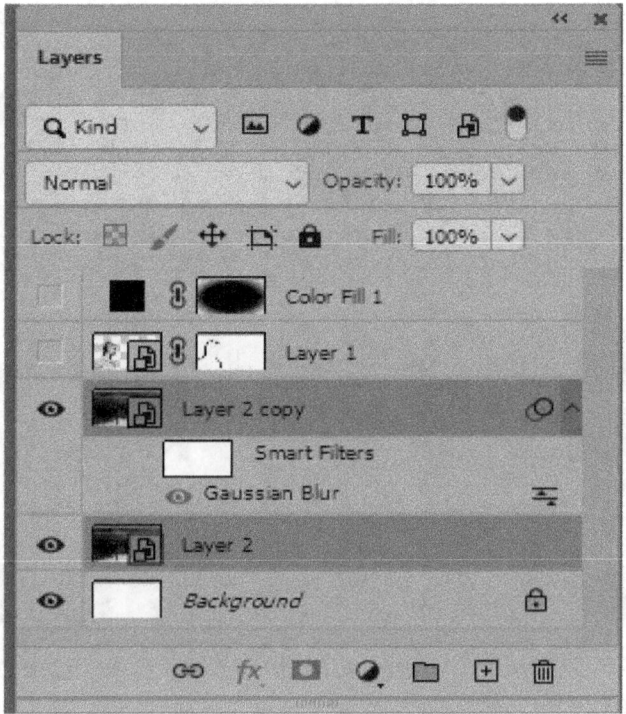

Figure 6-124. *Layers panel with both layers selected*

Drag the Blue Playback slider to about the 7 second mark. You can see this below, to the left of the frame rate. Refer to Figure 6-125.

CHAPTER 6   CREATING A PARALLAX: BRING YOUR VINTAGE OR HISTORICAL PHOTOS TO LIFE

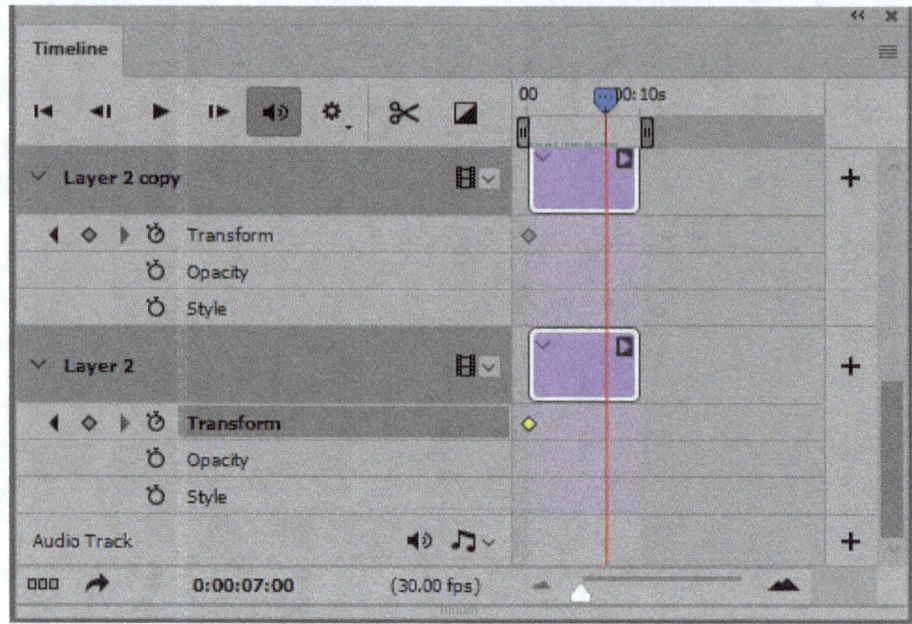

Figure 6-125. *Timeline panel with both players selected and moving the playhead*

Now go to Edit ➤ Free Transform. In this case, because a smart filter was applied to a layer, you may get a warning message that that filter will be turned off until the transformation is committed. That is why we turned the visibility of the filter off before we started. Click OK to proceed. Refer to Figure 6-126.

CHAPTER 6 CREATING A PARALLAX: BRING YOUR VINTAGE OR HISTORICAL PHOTOS TO LIFE

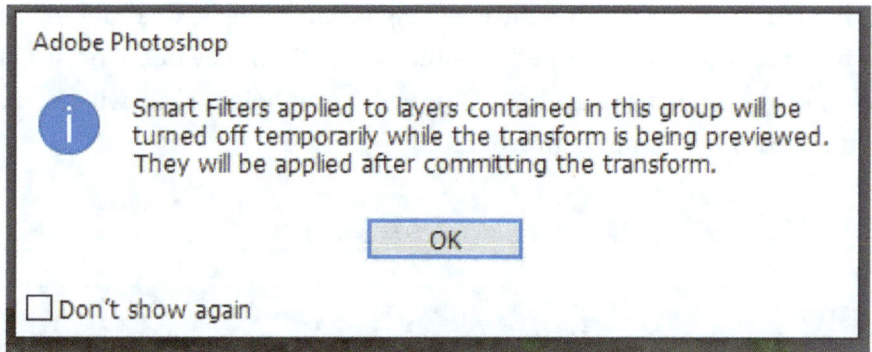

Figure 6-126. *Warning message that may appear if Smart filters are applied to a Smart Object Layer*

In the Options Bar panel, the image is currently at 100%. Refer to Figure 6-127.

Figure 6-127. *Free Transform Options bar panel and Image to be scaled*

925

CHAPTER 6   CREATING A PARALLAX: BRING YOUR VINTAGE OR HISTORICAL PHOTOS TO LIFE

First, to scale, drag using the lower right bounding box handle. To set the width to touch the lower edge of the canvas. You may need to use Ctrl/CMD++ to zoom in as you adjust. This width and height scale will need to be about 81.6%. Refer to Figure 6-128.

Figure 6-128. *Free Transform Options bar panel and Image partially scaled*

Now drag to scale from the upper right bounding box handle to affect the width again. The final width and height will be about 49.16% and should touch the edges of the canvas on the left, right, and bottom as shown here. Refer to Figure 6-129.

CHAPTER 6   CREATING A PARALLAX: BRING YOUR VINTAGE OR HISTORICAL PHOTOS TO LIFE

Figure 6-129. Free Transform Options bar panel and Image fully scaled and committed

It's OK if some of the image is cut off at the top as we will adjust that later as part of the animation.

The main thing as you scale is that no white from the background layer appears as a border near the edges of the canvas.

For now, just click the Check in the Options bar panel to Commit and review the scene so far.

New keyframes have been added for each layer in the transform area of the Timeline.

927

You can move the blue playhead back and forth to see how this appears. Refer to Figure 6-130.

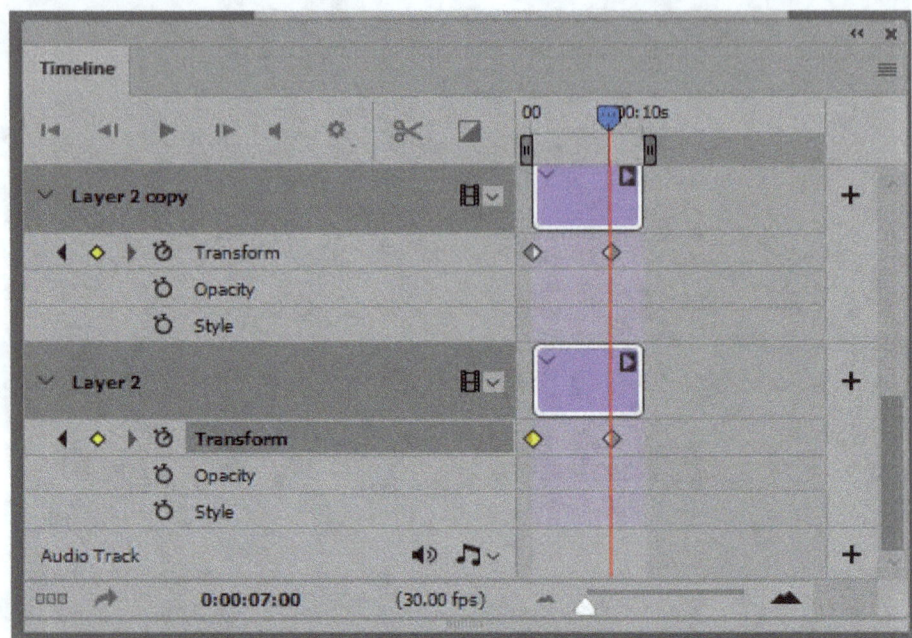

Figure 6-130. *Timeline panel new keyframes added to both layers at once*

However, make sure to keep both layers selected as you work and then move the playhead to the 9 second mark. Refer to Figure 6-131.

CHAPTER 6 CREATING A PARALLAX: BRING YOUR VINTAGE OR HISTORICAL PHOTOS TO LIFE

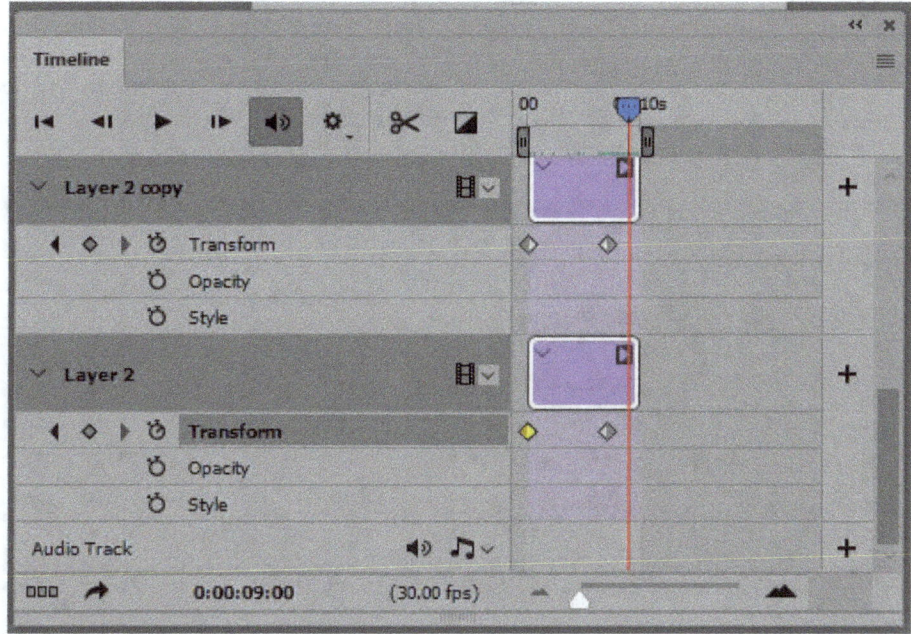

Figure 6-131. *Timeline panel moving the playead for the next transformation*

This time, select the Move Tool, and with the down arrow key on your keyboard pressing, several times, move both selected images until you can see more of the sky and now just a bit of the bank. Refer to Figure 6-132.

CHAPTER 6 CREATING A PARALLAX: BRING YOUR VINTAGE OR HISTORICAL PHOTOS TO LIFE

Figure 6-132. *Use the Move Tool and the arrow keys for the next transformation to move the image down*

This now adds another keyframe and then you can use the blue playhead to observe the movements as the scene becomes more centered. Refer to Figure 6-133.

CHAPTER 6   CREATING A PARALLAX: BRING YOUR VINTAGE OR HISTORICAL PHOTOS TO LIFE

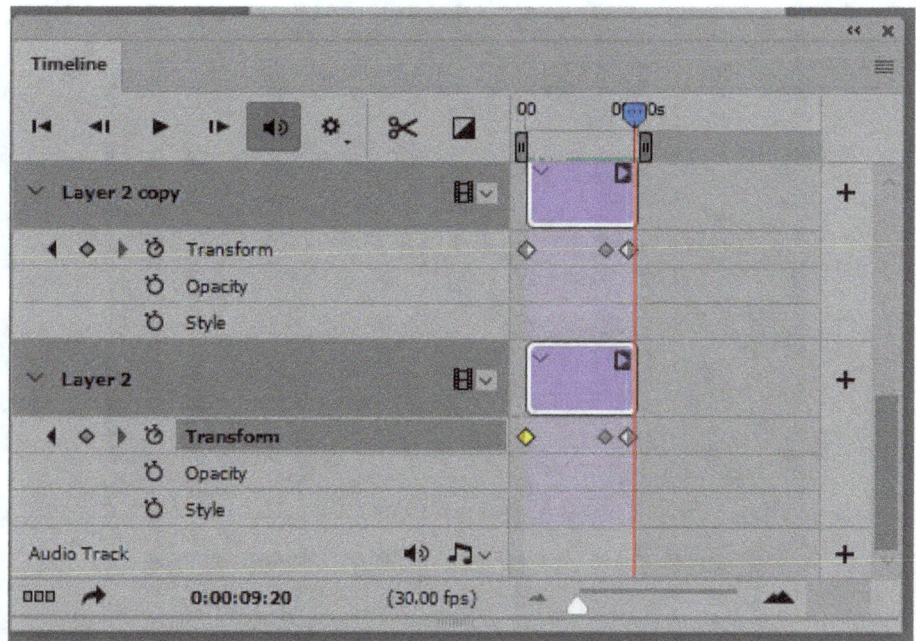

Figure 6-133. Timeline panel new keyframes added to both layers at once

Later, if you need to adjust these movements, make sure to keep both keyframes in unison parallel and also keep the layers selected as you work to avoid one transforming differently than the other.

Now move the playhead back to the 0 point on the left and just select the layer Layer 2 copy, and in the Layers panel, turn the smart filter's visibility back on so that the Gaussian Blur is visible. Refer to Figure 6-134.

CHAPTER 6 CREATING A PARALLAX: BRING YOUR VINTAGE OR HISTORICAL PHOTOS TO LIFE

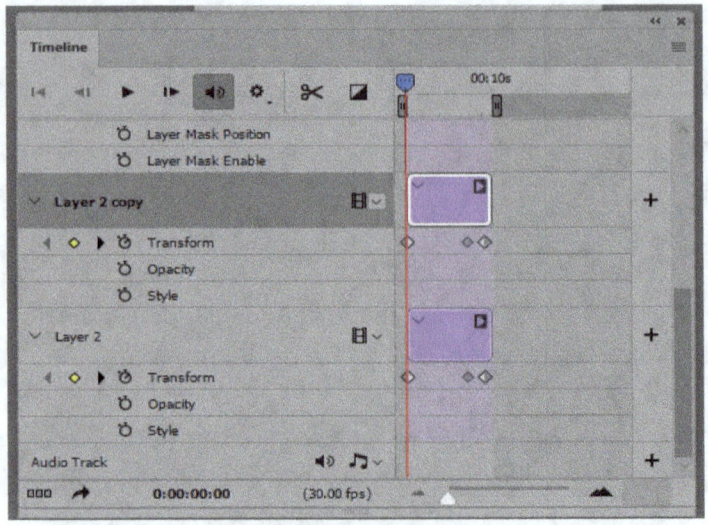

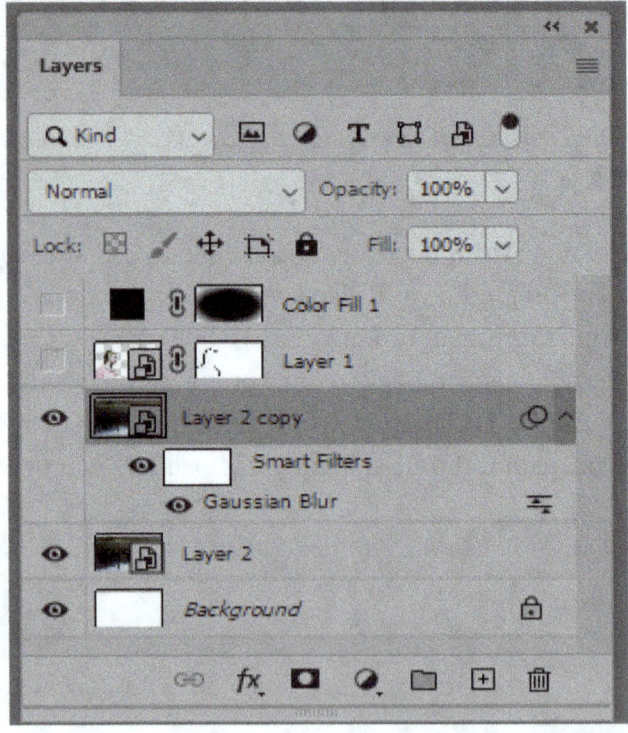

Figure 6-134. Timeline panel with only the Layer 2 copy blur layer selected

Adjust Blur and Opacity

This time, for this layer, only set a keyframe for opacity by clicking the Opacity stopwatch. Refer to Figure 6-135.

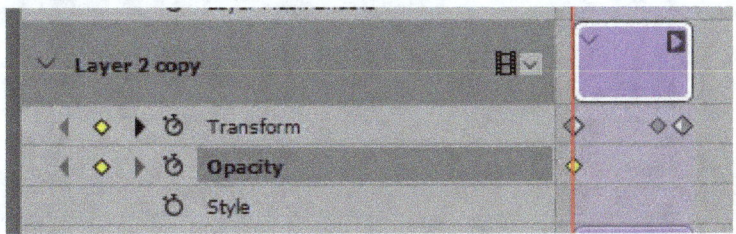

Figure 6-135. *Timeline panel adding a keyframe for opacity*

Currently, the Gaussian blur is at 100% opacity, and now, we are going to alter it at the 7 second mark to 0%, where the full scene comes into focus.

Drag the playhead to the 7 second mark. Refer to Figure 6-136.

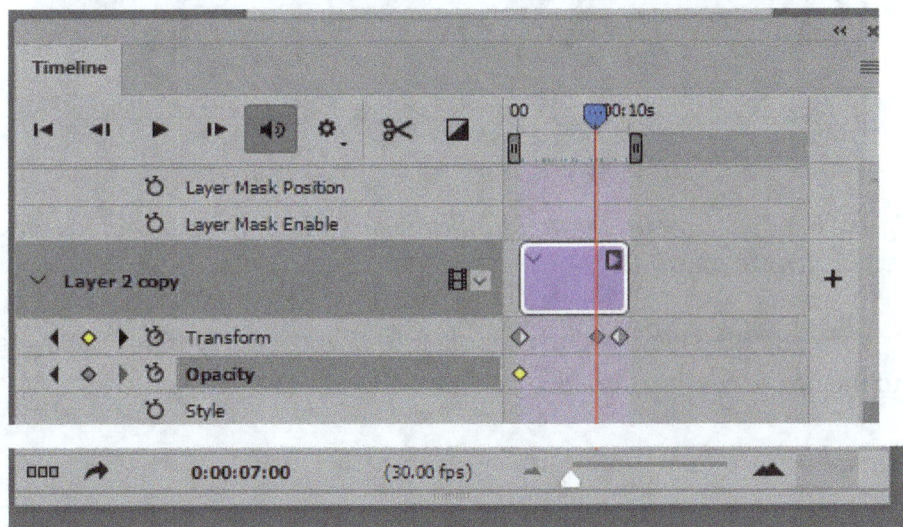

Figure 6-136. *Timeline panel moving the playhead for the next keyframe for opacity*

Now on Layer 2 copy, lower the opacity to 0% and a new keyframe is added. Refer to Figure 6-137.

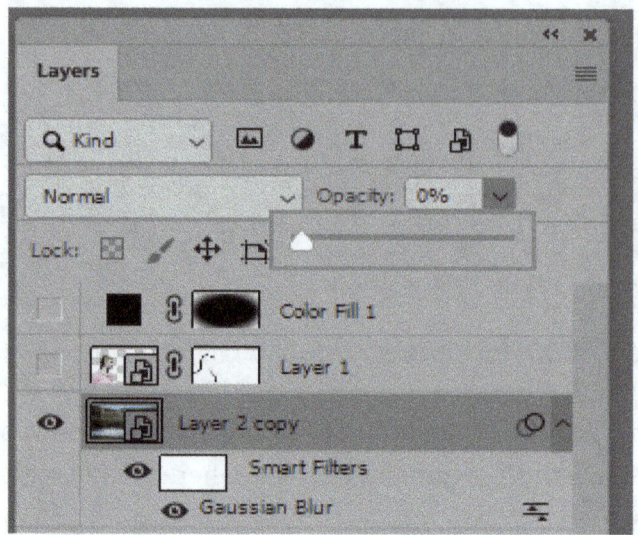

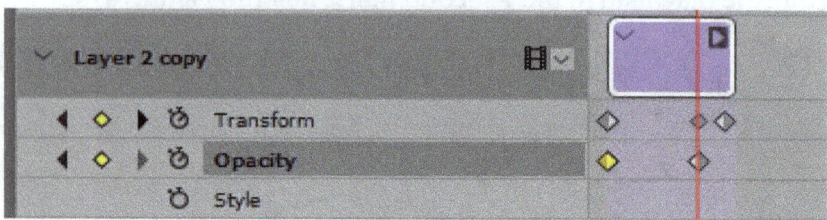

Figure 6-137. *Timeline panel moving using the Layers panel to add next keyframe for opacity*

Move the Blue Playhead to observe the effects of the blur disappearing and the image coming into focus. Refer to Figure 6-138.

CHAPTER 6 CREATING A PARALLAX: BRING YOUR VINTAGE OR HISTORICAL PHOTOS TO LIFE

Figure 6-138. *Opacity at set keyframe is now reduced for this layer.*

Simple animations like this can take time so don't expect to do this all in 1 hour.

File ➤ Save your work so far. Next, we will now add the girl back into the image.

Tip You can use the lower white slider to the right of your frames per second indicator (fps) if you need to get a more detailed look at the precise location of keyframes if you do not have them in the exact location or need to drag and move them around or see a preview image of the frame itself. However, I usually keep it at the small left side, as the preview movement could slow down my work. Refer to Figure 6-139.

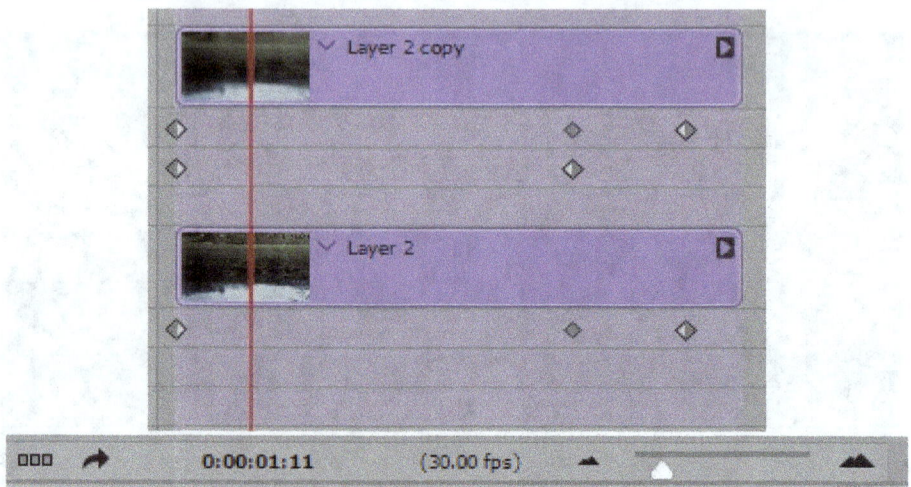

Figure 6-139. *When working in the timeline, you can view tracks better by adjusting the scaling slider or icons in the lower area of the panel to zoom out or in on the Timeline panel*

Adding Movement to Other Layers

In your current project, move the playhead back to the left 0 mark. Make sure that Layer 1 containing the girl is visible and selected in the Layers panel.

In her case, a few transformations may have to take place to get the scaling and movement correct. Refer to Figure 6-140 and Figure 6-141.

CHAPTER 6   CREATING A PARALLAX: BRING YOUR VINTAGE OR HISTORICAL PHOTOS TO LIFE

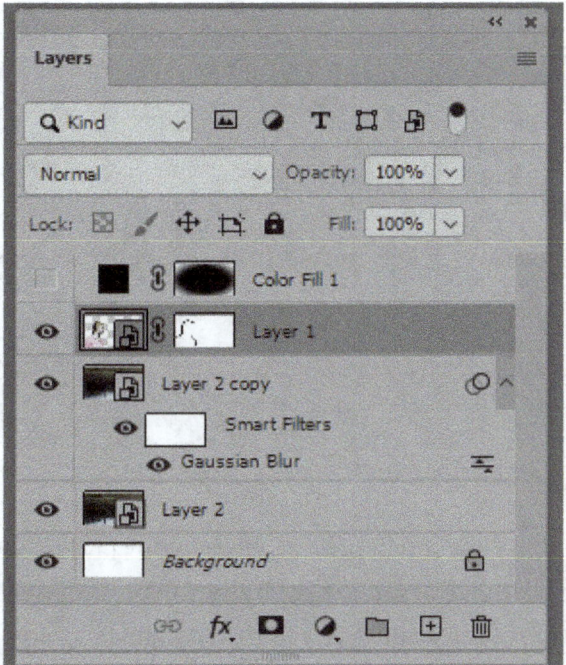

Figure 6-140. *Select Layer 1 in the Layers panel to work with the image of the girl*

937

CHAPTER 6   CREATING A PARALLAX: BRING YOUR VINTAGE OR HISTORICAL PHOTOS TO LIFE

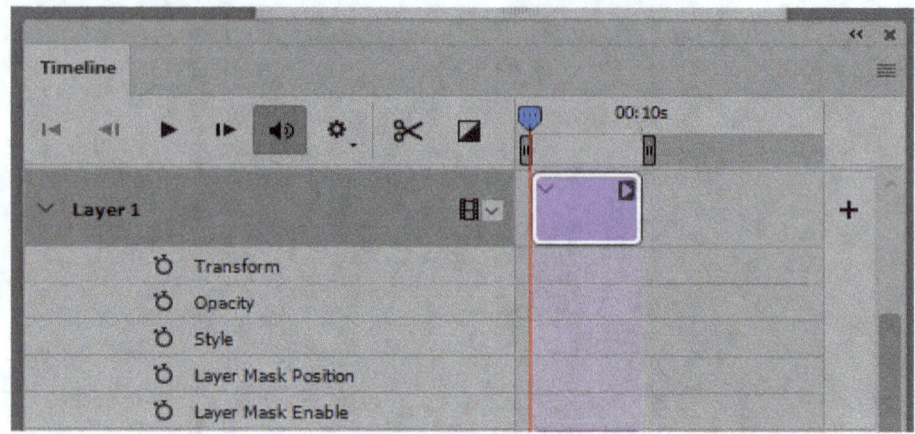

Figure 6-141. Timeline panel Layer 1 selected

However, at this point I will note that while this layer does contain an external layer mask that does allow keyframes to control position, you will not be able to control the scaling (transform) of the layer mask for both keyframes as it transitions.

So, at this point, I would recommend converting this layer again to a smart object layer so that the mask is now internal. Refer to Figure 6-142.

Figure 6-142. Layers panel converting Layer 1 to a smart object layer to internalize the mask

CHAPTER 6   CREATING A PARALLAX: BRING YOUR VINTAGE OR HISTORICAL PHOTOS TO LIFE

Doing so will remove the options of Layer Mask Position and Layer Mask Enabled from your choices, but that is OK in this case as Transform scaling everything at one time is what we really want.

Again, here you will want to set a keyframe for the transform as the starting point 0 for Layer 1. Refer to Figure 6-143.

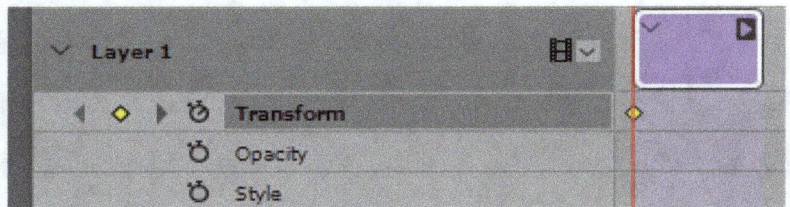

Figure 6-143. *Select Layer 1 and create a starting keyframe*

Move the slider to about the 7 second mark. The girl is currently blocking the scene. We want to scale her and move her into place too. However, to do that while we have a start point and will now create an endpoint, additional keyframes in between may be required. Refer to Figure 6-144.

CHAPTER 6　CREATING A PARALLAX: BRING YOUR VINTAGE OR HISTORICAL PHOTOS TO LIFE

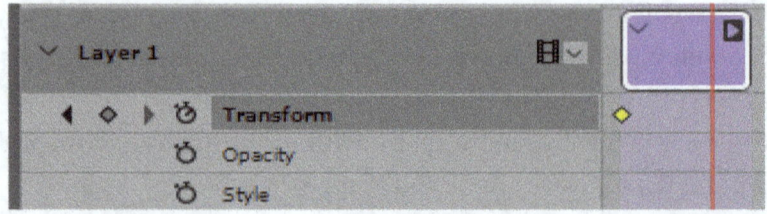

Figure 6-144. *Dragging the Playhead to the next point to add a keyframe*

Go to Edit ➤ Free transform and then move and scale the girl into place, similar to how she is placed here. Refer to Figure 6-145.

CHAPTER 6 CREATING A PARALLAX: BRING YOUR VINTAGE OR HISTORICAL PHOTOS TO LIFE

Figure 6-145. *Use the Free Transform panel to scale and move the girl to her new location*

Currently, she is about 16.17% in width and height. Now click the check in the Options bar panel to confirm. Refer to Figure 6-146.

Figure 6-146. *Free Transform panel; click the check to confirm the Transformation*

The keyframe is now added to second 7 in the transform. Refer to Figure 6-147.

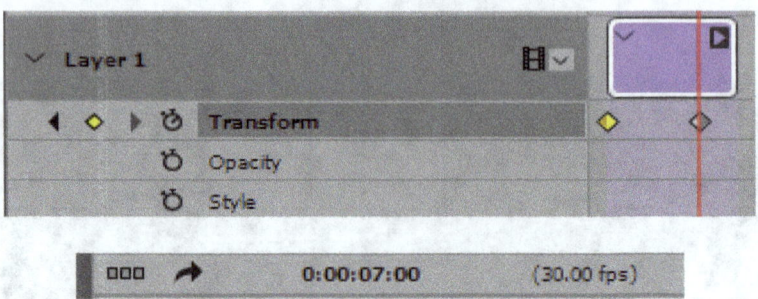

Figure 6-147. *Timeline panel; a new transform keyframe is added to the Timeline*

Now drag the blue playhead and play/preview the animation to see now the movement is affected on the canvas as you reach 7 seconds. The movement, in this case, up to here is good and does not require any additional midpoint movements and scaling. However, in your own projects, you may need to adjust for this.

However, after 7 seconds, the scene moved down and so the girl must move down too.

Move the sider to the 9 second mark. Currently, the girl is in the air levitating over the water which is definitely not natural. Refer to Figure 6-148.

CHAPTER 6   CREATING A PARALLAX: BRING YOUR VINTAGE OR HISTORICAL PHOTOS TO LIFE

Figure 6-148. *When I drag the playhead to the end of work area, the girl now appears in the air because we panned the background up*

As you did with the background layers, you need to, with the Move tool, move nudge her downward with the down arrow key. Refer to Figure 6-149.

CHAPTER 6 CREATING A PARALLAX: BRING YOUR VINTAGE OR HISTORICAL PHOTOS TO LIFE

Figure 6-149. At the new location nudge the girl downward so she appears like she is moving with the scene

This may take a bit of nudging up and down and then moving back to the previous keyframe 7 to compare, to get the downward movement correct. A new keyframe is added to the transform area of the track. Refer to 6-150.

Figure 6-150. A new transform keyframe appears on the Timeline

File ➤ Save your work so far.

944

Custom Rotations

Earlier, when we discussed adding motions, I noted that a preset rotation can be created. However, for custom rotations and scaling, remember, you can also use your Edit ➤ Free Transform to create the rotation as well using your bounding box handles to adjust while in Free Transform. While this current animation does not have any rotation. Rotation animations that you could consider could be objects like wheels spinning or to give the impression that something is falling off a shelf to the ground. Rotation could also be used in the sky along with expansion to give a different movement to clouds, as you can see in this example of the soldier at the castle that you may want to explore on your own after we have completed the current project. Refer to file **castle_sky_parallax.psd**. Refer to Figure 6-151.

CHAPTER 6   CREATING A PARALLAX: BRING YOUR VINTAGE OR HISTORICAL PHOTOS TO LIFE

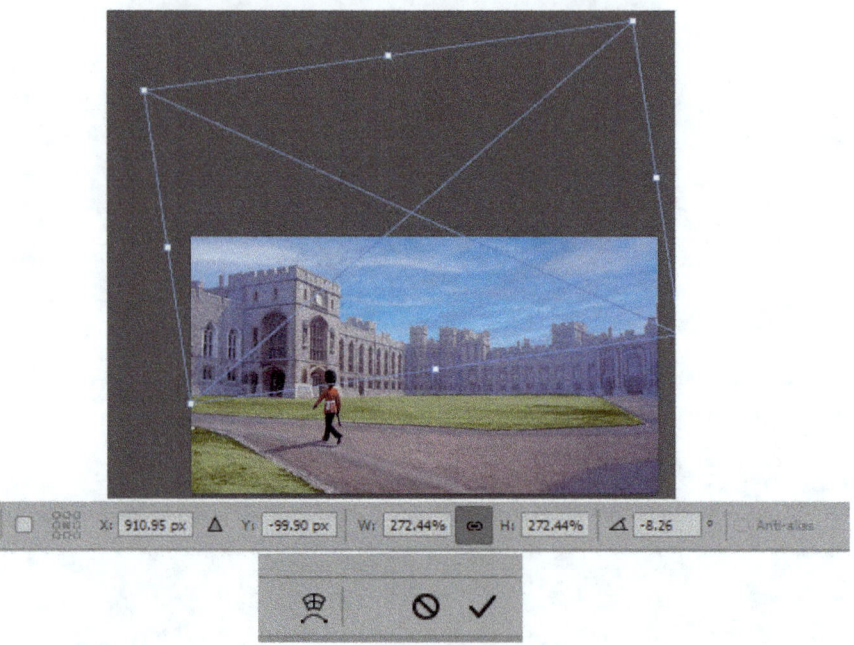

Figure 6-151. *Rotation for the sky can also be achieved with the Free Transform panel*

CHAPTER 6　CREATING A PARALLAX: BRING YOUR VINTAGE OR HISTORICAL PHOTOS TO LIFE

Like the current project, most animation action occurs using the Transform keyframes, as seen in the Timeline panel. Refer to Figure 6-152.

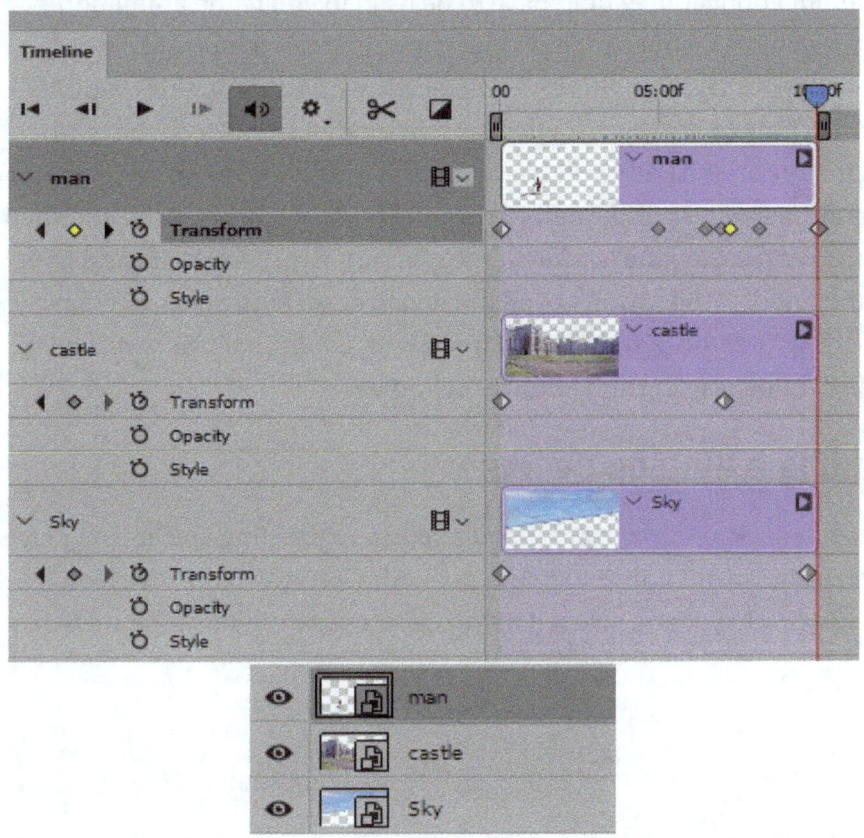

Figure 6-152. *Timeline panel with multiple keyframes for transform in the Timeline panel and the layers in the Layers panel*

We zoom out to see the castle; the sky slightly shrinks and moves at an angle to give the impression that the clouds are changing as the wind moves them. The solider can be scaled moved along the path as well, as it is possible he may have moved by the time the camera fully zoomed out. However, because he is a static photo, he only slides along.

To animate him more accurately, you would need additional photos of his leg and arm movements, or if you had animation knowledge, a different application would have to be used to create the animation and rigging of the joints. That kind of animation is a more advanced topic not discussed in this book; however, we can see in this example that keyframes of transform do need to be adjusted to keep the man accurately on the path with his shadow. In this case, the man's movement was animated last, and I started with the keyframe at 0 second and then moved and scaled the last keyframe near the 10 second mark and then in the middle keyframes moved him again at set keyframes where he diverges from the path; this required about additional five keyframes between the starting and ending keyframes.

Adding a Vintage Overlay

Coming back to our current project, return to timeline and set the playback to 0 seconds, and now make sure to put the Layer Visibility back on for the Color Fill 1 Layer and select it in the Layers panel. Refer to Figure 6-153.

CHAPTER 6   CREATING A PARALLAX: BRING YOUR VINTAGE OR HISTORICAL PHOTOS TO LIFE

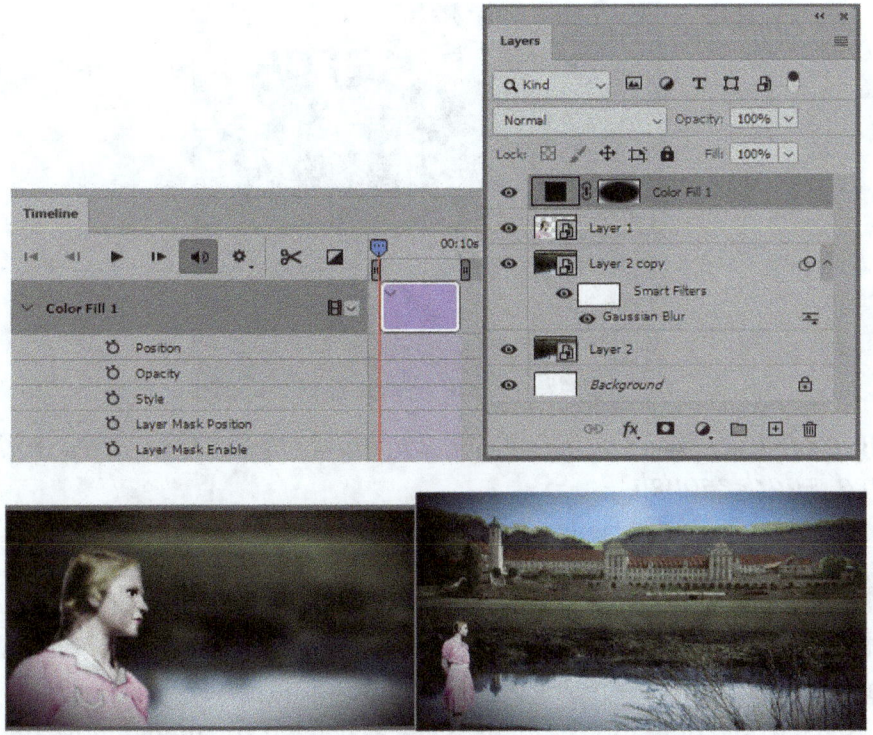

Figure 6-153. *Adding the color fill vignette to the image*

This layer will have no keyframes added to it. It is simply an overlay to give a vintage look, as you might see in historical tv shows. However, I will add a fade effect to this layer in a moment.

File ➤ Save you work so far.

Tip   For your own projects, make sure to include ground shadows for people behind the individuals, if required, especially if they are standing and their feet are visible. In this example, the ground where the girl was standing was only seen very briefly, and most of that area where the shadow would be is covered by the vignette, so it was not necessary to add in this instance. Refer to Figure 6-154.

CHAPTER 6 CREATING A PARALLAX: BRING YOUR VINTAGE OR HISTORICAL PHOTOS TO LIFE

Figure 6-154. *No extra shadow below the girl's feet is required as this area is dark enough*

As a suggestion, you could create a shadow on a blank layer, paint with black using your Brush tool with a soft brush, and set the blending mode of that layer to Multiply and an Opacity of 30 % and place the layer behind the person. You could then, using your keyframes, adjust the opacity as required so that it would only appear on the scene as needed and then remove the shadow as required. If there is movement in the scene, make sure to use the Position keyframes to adjust its placement or convert that layer to a smart object layer and use the Transform keyframes to adjust accordingly.

Duration and Frame Rate

While working with a video animation, we need to consider such things as FPS or frames per second, also known as frame rate. Various film recorders like your smartphone or digital camera take many pictures quickly when creating a video, in every second. Depending on the camera, it can be between 24 and 30 (29.97) frames (photos) per second. When incorporating vintage film that has been digitized for you, this can be important to how the film will display. And in the case of the Parallax, this can affect the speed of the animation as well as rendering time. In this case, we are working with 30 frames per second, but I want the entire video

CHAPTER 6 CREATING A PARALLAX: BRING YOUR VINTAGE OR HISTORICAL PHOTOS TO LIFE

to last about 10 seconds, just to keep the animation short. You may want it shorter or longer depending on its complexities or the speed you require, but you need to have a common frame rate. Refer to Figure 6-155.

Figure 6-155. *Timeline panel with FPS settings*

Frame rate can be checked or adjusted as well. From the Timeline panel menu, use "Set Timeline Frame Rate" if you need to adjust this for your own projects. You can set between 10 and 60 fps from the list, and altering this number can affect the speed overall at which the animation plays, but I will leave this on the default settings that I chose of 30. Refer to Figure 6-156.

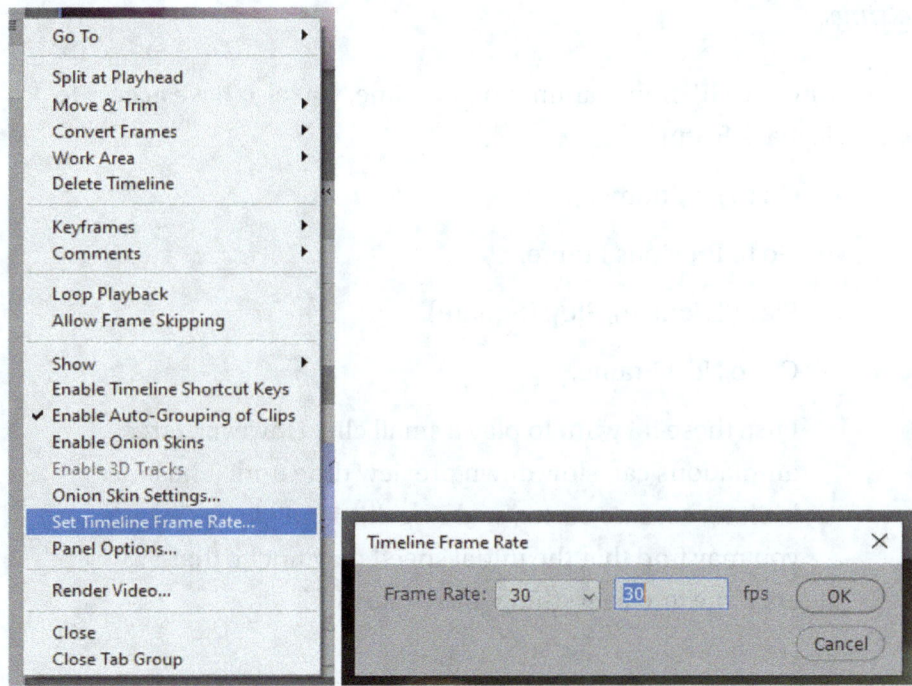

Figure 6-156. *Timeline panel use the menu to access the Timeline Frame Rate dialog box*

Additional menu items can be accessed as well, and if you need more information on many of these advanced options, you can refer to the link at the end of this section.

Playback and Sound Options

Before we render, I will just go over a few more options and considerations that you may want to add to your own projects. Refer to the upper area of the Timeline panel. Refer to Figure 6-157.

Figure 6-157. *Timeline panel playback options and additional settings*

As with the GIF frame animation timeline, you also have access to some playback features.

- Go to first frame.
- Go to Previous Frame.
- Play (Triangle)/Stop (Square).
- Go to Next Frame.

    I use these if I want to play a small clip. However, large animations can slow down preview time until it has built up a frame cache, so doing this kind of preview, you may find that the initial speed may not be that accurate and everything moves slowly.

CHAPTER 6 CREATING A PARALLAX: BRING YOUR VINTAGE OR HISTORICAL PHOTOS TO LIFE

- The speaker icon lets you enable or mute audio playback if it is present. In this case, there is currently no sound, so it does not matter that it is by default on. Refer to Figure 6-158.

Figure 6-158. *Timeline panel turning auto on and off while playing*

The next settings under the gear allow you to set additional playback options which includes Resolution set to a default of 50% as a lower setting can play back faster and Loop Playback which is disabled if you do not want the video to play again when it reaches the end. Refer to Figure 6-159.

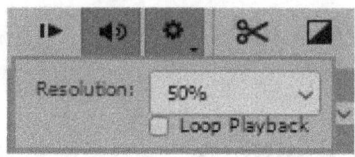

Figure 6-159. *Timeline panel settings resolution while previewing playback*

Split at Playhead

This icon resembles a scissor you can use with layers and video clips if you need to split a clip/track at a place where the playhead is sitting and move that part of the track to a new location, such as maybe an object will appear elsewhere later. For Layers in the Layers panel, this automatically creates a duplicate copy of the layer. Refer to Figure 6-160. Use your History panel if you need to undo this step.

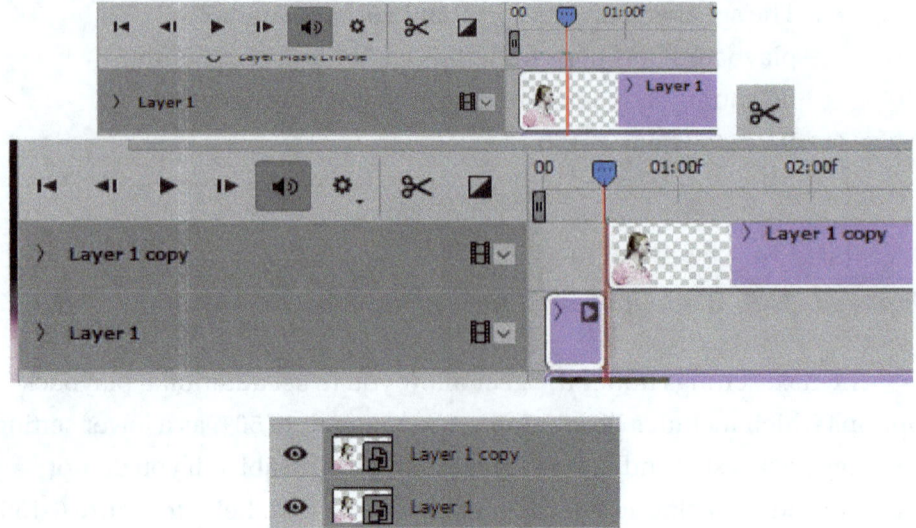

Figure 6-160. Splitting Layers at playhead results in two duplicate images

Adding a Fade (Transition)

Other things you may want to try is adding a fade at the beginning or end of the animation, known as a fade in or fade out. This is often useful when you plan to incorporate the video with other footage clips later and you are transitioning to the next scene or ending the video. Refer to Figure 6-161.

CHAPTER 6   CREATING A PARALLAX: BRING YOUR VINTAGE OR HISTORICAL PHOTOS TO LIFE

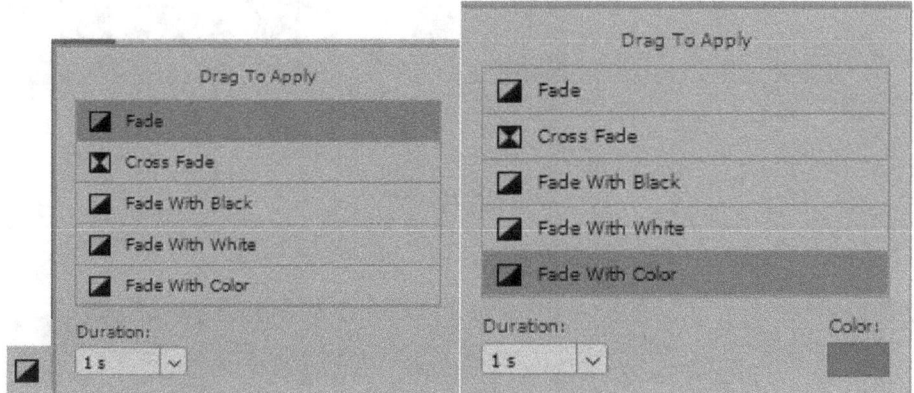

Figure 6-161. *Timeline panel adding a fade transition*

However, it can be added to the beginning or end of a layer track as well including fill layers. Some options you can try are Fade, Cross Fade, Fade with Black, Fade with White, or Fade with Color for a custom look. The duration can be set of 0.25–10 seconds. Choose one and then drag it onto the tracks beginning or end. And adjust the fade using the three prong arrow pointer while on the Layer track to edit the Duration, and you can right-click the Transition if you need to edit as well. Refer to **parallax_zoom_out_final.psd** where I have added a short fade at the beginning of the color fill layer of 2 seconds. Refer to Figure 6-162.

CHAPTER 6   CREATING A PARALLAX: BRING YOUR VINTAGE OR HISTORICAL PHOTOS TO LIFE

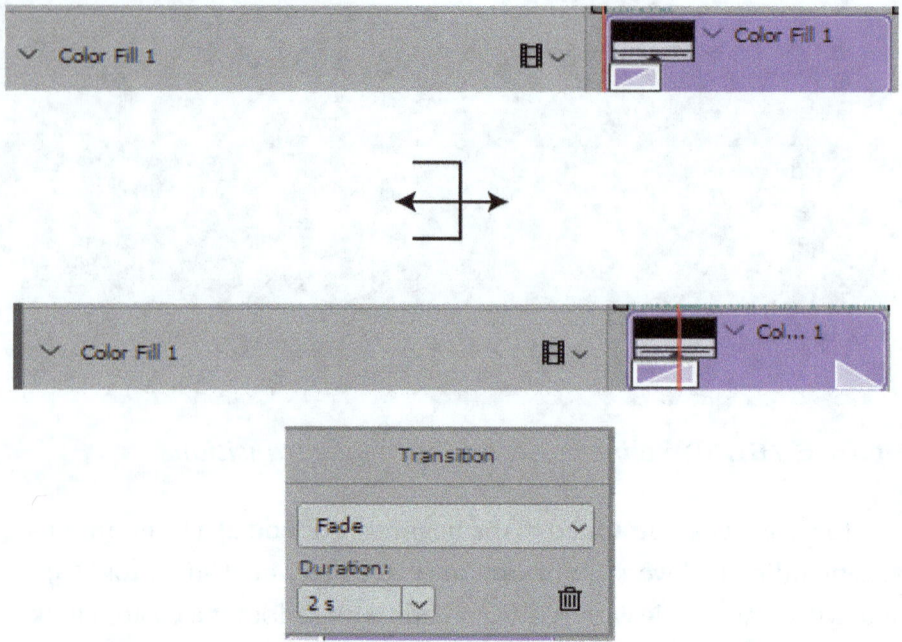

Figure 6-162. *Timeline panel with fade added to start of vignette and, if required, to the end as well*

Here we can test how a fade might look at the start of an animation. Refer to Figure 6-163.

CHAPTER 6   CREATING A PARALLAX: BRING YOUR VINTAGE OR HISTORICAL PHOTOS TO LIFE

Figure 6-163. *Vignette hidden at start of animation then gradually appears*

However, note that Cross Fades can only be used when two layers are part of a video group, as in when two duplicate layers are split and then added to the same track. Refer to Figure 6-164.

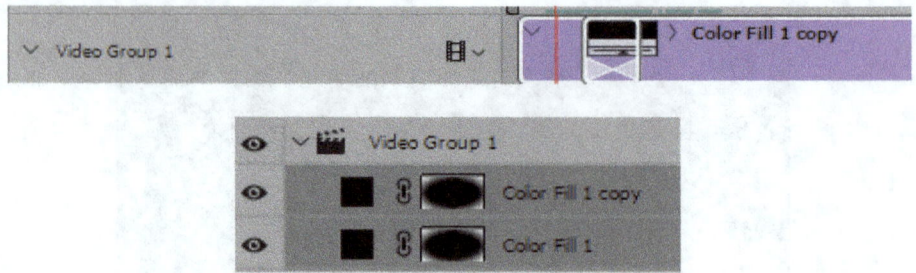

Figure 6-164. *Cross fades in the Timeline will only work if the layers are converted to a Video group*

In this example, we are not using a cross fade.

Adding Sound

While video track is important, you can also incorporate audio in the form of narration, music, or sound effects to the scene as well. This is not possible with GIF animation, but with video, separate audio tracks can be added in the form of .mp3 and other audio files. The audio, once it is added and you right-click the track, can also be turned on and off or the volume lowered or faded in or out if two sounds are occurring at once. And then you can turn audio on or off or mute the audio. Refer to Figure 6-165.

CHAPTER 6   CREATING A PARALLAX: BRING YOUR VINTAGE OR HISTORICAL PHOTOS TO LIFE

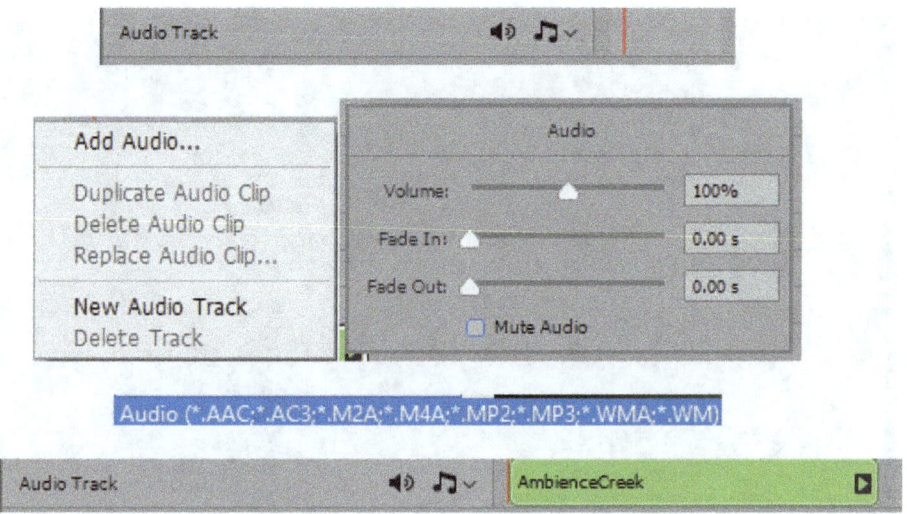

Figure 6-165. *Timeline panel adding an Audio track*

Here I have also added some audio to a copy of the file. In this case, you would want to adjust the Set End of Work area slider back to the 10 second frames because the audio, being longer than the video, would continue to play after the video had stopped. Be aware of this as you add, edit, or delete sounds. See **parallax_zoom_out_sound.psd** for reference and **AmbienceCreek.mp3**. Note that the sound I used was extracted from a file that I created with the Adobe Animate application. Animate has a sound clip asset library which is very useful for when you need some test sounds to practice with in Photoshop. Refer to Figure 6-166.

CHAPTER 6   CREATING A PARALLAX: BRING YOUR VINTAGE OR HISTORICAL PHOTOS TO LIFE

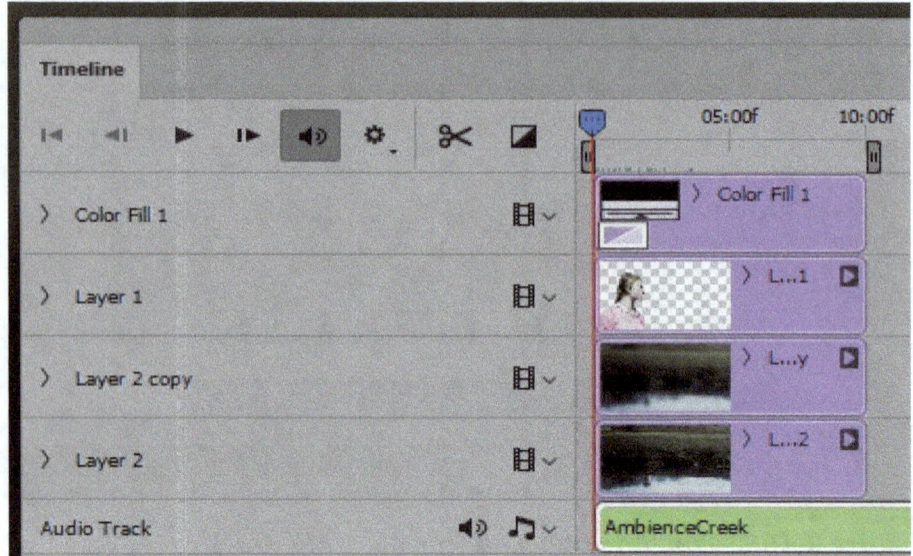

Figure 6-166. Timeline panel adjusting the work areas for a lengthy audio track

On you own project, continue from this point to test and make adjustments.

Deleting a Timeline

If you ever do need to delete the Timeline using the Timeline Panel menu to revert, make sure to do this on an Image ➤ Duplicate as you will lose all the work you did so far and you will need to use Edit ➤ Undo or your History panel immediately if you made this mistake. Refer to Figure 6-167.

CHAPTER 6 CREATING A PARALLAX: BRING YOUR VINTAGE OR HISTORICAL PHOTOS TO LIFE

Figure 6-167. *Use the Timeline panel menu when you need to make additional and advanced adjustments*

Note that additional options can be found in the Timeline panel menu if you are looking for an additional setting for keyframes, showing types of video clips/tracks, and other related video settings:

https://helpx.adobe.com/photoshop/using/creating-timeline-animations.html

Can a Video Animation Be Turned Back into a GIF Animation?

Yes, though sound will not be available. If you need to do this, always work on a copy of the file in case you decide later to switch back, as some settings would be lost.

CHAPTER 6 CREATING A PARALLAX: BRING YOUR VINTAGE OR HISTORICAL PHOTOS TO LIFE

I would not recommend, however, creating a GIF animation over a minute or two long as this would create a buildup of too many frames and may be too large a file size and be difficult to render. And keep to very simple movements and not using high color images as we saw with the gallery, as color quality could be lost.

Click the Convert to Frame animation button. Refer to Figure 6-168.

Figure 6-168. Converting a Timeline animation to a frame animation using the Timeline panel

Then when you see the Alert message regarding frame conversion, click Continue to see a frame by frame version. Refer to Figure 6-169.

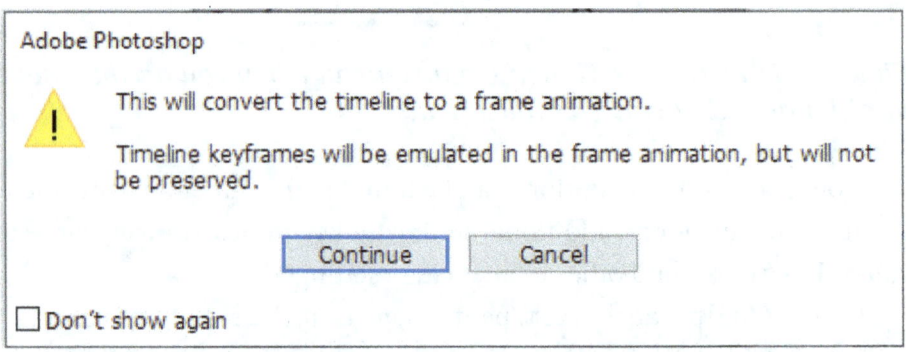

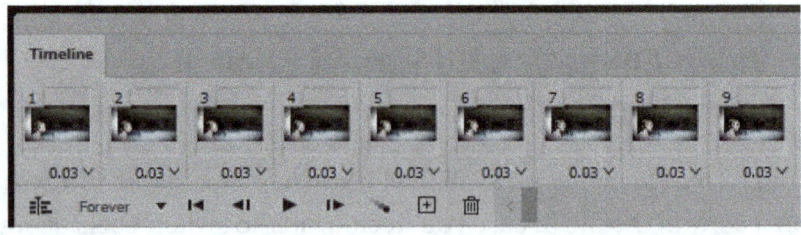

Figure 6-169. Warning that may appear before you convert your video timeline to a frame animation and the result in the Timeline panel

Then refer to the File ➤ Export ➤ Save for Web (Legacy) instruction that I describe earlier in the chapter to Output a GIF animation.

In this example, in the Save for Web (Legacy) dialog box, optionally you could use lower width and height percentage as the GIF animation would likely not be as large as a video. But make sure to observe your compression settings to see how they affect quality when you do so. Refer to Figure 6-170.

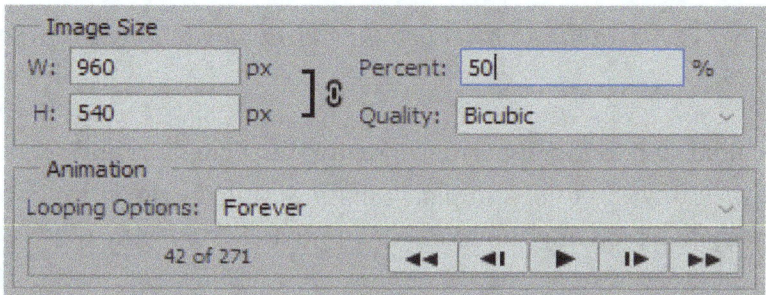

Figure 6-170. Save for Web dialog box GIF animation adjustment Image Size settings

Likewise, you can turn your GIF animation into a video, but beware that with any converting back and forth, certain animation settings will be lost and not appear as the original work. Refer to Figure 6-171.

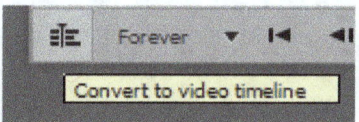

Figure 6-171. Use the Timeline panel to convert a Frame Animation to a video timeline

So, making the decision on the type of animation you want in the beginning is best.

CHAPTER 6   CREATING A PARALLAX: BRING YOUR VINTAGE OR HISTORICAL PHOTOS TO LIFE

Render the Video File

Returning back to our video timeline example, we will now look at the render option and the dialog box. Click the following Arrow button, or choose Render Video from the Timeline panel menu. Refer to Figure 6-172.

Figure 6-172. *Timeline panel use the arrow key to begin rendering the Video*

The final step to Render is to work with the dialog box and set the following settings. In this example, I am rendering the **parallax_zoom_out_final.psd** which does not contain audio. Refer to Figure 6-173.

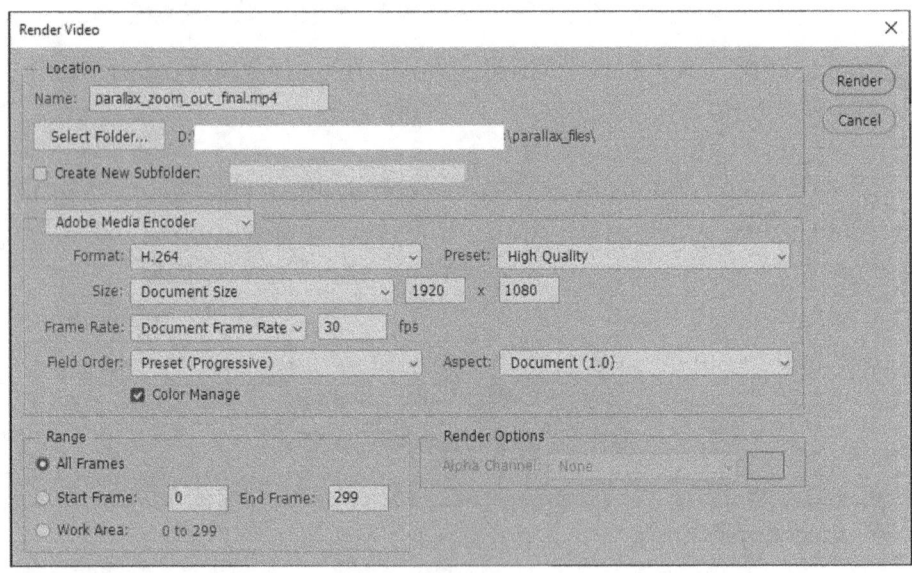

Figure 6-173. *Render Video dialog box*

Location: Name your .mp4 file.

964

CHAPTER 6 CREATING A PARALLAX: BRING YOUR VINTAGE OR HISTORICAL PHOTOS TO LIFE

Select folder that you would like to output to and optionally create new subfolder if required.

Use Adobe Media Encoder from the list, not the other option Photoshop Image Sequence.

For now, use the default settings:

- Format: H.264. Other options are DPX and Quick time which we are not using.

- Preset: High quality. There are other options you can choose from the list to adjust the quality level.

- Size: Leave at the Document Size of 1920 x 1800 to avoid distortion.

- Frame rate: Leave at the Document Frame Rate of 30 fps.

- Field order: Leave on the Preset of (Progressive) and keep Color Manage check box enabled.

- Pixel aspect radio: Leave on the default setting of Document (1.0) which is the same as square.

- Range: Use the setting of All Frames. However, if you need to set a range, you can use Start Frame number and End Frame number or Work Area if different than the number of frames, for example, in the case of the file containing audio **parallax_zoom_out_sound.psd**. To clip the video correctly, you would choose Work Area instead as All Frames would create 2705 frames rather than 299. Refer to Figures 6-173 and 6-174.

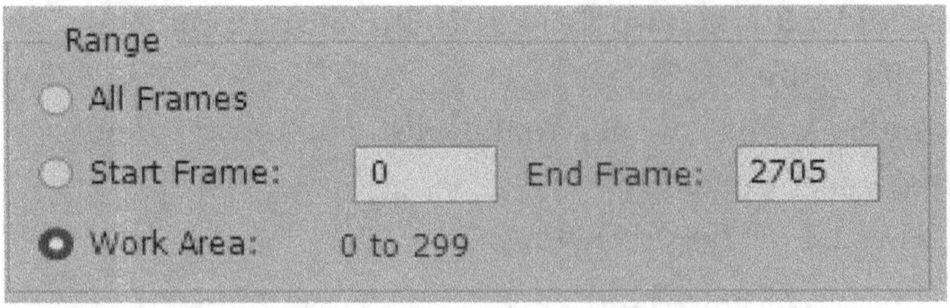

CHAPTER 6 CREATING A PARALLAX: BRING YOUR VINTAGE OR HISTORICAL PHOTOS TO LIFE

Figure 6-174. *Alter your Render Range setting if required to only the Work Area*

- Render options: Leave these at the default settings. In this case, there is no Alpha Channel being used, and there is no 3D options as they were removed recently from the dialog box. Refer to Figure 6-173.

Note that because we are working with a small file, the rendering should happen quickly. Larger files will render very slowly, and if your computer does not have enough RAM, it could cause the Application to crash, so make sure that when you render your file not to have any other applications, open other than Photoshop until the process is complete. Check RAM usage under Edit ➤ Preferences ➤ Performance.

In the Render Video dialog box, then click the Render button. This may take a few minutes depending on your file's length. Refer to Figure 6-175.

CHAPTER 6   CREATING A PARALLAX: BRING YOUR VINTAGE OR HISTORICAL PHOTOS TO LIFE

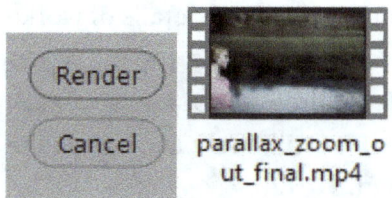

Figure 6-175. *Click render and create your video*

A file then will be created based on your settings in the folder location that you choose. In my case, refer to my files **parallax_zoom_out_final.mp4** and **parallax_zoom_out_sound.mp4** for review. You can also refer to the file **castle_sky_parallax.mp4**.

Later, if you choose, you can edit further in Adobe Media Encoder. While not required for this project I will just give a brief overview of the application of certain features you may want to use with your MP4 file. Use **parallax_color.mp4** for practice.

Media Encoder Settings

If your .mp4 files do not open automatically in Media Encoder, you can still use this application to do some final editing to the color. Use the Creative Cloud desktop console to download and then Open Media Encoder. Refer to Figure 6-176.

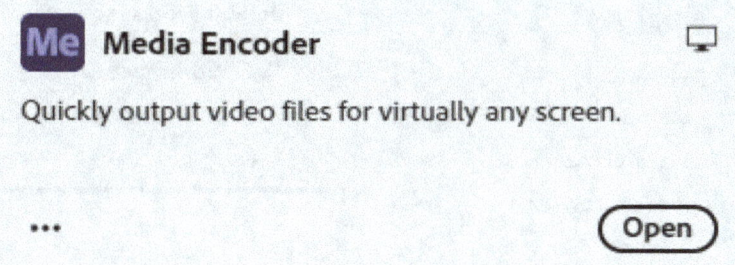

Figure 6-176. *Creative Cloud Desktop Media Encoder Application access*

CHAPTER 6   CREATING A PARALLAX: BRING YOUR VINTAGE OR HISTORICAL PHOTOS TO LIFE

While I am not going into all the details of working with Media Encoder for the Window ➤ Default Workspace, the main panels that you should see open are Tool area, Media Browser, Queue, Preset Browser, and Encoding panels. In this example, we will not be looking at the Watch Folders. Refer to Figure 6-177 and Figure 6-178.

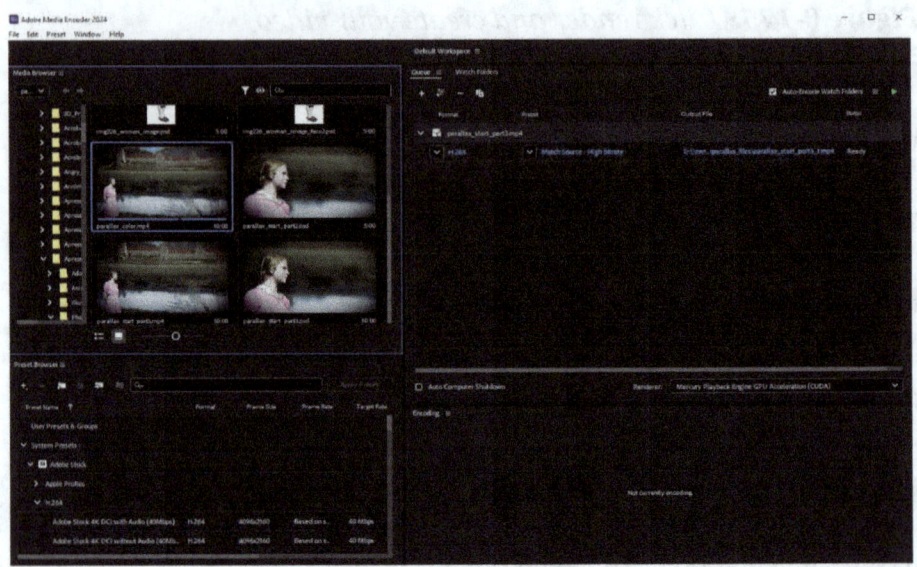

Figure 6-177. *Media Encoder Application Open*

Figure 6-178. *Make sure the Default Workspace is active*

968

CHAPTER 6 CREATING A PARALLAX: BRING YOUR VINTAGE OR HISTORICAL PHOTOS TO LIFE

If the file is not already found in the Queue, you would use the Media Browser panel to locate the file using your folder and add it to the Queue panel by dragging it over, as I did with my file **parallax_color.mp4**. Refer to Figure 6-179.

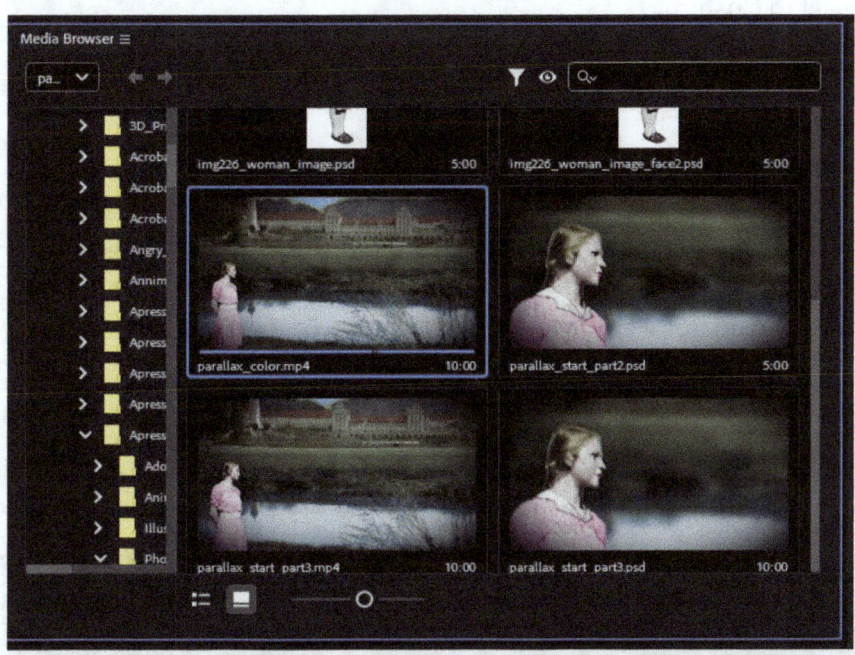

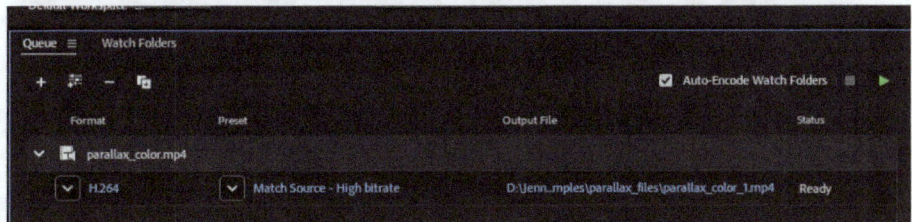

Figure 6-179. *Find files to add to Media Encoder using the Media Browser panel and drag to Queue panel*

Once in the Queue Panel, make sure that the file is set to Format H.264 which is the same as an .mp4 file, which can include audio if present. You can, at this point, view and edit various custom settings, if required. Click on the Preset Match source High bitrate link and if adjusted this will reset the preset to Custom.

While I will not be going through all the settings, here are a few you may want to observe or edit.

Export Settings

This dialog box controls the settings for the Source Document and the file you want to Output, in this case you are creating a copy to the Output file folder. We do not want to edit the Source file or use the Compare tab so stay on the Output Tab you can Leave the settings of Source Scaling as Scale To Fit and you want to keep the Source Rotation the same, so leave at None (0). Refer to Figure 6-180.

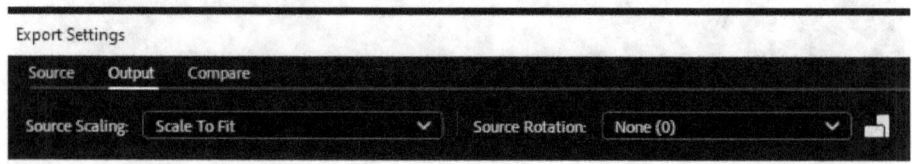

Figure 6-180. Export Settings dialog box

On the right are further Export settings. These are the current Format, the Preset which will become custom as it is edited, an area for comments and the output name of the file.

In this case for the .mp4 file, we want to make sure that Export Video and Export Audio are enabled. Likewise, for some projects you may want to exclude the audio or just export audio so you can check either of these off or on. Refer to Figure 6-181.

CHAPTER 6   CREATING A PARALLAX: BRING YOUR VINTAGE OR HISTORICAL PHOTOS TO LIFE

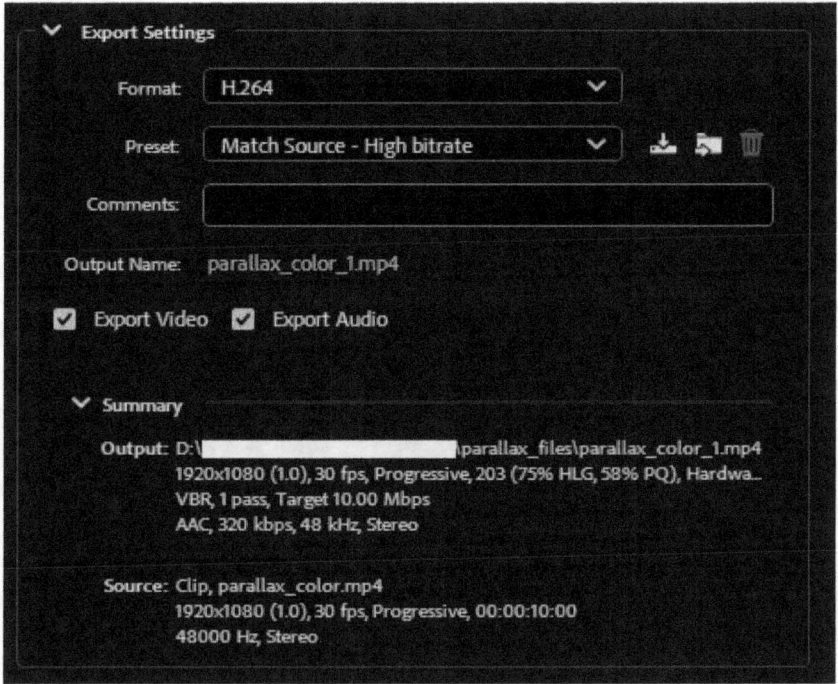

Figure 6-181. *Export Settings dialog box options*

Summary settings

This is a text version of your overall settings changes for both output and source. This can tell us such things as Size of file, frames per second, and any other settings that were added during previous rendering, editing or capturing of video.

The next section controls additional edits that you can make to the output video. They are divided into separate tabs, and each section under those tabs can be expanded using the arrow and reveal more settings. Some, in this case, are not relevant and too advanced for this project, but I will briefly mention the purpose of each tab and some specific settings, as well as a link to more information at the end of the section.

CHAPTER 6   CREATING A PARALLAX: BRING YOUR VINTAGE OR HISTORICAL PHOTOS TO LIFE

Effects

This tab controls some of the rudimentary effects that you can apply to a video. These include the following sections: Tone Mapping, Lumetri Look/LUT, SDR Conform, Image Overlay, Text Overlay, Time Code Overlay (watermark), Time Tuner, Video Limiter, and Loudness Normalization. Refer to Figure 6-182.

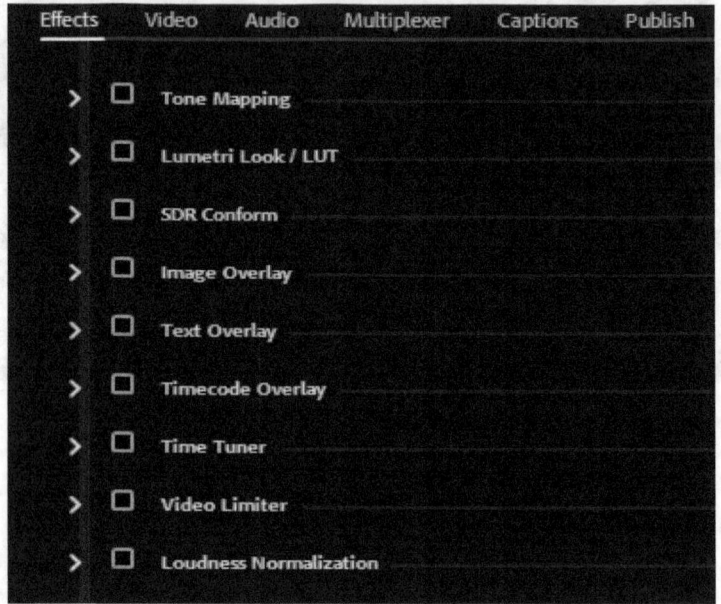

Figure 6-182. *Export Settings dialog box Effects tab*

The main setting adjustment that I want to point out here that you may want to adjust is under Lumetri Look/LUT. Under the area called Applied, currently this area is set to None. However, as we saw in Chapter 1 when we create the adjustment layer Color Lookup files, here again can we reuse them, when we choose to enable the check of that option. From the applied list, choose either a loaded preset option or choose Select and locate and choose a file format option listed of Looks and LUTs. Use the folder Looks if you need a file to test. Refer to Figure 6-183.

CHAPTER 6   CREATING A PARALLAX: BRING YOUR VINTAGE OR HISTORICAL PHOTOS TO LIFE

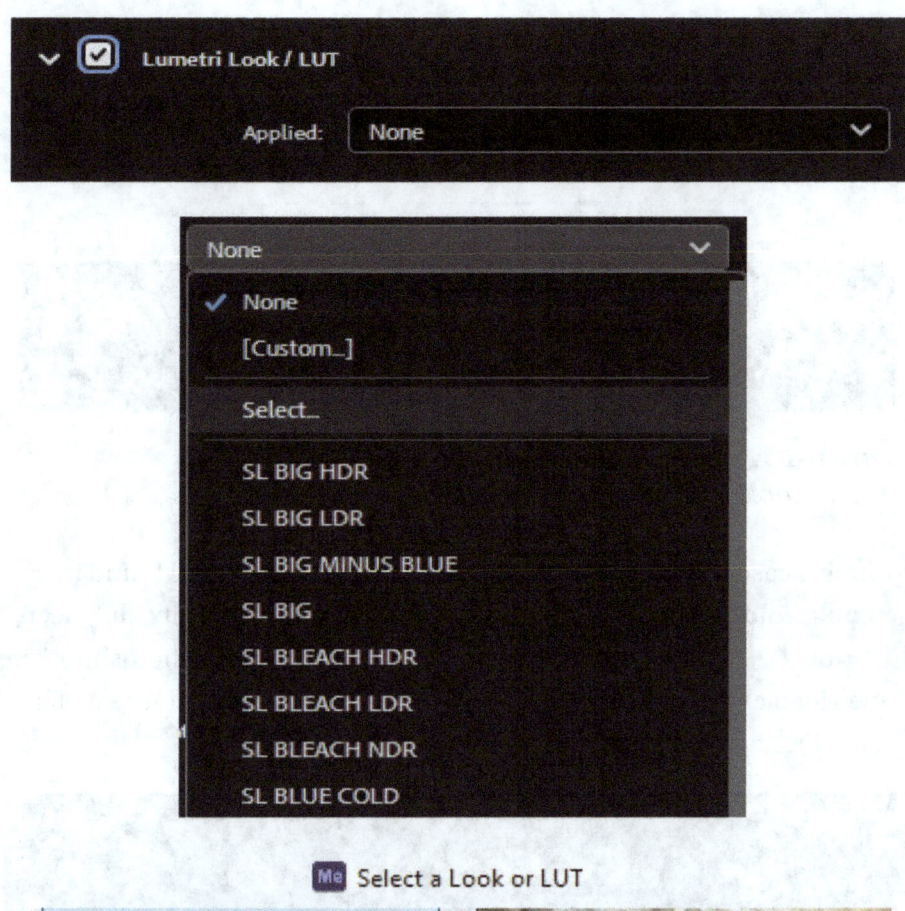

Figure 6-183. *Export Settings dialog box Effects tab set Lumetri Look/LUT*

CHAPTER 6   CREATING A PARALLAX: BRING YOUR VINTAGE OR HISTORICAL PHOTOS TO LIFE

Then click the open button to load a (.CUBE) file. Refer to Figure 6-184.

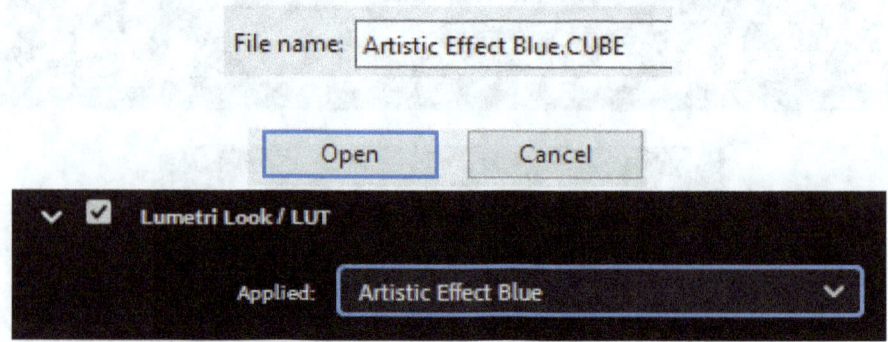

Figure 6-184. *Export Settings dialog box Effects tab set Lumetri Look/LUT from custom file*

In this case from Photoshop, I could use the .cube or .3dl found in the **Looks folder.** Other formats that can be used are .look, .itx, .lut, .fccp, .ilut, irlut, .txt, .cc, and .cdl, but these are not all created in Photoshop. The whole video clip, if this setting is applied, will have a blue color cast effect. Refer to Figure 6-185.

Figure 6-185. *Preview of Lumetri Look/LUT*

To remove or preview the option, just turn the check box off and then on again. Refer to Figure 6-186.

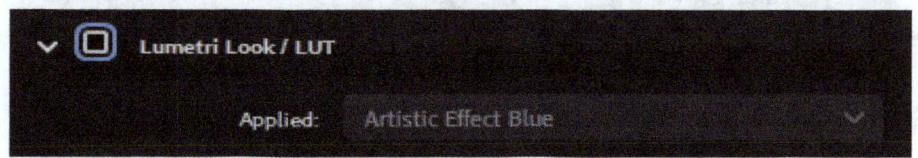

Figure 6-186. *Export Settings dialog box Effects tab disable Lumetri Look/LUT from custom file*

Tip If you do not want to create this effect in Media Encoder and prefer using Photoshop to have greater control over where color is altered, in your video, alternatively add an adjustment layer like Hue/Saturation with the colorize setting enable over your current layers in your .psd file before you render the file.

Video

This area controls various video settings and notes the settings of the source video. The main area to look at here is the Basic Video settings which control the Width (1920) and Height (1080) of the document which linked to maintain aspect ratio, Fame Rate (30), Field Order (progressive), and Aspect (ratio) (square pixels) (1.0) currently defaulted to Match source. The setting Render at Maximum Depth is disabled. Refer to Figure 6-187.

CHAPTER 6   CREATING A PARALLAX: BRING YOUR VINTAGE OR HISTORICAL PHOTOS TO LIFE

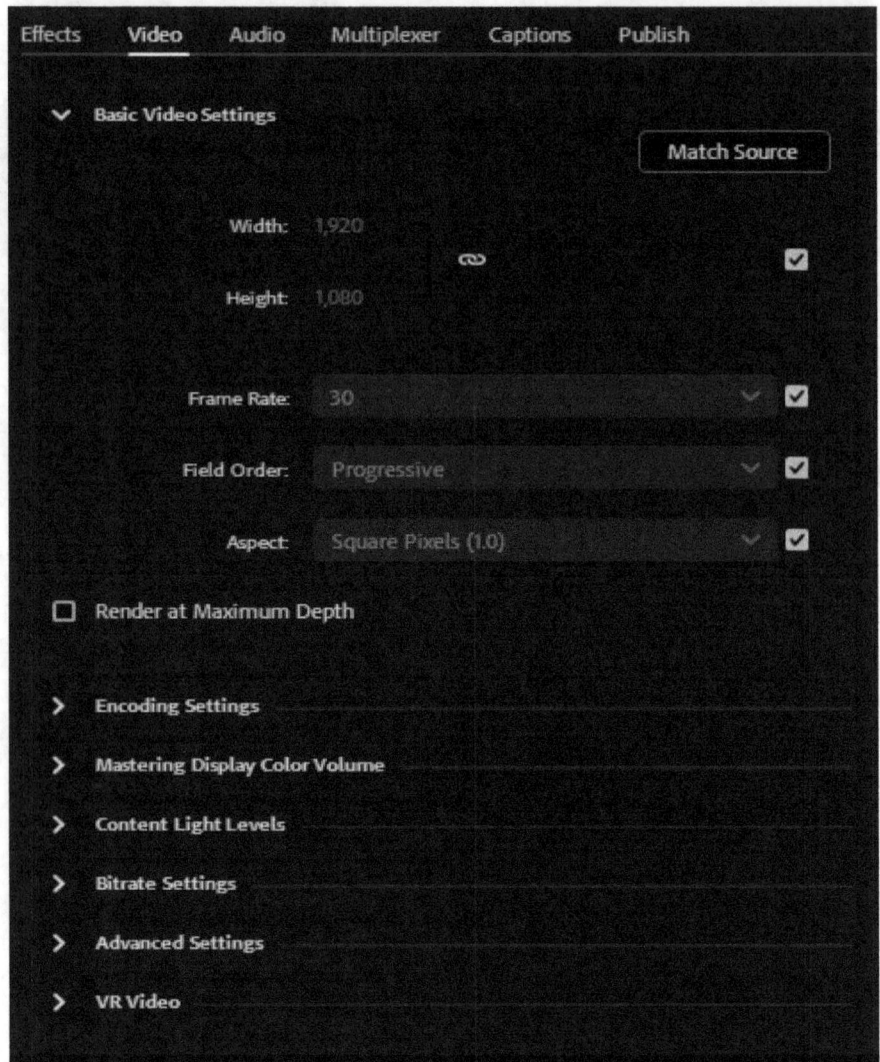

Figure 6-187. *Export Settings dialog box Video Tab*

Other additional selections in this area include Encoding Settings, Mastering Display Color Volume, Content Light Levels, Bitrate Settings, Advanced Settings for Keyframes, and VR Video.

CHAPTER 6   CREATING A PARALLAX: BRING YOUR VINTAGE OR HISTORICAL PHOTOS TO LIFE

Audio

This area controls the various audio settings for the Video which fall under the sections of Audio Format Settings, Basic Audio, and Bitrate Settings. If your video has no audio or you do not plan to adjust any default settings, you can ignore this area. Refer to Figure 6-188.

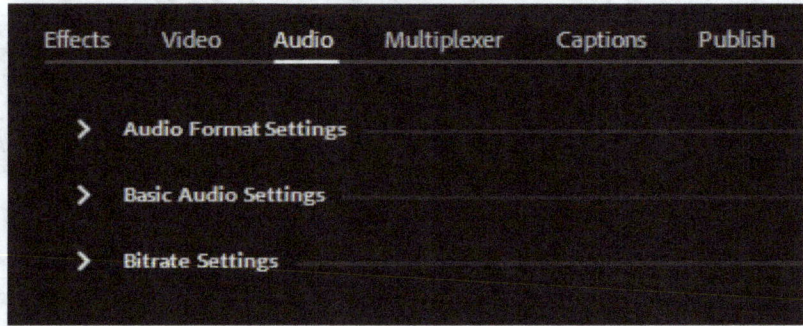

Figure 6-188.   Export Settings dialog box Audio Tab

Multiplexer

It is an advanced area that is used for data selection for the output of the video. However, basic settings for the MP4 file can be adjusted here. Refer to Figure 6-189.

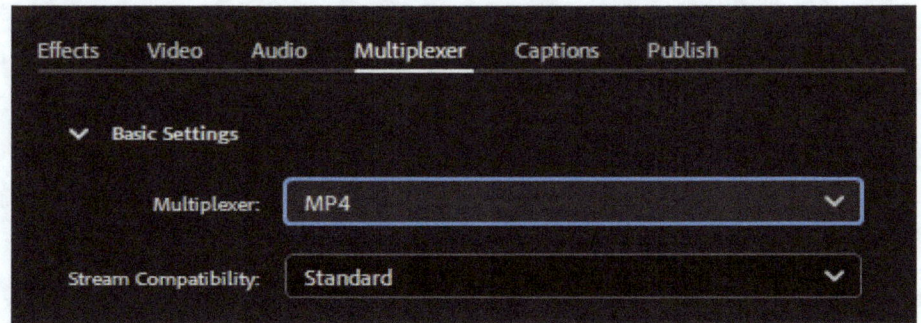

Figure 6-189.   Export Settings dialog box Multiplexer Tab

Captions

If your video requires captions, this information is set here. However, for this format, the settings are disabled and cannot be adjusted. Refer to Figure 6-190.

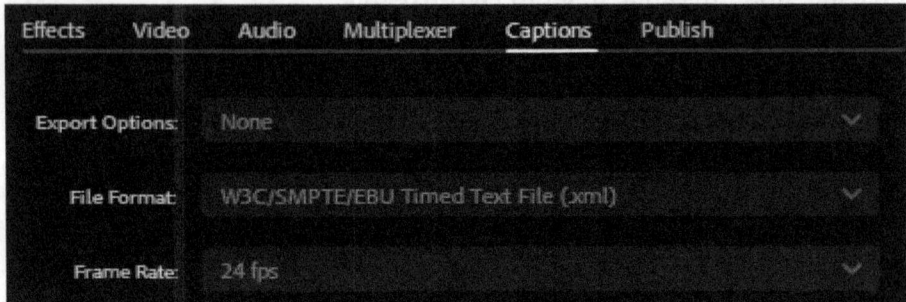

Figure 6-190. *Export Settings dialog box Captions Tab*

Publish

This option in Media Encoder is a quick way to set up the publishing of your video to multiple social media sites that include Behance, Facebook, FTP (your personal website), X (formerly Twitter), Vimeo, YouTube, and TikTok. Refer to Figure 6-191.

CHAPTER 6 CREATING A PARALLAX: BRING YOUR VINTAGE OR HISTORICAL PHOTOS TO LIFE

Figure 6-191. Export Settings dialog box Publish Tab

For example, if you choose to upload to YouTube, you would need to sign in and set various parameters in the area of the dialog box before you could upload the file. Refer to Figure 6-192.

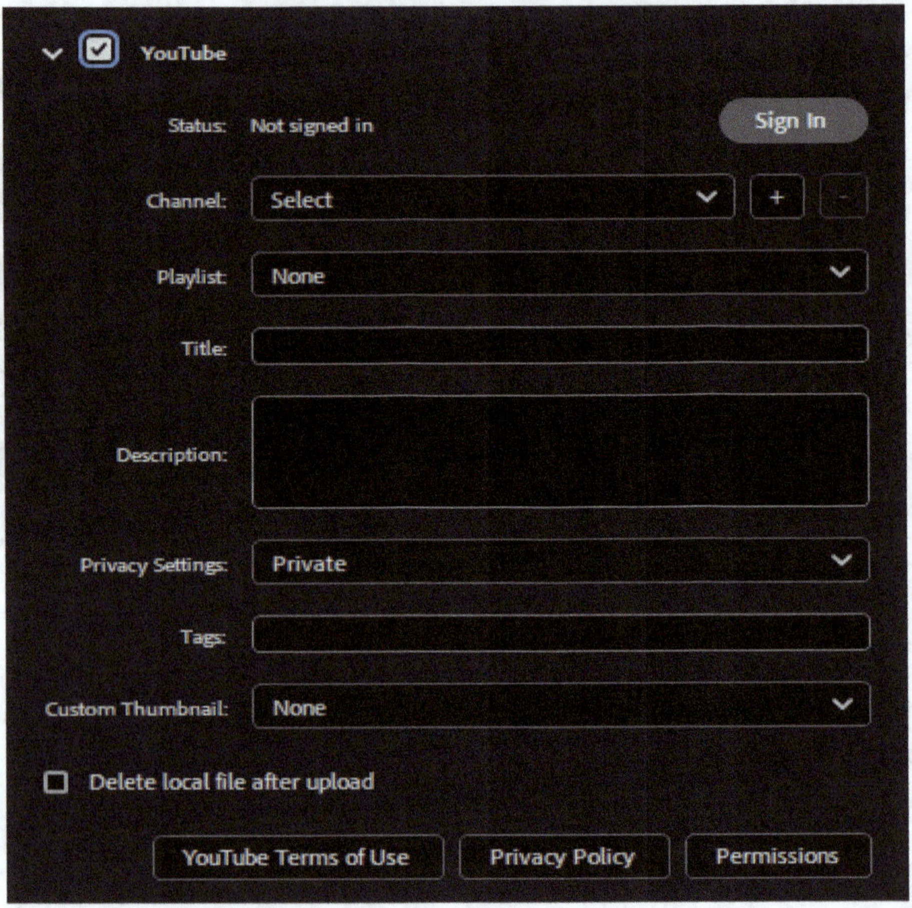

CHAPTER 6   CREATING A PARALLAX: BRING YOUR VINTAGE OR HISTORICAL PHOTOS TO LIFE

Figure 6-192. Export Settings dialog box Publish Tab YouTube

In this case, I will leave the setting disabled as I am just saving to my folder on my desktop.

Each social media site has different parameters that you need to review. Also, you need to check which sites you can upload to based on the type of file format you choose to render if it is something other than .MP4. In this case, .mp4 is available for all the listed social media sites.

CHAPTER 6   CREATING A PARALLAX: BRING YOUR VINTAGE OR HISTORICAL PHOTOS TO LIFE

Additional settings that can be set include the following:

Use Maximum Render Quality, Use Previews, Use Proxies, Set Start Timecode, and Render Alpha Channel only. These options are disabled. Time interpolation which set to Frame Sampling.

Estimated File Size: This will vary based on the project and Maximum File Size which is also disabled. The Meta data button lets you add additional metadata information if required. Refer to Figure 6-193.

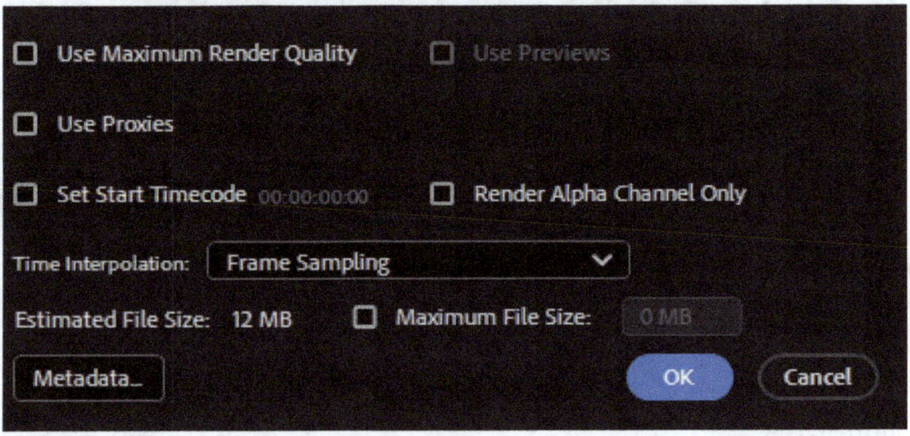

Figure 6-193. Export Settings dialog box additional settings for output file

On the left, below the preview, note that you can Clip the video's start and end area using the lower triangle sliders to remove those parts from the entire clip. Drag the blue slider playhead to preview the video by moving the blue dial. You can also fit the zoom level of the preview or toggle on and off aspect ratio correction. Source Range is set to Custom. Refer to Figure 6-194.

CHAPTER 6   CREATING A PARALLAX: BRING YOUR VINTAGE OR HISTORICAL PHOTOS TO LIFE

Figure 6-194. *Export Settings dialog box adjusting the length of the clip to output if required*

Click OK to exit this dialog box if you have made changes. Refer to Figure 6-195.

Figure 6-195. *Export Settings dialog box OK and cancel dialog box and return to the Queue panel*

The preset is now Custom. Click on the Output File line to set an output file location for the file; in this case, it will have a "_1" or the next number in the sequence at the end so that the source is not overwritten, and observe the status as it is set to Ready. Refer to Figure 6-196.

CHAPTER 6   CREATING A PARALLAX: BRING YOUR VINTAGE OR HISTORICAL PHOTOS TO LIFE

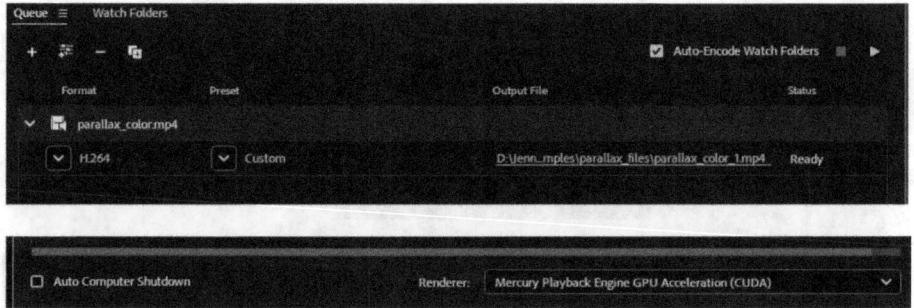

Figure 6-196. *Media Encoder Queue Panel settings*

Note Media Encoder is limited in how it combines video clips, and as this application does not have timeline tracks, it can however merge two or more clips together. In these examples, because we were working with still photos, we did not use all the options found in this area of the Queue panel, but if you would like to know more about these options, you can refer to the following links at the end of the chapter.

In this case, click the green triangle play button to start rendering the new file, but before you do that, make sure that auto computer shutdown is not checked as you do not want this to happen. The renderer, in my case, is set to Mercury Playback Engine GPU Acceleration (CUDA) but you may have a different Engine. Refer to Figure 6-196.

When you click the Green Play arrow. This will allow you to complete the process. Then you would render, and the completed file will appear in the Encoding panel until it is completed and it will then read "Done" in the queue. This rendered for me the file **parallax_color_1.mp4**

Refer to Figure 6-197.

CHAPTER 6   CREATING A PARALLAX: BRING YOUR VINTAGE OR HISTORICAL PHOTOS TO LIFE

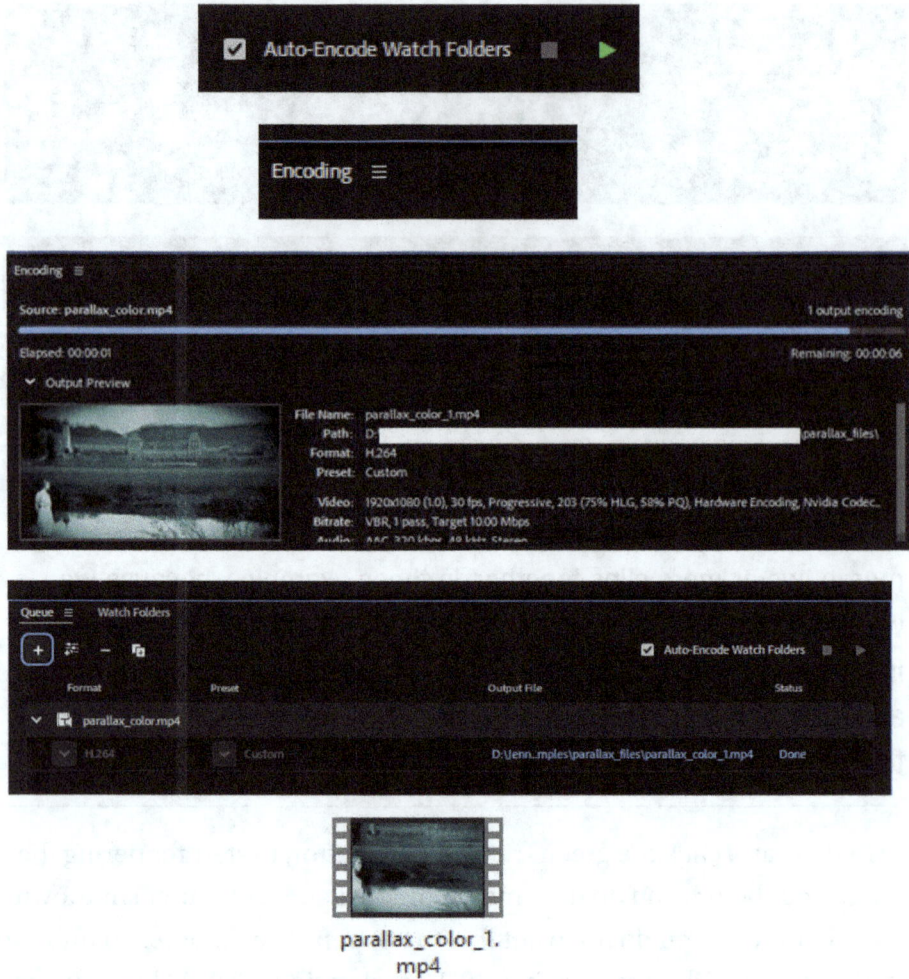

Figure 6-197. *Media Encoder Queue Panel and Encoding panel settings and final render*

If you need to render the same file again, you can right click the name in the Queue and choose Reset Status, from the pop-up list.

You can then close the Media Encoder application. File ➤ Exit (Ctrl/CMD+Q).

984

In Photoshop, remember to File ➤ Save your work. You can now close any .psd files and play any .mp4 files you have created in your computer's video viewer to review your work.

More on the topic of Media Encoder can be found at the following link:

https://helpx.adobe.com/media-encoder/get-started.html

https://helpx.adobe.com/media-encoder/using/overview-media-encoder-user-interface.html

Summary

In this chapter, we reviewed the Timeline panel and how it can be used to create either a GIF Frame Animation or render a video timeline animation as a MP4 file. We also briefly looked at Media Encoder, should you want to try some additional edits. In the final chapter, we will look at what your next steps are, using other Adobe Creative Cloud and Microsoft apps, as you continue to work on your photo restoration project.

CHAPTER 7

What Is the Next Step in Your Photo Restoration Project?

So far, the focus of this book has been mainly on Photoshop for photo restoration. However, after the photo has been restored, what are some of the next steps that you should consider as you work on your project? How do you intend to display your photos? In print, as part of a scrapbook, maybe online, or part of a slideshow as a memorial for a friend? What other applications would you use that are part of the Adobe Creative Cloud or maybe a Microsoft application? In this chapter, we will briefly look at several applications and suggestions.

> Note that this chapter does contain projects found in the Volume 2 Chapter 7 folder. There are various folders you can review, based on the application discussed.

© Jennifer Harder 2024
J. Harder, *A Beginner's Guide to Digital Image Repair in Photoshop: Volume 2*,
https://doi.org/10.1007/979-8-8688-0763-3_7

CHAPTER 7   WHAT IS THE NEXT STEP IN YOUR PHOTO RESTORATION PROJECT?

Photoshop

In this chapter, before we conclude the topic on working in Photoshop. Here are a few remaining things you can do to complete your work should you want to export your images for other projects.

Some tips and tricks about online viewing can be found here for online work and color management:

https://helpx.adobe.com/photoshop/using/color-managing-documents-online-viewing.html

For this section, you can refer to the **Photoshop Projects Folder** for files you can edit and open if you want to experiment and follow along.

Saving RGB Files for the Web or Email

Also, remember that if you plan to save your files for the Web in RGB color mode, as mentioned before, for optimum color quality online, I recommend using .jpeg and .png files.

As you saw with the .GIF animation file, you can use File➤ Export ➤Save for Web (Legacy). This will offer you alternative options for saving your files as either a .jpg or .png format when you choose that file format from the optimize file format list (JPEG, PNG, PNG-24) or choose a preset. Once a format is chosen, then you can set similar settings as you did for the animation but this time for the static image, such as adjust quality levels and transparency. Note that some file formats may have less options than others. For example, JPEG do have a setting for Low, Medium, High, Very High, and Maximum. However, you can use the Quality and Blur sliders for greater control of quality as well. You can refer back to Chapter 6 if you need more details or need to compare. Refer to Figure 7-1 and Figure 7-2.

CHAPTER 7   WHAT IS THE NEXT STEP IN YOUR PHOTO RESTORATION PROJECT?

***Figure 7-1.** Save for Web dialog box*

CHAPTER 7   WHAT IS THE NEXT STEP IN YOUR PHOTO RESTORATION PROJECT?

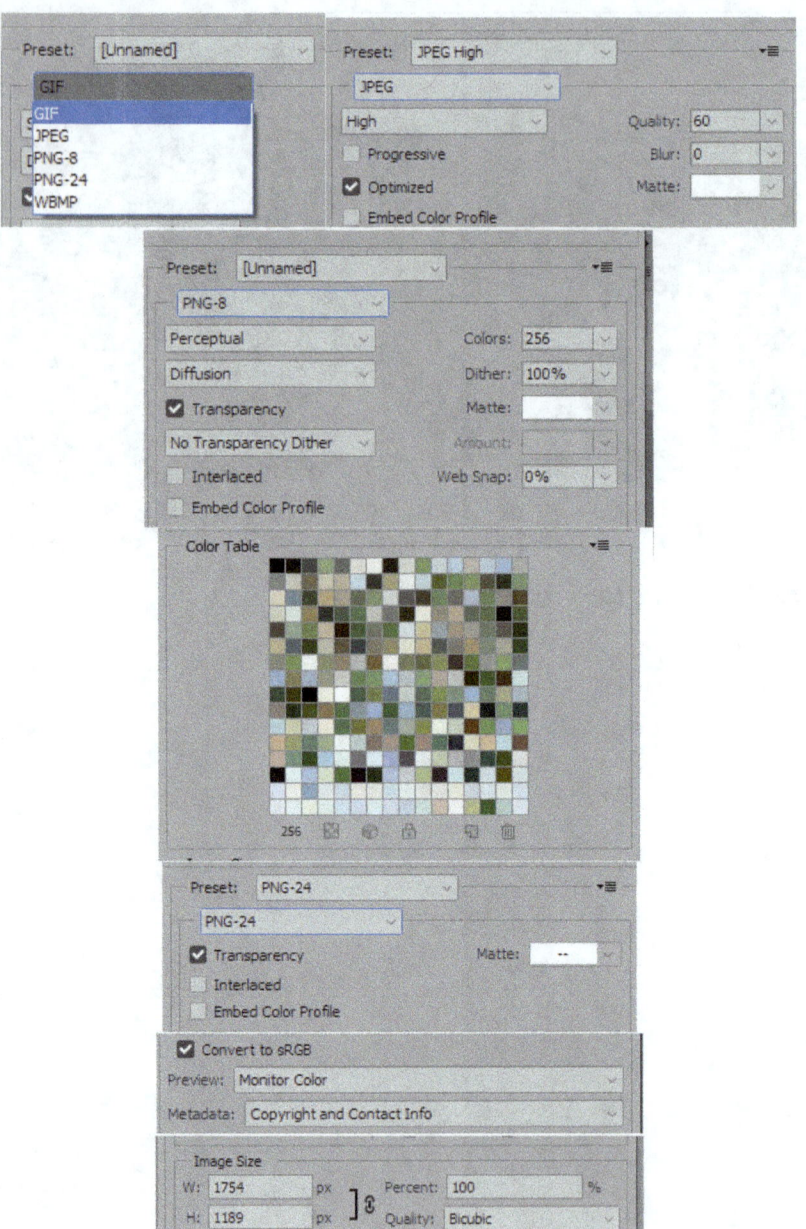

Figure 7-2. *Save for Web dialog box settings for other file formats*

CHAPTER 7   WHAT IS THE NEXT STEP IN YOUR PHOTO RESTORATION PROJECT?

Likewise, JPEG will not allow for any transparent areas while the PNG formats will.

After choosing a JPEG, PNG-8, or PNG-24 option, you would then save the file. In the Format of Images Only, Settings: Default settings, and save the file to a new location. Refer to Figure 7-3.

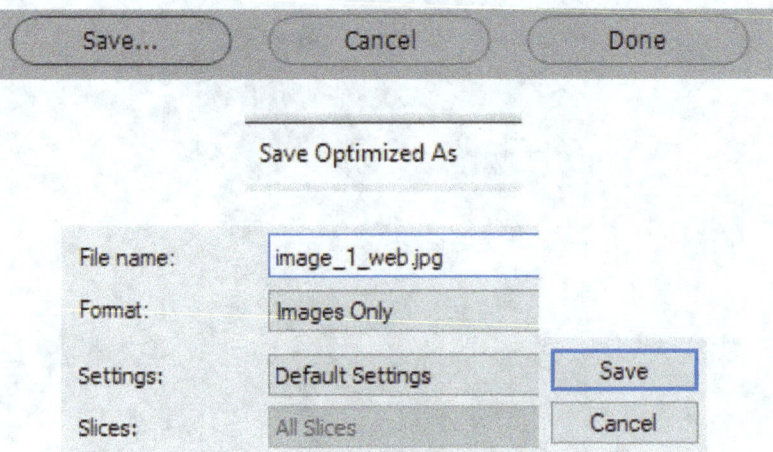

Figure 7-3. *Saving a jpeg file for Output*

If the image was 300ppi, it will automatically convert the image in 72ppi.

However, when you need to save in multiple size formats of the same file in either JPEG, PNG, or GIF (static only) at once, I recommend using File Export ➤ Export As dialog box. Refer to Figure 7-4.

CHAPTER 7   WHAT IS THE NEXT STEP IN YOUR PHOTO RESTORATION PROJECT?

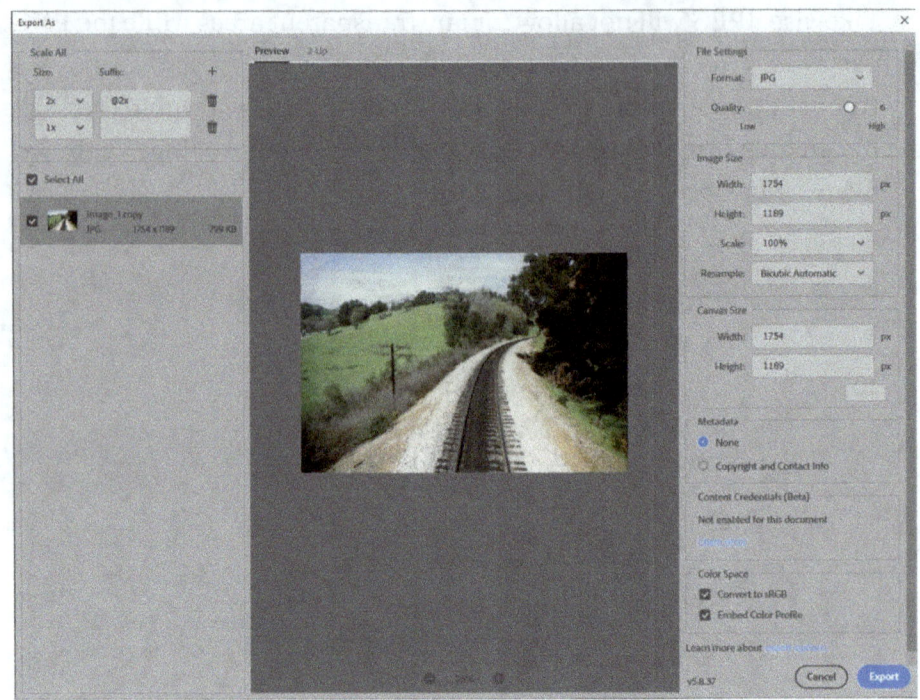

Figure 7-4. *Export as dialog box and resulting files*

You can learn more about this dialog box and other export options from the following links:

https://helpx.adobe.com/photoshop/using/export-artboards-layers.html

https://helpx.adobe.com/photoshop/using/content-credentials.html

File Options and Tips for Saving Your Photo for Print

In most of the book, we have been working with our images in RGB color mode. However, when you are ready to print your images, you may want to convert your images to CMYK.

Note that with some inkjet printers, you can leave the format in RGB, and the image will print out very nicely as the printer's software does its own conversions. However, if a printing company has asked you to convert the image to CMYK, here are a few tips to consider.

Before converting the file to CMYK, you can use the View➤ Proof Setup and View ➤Gamut Warning options, as were discussed in Chapter 2. If the changes are minor, you may prefer not to make any adjustments, or you may want to use one of the adjustment layers like Hue/Saturation, to make some adjustments to select areas, using a layer mask selection. Refer to Figure 7-5.

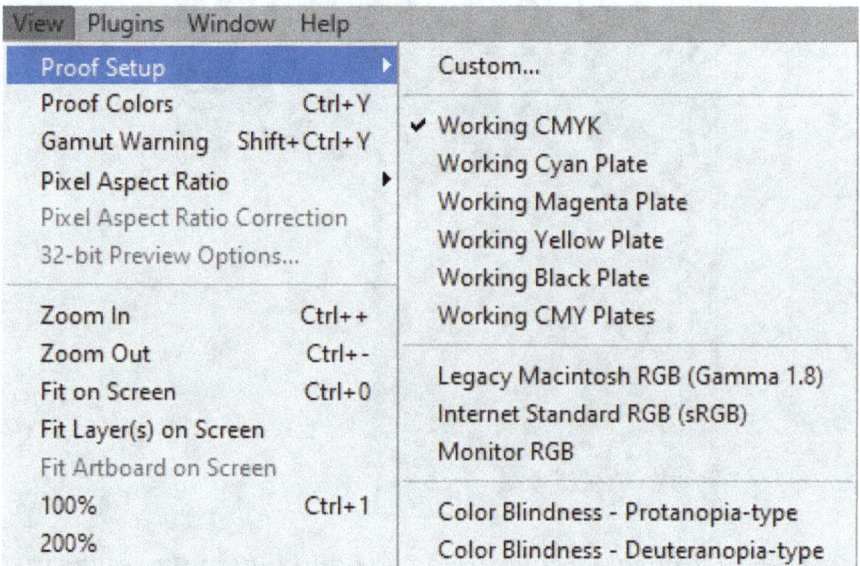

Figure 7-5. View menu settings

CHAPTER 7   WHAT IS THE NEXT STEP IN YOUR PHOTO RESTORATION PROJECT?

As always, make sure to work on an Image➤ Duplicate of the file so you do not destroy the original RGB document. Then make sure to Layer ➤ Flatten the image using your Layers panel menu if there are additional layers. Refer to Figure 7-6.

Figure 7-6. *Duplicate image dialog box and flatten the image in Photoshop*

However, for more technical information on exact color adjustments, as we discussed in Chapters 1 and 2, you can also refer to the following link:

https://helpx.adobe.com/photoshop/using/color-adjustments.html

Once you have flattened the image, then Choose Image ➤ Mode ➤ CMYK Color. You will get a warning message that you are making a color conversion. Click OK. Refer to Figure 7-7.

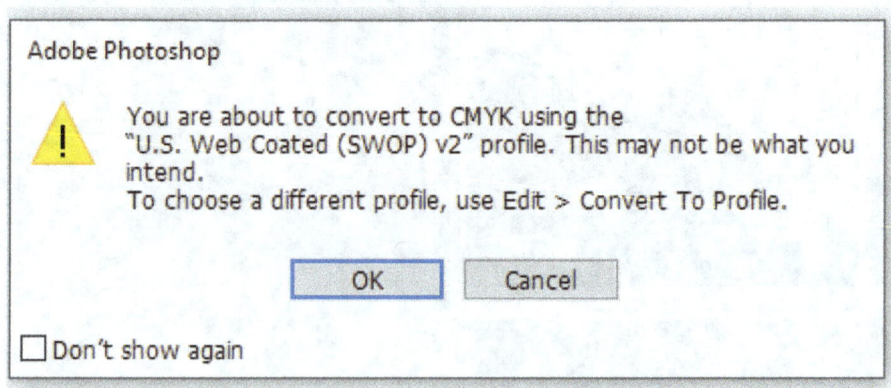

Figure 7-7. *Photoshop warning message*

You may also notice a color conversion on the screen when you do this. This is because RGB has a wider range of colors than CMYK. However, CMYK inks are how files are printed, by, for example, an offset printer or press. Yet the colors can appear duller, as we discussed earlier in Chapter 2, because you are now printing in pigment and not viewing in the light of your screen.

Here are some printing tips to note: When you go to File ➤ Print your document,

- Become aware not only of your screen profiles but also printer profiles for the hardware you work with. Knowing and understanding what kind of quality your inkjet or laser printer can output is important and can be reviewed for each printer under the Print Settings dialog box. You can discover such things as what kind of paper or paper sizes it can or cannot accept before you click print. Also, you may want to consult the print company or your home printer's online manual as well. Refer to Figure 7-8.

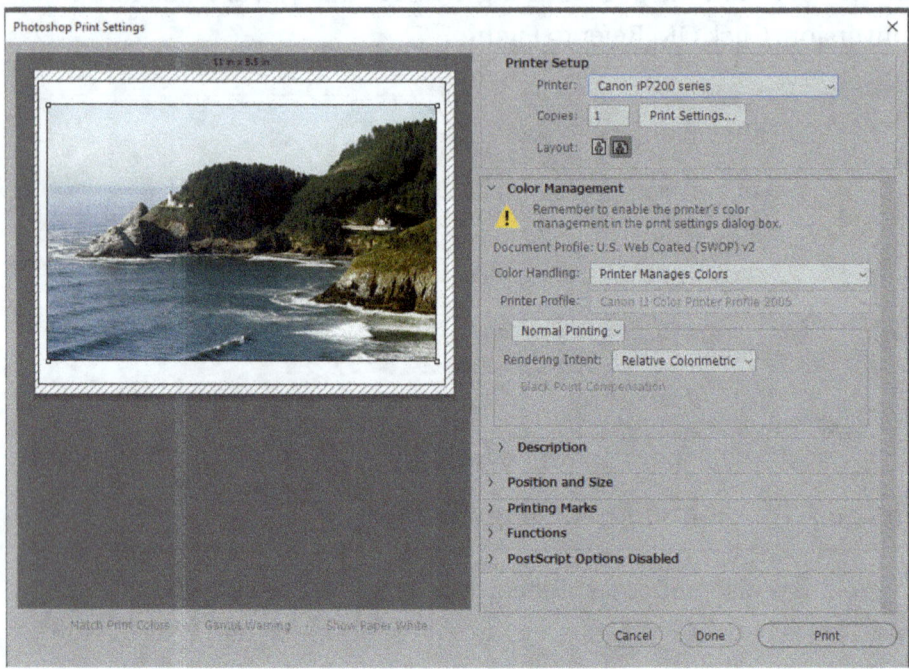

Figure 7-8. *Photoshop Print Settings dialog box*

When choosing a paper, consider the following:

- Glossy paper will often produce a better color result which is ideal for photos.

- Matte paper is good for situations where there is a combination of images and text.

- If you are going for a more artistic effect, you may want to look at canvas options for pictures you plan to frame.

- For optimum results of any paper that you use, make sure it is compatible with your inkjet or laser printer and the color is a bright white, as paper that has a dull yellow or another color will affect printing results as well.

- Always have a few extra sheets of the paper available, and ensure that the toner or inkjet cartridges are not running low if you must run a few test prints.

CMYK Filter Adjustments for a Specific Channel

One recommendation, after converting to CMYK and before printing, is to use a sharpen filter for a final touch-up before printing.

A bit of sharpening is always helpful as you can use an Unsharp Mask or the Smart Sharpen filter, as we saw in Chapter 3. It was mentioned that sharpening can improve the image if it has gone through an image size conversion and been enlarged after using Image ➤ Image Size. Refer to Figure 7-9.

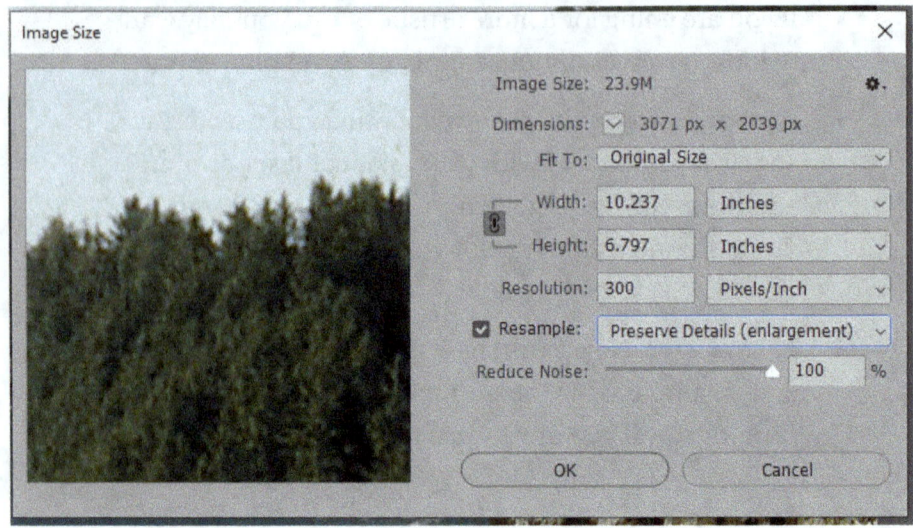

Figure 7-9. *Image size dialog box in the process of enlarging an image*

When in RGB color mode, you saw that you could do an overall sharpening. However, while in CMYK mode, this might make some colors shift or create some unwanted noise. However, in the Channels panel, by just selecting Black channel and applying the Sharpening filter of unsharp mask to it, this may be adequate. Refer to Figure 7-10.

CHAPTER 7 WHAT IS THE NEXT STEP IN YOUR PHOTO RESTORATION PROJECT?

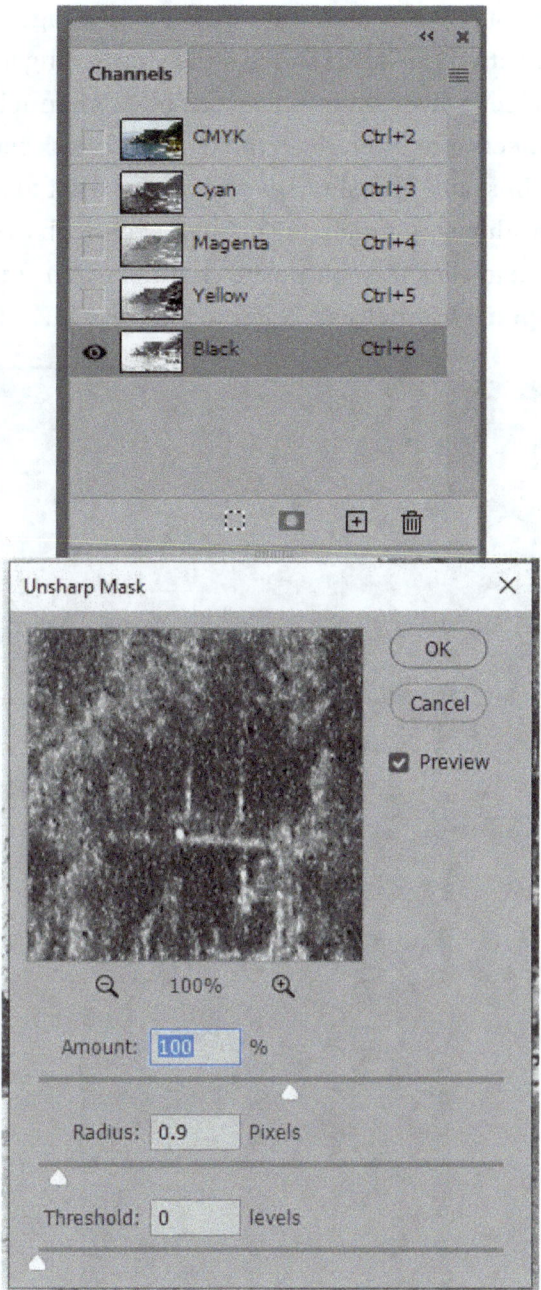

***Figure 7-10.** Channels panel and Unsharp Mask filter*

CHAPTER 7   WHAT IS THE NEXT STEP IN YOUR PHOTO RESTORATION PROJECT?

To compare results, you can always work on an image duplicate of your layer before you flatten the layers to see if the sharpening took effect as you intended. Select a layer, then select your black channel, and apply the filter so it only affects that layer. Keep the Unsharp mask settings low for the Amount, Radius, and Threshold as you do not want to over sharpen the channel and introduce too much noise, but just enough to still reveal some details. Make sure to click the composite channel when you are done. See file **image_sharpen_channel.psd**. Refer to Figure 7-11.

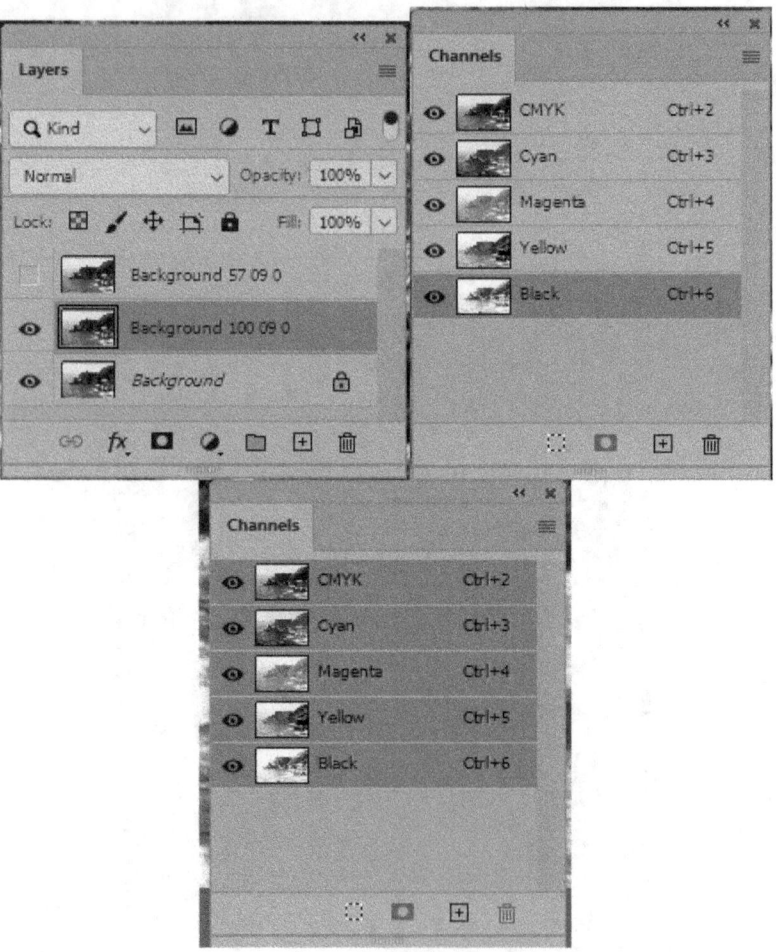

Figure 7-11. *Layers renamed with my settings and channels panel*

CHAPTER 7 WHAT IS THE NEXT STEP IN YOUR PHOTO RESTORATION PROJECT?

Warning Do not convert a CMYK document back to RGB as with each conversion you will lose information. Always keep a copy of your RGB original as a backup.

Saving Your File for Print

Then, for the print company, you can flatten the image copy and File ➤ Save your images as a .tif as this format will keep the image's quality and not compress the file further, as a .jpeg would. Refer to Figure 7-12.

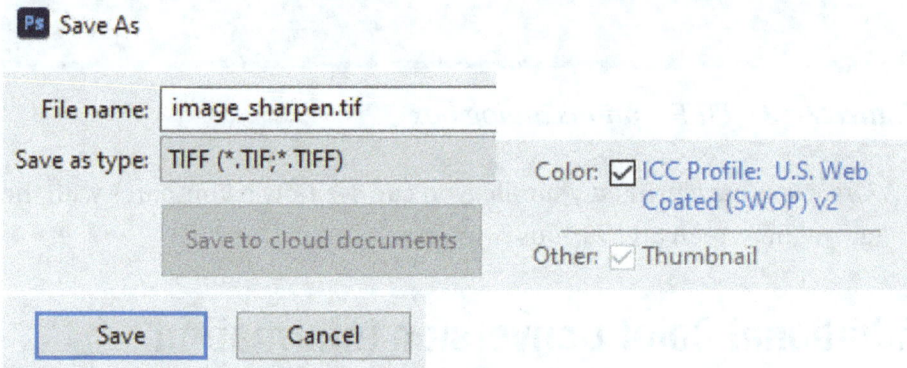

Figure 7-12. Save as dialog box save image as a TIFF file

In the dialog box, I used the settings of Image Compression None. I left the Save Image Pyramid option disabled, left Pixel order at Interleaved (RGBRGB), and the Byte Order at IMB PC, but for your files it may be Macintosh. There are no extra layers in this file so the Layer Compression options were not required and I clicked OK, to complete the save. Refer to Figure 7-13.

1001

CHAPTER 7   WHAT IS THE NEXT STEP IN YOUR PHOTO RESTORATION PROJECT?

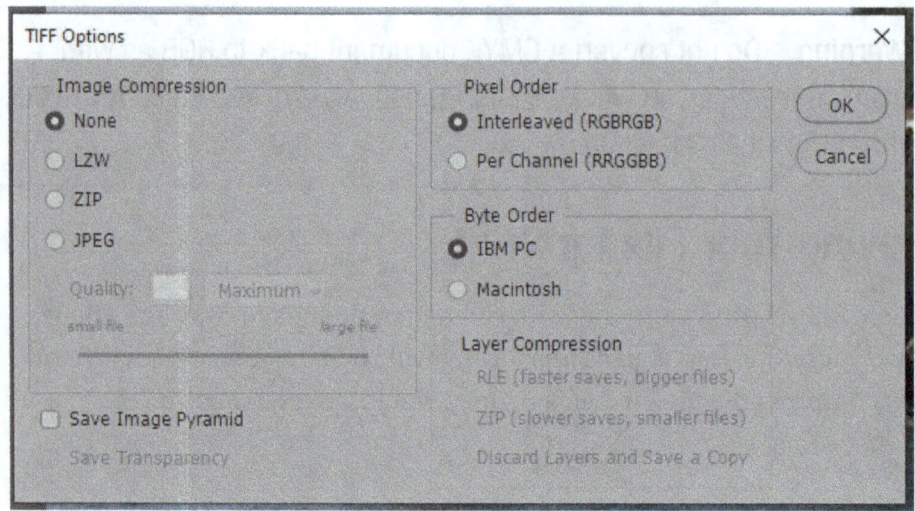

Figure 7-13. *TIFF Options dialog box*

Once you have printed your file, you can see how it compares with the image on the screen and various printers.

Additional Color Conversion Information

If the conversion is not ideal and you need to have your images professionally printed, then you may need to consult with your print company as to what kind of color settings and profile you should be using. This is a more advanced topic, but you can find these settings here in the Edit menu as well. Use them in combination with the View ➤ Proof Setup and Gamut Warning menu as you consult with the print company you are working with. Refer to Figure 7-14.

Figure 7-14. *Edit menu color stings options*

CHAPTER 7   WHAT IS THE NEXT STEP IN YOUR PHOTO RESTORATION PROJECT?

Edit ➤ Color Settings

This dialog box will give you information on the current color settings that Adobe is using for your Working spaces of RGB, CMYK, Gray, and Spot as well as Conversion Options, Color Management Policies, and Advanced controls. Refer to Figure 7-15.

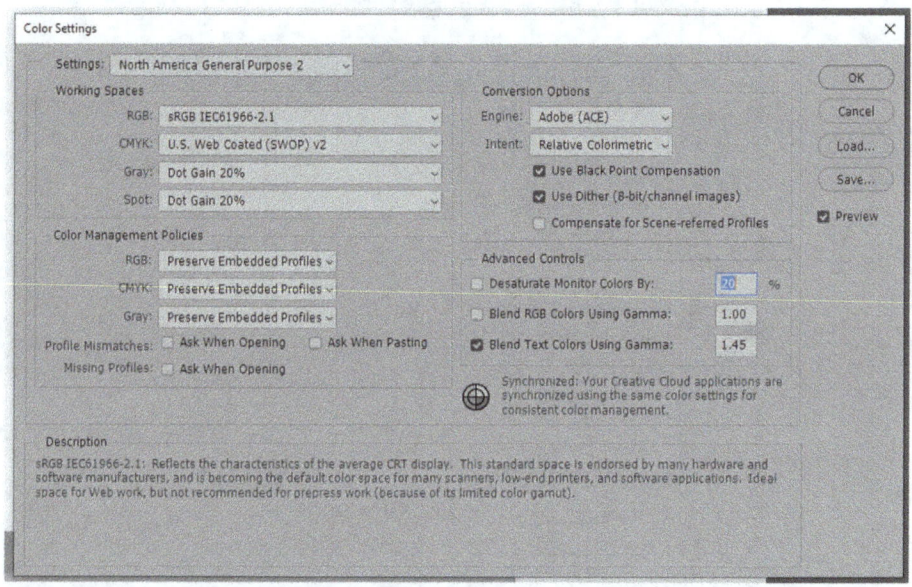

Figure 7-15. *Color Settings dialog box*

You can hover over any of these items if you need a more detailed description. The ideal workspace, as seen for the RGB color mode mentioned here, is sRGB which has a limited color gamut but is OK for my inkjet printers. However, if you are working with professional prints and photography, your instructor or print company may suggest a different workspace like Adobe RGB (1998) or another printer profile. Some print companies may even supply you with their custom profile and give instructions on how to load for one of your Workspaces like RGB or CMYK. Refer to Figure 7-16.

1003

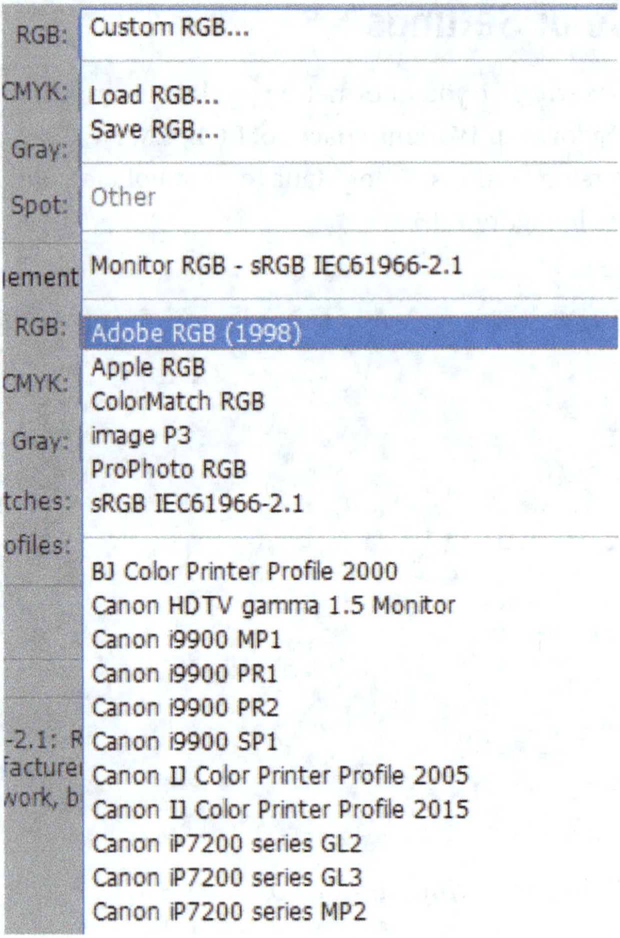

CHAPTER 7   WHAT IS THE NEXT STEP IN YOUR PHOTO RESTORATION PROJECT?

Figure 7-16. Color settings dialog box reviewing Working Spaces from the list

For now, if you do not want to make changes, just click Cancel and exit this dialog box. If you need more detailed information on this topic, you can refer to the following link:

https://helpx.adobe.com/photoshop/using/color-settings.html

- Edit ➤ Assign Profile: Can be used to assign a profile to a document if it does not currently have it and you are receiving a warning or you want to switch the profile because maybe it was not assigned correctly. Likewise, you can choose not to color mange the document or just quickly view what the current profile is. Refer to Figure 7-17.

Figure 7-17. Assign Profile dialog box

- Edit ➤ Convert to Profile: This can be set to an advanced or basic setting to convert to a specific destination profile. Consult with your printing company if they require you to make any changes in this dialog box. Refer to Figure 7-18.

CHAPTER 7 WHAT IS THE NEXT STEP IN YOUR PHOTO RESTORATION PROJECT?

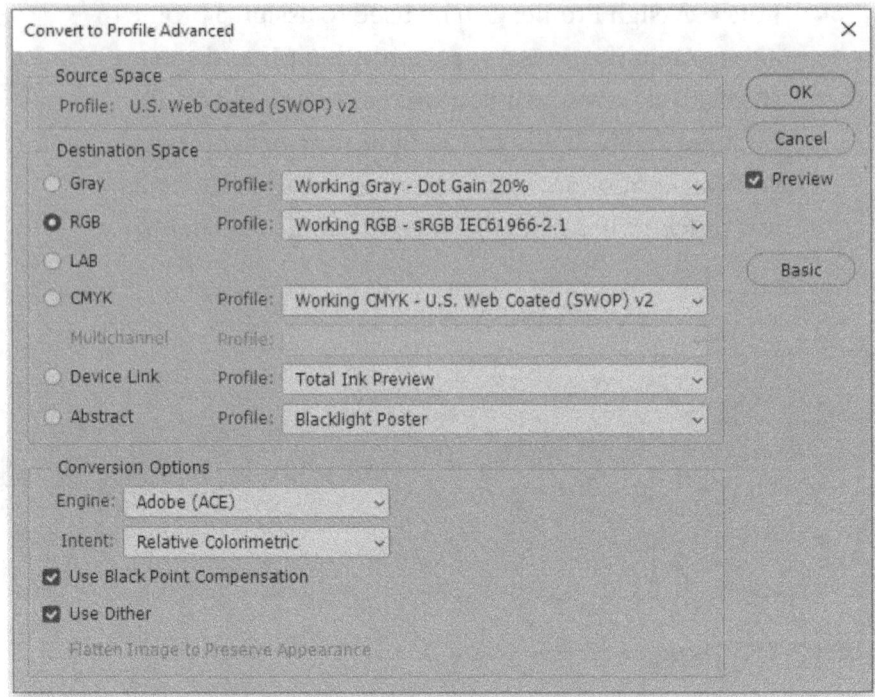

Figure 7-18. *Convert to Profile Advanced settings dialog box*

Note that many of these color settings will also be synchronized with your other Adobe applications like Illustrator and InDesign.

Online Projects (PDF Presentation)

If you are planning to present a few images in a gallery format other than a GIF animation, as mentioned in Chapter 6, another option is to create a PDF Presentation which you can do directly from Photoshop using File ➤ Automate ➤ PDF presentation. In the dialog box, you can Browse and then add various source files, organize them, duplicate, remove, or sort by name and then create a presentation with various transition options.

Make sure, when you do this, that the width and height of each is the same orientation (portrait or landscape). They do not have to be the exact same dimension, but this can make a better presentation. Add open files or browse for files you want to add to the list. Refer to Figure 7-19.

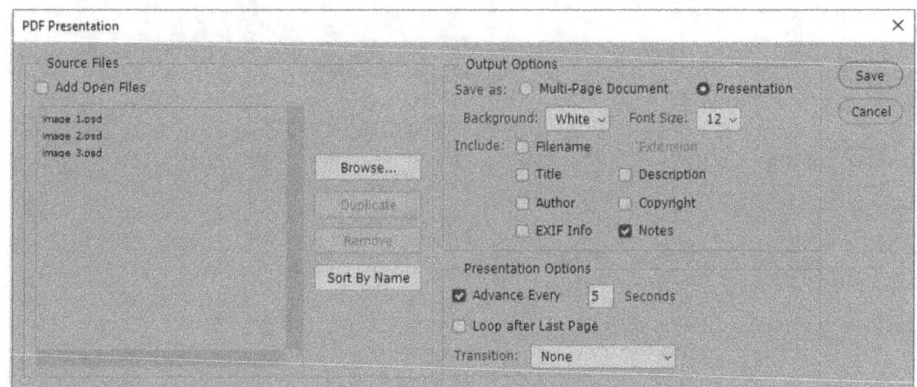

Figure 7-19. *PDF Presentation dialog box*

Choose your output options and change Save As: from Multi-Page Document to Presentation. Set the background if it shows up in the final output to white, gray, or black. Set the font size to 6–16pt should you plan to include information in the Presentation, such as Filename, Extension, Title, Description, Author, Copyright, EXIF Info, and Notes. Remember, as mentioned in Chapter 6, most if this information is found in File ➤ File Info area of each document, some of which may have been auto entered when each file was created or later by yourself. In this case, I have only left only the Notes checkbox enabled.

In the Presentation Options, you can set a duration of Advance Every 5 or more seconds if you want to play the animation automatically. You can also set it to Loop after the last page or leave that option disabled to stop after the last page. Then set a Transition for the slide if you want a type of transition animation. Currently, it is set to None. Each transition can have a different effect. Try another option like Fade or Randon, and edit that setting afterward in Acrobat Pro. Refer to Figure 7-20.

CHAPTER 7   WHAT IS THE NEXT STEP IN YOUR PHOTO RESTORATION PROJECT?

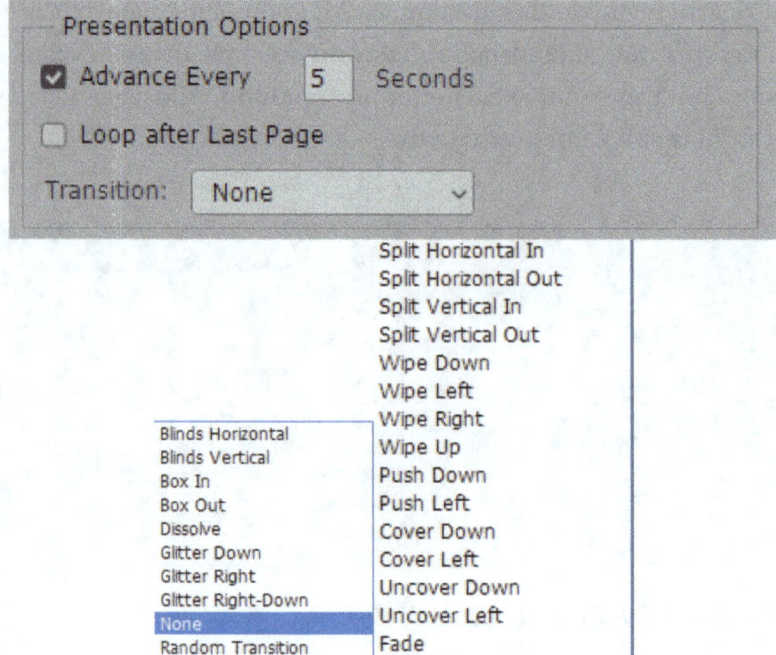

Figure 7-20. *PDF Presentation dialog box Presentation Options*

Click Save and locate a location to save the file in the Save As dialog box. Then click the next Save button. Refer to Figure 7-21.

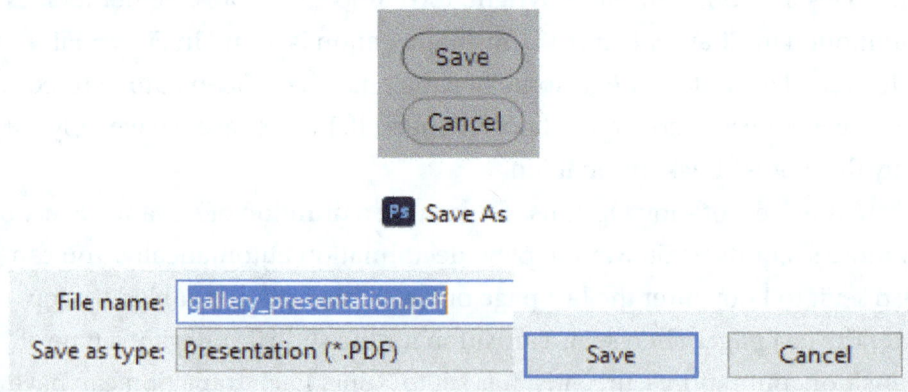

Figure 7-21. *Save As dialog box and saving the file*

CHAPTER 7   WHAT IS THE NEXT STEP IN YOUR PHOTO RESTORATION PROJECT?

This will then switch to the Save Adobe PDF dialog box. In this case, you can adjust the Quality of your Adobe PDF Preset from High Quality Print to another setting; set a Standard and Compatibility Level. In this case, I left the standard at none and the compatibility at Acrobat 5 (PDF 1.4).

The General area will give a description of those current choices. In this case, the presentation could have a dual purpose, both for presentation and print. Refer to Figure 7-22.

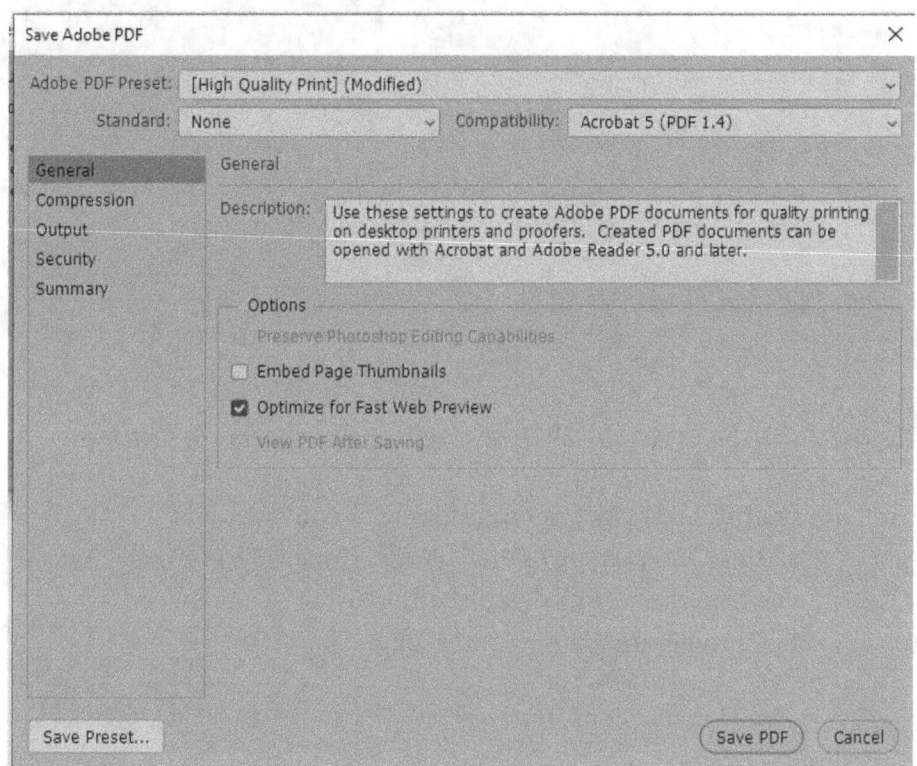

Figure 7-22. *Save Adobe PDF dialog box General settings*

The General tab also lets you set additional viewing options once the file is saved.

Other tabs in this section include

- Compression: For setting additional image compression options and image quality for all the images as well as conversion of images from 16 Bit/Channel to 8 Bits/Channel. Refer to Figure 7-23.

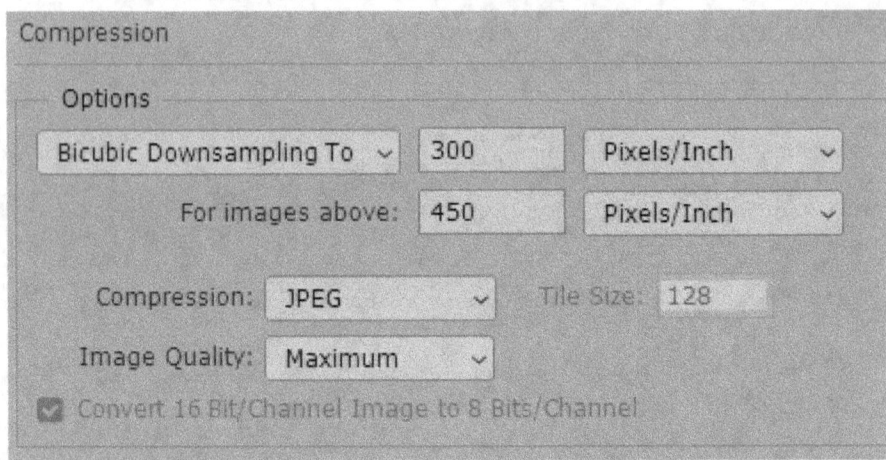

Figure 7-23. *Save Adobe PDF dialog box Compression settings*

- Output: Advanced settings for Color conversion or settings for the type of PDF profile. Generally, you can leave this area at its default settings of No Conversion. Refer to Figure 7-24.

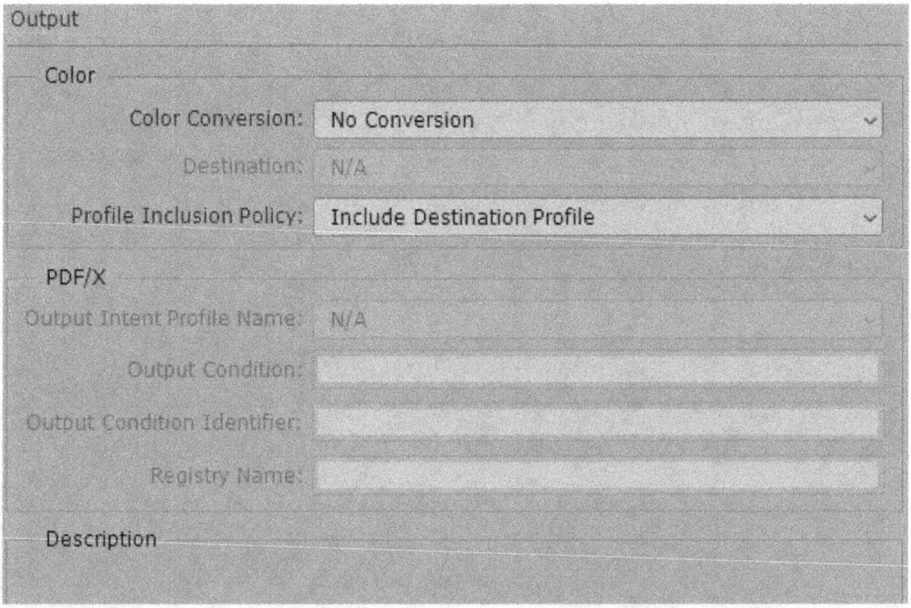

Figure 7-24. Save Adobe PDF dialog box Output settings

- Security: If you plan to have the PDF on your website, you may want to alter these settings so that people can't change or edit your PDF and need a Password to do so. In this case, I did not set this area as I might want to print images, or it will be on my laptop which no one else will access during the presentation. Refer to Figure 7-25.

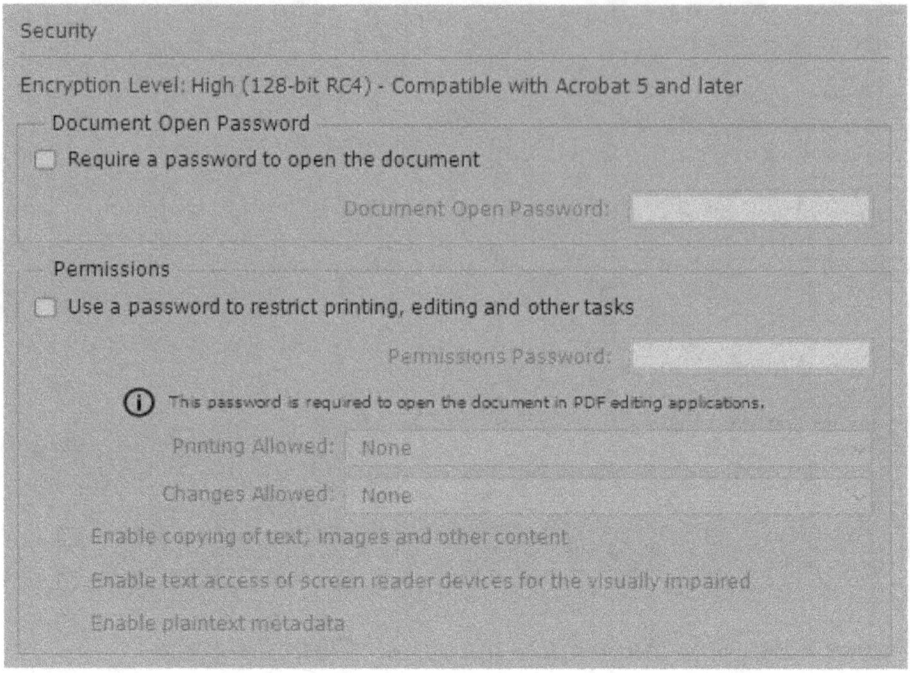

CHAPTER 7   WHAT IS THE NEXT STEP IN YOUR PHOTO RESTORATION PROJECT?

Figure 7-25. Save Adobe PDF dialog box Security Settings

- Summary: This is just an overview of the settings and warnings chosen and no changes can be made here. Refer to Figure 7-26.

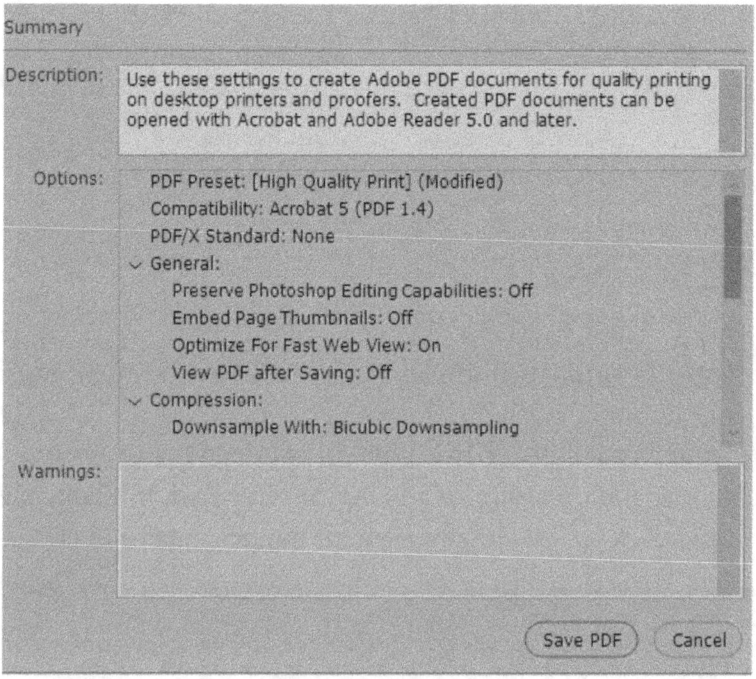

CHAPTER 7   WHAT IS THE NEXT STEP IN YOUR PHOTO RESTORATION PROJECT?

Figure 7-26. Save Adobe PDF dialog box Summary Options

Click Save PDF button. The output is a PDF file. See file **gallery_presentation.pdf** found in the **gallery_PDF_presentation folder**.

Edit in Acrobat Pro

This is a good option if you do not have access to Microsoft PowerPoint, as the files can be opened in the free Application Acrobat Reader or from the Creative Cloud Application Acrobat Pro. In Pro, you can edit your transitions further. Then display using presentation mode when opened. Refer to Figure 7-27.

CHAPTER 7   WHAT IS THE NEXT STEP IN YOUR PHOTO RESTORATION PROJECT?

Figure 7-27. *Creative Cloud Desktop Adobe Acrobat Open Menu*

For example, when the PDF is open in Acrobat Pro, it will automatically display in Presentation Mode, or you may receive a warning that it will do so. Agree and click yes and let the presentation play. Refer to Figure 7-28.

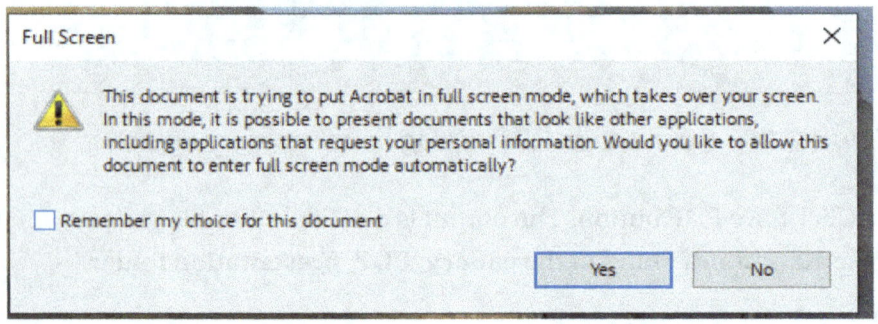

Figure 7-28. *Adobe Acrobat Full Screen warning message*

To exit this Presentation Mode, you can press the Esc button on your keyboard.

Tip to edit your transition settings in Acrobat Pro under the All Tools section of the New Acrobat Display, locate the Organize Pages Tool and click it. Refer to Figure 7-29.

CHAPTER 7   WHAT IS THE NEXT STEP IN YOUR PHOTO RESTORATION PROJECT?

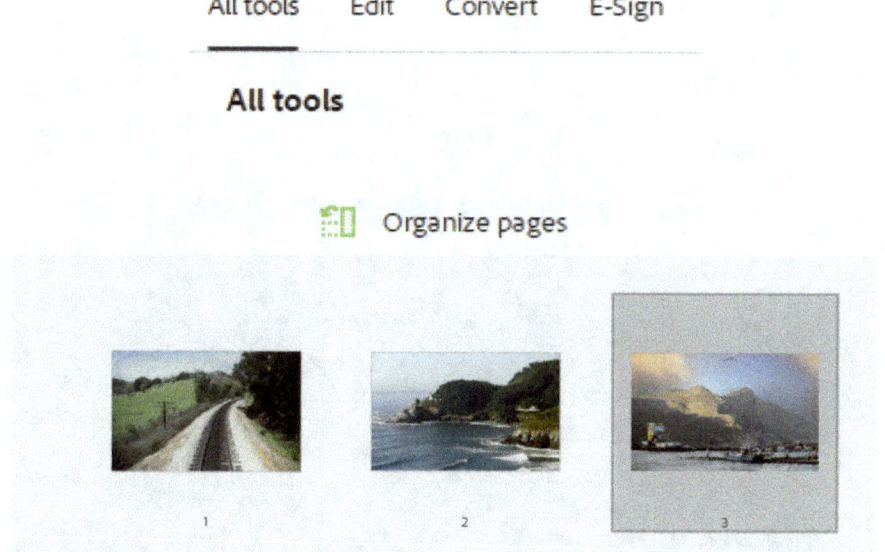

Figure 7-29. Adobe Acrobat menu to get to the Tool Organize Pages

Then Locate the sub-tool options Page Transitions, and click it to access the dialog box. Refer to Figure 7-30.

Page transitions

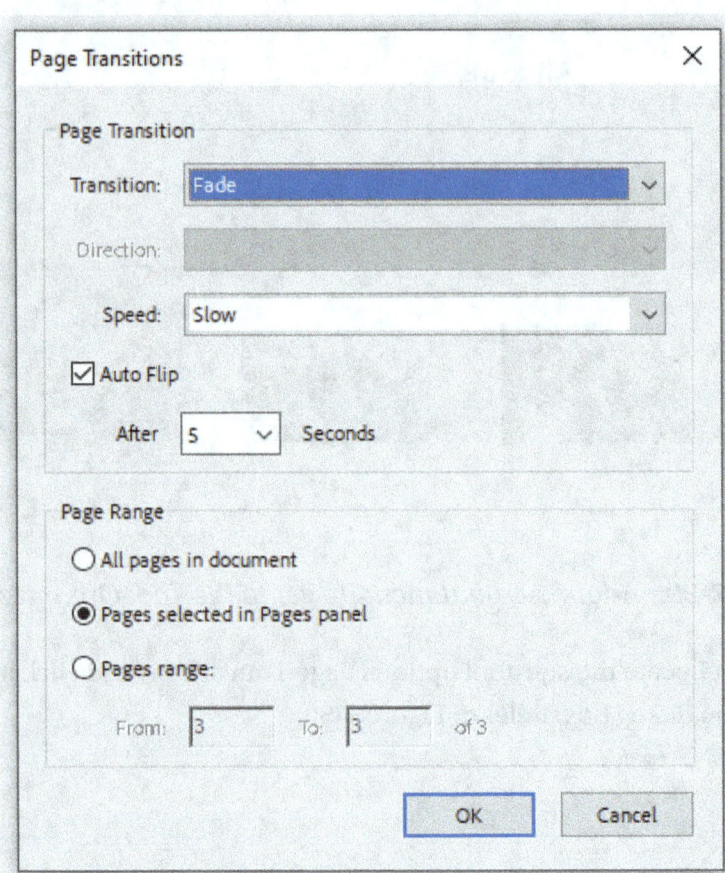

Figure 7-30. Adobe Acrobat working with Page Transitions and options in the dialog box

Besides similar transition options which you can choose from the list, you can set, for some, the direction and also a speed (slow, medium, or fast) and Auto flip after every 5 seconds. Alternatively, you can also set a page range for All pages in the document, Pages that are selected in the panel, or a Page range. Once you have made your choices and adjustments, click OK.

CHAPTER 7   WHAT IS THE NEXT STEP IN YOUR PHOTO RESTORATION PROJECT?

From the main menu, choose Save and then exit the Organize Pages tool by clicking the back arrow. Refer to Figure 7-31.

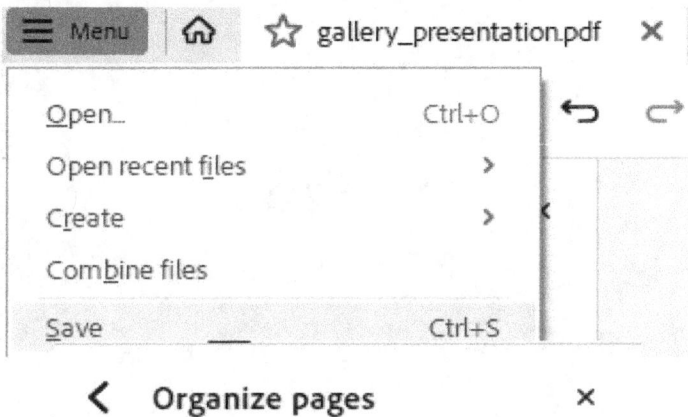

Figure 7-31. *Adobe Acrobat menu Options and exiting the Organize pages tool*

Make sure to return your presentation to the first page. And then from the menu, choose View ➤ Full Screen mode if you want to view your presentation with the changes. Refer to Figure 7-32.

CHAPTER 7   WHAT IS THE NEXT STEP IN YOUR PHOTO RESTORATION PROJECT?

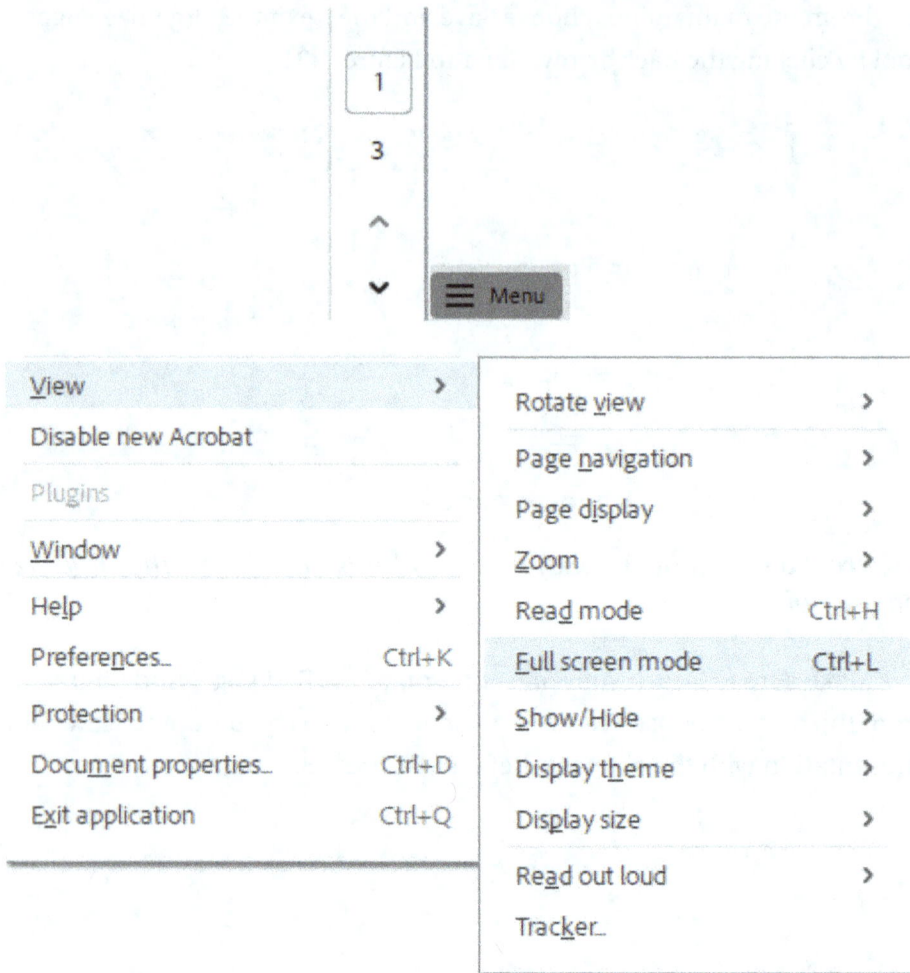

Figure 7-32. *Resetting the page number and then viewing in full screen mode*

Later you can close the file and use the Menu to exit the Acrobat Application.

If your PDF Presentation will also have extra text descriptions, you can add the Type using Photoshop, or alternatively, I would recommend creating the Interactive presentation instead, in Adobe InDesign, which I will briefly mention next.

Remember, if you are just planning to upload your images to the Web separately, then keep them in RGB Color mode and a .jpeg file is fine as we saw earlier in the chapter.

InDesign

The InDesign Application is a good application to learn if you are planning to create a booklet for Print exported as a PDF or to export an interactive PDF for a presentation like the one mentioned earlier for Photoshop. Refer to Figure 7-33.

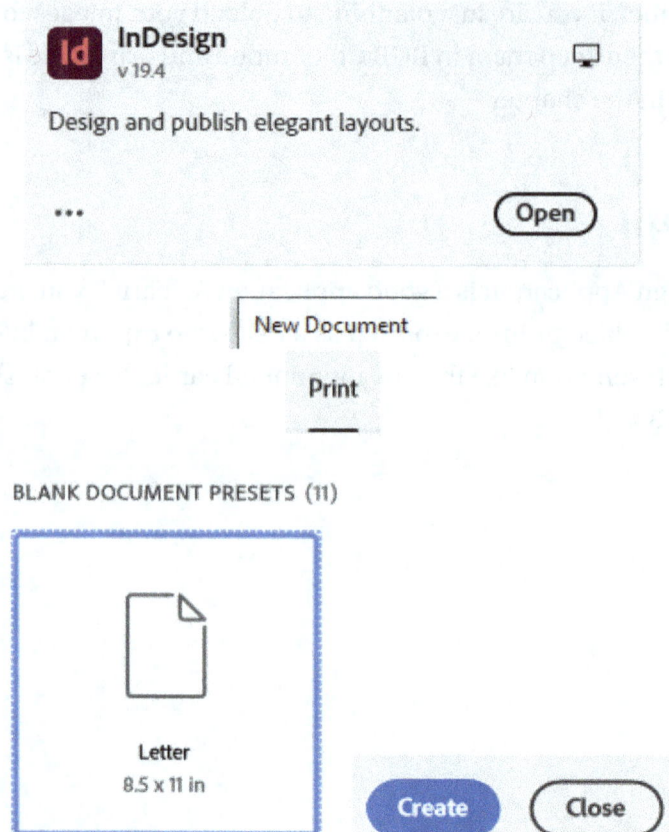

Figure 7-33. Creative Cloud Desktop InDesign Application

The steps to creating an interactive PDF and print PDFs using InDesign are a bit more complex than in Photoshop, due to the fact you are working with Text as well as multiple graphics on separated pages. For this section, you can refer to the **InDesign Project Folder** for files you can edit and open and review. See files **Digital_Scrapbook_Layout_Example.indd** and **page_transitions.indd**.

CHAPTER 7   WHAT IS THE NEXT STEP IN YOUR PHOTO RESTORATION PROJECT?

InDesign's purpose is not to correct photos but only for layout and display. Various forms of digital scrapbooking have become popular in recent years. If you have not added effects like a drop shadow or transparency, you can add these effects to your photos afterward in InDesign and add some surrounding text or additional shapes and enmeshment to tell your story.

Print Presentation

Here are a few layout ideas on 8.5x11 inch (Letter-size) pages to get you started. Refer to Figure 7-34 and Figure 7-35.

Figure 7-34. *InDesign Page Layout ideas with rectangular frames and text*

CHAPTER 7   WHAT IS THE NEXT STEP IN YOUR PHOTO RESTORATION PROJECT?

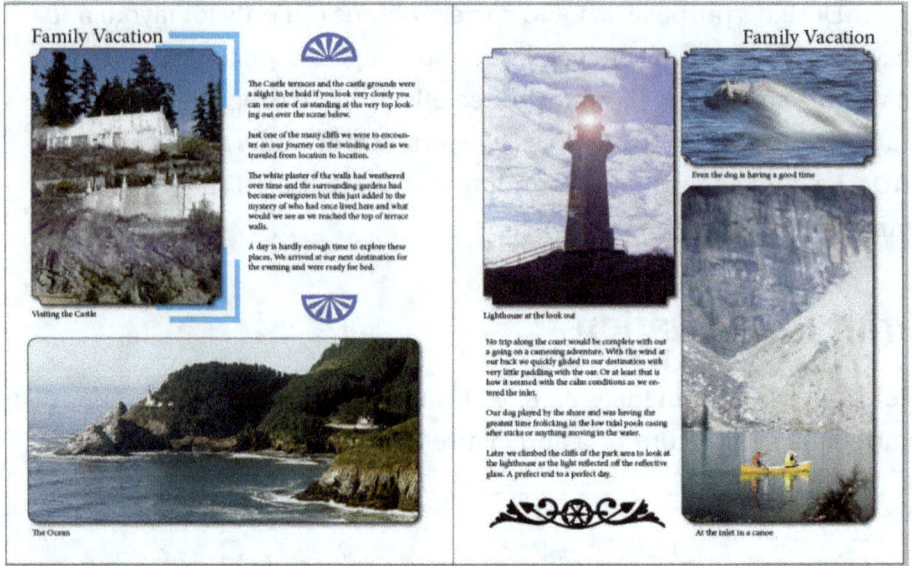

Figure 7-35. *InDesign Page Layout ideas with different borders and drop shadow effects*

These images which are stored in the "images" folder are added using File ➤ Place and linked to the (.indd) file. You can view there linkage via the Links panel and the Pages panel as they appear on individual pages or spreads. Using the frames of your images, you can then cover areas and enlarge or decrease the images within the frames as well as apply effects and border style strokes to the frames using the Tools, Control, and Effects panels. Refer to Figure 7-36.

CHAPTER 7   WHAT IS THE NEXT STEP IN YOUR PHOTO RESTORATION PROJECT?

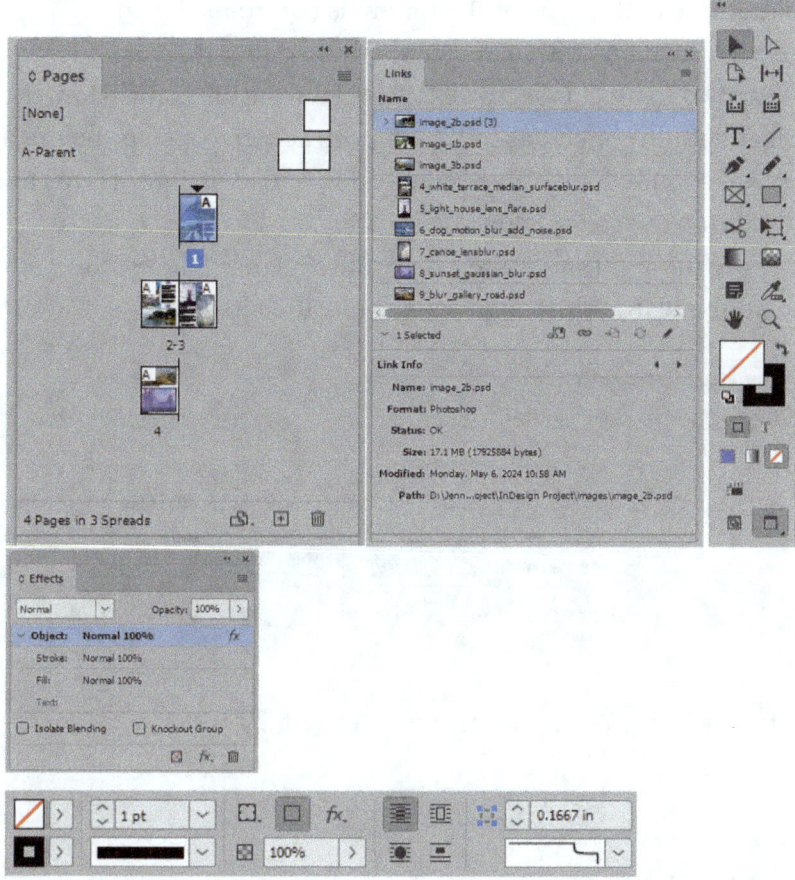

Figure 7-36. *InDesign Page panel, Links Panel, Tools Panel, Effects panel, and Part of the Control panel*

While the purpose of this book is not to go into any detail on InDesign layout, you can learn more about the application in the following links:

https://helpx.adobe.com/support/indesign.html
https://helpx.adobe.com/indesign/using/exporting-publishing-pdf.html

CHAPTER 7   WHAT IS THE NEXT STEP IN YOUR PHOTO RESTORATION PROJECT?

Color mode in this type of Document is controlled by Edit ➤Transparency Blend Space and can only be either RGB or CMYK for print files. By default, it is set to CMYK and during file conversion, the RGB image files should convert as well. For more accurate results, before linking images, you should do this color conversion ahead of time, as well as set your resolution to at least 300ppi.

After saving your (.indd) file, you could then use File ➤Export and choose Adobe PDF (Print) and Save the file. Refer to Figure 7-37.

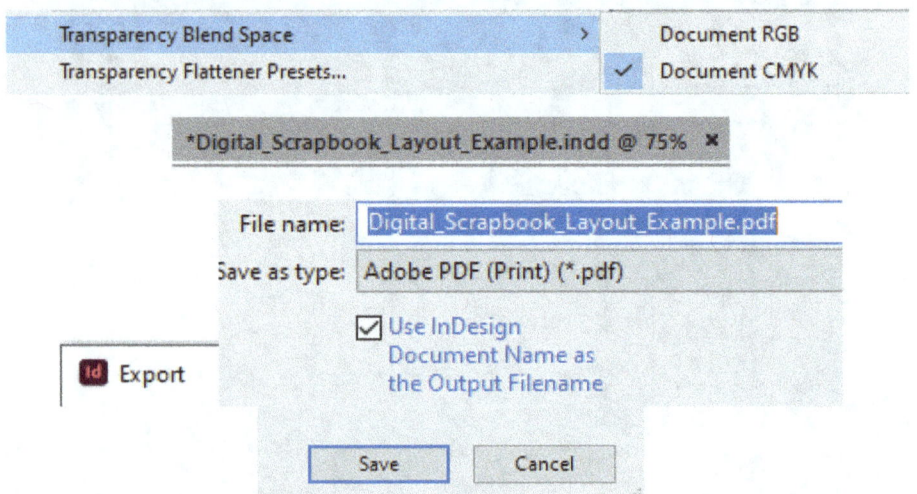

Figure 7-37. Export Options dialog box

In the Export as PDF, most settings are very similar to the ones located in Photoshop's dialog box and can be left at default if you choose High Quality Print. Adjust the General area to set quality as well as page order and viewing settings. The Compression area, as before, controls the quality of image output, and the Output area controls Color and additional PDF settings.

CHAPTER 7   WHAT IS THE NEXT STEP IN YOUR PHOTO RESTORATION PROJECT?

However, additional settings and tabs such as Marks and Bleeds and Advanced for Fonts and Transparency may be areas that you are not familiar with, so if you are not familiar with these settings, you may want to review the help link listed earlier as well as consult with your print company if these are settings that you would need to include when exporting a PDF. As mentioned earlier for Print Documents, do not alter the Security Tab settings, and leave the protection off. Refer to Figure 7-38.

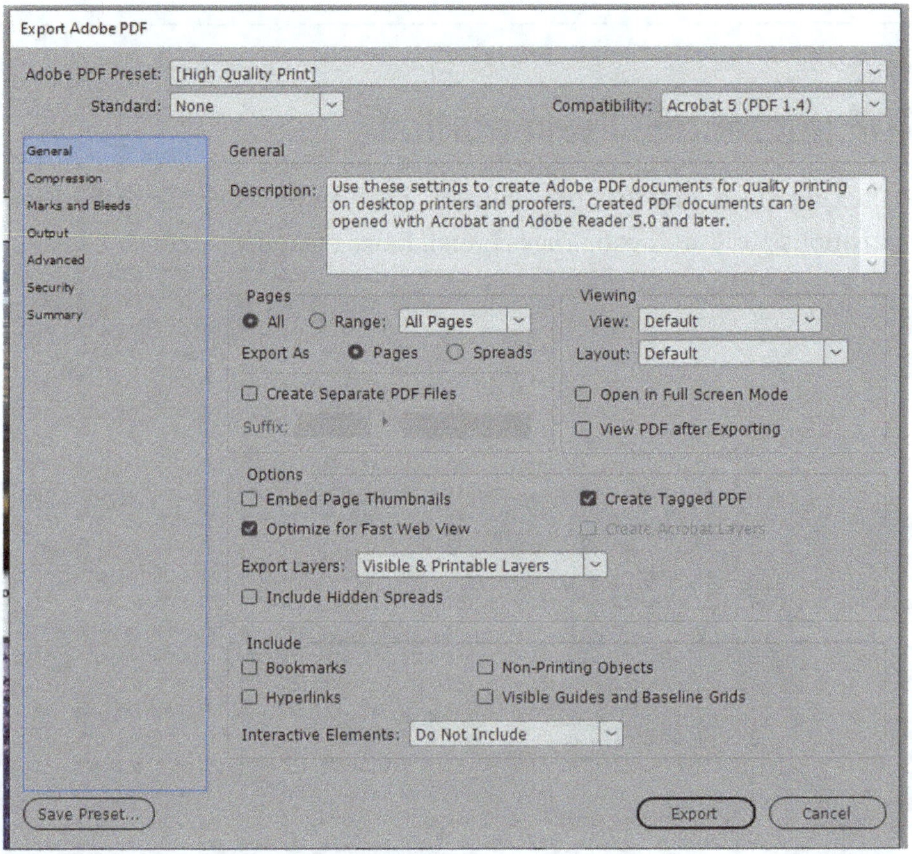

Figure 7-38. Export to PDF dialog box

Then click the Export button to save the PDF file.

And you can then Print your files using Adobe Acrobat Pro.

Note If you are creating a printed album, make sure to check what kind of paper options you could use. Additionally, if placing images in an album that you have printed out with your laser or inkjet printer, make sure to use acid-free glue and picture mounts.

PDF Interactive Presentation

In the case of a digital PDF presentation, this can be set up using the Page Transitions panel and your Pages panel. Refer to Figure 7-39.

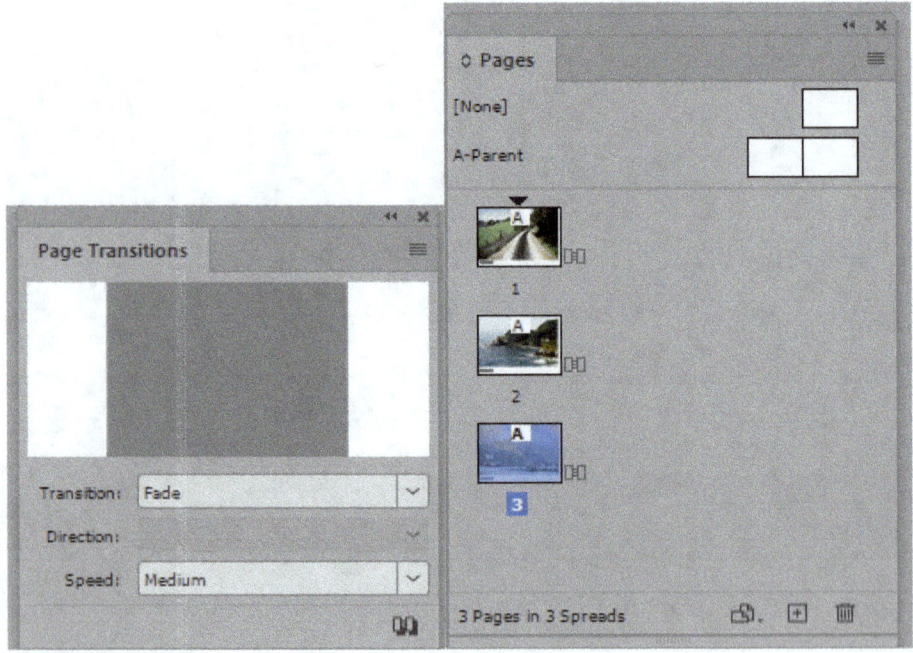

Figure 7-39. Page Transitions panel and Pages panel with transition applied

Then you would access the PDF settings under File ➤ Export. Choose the option of Adobe PDF interactive. Click Save. Refer to Figure 7-40.

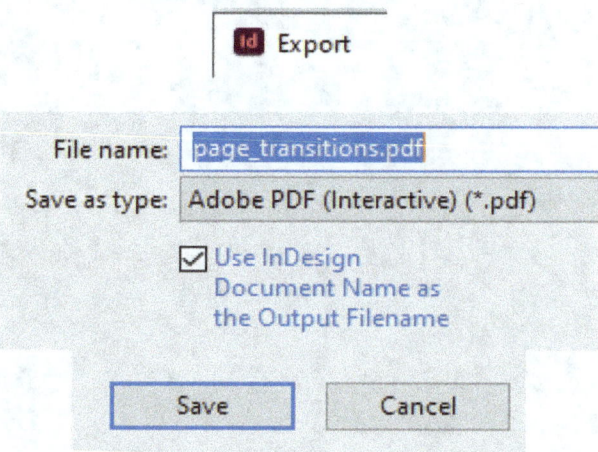

Figure 7-40. *Export options dialog box*

The dialog box Export to interactive PDF appears. The General Tab lets you set how many pages you want to have appear in your presentation. In the Viewing area, look for the sections of View, Layout, and Presentation, and then finally review the Page Transitions options that were already chosen earlier as you built the Document. Refer to Figure 7-41.

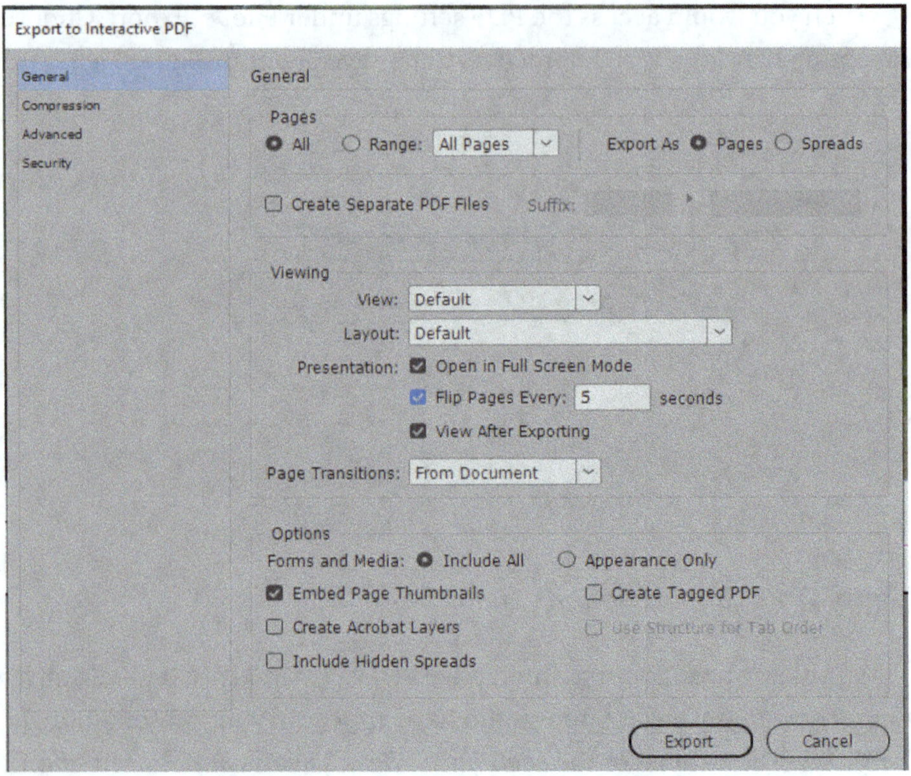

CHAPTER 7   WHAT IS THE NEXT STEP IN YOUR PHOTO RESTORATION PROJECT?

Figure 7-41. *Export to Interactive PDF dialog box*

This dialog box also lets you set additional image compression, advanced accessibility options, and security options.

After you have adjusted your settings, you would then click the Export button to create the PDF file, now complete with the transition option of your choice, and again, the file could be further adjusted in Acrobat Pro if required, such as adding a timed flipping for pages.

More information about working with InDesign and Interactive PDFs can be found in the following links:

https://helpx.adobe.com/indesign/using/dynamic-pdf-documents.html

https://helpx.adobe.com/indesign/using/page-transitions.html#page_transitions

Microsoft PowerPoint Presentation

After you have created a JPEG version of your images, if you need to create a PowerPoint presentation for a celebration or memorial, consider using PowerPoint to create a presentation. For this section, you can refer to the **PowerPoint Project** Folder for files you can edit and open. Refer to Figure 7-42.

Figure 7-42. *PowerPoint Application logo*

You can learn more about PowerPoint from the following link:

https://support.microsoft.com/en-us/office/basic-tasks-for-creating-a-powerpoint-presentation-efbbc1cd-c5f1-4264-b48e-c8a7b0334e36

Inserting an Image or GIF Animation

However, if you need to insert a basic image into PowerPoint, you can do the following:

Open your blank or currently created new presentation file. Refer to Figure 7-43.

CHAPTER 7 WHAT IS THE NEXT STEP IN YOUR PHOTO RESTORATION PROJECT?

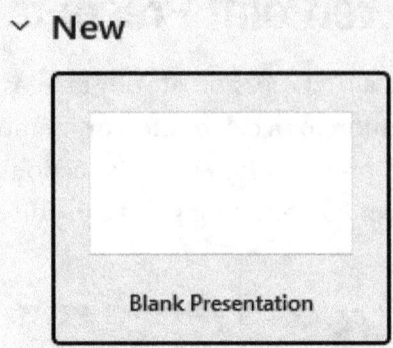

Figure 7-43. *Create a New blank presentation file using PowerPoint*

With PowerPoint open, from the Ribbon go to Insert ➤ Pictures and Choose to Insert Pictures From ➤ this device, then locate the image in the folder that you want to insert, and in the dialog box, click Insert. Refer to Figure 7-44.

CHAPTER 7   WHAT IS THE NEXT STEP IN YOUR PHOTO RESTORATION PROJECT?

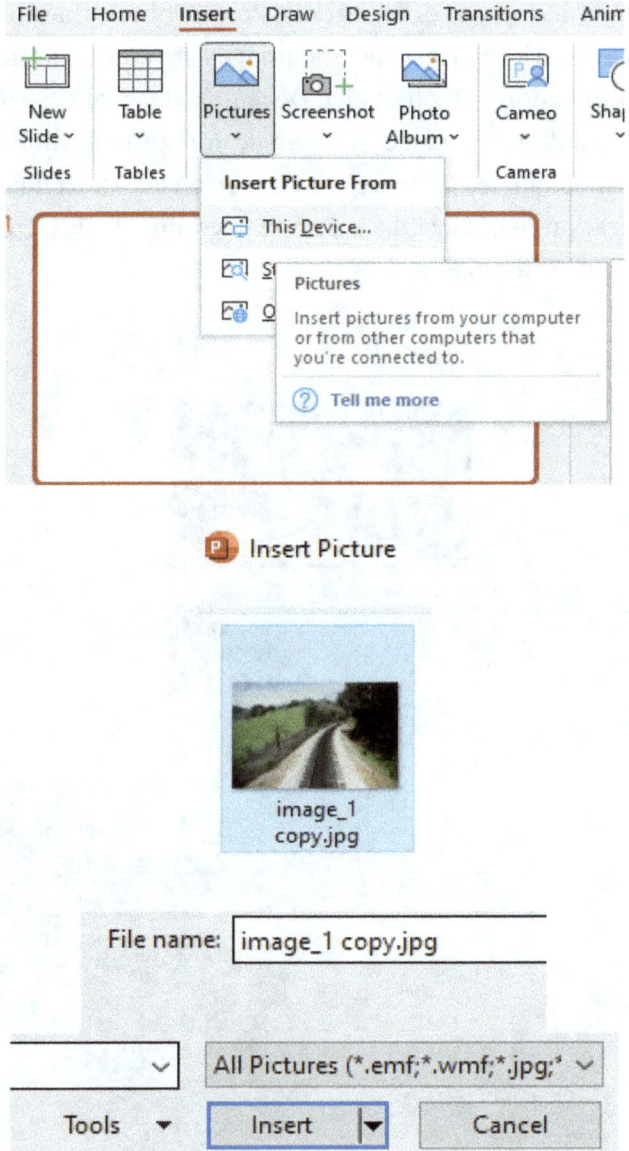

Figure 7-44. *Locate and Insert a Picture into your PowerPoint file*

CHAPTER 7   WHAT IS THE NEXT STEP IN YOUR PHOTO RESTORATION PROJECT?

One of the things that I do like about PowerPoint is that they have a lot of templates. Also when one or several images are copied or inserted onto a slide, the application will often give Designer Ideas for how to arrange those slides, and then you can choose an option and the slide is updated. This can be especially useful when you are on a very short deadline, such as for a celebration of life event, and need to come up with a presentation in a week or two. Refer to Figure 7-45.

Figure 7-45. *Use PowerPoint Designer to Quickly create a professional presentation*

CHAPTER 7   WHAT IS THE NEXT STEP IN YOUR PHOTO RESTORATION PROJECT?

Likewise, you can use the same process if you need to insert a GIF animation that will play in the presentation as well.

Video Applications and Considerations

In Chapter 6, we reviewed how we could create a Parallax animation using Photoshop's Timeline panel along with Media Encoder to render the video. However, if you are interested in incorporating this animation with other video footage, here are a few other Adobe Applications that are part of the Creative Cloud collection you may want to look at in more detail for your digital restoration projects.

Premiere Pro can be used to edit your video footage which as mentioned in Volume 1 Chapter 1 you may have had converted from film or tape to a digital file. Along with these videos, you could incorporate your parallax file from Chapter 6 and create a new film. Premiere Pro also has color correction options for videos. Refer to Figure 7-46.

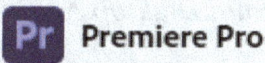

Figure 7-46. Adobe Creative Cloud Desktop Premiere Pro

More details on this application can be found in the following link:

https://helpx.adobe.com/support/premiere-pro.html

After Effects can be used in combination with Premiere Pro to add special effects to your work. Refer to Figure 7-47.

1033

CHAPTER 7   WHAT IS THE NEXT STEP IN YOUR PHOTO RESTORATION PROJECT?

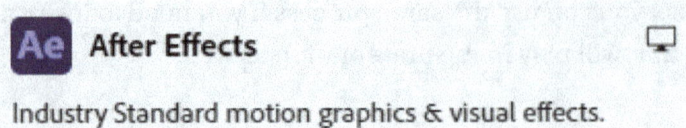

Figure 7-47. *Adobe Creative Cloud Desktop After Effects*

More details on this application can be found in the following link:

https://helpx.adobe.com/support/after-effects.html

Audition can be used in combination with Premiere Pro to create and edit sounds and audio that would be a part of your video. Refer to Figure 7-48.

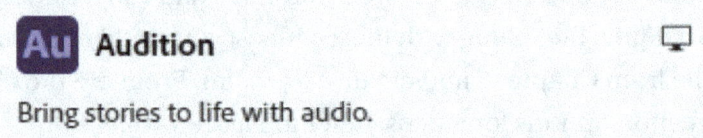

Figure 7-48. *Adobe Creative Cloud Desktop Audition*

More details on this application can be found in the following link:

https://helpx.adobe.com/support/audition.html

Parallax and Animation

While not specifically for Photo restoration, you can paste high or low resolution images into another Adobe Animation application that works with a very similar timeline panel, in this case Adobe Animate.

For this section, you can refer to the **Animate Project Folder** for files you can edit and open and review in regard to this chapter. Refer to Figure 7-49.

CHAPTER 7   WHAT IS THE NEXT STEP IN YOUR PHOTO RESTORATION PROJECT?

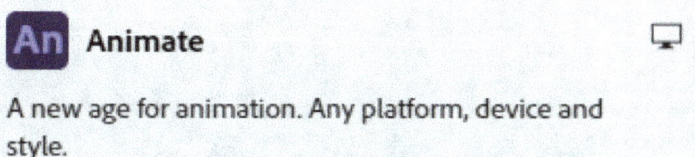

Figure 7-49. *Adobe Creative Cloud Desktop Animate*

While more for artistic animations for the Web, you can incorporate your image that you edited in Photoshop into the background of your animations projects. These files are saved in a (.fla) (HTML 5 Canvas) file before you publish the file from Animate as in this case of a .HTML5 canvas or another format. Refer to Figure 7-50.

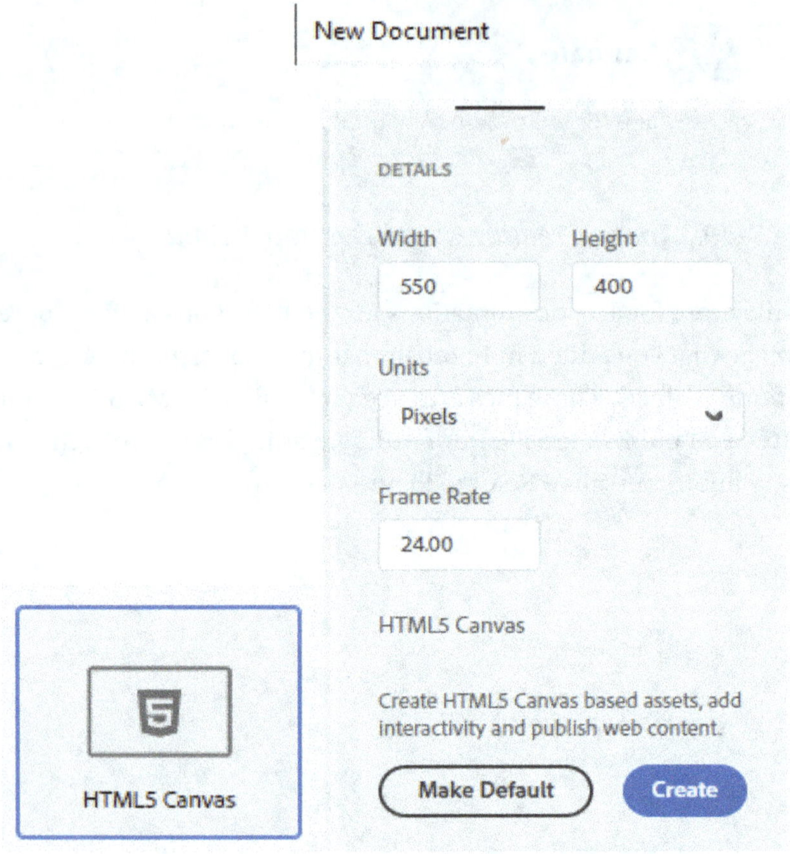

CHAPTER 7   WHAT IS THE NEXT STEP IN YOUR PHOTO RESTORATION PROJECT?

Figure 7-50. *Create an HTML Animation in the New Document dialog box*

In Photoshop one quick way to export an image to another file or application as we have seen is to use Select ➤ All (Ctrl/CMD+A) and then Edit ➤ Copy. Once the Animate canvas is open, image can be directly pasted (Ctrl/CMD+V) directly on to an open timeline layer keyframe. Refer to Figure 7-51 and Figure 7-52.

CHAPTER 7   WHAT IS THE NEXT STEP IN YOUR PHOTO RESTORATION PROJECT?

Figure 7-51. *Add images from Photoshop to Animate, but they may be larger than the canvas after export and require scaling*

CHAPTER 7   WHAT IS THE NEXT STEP IN YOUR PHOTO RESTORATION PROJECT?

Figure 7-52. *Animate Timeline*

This image is also stored in the Library panel for use in other keyframes. Refer to Figure 7-53.

Figure 7-53. *Animate Library and Tools panels and the image scaled*

CHAPTER 7   WHAT IS THE NEXT STEP IN YOUR PHOTO RESTORATION PROJECT?

Changes to scaling and sizing are made to the image using the Properties panel and Tools found in the Tool panel, such as the Free Transform tool. Refer to Figure 7-54.

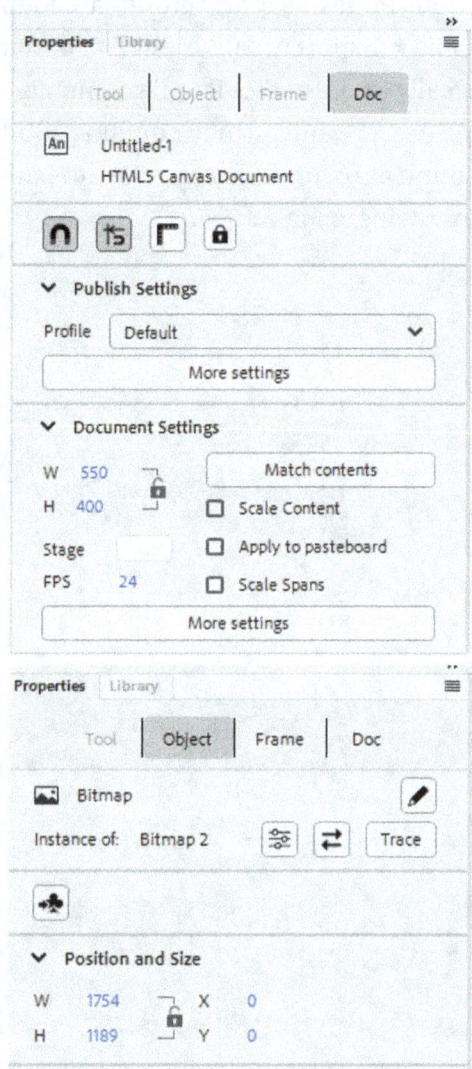

Figure 7-54. Animate Properties panel settings when the Document or Object is selected

CHAPTER 7   WHAT IS THE NEXT STEP IN YOUR PHOTO RESTORATION PROJECT?

While I will not be going into any detail here about animation, I just want to mention that this application is great for creating basic GIF animations with more control over movement, such as rotation and scaling. The various Publish export settings are found using the application's menu File ➤Export or File ➤Publish options.

If you are specifically interested in Parallax animation, it has a number of panels, such as the Assets panel, which contains additional animations, static images, and sound clips, and the Layer Depth panel if working with distances and depths. Refer to Figure 7-55.

CHAPTER 7 WHAT IS THE NEXT STEP IN YOUR PHOTO RESTORATION PROJECT?

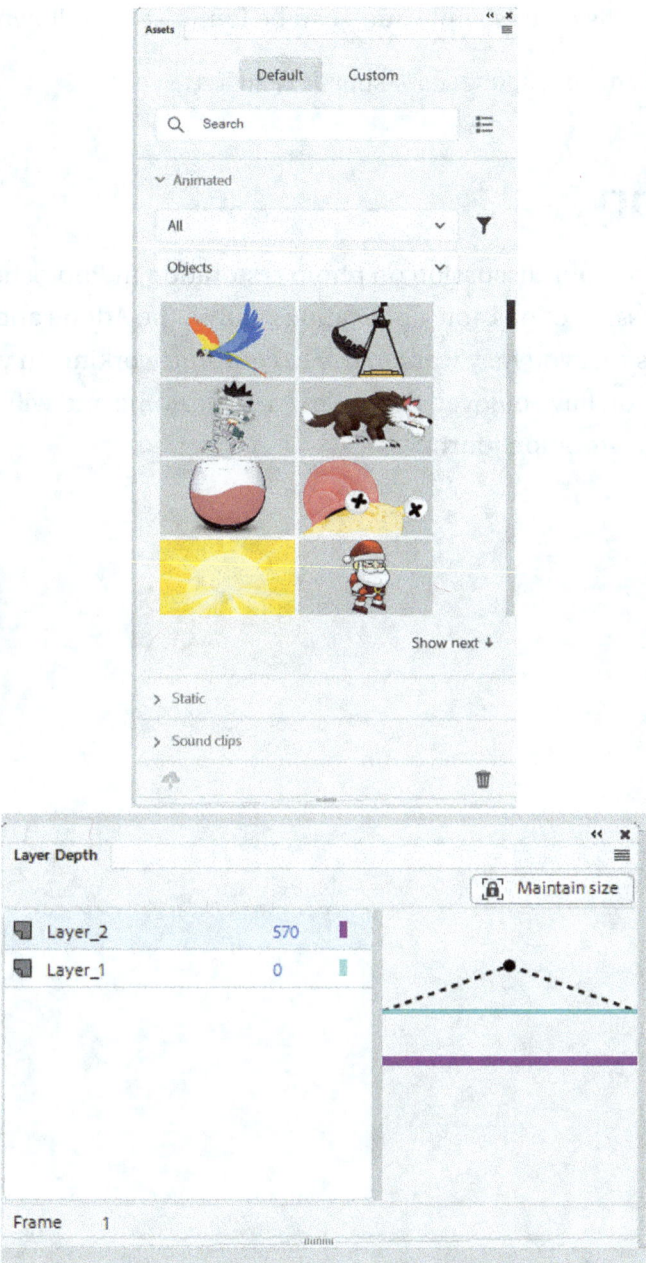

Figure 7-55. *Animate Assets and Layer Depth panel*

CHAPTER 7   WHAT IS THE NEXT STEP IN YOUR PHOTO RESTORATION PROJECT?

More details on this application can be found at the following link:

https://helpx.adobe.com/support/animate.html

Summary

This concludes our discussion on photo restoration in Photoshop as well as our discussion of possible applications within the Adobe and Microsoft applications that you may want to use to continue working on your project. I hope that you have enjoyed the topics in this volume and will continue your photo restoration journey.

Index

A

Additional selection-related tools, 2
Add Noise, 457
Add Noise dialog box, 456
Adjustment layers, 153, 211, 220, 221, 227, 238, 239
    clipping masks, 250–252
    damaged image, 237
    Hue/Saturation adjustments, 240
    layer masks, 248
        copying, 234, 235
        deletion, 236
        painting, 235
    opacity, 292, 293
    repaired image, 237, 238
Adjustments panel, 65, 66, 86, 89, 154, 155, 226, 228, 229
Adobe Illustrator, 719
Adobe Lightroom Classic application, 562, 563
Adobe Media Encoder, 814
Adobe substance collection, 511
After effects, 814, 1033, 1034
Animate, 1035
    add images from Photoshop, 1037
    animate project folder, 1034
    assets and layer depth panel, 1040, 1041
    canvas, 1036
    HTML animation, 1035, 1036
    library and tools panels, 1038
    properties panel settings, 1039
    timeline, 1038
Animations, 815, 816
Audition, 1034

B

Basic tab, 497
Blending modes, 291
    brushes, 288, 289
    color shifts, 286
    difference/exclusion/subtract/divide, 283, 285
    dissolve/darken/multiply/color burn/linear burn/darker color, 282
    group folders, 292
    Hue/Saturation, 279–281

INDEX

Blending modes (*cont.*)
    Hue/Saturation/Color/
        Luminosity, 285, 286
    human's/animal's eye color,
        286, 287
    layers, 278, 279
    Lighten/Screen/Color Dodge/
        Linear Dodge (Add)/
        Lighter Color, 282, 283
    options, 282, 286
    overlapping pixels, 288, 289
    Overlay/Soft Light/Hard Light/
        Vivid Light/Linear Light/
        Pin Light/Hard Mix,
        283, 284
    painting, 287, 288, 290, 291
Blur filter menu, 379
    dialog box settings, 381
    digital photo repair, 379
    mask, 380, 383
    photo repair, 381
    shape Blur dialog box, 384
    submenu list, 379
    subtle blur, 382
Blur filters, 514
Blur Focal Distance slider, 399
Blur Gallery, 423, 428, 441–446,
    450, 455
    Blur tools panel, 425
    channels panel, 429
    options bar panel, 425
    panel layer mask, 426
    preview, 430, 431
    submenu, 424

Blur Gallery Blur Tools panel, 451
Blur Gallery Effects, 447
Blur Gallery Motion Effects, 437
Blur Gallery Tilt-Shift, 452
Blur slider, 432, 443
Blur Tools panel, 432, 442, 448
    corner field, 434
    dragging, 449
Brightness/contrast
    additional adjustments, 152
    adjustment layer, 143
    Cyan-Red slider, 150
    legacy behavior, 143
    magenta–green slider, 151
    midtones, 146
    photoshop, 149
    properties panel settings, 142
    settings, 143
    yellow–blue slider, 151
Brush-related tools, 374

C

Camera raw filter, 561
    adaptive wide angle filter, 689
        additional options, 717
        auto, 714, 715
        constrain tool, 708, 709
        crop factor, 713
        crop tool, 715, 716
        details, 717
        distortion, 710, 711
        fisheye lens, 711, 712
        focal length, 712

INDEX

full spherical, 715
hand tool, 710
ideal project/correction model, 711
image distortions, 706, 707
move tool, 710
navigation/preview, 710
OK/cancel button, 717, 718
perspective, 713, 714
polygon constraint tool, 710
rounded distortion, 716
scale, 712
as shot, 713
tools, 707, 708
zoom tool, 710
Adobe Lightroom Classic application, 562
color alteration, 646, 647
color sampler tool, 568
and creative clould Bridge, 561, 562
edit panel, 573
flower bed, 563, 564
geometry panel, 634, 635
   auto, 635, 636
   content-aware fill, 641, 642
   full, 637, 638
   guided, 638, 639
   layer panel, 642, 643
   level, 636
   magenta guides, 639, 640
   manual transformations, 643, 644
   OK button, 645
   savings changes options, 645, 646
   text guides, 640, 641
   upright, 635, 637
   vertical, 636, 637
   zooming out, 641
healing panel, 647
   clone tool, 652
   content-aware remove tool, 648, 649
   healing tool, 650, 651
   refresh button, 650
   show overlay, 649
   tools, 647
   visualize spots, 653
   waterfall image, 654
histogram panel, 570, 572
layout/options, 565
lens correction filter, 689, 690
masking panel, 655
   background, 659
   brush, 663–665
   color adjustment, 673, 674
   color mixer tab, 675
   color tab, 675
   curve tab, 676
   depth range, 671
   detail tab, 676
   effect tab, 675
   help charts, 677
   and layer panel, 655, 656
   light tab, 675
   linear gradient, 665, 666

INDEX

Camera raw filter (*cont.*)
    luminance range, 670
    mask editing/creation, 671, 672
    mask options, 657
    objects, 662
    overlay options, 673
    people, 660
    person, 660, 661
    preset options, 673
    radial gradient, 667, 668
    range, 669
    red mask, 673
    reset sliders, 676
    sky, 658
    subject, 657, 663
  navigation tools, 567, 568
  overlay tool options, 569
  panel options, 634
  presets, 684, 685, 687
  preview preferences, 565, 567
  red eye panel
    color corrections, 678
    color fill layer, 682, 683
    options, 678, 679
    pet eye, 681
    red eye, 679, 680
    reset button, 682
    uses, 678
  saving/preferences/full-screen mode options, 569
  settings, 688
  viewing icons, 567
  view settings, 565, 566

Channel mixer, 178–180, 182, 184–189
Channel mixer adjustment, 181
Clipping masks
  adjustment layers, 250–252
  image, affect color, 252
  layers panel, 251–253
Clone stamp tool, 15, 521, 815, 819, 899
Cloud desktop for stock
  and marketplace, 808, 811
  search/filter, 809
CMYK color mode, 209
Color balance, 144, 151
  adjustment layer, 145
  faded image, 145
  properties panel settings, 147
  properties settings, 146
Colorize filter, 737
  activation, 742
  adjustment layers, 741
  adjustments, 750, 751
  applied color, 755, 756
  apply color
    automatically, 742, 743
    manually, 745
  auto color Image, 748
  color layer, 755
  color picker, 746
  download, 738, 739
  focal points
    addition, 748
    and applied colors, 746, 747

INDEX

final colorized image, 753, 754
multiple colors, 748, 749
preview, 750
Hue/Saturation, 755
installation, 739, 740
OK/cancel button, 740
output options, 755, 756
profile options, 752
re-colorization, 741
scratches, 741
selection, 737, 738
settings, 743, 744
slider options, 752, 753
smart object layer, 741, 742
updates, 741
Color Lookup, 190–192, 194, 195, 207
Color Lookup file, 197, 199, 208
Color-managed environment, 8
Color mode, RGB, 816, 817, 824
Color reduction algorithm, 861–863, 873
Color Sampler Tool, 78
  Ctrl/CMD key, 79
  dropdown menus, 82
  hand tool and zoom tool, 81
  markers, 80
Color transfer filter, 762
  Hue/Saturation, 767
  lab color space, 763, 764
  luminance slider, 765, 766
  preserve luminance, 765
  presets, 763
  RGB color space, 763, 764, 767
  settings, 766, 767
  smart filter, 767
Content-Aware Move tool, 176
Cross fades, 957, 958
Curves, 102
  adjustment, 102
  current garden image, 125
  default settings, 108
  eyedroppers, 113
  layers panel, 104
  midpoint, 117
  properties panel settings, 106, 108, 114, 117, 120
  S curve, 124
  values button, 114
Cyan, magenta, yellow, and black (CMYK), 78
  black-and-white photos, 8
  monochrome image, 10
  pigments, 5
  printer, 7
  properties panel settings, 122
  subtractive print colors, 6
Cyan–Red slider, 150

D

Digital camera, 471
Digital photos, 16, 542, 562, 692
Digital scrapbooking, 1021
Digital scrapbook projects, 495
Dither algorithm, 864–867
Drop shadow, 495, 503
Dust & Scratches, 458, 459, 461–463

INDEX

E

Edit panel, Camera Raw Filter, 573, 574
   activation, 579
   basic color settings, 574
   calibration tab, 632, 633
   color grading tab, 603
      adjustments, 603, 604
      balance, 606
      blending, 606
      histogram, 606
      preview, 607
      shadows/global, 605
   color mixer tab/B&W mixer, 596
      adjust options, 596, 598
      point color, 598–603
   Color tab, 582–584
   Curve tab, 589, 590
      adjust options, 590, 591
      highlights, 590
      parametric curve targeted adjustment tool, 594, 595
      point curve, 592, 593
   detail tab, 608–610
   effects tab
      clarity, 586
      dehaze, 586
      grain, 588, 589
      preview, 589
      sliders adjustments, 584, 585
      style, 588
      texture, 585
      vignette, 586–588
   HDR option, 575
   Lens Blur tab, 621
      apply, 621
      auto mask, 630
      blur amount, 622
      bokeh, 623
      boost, 624
      brush, 629
      bubble, 624
      depth settings, 628
      focal range, 625
      focus amount, 630
      painting, 631
      point/area focus, 625, 626
      preview, 631, 632
      range depth values, 627
      settings, 621, 622, 630
      visualize depth, 628, 629
   light tab, 579–581
   optics tab, 611, 612
      defringe settings, 617, 618, 620
      distortion, 612–615
      Hue/Saturation, 619
      vignette, 615, 616
   profile, 576
      categories, 576
      color setting, 578
      options, 576, 577
      setting, 578
Effects panel
   Bokeh, 435, 436
   settings, 437
Eraser tool, 32, 33, 133

INDEX

Export color lookup, 204
Export color lookup dialog box, 205
Export color lookup tables dialog box, 203
Eyedropper tool, 75

F

Fade in/fade out, 954
Field Blur, 432, 437
Filters, 511, 522
    dialog box, 513–516
    linear light, 513
    radius, 512
Frame dialog box, 497–499
Frame rate, 851, 923, 950, 951
Frames per second (FPS), 950, 951
Free transform panel, 834–836, 917, 924–927, 941, 945, 946

G

Gaussian Blur, 387, 414, 484, 514
    curve, 390
    dialog box, 385, 388
    experiment, 392
    filter mask active, 392
    layer mask, 385, 386
    layers panel, 389
    properties panel, 391
GIF animation
    create frame animation, 822
    create new document
        add images to layer panel, 828–830
    confirm scale settings, 834, 835
    convert layers to smart object layer, 832, 833
    to custom settings, 825
    dialog box settings, 824
    gallery_animation_start.psd, 827
    images to use, sequence order, 827, 828
    match new canvas, 831, 832
    rasterize layer command, 839
    reorder layer panel, 830, 831
    scale image using transform panel, 833, 834
    scaling adjust and visibility return, 836, 837
    select next layer to free transform, 835, 836
    use move tool and keyboard to nudge images, 838
    with and without guides and Layers panel, 826
gallery, 822
Image Size Dialog box settings, 823
looping options and preview
    file animation_gallery_final.gif, 879
    final GIF animation file, 880
    save optimized as, 878, 879
    timeline panel adjust time settings, 877, 878

INDEX

GIF animation (*cont.*)
    Web dialog box animation options, 877
    Web dialog box Animation preview settings, 878
    Web dialog box option buttons, 877
  preparation considerations, 816, 817
  save for Web dialog box, 856
    color reduction algorithm options, 861–863
    color reduction options, 863, 864
    color table and menu, 873, 874
    convert to sRGB options, 871
    Dither algorithm, 864–867
    File Info Dialog box, 872, 873
    GIF animation settings, 861
    image options, 875, 876
    interlaced options, 869
    Lossy options, 870, 871
    Matte setting, 868
    menu settings, 858, 859
    metadata options, 872
    overview, 857
    preset settings, 857, 858
    preview original and optimize setting summary, 860
    tools and navigation, 859
    transparency, 867–869
    Web Snap options, 869, 870
  with timeline panel
    add frame and adjust layer visibility, 845
    additional frame settings, 855
    adjust looping, 849
    adjust timing, 848, 849
    deletes selected frames, 844
    duplicates selected frames, 841
    and extra tween frames, 852
    first frame, 848
    frames selection and create new tween, 853
    layers panel hiding layer, 841, 842
    and Layers panel with changes, 842, 843
    layers panel with frame animation set, 839, 840
    optimize animation dialog box, 855
    panel settings, 850
    panel with time settings and final frame, 853, 854
    play animation, 854
    return first frame, 856
    and select frames, 852
    stop and start animation, 844
    timeline menu and adjustments with History panel, 846, 847

INDEX

tween dialog box and
settings, 850, 851
tweening, 850
GIF animation file, 988
GIF animations, 817
GIF Photo Gallery, 813
Gradient editor, 47, 48, 53
Gradient fill, 52, 54, 56
Gradient fill dialog box, 44, 45, 47, 51, 55
Gradient interpolation method, 46
Gradient Map, 44, 222–224
Gradients, 39, 41, 50
Gradient tool, 41, 52, 226

H

Hardware, 3
Harmonization filter
    layer, mask/transparency, 756
    layer panel, 756, 757
    output, 760, 761
    reference image, 757, 758
    settings, 758, 759
    sliders, 760
High Dynamic Range (HDR), 17, 160
    effect, 169
    exposure, 162
    gamma correction, 164, 166
    properties settings, 163
High Dynamic Range (HDR) images
    HDR Pro dialog box, 338

HDR Pro workspace options
    confirm settings, 341
    current image collection, 340
    ideal photo, 339
HDR toning, 327
    adjustment layer, 329
    advanced settings, 329, 333, 334
    alert message, 327, 328
    automated option, 329
    dialog box, 330
    edge glow, 332
    flattened to single layer, 329
    method, 331, 332
    presets, 330, 331
    tone and detail, 333
    toning curve and histogram, 334–338
    identical images, 326
    remove ghosts, 341
Histogram, 120
Histogram panel, 68, 70, 74, 318
    image, 73
    levels, 85
    and menu, 68
    settings, 69
Hold Interpolation keyframe, 920
Hue/Saturation, 145, 174, 189
    adjustment layer, 126, 134
    CMYK, 139
    color adjustments to skin tone, 128
    colorize check box, 133
    color options, 129

Hue/Saturation (*cont.*)
   color range, 131
   dragging, 138
   eyedropper, 130, 132
   inner sliders, 137
   lightness slider, 131
   presets, 129
   properties panel settings, 127, 133, 136, 139
   saturation slider, 131
Hue, Saturation, and Brightness (HSB), 518
Hue, Saturation, and Luminosity (HSL), 518

I

Image adjustment options
   adjustment layer, 25
   apply image
      blending modes, 352
      dialog box, 351
      duplication, 355, 356
      faded images, 353, 354
      mask options, 352, 353
      source file, 351
   calculations, 357–359
   color adjustments, 21
   color correction, 17, 20
   layers panel, 24
   sRGB profile, 18
Image adjustment settings
   auto correction, 323, 325
   desaturate, 326

equalize, 325, 326
HDR images, 326
match color, 342
   check box, 345
   dialog box, 342, 343
   image options, 343
   image statistics, 344
   settings, 345, 346
   target, 342
replace color
   Adobe mentions, 349
   Alt/Option key, 349
   dialog box, 347, 348
   locate image, 347
   select sections, 350
   settings, 348, 349
   uses, 347
Image/GIF animation, 1029–1033
image repair review
   color correction, 15
   nondestructive way., 15
InDesign application, 1019
   compression area, 1024
   creative Cloud Desktop, 1020
   digital scrapbooking, 1021
   export options, 1024
   export PDF dialog box, 1025
   InDesign Page Layout ideas
      color mode, 1024
      with different borders and drop shadow effects, 1022
      with rectangular frames and text, 1021

Tools, Control and Effects panels, 1022, 1023
PDF interactive presentation, 1026–1028
Info panel, 75, 76, 78, 83
Interactive PDFs, 1019, 1020, 1027, 1028
Invert, 216, 217
Iris Blur, 442, 445

J, K

JPEG Artifact, 471
jpg/.png format, 988

L

Lab color *vs*. RGB color, 364
Landscape Mixer (Beta) filter
   activation, 795
   output, 801
   preserve subject, 800
   presets, 796–798
   settings, 800
   sliders, 798
   unique image, 799
Layer adjustments, 63
Layer masks
   add/selection, 240, 241
   adjustments, 242, 243
   feathered edge, 243, 244
   fill layers, 241, 242, 245, 246
   invert selection, 246, 247
   layer order, 244

move tool, 244
   selection, without mask, 245
   solid fill color layer, 246, 248
   vignettes, 242
Layers menu, Convert to Smart Object, 309, 310
Layers panel, 67, 95
   badges, 277, 278
   deletion, 276, 277
   fill/opacity, 294
   parametric filter, 724
Layers panel fill, 64
   adjustments panel, 26
   blending modes, 36
   CMYK compatible, 38
   color fill, 27
   fill options, 25
   layer mask, 29
   pattern, 57, 59
Layers panel list, 28
Layer style dialog box, 502
   blending options, 297
      advanced blending, 298, 299
      effects, 302, 303
      general blending, 298
      gray/red, 299, 300
      sliders, 300, 301
      splitting, 301, 302
Layer styles, 294
   drop shadow effect, 304, 305
   fill/adjustment layer, 308
   make default button, 306
   opacity/fill, 295, 296
   options, 294, 295, 307

INDEX

Layer styles (*cont.*)
    settings, 305, 307
    storing/locating, 307
    stroke, 305, 306
Lens Blur, 393
    blade curvature
        adjustments, 403
    canvas, 399
    channels panel, 397
    current settings, 408
    Iris radius adjustments, 402
    Iris settings, 400
    layers panel, 393
    lens Blur workspace, 394
    noise settings, 405–407
    OK and cancel buttons, 409
    specular highlights options, 404
    transparency and layer
        mask, 396
    workspace options, 395
Lens correction filter
    auto correction tab, 695–698
    custom tab, 698, 699
        chromatic aberration, 702
        final image, 704, 705
        geometric distortion,
            700, 701
        settings, 700
        transform, 703, 704
        vignette, 702, 703
    digital photos, 692
    hand tool, 695
    lens distortion, 690, 691
    move grid, 694, 695
    remove distortion tool, 694
    straighten tool, 694
    tools, 692, 693
    workspace, 691, 692
    zoom tool, 695
Lens flare, 504–506
    dialog box, 506
    filter, 507, 508
Levels adjustments, 88
Levels histogram, 94
Linear Interpolation keyframes,
    918, 920
Liquify filter, 528
    bloat tool (B), 531, 532
    brush reconstruct options,
        541, 542
    brush tool options, 534
    Face-Aware Liquify options, 547
        eyes, 550, 552
        face/multiple faces, 547, 548
        face shape, 557, 558
        mouth, 554–556
        nose, 553, 554
    face tool
        Hue/Saturation layers,
            544, 545
        layers panel, 546
        mannequin faces, 543
        uses, 542
        warning message, 542, 543
        women's faces, 543, 544
    final results, 559, 560
    Forward Warp Tool (W), 529
    Freeze Mask Tool (F), 532, 533

INDEX

Hand and Zoom tools, 535
Load Mesh options, 536, 537
mannequin faces, 528
Mask options, 537, 539
OK/Cancel button, 559
Pucker tool (S), 531
Push left tool (O), 532
reconstruct tool (R), 529, 530
smooth tool (E), 530
Thaw Mask Tool (D), 533
Twirl Clockwise Tool (C), 531
View options, 539, 548, 549
    layer panel, 541
    Show Backdrop, 540, 541
Lumetri Look Up Table (LUT), 190, 972–975

M

Media encoder, 814
    application access, 967
    application open, 968
    export settings, 970
        additional settings, 981
        audio settings, 977
        captions, 978
        dialog box options, 971
        effects tab, 972–975
        multiplexer, 977
        publish, 978–980
        queue panel, 982–984
        video settings, 975, 976
    queue panel, 969, 970
    using Media Browser panel, 969
    Workspace, 968
Microsoft PowerPoint, 1013–1017
Monochromatic, 407
Monochromatic setting, 408
Monochrome, 183
Motion Blur, 484
    dialog box, 410, 411
    distance, 411
    effect of movement, 409
    properties panel, 413
    smart filter mask, 412

N

Neural filters, 728
    colorize filter, 737
    color transfer, 762
    depth blur filter
        adjustments, 793, 794
        focal distance, 792
        focal point, 791
        output, 794, 795
        settings, 790, 793
    filters menu, 727
    harmonization, 756
    JPEG Artifacts Removal filter, 773
    Landscape Mixer (Beta), 795
    photo restoration, 768
    portrait (facial adjustments), 773
    style transfer, 801
    super zoom filter, 788, 789
    wait list options, 806, 807
    workspace list, 728, 729

INDEX

Neural filter workspace tools, 730
    add to selection, 730, 731
    categories, 735, 736
    GPU, 735
    hand tool, 732
    key commands, 733
    layer preview, 733, 734
    OK/cancel button, 734, 735
    output options/list, 734
    preview button, 733
    show original artwork, 733
    smart filters, 736, 737
    subtract from selection, 731, 732
    toggle button, 735
    zoom tool, 732, 733
Noise correction filters, 453
    color changes, 457
    RGB channels, 453
Noise filter, 454
Noise panel, 446, 450
    Blur Gallery, 440, 447
    custom adjustments, 438
    grain setting, 439
    grain texture, 441
    settings, 438, 451
Non-floral frames, 499

O

On-image Targeted Adjustment Tool, 110
Opacity, 851, 883, 892, 911, 933–935, 950
Out-of-gamut colors
    CMYK process, 364
    color picker, 361, 362
    color range, 362, 363
    preview, 360, 361
    test print, 364
    view menu, 360

P

Panorama, 716
Parallax animation, 883, 1033, 1040
    add layers/tracks, 901–904
    add motions and keyframes, 904–906
    add movement to other Layers, 936–944
    add vintage overlay, 949–951
    adjust Blur and Opacity, 933–935
    create GIF animation, 962, 963
    create new document, 885
    colorized image, 897
    create video timeline, 899, 900
    dialog box settings, 885–887
    Elliptical Marquee Tool, 893
    Gaussian blur applied, 895
    Gaussian Blur dialog box, 894
    with guides, 887, 888
    hiding and locking guides, 888, 889
    layer renamed, 892
    layers panel, 891

organize layers, 899
place image, 890
reference images, 895, 896
remove figures from image, 897, 898
save file, 889, 890
Smart Object Layers, 892
tools and workspaces, 899
custom rotations, 945–948
duration and frame rate, 950–952
fade transition, 954–957
file landscape_final.psd, 883
flatten image, 884
to frame animation, 962, 963
GIF animation gallery, 881
layer panel will separate layers, 883, 884
main images, 882
playback and sound options, 952, 953
preset motion options, 912
    free transform options, 925–927
    keyframes, 918, 919
    layers panel, 923
    linear Interpolation keyframes, 920
    motion option menu, 912
    options from list, 913
    pan/move, 913–915
    rotate and zoom, 918, 944
    set to No Motion, 920, 921
    single layer selected, 921
    start keyframe for transform, 922
    timeline panel new keyframes, 928, 931
    transformation, 929
    use Move Tool, 929, 930
    warning message, 925
    zoom in/zoom out, 916
render video file, 964–967
sound effects, 958–961
split layers at playhead, 953, 954
timeline panel lengthening track, 907–909
timeline track and Layer panel, 901
track removal and other Video options, 906, 907
transitions and interpolations, 910–912
video timeline panel layout, 900
Parallax effect, 813
Parametric filter
    add filters, 724, 725
    background patterns, 723
    blending options, 720, 721
    layers panel, 724
    and neural filters, 725
    parametric properties panel, 722, 723
Paths panel, 255
Pattern Fill, 63
Pattern Fill dialog box, 58

INDEX

PDF Presentation, photo
    restoration, 1006, 1007
  compression, 1010
  dialog box, 1007
  edit in Acrobat Pro, 1013
    all tools section, 1014, 1015
    Cloud Desktop Adobe
      Acrobat Open Menu, 1014
    full screen warning
      message, 1014
    menu options and exit
      Organize pages tool, 1017
    page transitions, 1015, 1016
    view full screen mode,
      1017, 1018
  interactive presentation, 1018
  multi-page document, 1007
  output, 1010
  presentation options, 1007, 1008
  save Adobe PDF, 1009
  save file, 1008
  security, 1011, 1012
Photo filter
  adjustments panel, 174
  color theory, 173
  custom color filter, 175
Photo project
  adjustment layer
    black & white, 367
    color stain, 366
    Hue/Saturation, 368, 369
  adjustment layers, 364
  clone stamp tool, 367
  color correction, 368

  layer mask, 365
  stamp tool, 366
Photo projects, 812
Photo restoration
  CMYK filter adjustments
    channels panel and unsharp
      mask filter, 998, 999
    image size dialog box,
      997, 998
    layers renamed and
      channels panel, 1000
  color conversion, 1002
  color settings, 1003
    assign profile dialog
      box, 1005
    convert to profile advanced
      settings, 1005, 1006
    dialog box, 1003
    RGB color mode, 1003
    workspaces, RGB/CMYK,
      1003, 1004
  color stings options, 1002
  export, dialog box and resulting
    files, 992
  file options for save photo
    choose paper, 996
    duplicate image dialog
      box, 994
    file to CMYK, 993
    flatten image, 994
    photoshop warning
      message, 995
    print settings dialog box, 996
    view menu settings, 993

INDEX

InDesign, 1019
online viewing, 988
and parallax animation, 1040–1043
PDF presentation, 1006
Photoshop Projects Folder, 988
PowerPoint presentation, 1029–1033
save image as TIFF file, 1001
save jpeg files for output, 991
save RGB files for Web/Email, 988–992
TIFF Options dialog box, 1001, 1002
video applications, 1033, 1034
Photo Restoration filter, 768, 769
   clone stamp tool, 772
   color noise reduction, 771
   damaged color images, 772
   dust particles and scratches, 768
   Halftone artifact reduction, 771
   JPEG artifact reduction, 771
   noise reduction, 771
   photo enhancement, 770
   scratch reduction, 771
   settings, 770
   smart filter, 771
Photoshop, 1, 2, 9, 12, 242, 306, 327, 727
   Camera Raw Filter, 562, 563
   crop tools, 562
   filters, 526, 527
   locate filters, 809, 810
   materials panel, 720
   plugin menu, 808, 811
   plugins panel, 811
   Photoshop main menu, 510
   Photoshop's basic filters, 375
   Blur filter, 379
   digital photo repair, 376
   layer masks and channels, 375
   layers panel, 377
   object layers, 376
   photo correction, 378
   RGB color mode, 378
Polygonal Lasso Tool, 30
Portrait filters (facial adjustments)
   makeup transfer, 786, 787
   skin smoothing, 784, 785
   smart portrait expressions, 779, 780, 783
   eye direction, 778, 779
   facial age, 776, 777
   global controls, 781
   hair thickness, 777, 778
   happiness, 776
   preview, 774
   settings, 775, 782, 783
   smart filter, 784
Position keyframes, 950
Posterization, 219
Posterize effect, 218
PowerPoint Designer, 1032
PowerPoint presentation, 1029–1033

INDEX

Premiere Pro, 814, 1033, 1034
Properties panel, 83, 86, 97, 98
   algorithms, 90
   bottom of panel, 100
   CMYK, grayscale, 84
   eyedropper and color picker, 101
   eyedroppers, 91, 92
   gray midpoint, 92, 93
   histogram warning, 99
   and menu options, 84
   menu options of Levels, 101
   settings for levels channels, 89
   settings for levels presets, 89
   shadow and highlight, 99
   adjustment layer, 249, 250
   clipping masks, 250
   icons, 248, 249
   layer mask, 249
   layer options, 249
   layers masks, 240
   smart filter mask, 322
   vector masks, 255

Q

Quality grid points, 204
Queue panel, 969, 970, 982

R

Rectangular Marquee Tool, 427, 496
Reduce color noise, 470
Reduce noise, 467, 469
Reduce noise dialog box, 471, 473
Reduce noise filter, 475
Render submenu, 495
RGB channel
   curves, 107
   level, 69
RGB profile, 4

S

Set black point, 115
Shadows/highlights command
   adjustments, 313
   adjustment sliders, 316, 317
   blending options, 320, 321
   check boxes and buttons, 317
   dialog box, 313, 314, 318
   filters, 319
   outdoor images, 322
   sliders, 315, 316
   sunset image, 308, 309, 319
   uses, 313
Shape creation, 278
Sharpen filters, 475
   dialog box, 477–480, 483
   legacy settings, 478
   setting, 475
   shadows and highlights, 476, 484
   sharpening effect, 481
   submenu, 476
Smart Blur, 414
   dialog box, 415–418

and Gaussian Blur, 419
    mask selection, 416
Smart filter mask paint, 521
Smart object layers, 510
    adjustment dialog box, 311, 312
    adjustment layers, 312
    filters, 319
    multiple adjustments, 310, 311
Smart Sharpen dialog box, 485
Smart Sharpen filter, 487, 997
Solid color, 27, 37
Static digital photos, 813
Style transfer filter
    artist styles/preview, 801, 802
    image styles/preview, 801, 803
    options, 803, 804
    output, 806
    preserve color/preview, 804, 805
Substance collection applications, 719
Subtractive color mode, 5
Surface Blur, 419
    dialog box, 420, 421, 466
    layers panel, 423
    settings, 422

T

Targeted Adjustment Tool, 137
Tilt-shift lens, 447, 448
Timeline panel, 822
    animations, 815, 816
    create Frame Animation, 822
    create new file for animation, 820, 821
    GIF animation preparation, 816, 817
    GIF Photo Gallery, 813
    GIF photo gallery project, 822
    media encoder, 967
    and menu, 814, 815
    video animation parallax project, 880
    video parallax animation preparation, 817–820
Transform keyframes, 947
Tweening, 850, 851, 919

U

Unsharp mask, 488, 489, 493, 997
    Alt/option key, 490
    color correction, 489, 492
    dialog box, 490
    enlargement, 493
    high-resolution printed images, 489
    a low-resolution image, 493
    pixels, 490
    scanning, 495
    selections, 493
    sharpen filter, 491
    sharpening, 495
    sharpening adjustments, 494
    sharper image, 489
    smart filter, 491
    threshold value, 490

V

Vector masks, 278
 alteration, 258
 layer mask, 256
 loading path, 256, 257
 multiple masks, 275–278
 paths panel, 255, 259
 pen tool, 259
  Add/Delete Anchor Point Tool, 266
  add/remove points, 266, 267
  clicking, 261
  closing path, 264, 265
  completed path, 263, 264
  convert point tool, 267, 268
  curved line, 262
  direct selection tool, 268, 269
  drawing path, 260
  frame selection, 260
  inverse vector path, 274, 275
  invert selection, 274
  layer mask, 269, 270
  options bar panel, 260
  path mode, 261
  path operations, 261, 262
  path selection tool, 268, 269
  saving path, 265
  shift key, 262
  straight line, 262, 263
  vector mask, 271, 272
 renaming path/save, 255, 256
 selection, channels panel, 253, 254
Vibrance, 169–171, 173
Video footage, 1033
Video Parallax Project, 818

W, X, Y, Z

Wood pattern, 59

GPSR Compliance
The European Union's (EU) General Product Safety Regulation (GPSR) is a set of rules that requires consumer products to be safe and our obligations to ensure this.

If you have any concerns about our products, you can contact us on

ProductSafety@springernature.com

In case Publisher is established outside the EU, the EU authorized representative is:

Springer Nature Customer Service Center GmbH
Europaplatz 3
69115 Heidelberg, Germany

www.ingramcontent.com/pod-product-compliance
Lightning Source LLC
LaVergne TN
LVHW020409070526
838199LV00054B/3568